Brief Contents

Real
Writing
with Readings

Seventh Edition

Real
Writing

with Readings

**Paragraphs and Essays for Success in
College, Work, and Everyday Life**

Susan Anker

with **Nicole Aitken**
Illinois Central College

Bedford/St.Martin's
A Macmillan Education Imprint
Boston   •   New York

For Bedford/St. Martin's

Vice President, Editorial, Macmillan Higher Education Humanities: Edwin Hill
Editorial Director for Literature and Music: Karen S. Henry
Publisher for Composition, Business and Technical Writing,
    and Developmental Writing: Leasa Burton
Executive Editor: Vivian Garcia
Senior Developmental Editor: Jill Gallagher
Production Editors: Annette Pagliaro Sweeney, Louis C. Bruno Jr.
Publishing Services Manager: Andrea Cava
Senior Production Supervisor: Jennifer Wetzel
Project Management: Graphic World, Inc.
Director of Rights and Permissions: Hilary Newman
Senior Art Director: Anna Palchik
Text Design: Claire Seng-Niemoeller
Cover Design: William Boardman
Cover Art: © Murray Lee / Getty Images
Composition: Graphic World, Inc.
Printing and Binding: RR Donnelley and Sons

Manufactured in the United States of America.
0   9   8   7   6   5
f   e   d   c   b   a

For information, write: Bedford/St. Martin's, 75 Arlington Street, Boston, MA 02116
(617-399-4000)

ISBN 978-1-319-00319-7 (Student Edition)
ISBN 978-1-319-00321-0 (Loose-leaf Edition)
ISBN 978-1-319-00323-4 (Instructor's Annotated Edition)

A note to students from Susan Anker

For the last twenty years or so, I have traveled the country talking to students about their goals and, more important, about the challenges they face on the way to achieving those goals. Students always tell me that they want good jobs and that they need a college degree to get those jobs. I designed *Real Writing* with those goals in mind — strengthening the writing, reading, and editing skills needed for success in college, at work, and in everyday life.

Here is something else: good jobs require not only a college degree but also a college education—knowing not only how to read and write but how to think critically and learn effectively. So that is what I stress here, too. It is worth facing the challenges. All my best wishes to you, in this course and in all your future endeavors.

A note to students from Nicole Aitken

I've been working in both the university and community college environments since 2001, and I've had the opportunity to be a student in all different types of situations as well, including a large university, a small private college, and community colleges. I understand how your surroundings affect the way you learn and how important it is to be comfortable in those surroundings. What you bring with you to the classroom is as important to the learning experience as the material you learn in that classroom.

What does that mean? It means that you, as a student, have something to say and something to contribute. Every day you are thinking, reading, and writing in a critical way that is valuable to the college classroom, but you may not be aware of how to access those thoughts or skills in a meaningful way just yet. Although this book may introduce you to some new words and concepts, chances are good that many of these concepts or methods are ones you use regularly. Every day you are writing. You are texting, emailing, and sending messages, and you are communicating through written or spoken language. When you read or hear someone speak to you, you are analyzing what was said or written and interpreting those words; that is all a part of thinking critically and being a receptive audience.

Come to the classroom ready to share what you already know and understand that a concept we may call by a new and foreign term is actually something that may already be commonplace to you. Let's share our knowledge and ideas. While this book can guide you and help you make the choices you need to be successful in your careers and in college, you are also already an expert: you are the expert in your life, your technologies, and your own experiences. A writing community asks that we all share our experiences to increase the knowledge of the group: join our writing community and increase our collective knowledge.

Contents

Thematic Contents

Preface

The first aim of *Real Writing with Readings* has always been to communicate to students that good writing skills are both *essential* and *attainable*. When they have this, perspective, students can start fresh, reframing the writing course for themselves not as an irrelevant hoop to jump through but as a central gateway — a potentially life-changing opportunity, worthy of their best efforts. In large and small ways, this book is designed to help students prepare for their futures. It connects the writing class to their other courses, to their real lives, and to the expectations of the larger world.

Real Writing underscores this powerful message in its initial chapter, "Critical Thinking, Reading, and Writing"; in its practical advice on writing different kinds of essays; and in its step-by-step grammar sections, which build confidence and proficiency by focusing first on the most serious errors students commonly make. A diverse collection of both student and professional readings further encourages students to see the big picture, giving them a context for what they are learning. Profiles of Success provide inspirational portraits of former students, now in the workplace, who reflect on the varied, important ways they use writing in their work. These profiles are accompanied by real samples of the kinds of writing these professionals use in the workplace.

Real Writing shares this practical, real-world approach with its companion texts — *Real Essays, Real Skills,* and *Real Reading and Writing,* an integrated reading and writing text. All four books put writing in a real-world context and link writing skills to students' own goals in and beyond college.

Core Features

Successful and popular features of earlier editions of *Real Writing* have been carried over to this edition, with revisions based on suggestions from many insightful instructors and students.

A Comprehensive Teaching and Learning Package: *Real Writing* combines carefully curated readings, writing samples, writing assignments, grammar instruction, critical thinking and reading coverage, and online practice in one convenient volume, allowing instructors to focus on their students.

Writing Practice: Not only does *Real Writing* feature a number of student model paragraphs and essays, workplace writing, and professional readings, it asks students to write their own paragraphs and essays in multiple assignments throughout the book. These assignments aid students in translating their writing skills to the real world, asking them to practice concepts through the

WRITING ABOUT IMAGES

Study the photograph below, and complete the following steps.

1. **Read the image** Ask yourself: What details does the photographer focus on? How do the colors and lights affect you as a viewer? What main impression does the picture make? (For more information on reading images, see Chapter 1.)

2. **Write an illustration** The photograph shows a luxury liner whose bright, colorful lights attract onlookers and potential customers. Write an illustration paragraph or essay about businesses that draw customers with colorful displays, loud music, or some other appeal to the senses. Include the types of details you examined in step 1.

Profile of Success
Process Analysis in the Real World

Monique Rizer
Chief of Staff

Background   I was the oldest of six children, and before my mother married my stepfather, she was on welfare. She homeschooled me for five years until I begged her to let me go to a public high school. There I made friends with some people who expected to go to college, and I realized I wanted to go, too. I started at Green River Community College, but just then my parents' financial situation got really bad, and the eight of us had to move to a trailer. I stopped going to school until I met my future husband, who was going to a community college and encouraged me to go back. Several months later, I became pregnant with my first son. I was determined to stay in college, so I completed one year at Highline Community College. That summer, I had my son, got married, and found loans to transfer to Pacific Lutheran University. While there, I received a Gates Millennium Scholarship, which made continuing college possible. Although I moved a few times, I graduated from college and went on to graduate school. After I finished graduate school, I had another son.

Degrees/Colleges   B.A., Gonzaga University; M.S., Syracuse University

Employer   Be the Change, Inc.

Writing at Work   Writing is the one skill I use every day at work. As chief of staff, I'm responsible for supporting our fundraising efforts, managing our board, leading staff meetings, and other special projects. So, I am often writing to staff within the organization, my leadership, our board members, or people outside our organization with whom we are developing a relationship. I usually communicate through e-mail and I've learned it's so important to keep an e-mail short and to the point, but also friendly. Write, "Good morning" or write "Thank you" or "My best." These are small ways to keep e-mail communication personal through what can be a very impersonal technology, especially with people you don't see very often. Also, when I have to e-mail someone with a criticism or difficult message, I always try to start that e-mail with a positive note or thanks. Finally, I think very carefully about sending an e-mail when a phone call or face-to-face conversation is better. We rely on e-mail and text a lot, and we have to really try to keep those writing forums professional. But sometimes a phone call or a face-to-face conversation is more appropriate depending on the message or purpose. As I've grown in my career, I find my writing to be more important. I also have been responsible for hiring new staff and I pay close attention to how they represent themselves in writing.

I represent my leaders often in writing and so I'm very careful about what I am writing and how it will reflect on them and my organization. Sometimes I'll also write or edit something in the voice of my leadership as well. So, reading their writing and learning their "voice" has become an important skill along with writing. Finally, I draft my writing and have someone look it over or let it sit and look at it later—even a few minutes—just to get some distance and look at it with fresh eyes. Getting some distance or having a fresh view almost always improves my writing.

Four Basics of Critical Thinking

1. Be alert to assumptions made by you and others.
2. Question those assumptions.
3. Consider and connect various points of view, even those different from your own.
4. Do not rush to conclusions but instead remain patient with yourself and others and keep an open mind.

2PR   The Critical Reading Process

Preview the text.

Read the text, looking for the main idea and support.

Pause to question and interpret the text, taking notes as you read.

Review the text and your notes, and **Respond** to it.

---

lens of tasks they will need to complete in college and beyond, such as analyzing monthly expenses, evaluating instructors, and creating a résumé. Each rhetorical mode chapter also features a step-by-step writing guide and checklist that students can refer to when completing their writing assignments.

Profiles of Success: These profiles feature former students who regularly use writing in their careers, highlighting their background and the ways in which they use writing beyond the classroom. These inspirational stories give students an idea of the diverse range of careers in which writing skills are valuable — from auto technician to chief of police — and how they, too, can hope to reach their career goals.

The Four Basics and Four Most Serious Errors: This approach breaks the writing process down into logical steps, focusing on the four basics of each rhetorical mode as well as the four most serious errors in grammar. This lets students digest information at their own pace, helping them really understand each concept before starting a new one.

2PR Critical Reading Process: Appearing throughout the book, this process helps students tackle readings using critical thinking skills, asking them to preview, read, pause, review, and respond to each reading. Students can use this process not only with the readings in this course, but those in all of their college courses.

New to This Edition

This edition includes carefully developed new features to help students become better readers and writers in college and beyond.

Expanded Reading Coverage: Every chapter in Parts 1 and 2 of the book features Learning Objectives, Key Terms, and a Reading Roadmap that help students zero in on the skills they should be learning in each chapter. Reflecting on the Journey, at the end of these chapters, allows students to track their own progress on those skills. Together, these new features help students become stronger readers by pointing them precisely where they need to focus.

Updated Readings: This new edition features new relevant and relatable readings on themes such as military service, climate change, the language of hip-hop, and issues of class and gender. Nearly all of the student writing and Profiles of

Success came to us from our users — instructors and students who have used the book in their own classrooms.

Emphasis on Situational Writing: Real writing samples from the workplace, including a police report, a blog post, a professional and student résumé, an auto repair form, and a program e-mail showcase the various ways in which students will use writing skills beyond the classroom, encouraging them to apply what they learn in their future college courses and in their daily lives.

Redesigned Interior: A streamlined design allows students to focus on the most important elements of the text, getting rid of the clutter of additional features while still being visually appealing.

A Slimmer Book: Working from instructor feedback, this edition has been carefully edited to sharpen the instructional content, making the concepts easier for students to absorb and simpler for instructors to teach. Writing process chapters have been condensed, and all readings are now integrated into the rhetorical modes chapters instead of appearing in a separate chapter at the end of the book.

Calysta Will

555 N. Oak Terrace, Normal, IL 60052 | (111) 555-5678 | cwill@ilstu.edu

Education
Bachelor of Arts | May 2015 | Illinois State University
Major: Public Relations
Lorenze de' Medici University | Spring 2013 | Florence, Italy

Skills & Abilities
Communication and computer skills
Microsoft Word and Power Point: Proficient
Excel: Intermediate
Spanish: Proficient
Italian: Basic, conversational, and reading

Leadership
Social Chair, Public Relations Student Society of America, Illinois State University
August 2014–May 2015

Experience
Academic Peer Advisor | Illinois State University—University College | May 2014–Present
- Advise first-year students with academic planning and major exploration in partnership with a University College Professional Advisor
- Assist in the delivery of University College programs and services
- Maintain accurate, detailed record of all advising contacts
Marketing and Communications Intern | Special Olympics Illinois | January–May 2014
- Created various publications for Special Olympics events
- Planned and executed Special Olympics events
- Facilitated creative projects to be featuring Special Olympics Illinois athletes
- Supported and promoted accomplishments of Special Olympics athletes
Communications Intern | Illinois State University Dean of Students | January–May 2014
- Conducted research to define needs of members of the Student Government Association
- Reconstructed operations manual for Student Government Association
- Edited and condensed various documents included in the operations manual
Peer Instructor | Illinois State University Success 101 Program | August 2012–January 2014
- Provided academic support to first-year students
- Created lesson plans focused on important skills necessary to being successful in higher education
- Planned and facilitated social events for students

Support for Instructors and Students

Real Writing is accompanied by comprehensive teaching and learning support.

STUDENT RESOURCES

LaunchPad Solo for Readers and Writers includes multimedia content and assessments, including diagnostics on grammar and reading and LearningCurve adaptive quizzing, organized into pre-built, curated units for easy assigning and monitoring of student progress. For critical reading practice, twenty-five reading selections with quizzes are also included. Get all our great resources and activities in one fully customizable space online; then assign and mix our resources with yours. *LaunchPad Solo for Readers and Writers* **can be packaged at a significant discount.** Order ISBN 978-1-319-03616-4 to ensure your students can take full advantage. Visit **macmillanhighered.com/readwrite** for more information.

LearningCurve for Readers and Writers: LearningCurve, Bedford/St. Martin's adaptive quizzing program, quickly learns what students already know and helps them practice what they don't yet understand. Game-like quizzing motivates students to engage with their course, and reporting tools help teachers discern their students' needs.

With LearningCurve, students receive as much practice as they need to master a given concept and are provided with immediate feedback and links back to online instruction. A personalized study plan with suggestions for further practice completes Bedford's plan to give your students just what they need to be successful in the college classroom. To order *LearningCurve for Readers and Writers* packaged with *Real Writing*, please use the following package ISBN: 978-1-319-03615-7.

Please note: *LearningCurve for Readers and Writers* is included with *LaunchPad Solo for Readers and Writers*.

The *Bedford/St. Martin's Planner* includes everything that students need to plan and use their time effectively, with advice on preparing schedules and to-do lists plus blank schedules and calendars (monthly and weekly). The planner fits easily into a backpack or purse, so students can take it everywhere. Free when packaged with the print text. ISBN: 978-0-312-57447-5

The *Bedford/St. Martin's ESL Workbook,* **Second Edition,** by Sapna Gandhi-Rao, Maria McCormack, and Elizabeth Trelenberg provides ESL students with a broad range of exercises. This outstanding resource covers grammatical issues for multilingual students with varying English-language skills and cultural backgrounds. To reinforce each lesson, instructional introductions are followed by examples and exercises. ISBN: 978-0-312-54034-0

E-BOOK OPTIONS

Real Writing e-book. Available in several formats for use with computers, tablets, and e-readers — visit **macmillanhighered.com/catalog/ebookpartners** for more information.

FREE INSTRUCTOR RESOURCES

The *Instructor's Annotated Edition of Real Writing* gives practical page-by-page advice on teaching with *Real Writing* and answers to exercises. It includes discussion prompts, strategies for teaching ESL students, ideas for additional classroom activities, suggestions for using other print and media resources, and cross-references useful to teachers at all levels of experience. ISBN: 978-1-319-00323-4

Instructor's Manual for Real Writing provides helpful information and advice on teaching integrated reading and writing. It includes sample syllabi, reading levels scores, tips on building students' critical thinking skills, resources for teaching nonnative speakers and speakers of nonstandard dialects, ideas for assessing students' writing and progress, and up-to-date suggestions for using technology in the writing classroom and lab. Available for download; see **macmillanhighered .com/realwriting/catalog**.

Teaching Developmental Reading: Historical, Theoretical, and Practical Background Readings, **Second Edition,** is a professional development resource edited by Sonya L. Armstrong, Norman A. Stahl, and Hunter R. Boylan. It offers a wealth of readings from the historical foundations of the developmental reading field to the latest scholarship. ISBN: 978-1-4576-5895-2

Teaching Developmental Writing: Background Readings, **Fourth** Edition, is a professional resource edited by Susan Naomi Bernstein, former co-chair of the Conference on Basic Writing. It offers essays on topics of interest to basic writing instructors, along with editorial apparatus pointing out practical applications for the classroom. ISBN: 978-0-312-60251-2

The Bedford Bibliography for Teachers of Basic Writing, **Third Edition** (also available online at **macmillanhighered.com/basicbib**), has been compiled by members of the Conference on Basic Writing under the general editorship of Gregory R. Glau and Chitralekha Duttagupta. This annotated list of books, articles, and periodicals was created specifically to help teachers of basic writing find valuable resources. ISBN: 978-0-312-58154-1

ORDERING INFORMATION

To order any of these ancillaries for *Real Writing* contact your local Bedford/St. Martin's sales representative; send an e-mail to **sales_support@macmillan.com**; or visit our Web site at **macmillanhighered.com**.

Acknowledgments

Like every edition that preceded it, this book grew out of a collaboration with teachers and students across the country and with the talented staff of Bedford/St. Martin's. I am grateful for everyone's thoughtful contributions.

REVIEWERS

I would like to thank the following instructors for their many good ideas and suggestions for this edition. Their insights were invaluable.

Lauren Birdsong, Atlantic Cape Community College
Polly Hawk, Kansas City Kansas Community College
Vickie Kelly, Hinds Community College
Loren Kleinman, Passaic County Community College
Rebekah Lewis, Miami Dade College, North Campus
Katherine Lott, College of Southern Maryland
Sonya McCoy-Wilson, Atlanta Technical College
Susan Monroe, Housatonic Community College
John Mravik, Elgin Community College
Clarence Nero, Baton Rouge Community College
Lonetta Oliver, St. Louis Community College — Florissant Valley
Regina Peters, Blinn College
Anne Marie Prendergast, Bergen Community College
Tara Ronda, Atlantic Cape Community College
Lori Smalley, Greenville Technical College
Lisa Tittle, Hartford Community College
Debbie Wilke, Daytona State College

STUDENTS

Many current and former students have helped shape this edition of *Real Writing* and I am grateful for all their contributions.

Among the students who provided paragraphs and essays for the book are Jelani Lynch, Arianna Morgan, Casandra Palmer, Alessandra Cepeda, Brian Healy, Charton Brown, Daniel Bird, Lorenza Mattazi, Kelly Hultgren, Corin Costas, Said Ibrahim, Armand Powell-Archie, Caitlin Prokop, Stephanie Alaimo, and Mark Koester.

CONTRIBUTORS

Art researcher Connie Gardner, working with Martha Friedman, assisted with finding and obtaining permission for the many new, thought-provoking images included in the book.

Kathleen Karcher, working with Kalina Ingham, successfully completed the large and essential task of clearing text permissions.

I am also deeply grateful to designer Claire Seng-Niemoeller, who freshened the look of the book's interior.

BEDFORD/ST. MARTIN'S

I have been extremely fortunate to work with the incredibly talented staff of Bedford/St. Martin's, whose perceptiveness, hard work, and dedication to everything they do are without parallel.

Thanks to Edwin Hill, Vice President of Humanities for Macmillan Education; Leasa Burton, Publisher for Composition; and Vivian Garcia, Executive Editor for Developmental English. Editorial assistant Eliza Kritz helped with innumerable tasks, from running review programs to assisting with manuscript preparation. We were very fortunate to have Annette Pagliaro Sweeney and Louis Bruno, production editors, shepherding *Real Writing* through production, as well as Matt Rosenquist at Graphic World. Overseeing and thoughtfully contributing to all aspects of the design was Anna Palchik, senior art director. Thanks to Billy Boardman for his work on the cover design. I must also extend tremendous gratitude to the sales and marketing team. Christina Shea, senior marketing manager, has been a great advocate for all my books and has helped me to forge greater connections with the developmental market and to stay up to date on its needs. And I continue to be deeply thankful for the hard work and smarts of all the sales managers and representatives.

This book would not have reached its fullest potential without the input and attention it received, from the earliest stages of development, from executives and long-time friends in the Boston office. Thanks also to my editor, Jill Gallagher, for developing this edition.

As he has in the past, to my great good fortune, my husband Jim Anker provides assurance, confidence, steadiness, and the best companionship throughout the projects and the years. His surname is supremely fitting.

— *Susan Anker*

In addition to the names already mentioned, I wanted to thank Alexis Walker, former Executive Editor for Developmental Studies at Bedford/St. Martin's, for asking me to be involved in this project. Although it was initially a bit of a surprise to be contacted to work on this project, it has been a very insightful and rewarding experience. It was a delight to collaborate with Alexis and Martha Bustin, my initial contacts at Bedford/St. Martin's, and I am grateful for their trust in letting me work with Susan Anker's time-tested materials. I would also like to acknowledge Jill Gallagher, who walked me through the book's development. Jill was certainly one of the most valuable assets to me in this process, and I owe her a great debt of thanks. She has made the process of editing this book one of pure joy and discovery; her assistance and insights were undoubtedly crucial to the finished product.

I need to also express my gratitude to colleagues, students, and friends who stepped in and assisted me along the way whenever I asked for help. There were several people in the Department of English, Humanities, and Language Studies at Illinois Central College as well as friends and colleagues working in developmental studies and transfer-level courses who were willing to provide any assistance I needed. I also need to thank the friends and colleagues who offered up writing samples within a day when asked. I'm blessed to have such a strong group of writers and colleagues ready to step up and offer their work and support.

Finally, I want to thank my family. My husband, Brian Aitken, has been endlessly patient and supportive through this entire process. There have been quite a few times when his encouragement has been my rock, and that was certainly crucial to my success. I also thank my amazing daughters, Katie and Hope, who have adjusted their schedules at times to allow me to work on this book. I hope that they will see this work as something that they can be proud of as well, since they are the reason I work so hard on everything I do. Thank you to my entire family for supporting me and believing in me; you are all a blessing to me.

— *Nicole Aitken*

Part 1

How to Write Paragraphs and Essays

"I write ideas and summaries. Writing is a tool in my creative process."

Tate Brown-S., student

Critical Thinking, Reading, and Writing
Making Connections

READING ROADMAP

Learning Objectives

Chapter Goal: Learn how to become a prepared and active student as well as a critical thinker, reader, and writer.

Tools to Achieve the Goal:
- Student Preparedness Checklist (p. 5)
- Four Basics of Critical Thinking (p. 11)
- 2PR: The Critical Reading Process (p. 13)
- Writing Critically about Readings (p. 21)
- Writing Critically about Visuals (p. 25)
- Problem Solving (p. 28)

Key Terms

Skim Chapter 1 before reading. Find these words or terms in **bold** type. Put a check mark next to each once you locate it.

____ critical thinking   ____ main idea
____ making   ____ purpose
connections
____ assumptions   ____ support
____ biases, critical   ____ summary
reading   ____ analysis
____ boldface   ____ synthesis
____ guiding question   ____ evaluation
    ____ Z pattern

Guided Reading for Chapter 1

Fill out the following chart before you begin reading. For each skill, write what you know about the skill and what you would like to know upon completing the chapter. At the end of the chapter, you will be asked to share what you learned about each skill.

Skill	When I have used this skill	What I want to know about this skill
Preparing for success		
Thinking critically		
Using the critical reading process		
Writing critically about readings		
Writing critically about visuals		
Problem solving		

⚠ LaunchPad Solo

Visit **LaunchPad Solo for Readers and Writers > Reading** for more tutorials, videos, and practice with critical reading.

Understanding College Success

If you are reading this chapter, you probably just started a college writing course, and you might not know what to expect. What will the teacher require? What will class be like? How do I get through it—and all my courses—successfully?

Students come to college from all walks of life and with different types of experiences and backgrounds. What may be common knowledge to you about how to be a successful student may be a new idea to another student, or it could even be a strategy that one of your classmates used at one time but has forgotten. Before starting any course, it is important not only to purchase your supplies and attend class but also to put yourself into a mind-set that will help create a successful college experience for you.

In the first section of this chapter, you will learn about common expectations that many college writing instructors have of their students. Some of these expectations may be familiar to you, and some may be new. It is important not only to be aware of these expectations, but also to set goals for yourself for the semester. Setting goals helps you focus your time in the classroom and identify what you want to learn in this class. The writing classroom, however, is a bit different from other classes you may enroll in because a writing class is a writing community. At times, you may find the experience of sharing your writing uneasy or uncomfortable, but learning to work with others to brainstorm, draft, revise, and edit papers will help you become a stronger writer. By understanding your role in that community and how that community will help you grow as a writer and a student, you will be better equipped to prepare for the semester and become a more successful student.

Teaching tip This chapter gives students a preview of what they can expect in your course, in later writing courses, and in other college courses. Helping students prepare for your course and set short- and long-term goals can help them understand their purpose in this writing community.

Becoming a Prepared and Active Student

All students can benefit from thinking carefully about the strategies that will help them become successful in class. During the first week of class, your instructor should distribute a syllabus or some other document with expectations and policies. Not all policies and expectations will be the same because every instructor and every course is different, but most share the baseline expectations outlined here. You should be aware of them as you start this course because your instructor will expect you to understand and adhere to them throughout the semester.

Teaching tip Ask students to discuss their preferences after going over the student preparedness checklist. Which of these tips work for them and why? Which haven't they tried? How might trying those particular tips help them learn?

Teaching tip Go over your own expectations for the course and demonstrate where they can be found in the syllabus.

Teaching tip It can be beneficial to put students in groups that rotate throughout the semester. Giving them some sense of consistency or familiarity can help build confidence.

> **PRACTICE 1** **Learn more about your own preparedness**
>
> Take a few minutes to go through the list of items on the next page that make a student more prepared and mentally ready to engage with the course. How many of these items are ones that you already employ? Why have you chosen to use them? If you haven't used one of them, why not? Would you be willing to try? Why or why not?
>
> After writing about your own preferences, interview one or two other students in the class—preferably those who are not sitting in the same general area as you. What did they write in their own responses? Why did they make the choices they did? What does this tell you about the way different people learn and participate in a class?

Student Preparedness Checklist

Item	What it means	Do you do this?
Treat your course as seriously as you would a job.	Your boss does not *give* you money—you *earn* it, through hard work and professional behavior. Likewise, your instructor does not *give* you a grade. You *earn* the grade you get. Think of your coursework as a job that can lead to bigger and better things—if you work hard and perform well.	
Come to class on time, and stay until your instructor dismisses you.	Again, going to class is like going to a job—you have to come and go on the boss's schedule, not your own. When you arrive late or leave early, you not only disrupt other students, you might miss instructions for the day's work, and you may miss additional instructions for homework to prepare for the next day.	
Come to class prepared.	You have to do your homework or expect to fail. Even if you have never regularly done homework before and have managed to pass, you will not pass in college. You will also likely have points taken off for late homework. Some instructors may even ask you to leave class or count you as absent if you do not have your homework completed.	
Connect to others in class.	Students often sit in the same places for each class. Exchange names, phone numbers, and e-mail addresses with at least one student who sits near you. That way, if you miss a class, you can find out from that person what you missed. You might also want to study with that person.	
Let your instructor know if you know you are going to miss class, and contact him or her about the work you missed.	Be a good communicator. Instructors can help you make up what you have missed—but only if you have made a connection and communicate in a clear, respectful way. Send an e-mail or call your instructor to find out what you missed, and make sure you write in clear language—not texting language.	
Read the syllabus carefully and hang onto it the entire semester.	Your instructor will expect you to know what the homework is and when assignments are due: Your syllabus will tell you. Always bring your syllabus to class, in case your instructor announces updates or reminders.	
Get to know your instructor.	Communication is important. If you get a low grade or do not understand something, ask in class, via e-mail, or visit your instructor during office hours. It is up to you to take steps to clear up anything you do not understand.	
Participate in class: ask questions, answer questions, and make comments.	Do not be afraid of making a stupid comment or giving the wrong answer. That is part of the learning process. Plus, many instructors grade on participation. ▶	

Item	What it means	Do you do this?
Listen and take notes.	When the instructor is talking, listen carefully, but do not try to write down every word he or she says. To figure out what you should make a note of, look at the instructor. Important points are often signaled with a hand gesture, a note on the board, or a change in the tone of the instructor's voice.	
Don't hide.	The further back in the classroom you sit, or the closer you are to a back corner, the more tempting it is to let your mind wander or to stop focusing on class material. If you want to keep your mind focused on the task at hand, try to get a seat near the front of the class.	
Schedule your time wisely.	If you choose to wait until the last minute to work on a large project, you will either not be able to finish or you will do a bad job and get a bad grade. Part of being a successful student is the ability to schedule your time.	

Teaching tip Ask students to work with students they do not already know or who are sitting in a different area of the classroom. This will give them the chance to not only meet and interact with more of their classmates, creating a close-knit writing community, but will also give them the chance to experience other views and ideas about a topic.

Setting Goals

You may already know what kind of degree you want to pursue in college and what type of job you want in the future. With these long-term goals in mind, you also need shorter-term goals—steps that help you get where you want to go. To be successful in any course, it is important to identify both your long-term and short-term goals. These goals give you a reason to attend class and a tangible goal to work toward. Consider each of the following as you start this new semester.

PRACTICE 2   **Look ahead to writing goals**

List at least four writing goals—skills you want to learn, practice, or improve in this course. Be as specific as possible. For example, "Learn to write better" is too general to help you focus on what you need to do. A better example could be "Learn how to write clear thesis statements." Throughout the course, refer to these goals, changing or updating them as needed. As you progress through the semester, you may find that your goals become more specific. The list will give you a way to reflect on the skills and abilities that you are actively developing.

1. _____

2. _____

3. _____

4. _____

PRACTICE 3   **Look ahead to reading goals**

Identify at least four reading goals—skills you want to learn, practice, or improve in this course. Be as specific as possible. For some people, this is not as easy to identify or articulate as their writing goals because we don't often think about our reading as a process. Do your best to think about what happens when you, personally, sit down to read. Do you need to work on limiting distractions when you read? Do your best to identify what, exactly, you would like to improve. Then, throughout the course, refer to this list of skills and abilities to help you refine what you've learned.

1. _____

2. _____

3. _____

4. _____

PRACTICE 4   **Looking ahead to degree goals**

Whether or not you have decided what you want to major in, you should still ask yourself some questions now. Which majors interest me? Which courses would I need to take to complete the major(s) that interest me? What are the required core courses that every student must take to graduate, and when should I take those courses?

Course requirements for each major are listed in the college bulletin and on the college Web site. It's a good idea, though, to sit down with your academic adviser as soon as possible to plan a sequence of courses. If you are like most students, you are juggling a lot of important priorities, and having a plan to reach your goals will help you achieve them. Write your tentative plans in the spaces provided.

I (might) want to major in _____.

Courses I will need for that major (If you do not know your major yet, list the courses required for all students.)

_____

_____

_____

_____

_____

_____

_____

Number of courses I can take next term _____

Courses I should take if they fit into my schedule (Remember, certain courses have other courses as prerequisites.)

_____

PRACTICE 5   **Looking ahead to career goals**

You may or may not know what your career goals are at this point. Even if you do not yet have clear goals, try answering the following questions to jump-start your thinking.

What field might I like to work in after completing my college coursework?

_____

What kinds of additional degrees or certifications might I need to obtain to work in that field? (If you need additional coursework beyond your current degree or certificate program, list them here.)

_____

_____

In this field, how is writing used? (Reports? Memos? Charts?)

_____

_____

In this field, how is reading used? (Computer records? Articles? Guidebooks?)

_____

_____

Becoming a Critical Thinker

"To be successful, be a critical thinker." This statement is becoming more and more common, and it is true. College courses require critical thinking. Workplaces require it. Life requires it. The good news is, you already practice critical thinking, and it is a skill you can strengthen, as you will learn in this chapter.

Take a closer look at a type of critical thinking with which you are already familiar: making judgments about what to buy, or not to buy, based on product labels and advertising. First, **study** the picture to the right. **Ask yourself:**

• Why did the designers of this label make the choices that they did?

COURTESY OF BETH CASTRODALE

- What textual and visual elements of the label suggest health and purity?
- **Make a connection** to your daily life: Are you any more likely to purchase Pure Health Water or any type of bottled water based on this label? Why or why not?

Now, **study** this advertisement from Tappening, an environmental group. **Ask yourself:**

- What is this ad's main message?
- What is the message behind the **boldface** note in the lower left corner of the ad?
- **Make a connection** to the previous label: How would the creator of the Tappening ad respond to the way the bottled-water company presents its product?

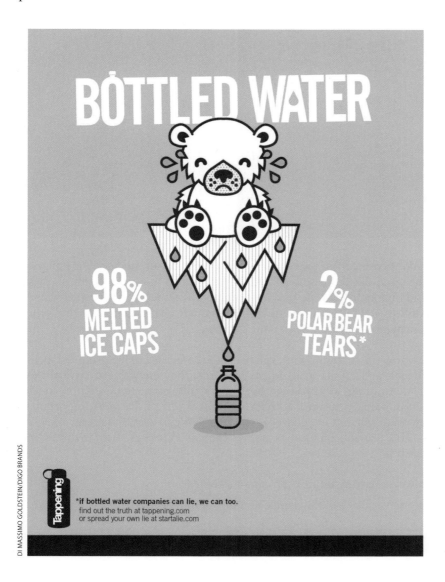

- **Make a connection** to your daily life: Does the Tappening ad make bottled water any less appealing to you? Why or why not?

Finally, **study** the labels below. **Ask yourself:**

- What do these bottled-water labels say about the companies that produced them?
- **Make a connection** to the previous advertisement: How do these labels respond to the main message of the Tappening advertisement?

- **Make a connection** to your daily life: Reflect on all the previous images—the labels and the Tappening ad. Do they make you think differently about what kind of bottled water to purchase or about whether to buy bottled water at all? In what ways have product labels, your own experiences, and other information contributed to your decision?

The previous activities took you beneath the surface of the product labeling and beyond quick reactions to it. In other words, they encouraged **critical thinking**, actively questioning what you see, hear, and read to come to thoughtful conclusions about it. Building your critical thinking skills is one of the most important things you can do to succeed in college, at work, and in everyday situations.

As the previous activities show, critical thinking also involves **making connections**

- between existing impressions and new ones
- among various beliefs, claims, and bits of information.

In the following sections, we will take a closer look at critical thinking strategies. Also, we will explore the connections among critical thinking, reading, and writing.

What Is Critical Thinking?

Imagine you are the supervisor at a small, family-owned business. Recently, one of the owners hired a new employee that you are asked to train during your shift. When the shift begins, the new employee still has not shown up. In fact, she shows up fifteen minutes late. When she does finally arrive, her uniform is a bit sloppy, and she doesn't seem in any hurry to find you or anyone else so that she can start her shift.

What do you think to yourself about this person? What assumptions have you made about her? What kind of employee will she be? Why do you think that?

Everything you know is based on a first impression—an assumption or guess. You don't have any facts, but you are using what you see on the surface to judge this new employee's overall performance. This is something everyone does from time to time; however, in college we need to learn to move beyond assumptions and quick judgments and to think more critically. Critical thinking asks us to explore the reasons behind something and not to rely on our snap judgments and assumptions.

Teaching tip Ask students what questions they would have for a new employee who is late for her or his first day of work. How would they approach the situation?

Four Basics of Critical Thinking

1. Be alert to assumptions made by you and others.
2. Question those assumptions.
3. Consider and connect various points of view, even those different from your own.
4. Do not rush to conclusions but instead remain patient with yourself and others and keep an open mind.

Assumptions—ideas or opinions that we do not question and that we automatically accept as true—can get in the way of clear, critical thinking. Here are some assumptions you would probably make about the new employee:

> The new employee is careless because she is late.
>
> The new employee is sloppy because her uniform is a mess.
>
> The new employee is unreliable because she didn't contact anyone before coming in late.
>
> The new employee will not be a good employee because she didn't immediately apologize for her tardiness.

In college, work, and everyday life, we often hold assumptions that we are not even aware of. By identifying these assumptions, stating them, and questioning them, we stand a better chance of seeing reality and acting more effectively.

In the case of the new employee, perhaps she had not realized her shift started fifteen minutes before she arrived. Perhaps she thought she was fifteen minutes early. In that case, she would have had plenty of time to straighten out her uniform and introduce herself. She still should have double-checked the schedule and straightened her uniform before entering the workplace, but it's possible that all, or at least some, of these assumptions are entirely incorrect.

When questioning assumptions, it can help to try to get a bit of distance from them. Imagine what people with entirely different points of view might say. You might even try disagreeing with your own assumptions. Take a look at the following examples.

Questioning Assumptions

Situation	Assumption	Questions
COLLEGE: I saw from the syllabus that I need to write five essays for this course.	This course may be too difficult for me.	Other students have passed this course; what makes me think I cannot? What obstacles might be getting in my way? What might be some ways around those obstacles? What have others done in this situation?
WORK: Two of my coworkers just got raises.	My own raise is just around the corner.	Did my coworkers accomplish anything I did not? When were their last raises, and when was mine?
EVERYDAY LIFE: My friend has been acting strangely toward me lately.	I must have done something wrong.	Is it possible it has nothing to do with me? Maybe he is going through something really difficult in his life.

Tip In every situation, try to be open to different points of view. Listen and think before responding or coming to any conclusions. Although you may not agree with other points of view, you can learn from them.

You need to be aware not only of your own assumptions but also of those in what you read, see, and hear. For example, bottled-water labels and advertising might suggest directly or indirectly that bottled water is better than tap water. Think carefully about the evidence they provide to support this assumption. What other sources of information could be consulted to either support, disprove, or call into question this assumption? However confidently a claim is made, never assume it is 100% correct and cannot be questioned.

Teaching tip Students might do Practice 6 in small groups, first discussing assumptions behind the images and then coming up with questions about the assumptions. One group member should write down key points of the discussion.

PRACTICE 6   **Thinking critically**

What assumptions are behind each of the images on pages 8–10? Write down as many as you can identify. Then, write down questions about these assumptions, considering different points of view.

In addition to assumptions, be aware of **biases**, one-sided and sometimes prejudiced views that may blind you to the truth of a situation. Here is just one example:

No one older than age fifty can pick up new skills quickly.

Others could contradict this extreme statement with their own experiences, exceptions, and insights or with additional information that could show reality is more nuanced or complicated than this statement allows.

Be on the lookout for bias in your own views and in whatever you read, see, and hear. When a statement seems one-sided or extreme, ask yourself what facts or points of view might have been omitted.

What Is Critical Reading?

Critical reading is paying close attention as you read and asking yourself questions about the author's purpose, his or her main idea, the support he or she gives, and how good that support is. It is important to think critically as you read, looking out for assumptions and biases (both the writer's and your own). You should also consider whether you agree or disagree with the points being made.

Here are the four steps of the critical reading process:

2PR   The Critical Reading Process

Preview the text.

Read the text, looking for the main idea and support.

Pause to question and interpret the text, taking notes as you read.

Review the text and your notes, and **Respond** to it.

2PR   *Preview the Text*

Before reading any piece of writing, skim the whole thing, using the following steps.

READ THE TITLE, HEADNOTE, AND INTRODUCTORY PARAGRAPHS

The title of a chapter, an article, or any other document usually gives you some idea of what the topic is. Some documents are introduced by headnotes, which summarize or provide background about the selection. If there is a headnote, read it. Whether or not there is a headnote, writers often introduce their topic and main idea in the first paragraphs, so read those and make a note stating what you think is the main idea.

READ HEADINGS, KEY WORDS, AND DEFINITIONS

Textbooks and magazine articles often include headings to help readers follow the author's ideas. These headings (such as "Preview the Text" above) tell you what the important subjects are within the larger piece of writing.

Any terms in **boldface** type are especially important. In textbooks, writers often use boldface for key words that are important to the topic.

LOOK FOR SUMMARIES, CHECKLISTS, AND CHAPTER REVIEWS

Many textbooks (such as this one) include features that summarize or list main ideas. Review summaries, checklists, or chapter reviews to make sure you have understood the main ideas.

READ THE CONCLUSION

Writers usually review their main idea in their concluding paragraphs. Read the conclusion, and compare it with the note you made after you read the introduction and thought about what the main idea might be.

ASK A GUIDING QUESTION

As the final step in your preview of a text, ask yourself a **guiding question**—a question you think the text might answer. This question will give you a purpose for reading and help keep you focused. Sometimes, you can turn the title into a guiding question. For example, read the title of this chapter, and write a possible guiding question.

2PR   *Read the Text: Find the Main Idea and Support*

After previewing, begin reading carefully for meaning, trying especially to identify a writer's main idea and the support for that idea.

MAIN IDEA AND PURPOSE

For more on main ideas, see Chapter 3.

The **main idea** of a text is the central idea the author wants to communicate. The main idea is related to the writer's **purpose**, which can be to explain, to demonstrate, to persuade, or to entertain. Writers often introduce their main idea early, so read the first few paragraphs with special care. After reading the first paragraph (or more, depending on the length of the reading selection), stop and write down—in your own words—what you think the main idea is. If the writer has stated the main idea in a single sentence, double-underline it.

Teaching tip   Practice 7 works well as a group activity.

> **PRACTICE 7**   **Finding the main idea**

Read each of the following paragraphs. Then, write the main idea in your own words in the spaces provided.

1. Making a plan for your college studies is a good way to reach your academic goals. The first step to planning is answering this question: "What do I want to be?" If you have only a general idea—for example, "I would like to work in the health-care field"—break this large area into smaller, more specific subfields. These subfields might include working as a registered nurse, a nurse practitioner, or a physical therapist. The second step to planning is to meet with an academic adviser to talk about the classes you will need to take to get a degree or certificate in your chosen field. Then, map out the courses you will be taking over the next couple of semesters. Throughout the process, bear in mind the words of student mentor Ed Powell: "Those who fail to plan, plan to fail." A good plan boosts your chances of success in college and beyond.

   Main idea: *Answers will vary but should refer to the benefits of planning a course of study in college.*

2. Networking is a way businesspeople build connections with others to get ahead. Building connections in college also is well worth the effort. One way to build connections is to get to know some of your classmates and to exchange names, phone numbers, and e-mail addresses with them. That way, if you cannot make it to a class, you will know someone who can tell you what you missed. You can also form study groups with these other students. Another way to build connections is to get to know your instructor. Make an appointment to visit your instructor during his or her office hours. When you go, ask questions about material you are not sure you understood in class or problems you have with other course material. You and your instructor will get the most out of these sessions if you bring examples of specific assignments with which you are having trouble.

   Main idea: <u>*Answers will vary but should refer to the benefits of networking in*</u>

   <u>*college.*</u>

SUPPORT

Support is the details that show, explain, or prove the main idea. The author might use statistics, facts, definitions, and scientific results for support. Or he or she might use memories, stories, comparisons, quotations from experts, and personal observations.

For more on support, see Chapter 4.

> **PRACTICE 8**　**Identifying support**
>
> Go back to Practice 7 (p. 14), and underline the support for the main ideas of each passage in the practice.

Teaching tip Ask students if they can identify the main idea and support in any of the essays in Chapters 6–14.

Not all support that an author offers in a piece of writing is good support. When you are reading, ask yourself: What information is the author including to help me understand or agree with the main idea? Is the support (evidence) valid and convincing? If not, why not?

2PR *Pause to Think*

Taking notes and asking questions as you read will help you understand the author's points and develop a thoughtful response. As you read, do the following:

- Double-underline or write the main idea in the margin.
- Note the major support points by underlining them.
- Note ideas that you agree with by placing a check mark next to them (✓).
- Note ideas that you do not agree with or that surprise you with an ✗ or !, and ideas you do not understand with a question mark (?).
- Note any examples of an author's or expert's bias.
- Jot any additional notes or questions in the margin.
- Consider how parts of the reading relate to the main idea.

2PR   *Review and Respond*

After reading, it is important to take a few minutes to look back and review. Go over your guiding question, your marginal notes, and your questions—and *connect yourself to what you have read*. Consider, "What interested me? What did I learn? How does it fit with what I know from other sources?" When you have reviewed your reading in this way and fixed it well in your mind and memory, it is much easier to respond in class discussions and writing assignments. To write about a text, you need to generate and organize your ideas, draft and revise your response, and, above all, use your critical thinking skills (see p. 11).

A Critical Reader at Work

Read the following piece. The notes in the margins show how one student applied the process of critical reading to an essay on bottled water.

Amanda Jacobowitz

A Ban on Water Bottles: A Way to Bolster the University's Image

Amanda Jacobowitz is a student at Washington University and a columnist for the university's publication *Student Life,* in which the following essay appeared.

Guiding question: What does the author think about the ban on bottled water?

Larger main idea (not stated directly): (1) the ban is ineffective, and (2) there are better ways to protect the environment.

Why not just drink from a water fountain? You don't have to have a bottle.

1   Lately, I am always thirsty. Always! I could not figure out why until I realized that the bottled water I had purchased continuously throughout my day had disappeared. At first I was just confused. Where did all the water bottles go? Then I learned the simple explanation: The University banned water bottles in an effort to be environmentally friendly.

2   Ideally, given the ban on selling water bottles, every student on campus should now take the initiative to carry a water bottle, filling it up throughout the day at the water fountains on campus. Realistically, we know this has not and will not happen. I have tried to bring a water bottle with me to classes—I do consider myself somewhat environmentally conscious—but have rarely succeeded in this effort. Instead, although I have never been too much of a soda drinker, I find myself reaching for a bottle of Coke out of pure convenience. We can't buy bottled water, but we can buy soda, juice, and other drinks, many of which come in plastic bottles. I am sure that for most people—particularly those who give very little thought to being environmentally conscientious—convenience prevails and they purchase a drink other than water. Wonderful result. The University can pride itself on being more environmentally friendly, with the fallback that its students will be less healthy!

Examples of other common forms of waste

3   Even if students are not buying unhealthy drinks, any benefit from the reduction of plastic water bottles could easily be offset by its alternatives.

Students are not using their hands to drink water during meals. They are using plastic cups—cups provided by the University at every eatery on campus. Presumably no person picks up a cup, drinks their glass of water, and then saves that same cup for later in the day. That being said, how many plastic cups are used by a single student, in a single day? How many cups are used by the total campus-wide population daily, yearly? This plastic cup use must equate to an exorbitant amount of waste as well.

Examples of other common forms of waste

4   My intent is not to have the University completely roll back the water bottle ban, nor is my intent for the University to level the playing field by banning all plastic drink bottles. I'm simply questioning the reasons for specifically banning bottled water of all things. Why not start with soda bottles—decreasing the environmental impact, as well as the health risks? There are also many other ways to help the environment that seem to be so easily overlooked.

Examples of other ways to protect the environment

5   Have you ever noticed a patch of grass on campus that's not perfectly green? I can't say that I have. The reason: the sprinklers. Now, I admit that I harbor some animosity when it comes to the campus sprinklers; I somehow always manage to mistakenly and inadvertently walk right in their path, the spray of water generously dousing my feet. However, my real problem with the sprinklers is the waste of water they represent. Do we really need our grass to be green at all times?

6   The landscaping around our beloved Danforth University Center (Gold LEED Certified) is irrigated with the use of rainwater. There is a 50,000-gallon rainwater tank below the building to collect rain! I admit, this is pretty impressive, but what about the rest of the campus? What water is used to irrigate and keep green the rest of our 169 acres on the Danforth campus?

Town/city water, I assume.

7   I understand that being environmentally conscious is difficult to do, particularly at an institutional level. I applaud the Danforth University Center and other environmental efforts the University has initiated. However, I can't help but wonder if the University's ban on the sale of water bottles is more about appearance and less about decreasing the environmental impact of our student body. The water bottle ban has become a way to build the school's public image: We banned water bottles; we are working hard to be environmentally friendly! In reality, given the switch to plastic cups and the switch to other drinks sold in plastic bottles, is the environmental impact of the ban that significant? Now that the ban has been implemented, I certainly don't see the University retracting it. However, I hope that in the future the University focuses less on its public image and more on the environment itself when instituting such dramatic changes.

Is it really about public image? What would a university administrator say?

| PRACTICE 9 | **Making connections** |

Look back at the images on pages 8–10. Then, review the reading by Amanda Jacobowitz. What assumptions does she make about bottled water? What evidence, if any, is provided to support these assumptions? On the basis of your observations, would you like to see bottled water not banned or banned at your college? Why or why not?

Read Real-World Documents Critically

Careless reading in your everyday life can cause minor problems such as a ruined recipe, but it can also have more serious consequences. For example, if you overlook the fine print in a loan offer, you might end up agreeing to a high interest rate and, therefore, more debt.

To read real-world documents closely and carefully, try the **2PR** strategy, especially for longer documents. Also, when you see a document or sign that makes a claim, ask yourself: Does this claim look too good to be true? If so, why?

> **Teaching tip** You might also have students apply the 2PR strategy to essays or articles that you bring in (or ones from this book) or to textbooks for this or other classes.

> **PRACTICE 10**   **Reading real-world documents**
>
> Working by yourself or with other students, read the following documents from college and everyday life, and answer the critical reading questions. *Answers may vary. Possible answers are shown.*

1. What is the writer's purpose? *The e-mail advertisement is attempting to sell something, the electric bill lists all charges owed for a specific address, the nutrition label provides material about all the ingredients in the item so that an informed consumer can determine the nutritional value, and the college catalog lists available courses in which students may enroll.*

2. Is the writer biased? *In the e-mail advertisement, yes. In the others, no.*

3. What are the key words or major claims? *Answers could include any words in headlines or boldface type.*

4. What is in the fine print? *See "for those who qualify" in the e-mailed advertisement.*

5. What do you think of what you have read? Why? Does anything seem odd, unrealistic, or unreliable? Give specific examples. *The claims in the e-mailed advertisement cannot be true.*

College: An E-mailed Advertisement

GET A COLLEGE DEGREE IN *TWO* WEEKS!

Are a few letters after your name the only thing that's keeping you from your dream job? Degree Services International will grant you a B.A., M.A., M.S., M.B.A., or Ph.D. from a prestigious nonaccredited institution based on what you already know!

NO CLASSES, EXAMS, OR TEXTBOOKS ARE REQUIRED
for those who qualify

If you order now, you'll receive your degree within two weeks.

CALL 1-800-555-0021

HURRY! Qualified institutions can grant these diplomas only because of a legal loophole that may be closed within weeks.

Everyday Life: Electric Bill

12 8 0000005360 0   80 2106 178   H

Account Number

Please Pay By
Oct. 26, 2014

Please Pay Amount
$53.60

ᵢₗᵢᵗₗᵢₗᵢₗₗₗᵢᵢₗₗᵢᵢₗᵢₗₗₗᵢᵢₗᵢₗᵢₗₗᵢₗᵢₗᵢₗ

NSTAR Electric

MOVING? PLEASE LET US KNOW. OTHERWISE YOU MAY BE RESPONSIBLE FOR ENERGY USE AFTER YOU MOVE.

Service Provided To:

Electric Bill Summary

Account Number	I06 178

Please Pay By	**Please Pay Amount**
October 26, 2014	$53.60

Current Bill Date	**Next Meter Read Date**
October 8, 2014	November 6, 2014

Electric Bill Comparison

	Current Month	Last Month	Last Year
Electric Charges	$53.60	$64.11	
Total Electricity Use (kWh)	265	324	
Delivery Charges (per kWh) *Cost to deliver electricity to your home.*	10.8¢	10.4¢	
Delivery Charges Total	$28.75	$33.72	
Generation Charges (per kWh) *Cost to purchase electricity on your behalf.*	9.3¢	9.3¢	
Generation Total	$24.85	$30.39	

Bill Analysis

Billing Days	28	29
Avg. Daily Electric Use (kWh)	9.4	11.1
Avg. Daily Temp (degrees)	64	73

Highlights From This Month's Billing Period

September 5, 2014 to October 3, 2014

Amount of Your Last Bill	$64.11
Payment - Thank You	-$64.11
Previous Balance	$0.00
Adjustments	$0.00
Delivery Charges Total	$28.75
Generation Charges	$24.85
Total Charges for Electricity	$53.60
Please Pay Amount	$53.60

NSTAR Green is an exciting option available for residential and small business customers looking to support renewable energy in the region and reduce greenhouse gas emissions.

By signing up, you can choose to have all (NSTAR Green 100) or half (NSTAR Green 50) of your electric use support wind energy. There is an additional premium for NSTAR Green.

More information about NSTAR Green, including pricing and an online enrollment form, is available on NSTAR.com.

Your Electricity Use By Month At A Glance

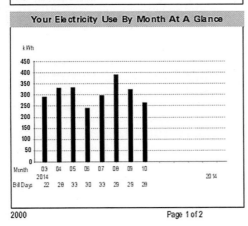

Month	03 2014	04	05	06	07	08	09	10	2014
Bill Days	22	28	33	30	33	29	29	29	

www.nstar.com

800-592-2000

Everyday Life: Nutrition Label

CHRIS SADOWSKI/GETTY IMAGES

Nutrition Facts

Serving Size 2/3 cup (51g)
Servings Per Container About 9

Amount Per Serving	Cereal	Cereal with 1/2 cup Skim Milk
Calories	240	280
Calories from Fat	70	70

	% Daily Value**	
Total Fat 8g*	**12%**	**12%**
Saturated Fat 2.5g	**13%**	**13%**
Trans Fat 0g		
Cholesterol 0mg	**0%**	**0%**
Sodium 50mg	**2%**	**5%**
Total Carbohydrate 37g	**12%**	**14%**
Dietary Fiber 3g	**12%**	**12%**
Sugars 13g		
Protein 4g	**8%**	**16%**
Vitamin A	0%	4%
Vitamin C	0%	0%
Calcium	2%	15%
Iron	6%	6%

College: Course Catalog

BUS 121

PRINCIPLES OF CUSTOMER SERVICE

Credit Hours: 3.0
*Tuition: $375.00

This course focuses on the importance of customer service, perception, and satisfaction, and the application of various customer relation systems in the marketplace. The course is designed to promote an understanding of the principles of customer service in general and how the application of customer service specifically contributes to positive customer perception and the success of business. Emphasis is placed on the importance of excellence in service to retain customers and gain a competitive advantage.

Class #	Days	Time	Location	Instructor	Details
2996	wed	06:00-08:50 pm	Technology Cent	Dewey	Lecture

BUS 151

JOB ORIENTATION

Credit Hours: 2.0
*Tuition: $250.00

This course employs a series of activities designed to identify and improve skills sought by employers of job candidates and current employees in the workplace. Presented in a workshop format, each session is devoted to one or more group activities focused on the development and/or refinement of a specific job skill. The class culminates in group presentations that require the members of each group to use all of the skills practiced during the course. Targeted skills include, but are not limited to: communication; teamwork; problem-solving; decision-making; and data analysis and presentation.

Class #	Days	Time	Location	Instructor	Details
1288	mon	06:00-07:15 pm	E Peo Academic	Dewey	Lecture
1288	mon	06:00-07:15 pm	E Peo Academic	Dewey	Lecture

COURTESY OF ILLINOIS CENTRAL COLLEGE

What Is Writing Critically about Readings?

Being able to write critically about what you read is a key college skill because it shows your deep understanding of course content. When you write critically about readings, you summarize, analyze, synthesize, and evaluate, and, in doing so, you answer the following questions.

Reading and Writing Critically

Summarize

- What is important about the text?
- What is the purpose, the big picture?
- What are the main ideas and key support?

Analyze

- What elements have been used to convey the main idea?
- Do any elements raise questions? Do any key points seem missing or undeveloped?

Synthesize

- What do other sources say about the topic of the text?
- How does your own (or others') experience affect how you see the topic?
- What new point(s) might you make by bringing together all the different sources and experiences?

Evaluate

- Based on your application of summary, analysis, and synthesis, what do you think about the material you have read?
- Is the work successful? Does it achieve its purpose?
- Does the author show any biases? If so, do they make the piece more effective or less effective?

Summary

A **summary** is a condensed, or shortened, version of something—often, a longer piece of writing, a movie or television show, a situation, or an event. In writing a summary, you give the main ideas and key support in your own words.

The following is an excerpt from the *Textbook of Basic Nursing* by Caroline Bunker Rosdahl and Mary T. Kowalski. It comes from a chapter that discusses some of the stresses that families can face, including divorce.

Adults who are facing separation from their partners—and a return to single life—may feel overwhelmed. They may become preoccupied with their own feelings, thereby limiting their ability to handle the situation effectively or to be strong for their children. The breakdown of the family system may require a restructuring of responsibilities, employment, childcare, and housing arrangements. Animosity between adults may expose children to uncontrolled emotions, arguments, anger, and depression.

Children may feel guilt and anxiety over their parents' divorce, believing the situation to be their fault. They may be unable to channel their conflicting emotions effectively. Their school performance may suffer, or they may engage in misbehavior. Even when a divorce is handled amicably, children may experience conflicts about their loyalties and may have difficulties making the transition from one household to another during visitation periods. . . .

Experts estimate that approximately 50% of all children whose parents divorce will experience another major life change within 3 years: remarriage. The arrival of a stepparent in the home presents additional stressors for children. Adapting to new rules of behavior, adjusting to a new person's habits, and sharing parents with new family members can cause resentment and anger. When families blend children, rivalries and competition for parental attention can lead to repeated conflicts.

Now, here is a summary of the textbook excerpt. The main idea is double-underlined, and the support points are underlined.

Although divorce seriously affects the people who are splitting up, Rosdahl and Kowalski point out that the couple's children face equally difficult consequences, both immediately and in the longer term. In the short term, according to the authors, children may blame themselves for the split or feel that their loyalty to both parents is divided. These negative emotions can affect their behavior at school and elsewhere. Later on, if one or both of the parents remarry, the children may have trouble adjusting to the new family structure.

Analysis

An **analysis** breaks down the points or parts of something and considers how they work together to make an impression or convey a main idea. When writing an analysis, you might also consider points or parts that seem to be missing or that raise questions in your mind.

Here is an analysis of the excerpt from the *Textbook of Basic Nursing*. The main idea is double-underlined, and the support points are underlined.

We all know that divorce is difficult for the people who are splitting up, but Rosdahl and Kowalski pay special attention to the problems faced by children of divorce, both right after the split and later on. The authors mention several possible outcomes of divorce on children, including emotional and behavioral difficulties and trouble in school. They also discuss the stresses that remarriage can create for children.

The authors rightly emphasize the negative effects that divorce can have on children. However, I found myself wondering what a divorcing couple could do to help their children through the process. Also, how might parents and stepparents

Teaching tip Ask students to read and write down questions about a reading from this book or from some other source. Then, have them write a brief analysis that poses these questions.

help children adjust to a remarriage? I would like to examine these questions in a future paper.

[Note how the writer raises questions about the textbook excerpt.]

Synthesis

A **synthesis** pulls together information from additional sources or experiences to make a new point. Here is a synthesis of the textbook material on divorce. Because the writer wanted to address some of the questions she raised in her analysis, she incorporated additional details from published sources and from people she interviewed. Her synthesis of this information helped her arrive at a fresh conclusion.

In the *Textbook of Basic Nursing*, Rosdahl and Kowalski focus on the problems faced by children of divorce, both right after the split and later on. According to the authors, immediate problems can include emotional and behavioral difficulties and trouble in school. Later on, parents' remarriage can create additional stresses for children. Although the authors discuss the impact of divorce on all parties, they do not suggest ways in which parents or stepparents might help children through the process of divorce or remarriage. However, other sources, as well as original research on friends who have experienced divorce as children or adults, provide some additional insights into these questions.
First source

A Web site produced by the staff at the Mayo Clinic recommends that parents come together to break the news about their divorce to their children. The Web site also suggests that parents keep the discussion brief and free of "ugly details." In addition, parents should emphasize that the children are in no way to blame for the divorce and that they are deeply loved. As the divorce proceeds, neither parent should speak negatively about the other parent in the child's presence or otherwise try to turn the child against the ex-spouse. Finally, parents should consider counseling for themselves or their children if any problems around the divorce persist.
Second source

The Web site of the University of Missouri Extension addresses the problems that can arise for children after their parents remarry. Specifically, the Web site describes several things that stepparents can do to make their stepchildren feel more comfortable with them and the new family situation. One strategy is to try to establish a friendship with the children before assuming the role of a parent. Later, once stepparents have assumed a more parental role, they should make sure they and their spouse stand by the same household rules and means of discipline. With time, the stepparents might also add new traditions for holidays and other family gatherings to help build new family bonds while respecting the old ones.
Third source

To these sources, I added interviews with three friends—two who are children of divorce and one who is both a divorced parent and a stepparent. The children of divorce said that they experienced many of the same difficulties and stresses that Rosdahl and Kowalski described. Interestingly, though, they also reported that they
Fourth source

felt guilty, even though their parents told them not to, just as the Mayo Clinic experts recommend. As my friend Kris said, "For a long time after the divorce, every time me and my dad were together, he seemed distracted, like he wished I wasn't there. I felt bad that I couldn't just vanish." Dale, the stepparent I interviewed, liked the strategies suggested by the University of Missouri Extension, and he had actually tried some of these approaches with his own stepchildren. However, as Dale told me, "When you're as busy as most parents and kids are these days, you can let important things fall by the wayside—even time together. That's not good for anyone."

Fresh conclusion

Thinking back on Kris's and Dale's words and everything I've learned from the other sources, I have come to conclude that divorced parents and stepparents need to make sure they build "together time" with their own children and/or stepchildren into every day. Even if this time is just a discussion over a meal or a quick bedtime story, children will remember it and appreciate it. This approach would help with some of the relationship building that the University of Missouri Extension recommends. It would also improve communication, help children understand that they are truly loved by *all* their parents, and assist with the process of postdivorce healing.

Works Cited

Leigh, Sharon, Maridith Jackson, and Janet A. Clark. "Foundations for a Successful Stepfamily." U of Missouri Extension, Apr. 2007. Web. 13 Oct. 2015.

Mayo Clinic Staff. "Children and Divorce: Helping Kids after a Breakup." *Mayo Clinic.* Mayo Clinic, 14 May 2011. Web. 12 Oct. 2015.

Rosdahl, Caroline Bunker, and Mary T. Kowalski. *Textbook of Basic Nursing.* 9th ed. Philadelphia: Lippincott Williams & Wilkins, 2008. 92. Print.

Evaluation

An **evaluation** is your *thoughtful* judgment about something based on what you have discovered through your summary, analysis, and synthesis. To evaluate something effectively, apply the questions from the Reading and Writing Critically box on page 21. You will want to refer to these questions as you work through later chapters of this book and through readings from other college courses.

Here is an evaluation of the excerpt from the *Textbook of Basic Nursing:*

In just a few paragraphs, Rosdahl and Kowalski give a good description of the effects of divorce, not only on the former spouses but also on their children. The details that the authors provide help to clearly communicate the difficulties that such children face. In the short term, these difficulties can include emotional and behavioral problems and trouble in school. In the longer term, if one or both of a child's parents remarry, the child faces the stress of dealing with a new and different family. Although the authors do not specifically address ways that parents and stepparents can ease children into divorce and/or new families, other sources—such as the Web sites of the University of Missouri Extension and the Mayo Clinic, as well as people I interviewed—do get into these issues. In the end, I think that Rosdahl and Kowalski present a good overview of their subject in a short piece of writing that was part of a larger discussion on family stresses.

> **PRACTICE 11** **Making connections**
>
> As you work through this exercise, refer to the Reading and Writing Critically box on page 21.
>
> 1. **Summary:** Summarize Amanda Jacobowitz's essay on pages 16–17.
> 2. **Analysis:** Whether you agree or disagree with Jacobowitz, write a paragraph analyzing the points she presents.
> 3. **Synthesis:** Read additional opinion pieces or blog postings about bottled water. In one paragraph, state your position on the subject according to your reading of these materials. Also, explain the range of opinions on the subject.
> 4. **Evaluation:** Write a paragraph that evaluates Jacobowitz's essay.

What Is Writing Critically about Visuals?

Images play a huge role in our lives today, and it is important to think critically about them just as you would about what you read or hear. Whether the image is a Web site, a photograph or illustration, a graphic, or an advertisement, you need to be able to "read" it. You can apply the same critical reading skills of summary, analysis, synthesis, and evaluation to read a visual.

Look carefully at the advertisement from Tappening on page 9. Then, consider how to read a visual using the critical thinking skills you have learned.

Teaching tip Bring in additional advertisements or other visuals and ask students to summarize, analyze, synthesize, and evaluate them.

Summary

To summarize a visual, ask yourself what the big picture is: What is going on? What is the main impression or message (the main idea)? What is the purpose? How is this purpose achieved (the support)? To answer these questions, consider some strategies used in visuals.

DOMINANT ELEMENTS

Artists, illustrators, and advertisers may place the most important object in the center of an image. Or, they may design visuals using a **Z pattern**, with the most important object in the top left and the second most important object in the bottom right. In English and many other languages, people read printed material from left to right and from top to bottom, and the Z pattern takes advantage of that pattern. Because of these design strategies, the main idea of a visual can often be determined by looking at the center of the image or at the top left or bottom right.

FIGURES AND OBJECTS

The person who creates an image has a purpose (main idea) and uses visual details to achieve (or support) that purpose. In a photograph, illustration, or painting, details about the figures and objects help create the impression the artist wants to convey. (Here, the term *figures* refers to people, animals, or other forms that can show action or emotion.) When studying any image, ask yourself the following questions:

- Are the figures from a certain period in history?
- What kind of clothes are they wearing?
- What are the expressions on their faces? How would I describe their attitudes?
- Are the figures shown realistically, or are they shown as sketches or cartoons?
- What important details about the figures does the creator of the image want me to focus on?

PUT DOWN THE PHONE AND NO ONE GETS HURT.

COURTESY OF THE NATIONAL SAFETY COUNCIL, NEBRASKA

PRACTICE 12   **Summarizing a visual**

Focus on the public service announcement from the Nebraska Safety Council above, and answer the following questions. *Answers will vary. Possible answers are shown.*

1. What is the big picture? What is going on? *There is a cell phone strapped to a bundle of dynamite.*

2. What is at the center of the ad? *The dynamite.*

3. What is the ad's purpose? *To educate people about the dangers of using a*
   cell phone while driving.

4. What details do you notice about the ad? Include as many as you can.
   Answers will vary, but can include: The dynamite is marked with numbers;
   the cell phone is a Blackberry with a red screen; there is a set of car keys; the
   fuse from the dynamite is connected to the cell phone.

Analysis

To analyze a visual, focus on the parts of it (figures, objects, type), and ask yourself how they contribute to the message or main impression. Consider the background, the use of light and dark, and the various elements' colors, contrasts, textures, and sizes.

> **PRACTICE 13** **Analyzing a visual**
>
> Focus on the public service announcement from the Nebraska Safety Council on page 26, and answer the following questions. *Answers will vary. Possible answers are shown.*
>
> 1. What elements are placed in large type? Why? *"Put down the phone and*
>   *no one gets hurt" is a play on something a terrorist negotiator would say*
>   *in a hostage situation. It's trying to bring awareness to the dangers of cell*
>   *phone use while driving.*
>
> 2. How do all the features in the ad contribute to the main impression? *The*
>   *use of sticks of dynamite connotes explosions and danger and terror, which*
>   *are meant to spark an association with the use of cell phones.*

Synthesis

To synthesize your impressions of a visual, ask yourself what the message seems to be, using your summary and analysis skills. Consider how this message relates to what else you know from experience and observation.

> **PRACTICE 14** **Synthesizing your impressions of a visual**
>
> Focus on the public service announcement from the Nebraska Safety Council on page 26, and answer the following questions. *Answers will vary. Possible answers are shown.*
>
> 1. What is the ad's central message? *That using a cell phone while you're*
>   *driving is as dangerous as dynamite.*

2. How does this message relate to what you already know or have heard or experienced? _Answers will vary._

Evaluation

To evaluate an image, ask yourself how effective it is in achieving its purpose and conveying its main idea or message. What do you think of the image, using your summary, analysis, and synthesis skills? Consider any biases or assumptions that may be working in the image.

> **PRACTICE 15** **Evaluating a visual**
>
> Focus on the public service announcement from the Nebraska Safety Council on page 26, and answer the following questions. _Answers will vary._
>
> 1. What do you think about the ad, especially its visual elements? _Answers will vary._
>
> 2. Does the creator of the ad seem to have any biases? Why or why not?
>
> 3. Is the ad effective, given its purpose and the main idea it is trying to make? Why or why not?

What Is Problem Solving?

In college, at work, and in everyday life, we often need to "read" situations to make important decisions about them. This process, known as problem solving, can also involve summarizing, analyzing, synthesizing, and evaluating. Let's look at key steps in the process.

1. Summarize the problem.

   Try to describe it in a brief statement or question.

   EXAMPLE: My ten-year-old car needs a new transmission, which will cost at least $1000. Should I keep the car or buy a new one?

2. Analyze the problem.

   Consider possible ways to solve it, examining any questions or assumptions you might have.

EXAMPLES

Assumption: I need to have a reliable car.

Question: Is this assumption truly justified?

Answer: Yes. I can't get to school or work without a reliable car. I live more than fifteen miles from each location, and there is no regular public transportation to either place from my home.

POSSIBLE SOLUTIONS

- Pay for the transmission repair.
- Buy a new car.

3. Synthesize information about the problem.

   Consult various information sources to get opinions about the possible solutions.

   EXAMPLES

   - My mechanic
   - Friends who have had similar car problems
   - Car advice from print or Web sources
   - My past experience with car repairs and expenses

4. Evaluate the possible solutions, and make a decision.

   You might consider the advantages and disadvantages of each possible solution. Also, when you make your decision, you should be able to give reasons for your choice.

   EXAMPLES (considering only advantages and disadvantages)

- Pay for the transmission repair.

  Advantage: This option would be cheaper than buying a new car.

  Disadvantage: The car might not last much longer, even with the new transmission.

- Buy a new car.

  Advantage: I will have a reliable car.

  Disadvantage: This option is much more expensive than paying for the repair.

  FINAL DECISION: Pay for the transmission repair.

  REASONS: I do not have money for a new car, and I do not want to take on more debt. Also, two mechanics told me that my car should run for three to five more years with the new transmission. At that point, I will be in a better position to buy a new car.

> **PRACTICE 16**   **Solving a problem**
>
> Think of a problem you are facing now—in college, at work, or in your everyday life. On a separate sheet of paper, summarize the problem. Next, referring to the previous steps, write down and analyze possible solutions,

considering different sources of information. Then, write down your final decision or preferred solution, giving reasons for your choice.

Chapter Review

1. What are the four basics of critical thinking? *Be alert to assumptions made by you and others. Question those assumptions. Consider and connect various points of view. Do not rush to conclusions.*

2. What are the four major steps of the critical reading process? *Preview, read, pause, review*

3. Why is it important to read real-world documents critically? *Because not doing so can cause problems in everyday life*

4. What are the four major steps of writing critically about readings and visuals? *Summarize, analyze, synthesize, evaluate*

5. Without looking back in the chapter, define the task of synthesizing in your own words. *Answers will vary, but should mention pulling together various bits of information to come to a fresh conclusion.*

REFLECTING ON THE JOURNEY

Skills Learned

Now that you've completed the chapter, share what you've learned about each skill by completing the following chart.

Skill	What I learned about this skill
Preparing for success	
Thinking critically	
Using the critical reading process	
Writing critically about readings	
Writing critically about visuals	
Problem solving	

Writing Basics

Audience, Purpose, and Process

Learning Objectives

Chapter Goal: Learn what audience and purpose are and how they affect the writing process.

Tools to Achieve the Goal:

- Four Basics of Good Writing (p. 32)
- Understand Audience and Purpose (p. 32)
- Understand the Writing Process (p. 36)
- Understand Grading Criteria (p. 37)
- Relationship between Paragraphs and Essays (p. 38)

Key Terms

Skim Chapter 2 before reading. Find these words or terms in **bold** type. Put a check mark next to each once you locate it.

_____ audience	_____ essay
_____ purpose	_____ introduction
_____ paragraph	_____ thesis
_____ topic sentence	_____ support paragraphs
_____ main idea	
_____ body	_____ conclusion
_____ support sentences	_____ writing process
_____ concluding sentence	_____ rubric

Guided Reading for Chapter 2

Fill out the following chart before you begin reading. For each skill, write what you know about the skill and what you would like to know upon completing the chapter. At the end of the chapter, you will be asked to share what you learned about each skill.

Skill	When I have used this skill	What I want to know about this skill
Identify a specific audience		
Identify a specific purpose		
Consider the needs and expectations of the audience		
Use a clear writing process to develop and revise a draft		
Make a clear, definite point		
Provide support that shows, explains, or proves the main idea		
Read and understand a rubric		

Four elements are key to good writing. Keep them in mind whenever you write.

Four Basics of Good Writing

> **1** It considers what the audience knows and needs.
>
> **2** It fulfills the writer's purpose.
>
> **3** It includes a clear, definite point.
>
> **4** It provides support that shows, explains, or proves the main idea.

LaunchPadSolo

Visit **LaunchPad Solo for Readers and Writers** > **Writing Process** > **Purpose, Audience, and Topic** for more practice with writing basics.

This chapter discusses the four basics in more detail. It also outlines the writing process, previewing steps that are covered more thoroughly in the next three chapters. Finally, it gives you some typical grading criteria and shows how they are applied to assess unsatisfactory, satisfactory, and excellent paragraphs.

Understand Audience and Purpose

Your **audience** is the person or people who will read what you write. In college, your audience is usually your instructors. Whenever you write, always have at least one real person in mind as a reader. Think about what that person already knows and what he or she will need to know to understand your main idea.

Your **purpose** is your reason for writing. Let's take a look at some different audiences and purposes.

Audience and Purpose

Type of writing	Audience	Purpose	Tips
College: A research essay about the environmental effects of "fracking": fracturing rock layers to extract oil or natural gas	The professor of your environmental science class	• To complete an assignment according to your professor's instructions and any research methods discussed in class • To show what you have learned about the topic	When writing to fulfill a course assignment, never make assumptions such as, "My instructor already knows this fact, so what's the point of mentioning it?" By providing plenty of relevant examples and details, you demonstrate your knowledge of a subject and make your writing more effective.
Work: An e-mail to coworkers about your company's new insurance provider	Fellow workers	To make sure that coworkers understand all the important details about the new provider	Define or explain any terminology or concepts that will not be familiar to your audience.
Everyday Life: A text message to your recreational softball league informing them about a time change for this week's game	The members of your softball team	To make sure your team knows what time to show up for their game this week	Although informal, texting still requires you to provide all the necessary information and to make sure you don't assume that everyone on that list understands every texting abbreviation. You may need to spell out some of the words you may not usually spell out with your friends.

The tone and content of your writing will vary depending on your audiences and purposes. Read the following three notes, which describe the same situation but are written for different audiences and purposes.

> **Situation:** Marta woke up one morning feeling strange, and her face was swollen and red. Marta immediately called her doctor's office and made an appointment. Marta's mother was coming to stay with Marta's children in a few minutes, so Marta asked a neighbor to watch the children until her mother got there. Marta then texted her mother explaining why she had already left. When she got to the doctor's office, she was feeling better, and, since the doctor was running late, she decided not to wait. The nurse asked her to write a brief description of her symptoms for the doctor to read later. Before leaving the doctor's office, however, Marta also wanted to make sure that her office knew that she would be at work sooner than she expected. She sent a quick e-mail to her office to let them know she would be there on time.

Marta's text to her mother

Nt feelng well; going 2 DR. I'm OK. Don't wry. Thx for watching kds 4 me.

Marta's note to the doctor

When I woke up this morning, my face was swollen, especially around the eyes, which were almost shut. My lips and skin were red and dry, and my face was itchy. However, the swelling seemed to go down quickly.

Marta's e-mail to work

Mrs. Smith,
After calling in this morning to let you know that I would be a bit late due to a potential illness, I realized that I am now feeling better and will manage to make it in to work on time. I am leaving the doctor's office right now and should be at the office very shortly. I apologize for any inconvenience this may cause and will make sure to make up for any missed time.
Sincerely,
Marta

> **PRACTICE 1**   **Comparing Marta's notes**

Read Marta's three notes, and answer the following questions. *Answers will vary. Possible answers are shown.*

1. How does Marta's note to her mother differ from the one to the doctor?

   How does the one to the doctor differ from the one to work? <u>The note to</u>
   <u>the doctor is more specific and more formal, while the text message is very</u>
   <u>informal and full of abbreviations. The e-mail to work is more businesslike in</u>
   <u>tone and contains no detailed information about her condition, which would</u>
   <u>not be appropriate.</u>

2. How do the different audiences and purposes affect what the notes say (the content) and how they say it (the tone)? *Marta does not want to worry her mother, so she is general, and she is also informal. Marta wants the doctor to know exactly what happened, so she provides more specifics. She also writes more formally. Marta wants her boss to know that she is mindful of her job and attempting to make it work on time. It is even more formal than the other two examples are.*

3. Which note has more detail, and why? *The one to the doctor because Marta wants the doctor to know the symptoms she had.*

As these examples show, we communicate with family members and friends differently than we communicate with people in authority (like employers, instructors, or other professionals)—or we should. Marta's text to her mother is extremely informal; it not only uses incomplete sentences but also incomplete words because the two women know each other well and are used to speaking casually to each other. Because Marta's purpose is to get quick information to her mother and to reassure her, she does not need to provide a lot of details. On the other hand, Marta's note to her doctor is more formal, with complete sentences, because the relationship is more formal. Also, the note to the doctor is more detailed because the doctor will be making treatment decisions based on it. Finally, the e-mail to work is the most formal because it requires Marta to be professional and businesslike. Anything less would not be acceptable in that environment.

In college, at work, and in your everyday life, when you are speaking or writing to someone in authority for a serious purpose, use formal English; people will take you seriously.

Teaching tip Bring in samples of e-mails, texts, or other notes that you have received, or have students do the same. Remove names and have the students compare the language to determine who the audience is and whether the language is appropriate for that audience. Ask the students to take a message that doesn't fit an audience and rewrite it to make it fit.

> **PRACTICE 2** **Writing for a formal audience**
>
> A student, Terri Travers, sent the following e-mail to a friend to complain about not getting into a criminal justice course. Rewrite the e-mail as if you were Terri and you were writing to Professor Widener. The purpose is to ask whether the professor would consider allowing you into the class given that you signed up early and have the necessary grades.
>
> To: Miles Rona
> Fr: Terri Travers
> Subject: Bummin
>
> Seriously bummin that I didn't get into Prof Widener's CJ class. U and Luis said it's the best ever, lol. Wonder why I didn't . . . I signed up early and I have the grades. Sup w/that?
>
> C ya,
> TT

Understand Paragraph and Essay Form

In this course (and in the rest of college), you will write paragraphs and essays. Each kind of writing has a basic structure.

PARAGRAPH FORM

A **paragraph** has three necessary parts: the topic sentence, the body, and the concluding sentence.

Paragraph Part	Purpose of the Paragraph Part
1. The **topic sentence**	states the **main idea**. The topic sentence is often the first sentence of the paragraph.
2. The **body**	supports (shows, explains, or proves) the main idea with **support sentences** that contain facts and details.
3. The **concluding sentence**	reminds readers of the main idea and often makes an observation.

Read the paragraph that follows with the paragraph parts labeled.

Following a few basic strategies can help you take better notes, an important — Topic sentence
skill for succeeding in any course. First, start the notes for each class session on a fresh page of your course notebook, and record the date at the top of the page. Next, to improve the speed of your note taking, abbreviate certain words, especially ones your instructor uses regularly. For example, abbreviations for a business course might include *fncl* for financial, *svc* for service, and *mgt* for management. However, don't try to write down every word your instructor says. Instead, look for ways to boil down extended explanations into short phrases. For instance, imagine that a business instructor says the following: "A profit-and-loss statement is a report of an organization's revenue and expenses over a specific financial period. Often, P-and-L's are used to determine ways to boost revenue or cut costs, with the — Body (with support sentences)
goal of increasing profitability." The note taker might write down something like, "P&L: rpt of revenue + expenses over a specific period. Used to boost rev or cut costs." Although you do not need to record every word of a lecture, listen for clues that indicate that your instructor is making a point important enough to write down. At such times, the instructor might raise his or her voice, or he or she might introduce key information with such phrases as "It's important to remember" or "Bear in mind." In addition, if the instructor has made a certain point more than once, it is a good indication that this point is important. By carefully listening to and recording information from your instructor, you are not just getting good — Concluding sentence
notes to study later; you are already beginning to seal this information into your memory.

ESSAY FORM

Teaching tip Have students interview a second- or third-year student in their major to find out what kind of writing that person does for his or her classes.

An **essay** is a piece of writing that examines a topic in more depth than a paragraph. A short essay may have four or five paragraphs, totaling three hundred to six hundred words. A long essay may be many pages long, depending on what the essay needs to accomplish, such as persuading someone to do something, using research to make a point, or explaining a complex concept.

An essay has three necessary parts: the introduction, the body, and the conclusion.

Essay Part	Purpose of the Essay Part
1. The **introduction**	states the main idea, or **thesis**, generally in a single, strong statement. The introduction may be a single paragraph or multiple paragraphs.
2. The **body**	supports (shows, explains, or proves) the main idea. It generally has at least three **support paragraphs**, each containing facts and details that develop the main idea. Each support paragraph has a topic sentence that supports the thesis statement.
3. The **conclusion**	reminds readers of the main idea and makes an observation. Often, it also summarizes and reinforces the support.

Teaching tip For some students, it helps to present visual analogies. Explain that just as a skyscraper needs more substantial support than a three-story apartment building, an essay needs more detailed support than a paragraph.

Paragraph		Essay
Topic sentence	→	Thesis statement
Support sentences	→	Support paragraphs
Concluding sentence	→	Conclusion

Teaching tip The *Instructor's Manual for Real Writing* contains reproducible forms that students can use to plan their paragraphs and essays.

The diagram on pages 38–39 shows how the parts of an essay correspond to the parts of a paragraph.

Understand the Writing Process

Teaching tip Have students practice the skills they learned in the previous chapter. After reading the essay on Millennials, ask them to practice summary, analysis, or evaluation in a brief paragraph response to work on their critical thinking and reading skills.

The chart that follows shows the four stages of the **writing process**. These are all the steps you need to follow to write well. The rest of the chapters in Part 1 cover every stage except editing (presented later in the book). You will practice each stage, see how another student completed the process, and write your own paragraph or essay. Keep in mind that you may not always go in a straight line through the four stages; instead, you might circle back to earlier steps to further improve your writing.

Teaching tip Ask students to describe a process related to their college experience, such as registering for classes, buying books, or applying for financial aid.

Some writing strategies—such as finding and exploring a topic, coming up with a main idea, and revising—are similar for both paragraphs and essays. In these cases, this book discusses the strategies for paragraphs and essays together. (See Chapters 3, 4, and 5.) However, other activities, such as supporting main ideas or drafting individual parts of paragraphs or essays, are somewhat different for the two

---

The Writing Process

Generate ideas

Consider: What is my purpose in writing? Given this purpose, what interests me? Who will read this paper? What do they need to know?

- Find and explore your topic (Chapter 3).
- Make your point (Chapter 3).
- Support your point (Chapter 4).

Draft

Consider: How can I organize my ideas effectively and show my readers what I mean?

- Arrange your ideas, and make an outline (Chapter 5).
- Write a draft, including an introduction that will interest your readers, a strong conclusion, and a title (Chapter 5).

Revise

Consider: How can I make my draft clearer or more convincing to my readers? How do I avoid plagiarism? How do I meet the requirements of the grading rubric?

- Look for ideas that do not fit (Chapter 5).
- Look for ideas that could use more detailed support (Chapter 5).
- Connect ideas with transitional words and sentences (Chapter 5).

Edit

Consider: What errors could confuse my readers and weaken my point?

- Find and correct errors in grammar (Chapters 15-26).
- Look for errors in word use (Chapters 27 and 28), spelling (Chapter 29), and punctuation and capitalization (Chapters 30–34).

---

types of writing. In those cases, this book makes greater distinctions between paragraphs and essays.

Understand Grading Criteria

Your instructor may use a **rubric**—a list of the elements on which your papers will be graded. If your instructor uses a rubric, it may be included in the course syllabus, and you should refer to it each time you write. Also, use the rubric to revise your writing.

Relationship between Paragraphs and Essays

For more on the important features of writing, see the Four Basics of Good Writing on page 32.

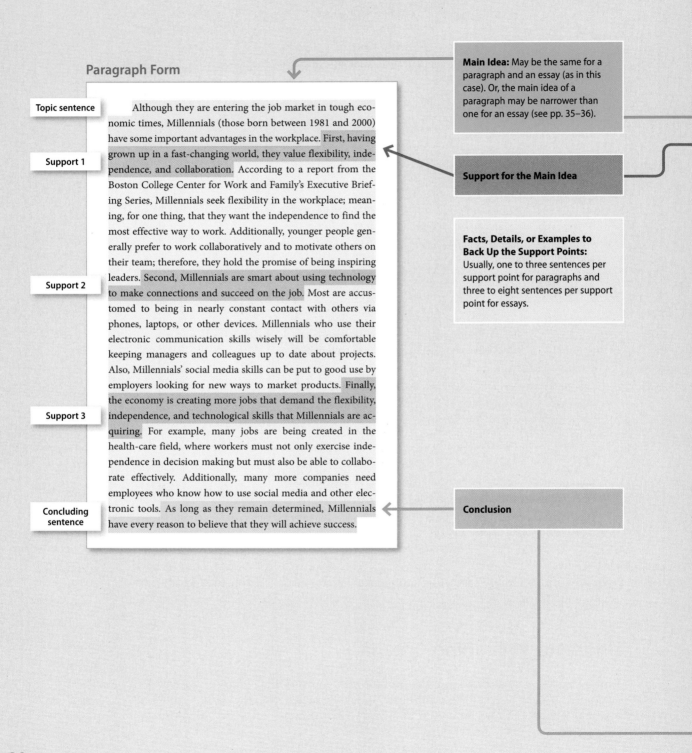

Paragraph Form

Topic sentence

Although they are entering the job market in tough economic times, Millennials (those born between 1981 and 2000) have some important advantages in the workplace. First, having grown up in a fast-changing world, they value flexibility, independence, and collaboration. According to a report from the Boston College Center for Work and Family's Executive Briefing Series, Millennials seek flexibility in the workplace; meaning, for one thing, that they want the independence to find the most effective way to work. Additionally, younger people generally prefer to work collaboratively and to motivate others on their team; therefore, they hold the promise of being inspiring leaders. Second, Millennials are smart about using technology to make connections and succeed on the job. Most are accustomed to being in nearly constant contact with others via phones, laptops, or other devices. Millennials who use their electronic communication skills wisely will be comfortable keeping managers and colleagues up to date about projects. Also, Millennials' social media skills can be put to good use by employers looking for new ways to market products. Finally, the economy is creating more jobs that demand the flexibility, independence, and technological skills that Millennials are acquiring. For example, many jobs are being created in the health-care field, where workers must not only exercise independence in decision making but must also be able to collaborate effectively. Additionally, many more companies need employees who know how to use social media and other electronic tools. As long as they remain determined, Millennials have every reason to believe that they will achieve success.

Support 1

Support 2

Support 3

Concluding sentence

Main Idea: May be the same for a paragraph and an essay (as in this case). Or, the main idea of a paragraph may be narrower than one for an essay (see pp. 35–36).

Support for the Main Idea

Facts, Details, or Examples to Back Up the Support Points: Usually, one to three sentences per support point for paragraphs and three to eight sentences per support point for essays.

Conclusion

Essay Form

Introductory paragraph

1

Fairly often, I hear older people saying that Millennials (those born between 1981 and 2000) are spoiled, self-centered individuals who have much less to contribute to the workplace than previous generations did. Based on my own experiences an **Thesis statement** I must disagree. Although they are entering the job market in tough economic times, Millennials have some important advantages in the workpla **Topic sentence 1**

First, having grown up in a fast-changing world, they value flexibility, independence, and collaboration. Unlike their parents and grandparents, Millennials never knew a world without personal computers, and the youngest of them never knew a world without the Internet or ever-changing models of smartphones. They are used to rapid change, and most of them have learned to adapt to it. Consequently, Millennials, for the most part, expect workplaces to adapt to them. According to a report from the Boston College Center for Work and Family's Executive Briefing Series (EBS), Millennials seek flexibility in the workplace—for example, in when and where they work. This attitude

2

does not mean that they are looking out for themselves alone. Instead, they want the independence to find the most effective and productive way to work. Additionally, according to the EBS report, Millennials are more likely than older workers to reject old-fashioned business hierarchies in which managers tell lower-ranking employees what to do, and there is no give-and-take. In general, younger people prefer to work collaboratively and to do what they can to motivate others on their team; therefore, they hold the promise of being inspiring leaders. **Topic sentence 2**

Second, Millennials are smart about using technology to make connections and succeed on the job. Most of them are accustomed to being in nearly constant contact with others via phones, laptops, or other devices. Although some people fear that **Support paragraphs** nectedness can be a distraction in the workplace, these technologies can be used productively and allow effective multitasking. For instance, over the course of a day, Millennials who have learned to use their electronic communication skills wisely will be comfortable

3

keeping managers and colleagues up to date about projects and responding to questions and requests as they arise. Furthermore, most Millennials are open to continuing such electronic exchanges during evenings and weekends if they feel they are collaborating with colleagues to meet an important goal. Also, many Millennials are skilled in using social media to reach out to and remain connected with others; in fact, some people refer to them as "the Facebook generation." Employers can put these skills to good use as they look for new ways to market their products and find new customers. **Topic sentence 3**

Finally, the economy is creating more jobs that demand the flexibility, independence, and technological skills that Millennials are acquiring. For example, many jobs are being created in the health-care field, where workers, such as nurses and physician assistants, must not only exercise independence in decision making but must also be able to collaborate effectively. Additionally, many more companies need employees who know how to use social media and

4

other electronic tools for marketing purposes. Similarly, Millennials with social media skills may have an advantage in finding work in the marketing and advertising industries specifically. There is also always a need for independent-minded people to create new businesses and innovations. Thus, Millennials can play a valuable role in helping the economy grow.

As long as they remain determined and confident, Millennials have every reason to believe that they will achieve career success. According to the EBS report and other sources, meaningful, challenging work is more important to this generation than having a high salary. In the long term, workers with those types of values will always be in demand. **Concluding paragraph**

The following sample rubric shows you some of the elements you may be graded on. Many rubrics include how each element is weighted; because that practice differs among instructors and courses, the example does not specify percentages of importance or points.

Sample Rubric

Element	Grading criteria	Point range
Appropriateness	• Did the student follow the assignment directions?	0–5
Main idea	• Does the paper clearly state a strong main idea in a complete sentence?	0–10
Support	• Is the main idea developed with specific support, including specific details and examples? • Is enough support presented to make the main idea evident to the reader? • Is all the support directly related to the main idea?	0–10
Organization	• Is the writing logically organized? • Does the student use transitions (e.g., *also, for example, sometimes,* and *so on*) to move the reader from one point to another?	0–10
Conclusion	• Does the conclusion remind the reader of the main point? • Does it make an observation based on the support?	0–5
Grammar	• Is the writing free of the four most serious errors? (See Chapters 16–19) • Is the sentence structure clear? • Does the student choose words that clearly express his or her meaning? • Are the words spelled correctly? • Is the punctuation correct?	0–10

The paragraph that follows shows how rubrics are applied to a piece of writing. For a key to the correction symbols used, see the Useful Editing and Proofreading Marks chart at the back of this book.

Assignment: Write a paragraph about something you enjoy doing. Make sure you give enough details about the activity so that a reader who knows little about it will have an idea of why you enjoy it.

Paragraph

In my spare time, I enjoy talking with my friend Karen. I know Karen since we ten, *tense*   *tense*
so we have growed up together and been through many things. Like a sister. We can
tense   *frag*

talk about anything. Sometimes we talk about problems. Money problems, problems
frag   *frag*
with men. When I was in a difficult relationship, for example. Now we both have
                                                          sp   *sp*   *tense*
children and we talk about how to raise them. Things are diffrent then when we kids.
                                                wc
Talking with a good friend helps me make good decisions and patience. Especially
              frag   *punc*
now that my son is a teenager. We also talk about fun things, like what were going
         run-on
to do on the weekend, what clothes we buy. We tell each other good jokes and make

each other laugh. These conversations are as important as talking about problems.

Analysis of paragraph: This paragraph would receive an average grade (not an A or B), for the following reasons.

Teaching tip Have students work together to rewrite the paragraph to improve the score. Have them look closely at the comments on the rubric and to think about what exactly needs to be changed or edited to improve the paper. Then, have groups either switch papers and grade them or grade them together as a group using the same rubric, discussing why each paper would earn the grade it did.

Sample Rubric

Element	Grading criteria	Point: Comment
Appropriateness	• Did the student follow the assignment directions?	5/5: Yes.
Main idea	• Does the paper clearly state a strong main idea in a complete sentence?	10/10: Yes.
Support	• Is the main idea developed with specific support, including specific details and examples? • Is there enough support to make the main idea evident to the reader? • Is all the support directly related to the main idea?	5/10: The paragraph has some support and detail, but it could use more.
Organization	• Is the writing logically organized? • Does the student use transitions (e.g., *also, for example, sometimes,* and *so on*) to move the reader from one point to another?	6/10: The student uses a few transitions (*sometimes, when, for example, now*).
Conclusion	• Does the conclusion remind the reader of the main idea? • Does it make an observation based on the support?	3/5: The conclusion relates back to the main idea, but the observation is weak.
Grammar	• Is the writing free of the four most serious errors? (See Chapters 16–19.) • Is the sentence structure clear? • Does the student choose words that clearly express his or her meaning? • Are the words spelled correctly? • Is the punctuation correct?	6/10: The writing has some major grammar errors. **TOTAL POINTS: 35/50**

Teaching tip If you are interested in having your students keep writing portfolios, see the *Instructor's Manual for Real Writing*.

PRACTICE 3 **Analyzing the paragraph**

Referring to the sample paragraph, answer the following questions.
Some answers will vary. Possible answers are shown.

1. Which sentence is the topic sentence? *Sentence 1*

2. Underline some of the added details that make Paragraph 3 stronger than the first two paragraphs, and note those details here. *Answers will vary.*

3. Circle the transitions, and write them here. *long ago, over the years, when, now, for example, also, throughout*

4. In what way is the last sentence a good concluding sentence? *The topic sentence specifically notes that the author enjoys talking to her friend Karen. The concluding sentence refers back to that statement with a reference to those conversations.*

Chapter Review

1. In your own words, define *audience*. *the person or people who will read what I write*

2. In college, who is your audience likely to be? *my instructors*

3. What are the stages of the writing process? *generating ideas, drafting, revising, editing*

4. Think of other courses in which you have written papers or taken tests. What purposes has that writing had? *showing knowledge of the material, arguing for my point of view*

5. What are four of the elements often evaluated in rubrics? *appropriateness, main idea, support, organization, conclusion, grammar*

REFLECTING ON THE JOURNEY

Skills Learned

Now that you've completed the chapter, share what you've learned about each skill by completing the following chart.

Skill	What I learned about this skill
Identify a specific audience	
Identify a specific purpose	
Consider the needs and expectations of the audience	
Use a clear writing process to develop and revise a draft	
Make a clear, definite point	
Provide support that shows, explains, or proves the main idea	
Read and understand a rubric	

3

Finding Your Topic and Writing Your Thesis Statement

Making a Point

Learning Objectives

Chapter Goal: Learn how to identify, narrow, and explore your topic and then learn how to write thesis statements and topic sentences.

Tools to Achieve the Goal:

- Understand What a Topic Is (p. 45)
- Practice Narrowing a Topic (p. 45)
- Practice Exploring Your Topic (p. 48)
- Write Your Own Topic and Ideas (p. 52)
- Understand What a Topic Sentence and a Thesis Statement Are (p. 52)
- Practice Developing a Good Topic Sentence or Thesis Statement (p. 55)
- Write Your Own Topic Sentence or Thesis Statement (p. 64)

READING ROADMAP

Key Terms

Skim Chapter 3 before reading. Find these words or terms in **bold** type. Put a check mark next to each once you locate it.

_____ topic	_____ peer review
_____ narrow	_____ clustering
_____ prewriting techniques	_____ mapping
_____ freewriting	_____ main idea
_____ listing	_____ topic sentence
_____ brainstorming	_____ thesis statement
	_____ peer review

Guided Reading for Chapter 3

Fill out the following chart before you begin reading. For each skill, write what you know about the skill and what you would like to know upon completing the chapter. At the end of the chapter, you will be asked to share what you learned about each skill.

Skill	When I have used this skill	What I want to know about this skill
Understand the difference between a topic and a main idea		
Explore and narrow a topic		
Write a thesis statement		
Write topic sentences		

Understand What a Topic Is

A **topic** is who or what you are writing about. It is the subject of your paragraph or essay.

Questions for finding a good topic

- Does this topic interest me? If so, why do I care about it?
- Do I know something about the topic? Do I want to know more?
- Can I get involved with some part of the topic? Is it relevant to my life in some way?
- Is the topic specific enough for the assignment (a paragraph or a short essay)?

Choose one of the following topics or one of your own and focus on one part of it that you are familiar with. (For example, focus on one personal goal or a specific problem of working students that interests you.)

Music/group I like	Sports
Problems of working students	My favorite vacation
An activity/group I am involved in	A personal goal
My proudest moment	A time when I took a big risk
An issue in the news	My ideal job
Relationships	A current trend

PRACTICE 1   **Finding a good topic**

Ask the "Questions for Finding a Good Topic" about the topic you have chosen. If you answer "no" to any of them, keep looking for another topic or modify the topic.

My topic: _Answers will vary._

With the general topic you have chosen in mind, read this chapter and complete all the practices. When you finish the chapter, you will have found a good topic to write about and explored ideas related to it.

Practice Narrowing a Topic

If your instructor assigns a general topic, it may at first seem uninteresting, unfamiliar, or too general. It is up to you to find a good, specific topic based on the general one. Whether the topic is your own or assigned, you next need to narrow and explore it. To **narrow** a general topic, focus on the smaller parts of it until you find one that is interesting and specific.

LaunchPadSolo

Visit **LaunchPad Solo for Readers and Writers > Writing Process** for more tutorials, videos, and practice with prewriting, topics, and main ideas.

Teaching tip To give students an example of what narrowing a topic is like, use a camera analogy. The general topic is similar to using a wide-angle lens. Narrowing it is like zooming in closer so that you can examine or focus on smaller elements of your subject.

Here are some ways to narrow a general topic.

DIVIDE IT INTO SMALLER CATEGORIES

THINK OF SPECIFIC EXAMPLES FROM YOUR LIFE

General Topic **Crime**

Stolen identities (how does it happen?)

When I had my wallet stolen by two kids (how? what happened?)

The e-mail scam that my grandmother lost money in (how did it work?)

General Topic **Social media**

Twitter (which feeds do I follow regularly? what do I get from them?)

Facebook (what features are fun or useful? what feels like a waste of time?)

Instagram (why do people feel the need to document their every move with pictures and post them online?)

THINK OF SPECIFIC EXAMPLES FROM CURRENT EVENTS

General Topic **Job-creation ideas**

Tax breaks for businesses

Training of future entrepreneurs in growth areas, like solar or wind energy

A special fund for public projects that will employ many people

General Topic **Heroism**

The guy who pulled a stranger from a burning car

My aunt, who volunteers at a homeless shelter for ten hours a week

Teaching tip Instructor James Grenier offers this advice to students: "Begin with ideas." As students start working on a paper, you might share this quotation with them. Alternatively, read this reflection by E. L. Doctorow: "Writing is an exploration. You start from nothing and learn as you go."

QUESTION YOUR ASSUMPTIONS

Questioning assumptions—an important part of critical thinking (see Chapter 1)—can be a good way to narrow a topic. First, identify any assumptions you have about your topic. Then, question them, playing "devil's advocate"; in other words, imagine what someone with a different point of view might say. For example, imagine that your general topic is the pros or cons of letting kids play video games.

Possible assumptions	Questions
Video game pros: Kids get rewarded with good scores for staying focused. → Video games can teach some useful skills. →	Does staying focused on a video game mean that a kid will stay focused on homework or in class? Like what? How am I defining "useful"?
Video game cons: They make kids more violent. → They have no real educational value. →	Is there really any proof for that? What do experts say? Didn't my niece say that some video game helped her learn to read?

Next, ask yourself what assumptions and questions interest you the most. Then, focus on those interests.

When you have found a promising topic for a paragraph or essay, be sure to test it by using the Questions for Finding a Good Topic at the beginning of this chapter. You may need to narrow and test your ideas several times before you find a topic that will work for the assignment.

A topic for an essay can be a little broader than one for a paragraph because essays are longer than paragraphs and allow you to develop more ideas. But be careful: Most of the extra length in an essay should come from developing ideas in more depth (giving more examples and details, explaining what you mean), not from covering a broader topic.

Read the following examples of how a general topic was narrowed to a more specific topic for an essay and an even more specific topic for a paragraph.

Teaching tip Have students work in small groups to identify and question each other's assumptions.

General topic		Narrowed essay topic		Narrowed paragraph topic
Internships	→	How internships can help you get a job	→	One or two important things you can learn from an internship
Social media	→	Popularity of social media among preteens	→	Should there be an age limit to use social media?
A personal goal	→	Getting healthy	→	Eating the right foods
A great vacation	→	A family camping trip	→	What I learned on our family camping trip to Michigan

Teaching tip Give students examples of questions they might be asked that are too "big" to answer in a paragraph or essay. Have them figure out how to narrow the question or assignment.

PRACTICE 2	**Narrowing a general topic**

Use one of the four methods on page 47 to narrow your topic. Then, ask yourself the Questions for Finding a Good Topic. Write your narrowed topic below.

My narrowed topic: *Answers will vary.*

_____

Practice Exploring Your Topic

Tip Scholar and writer Mina Shaughnessy said that a writer "gets below the surface of a topic." When it comes to exploring a topic, what do you think getting "below the surface" means?

Prewriting techniques can give you ideas at any time during your writing: to find a topic, to get ideas for what you want to say about it, and to support your ideas. Ask yourself: What interests me about this topic? What do I know? What do I want to say? Then, use one or more of the prewriting techniques to find the answers. No one uses all those techniques; writers choose the ones that work best for them.

Prewriting Techniques

- Freewriting
- Listing/brainstorming
- Discussing
- Clustering/mapping
- Using the Internet
- Keeping a journal

When prewriting, your goal is to come up with as many ideas as possible. Do not say, "Oh, that's stupid" or "That won't work." Just get your brain working by writing down all the possibilities.

A student, Chelsea Wilson, was assigned to write a short essay. She chose to write on the general topic of a personal goal, which she narrowed to "Getting a college degree." The following pages show how she used the first five prewriting techniques to explore her topic.

Freewriting

Tip If you are writing on a computer, try a kind of freewriting called "invisible writing." Turn the monitor off, or adjust the screen so that you cannot see what you are typing. Then, write quickly for five minutes without stopping. After five minutes, read what you have written. You may be surprised by the ideas that you can generate this way.

Freewriting is like having a conversation with yourself, on paper. To freewrite, just start writing everything you can think of about your topic. Write nonstop for five minutes. Do not go back and cross anything out, and do not worry about using correct grammar or spelling; just write. Here is Chelsea's freewriting:

> So I know I want to get a college degree even though sometimes I wonder if I ever can make it because it's so hard with work and my two-year-old daughter and no money and a car that needs work. I can't take more than two courses at a time and even then I hardly get a chance to sleep if I want to do any of the assignments or study. But I have to think I'll get a better job because this one at the restaurant is driving me nuts and doesn't pay much so I have to work a lot with a boss I can't stand and still wonder how I'm gonna pay the bills. I know life can be better if I can just manage to become a nurse. I'll make more money and can live anywhere I want because everyplace needs nurses. I won't have to work at a job where I am not respected by anyone. I want respect, I know I'm hardworking and smart and good with people and deserve better than this. So does my daughter. No one in my family has ever graduated from college even though my sister took two courses, but then she stopped. I know I can do this, I just have to make a commitment to do it and not look away.

Listing/Brainstorming

Listing (or **brainstorming**) is when you list all the ideas about your topic that you can think of. Write as many as you can in five minutes without stopping.

GETTING A COLLEGE DEGREE

want a better life for myself and my daughter

want to be a nurse and help care for people

make more money

not have to work so many hours

could live where I want in a nicer place

good future and benefits like health insurance

get respect

proud of myself, achieve, show everyone

be a professional, work in a clean place

Discussing

Many people find it helpful to discuss ideas with another person before they write. As they talk, they get more ideas and immediate feedback.

If you and your discussion partner both have writing assignments, first explore one person's topic and then explore the other's. The person whose topic is being explored is the interviewee; the other person is the interviewer. The interviewer should ask questions about anything that seems unclear and should let the interviewee know what sounds interesting. In addition, the interviewer should identify and try to question any assumptions the interviewee seems to be making (see page 46). The interviewee should give thoughtful answers and keep an open mind. He or she should also take notes.

Part of learning to be a successful writer is learning how to become a part of a writing community. Most composition classes will use a process called peer review at some point. **Peer review** asks a fellow student to read your paper and respond as a reader and writer, but it can also occur without a finished paper. To create a successful peer review experience, keep the following in mind:

- Know what questions you want to ask your peer. Try to avoid simple yes or no questions because they may not give you enough information to move forward in your writing process.

- Don't feel shy about asking for help. If you don't understand something or you are having trouble with something, ask about it during the peer review process. Your peers may have the same writing assignment that you do, so they may be able to explain it to you in a way that makes more sense. If not, you may feel better knowing someone else is also confused and the two of you can ask for clarification from the instructor.

- When responding to another person's paper, avoid being overly harsh and critical with your word choices. The purpose is to give helpful feedback in a constructive manner. However, you should also avoid being too general or too positive. Telling other writers that "everything looks good" doesn't help them improve their paper.

- Most important, when you receive feedback on your paper or your ideas, try to think about them objectively. It is up to you what ideas you choose to use or how you want to revise or approach your assignment. Peer review is a process meant to help you and give you an additional set of eyes.

Tip If you find that talking about your ideas with someone is a good way to get going, you might want to ask another student to be your regular partner and discuss ideas before beginning any paragraph or essay assignment.

By keeping these factors in mind, the peer review process can be beneficial for all involved and help create a supportive writing community within the classroom and beyond.

> **PRACTICE 3**   **Exploring your narrowed topic**
>
> Use two or three prewriting techniques to explore your narrowed topic.

Clustering/Mapping

Tip For online mapping tools, visit **http://bubbl.us**.

Teaching tip A clustering form for students is provided in the *Instructor's Manual for Real Writing*.

Clustering, also called **mapping**, is like listing except that you arrange your ideas visually. Start by writing your narrowed topic in the center. Then, answer the following questions around the narrowed topic: Why? What interests me? and What do I want to say? Using Chelsea's clustering below as a model, write three answers to these questions. Keep branching out from the ideas until you feel you have fully explored your topic. Note that when Chelsea filled in "Why?" "What interests me?" and "What do I want to say?" she had lots of reasons and ideas that she could use in her writing assignment.

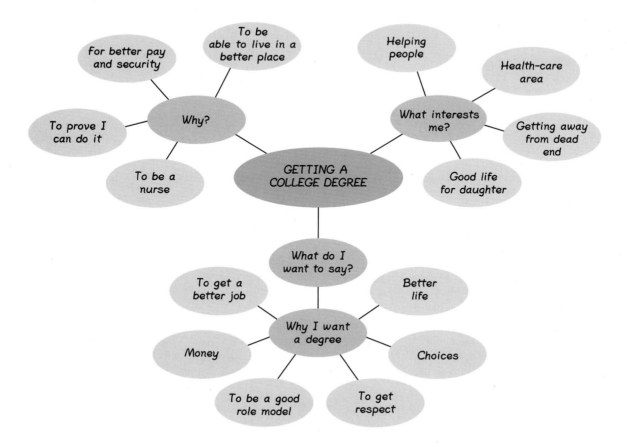

Using the Internet

Go to www.google.com and type in specific key words about your topic. The search will provide more results than you can use, but it will help you with ideas for your paper. Be sure to make your search terms as specific as possible so that the results are targeted and relevant to your topic. For example, Chelsea typed in "reasons to get a college degree" and got lots of information about aspects of her topic that she did not know much about, such as what a college degree is worth. Make notes about important or useful ideas you get from the Internet.

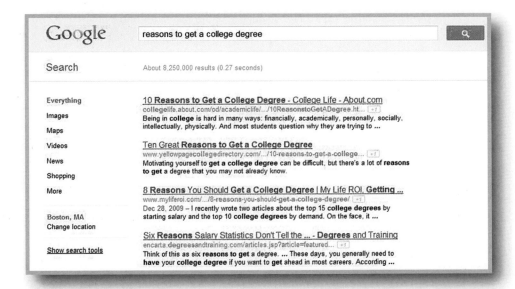

Keeping a Journal

Setting aside a few minutes on a regular schedule to write in a journal will give you a great source of ideas when you need them. What you write does not need to be long or formal. You can use a journal in several ways:

- To record and explore your personal thoughts and feelings
- To comment on things that happen, to you personally or in politics, in your neighborhood, at work, in college, and so on
- To explore situations you do not understand (as you write, you may figure them out)
- To keep track of your opinions on movies you have seen, tv shows you watch, music you've listened to, or books you have read.

Teaching tip For tips on helping students keep journals, see the *Instructor's Manual for Real Writing*.

One student, Jack, did all these things in the following journal entry.

Tip If you start keeping a journal, you might use some of the strategies described by writer Joan Didion. She says, "I write entirely to find out what I'm thinking, what I'm looking at, what I see and what it means. What I want and what I fear."

> *Been feeling a little confused about school lately. Doing OK in my classes and still liking the construction tech program. But having some doubts. Elena, another student in my English class, is studying to be a solar tech in a new program at the school. She's going to learn how to install and repair solar energy systems at a facility near campus, and that's pretty cool. Solar seems kind of sci-fi, and I love sci-fi movies. But seriously I'm truly interested in the technology, and some of the skills I've been learning in construction tech would probably transfer. And maybe I'd have a better chance of getting a job in solar energy since it's a field that seems to be growing? Not sure, but something to investigate. Bottom line: I can't get this new idea out of my mind, even though I thought I was sure about construction tech. I guess I'll keep talking with Elena about the solar tech program. And maybe I should meet with one of the instructors in the program? Or visit the solar facility?*

Write Your Own Topic and Ideas

You should have both your narrowed topic (recorded in Practice 2) and ideas from your prewriting. Now is the time to make sure your topic and ideas about it are clear. Use the checklist that follows to make sure you have completed this step of the writing process.

CHECKLIST

Evaluating Your Narrowed Topic

☐   This topic interests me.
☐   My narrowed topic is specific.
☐   I can write about it in a paragraph or an essay (whichever you have been assigned).
☐   I have generated some things to say about this topic.

Now that you have focused your topic, you are ready to create a clear and forceful thesis statement and topic sentences.

Understand What a Topic Sentence and a Thesis Statement Are

Every good piece of writing has a **main idea**—what the writer wants to get across to the readers about the topic or the writer's position on that topic. A **topic sentence** (for a paragraph) and a **thesis statement** (for an essay) express the writer's main idea. To see the relationship between the thesis statement of an essay and the topic sentences of paragraphs that support a thesis statement, see the diagram on pages 56–57.

In many paragraphs, the main idea is expressed in either the first or last sentence. In essays, the thesis statement is usually one sentence (often the first or last) in an introductory paragraph that contains several other sentences related to the main idea.

A good topic sentence or thesis statement has several basic features.

Basics of a good topic sentence or thesis statement

- It fits the size of the assignment.
- It states a single main idea or position about a topic.
- It is specific.
- It is something you can show, explain, or prove.
- It is forceful.

ESL tip Some cultures (particularly Asian cultures) avoid making direct points in writing. You may need to explain that in English, the rhetorical convention is that the writer make a clear, direct point. Ask students if writing conventions in their countries approach the main idea differently.

Weak   Giving children chores teaches them responsibility, and I think doing chores as a kid made me a better adult.

[This statement has more than one point (how chores teach responsibility and how they made the writer a better adult); it is not specific (what is "responsibility"? what does it mean to be a "better adult"?); and it is not forceful (the writer says, "I think").]

Good   Giving children chores teaches them the responsibilities of taking care of things and completing assigned tasks.

Being assigned chores as a child helped teach me the important adult skills of teamwork and attention to detail.

One way to write a topic sentence for a paragraph or a thesis statement for an essay is to use this basic formula as a start:

Narrowed topic   +   Main idea/Position   =   Topic sentence or Thesis statement

The tutoring center has helped me improve my writing.

If you have trouble coming up with a main idea or position, look back over the prewriting you did. For example, when the student Chelsea Wilson looked over her prewriting about getting a college degree (see pp. 48–50), she realized that several times she had mentioned the idea of more options for employment, living places, and chances to go on and be a nurse. She could also have chosen to focus on the topic of respect or on issues relating to her young daughter, but she was most drawn to write about the idea of *options*. Here is how she stated her main idea:

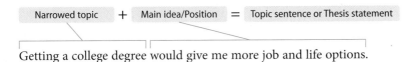

Narrowed topic   +   Main idea/Position   =   Topic sentence or Thesis statement

Getting a college degree would give me more job and life options.

PRACTICE 4   **Finding the topic sentence and main idea**

Read the paragraph that follows, and underline the topic sentence. In the spaces below the paragraph, identify the narrowed topic and the main idea.

A recent survey reported that employers consider communication skills more critical to success than technical skills. Employees can learn technical skills on the job and practice them every day. But they need to bring well-developed communication skills to the job. They need to be able to make themselves understood to colleagues, both in speech and in writing. They need to be able to work cooperatively as part of a team. Employers cannot take time to teach communication skills, but without them an employee will have a hard time.

Narrowed Topic: _communication skills_

Main Idea: _Employers consider communication skills more critical to success than technical skills._

PRACTICE 5   **Identifying topics and main ideas**

In each of the following sentences, underline the topic and double-underline the main idea about the topic.

Example: Rosie the Riveter was the symbol of working women during World War II.

1. Discrimination in the workplace is alive and well.

2. The oldest child in the family is often the most independent and ambitious child.

3. Gadgets created for left-handed people are sometimes poorly designed.

4. Presidential campaigns bring out dirty politics.

5. Walking away from a mortgage has become a financial survival strategy for some homeowners.

6. The magazine _Consumer Reports_ can help you decide which brands or models are the best value.

7. According to one study, dogs might be trained to detect signs of cancer on people's breath.

8. Status symbols are for insecure people.

9. Some song lyrics <u>have serious messages about important social issues.</u>

10. The Puritans came to America to escape religious intolerance, but <u>they were intolerant themselves.</u>

As you get further along in your writing, you may go back several times to revise the topic sentence or thesis statement based on what you learn as you develop your ideas. Look at how one student revised the example sentence on page 53 to make it more detailed:

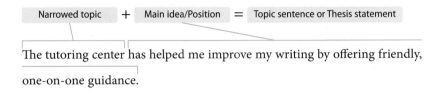

The tutoring center has helped me improve my writing by offering friendly, one-on-one guidance.

Practice Developing a Good Topic Sentence or Thesis Statement

The explanations and practices in this section, organized according to the "basics" described previously, will help you write good topic sentences and thesis statements.

It Fits the Size of the Assignment

As you develop a topic sentence or thesis statement, think carefully about the length of the assignment.

Sometimes, a main-idea statement can be the same for a paragraph or essay.

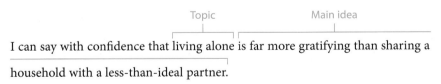

I can say with confidence that living alone is far more gratifying than sharing a household with a less-than-ideal partner.

If the writer had been assigned a paragraph, she might follow the main idea with support sentences and a concluding sentence like those in the "paragraph" diagram on pages 56–57.

If the writer had been assigned an essay, she might develop the same support, but instead of writing single sentences to support her main idea, she would develop each support point into a paragraph. The support sentences she wrote in a paragraph might be topic sentences for support paragraphs. (For more on providing support, see Chapter 4.)

Often, however, a topic sentence for a paragraph is much narrower than a thesis statement for an essay, simply because a paragraph is shorter and allows less development of ideas.

Relationship between Paragraphs and Essays

For more on the important features of writing, see the Four Basics of Good Writing on page 32.

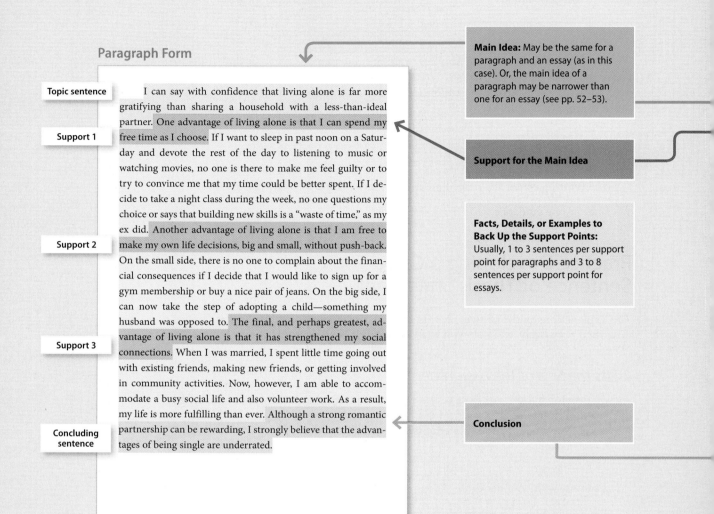

Paragraph Form

Topic sentence	I can say with confidence that living alone is far more gratifying than sharing a household with a less-than-ideal partner. One advantage of living alone is that I can spend my free time as I choose. If I want to sleep in past noon on a Saturday and devote the rest of the day to listening to music or watching movies, no one is there to make me feel guilty or to try to convince me that my time could be better spent. If I decide to take a night class during the week, no one questions my choice or says that building new skills is a "waste of time," as my ex did. Another advantage of living alone is that I am free to make my own life decisions, big and small, without push-back. On the small side, there is no one to complain about the financial consequences if I decide that I would like to sign up for a gym membership or buy a nice pair of jeans. On the big side, I can now take the step of adopting a child—something my husband was opposed to. The final, and perhaps greatest, advantage of living alone is that it has strengthened my social connections. When I was married, I spent little time going out with existing friends, making new friends, or getting involved in community activities. Now, however, I am able to accommodate a busy social life and also volunteer work. As a result, my life is more fulfilling than ever. Although a strong romantic partnership can be rewarding, I strongly believe that the advantages of being single are underrated.

Support 1

Support 2

Support 3

Concluding sentence

Main Idea: May be the same for a paragraph and an essay (as in this case). Or, the main idea of a paragraph may be narrower than one for an essay (see pp. 52–53).

Support for the Main Idea

Facts, Details, or Examples to Back Up the Support Points: Usually, 1 to 3 sentences per support point for paragraphs and 3 to 8 sentences per support point for essays.

Conclusion

Essay Form

1

As a young woman, I saw being single as a temporary—and undesirable—condition. When, at twenty-four, I married, I considered myself extremely lucky. That was until I spent years in an increasingly unsatisfying relationship that ultimately ended in divorce. Since the divorce, however, my life h **Thesis statement** for the better in many ways. I can now say with confidence that living alone is far more gratifying than sharing a household with a less-than-ideal **Topic sentence 1**

One advantage of living alone is that I can spend my free time as I choose. If I want to sleep in past noon on a Saturday and devote the rest of the day to listening to music or watching movies, no one is there to make me feel guilty or to try to convince me that my time could be better spent. If I decide to take a night class during the week, no one questions my choice or says that building new skills is a "waste of time," as my ex did. Also, when I am able to take vacation days, I can spend them relaxing at home, visiting out-of-state family members, or doing something more adventurous. In other words, I can set my own agenda, all the time.

2

Another advantage of living alone is **Topic sentence 2** free to make my own life decisions, big and small, without push-back. On the small side, there is no one to complain about the financial consequences if I decide that I would like to sign up for a gym membership or buy a nice pair of jeans. On the big **Support paragraphs** now take the step of adopting a child—som husband was opposed to. I realize that making all my own decisions requires personal responsibility and the ability to take some risks. But, to me, the benefits of independence far outweigh the challenges. **Topic sentence 3**

The final, and perhaps greatest, advantage of living alone is that it has strengthened my social connections. When I was married, I spent little time going out with existing friends, making new friends, or getting involved in community activities. If I did not spend nearly all of my free time with my husband, he would complain. Now, however, I am able to accommodate a busy social life and also volunteer work in my community. As a result, my life is more fulfilling than ever.

3

Although a strong romantic partnership can be rewarding, I strongly believe that the advantages of being single are underrated. Consequentl **Concluding paragraph** like to offer one piece of advice to partne Do not feel sorry for your single friends. One day, you may join their ranks and find that you have never been happier.

Consider how one general topic could be narrowed into an essay topic and into an even more specific paragraph topic.

General topic		Narrowed essay topic		Narrowed paragraph topic
Internships	→	How internships can help you get a job	→	One or two important things you can learn from an internship

Possible thesis statement (essay) — The skills and connections you gain through a summer internship can help you get a good job after graduation.

[The essay would discuss several benefits of internships, describing the various skills they can teach and the professional connections they can offer to interns.]

Possible topic sentence (paragraph) — A summer internship is a good way to test whether a particular career is right for you.

[The paragraph would focus on one benefit of internships: They are a way to test out a career. The paragraph might go on to discuss signs that a certain type of work is or is not passing the test.]

PRACTICE 6   **Writing sentences to fit the assignment**

Using the following example as a guide, write a thesis statement for the narrowed essay topic and a topic sentence for the narrowed paragraph topic.

Example:

Topic: Sports

Narrowed for an essay: Competition in school sports

Narrowed for a paragraph: User fees for school sports

Possible thesis statement (essay): _Competition in school sports has reached dangerous levels._

Possible topic sentence (paragraph): _This year's user fees for participation in school sports are too high._

1. **Topic:** Public service opportunities

   Narrowed for an essay: Volunteering at a homeless shelter

   Narrowed for a paragraph: My first impression of the homeless shelter

   Possible thesis statement (essay): _Answers will vary._

   _____

   Possible topic sentence (paragraph):_____

   _____

2. **Topic:** A personal goal

   Narrowed for an essay: Getting healthy

   Narrowed for a paragraph: Eating the right foods

   Possible thesis statement (essay): _____

   _____

   Possible topic sentence (paragraph): _____

   _____

3. **Topic:** A great vacation

   Narrowed for an essay: A family camping trip

   Narrowed for a paragraph: A lesson I learned on our family camping trip

   Possible thesis statement (essay): _____

   _____

   Possible topic sentence (paragraph): _____

   _____

Teaching tip When students write on the computer, have them use boldface type for their topic sentence or thesis statement. Boldface type helps you see what they consider their main idea and helps them stay focused as they provide support.

Some topic sentences or thesis statements are too broad for either a short essay or a paragraph. A main idea that is too broad is impossible to show, explain, or prove within the space of a paragraph or short essay.

Too broad   Art is important.

[How could a writer possibly support such a broad concept in a paragraph or essay?]

Narrower   Art instruction for young children has surprising benefits.

A topic sentence or thesis statement that is too narrow leaves the writer with little to write about. There is little to show, explain, or prove.

Too narrow   Buy rechargeable batteries.

[OK, so now what?]

Broader   Choosing rechargeable batteries over conventional batteries is one action you can take to reduce your effect on the environment.

PRACTICE 7   **Writing topic sentences that are neither too broad nor too narrow**

In the following five practice items, three of the topic sentences are either too broad or too narrow, and two of them are OK. In the space to the left of each item, write "B" for too broad, "N" for too narrow, or "OK" for just right.

Rewrite the three weak sentences to make them broader or narrower as needed.

Example: ___B___ **Life can be tough for soldiers when they come home.**

We are not providing our returning soldiers with enough help in readjusting to

civilian life.

1. ___N___ I take public transportation to work.
   Answers will vary.

   _____

2. ___OK___ Because of state and national education budget cuts, schools are having to lay off teachers and cut important programs.

   _____

   _____

3. ___B___ College is challenging.

   _____

   _____

4. ___B___ I would like to be successful in life.

   _____

   _____

5. ___OK___ Having a positive attitude improves people's ability to function, improves their interactions with others, and reduces stress.

   _____

   _____

It Contains a Single Main Idea

Your topic sentence or thesis statement should focus on only one main idea. Two main ideas can split and weaken the focus of the writing.

TOPIC SENTENCE WITH TWO MAIN IDEAS

High schools should sell healthy food instead of junk food, and they should start later in the morning.

The two main ideas are underlined. Although both are good main ideas, together they split both the writer's and the readers' focus. The writer would need to give reasons to support each idea, and the ideas are completely different.

TOPIC SENTENCE WITH A SINGLE MAIN IDEA

High schools should sell healthy food instead of junk food.

OR

High schools <u>should start later in the morning</u>.

> **PRACTICE 8**   **Writing sentences with a single main idea**
>
> In each of the following sentences, underline the main idea(s). Identify the sentences that have more than a single main idea by marking an *X* in the space provided to the left of that item. Put a check mark (✓) next to sentences that have a single main idea.

Example: <u>X</u> **Shopping at secondhand stores is a fun way to save money,** and <u>you can meet all kinds of interesting people as you shop</u>.

1. <u>✓</u> My younger sister, the baby of the family, <u>was the most adventurous of my four siblings</u>.

2. <u>X</u> <u>Servicing hybrid cars is a growing part of automotive technology education</u>, and <u>dealers cannot keep enough hybrids in stock</u>.

3. <u>X</u> <u>My brother, Bobby, is incredibly creative</u>, and <u>he takes in stray animals</u>.

4. <u>X</u> <u>Pets can actually bring families together</u>, and <u>they require lots of care</u>.

5. <u>✓</u> Unless people conserve voluntarily, <u>we will deplete our water supply</u>.

It Is Specific

A good topic sentence or thesis statement gives readers specific information so that they know exactly what the writer's main idea is.

General   Students are often overwhelmed.

[How are students overwhelmed?]

Specific   Working college students have to learn how to juggle many responsibilities.

One way to make sure your topic sentence or thesis statement is specific is to make it a preview of what you are planning to say in the rest of the paragraph or essay. Just be certain that every point you preview is closely related to your main idea.

Preview: Working college students have to learn how to juggle many responsibilities: doing a good job at work, getting to class regularly and on time, being alert in class, and doing the homework assignments.

Preview: I have a set routine every Saturday morning that includes sleeping late, going to the gym, and shopping for food.

| PRACTICE 9 | **Writing sentences that are specific** |

In the space below each item, revise the sentence to make it more specific. There is no one correct answer. As you read the sentences, think about what would make them more understandable to you if you were about to read a paragraph or essay on the topic.

Example: Marriage can be a wonderful thing. *Marriage to the right person can add love, companionship, and support to life.*

1. My job is horrible.
   Answers will vary.

2. Working with others is rewarding.

3. I am a good worker.

4. This place could use a lot of improvement.

5. My science class was challenging.

It Is an Idea You Can Show, Explain, or Prove

If a main idea is so obvious that it does not need support or if it states a simple fact, you will not have much to say about it.

Obvious   The Toyota Prius is a top-selling car.

Many people like to take vacations in the summer.

Revised   Because of rising gas costs and concerns about the environmental impact of carbon emissions, the Toyota Prius is a top-selling car.

The vast and incredible beauty of the Grand Canyon draws crowds of visitors each summer.

Fact   Employment of medical lab technicians is projected to increase by 14 percent between 2008 and 2018.

Three hundred cities worldwide have bicycle-sharing programs.

Revised   Population growth and the creation of new types of medical tests mean the employment of lab technicians should increase by 14 percent between 2008 and 2018.

Bicycle-sharing programs are popular, but funding them long-term can be challenging for cities with tight budgets.

PRACTICE 10   **Writing sentences with ideas you can show, explain, or prove**

Revise the following sentences so that they contain an idea you could show, explain, or prove.

Example: Leasing a car is popular.

Leasing a car has many advantages over buying one.

1. Texting while driving is dangerous.

    Answers will vary.

2. My monthly rent is $750.

    _____

3. Health insurance rates rise every year.

    _____

4. Many people in this country work for minimum wage.

    _____

5. Technology is becoming increasingly important.

    _____

It Is Forceful

A good topic sentence or thesis statement is forceful. Do not say you *will* make a point; just make it. Do not say "I think." Just state your point.

Weak   In my opinion, everyone should exercise.

Forceful   Everyone should exercise to reduce stress, maintain a healthy weight, and feel better overall.

Weak   I think student fees are much too high.

Forceful   Student fees need to be explained and justified.

PRACTICE 11   **Writing forceful sentences**

Rewrite each of the following sentences to make them more forceful. Also, add details to make the sentences more specific. *Answers will vary. Possible answers given.*

Example: Jason's Market is the best.

Jason's Market is clean, organized, and filled with quality products.

1. I will prove that drug testing in the workplace is an invasion of privacy.

    Drug testing in the workplace is an invasion of privacy.

2. This school does not allow cell phones in class. _Because cell phones are disruptive, this school does not allow them in class._

3. I strongly think I deserve a raise. _I deserve a raise based on my strong performance over the past year._

4. Nancy should be the head of the Students' Association. _Because she is hardworking and concerned about campus issues, Nancy should be the head of the Students' Association._

5. I think my neighborhood is nice. _My neighborhood is safe, close to stores, and diverse._

Write Your Own Topic Sentence or Thesis Statement

If you have worked through this chapter, you should have a good sense of how to write a topic sentence or thesis statement that includes the five features of a good one (see p. 53).

Before writing your own topic sentence or thesis statement, consider the process that Chelsea Wilson used. First, she narrowed her topic.

General Topic: _a personal goal_
Narrowed topic (for a paragraph): _why I want to get a nursing degree_
Narrowed topic (for an essay): _the many benefits of getting a college degree_

Then, she did prewriting to get ideas about her topic.

For a paragraph: _why I want to get a nursing degree_
   make more money
   get a better job
   become a respected professional
   live where I want
For an essay: _the many benefits of getting a college degree_
   get a job as a nurse
   make more money
   be a good role model for my daughter
   be proud of myself

Next, she was ready to write the statement of her main idea.

Topic sentence (paragraph): _My goal is to get a nursing degree._
Thesis statement (essay): _My goal is to get a college degree._

Finally, Chelsea revised this statement to make it more forceful.

> **Topic sentence:** *My goal is to become a registered nurse.*
>
> **Thesis statement:** *I am committed to getting a college degree because it will give me many good job and life options.*

You may want to change the wording of your topic sentence or thesis statement later, but following a sequence like Chelsea's should start you off with a good basic statement of your main idea.

WRITING ASSIGNMENT

Write a topic sentence or thesis statement using the narrowed topic you developed earlier in the chapter or one of the following topics (which you will have to narrow).

Community service	A holiday or family tradition
A controversial issue	A strong belief
Dressing for success	Bullying
Movies	Exciting experiences
Saving money	Juggling many responsibilities
Interviewing for jobs	Friendship
Music	Learning/teaching cooking skills

Teaching tip Even if you aren't reading a student's entire first draft, it always helps to check the topic sentence or thesis statement because you can clear up numerous potential problems before you have to give a grade.

After writing your topic sentence or thesis statement, complete the checklist that follows.

CHECKLIST

Evaluating Your Main Idea
- ☐ It is a complete sentence.
- ☐ It fits the assignment.
- ☐ It includes my topic and the main idea I want to make about it.
- ☐ It states a single main idea.
- ☐ It is specific.
- ☐ It is something I can show, explain, or prove.
- ☐ It is forceful.

Coming up with a good working topic sentence or thesis statement is the foundation of the writing you will do. Now that you know what you want to say, you are ready to learn more about how to show, explain, and prove your main idea to others. The next chapter, "Supporting Your Point," helps you make a strong case, consider what your readers need to know, and provide sufficient details and examples in your paragraph or essay.

Chapter Review

1. What are four questions that can help you find a good topic? _Does it interest me? Do I know something about it? Can I get involved with some part of it? Is it specific enough for the assignment?_

2. How can you narrow a topic that is too broad or general? _Divide the topic into smaller categories, think of specific examples, and question your assumptions._

3. What are some prewriting techniques? _freewriting, listing/brainstorming, discussing, clustering/mapping, using the Internet, keeping a journal_

4. Write for one minute on "Topics I would like to know more about."

5. The main idea of a piece of writing is _what the writer wants to get across to the readers about the topic._

6. One way to write a topic sentence or a thesis statement is to include the narrowed topic and _the main idea/position about the topic._

7. The basics of a good topic sentence or thesis statement are _It fits the size of the assignment. It states a single main idea or position about a topic. It is specific. It is something you can show, explain, or prove. It is forceful._

8. Write for one minute about "What questions I should ask my instructor."

REFLECTING ON THE JOURNEY

Skills Learned

Now that you've completed the chapter, share what you've learned about each skill by completing the following chart.

Skill	What I learned about this skill
Understand the difference between a topic and a main idea	
Explore and narrow a topic	
Write a thesis statement	
Write topic sentences	

Supporting Your Point
Finding Details, Examples, and Facts

Learning Objectives

Chapter Goal: Learn to support your main idea by presenting strong evidence and details.

Tools to Achieve the Goal:
- Key Features of Good Support (p. 68)
- Three Quick Strategies for Generating Support (p. 70)
- Write Your Own Support (p. 72)

READING ROADMAP

Key Terms

Skim Chapter 4 before reading. Find these words or terms in **bold** type. Put a check mark next to each once you locate it.

____ support
____ primary support points
____ secondary support

Guided Reading for Chapter 4

Fill out the following chart before you begin reading. For each skill, write what you know about the skill and what you would like to know upon completing the chapter. At the end of the chapter, you will be asked to share what you learned about each skill.

Skill	When I have used this skill	What I want to know about this skill
Write primary support points		
Write secondary support points		
Generate support		
Relate support directly to the main idea		

Understand What Support Is

Support is the collection of examples, facts, or evidence that shows, explains, or proves your main idea. **Primary support points** are the major ideas that back up your main idea, and **secondary support** gives details to back up your primary support.

Key Features of Good Support

Without support, you *state* the main idea, but you do not *make* the main idea. Consider these unsupported statements:

> The amount shown on my bill is incorrect.
>
> I deserve a raise.
>
> I need a vacation.

The statements may be true, but without good support, they are not convincing. If you sometimes get papers back with the comment "You need to support/develop your ideas," the suggestions in this chapter will help you.

Also, keep in mind that the same point repeated several times is not support. It is just repetition.

Repetition, Not Support	The amount shown on my bill is incorrect. You overcharged me. It didn't cost that much. The total is wrong.
Support	The amount shown on my bill is incorrect. I ordered the bacon-cheeseburger plate, which is $6.99 on the menu. On the bill, the order is correct, but the amount is $16.99.

As you develop support for your main idea, make sure it has these three features.

Tip Showing involves providing visual details or other supporting observations. Explaining involves offering specific examples or illustrating aspects of the main idea. Proving involves providing specific evidence, sometimes from outside sources.

Basics of good support

- It relates directly to your main idea. Remember that the purpose of support is to show, explain, or prove your main idea.
- It considers your readers and what they will need to know.
- It gives readers enough specific details, particularly through examples, so that they can see what you mean.

Support in Paragraphs versus Essays

Again, primary support points are the major ideas that back up your main idea. In paragraphs, your main idea is expressed in a topic sentence. In both paragraphs and essays, it is important to add enough details (secondary support) about the primary support to make the main idea clear to readers.

In the following paragraph, the topic sentence is underlined twice, the primary support is underlined once, and the details for each primary support point are in italics.

When I first enrolled in college, I thought that studying history was a waste of time. <u>But after taking two world history classes, I have come to the conclusion that these courses count for far more than some credit hours in my college record.</u> <u>First, learning about historical events has helped me put important current events in perspective.</u> *For instance, by studying the history of migration around the world, I have learned that immigration has been going on for hundreds of years. In addition, it is common in many countries, not just the United States. I have also learned about ways in which various societies have debated immigration, just as Americans are doing today.* <u>Second, history courses have taught me about the power that individual people can have, even under very challenging circumstances.</u> *I was especially inspired by the story of Toussaint L'Ouverture, a former slave who, in the 1790s, led uprisings in the French colony of Saint-Domingue, transforming it into the independent nation of Haiti. Although L'Ouverture faced difficult odds, he persisted and achieved great things.* <u>The biggest benefit of taking history courses is that they have encouraged me to dig more deeply into subjects than I ever have before.</u> *For a paper about the lasting influence of Anne Frank,[1] I drew on quotations from her famous diary, on biographies about her, and on essays written by noted historians. The research was fascinating, and I loved piecing together the various facts and insights to come to my own conclusions.* To sum up, I have become hooked on history, and I have a feeling that the lessons it teaches me will be relevant far beyond college.

1. **Anne Frank (1929-1945):** a German Jewish girl who fled to the Netherlands with her family after Adolf Hitler, leader of the Nazi Party, became chancellor of Germany. In 1944, Anne and her family were arrested by the Nazis, and she died in a concentration camp the following year.

In an essay, each primary support point, along with its supporting details, is developed into a separate paragraph. (See the diagram on pages 56–57.) Specifically, each underlined point in the previous paragraph could be turned into a topic sentence that would be supported by the italicized details. However, in preparing an essay on the preceding topic, the writer would want to add more details and examples for each primary support point. Here are some possible additions:

- **For primary support point 1:** more connections between history and current events (one idea: the rise and fall of dictators in past societies and in the modern Middle East)

- **For primary support point 2:** more examples of influential historical figures (one idea: the story of Joan of Arc, who, in the fifteenth century, led the French to victories over English armies)

- **For primary support point 3:** more examples of becoming deeply engaged in historical subjects (one idea: fascination with reprinted diaries or letters of World War II soldiers)

Practice Supporting a Main Idea

Generate Support

To generate support for the main idea of a paragraph or essay, try one or more of the following strategies.

Three quick strategies for generating support

1. *Circle an important word or phrase* in your topic sentence (for a paragraph) or thesis statement (for an essay), and write about it for a few minutes. As you work, refer back to your main idea to make sure you're on the right track.

2. *Reread your topic sentence or thesis statement, and write down the first thought you have.* Then, write down your next thought. Keep going.

3. *Use a prewriting technique* (freewriting, listing, discussing, clustering, and so on) while thinking about your main idea and your audience. Write for three to five minutes without stopping.

Teaching tip Emphasize to students that prewriting can help them at every stage of the writing process, whenever they need to develop ideas further or provide more detail.

Teaching tip Have each student write down their topic or main idea on their computer screen or a piece of paper. Then, either have students get up and move from seat to seat or pass around the papers. When they sit down at a new computer or receive the paper, ask them to write down three support points that they might use if this were their own paper. Complete the exercise three or four times. Ask students to return to their seats or to find their paper and read through the responses. Discuss what types of support points others suggested and if they were helpful. Were there good thoughts that the writer didn't originally think about?

> **PRACTICE 1**   **Generating supporting ideas**
>
> Choose one of the following sentences, or your own topic sentence or thesis statement, and use one of the three strategies to generate support just mentioned. Because you will need a good supply of ideas to support your main idea, try to find at least a dozen possible supporting ideas. Keep your answers because you will use them in later practices in this chapter. *Answers will vary.*
>
> 1. Some television shows challenge my way of thinking instead of numb my mind.
>
> 2. Today there is no such thing as a "typical" college student.
>
> 3. Learning happens not only in school but throughout a person's life.
>
> 4. Practical intelligence can't be measured by grades.
>
> 5. I am an excellent candidate for the job.

Select the Best Primary Support

After you have generated possible support, review your ideas; then, select the best ones to use as primary support. Here you take control of your topic, shaping the way readers will see it and the main idea you are making about it. These ideas are *yours*, and you need to sell them to your audience.

The following steps can help.

Tip For a diagram showing the relationship between topic sentences and support in paragraphs, and thesis statements and support in essays, see pages 56–57 of Chapter 3.

1. Carefully read the ideas you have generated.

2. Select three to five primary support points that will be clearest and most convincing to your readers, providing the best examples, facts, and observations to support your main idea. If you are writing a paragraph, these points will become the primary support for your topic sentence. If

you are writing an essay, they will become topic sentences of the individual paragraphs that support your thesis statement.

3. Cross out ideas that are not closely related to your main idea.

4. If you find that you have crossed out most of your ideas and do not have enough left to support your main idea, use one of the three strategies from page 70 to find more.

Teaching tip Remind students that just because they find a point interesting does not necessarily mean they should include it in their writing. It must support their main idea.

> **PRACTICE 2**   **Selecting the best support**
>
> Refer to your response to Practice 1 (p. 70). Of your possible primary support points, choose three to five that you think will best show, explain, or prove your main idea to your readers. Write your three to five points in the space provided.
>
> *Answers will vary.*

Add Secondary Support

Once you have selected your best primary support points, you need to flesh them out for your readers. Do this by adding **secondary support**, specific examples, facts, and observations to back up your primary support points.

> **PRACTICE 3**   **Adding secondary support**
>
> Using your answers to Practice 2, choose three primary support points, and write them in the spaces indicated below. Then, read each of them carefully, and write down at least three supporting details (secondary support) for each one. For examples of secondary support, see the example paragraph on page 69. *Answers will vary.*
>
> Primary support point 1:
>
> _____
>
>   Supporting details: _____
>
> _____
>
> Primary support point 2:
>
> _____
>
>   Supporting details: _____
>
> _____
>
> Primary support point 3:
>
> _____
>
>   Supporting details: _____
>
> _____

Teaching tip Tell students to ask themselves the kinds of questions their readers will ask: Such as? In what way? For example? If their support points answer those questions, readers should understand their main idea.

Write Your Own Support

Before developing your own support for a main idea, look at how Chelsea developed support for her paragraph.

> **Topic sentence:** *My goal is to get a nursing degree.*

First, she did some prewriting (using the listing technique) and selected the best primary support points, while eliminating ones she didn't think she would use.

Primary support points

GETTING AN LPN DEGREE
nurses help people and I want to do that
jobs all over the country
good jobs with decent pay
~~*good setting, clean*~~
a profession, not just a job
opportunity, like RN
bigger place, more money
treated with respect
role model
pride in myself and my work, what I've done
~~*good benefits*~~
~~*nice people to work with*~~
may get paid to take more classes—chance for further professional development
~~*uniform so not lots of money for clothes*~~
~~*I'll be something*~~

Teaching tip Have students first type in possible support and then cut and paste to group it. They can easily move the points around to try new groupings.

Chelsea noticed that some of her notes were related to the same subject, so she arranged them into related clusters, with the smaller points indented under the larger ones.

Organized list of support points

good job
  decent pay
  jobs all over the country
a profession, not just a job
  treated with respect
  opportunity for the future (like RN)
  maybe get paid to take more classes?

pride/achievement
  a job that helps people
  I would take pride in my hard work
  I'd be a role model

Then, she took the notes she made and organized them into primary support and supporting details. Notice how she changed and reorganized some of her smaller points.

Primary support: *Being an LPN is an excellent job.*

> **Supporting details:** *The pay is regular and averages about $40,000 a year.*
>
> *I could afford to move to a bigger and better place with more room for my daughter and work fewer hours.*

Primary support: *Nursing is a profession, not just a job.*

> **Supporting details:** *Nurses help care for people, an important job, giving to the world.*
>
> *Future opportunities, like becoming an RN with more money and responsibility.*
>
> *People respect nurses.*

Primary support: *Being a nurse will be a great achievement for me.*

> **Supporting details:** *I will have worked hard and met my goal.*
>
> *I will respect myself and be proud of what I do.*
>
> *I will be a good role model for my daughter.*

WRITING ASSIGNMENT

Develop primary support points and supporting details using your topic sentence or thesis statement from Chapter 3 or one of the following topic sentences/thesis statements.

> Wearing seatbelts in cars should be/should not be mandatory
>
> The drinking age should/should not be lowered.
>
> Going to college is/is not essential.
>
> People who do not speak "proper" English are discriminated against.
>
> Most people in the United States could/could not live without technology today.

After developing your support, complete the following checklist.

CHECKLIST

Evaluating Your Support

- ☐ It is directly related to my main idea.
- ☐ It uses examples, facts, and observations that will make sense to my readers.
- ☐ It includes enough specific details to show my readers exactly what I mean.

Once you have pulled together your primary support points and secondary supporting details, you are ready for the next step: drafting a paragraph or essay based on a plan. For more information, go on to the next chapter.

Chapter Review

1. Support points are examples, facts, or evidence that ____*show*____, ____*explain*____, or ____*prove*____ your main idea.

2. Three basics of good support are: *It relates directly to your main idea.*

   It considers your readers.

   It gives specific details.

3. To generate support, try these three strategies: *Circle an important word or phrase in your topic sentence or thesis statement, and write about it.*

   Reread your topic sentence or thesis statement, and write down the first thought you have, then your second, and so on.

   Use a prewriting technique.

4. When you have selected your primary support points, what should you then add? *secondary support (or supporting details)*

5. Write for one minute about "What questions I should ask my instructor."

REFLECTING ON THE JOURNEY

Skills Learned

Now that you've completed the chapter, share what you've learned about each skill by completing the following chart.

Skill	What I learned about this skill
Write primary support points	
Write secondary support points	
Generate support	
Relate support directly to the main idea	

Drafting and Revising

The Writing Process

READING ROADMAP

Learning Objectives

Chapter Goal: Learn how to draft a full paragraph or essay and revise and edit it.

Tools to Achieve the Goal:

- Basics of a Good Draft (p. 76)
- Sample Outline for a Paragraph and Essay (p. 79)
- Basics of a Good Introduction (p. 84)
- Basics of a Good Conclusion (p. 86)
- Tips for Revising Your Writing (p. 91)
- Checklist for Revision (pp. 91–92)
- Special Note on Plagiarism (pp. 98–100)

Key Terms

Skim Chapter 5 before reading. Find these words or terms in **bold** type. Put a check mark next to each once you locate it.

____ draft	____ title
____ order	____ revising
____ space order	____ editing
____ time order	____ unity
____ order of importance	____ coherence
____ outline	____ transitions
____ concluding sentence	____ key word
	____ plagiarism

Guided Reading for Chapter 5

Fill out the following chart before you begin reading. For each skill, write what you know about the skill and what you would like to know upon completing the chapter. At the end of the chapter, you will be asked to share what you learned about each skill.

Skill	When I have used this skill	What I want to know about this skill
Use an outline to draft a paragraph or essay		
Draft a paragraph or essay with a thesis statement and/or topic sentences		
Draft an effective introduction		
Draft an effective conclusion		
Revise for unity, coherence, and detail		
Avoid plagiarism		

LaunchPadSolo

Visit **LaunchPad Solo for Readers and Writers > Writing Process** for more tutorials, videos, and practice with drafting and revising.

Understand What a Draft Is

A **draft** is the first whole version of all your ideas put together in a piece of writing. Do the best job you can in drafting but know that you can make changes later.

Basics of a good draft

- It has a topic sentence (for a paragraph) and a thesis statement (for an essay) that states a clear main idea.
- It has a logical organization of ideas.
- It has primary and secondary support that shows, explains, or proves the main idea.
- It has a conclusion that makes an observation about the main idea.
- It follows standard paragraph form (see p. 35) or standard essay form (see p. 36).

Two good first steps to drafting a paragraph or essay are (1) to arrange the ideas that you have generated in an order that makes sense and (2) to write out a plan for your draft. We will look at these steps next.

Arrange Your Ideas

In writing, **order** means the sequence in which you present your ideas: what comes first, what comes next, and so on. There are three common ways of ordering—arranging—your ideas: time order (also called chronological order), space order, and order of importance.

Read the paragraph examples that follow. In each paragraph, the topic sentences are underlined twice, the primary support points are underlined once, and the secondary support is in italics.

Use Time Order to Write about Events

Use **time order** (chronological order) to arrange points according to when they happened. Time order works best when you are writing about events. You can go from

- First to last or last to first
- Most recent to least recent or least recent to most recent

Example using time order

Teaching tip Call out different subjects to students (e.g., a wedding, a rescue, a vacation spot, a gathering place, a community controversy) and ask which type of order they would use to write about it.

Officer Meredith Pavlovic's traffic stop of August 23, 2011, was fairly typical of an investigation and arrest for drunk driving. First, at around 12:15 a.m. that day, she noticed that the driver of a blue Honda Civic was acting suspiciously. *The car was weaving between the fast and center lanes of Interstate 93 North near exit 12. In addition, it was proceeding at approximately 45 mph in a 55 mph zone.* Therefore, Officer Pavlovic took the second step of pulling the driver over for a closer investigation. *The driver's license told Officer Pavlovic that the driver was twenty-six-year-old Paul Brownwell. Brownwell's red eyes, slurred speech, and alcohol-tainted breath told Officer Pavlovic that Brownwell was very drunk.* But she had to be absolutely sure. Thus, as a next step, she tested his balance and blood alcohol level. *The results were that Brownwell could barely get out of the car, let alone stand on one foot. Also, a Breathalyzer test showed that his blood alcohol level was 0.13, well over the legal limit of 0.08.* These results meant an arrest for Brownwell, an unfortunate outcome for him, but a lucky one for other people on the road at that time.

What kind of time order does the author use? <u>first to last</u>

Use Space Order to Describe Objects, Places, or People

Use **space order** to arrange ideas so that your readers picture your topic the way you see it. Space order usually works best when you are writing about a physical object or place or a person's appearance. You can move from

- Top to bottom or bottom to top
- Near to far or far to near
- Left to right or right to left
- Back to front or front to back

Example using space order

I was gazing at my son's feet, in awe. There were ten toes, and they were no bigger than my fingernail. *How could something so small be moving so quickly?* Staring at those little toes squirming around as I tried to put socks on them, I had to laugh because the chubby little tree trunks that his dad and I call legs decided to get in on the action. Those full kicks that I had felt for the past several months and that had felt like someone performing kung-fu on my internal organs were now free and he clearly enjoyed that open space. Nothing, however, could prepare me for that tubby little belly. *So small, round, and smooth – yet it bounced up and down with each giggle, burp, and cry.* Two large sausage-like appendages turned into arms with long, slender fingers and fingernails that were no larger than the head of a pin, or so it appeared. But what did all that matter when the true beauty perched right atop his non-existent neck: *that gorgeous, round head covered with brown peach fuzz, sticking up in all directions.* Add all the pieces together, and all you see is love.

What type of space order does the example use? <u>Bottom to top</u>

Use Order of Importance to Emphasize a Particular Point

Use **order of importance** to arrange points according to their significance, interest, or surprise value. Usually, save the most important point for last.

Example using order of importance

Many parents today do not realize that there is a serious problem in their own home: prescription drug abuse. Unfortunately, we live in a day and age where the answer for many different problems is a prescription drug of some type. *We are prescribed drugs for pain, illness, mental disorders, sleep disorders, and even sexual problems.* With so many different disorders or problems that need treatment today, it is likely that any household has at least two or three active prescriptions at any one time, but who is actually using and taking those pills? News reports have shown that adults do not typically think to take the same precautions with prescriptions as they would with other dangerous substances, *namely weapons like guns or knives*; however, pills are just as deadly and far more addicting. If you are not keeping your prescriptions locked up, you are not keeping your home and your children safe.

What is the writer's most important point? *That parents are taking serious risks if they don't keep prescription medication locked away.*

Make a Plan

Tip Try using the cut-and-paste function on your computer to experiment with different ways to order support for your main idea. Doing so will give you a good sense of how your final paragraph or final essay will look.

When you have decided how to order your primary support points, it is time to make a more detailed plan for your paragraph or essay. A good, visual way to plan a draft is to arrange your ideas in an outline. An **outline** lists the topic sentence (for a paragraph) or thesis statement (for an essay), the primary support points for the topic sentence or thesis statement, and secondary supporting details for each of the support points. It provides a map of your ideas that you can follow as you write.

Outlining Paragraphs

Look at the outline Chelsea Wilson created with the support she wrote. She had already grouped together similar points and put the more specific details under the primary support (see p. 72). When she thought about how to order her ideas, the only way that made sense to her was by importance. If she had been telling the steps she would take to become a nurse, time order would have worked well. If she had been describing a setting where nurses work, space order would have been a good choice. However, because she was writing about why she wanted to get a college degree and become a nurse, she decided to arrange her reasons in order of importance. Notice that Chelsea also strengthened her topic sentence and made changes in her primary support and secondary support. At each stage, her ideas and the way she expressed them changed as she got closer to what she wanted to say.

Sample outline for a paragraph

> **Topic sentence:** *Becoming a nurse is a goal of mine because it offers so much that I value.*
>
> **Primary support 1:** *It is a good and practical job.*
>
> > **Supporting details:** *Licensed practical nurses make an average of $40,000 per year. That amount is much more than I make now. With that salary, I could move to a better place with my daughter and give her more, including more time.*
>
> **Primary support 2:** *Nursing is a profession, not just a job.*
>
> > **Supporting details:** *It helps people who are sick and in need. Being an LPN offers great opportunities, like the chance to go on to become a registered nurse, with more money and responsibility. People respect nurses.*
>
> **Primary support 3:** *I will respect and be proud of myself for achieving my goal through hard work.*
>
> > **Supporting details:** *I will be a good role model for my daughter. I will help her and others, but I will also be helping myself by knowing that I can accomplish good things.*
>
> **Conclusion:** *Reaching my goal is important to me and worth the work.*

Teaching tip You might point out to students that Chelsea has added a concluding sentence. It might change, but she is beginning to think about possible endings.

Outlining Essays

The outline that follows is for a typical five-paragraph essay, in which three body paragraphs (built around three topic sentences) support a thesis statement. The thesis statement is included in an introductory paragraph; the fifth paragraph is the conclusion. However, essays may include more or fewer than five paragraphs, depending on the size and complexity of the topic.

This example is a "formal" outline form, with letters and numbers to distinguish between primary supporting and secondary supporting details. Some instructors require this format. If you are making an outline just for yourself, you might choose to write a less formal outline, simply indenting the secondary supporting details under the primary support rather than using numbers and letters.

Sample outline for a five-paragraph essay

Thesis statement (part of introductory paragraph 1)

A. **Topic sentence for support point 1** (paragraph 2)

   1. Supporting detail 1 for support point 1

   2. Supporting detail 2 for support point 1 (and so on)

B. **Topic sentence for support point 2** (paragraph 3)

   1. Supporting detail 1 for support point 2

   2. Supporting detail 2 for support point 2 (and so on)

C. **Topic sentence for support point 3** (paragraph 4)

   1. Supporting detail 1 for support point 3

   2. Supporting detail 2 for support point 3 (and so on)

Concluding paragraph (paragraph 5)

> **PRACTICE 1**   **Making an outline**

Reread the paragraph on pages 76–77 that illustrates time order of organization. Then, make an outline for it in the space provided.

Topic sentence: *Officer Meredith Pavlovic's traffic stop of August 23, 2011, was fairly typical of an investigation and arrest for drunk driving.*

Primary support 1: *First, at around 12:15 a.m. that day, she noticed that the driver of a blue Honda Civic was acting suspiciously.*

1. **Supporting detail:** *The car was weaving between the fast and center lanes of Interstate 93 North near exit 12.*

2. **Supporting detail:** *In addition, it was proceeding at approximately 45 mph in a 55 mph zone.*

Primary support 2: *Therefore, Officer Pavlovic took the second step of pulling the driver over for a closer investigation.*

1. **Supporting detail:** *The driver's license told Officer Pavlovic that the driver was twenty-six-year-old Paul Brownwell.*

2. **Supporting detail:** *Brownwell's red eyes, slurred speech, and alcohol-tainted breath told Officer Pavlovic that Brownwell was very drunk.*

Primary support 3: *Thus, as a next step, she tested his balance and blood alcohol level.*

1. **Supporting detail:** *The results were that Brownwell could barely get out of the car, let alone stand on one foot.*

2. **Supporting detail:** *Also, a breathalyzer test showed that his blood alcohol level was 0.13, well over the legal limit of 0.08.*

Teaching tip If you are working with paragraphs only, ask students to read pages 80–82 and then move on to the sample draft paragraph and writing assignment on page 88, followed by the Chapter Review. If you are working with essays only, ask students to skip ahead to pages 82–87, then to the sample essay draft and writing assignment on page 90, and finally to the Chapter Review.

Practice Writing a Draft Paragraph

As you write your paragraph, you will need to go through the steps in the following sections. Also, refer to the Basics of a Good Draft on page 76.

Write a Draft Using Complete Sentences

Write your draft with your outline in front of you. Be sure to include your topic sentence, and express each point in a complete sentence. As you write, you may want to add support or change the order. It is OK to make changes from your outline as you write.

Read the following paragraph, annotated to show the various parts of the paragraph.

Parabens: Widely Used Chemicals Spark New Cautions ———————— Title

    Parabens, preservatives used in many cosmetics and personal-care products, —— Topic sentence
are raising concerns with more and more consumers. In some people, parabens
cause allergic reactions, but the effects of these chemicals may be more than skin
deep. After being applied to the face or body, parabens can enter the bloodstream,
where they have been found to mimic the hormone estrogen. Because long-term
exposure to estrogen can increase the risk of breast cancer, researchers have tried
to determine whether there is any link between parabens and breast cancer. So far,
the findings have been inconclusive. One study found parabens in the breast cancer
tissue of some research subjects. However, the study was small, and based on its
results, it cannot be said that parabens actually cause cancer. Nevertheless, some —— Support
consumers wish to reduce their use of paraben-containing products or to avoid
them altogether. To do so, they carefully read the labels of personal-care products,
looking out for ingredients like butylparaben, ethylparaben, methylparaben,
isopropyl, and propylparaben. All these chemicals are parabens. Consumers who
do not wish to give up parabens entirely might consider avoiding only those
paraben-containing products, like lotions and makeup, that stay on the skin for an
extended period. Products that are rinsed away quickly, like shampoos and soaps,
do not have as much time to be absorbed through the skin.

Although paragraphs typically begin with topic sentences, they may also begin
with a quote, an example, or a surprising fact or idea. The topic sentence is then
presented later in the paragraph. For examples of various introductory techniques,
see pages 83–86.

Tip For more on topic sentences, see Chapter 3.

Write a Concluding Sentence

A **concluding sentence** refers back to the main idea and makes an observation
based on what you have written. The concluding sentence does not just repeat the
topic sentence.

    In the preceding paragraph, the main idea, expressed in the topic sentence, is
"Parabens, preservatives used in many cosmetics and personal-care products, are
raising concerns with more and more consumers."

    A good conclusion might be, "Given the growing concerns about parabens and
uncertainties about their potential dangers, more research is clearly needed." This
sentence **refers back to the main idea** by repeating the words *parabens* and *concerns*. It **makes an observation** by stating, "more research is clearly needed."

    Concluding paragraphs for essays are discussed on pages 86–87.

Teaching tip Tell students that the concluding sentence gives them an opportunity to express a personal opinion based on the support they have provided, but they should not use it to introduce new, unrelated ideas.

Teaching tip Warn students about two common problems in endings of paragraphs: (1) stopping abruptly so that it seems as if the paragraph is unfinished or that the writer ran out of time and (2) changing focus so that readers are left wondering what the point is.

> **PRACTICE 2**   **Writing concluding sentences**
>
> Read the following paragraphs, and write a concluding sentence for each one.
>
>   1. One of the most valuable ways parents can help children is to read to
>   them. Reading together is a good way for parents and children to relax,

and it is sometimes the only "quality" time they spend together during a busy day. Reading develops children's vocabulary. They understand more words and are likely to learn new words more easily than children who are not read to. Also, hearing the words aloud helps children's pronunciation and makes them more confident with oral language. In addition, reading at home increases children's chances of success in school because reading is required in every course in every grade.

Possible concluding sentence: *Answers will vary but should include the idea that reading helps children in many ways or that it is an important activity for parents and children to share.*

2. Almost everyone uses certain memory devices, called mnemonics. One of them is the alphabet song. If you want to remember what letter comes after j, you will probably sing the alphabet song in your head. Another is the "Thirty days hath September" rhyme that people use when they want to know how many days are in a certain month. Another mnemonic device is the rhyme "In 1492, Columbus sailed the ocean blue."

Possible concluding sentence: *Answers will vary but should refer to the memory devices and how commonly they are used.*

Practice Writing a Draft Essay

The basics of a good essay draft are all listed on page 76. In addition,

- The essay should include an introductory paragraph that draws readers in and includes the thesis statement.
- The topic sentences for the paragraphs that follow the introduction should directly support the thesis statement. In turn, each topic sentence should be backed by enough support.
- The conclusion should be a full paragraph rather than a single sentence.

Let's start by looking at topic sentences and support for them.

Write Topic Sentences, and Draft the Body of the Essay

When you start to draft your essay, use your outline to write complete sentences for your primary support points. These sentences will serve as the topic sentences for the body paragraphs of your essay.

> **PRACTICE 3**   **Writing topic sentences**
>
> Each thesis statement that follows has support points that could be topic sentences for the body paragraphs of an essay. For each support point, write a topic sentence.

Example

Thesis statement: My daughter is showing definite signs of becoming a teenager.

Support point: constantly texting friends

> **Topic sentence:** _She texts friends constantly, even when they are sitting_ _with her while I'm driving them._

Support point: doesn't want me to know what's going on

> **Topic sentence:** _She used to tell me everything, but now she is secretive and_ _private._

Support point: developing an "attitude"

> **Topic sentence:** _The surest and most annoying sign that she is becoming a_ _teenager is that she has developed a definite "attitude."_

Thesis statement: The Latin American influence is evident in many areas of U.S. culture.

Support point: Spanish language used in lots of places

> **Topic sentence:** _Answers will vary._

Support point: lots of different kinds of foods

> **Topic sentence:** _____

Support point: new kinds of music and popular musicians

> **Topic sentence:** _____

Drafting topic sentences for your essay is a good way to start drafting the body of the essay (the paragraphs that support each of these topic sentences). As you write support for your topic sentences, refer back to your outline, where you listed supporting details. (For an example, see Chelsea Wilson's outline on page 79.) Turn these supporting details into complete sentences, and add additional support if necessary. (Prewriting techniques can help here; see Chapter 3.) Don't let yourself get stalled if you are having trouble with one word or sentence. Just keep writing. Remember that a draft is a first try; you will have time later to improve it.

Write an Introduction

The introduction to your essay captures your readers' interest and presents the main idea. Ask yourself: How can I sell my essay to readers? You need to market your main idea.

ESL tip Remind nonnative speakers that it is a convention of English to present the main idea in the first paragraph, stated explicitly.

Basics of a good introduction

- It should catch readers' attention.

- It should present the thesis statement of the essay, usually in the first or the last sentence of an introductory paragraph.

- It should give readers a clear idea of what the essay will cover.

Here are some common kinds of introductions that spark readers' interest. In each one, the introductory technique is in boldface. These introductions are not the only ways to start essays, but they should give you some useful models.

OPEN WITH A QUOTATION

A good, short quotation definitely gets people interested. It must lead naturally into your main idea, however, and not be there just for effect. If you start with a quotation, make sure you tell the reader who the speaker is.

> **"Never before had I truly felt such an extreme sense of estrangement and alienation,"** [a Vanderbilt student] says of his first few months. **"I quickly realized that although I may look the part, my cultural and socio-economic backgrounds were vastly different from those of my predominantly white, affluent peers. I wanted to leave."**
>
> —Liz Riggs, "What It's Like to Be the First Person in Your Family to Go to College"

GIVE AN EXAMPLE, OR TELL A STORY

People like stories, so opening an essay with a brief story or example often draws readers in.

> **The bank called today, and I told them my deposit was in the mail, even though I hadn't written a check yet.** It'd been a rough day. The baby I'm pregnant with decided to do aerobics on my lungs for two hours, our three-year-old daughter painted the living-room couch with lipstick, the IRS put me on hold for an hour, and I was late to a business meeting because I was tired.
>
> —Stephanie Ericsson, "The Ways We Lie"

START WITH A SURPRISING FACT OR IDEA

Surprises capture people's interest. The more unexpected and surprising something is, the more likely people are to notice it.

> **In some places, towns essentially shut down in the afternoon while everyone goes home for a siesta.** Unfortunately, in the U.S.—more bound to our corporate lifestyles than our health—a mid-day nap is seen as a luxury and, in some cases, a sign of pure laziness. But before you feel guilty about that weekend snooze or falling asleep during a movie, rest assured that napping is actually good for you and a completely natural phenomena in the circadian (sleep-wake cycle) rhythm.
>
> —Elizabeth Renter, "Napping Can Dramatically Increase Learning, Memory, Awareness, and More"

OFFER A STRONG OPINION OR POSITION

The stronger the opinion, the more likely it is that your readers will pay attention. Don't write wimpy introductions. Make your point and shout it!

> **Yes, money can buy happiness, but probably not in the way you imagined.** Spending it on yourself may not do much for your spirits, but spending it on others will make you happier, according to a report from a team of social psychologists in the new issue of *Science*.
>
> —John Tierney, "Yes, Money Can Buy Happiness"

ASK A QUESTION

A question needs an answer, so if you start your introduction with a question, your readers will need to read on to get the answer.

> **At the end of a tour of Catskill Animal Sanctuary last year, a visitor who'd just been kissed by cows and held chickens in his lap said to me, "OK. I get it. How do I start?"**
>
> —Kathy Stevens, "Ten Tips for Easing into Plant-Based Eating"

Tip If you get stuck while writing your introductory statement, try one or more of the prewriting techniques described in Chapter 3 on pages 48–52.

PRACTICE 4 **Marketing your main idea**

As you know from advertisements, a good writer can make just about anything sound interesting. For each of the following topics, write an introductory statement using the technique indicated. Some of these topics are purposely dull to show you that you can make an interesting statement about almost any subject, if you put your mind to it.

Example

Topic: Reality TV

Technique: Question

Exactly how many recent top-selling songs have been recorded by former

contestants of reality TV singing contests?

Teaching tip Remind students that because the introduction should catch readers' attention, they should consider who their readers are and what those readers would find interesting.

1. **Topic:** Credit cards

   Technique: Surprising fact or idea

   Answers will vary.

2. **Topic:** Role of the elderly in society

   Technique: Question

3. **Topic:** Stress

   Technique: Quote (You can make up a good one.)

PRACTICE 5   **Identifying strong introductions**

In a newspaper or magazine, an online news site, an advertising flier—or anything written—find a strong introduction. Bring it to class and explain why you chose it as an example.

Write a Conclusion

When they have finished the body of their essay, some writers believe their work is done—but it isn't quite finished. Remember that people usually remember best what they see, hear, or read last. Use your concluding paragraph to drive your main idea home one final time. Make sure your conclusion has the same energy as the rest of the essay, if not more.

Basics of a good essay conclusion

- It refers back to the main idea.
- It sums up what has been covered in the essay.
- It makes a further observation or point.

In general, a good conclusion creates a sense of completion. It brings readers back to where they started, but it also shows them how far they have come.

One of the best ways to end an essay is to refer directly to something in the introduction. If you asked a question, re-ask and answer it. If you started a story, finish it. If you used a quote, use another one—maybe a quote by the same person or maybe one by another person on the same topic. Or, use some of the same words you used in your introduction. Look again at one of the introductions you read earlier, and notice how the writer concluded her essay. Pay special attention to the text in boldface.

Ericsson's introduction

The bank called today, and I told them my deposit was in the mail, even though I hadn't written a check yet. It'd been a rough day. The baby I'm pregnant with decided to do aerobics on my lungs for two hours, our three-year-old daughter painted the living-room couch with lipstick, the IRS put me on hold for an hour, and I was late to a business meeting because I was tired.

— Stephanie Ericsson, "The Ways We Lie"

Ericsson's conclusion
Maybe if I don't tell the bank the check's in the mail I'll be less tolerant
of the lies told to me every day. A country song I once heard said it all for me,
"You've got to stand for something or you'll fall for anything."

— Stephanie Ericsson, "The Ways We Lie"

PRACTICE 6   **Finding good introductions and conclusions**

In a newspaper or magazine or anything written, find a piece of writing that
has a strong introduction and conclusion. (You may want to use what you
found for Practice 5.) Answer the questions that follow.

1. What method of introduction is used? _Answers will vary._ _____

2. What does the conclusion do? (Restate the main idea? Sum up the

   support? Make a further observation?) _____

   _____

3. How are the introduction and the conclusion linked? _____

   _____

Title Your Essay

Even if your **title** is the last part of the essay you write, it is the first thing readers
read. Use your title to get your readers' attention and to tell them, in a brief way,
what your paper is about. Use vivid, strong, specific words.

Basics of a good essay title

- It makes people want to read the essay.

- It hints at the main idea (thesis statement), but it does not repeat it.

One way to find a good title is to consider the type of essay you are writing. If
you are writing an argument (as you will in Chapter 14), state your position in your
title. If you are telling your readers how to do something (as you will in Chapter 9),
try using the term *steps* or *how to* in the title. This way, your readers will know
immediately not only what you are writing about but how you will discuss it.

PRACTICE 7   **Titling an essay**

Reread the paragraphs on pages 86–87, and write an alternate title for the
essay that they belong to.

Ericsson's introduction/conclusion: _Answers will vary._ _____

Teaching tip Cut out the
introductions and conclusions
that students bring in,
scramble them, and have the
students work in small groups
to match introductions and
conclusions.

Teaching tip Ask students
to name favorite television
shows, movies, or songs, and
write them on the board. Then,
invite students to discuss what
makes these titles interesting
or dull, topic-appropriate or
irrelevant. Can they think of
better alternatives?

Tip Center your title at the
top of the page before the
first paragraph. Do not put
quotation marks around it or
underline it.

Write Your Own Draft Paragraph or Essay

Before you draft your own paragraph, read Chelsea Wilson's annotated draft. It is based on her outline from page 79.

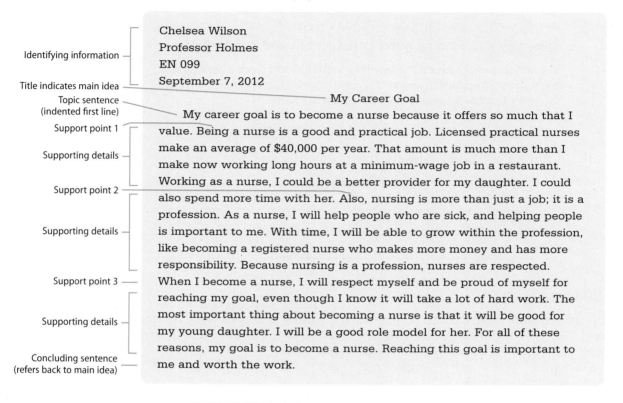

Identifying information

Title indicates main idea

Topic sentence (indented first line)

Support point 1

Supporting details

Support point 2

Supporting details

Support point 3

Supporting details

Concluding sentence (refers back to main idea)

Chelsea Wilson
Professor Holmes
EN 099
September 7, 2012

My Career Goal

My career goal is to become a nurse because it offers so much that I value. Being a nurse is a good and practical job. Licensed practical nurses make an average of $40,000 per year. That amount is much more than I make now working long hours at a minimum-wage job in a restaurant. Working as a nurse, I could be a better provider for my daughter. I could also spend more time with her. Also, nursing is more than just a job; it is a profession. As a nurse, I will help people who are sick, and helping people is important to me. With time, I will be able to grow within the profession, like becoming a registered nurse who makes more money and has more responsibility. Because nursing is a profession, nurses are respected. When I become a nurse, I will respect myself and be proud of myself for reaching my goal, even though I know it will take a lot of hard work. The most important thing about becoming a nurse is that it will be good for my young daughter. I will be a good role model for her. For all of these reasons, my goal is to become a nurse. Reaching this goal is important to me and worth the work.

WRITING ASSIGNMENT   **Paragraph**

Write a draft paragraph using what you have developed in previous chapters or one of the following topic sentences. If you use one of the topic sentences below, you may want to revise it to fit what you want to say.

Being a good _____ requires _____.

I can find any number of ways to waste my time.

So many decisions are involved in going to college.

The most important thing to me in life is _____.

After writing your draft paragraph, complete the following checklist.

> **CHECKLIST**
>
> Evaluating Your Draft Paragraph
>
> ☐ It has a clear, confident topic sentence that states my main idea.
>
> ☐ Each primary support point is backed up with supporting details, examples, or facts.

☐ The support is arranged in a logical order.

☐ The concluding sentence reminds readers of my main idea and makes an observation.

☐ The title reinforces the main idea.

☐ All the sentences are complete, consisting of a subject and verb, and expressing a complete thought.

☐ The draft is properly formatted:
  • My name, my instructor's name, the course, and the date appear in the upper left corner.
  • The first sentence of the paragraph is indented, and the text is double-spaced (for easier revision).

☐ I have followed any other formatting guidelines provided by my instructor.

Before you draft your own essay, read Chelsea Wilson's annotated draft of her essay.

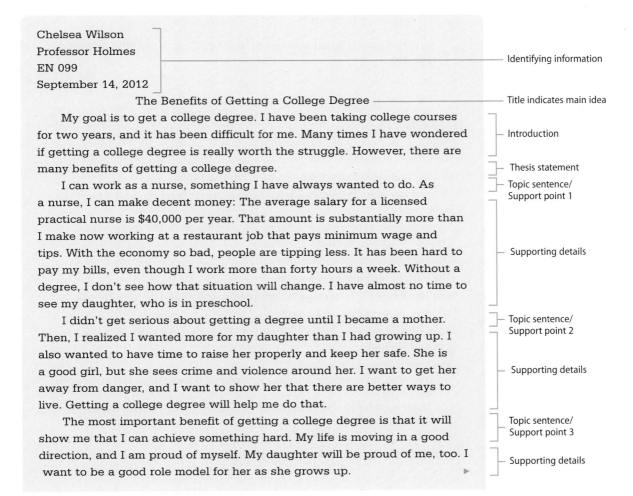

Chelsea Wilson
Professor Holmes
EN 099
September 14, 2012 ———————————————— Identifying information

The Benefits of Getting a College Degree ——— Title indicates main idea

My goal is to get a college degree. I have been taking college courses for two years, and it has been difficult for me. Many times I have wondered if getting a college degree is really worth the struggle. However, there are many benefits of getting a college degree. — Introduction / Thesis statement

I can work as a nurse, something I have always wanted to do. As a nurse, I can make decent money: The average salary for a licensed practical nurse is $40,000 per year. That amount is substantially more than I make now working at a restaurant job that pays minimum wage and tips. With the economy so bad, people are tipping less. It has been hard to pay my bills, even though I work more than forty hours a week. Without a degree, I don't see how that situation will change. I have almost no time to see my daughter, who is in preschool. — Topic sentence/Support point 1 / Supporting details

I didn't get serious about getting a degree until I became a mother. Then, I realized I wanted more for my daughter than I had growing up. I also wanted to have time to raise her properly and keep her safe. She is a good girl, but she sees crime and violence around her. I want to get her away from danger, and I want to show her that there are better ways to live. Getting a college degree will help me do that. — Topic sentence/Support point 2 / Supporting details

The most important benefit of getting a college degree is that it will show me that I can achieve something hard. My life is moving in a good direction, and I am proud of myself. My daughter will be proud of me, too. I want to be a good role model for her as she grows up. ▶ — Topic sentence/Support point 3 / Supporting details

Conclusion —
> Because of these benefits, I want to get a college degree. It will give me the chance to earn a better living, it will give my daughter and me a better life, and I will be proud of myself.

WRITING ASSIGNMENT   **Essay**

Write a draft essay using what you have developed in previous chapters or one of the following thesis statements. If you choose one of the thesis statements that follow, you may want to modify it to fit what you want to say.

Being successful at _____ requires _____.

Doing _____ gave me a great deal of pride in myself.

Training for a (job/marathon/sport/performance) requires a lot of discipline.

Some of the differences between men and women create misunderstandings.

After you have finished writing your draft essay, complete the following checklist.

CHECKLIST

Evaluating Your Draft Essay

☐ A clear, confident thesis statement states my main idea.

☐ The primary support points are now topic sentences that support the main idea.

☐ Each topic sentence is part of a paragraph, and the other sentences in the paragraph support the topic sentence.

☐ The support is arranged in a logical order.

☐ The introduction will interest readers.

☐ The conclusion reinforces my main idea and makes an additional observation.

☐ The title reinforces the main idea.

☐ All the sentences are complete, consisting of a subject and verb, and expressing a complete thought.

☐ The draft is properly formatted:
  • My name, my instructor's name, the course, and the date appear in the upper left corner.
  • The first sentence of each paragraph is indented, and the text is double-spaced (for easier revision).
  • The pages are numbered.

☐ I have followed any other formatting guidelines provided by my instructor.

Give yourself some time away from your draft, at least a few hours and preferably a day or two. Taking a break will allow you to return to your writing later with a fresher eye and more energy for revision, resulting in a better piece of writing—and a better grade. After your break, you will be ready to take the next step: revising your draft.

Understand What Revision Is

When you finish a draft, you probably wish that you were at the end: You don't want to have to look at it again. But a draft is just the first whole version, a rough cut; it is not the best you can do to represent yourself and your ideas. After taking a break, you need to look at the draft with fresh eyes to revise and edit it.

Revising is making your ideas clearer, stronger, and more convincing. When revising, you are evaluating how well you have made your point.

Editing is finding and correcting problems with grammar, word usage, punctuation, and capitalization. When editing, you are evaluating the words, phrases, and sentences you have used.

Most writers find it difficult to revise and edit well if they try to do both at once. It is easier to solve idea-level problems first (by revising) and then to correct smaller, word-level ones (by editing). This chapter focuses on revising. For editing help, use Chapters 15 through 34.

Tips for revising your writing

- Wait a few hours or, if possible, a couple of days before starting to revise.

- Read your draft aloud, and listen for places where the writing seems weak or unclear.

- Read critically and ask yourself questions, as if you were reading through someone else's eyes.

- Write notes about changes to make. For small things, like adding a transition (pp. 96–97), you can make the change on the draft. For other things, like adding or getting rid of an idea or reordering your support points, make a note in the margin.

- Get help from a tutor at the writing center, or get feedback from a friend (see the following section for information on peer review).

Even the best writers do not get everything right the first time. So, if you finish reading your draft and have not found anything that could be better, you are not reading carefully enough or are not asking the right questions. Use the following checklist to help you make your writing better.

Tip For more on reading critically, see Chapter 1.

Teaching tip As students begin revising their work, consider sharing this observation by writer Sophy Burnham: "[T]he only element I find common to all successful writers is persistence—an overwhelming determination to succeed." Explain that revising and editing, done thoughtfully and regularly, can be especially productive forms of persistence.

CHECKLIST

Revising Your Writing

☐ If someone else just read my topic sentence or thesis statement, what would he or she think the paper is about? Would the main point make a lasting impression? What would I need to do to make it more interesting?   ▶

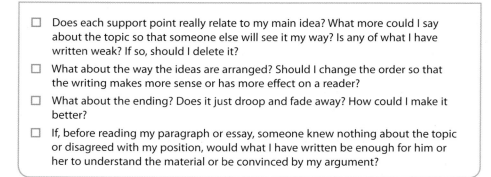

- ☐ Does each support point really relate to my main idea? What more could I say about the topic so that someone else will see it my way? Is any of what I have written weak? If so, should I delete it?
- ☐ What about the way the ideas are arranged? Should I change the order so that the writing makes more sense or has more effect on a reader?
- ☐ What about the ending? Does it just droop and fade away? How could I make it better?
- ☐ If, before reading my paragraph or essay, someone knew nothing about the topic or disagreed with my position, would what I have written be enough for him or her to understand the material or be convinced by my argument?

Tip Add transitions as you read to help move from one idea to the next.

Practice Revising for Unity, Detail, and Coherence

You may need to read what you have written several times before deciding what changes would improve it. Remember to consider your audience and your purpose and to focus on three areas: unity, detail, and coherence.

Revise for Unity

Unity in writing means that all the points you make are related to your main idea; they are *unified* in support of it. As you draft a paragraph or an essay, you may detour from your main idea without even being aware of it, as the writer of the following paragraph did with the underlined sentences. The diagram after the paragraph shows what happens when readers read the paragraph.

First, double-underline the main idea in the paragraph that follows to help you see where the writer got off-track.

Teaching tip Read the paragraph aloud to the class, and ask students to stop you as soon as they hear it detouring from the main idea.

If you want to drive like an elderly person, use a cell phone while driving. A group of researchers from the University of Utah tested the reaction times of two groups of people—those between the ages of sixty-five to seventy-four and those who were eighteen to twenty-five—in a variety of driving tasks. All tasks were done with hands-free cell phones. That part of the study surprised me because I thought the main problem was using only one hand to drive. I hardly ever drive with two hands, even when I'm not talking to anyone. Among other results, braking time for both groups slowed by 18 percent. A related result is that the number of rear-end collisions doubled. The study determined that the younger drivers were paying as much—or more—attention to their phone conversations as they were to what was going on around them on the road. The elderly drivers also experienced longer reaction times and more accidents, pushing most of them into the category of dangerous driver. This study makes a good case for turning off the phone when you buckle up.

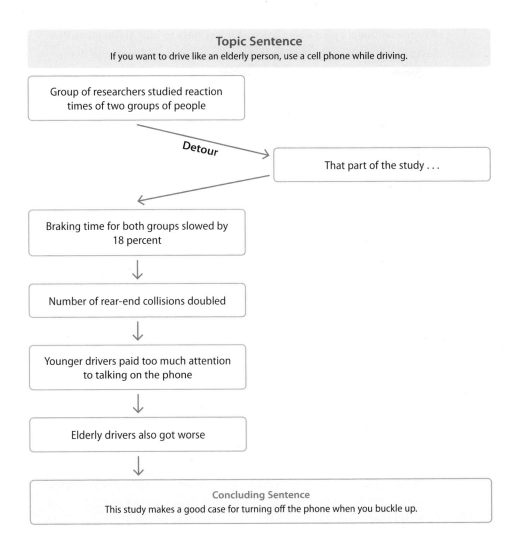

Topic Sentence
If you want to drive like an elderly person, use a cell phone while driving.

Group of researchers studied reaction times of two groups of people

Detour

That part of the study . . .

Braking time for both groups slowed by 18 percent

Number of rear-end collisions doubled

Younger drivers paid too much attention to talking on the phone

Elderly drivers also got worse

Concluding Sentence
This study makes a good case for turning off the phone when you buckle up.

Detours weaken your writing because readers' focus is shifted from your main idea. As you revise, check to make sure your paragraph or essay has unity.

PRACTICE 8   Revising for unity

Each of the following paragraphs contains a sentence that detours from the main idea. First, double-underline the main idea. Then, underline the detour in each paragraph.

Example: "Education is one of the few things people are willing to pay for and not get." When we buy something expensive, we make sure we take it home and use it. For example, we wouldn't think of spending a couple of hundred dollars on a new coat and shoes only to hide them away in a closet never to be worn. And we certainly wouldn't pay for those items and then decide to leave them at the store. <u>I once left a bag with three new shirts in it at the cash register, and I never got it back.</u> People pay a lot for education, but sometimes they look for ways to leave the "purchase" behind. They cheat themselves by not attending class, not paying attention, not studying, or not doing assignments. At the end of the term, they have a grade but didn't get what they paid for: education and knowledge. They have wasted money, just as if they had bought an expensive sound system and had never taken it out of the box.

1. <u>One way to manage time is to keep a print or electronic calendar or schedule.</u> It should have an hour-by-hour breakdown of the day and evening, with space for you to write next to the time. As appointments or responsibilities come up, add them on the right day and time. Before the end of the day, consult your calendar to see what's going on the next day. <u>For example, tomorrow I have to meet Kara at noon, and if I forget, she will be furious with me.</u> Once you are in the habit of using a calendar, you will see that it frees your mind because you are not always trying to think about what you're supposed to do, where you're supposed to be, or what you might have forgotten.

2. <u>As you use a calendar to manage your time, think about how long certain activities will take.</u> A common mistake is to underestimate the time needed to do something, even something simple. For example, when you are planning the time needed to get money from the cash machine, remember that a line of people may be ahead of you. <u>Last week in the line I met a woman I went to high school with.</u> When you are estimating time for a more complex activity, such as reading a chapter in a textbook, block out more time than you think you will need. If you finish in less time than you have allotted, so much the better.

Revise for Detail and Support

When you revise a paper, look carefully at the support you have developed. Will readers have enough information to understand and be convinced by the main idea?

In the margin or between the lines of your draft (which should be double-spaced), note ideas that seem weak or unclear. As you revise, build up your support by adding more details.

PRACTICE 9   **Revising for detail and support**

Read the following paragraphs, double-underline the main idea, and add at least three additional support points or supporting details. Write them in the spaces provided under each paragraph, and indicate where they should go in the paragraph by writing in a caret (^) and the number.

Example: <u>Sojourner Truth was a brave woman who helped educate</u> <u>people about the evils of slavery.</u> She was a slave herself in New York 1. ^ 2 After she had a religious vision, she traveled from place to place ^ giving speeches about how terrible it was to be a slave. 3 But even ^ after the Emancipation Proclamation was signed in 1863, slave owners did not follow the laws. Sojourner Truth was active in the Civil War, nursing soldiers and continuing to give speeches. She was active in the fight for racial equality until her death in 1883.

1. *and was not allowed to learn to read or write*

2. *Sojourner Truth ran away from her owner because of his cruelty.*

3. *Although she was beaten for her beliefs, she continued her work and was part of the force that caused Abraham Lincoln to sign the Emancipation Proclamation freeing the slaves.*

1. <u>Sports fans can turn from normal people into destructive maniacs.</u> After big wins, a team's fans sometimes riot. Police have to be brought in. Even in school sports, parents of the players can become violent. People get so involved watching the game that they lose control of themselves and are dangerous.

    1. *Answers will vary.*

    2. _____

    3. _____

2. <u>If a friend is going through a hard time, try to be as supportive as you can.</u> For one thing, ask if you can help out with any errands or chores. Also, find a time when you can get together in a quiet, nonstressful place. Here, the two of you can talk about the friend's difficulties or just spend time visiting. Let the friend decide how the time is spent. Just knowing that you are there for him or her will mean a lot.

    1. _____

    2. _____

    3. _____

Revise for Coherence

Coherence in writing means that all your support connects to form a whole. In other words, you have provided enough "glue" for readers to see how one point leads to another.

A good way to improve coherence is to use **transitions**—words, phrases, and sentences that connect your ideas so that your writing moves smoothly from one point to the next. The table on pages 96–97 shows some common transitions and what they are used for.

Here are two paragraphs, one that does not use transitions and one that does. Read them and notice how much easier the second paragraph is to follow because of the underlined transitions.

No transitions

It is not difficult to get organized—it takes discipline to stay organized. All you need to do is follow a few simple ideas. You must decide what your priorities are and do these tasks first. You should ask yourself every day: What is the most important task I have to accomplish? Make the time to do it. To be organized, you need a personal system for keeping track of things. Making lists, keeping records, and using a schedule help you remember what tasks you need to do. It is a good idea not to let belongings and obligations stack up. Get rid of possessions you do not need, put items away every time you are done using them, and do not take on more responsibilities than you can handle. Getting organized is not a mystery; it is just good sense.

Transitions added

It is not difficult to get organized—<u>although</u> it takes discipline to stay organized. All you need to do is follow a few simple ideas. You must decide what your priorities are and do these tasks first. <u>For example</u>, you should ask yourself every day: What is the most important task I have to accomplish? <u>Then</u>, make the time to do it. To be organized, you <u>also</u> need a personal system for keeping track of things. Making lists, keeping records, and using a schedule help you remember what tasks you need to do. <u>Finally</u>, it is a good idea not to let belongings and obligations stack up. Get rid of possessions you do not need, put items away every time you are done using them, and do not take on more responsibilities than you can handle. Getting organized is not a mystery; it is just good sense.

Common Transitional Words and Phrases

Indicating space

above	below	near	to the right
across	beside	next to	to the side
at the bottom	beyond	opposite	under
at the top	farther/further	over	where
behind	inside	to the left	

Indicating time

after	eventually	meanwhile	soon
as	finally	next	then
at last	first	now	when
before	last	second	while
during	later	since	

Indicating importance

above all	in fact	more important	most important
best	in particular	most	worst
especially			

Signaling examples

for example	for instance	for one thing	one reason

Signaling additions

additionally	and	as well as	in addition
also	another	furthermore	moreover

Signaling contrast

although	however	nevertheless	still
but	in contrast	on the other hand	yet
even though	instead		

Signaling causes or results

as a result	finally	so	therefore
because			

PRACTICE 10   **Adding transitions**

Read the following paragraphs. In each blank, add a transition that would smoothly connect the ideas. In each case, there is more than one correct answer.

Example

LifeGem, a Chicago company, has announced that it can turn cremated human ashes into high-quality diamonds. _After_ **cremation, the ashes are heated to convert their carbon to graphite.** _Then_ **, a lab wraps the graphite around a tiny diamond piece and again heats it and pressurizes it.** _After_ **about a**

week of crystallizing, the result is a diamond. ___*Because of*___ the time and labor involved, this process can cost as much as $20,000. ___*Although*___ the idea is very creative, many people will think it is also very weird. *Answers will vary.*

1. Frida Kahlo (1907–1954) is one of Mexico's most famous artists. From an early age, she had an eye for color and detail. ___*However*___, it was not until she was seriously injured in a traffic accident that she devoted herself to painting. ___*During*___ her recovery, she went to work on what would become the first of many self-portraits. ___*Eventually*___, she married the famous muralist Diego Rivera. ___*Because*___ Rivera was unfaithful to Kahlo, their marriage was difficult. ___*Nevertheless*___, Kahlo continued to develop as an artist and produce great work. Rivera may have summed up Kahlo's paintings the best, describing them as "acid and tender, hard as steel and delicate and fine as a butterfly's wing, lovable as a beautiful smile, and profound and cruel as the bitterness of life."

2. Many fast-food restaurants are adding healthier foods to their menus. ___*For example*___, several kinds of salads are now on most menus. These salads offer fresh vegetables and roasted, rather than fried, chicken. ___*However*___, be careful of the dressings, which can be very high in calories. ___*Also*___, avoid the huge soft drinks that have large amounts of sugar. ___*Finally*___, skip the french fries. They are high in fat and calories and do not have much nutritional value.

Another way to give your writing coherence is to repeat a **key word**—a word that is directly related to your main idea. For example, in the paragraphs on page 96, the writer repeats the word *organized* several times. Repetition of a key word is a good way to keep your readers focused on your main idea, but make sure you don't overdo it.

NOTE: AVOIDING PLAGIARISM

In all the writing you do, it is important to avoid **plagiarism**—using other people's words as your own or handing in information you gather from another source as your own. Your instructors are aware of plagiarism and know how to look for it. Writers who plagiarize, either on purpose or by accident, risk failing a course or losing their jobs and damaging their reputations.

To avoid plagiarism, take careful notes on every source (books, interviews, television shows, Web sites, and so on) you might use in your writing. When recording information from sources, take notes in your own words, unless you plan to use direct quotations. In that case, make sure to record the quotation word for word. Also, include quotation marks around it, both in your notes and in your paper. When you use material from other sources—whether you directly quote or put information in your own words (paraphrase)—you must name and give citation information about these sources.

Revise Your Own Paragraph

On page 88, you read Chelsea's draft paragraph. Reread that now as if it were your own, asking yourself the questions in the Checklist for Revising Your Writing on pages 91–92. Work either by yourself or with a partner or a small group to answer the questions about Chelsea's draft. Then, read Chelsea's revised paragraph that follows, and compare the changes you suggested with those she made. Make notes on the similarities and differences to discuss with the rest of the class.

Teaching tip If you are working with paragraphs only, ask students to read this section and then move on to the Chapter Review, pages 102–104. If you are working with essays only, skip this section and go to Revise Your Own Essay, pages 100–102.

Teaching tip You might challenge teams of students to find the most revisions to the paragraph.

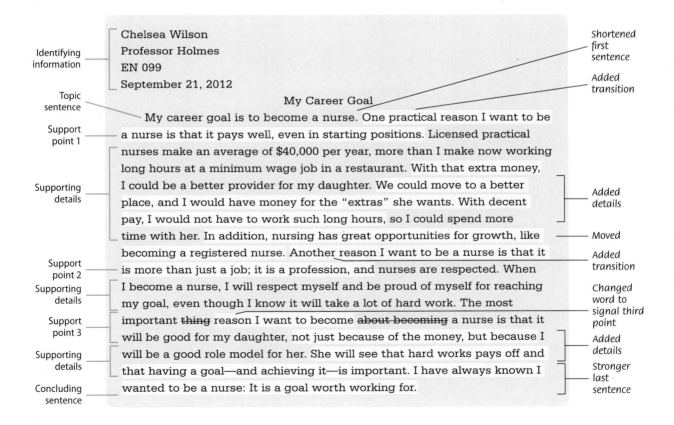

Identifying information

Chelsea Wilson
Professor Holmes
EN 099
September 21, 2012

Shortened first sentence

Added transition

Topic sentence

My Career Goal

Support point 1

My career goal is to become a nurse. One practical reason I want to be a nurse is that it pays well, even in starting positions. Licensed practical nurses make an average of $40,000 per year, more than I make now working long hours at a minimum wage job in a restaurant. With that extra money,

Supporting details

I could be a better provider for my daughter. We could move to a better place, and I would have money for the "extras" she wants. With decent pay, I would not have to work such long hours, so I could spend more time with her. In addition, nursing has great opportunities for growth, like becoming a registered nurse. Another reason I want to be a nurse is that it

Added details

Moved

Support point 2

is more than just a job; it is a profession, and nurses are respected. When

Added transition

Supporting details

I become a nurse, I will respect myself and be proud of myself for reaching my goal, even though I know it will take a lot of hard work. The most

Support point 3

important ~~thing~~ reason I want to become ~~about becoming~~ a nurse is that it

Changed word to signal third point

Supporting details

will be good for my daughter, not just because of the money, but because I will be a good role model for her. She will see that hard works pays off and that having a goal—and achieving it—is important. I have always known I

Added details

Stronger last sentence

Concluding sentence

wanted to be a nurse: It is a goal worth working for.

PRACTICE 11   **Revising a paragraph**

1. What major changes did you suggest for Chelsea's draft in response to the Checklist for Revising Your Writing?

    Answers will vary.

    _____

2. Did Chelsea make any of the suggested changes? Which ones?

    _____

    _____

3. Did Chelsea make any changes that were not suggested? Which ones? Were they good changes?

    _____

    _____

WRITING ASSIGNMENT   **Paragraph**

Revise the draft paragraph you wrote on page 88. After revising your draft, complete the following checklist.

CHECKLIST

Evaluating Your Revised Paragraph
- ☐ My topic sentence is confident, and my main idea is clear.
- ☐ My ideas are detailed, specific, and organized logically.
- ☐ My ideas flow smoothly from one to the next.
- ☐ This paragraph fulfills the original assignment.
- ☐ I am ready to turn in this paragraph for a grade.
- ☐ This paragraph is the best I can do.

After you have finished revising your paragraph, you are ready to edit it. See the Important Note about editing on page 102.

Revise Your Own Essay

Earlier in the chapter, you read Chelsea's draft essay (pp. 89–90). Reread that now as if it were your own, asking yourself the questions in the Checklist for Revising Your Writing on pages 91–92. Work either by yourself or with a partner or a small group to answer the questions about Chelsea's draft. Then, read Chelsea's revised essay that follows, and compare the changes you suggested with those that she made. Make notes on the similarities and differences to discuss with the rest of the class.

Identifying information

Chelsea Wilson
Professor Holmes
EN 099
September 28, 2012

Title, centered

The Benefits of Getting a College Degree

First line indented

Details

I have been taking college courses for two years, and it has been difficult for me. I have a full-time job, a young daughter, and a car that breaks down often. Many times as I have sat, late at night, struggling to stay awake to do homework or to study, I have wondered if getting a college degree is really worth the struggle. That is when I remind myself why getting a degree is so important: It will benefit every aspect of my life.

Added details

Thesis statement

Topic sentence/ Support point 1

One benefit of getting a degree is that I can work as a nurse, something I have always wanted to do. Even as a child, I enjoyed helping my mother care for my grandmother or take care of my younger brothers and sisters when they were sick. I enjoy helping others, and nursing will allow me to do so while making good money. The average salary for a licensed practical nurse is $40,000 per year, substantially more than I make now working at a restaurant. Without a degree, I don't see how that situation will change. Meanwhile, I have almost no time to spend with my daughter.

Added transition

Supporting details

Added transitions

Topic sentence/ Support point 2

Another benefit of getting a college degree is that it will allow me to be a better mother. In fact, I didn't get serious about getting a degree until I became a mother. Then, I realized I wanted more for my daughter than I had had: a safer place to live, a bigger apartment, some nice clothes, and birthday presents. I also wanted to have time to raise her properly and keep her safe. She is a good girl, but she sees crime and violence around her. I want to get her away from danger, and I want to show her that there are better ways to live. The job opportunities I will have with a college degree will enable me to do those things.

Supporting details

Topic sentence/ Support point 3

The most important benefit of getting a college degree is that it will show me that I can achieve something hard. In the past, I have often given up and taken the easy way, which has led to nothing good. The easy way has led to a hard life. Now, however, working toward a goal has moved my life in a good direction. I have confidence and self-respect. I can honestly say that I am proud of myself, and my daughter will be proud of me, too. I will be a good role model as she grows up, not only for her but also for her friends. She will go to college, just like her mother.

Added details

Supporting details

Conclusion

So why am I working so hard to get a degree? I am doing it because I see in that degree the kind of life I want to live on this earth and the kind of human being I want to be. Achieving that vision is worth all the struggles.

Conclusion strengthened with an observation

PRACTICE 12   **Revising an essay**

1. What major changes did you suggest for Chelsea's draft in response to the questions in the Checklist for Revising Your Writing?
   Answers will vary.
   _____

2. Did Chelsea make any of the suggested changes? Which ones?
   _____

3. Did Chelsea make any changes that were not suggested? Which ones? Were they good changes?
   _____

WRITING ASSIGNMENT   **Essay**

Revise the draft essay you wrote earlier in the chapter. After revising your draft, complete the following checklist.

Teaching tip Ask students to write you an informal letter and attach it to their papers. In the letter, they should comment on the assignment: whether it was easy or hard, interesting or not. They should also indicate what they might change about their own writing process if they were to do the assignment again.

CHECKLIST

Evaluating Your Revised Essay

- ☐ My thesis statement is confident, and my main idea is clear.
- ☐ My ideas are detailed, specific, and organized logically.
- ☐ My ideas flow smoothly from one to the next.
- ☐ This essay fulfills the original assignment.
- ☐ I am ready to turn in this essay for a grade.
- ☐ This essay is the best I can do.

Important note: After you have revised your writing to make the ideas clear and strong, you need to edit it to eliminate any distracting or confusing errors in grammar, word use, punctuation, and capitalization. When you are ready to edit your writing, turn to Part 3, the beginning of the editing chapters.

Chapter Review

1. A draft is *the first whole version of all your ideas put together in a piece of writing.*
   _____

2. List the basic features of a good draft paragraph or essay: _(Lists should include_
features on page 79.) _____

_____

_____

_____

_____

3. Three ways to order ideas are ___time___, ___space___, and ___importance___.

4. Making an ___outline___ is a useful way to plan your draft.

5. Five ways to start an essay are

_Open with a quotation._____

_Give an example or tell a story._____

_Start with a surprising fact or idea._____

_Offer a strong opinion or position._____

_Ask a question._____

6. Three features of a good essay conclusion are

_It refers back to the main idea._____

_It sums up what has been covered in the essay._____

_It makes a further observation or point._____

7. Two basic features of a good essay title are

_It makes people want to read the essay._____

_It hints at the main idea (thesis statement), but it does not repeat it._____

8. Revising is _making your ideas clearer, stronger, and more convincing._____

_____

9. Three basic features of useful feedback are

It is given in a positive way. It offers specific suggestions. It may be given in writing or

_orally._____

10. As you revise, make sure your paragraph or essay has these three things: ___unity___,
___detail /support___, and ___coherence___.

11. ___Unity___ means that all the points you make are related to your main idea.

12. Coherence means _that all your support connects to form a whole._____

13. An important way to ensure coherence in your writing is to *use transitions.*

14. Transitions are *words, phrases, and sentences that connect your ideas so that your writing moves smoothly from one point to the next.*

15. Write for one minute about "What questions I should ask my instructor."

REFLECTING ON THE JOURNEY

Skills Learned

Now that you've completed the chapter, share what you've learned about each skill by completing the following chart.

Skill	What I learned about this skill
Use an outline to draft a paragraph or essay	
Draft a paragraph or essay with a thesis statement and/or topic sentences	
Draft an effective introduction	
Draft an effective conclusion	
Revise for unity, coherence, and detail	
Avoid plagiarism	

Part 2

Writing Different Kinds of Paragraphs and Essays

"I write school essays, performance reviews, and letters to my daughter."

–Sam M., student

6

Narration

Writing That Tells Important Stories

Learning Objectives

Chapter Goal: Learn how to write a narrative paper.

Tools to Achieve the Goal:

- Four Basics of Good Narration (p. 108)
- Diagram: Paragraphs and Essays in Narration (pp. 112–13)
- Common Transitions in Narration (p. 115)
- Sample Narration Paragraph and Rubric (pp. 116–17)
- Student Narration Paragraph: Jelani Lynch, *My Turnaround* (p. 118)
- Student Narration Essay: Arianna Morgan, *The Time I Almost Lost My Baby Brother* (p. 119)
- Profile of Success and Workplace Narration: Alice Adoga (p. 121)
- Professional Narration Essay: Amy Tan, *Fish Cheeks* (p. 123)
- Checklist: How to Write Narration (p. 127)

READING ROADMAP

Key Terms

Skim Chapter 6 before reading. Find these words or terms in **bold** type. Put a check mark next to each once you locate it.

_____ narration

_____ main idea

_____ support

_____ time (chronological) order

_____ transitions

Guided Reading for Chapter 6

Fill out the following chart before you begin reading. For each skill, write what you know about that skill and what you would like to know upon completing the chapter. At the end of the chapter, you will be asked to share what you learned about each skill.

Skill	When I have used this skill	What I want to know about this skill
Write a story about myself or someone else		
Write a clear thesis statement or main idea for a narrative		
Generate support for a narrative paper		
Relate support directly to the main idea of the paper		
Read and analyze a narrative paper		

Visit **LaunchPad Solo for Readers and Writers > Reading > Patterns of Organization** for more tutorials, videos, and practice with patterns of organization.

Understand What Narration Is

Narration is writing that tells the story of an event or an experience.

Four Basics of Good Narration

1 It reveals something of importance to the writer (the main idea).

2 It includes all the major events of the story (primary support).

3 It brings the story to life with details about the major events (secondary support).

4 It presents the events in a clear order, usually according to when they happened.

In the following paragraph, the numbers and colors correspond to the Four Basics of Good Narration.

4 Events in time order

1 Last year, a writing assignment I hated produced the best writing I have done. **2** When my English teacher told us that our assignment would be to do a few hours of community service and write about it, I was furious. **3** I am a single mother, I work full time, and I am going to school—isn't that enough? **2** The next day, I spoke to my teacher during her office hours and told her that I was already so busy I could hardly make time for homework, never mind housework. My own life was too full to help with anyone else's life. **3** She said that she understood perfectly and that the majority of her students had lives as full as mine. Then, she explained that the service assignment was just for four hours and that other students had enjoyed both doing the assignment and writing about their experiences. She said they were all surprised and that I would be, too. **2** After talking with her, I decided to accept my fate. The next week, I went to the Community Service Club and was set up to spend a few hours at an adult day-care center near where I live. A few weeks later, I went to the Creative Care Center in Cocoa Beach, not knowing what to expect. **3** I found friendly, approachable people who had so many stories to tell about their long, full lives. **2** The next thing I knew, I was taking notes because I was interested in these people: **3** their marriages, life during the Depression, the wars they fought in, their children, their joys and sorrows. I felt as if I was experiencing everything they lived while they shared their history with me. **2** When it came time to write about my experience, I had more than enough to write about: **3** I wrote the stories of the many wonderful elderly people I had talked with. **2** I got an A on the paper, and beyond that accomplishment, I made friends whom I will visit on my own, not because of an assignment but because I value them.

You can use narration in many practical situations.

College	In a lab course, you are asked to tell what happened in an experiment.
Work	Something goes wrong at work, and you are asked to explain to your boss—in writing—what happened.
Everyday life	In a letter of complaint about service you received, you need to tell what happened that upset you.

In college, the word *narration* probably will not appear in writing assignments. Instead, an assignment might ask you to *describe* the events, *report* what happened, or *retell* what happened. Words or phrases that call for an *account of events* are situations that require narration.

Teaching tip Here and in the remaining chapters of Part 2, students are given examples of typical key words in assignments—key words that signal a need for narration, illustration, description, and so on. Show students sample assignments from your course and ask them to identify key words and the type of writing these words call for. To broaden the discussion, students might also bring in assignments from other courses.

Main Idea in Narration

In narration, the **main idea** is what is important about the story—to you and to your readers. To help you discover the main idea for your own narration, complete the following sentence:

Main idea in narration   **What is important to me about the experience is . . .**

The topic sentence (paragraph) or thesis statement (essay) usually includes the topic and the main idea the writer wants to make about the topic. Let's look at a topic sentence first.

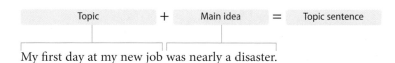

My first day at my new job was nearly a disaster.

Remember that a topic for an essay can be a little broader than one for a paragraph.

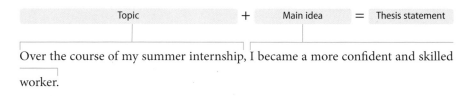

Over the course of my summer internship, I became a more confident and skilled worker.

Whereas the topic sentence is focused on just one workday, the thesis statement considers a season-long internship.

Tip Sometimes, the same main idea can be used for a paragraph and an essay, but the essay must develop this idea in more detail. (See pp. 68–69.)

PRACTICE 1   **Writing a main idea**

Look at the example narration paragraph on page 108. Fill in the diagram with the paragraph's topic sentence.

Topic	Main idea

A writing assignment produced the best writing I have done.

PRACTICE 2   **Deciding on a main idea**

For each of the following topics, write a main idea for a narration. Then, write a sentence that includes your topic and your main idea. This sentence would be your topic sentence (paragraph) or thesis statement (essay).

Example:

Topic: A fight I had with my sister

Important because: *it taught me something*

Main idea: *learned it is better to stay cool*

Topic sentence/Thesis: *After a horrible fight with my sister, I learned the value of staying calm.*

1. Topic: A powerful, funny, or embarrassing experience

    Important because: *Answers will vary.*

    Main idea: *Answers will vary.*

    Topic sentence/Thesis: *Answers will vary.*

2. Topic: A strange or interesting incident that you witnessed

    Important because: _____

    Main idea: _____

    Topic sentence/Thesis: _____

Support in Narration

Tip In an essay, the major events may form the topic sentences of paragraphs. The details supporting the major events then make up the body of these paragraphs.

In narration, **support** demonstrates the main idea—what's important about the story.

The paragraph and essay models on pages 112–13 use the topic sentence (paragraph) and thesis statement (essay) from the Main Idea section of this chapter. (The thesis statement has been revised slightly.) Both models include the support used in all narration writing—major events backed up by details about the events. In the essay model, however, the major support points (events) are topic sentences for individual paragraphs.

CHOOSING MAJOR EVENTS

When you tell a story to a friend, you can include events that are not essential to the story. In contrast, when you are writing a narration, you need to give more careful thought to which events you will include, selecting only those that most clearly demonstrate your main idea.

Teaching tip Ask students to write a narrative joke they have heard. Then, examine the structure of one or two of these jokes.

PRACTICE 3   **Choosing major events**

Choose two items from Practice 2, and write down the topic sentence or thesis statement you came up with for each. Then, for each topic sentence/thesis statement, write three events that would help you make your main idea.

Example:

Topic: A fight I had with my sister

Topic sentence/Thesis: _After a horrible fight with my sister, I learned the value of staying calm._

Events: _We disagreed about who was going to have the family party._

She made me so mad that I started yelling at her, and I got nasty.

I hung up on her, and now we're not talking.

1. Topic: A powerful, funny, or embarrassing experience

    Topic sentence/Thesis: _Answers will vary._

    _____

    _____

    Events: _Answers will vary._

    _____

    _____

    _____

2. Topic: A strange or interesting incident that you witnessed

    Topic sentence/Thesis: _____

    Events: _____

Paragraphs vs. Essays in Narration

For more on the important features of narration, see the Four Basics of Good Narration on page 108.

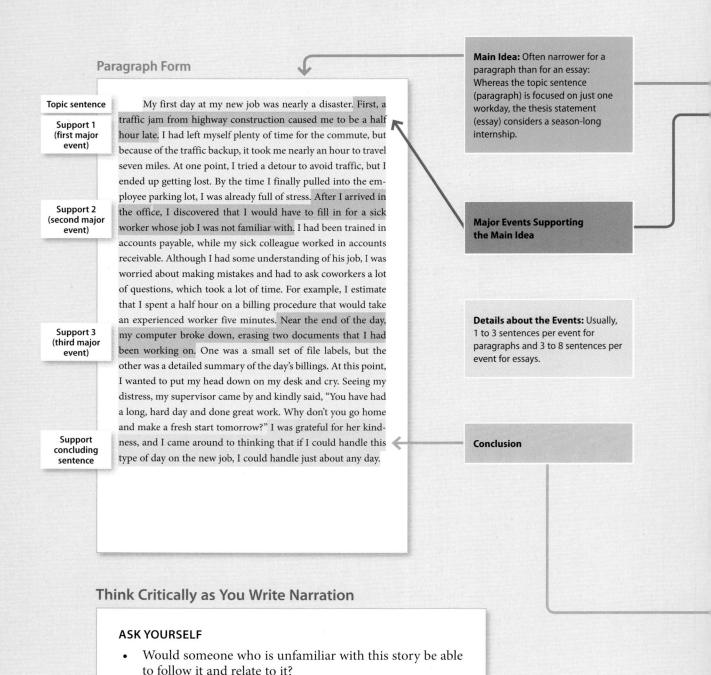

Paragraph Form

Topic sentence

My first day at my new job was nearly a disaster. First, a traffic jam from highway construction caused me to be a half hour late. I had left myself plenty of time for the commute, but because of the traffic backup, it took me nearly an hour to travel seven miles. At one point, I tried a detour to avoid traffic, but I ended up getting lost. By the time I finally pulled into the employee parking lot, I was already full of stress. After I arrived in the office, I discovered that I would have to fill in for a sick worker whose job I was not familiar with. I had been trained in accounts payable, while my sick colleague worked in accounts receivable. Although I had some understanding of his job, I was worried about making mistakes and had to ask coworkers a lot of questions, which took a lot of time. For example, I estimate that I spent a half hour on a billing procedure that would take an experienced worker five minutes. Near the end of the day, my computer broke down, erasing two documents that I had been working on. One was a small set of file labels, but the other was a detailed summary of the day's billings. At this point, I wanted to put my head down on my desk and cry. Seeing my distress, my supervisor came by and kindly said, "You have had a long, hard day and done great work. Why don't you go home and make a fresh start tomorrow?" I was grateful for her kindness, and I came around to thinking that if I could handle this type of day on the new job, I could handle just about any day.

Support 1 (first major event)

Support 2 (second major event)

Support 3 (third major event)

Support concluding sentence

Main Idea: Often narrower for a paragraph than for an essay: Whereas the topic sentence (paragraph) is focused on just one workday, the thesis statement (essay) considers a season-long internship.

Major Events Supporting the Main Idea

Details about the Events: Usually, 1 to 3 sentences per event for paragraphs and 3 to 8 sentences per event for essays.

Conclusion

Think Critically as You Write Narration

ASK YOURSELF

- Would someone who is unfamiliar with this story be able to follow it and relate to it?
- Have I provided enough detail to bring each event to life?

Essay Form

1

Several of my friends question whether summer internships are really worthwhile, especially if the pay is low or nonexistent. However, the right internship definitely pays off professionally in the l**Thesis statement** if it doesn't financially in the short run. The proof is in my own summer marketing internship, which made me a far more confident and skilled worker.

During the first two weeks of the internship, I received thorough training in every part of my job. **Topic sentence 1 (first major event)** For example, my immediate superviso_____ full days going over everything I would _____ help with e-mail campaigns, online marketing efforts, and other promotions. She even had me draft a promotional e-mail for a new product and gave me feedback about how to make the message clearer and more appealing. I also spent a lot of time with other staffers, who taught me everything from how to use the photocopier and printers to how to pull together marketing and sales materials for executive meetings. Most impressive, the president of the company took some time out of a busy afternoon to answer my questions about

2

how he got started in his career and what he sees as the keys to success in the marketing field. As I explained to a friend, I got a real "insider's view" of **Topic sentence 2 (second major event)** and its leadership.

Next, I got hands-on experience with listening to customers and addressing their needs. Specifically, I sat in on meetings with new clients and listened to them describe products and services they would like the company's help in promoting. They also discussed the message they would like to get across about their businesses. After the meetings, I sat in on brainstorming sessions with other staffers in which we came up with as many ideas as we could about campaigns to address the clients' needs. At first, I didn't think anyone would care about my ideas, but others listened to them respectfully and even ended up including some of them in the marketing plans that were sent back to the clients. I learned later that some of m_____ **Topic sentence 3 (third major event)** be included in the actual promotional ca_____

By summer's end, I had advanced my skills so much that I was asked to return next summer. My

3

supervisor told me that she was pleased not only with all I had learned about marketing but also with the responsibility I took for every aspect of my job. I did not roll my eyes about having to make photocopies or help at the reception desk, nor did I seem intimidated by bigger, more meaningful tasks. Although I'm not guaranteed a full-time job at the company after graduation, I think my chances are good. Even if I don't end up working there long term, I am grateful for how the job has helped me grow.

In the end, the greatest benefit of the internship might be the confidence it gave me. I have learned that no matter how challenging the task before me—at work or in real life—I can succeed at it by getting the right information and input on anything unfamiliar, working effectively with others, and truly dedicating myself to doing my best. My time this past summer was definitely well spent.

GIVING DETAILS ABOUT THE EVENTS

When you write a narration, include examples and details that will make each event easier to visualize and understand. You want your readers to share your point of view and see the same message in the story that you do.

PRACTICE 4 **Giving details about the events**

Teaching tip A fun way to encourage critical thinking in the context of narration is to ask students for examples of urban legends, ghost stories, or other "amazing stories" they have heard. Then, ask them what type of support would be needed to prove or disprove such stories. If you have Internet access, you might type students' examples into the search box at **www. snopes.com**, which provides evidence to prove or debunk popular stories and rumors.

Write down the topic sentence or thesis statement for each item from Practice 3. Then, write the major events in the spaces provided. Give a detail about each event.

Example:

Topic sentence/Thesis: _After a horrible fight with my sister, I learned the value of staying calm._

Event: _We disagreed about who was going to have the family party._

> **Detail:** _Even though we both work, she said she was too busy and I would have to do it._

Event: _She made me so mad, I started yelling at her, and I got nasty._

> **Detail:** _I brought up times in the past when she had tried to pass responsibilities off on me, and I told her I was sick of being the one who did everything._

Event: _I hung up on her, and now we are not talking._

> **Detail:** _I feel bad, and I know I will have to call her sooner or later because she is my sister. I do love her, even though she is a pain sometimes._

1. Topic sentence/Thesis: _Answers will vary._

   _____

   Event: _Answers will vary._

   > Detail: _____
   >
   > _____

   Event: _____

   > Detail: _____
   >
   > _____

   Event: _____

   > Detail: _____
   >
   > _____

2. Topic sentence/Thesis: _____

    _____

    Event: _____

        Detail: _____'_____

        _____

    Event: _____

        Detail: _____

        _____

    Event: _____

        Detail: _____

        _____

Organization in Narration

Narration usually presents events in the order in which they happened, which is referred to as **time (chronological) order**. As shown in the paragraph and essay models on pages 112–13, a narration starts at the beginning of the story and describes events as they unfolded.

    Transitions move readers from one event to the next.

Tip For more on time order, see pages 76–77.

Common Transitions in Narration

after	eventually	meanwhile	since
as	finally	next	soon
at last	first	now	then
before	last	once	when
during	later	second	while

PRACTICE 5   **Using transitions in narration**

Read the paragraph that follows, and fill in the blanks with time transitions. *Answers may vary. Possible answers are shown.*

    Some historians believe that as many as four hundred women disguised themselves as men so that they could serve in the U.S. Civil War (1861–1865). One of the best known of these women was Sarah Emma Edmonds. __*Once*__ the war began, Edmonds, an opponent of slavery, felt driven to join the Union Army, which fought for the free states. __*When*__ President Abraham Lincoln asked for army volunteers, she disguised herself as a man, took the name Frank Thompson, and enlisted in the infantry. ___During___ her military service, Edmonds worked as a male nurse and a messenger. ___While___ serving as a nurse, she learned that the Union general needed someone to spy on the Confederates. ___After___ extensive training, Edmonds took on this duty and, disguised as a slave, went behind enemy lines. Here, she learned about the Confederates' military strengths and weaknesses. ___Eventually___, she returned to the Union side and went back to work as a nurse. In 1863, Edmonds left the army after developing malaria. She was worried that hospital workers would discover that she was a woman. As a result of her departure, "Frank Thompson" was listed as a deserter. In later years, Edmonds, under her real name, worked to get a veteran's pension and to get the desertion charge removed from her record. ___At last___, in 1884, a special act of Congress granted her both of these wishes.

Evaluate Narration

Teaching tip If you have samples from a previous class, bring in full papers or paragraphs and ask the students to use either this rubric or the Four Basics of Good Narration to "grade" the assignments. When they have done so, ask them to pair up and work in groups to see whether they all came up with the same score and to determine the areas of consensus and disagreement.

To become a more successful writer, it is important not only to understand the Four Basics of Good Narration but to read and evaluate examples as well. In this section, you will have the opportunity to use a sample rubric to analyze or evaluate the samples of narrative writing provided. By using this rubric, you will gain a better understanding of how the components of good narration work together to create a successful paragraph or essay. Additionally, reading examples of narration will help you write your own.

Read the following sample narration paragraph. Using the Four Basics of Good Narration and the sample grading rubric, decide what grade this paragraph would earn. Explain your answer.

Assignment: Write a paragraph about one moment that made a significant difference in your week. You should use clear transitions to indicate the passage of time, and you should use enough detail to bring the story to life for your reader.

As I was driving to work the other day, I noticed that it was starting to rain. Normally, that would not be a problem, but on this day it was. I had no windshield wipers. They had broken the previous week and I had not had enough money to fix them yet. Although the rain never became overly heavy, it was enough to be annoying. Perhaps I should consider putting in new wipers when I get home. Without good windshield wipers, I am putting both myself and others in danger in poor weather.

Analysis of Sample Paragraph: *The sample paragraph is an average paragraph. Comments on each point may vary but should include the following:*

Sample rubric

Element	Grading criteria	Point: Comment
Appropriateness	• Did the student follow the assignment directions?	<u>3</u> /5: *Student followed some of the instructions, but the story is not very significant and doesn't show passage of time.*
Main idea	• Does the paper clearly state a strong main idea in a complete sentence?	<u>10</u> /10: *There is a clear main idea.*
Support	• Is the main idea developed with specific support, including specific details and examples? • Is there enough support to make the main idea evident to the reader? • Is all the support directly related to the main idea?	<u>7</u> /10: *There is a main idea, but it is not particularly important. The supporting details do not demonstrate a lot of significance.*
Organization	• Is the writing logically organized? • Does the student use transitions (*also, for example, sometimes,* and so on) to move the reader from one point to another?	<u>7</u> /10: *Writing appears in logical order but does not use transitions.*
Conclusion	• Does the conclusion remind the reader of the main idea? • Does it make an observation based on the support?	<u>5</u> /5: *The conclusion adds information that reinforces the main idea.*
Grammar	• Is the writing free of the Four Most Serious Errors? (See Chapters 16–19.) • Is the sentence structure clear? • Does the student choose words that clearly express his or her meaning? • Are the words spelled correctly? • Is the punctuation correct?	<u>7</u> /10: *The paper is free from the common errors but is not descriptive.*
		TOTAL POINTS: <u>39</u> /50

Read and Analyze Narration

The first two examples of narrative writing here come from students Jelani Lynch and Arianna Morgan. In the third example, a Profile of Success, Alice Adoga shows how she uses narration in her field of social work. The final example is a narration essay by Amy Tan, a professional writer. As you read these selections, pay attention to the vocabulary, and answer the questions in the margin. They will help you read critically.

Teaching tip Ask students to work individually, in pairs, or in groups to evaluate each of the following readings using the rubric provided above.

Student Narration Paragraph

Jelani Lynch

My Turnaround

integrity: honesty; having a sound moral code

mentor: a counselor, a teacher, an adviser

Predict What will Jelani's paragraph explain?

Vocabulary development Underline these words as you read Jelani's paragraph: *integrity, mentor.*

1   Before my big turnaround, my life was headed in the wrong direction.¹ I grew up in the city and had a typical sad story: broken home, not much money, gangs, and drugs. In this world, few positive male role models are available.² I played the game "Street Life": running the streets, stealing bikes, robbing people, carrying a gun, and selling drugs. The men in my neighborhood did not have regular jobs; they got their money outside the system. No one except my mother thought school was worth much.³ I had a history of poor school performance, a combination of not showing up and not doing any work when I did. My pattern of failure in that area was pretty strong. When I was seventeen, though, things got really bad.⁴ I was arrested for possession of crack cocaine. I was kicked out of school for good. ⁵During this time, I realized that my life was not going the way I wanted it to be. I was headed nowhere, except a life of crime, violence, and possibly early death. I knew that way of life, because I was surrounded by people who had chosen that direction. I did not want to go there anymore.⁶ When I made that decision, my life started to change.⁷ First, I met Shawn Brown, a man who had had the same kind of life I did. He got out of that life, though, by graduating from high school and college and getting a good job. He has a house, a wife, and children, along with great clothes. Shawn became my role model, showing me that with honesty, integrity, and hard work I could live a much better life.⁸ Since meeting Shawn, I have turned my life around. I started taking school seriously and graduated from high school, something I thought I would never do. Working with Shawn, I have read books and learned I enjoy writing. I have met the mayor of Boston and got a summer job at the State House. I have been part of an educational video and had many opportunities to meet and work with people who are successful. Now, I am a mentor with Diamond Educators, and I work with other young, urban males to give them a role model and help them make good choices. Now, I have a bright future with goals and plans. I have turned my life around and know I will be a success.

Reflect Have you ever made a decision that changed your life?

Summarize How did meeting Shawn change Jelani's life?

1. Underline the topic sentence.

2. What is important about the story? *Answers will vary. Possible answer: People can take control of their lives with the help of a mentor.*

3. Number the major events.

4. Circle the transitions.

5. Does Jelani's paragraph follow the Four Basics of Good Narration (p. 108)? Be ready to give specific reasons for your answer. _Answers will vary. Possible_ _answer: Yes. The story is important. It describes events and details in a clear time_ _order._

Student Narration Essay

Arianna Morgan

The Time I Almost Lost My Baby Brother

Arianna is a student at Illinois Central College pursuing a degree in Theater. She is currently employed by Right at School, and she is the site manager of Dunlap Grade. Arianna explains, This was one of my favorite essays I got to write. The writing process wasn't very difficult for me. I just wrote a story about a moment when I thought I was going to lose someone very close to me, and I revised it once. The day I wrote about was one of the hardest days of my life. I have never been more connected to a paper than I was with this one. When I wrote this, I wasn't just typing words onto a paper. Every word came from my heart, and I'm glad other people get to experience this moment with me now.

Predict What situation do you think Morgan's family faced?

Vocabulary development Underline these words as you see them in Morgan's essay: *Stevens-Johnson syndrome, Staph*

Stevens-Johnson syndrome: a rare disorder characterized by flu-like symptoms followed by painful blisters and rashes on the skin that then shed and die. This syndrome requires immediate hospital treatment and an often lengthy recovery.

Staph: short for *Staphylococcus*, a bacterium that can cause pus formations, especially in the skin and mucus membranes.

1   Just like any other summer day it was very warm and sunny out and I had stayed with my aunt and uncle the night prior. My Aunt Rosa and I were on our way home after going to the store, but when we walked inside, my uncle was standing in the kitchen, and I could tell by looking at him that something was wrong. He looked at me and said, "Grandpa called; they think they know what is wrong with Bryce. The doctors say that he has a 30 percent chance of living." Those words rang in my ears; I couldn't believe what was just said. We were just staring at him. None of us could comprehend the words my uncle just spoke. All of our minds were going crazy, but no one could speak, and we wished it could have been one of us rather than Bryce.

2   I just stood there because I could not believe what my uncle had just said, and I was thinking of what I could do to help my baby brother. Unfortunately, there was nothing I could do, and, as a big sister, that's the worst feeling, so I kept shaking my head as we were all crying. How could this happen to him? He was just fine and healthy last week. I didn't understand.

Reflect Have you ever had an experience that made you feel overwhelmed and powerless? What did you do to work through that situation or try to deal with it?

Summarize What particular ideas went through Arianna's mind as she tried to process the new information about her brother?

3   After what seemed like hours, I realized that I couldn't even create any words and I just had this blank stare with every kind of emotion running through my mind and body. Why did he have to get sick? Inside I was so angry. Why couldn't it have been one of the older kids? Someone more grown up could have fought it off, but he couldn't because he was so small. Terrified and alone, I just wanted to hold him in my arms again and tell him how much I loved him. I was so sad, hurt, and upset. This could not happen; I would not lose my little brother.

4   At this point I couldn't take it anymore. The tears and sadness were too much. Slamming the door behind me, I stormed out of the back door, bawling. All I could hear was my aunt yelling for me to come back in, but I couldn't because I was thinking to myself, "I just need fresh air and time alone to figure out what is going on." I could not even pray—which is something that I've always done when I had no one else to turn to. Everything around me made me upset. I wanted to hit something or scream at the top of my lungs, but I knew it wouldn't help.

5   My aunt came outside, but I kept running down the driveway until I couldn't run anymore. As I fell to my knees, my eyes filled with tears and I was sitting there crying like a little baby. Would I have to bury my baby brother? Would I have to be strong for my mom and little sister? Was I strong enough to do this? My aunt tried to pick me up off the ground, but I couldn't breathe, let alone get up. I couldn't feel anything other than the fact that I was in a deep dark black hole, and no one could do anything to pull me out.

6   My baby brother was going to die. I wouldn't be able to laugh or play with him ever again. All I wanted was to see my older brother and sister. I needed to see them, to hug them, and to tell them how much I loved both of them. Finally, my aunt picked me up and we went inside so I could calm down.

7   The doctors were wrong but we didn't find this out until much later. Bryce didn't have Stevens-Johnson syndrome; he had a staph infection and the doctors let us know later that he was going to live, but he would be in the hospital for a week or so.

8   After almost losing my brother so much changed. I learned to appreciate my family and everyone in it, and I don't take things for granted anymore. My baby brother is five years old now, and he's alive, healthy, and he's growing up into a little man. Any time I get annoyed with him I think about when I almost lost him, and I am just thankful he's here with us. Since this was such a life-changing experience, this moment will be a time I will always remember.

1. Underline the topic sentence.

2. What is important about the story? _Answers will vary. Possible answer: We should appreciate what we have before we are in a situation that makes us feel powerless to change it._

Profile of Success
Narration in the Real World

COURTESY OF ALICE ADOGA

Background: In January 2007, I moved from West Africa, Nigeria, to the United States at the age of eighteen to live with my stepmom and three siblings. Before my departure from Nigeria, I knew my life was going to change a great deal. However, I had no idea what these changes would be. In the fall of 2007, I was admitted into the twelfth grade at Franklin High School after taking many Standards of Learning Tests. Many were surprised that I could speak English or even articulate well. Not only did I have to deal with cultural differences, I also had to adjust to the educational system of this country. In my English classes, I was lacking in grammar and I had difficulties writing research papers. I was always self-conscious about my writing and panicked when asked to write a paper. After graduating from high school in 2008, I decided to further my education at Paul D. Camp Community College (PDCCC). While at PDCCC, I had to take developmental English, and I struggled through most English classes during my freshman year in college. I worked very closely with all my English teachers and professors in high school and college. I also had several tutors assist me with my papers. Although my grammar has improved, I am still learning how to be a better writer today. I have always had a passion for education. I believe that knowledge is power. The

many challenges I faced all these years have sparked my zeal to continue my academic journey no matter what it takes. I am currently seeking my master's degree online at Liberty University in Human Services Counseling with concentration in crisis response and trauma.

Degrees/Colleges: A.S., Paul D. Camp Community College; B.S. Psychology, George Mason University

Employer: City of Franklin Department of Social Services

Writing at work: My writing at work is an objective narrative of reports from mandated reporters and clients' documentation during intake assessment or investigations. My job requires accurate documentation of interactions with clients during interviews and any interactions carried out with child victims and anyone involved. Reports made to our agency need to be documented in the Online Automated Structured Information System (OASIS). Part of my job is to write out accurately what has been reported to me during interviews and investigation to help give the reader a better picture of what took place during the incident. After interviews with a client, I write a descriptive narrative of what was said to me without inclusion of personal thoughts or opinions.

Alice Adoga
Family Service Specialist

3. Double underline the major events.

4. Does Arianna's essay follow the Four Basics of Good Narration (p. 108)? Be ready to give specific reasons for your answer. *Answers will vary. Possible answer: Yes. The story is important. It describes events and details in a clear time order.*

121

Workplace Narration

Incident Descriptions (Hypothetical Example)

1   Caller, Ms. Joyce Baton, stated that she knows that Courtney Moses is leaving her seven-year-old daughter, Lilian Moses, at home alone in the evening several nights of the week and all day during the weekends without any food. Also, the apartment has been without power for the past three weeks. Caller informed this worker that she noted several times over the past month that Lilian has come over to their house after school and near dinner time to see their daughter, Melody Baton. Caller informed this worker that Lilian and her daughter Melody go to the same school and ride the same bus to and from school. Whenever she stops by their house, Lilian asks if she can join Melody for dinner because, "Mom doesn't have anything for me to eat." Ms. Baton stated that her daughter and Lilian "hang out" after school, and sometimes Lilian stays over for dinner. Ms. Baton says she always makes Lilian call her mother to get permission, and she has even talked with Ms. Moses about Lilian's frequent dinner requests. Ms. Baton reports that Ms. Moses does not mind that Lilian stays over and profusely thanks her for letting Lilian eat dinner with them. When this first began, Ms. Baton thought Lilian just didn't like what was being offered at home. However, Ms. Baton said she recently began to notice that Lilian "wolfs her food down" when she eats and is always finished earlier than her family. She has told her on a few occasions that, "we don't have any food left."

2   Ms. Baton stated that Melody is in the same class as Lilian. Melody told her that Lilian did not have food in her lunch bag several times last week. She also told her that Lilian asks other kids for food at school and on the bus. Ms. Baton has been to the Moses's home but has not been comfortable talking with Ms. Moses about the lack of food. Ms. Baton is concerned because her daughter has come home every day this week and reported that Lilian was begging for food. She has begun putting extra sandwiches and fruit in her daughter's lunch to share with Lilian. Ms. Baton informed this worker that she saw Lilian and her daughter get on the bus this morning. They use the same bus stop. Lilian is currently at All Kings Elementary School. The address is 1539 Lakeview Drive, Franklin, Virginia 23851. Ms. Baton stated that she wants to remain anonymous because no one knows she is calling us. She believes Ms. Moses knows about Lilian's behavior.

1. What is your main impression of what is happening in the Moses home?

    Lilian Moses's mother is typically not home to supervise her seven-year-old

    daughter and does not ensure that there is any food for her to eat.

2. Underline the primary details that support the main impression.

3. Double underline or circle any secondary details that help tell the story and give more information to the reader.

4. How is the description organized? *time (chronological) order*

Professional Narration Essay

Amy Tan

Fish Cheeks

Amy Tan was born in Oakland, California, in 1952, several years after her mother and father emigrated from China. She studied at San Jose City College and later San Jose State University, receiving a B.A. with a double major in English and linguistics. In 1973, she earned an M.A. in linguistics from San Jose State University. In 1989, Tan published her first novel, *The Joy Luck Club*, which was nominated for the National Book Award and the National Book Critics Circle Award. Tan's other books include *The Kitchen God's Wife* (1991), *The Hundred Secret Senses* (1995), *Saving Fish from Drowning* (2005), and *The Valley of Amazement* (2013). Her short stories and essays have been published in the *Atlantic, Grand Street, Harper's,* the *New Yorker,* and other publications.

In the following essay, Tan uses narration to describe an experience that taught her an important lesson.

Vocabulary development Underline these words as you read the narration essay: *prawns, appalling, clamor, murmured, belched.*

prawns: shrimp or shrimp-like creatures
appalling: horrifying
clamor: noise
murmured: spoke in low tones
belched: burped

1 I fell in love with the minister's son the winter I turned fourteen. He was not Chinese, but as white as Mary in the manger. For Christmas I prayed for this blond-haired boy, Robert, and a slim new American nose.

2 When I found out that my parents had invited the minister's family over for Christmas dinner, I cried. What would Robert think of our shabby Chinese Christmas? What would he think of our noisy Chinese relatives who lacked proper American manners? What terrible disappointment would he feel upon seeing not a roasted turkey and sweet potatoes but Chinese food?

Predict Based on the second paragraph, what do you think will happen?

3 On Christmas Eve I saw that my mother had outdone herself in creating a strange menu. She was pulling black veins out of the backs of fleshy prawns. The kitchen was littered with appalling mounds of raw food: A slimy rock cod with bulging eyes that pleaded not to be thrown into a pan of hot oil. Tofu, which looked like stacked wedges of rubbery white sponges. A bowl soaking dried fungus back to life. A plate of squid, their backs crisscrossed with knife markings so they resembled bicycle tires.

4 And then they arrived—the minister's family and all my relatives in a clamor of doorbells and rumpled Christmas packages. Robert grunted hello, and I pretended he was not worthy of existence.

Reflect Name an event during which you tried to make a good impression on someone.

5   Dinner threw me into despair. My relatives licked the ends of their chopsticks and reached across the table, dipping them into the dozen or so plates of food. Robert and his family waited patiently for platters to be passed to them. My relatives murmured with pleasure when my mother brought out the whole steamed fish. Robert grimaced. Then my father poked his chopsticks just below the fish eye and plucked out the soft meat. "Amy, your favorite," he said, offering me the tender fish cheek. I wanted to disappear.

6   At the end of the meal my father leaned back and belched loudly, thanking my mother for her fine cooking. "It's a polite Chinese custom to show you are satisfied," explained my father to our astonished guests. Robert was looking down at his plate with a reddened face. The minister managed to muster up a quiet burp. I was stunned into silence for the rest of the night.

Reflect Have you ever felt different on the outside than you did on the inside?

7   After everyone had gone, my mother said to me, "You want to be the same as American girls on the outside." She handed me an early gift. It was a miniskirt in beige tweed. "But inside you must always be Chinese. You must be proud you are different. Your only shame is to have shame."

8   And even though I didn't agree with her then, I knew that she understood how much I had suffered during the evening's dinner. It wasn't until many years later— long after I had gotten over my crush on Robert—that I was able to fully appreciate her lesson and the true purpose behind our particular menu. For Christmas Eve that year, she had chosen all my favorite foods.

Tip For reading advice, see Chapter 1.

1. What is Tan's purpose for writing? _Answers will vary. Possible answers: to amuse readers; to describe an important event in her life; to help readers learn from her experience._

2. Does she achieve it? _Answers will vary._

3. In your own words, state her main idea. _Answers will vary. Possible answer: It is important to take pride in your background, even if it is different from others' backgrounds._

4. How has Tan organized her essay? _time order_. Circle the transitional words and phrases that indicate this order.

Respond to one of the following assignments in a paragraph or essay.

1. Have you ever been embarrassed by your family or by others close to you? Write about the experience, and describe what you learned from it.

2. Write about a time when you felt different from other people. How did you react at the time? Have your feelings about the situation changed since then? If so, how?

3. Write about an experience that was uncomfortable at the time but funny later. Explain how you came to see humor in the situation.

Write Your Own Narration

In this section, you will write your own narration based on one of the following assignments. For help, refer to the "How to Write Narration" checklist on page 127.

ASSIGNMENT OPTIONS   **Writing about college, work, and everyday life**

Write a narration paragraph or essay on one of the following topics or on one of your own choice.

College
- Tell the story of how a teacher made a difference in your life.
- Write about a time when you achieved success or experienced a difficulty or success in school.
- Interview a college graduate about his or her educational experience. Questions might include the following: "Why did you go to college?" "What were your biggest challenges?" and "What were your greatest accomplishments?" Then, write that person's story.

Work
- Write about a situation or incident that made you decide to leave a job.
- Imagine a successful day or a frustrating day at your current or previous job. Then, tell the story of that day, including examples of successes.
- Write your own work history, guided by a statement that you would like to make about this history or your work style. Here is one example: "Being a people person has helped me in every job I have ever had." You might imagine that you are interviewing with a potential employer.

Everyday life
- Write about an experience that triggered a strong emotion: happiness, sadness, fear, anger, regret.
- Find a campus community service club that offers short-term assignments. Take an assignment and write about your experience.
- Tell the story of a community issue that interests you. One example is plans to create a bike lane on a major road. Discuss how the issue arose, and describe key developments. Research details by visiting a local newspaper's Web site.

| ASSIGNMENT OPTIONS | **Reading and writing critically** |

Complete one of the following assignments, which ask you to apply the critical thinking, reading, and writing skills discussed in Chapter 1.

WRITING CRITICALLY ABOUT READINGS

Tip For a reminder of how to summarize, analyze, synthesize, and evaluate, see the Reading and Writing Critically box on page 21.

Both Alice Adoga's "Incident Descriptions" (p. 122) and Celia Hyde's "Police Report" (p. 165) require the writer to carefully and deliberately tell a specific story, recording only the facts. Review both of these pieces. Then, follow these steps:

1. **Summarize** Briefly summarize the works, listing major events.

2. **Analyze** List any types of examples or details you wish had been included in Adoga's or Hyde's reports. Also, write down any questions that the pieces raise for you.

3. **Synthesize** Using examples from either Adoga's and Hyde's stories and from your own experience, write about an observation in your own life. Choose an event that was significant and write about it clearly and with detail.

4. **Evaluate** Which piece do you think is more effective? Why? To write your evaluation, look back on your responses to step 2.

WRITING ABOUT IMAGES

Study the photograph below, and complete the following steps.

PAUL BRADBURY/GETTY IMAGES

1. **Read the image** Ask yourself: What details does the photographer focus on? What seems to be the photo's message? (For more information on reading images, see Chapter 1.)

2. **Write a narration** Write a narration paragraph or essay about what has happened (or is happening) in the photograph. Be as creative as you like, but be sure to include details and reactions from step 1.

WRITING TO SOLVE A PROBLEM

Read or review the discussion of problem solving in Chapter 1 (pp. 28–30). Then, consider the following problem:

You have learned that a generous scholarship is available for low-income, first-generation college students. You really need the money to cover day-care expenses while you are taking classes (in fact, you had thought you would have to stop going to college for a while). Many people have been applying. Part of the application is to write about yourself and why you deserve the scholarship.

Assignment: Write a paragraph or essay that tells your story and why you should be considered for the scholarship. Think about how you can make your story stand out. You might start with the following sentence:

Even though you will be reading applications from many first-generation

college students, my story is a little different because _____

_____.

Tip Such scholarships really do exist. Go online or to the college financial aid office to find out about them. If you are pleased with what you have written for this assignment, you could use it as part of your application.

CHECKLIST

How to Write Narration

Steps	Details
☐ Narrow and explore your topic. See Chapter 3.	• Make the topic more specific. • Prewrite to get ideas about the narrowed topic.
☐ Write a topic sentence (paragraph) or thesis statement (essay). See Chapter 3.	• State what is most important to you about the topic and what you want your readers to understand.
☐ Support your point. See Chapter 4.	• Come up with examples and details to explain your main idea to readers.
☐ Write a draft. See Chapter 5.	• Make a plan that puts events or examples in a logical order. • Include a topic sentence (paragraph) or thesis statement (essay) and all the supporting events, examples, and details.
☐ Revise your draft. See Chapter 5.	• Make sure it has *all* the Four Basics of Good Narration. • Make sure you include transitions to move readers smoothly from one event or example to the next.
☐ Edit your revised draft. See Parts 3 through 6.	• Correct errors in grammar, spelling, word use, and punctuation.

Chapter Review

1. Narration is writing that _tells the story of an event or experience._

2. List the Four Basics of Good Narration. _It reveals something of importance to you. It includes all the major events of the story. It brings the story to life with details about the major events. It presents the events in a clear order, usually according to when they happened._

3. The topic sentence in a narration paragraph or the thesis statement in a narration essay usually includes what two things? _your narrowed topic; your main idea_

4. What type of organization do writers of narration usually use? _time order, also known as chronological order_

5. List five common transitions for this type of organization. _Answers will vary._

6. Write sentences using the following vocabulary words: *integrity, mentor, prawns, appalling, clamor, murmured,* and *belched. Answers will vary._

REFLECTING ON THE JOURNEY

Skills Learned

Now that you've completed the chapter, share what you've learned about each skill by completing the following chart.

Skill	What I learned about this skill
Write a story about myself or someone else	
Write a clear thesis statement or main idea for a narrative	
Generate support for a narrative paper	
Relate support directly to the main idea of the paper	
Read and analyze a narrative paper	

7

Illustration
Writing That Gives Examples

Learning Objectives

Chapter Goal: Learn how to write an illustration paper.

Tools to Achieve the Goal:
- Four Basics of Good Illustration (p. 130)
- Diagram: Paragraphs and Essays in Illustration (pp. 134–35)
- Sample Illustration Paragraph and Rubric (pp. 137–38)
- Student Illustration Paragraph: Casandra Palmer, *Gifts from the Heart* (p. 138)
- Student Illustration Essay: Sarah Bigler, *High School Is Not Preparing Us for College* (p. 139)
- Profile of Success and Workplace Illustration: John D'Urso (p. 141)
- Professional Illustration Essay: Andrea Whitmer, *When Poor People Have Nice Things* (p. 143)
- Checklist: How to Write Illustration (p. 149)

READING ROADMAP

Key Terms

Skim Chapter 7 before reading. Find these words or terms in **bold** type. Put a check mark next to each once you locate it.

____ illustration
____ main idea
____ support
____ order of importance
____ time order
____ transitions

Guided Reading for Chapter 7

Fill out the following chart before you begin reading. For each skill, write what you know about that skill and what you would like to know upon completing the chapter. At the end of the chapter, you will be asked to share what you learned about each skill.

Skill	When I have used this skill	What I want to know about this skill
Write a paper with one specific idea		
Identify the best possible support details to show, explain, or prove the main idea		
Provide examples to support the main idea		
Provides enough details and examples to get the idea across to the readers		

⚑ LaunchPad Solo

Visit **LaunchPad Solo for Readers and Writers > Reading > Patterns of Organization** for more tutorials, videos, and practice with patterns of organization.

Understand What Illustration Is

Illustration is writing that uses examples to support a point.

Four Basics of Good Illustration

1 It has a point.

2 It gives specific examples that show, explain, or prove the point.

3 It gives details to support the examples.

4 It uses enough examples to get the point across to the reader.

In the following paragraph, the numbers and colors correspond to the Four Basics of Good Illustration.

1 Many people would like to serve their communities or help with causes that they believe in, but they do not have much time and do not know what to do. Now, the Internet provides people with ways to help that do not take much time or money. 2 Web sites now make it convenient to donate online. With a few clicks, an organization of your choice can receive your donation or money from a sponsoring advertiser. For example, if you are interested in helping rescue unwanted and abandoned animals, you can go to www.theanimalrescuesite.com. 3 When you click as instructed, a sponsoring advertiser will make a donation to help provide food and care for the 27 million animals in shelters. Also, a portion of any money you spend in the site's online store will go to providing animal care. 2 If you want to help fight world hunger, go to www.thehungersite.com 3 and click daily to have sponsor fees directed to hungry people in more than seventy countries via the Mercy Corps, Feeding America, and Millennium Promise. Each year, hundreds of millions of cups of food are distributed to one billion hungry people around the world. 2 Other examples of click-to-give sites are www.thechildhealthsite.com, www.theliteracysite.com, and www.breastcancersite.com. 3 Like the animal-rescue and hunger sites, these other sites have click-to-give links, online stores that direct a percentage of sales income to charity, and links to help you learn about causes you are interested in. One hundred percent of the sponsors' donations go to the charities, and you can give with a click every single day. Since I have found out about these sites, I go to at least one of them every day. 1 I have learned a lot about various problems, and every day, I feel as if I have helped a little.

4 Enough examples to get the point across to the reader

It is hard to explain anything without using examples, so you use illustration in almost every communication situation.

College	An exam question asks you to explain and give examples of a concept.
Work	Your boss asks you to tell her what office equipment needs to be replaced and why.
Everyday life	You complain to your landlord that the building superintendent is not doing his job. The landlord asks for examples.

In college, the words *illustration* and *illustrate* may not appear in writing assignments. Instead, you might be asked to *give examples of* _____ or to *be specific about* _____. Regardless of an assignment's wording, to be clear and effective, most types of writing require specific examples. Include them whenever they help you make your point.

Main Idea in Illustration

In illustration, the **main idea** is the message you want your readers to receive and understand. To help you discover your main idea, complete the following sentence:

Main idea in illustration   **What I want readers to know about this topic is . . .**

The topic sentence (in a paragraph) or thesis statement (in an essay) usually includes the topic and the main idea the writer wants to make about the topic. Let's look at a topic sentence first.

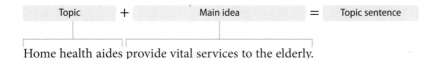

Home health aides provide vital services to the elderly.

Remember that a thesis statement for an essay can be a little broader than a paragraph topic.

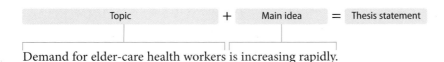

Demand for elder-care health workers is increasing rapidly.

Whereas the topic sentence is focused on just home health aides, the thesis statement considers elder-care careers in general.

Teaching tip Tell students that with illustration, examples often come to mind before the main idea does. For example, they might have several bad meals at the cafeteria before realizing that the cafeteria has a quality control problem.

Tip Sometimes, the same main idea can be used for a paragraph and an essay, but the essay must develop this point in more detail. (See pp. 68–69.)

> **PRACTICE 1** **Forming a main idea**

Each of the items in this practice is a narrowed topic. Think about each of them, and write a main idea about each topic in the space provided.

Example: The words to songs I like *relate closely to experiences I have had.*

1. A few moments alone *Answers will vary.*

2. A course I am taking _____

3. The busiest time at work _____

4. Being a parent of a newborn baby _____

5. Working with other people _____

Support in Illustration

The paragraph and essay models on pages 134–35 use the topic sentence (paragraph) and thesis statement (essay) from the Main Idea section of this chapter. Both models include the **support** used in all illustration writing: examples backed up by details about the examples. In the essay model, however, the major support points (examples) are topic sentences for individual paragraphs.

To generate good detailed examples, use one or more of the prewriting techniques discussed in Chapter 3. First, write down all the examples that come into your mind. Then, review your examples, and choose the ones that will best communicate your point to your readers.

> **PRACTICE 2** **Supporting your main idea with examples**

Read the following main ideas, and give three examples you might use to support each one.

Example: My boss's cheapness is unprofessional.

makes us bring in our own calculators

makes us use old, rusted paper clips

will not replace burned-out light bulbs

1. My (friend, sister, brother, husband, wife—choose one) has some admirable traits.

   Answers will vary.

   _____

   _____

   _____

2. This weekend is particularly busy.

_____

_____

_____

ESL teaching tip Tell students that if they are writing about something from their native country's culture, they have to think about what their readers may not be familiar with. They may need to give more details than they would need to provide for readers from their native culture.

PRACTICE 3 **Giving details about the examples**

In the spaces provided, copy your main ideas and examples from Practice 2. Then, for each example, write a detail that further shows, explains, or proves what you mean.

Example:

Main idea: My boss's cheapness is unprofessional.

Example: _makes us bring in our own calculators_

　　Detail: _Some people do not have a calculator._

Example: _makes us use old, rusted paper clips_

　　Detail: _They leave rust marks on important documents._

Example: _will not replace burned-out light bulbs_

　　Detail: _The dim light leads to more errors._

Teaching tip To encourage critical thinking in the context of illustration, give students examples of some of the characteristics of critical thinkers from **www.criticalthinking.org**. (Search for the article "Valuable Intellectual Traits.") Which characteristics do students see in themselves and others? Which traits would they like to work on developing?

1. Main idea: _Answers will vary._

　Example: _Answers will vary._

　　Detail: _Answers will vary._

　Example: _____

　　Detail: _____

　Example: _____

　　Detail: _____

2. Main idea: _____

　Example: _____

　　Detail: _____

　Example: _____

　　Detail: _____

　Example: _____

　　Detail: _____

Paragraphs vs. Essays in Illustration

For more on the important features of illustration, see the Four Basics of Good Illustration on page 130.

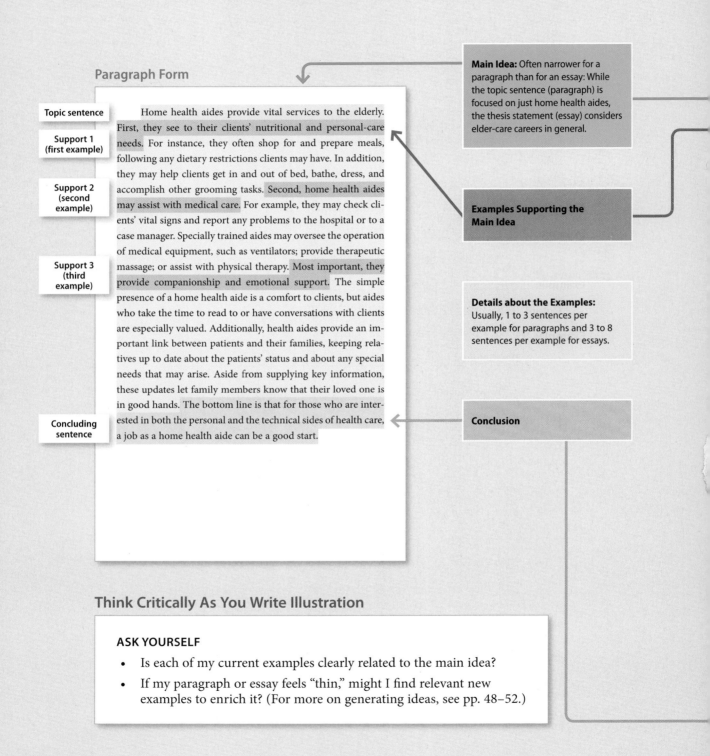

Paragraph Form

Topic sentence

Support 1 (first example)

Support 2 (second example)

Support 3 (third example)

Concluding sentence

Home health aides provide vital services to the elderly. First, they see to their clients' nutritional and personal-care needs. For instance, they often shop for and prepare meals, following any dietary restrictions clients may have. In addition, they may help clients get in and out of bed, bathe, dress, and accomplish other grooming tasks. Second, home health aides may assist with medical care. For example, they may check clients' vital signs and report any problems to the hospital or to a case manager. Specially trained aides may oversee the operation of medical equipment, such as ventilators; provide therapeutic massage; or assist with physical therapy. Most important, they provide companionship and emotional support. The simple presence of a home health aide is a comfort to clients, but aides who take the time to read to or have conversations with clients are especially valued. Additionally, health aides provide an important link between patients and their families, keeping relatives up to date about the patients' status and about any special needs that may arise. Aside from supplying key information, these updates let family members know that their loved one is in good hands. The bottom line is that for those who are interested in both the personal and the technical sides of health care, a job as a home health aide can be a good start.

Main Idea: Often narrower for a paragraph than for an essay: While the topic sentence (paragraph) is focused on just home health aides, the thesis statement (essay) considers elder-care careers in general.

Examples Supporting the Main Idea

Details about the Examples: Usually, 1 to 3 sentences per example for paragraphs and 3 to 8 sentences per example for essays.

Conclusion

Think Critically As You Write Illustration

ASK YOURSELF

- Is each of my current examples clearly related to the main idea?
- If my paragraph or essay feels "thin," might I find relevant new examples to enrich it? (For more on generating ideas, see pp. 48–52.)

Essay Form

1

During these difficult economic times, many students are looking to pursue careers in expanding fields with good long-term prospects. One~~~ **[Thesis statement]** they should seriously consider is elder care. Because the U.S. population is aging, demand for workers who specialize in the health of the elderly is increasing rapidly.

One set of workers in great demand consists of physical therapists, who help elderly patients improve their mobility and retain their independence. Some of these therapists are based at hospitals or nu~~~ **[Topic sentence 1 (first example)]** ties, others at clinics or private offices. Re~~~ where they work, they provide a variety of services to elderly patients, from helping stroke sufferers relearn how to walk and perform other daily activities to showing others how to live a more active life. Physical therapists can also help patients injured in falls reduce their reliance on painkillers, which can become less effective over time and in certain cases even addictive. According to the U.S. Department of Labor, employment of physical therapists will grow by 30 percent

2

over the next ten years, largely because of the increasing number of elderly Americans.

Also in demand are nutritionists who specialize in older people's dietary needs. These pr~~~ **[Topic sentence 2 (second example)]** may plan meals and provide nutrition advi~~~ pitals, nursing homes, and other institutions, or they may counsel individual patients on how to eat more healthfully or on how to prepare meals that meet certain dietary restrictions. For instance, elderly patients suffering from heart disease may need to eat foods that are low in salt and saturated fat. Other patients might have to avoid foods that interfere with the absorption of certain medications. Although the market for nutritionists is not expected to grow as quickly as that for physical therapists, it is projected **[Topic sentence 3 (third example)]** steadily as the population continues to age.

The highest-demand workers are those who provide at-home health care to the elderly. One subset of these workers consists of home nurses, who often provide follow-up care after patients are released from a hospital or other medical facility. These nurses help

3

patients transition from an institutional setting while making sure they continue to receive high-quality care. For instance, they track patients' vital signs, administer and monitor medications, and carry out specific tasks required to manage particular diseases. Another subset of home health workers is made up of home health aides, who assist nurses and other professionals with medical care, see to clients' nutritional and personal-care needs, and provide companionship and emotional support. Both home health aides and nurses provide an important link between patients and their families, keeping relatives up to date about the patients' status and about any special needs that may arise. In addition to supplying key information, these updates let family members know that their loved one is in good hands. Because of home health-care workers' vital role in serving the expanding elderly population, their employment is expected to grow significantly: o~~~ 30 to 40 percent over the next ten years.

Given the growing demand for elder-care workers, people pursuing these professions stand an excel-

4

lent chance of getting jobs with good long-term outlooks. Based on what I have learned about these professions, the best candidates are those who have a strong interest in health or medicine, a willingness to work hard to get the necessary qualifications, and, perhaps most important, an ability to connect with and truly care for others.

Organization in Illustration

Tip For more on order of importance and time order, see pages 76–78.

Illustration often uses **order of importance**, saving the most powerful example for last. This strategy is used in the paragraph and essay models on pages 134–35. Or, if the examples are given according to when they happened, it might be organized by **time order**.

Transitions in illustration let readers know that you are introducing an example or moving from one example to another.

Common Transitions in Illustration

also	first, second, and so on	for one thing/ for another	the most/the least
another	for example	in addition	one example/ another example
finally	for instance		

PRACTICE 4   **Using transitions in illustration**

Read the paragraph that follows, and fill in the blanks with transitions.
Answers may vary. Possible answers are shown.

Greek myths include many heroes, such as the great warriors Achilles and Herakles. __In addition__, the myths describe several monsters that tested the heroes' strength. __One example__ of these frightening creatures was the Hydra, a water serpent with many heads. When a warrior cut off one of these heads, two or more would sprout up in its place. __Another example__ of these mythical monsters was the Gorgons, three sisters who had snakes for hair. Any person who looked into the Gorgons' eyes would turn to stone. __The most__ terrifying monster was Cerberus, a three-headed dog with snapping jaws. He guarded the gates to the underworld, keeping the living from entering and the dead from leaving. Fortunately, some heroes' cleverness equaled the monsters' hideousness. __For instance__, Herakles discovered that by applying a torch to the wounds of the Hydra, he could prevent the creature from growing more heads. __Also__, Orpheus, a famous mythical musician, soothed Cerberus by plucking the strings of a lyre. In this way, Orpheus got past the beast and entered the underworld, from which he hoped to rescue his wife.

Evaluate Illustration

To become a more successful writer, it is important not only to understand the Four Basics of Good Illustration but to read and evaluate examples as well. In this section, you will have the opportunity to use a sample rubric to analyze or evaluate the samples of illustration provided. By using this rubric, you will gain a better understanding of how the components of good illustration work together to create a successful paragraph or essay. Additionally, reading examples of illustration will help you write your own.

Read the following sample illustration paragraph. Using the Four Basics of Good Illustration (p. 130) and the sample grading rubric, decide what grade this paragraph would earn. Explain your answer.

Teaching tip If you have samples from a previous class, bring in full papers or paragraphs and ask the students to use either this rubric or the Four Basics of Good Illustration to "grade" the assignments. When they have done so, ask them to pair up and work in groups to see whether they all came up with the same score and to determine where the areas of consensus and disagreement are.

> **Assignment:** Write a paragraph explaining why any one particular extracurricular activity is important.

> When I mention "marching band," it's pretty clear that most of my readers have already tuned out. In fact, I think that a lot of people reading this may not even consider it a true activity because it does not involve physical exercise, like any number of sporting activities; intense intellectual thought, as a chess or math team may require; or even individual performance, as you may see in theater. But to feel this way is to overlook activities like choir and band that not only keep students involved and out of trouble, but also help them learn leadership and teamwork skills that they may not find in other activities. As a member of a large group, every member of that group is always counting on them, so while it seems like it may be a "safety" activity where one can hide, I believe it is a significant and important activity.

> **Analysis of Sample Paragraph:** *The sample paragraph is an above-average paragraph. Comments on each point may vary but should include the following:*

Sample rubric

Element	Grading criteria	Point: Comment
Appropriateness	• Did the student follow the assignment directions?	__5__/5: *Student followed the instructions.*
Main idea	• Does the paper clearly state a strong main idea in a complete sentence?	__10__/10: *There is a clear main idea.*
Support	• Is the main idea developed with specific support, including specific details and examples? • Is there enough support to make the main idea evident to the reader? • Is all the support directly related to the main idea?	__8__/10: *The supporting details do demonstrate significance, but more examples would be helpful.* ▶

Element	Grading criteria	Point: Comment
Organization	• Is the writing logically organized? • Does the student use transitions (*also, for example, sometimes,* and so on) to move the reader from one point to another?	__8__/10: *Writing follows "order of importance." Transitions are not always clear, however.*
Conclusion	• Does the conclusion remind the reader of the main idea? • Does it make an observation based on the support?	__5__/5: *The conclusion adds information that reinforces the main idea.*
Grammar	• Is the writing free of the Four Most Serious Errors? (See Chapters 16–19.) • Is the sentence structure clear? • Does the student choose words that clearly express his or her meaning? • Are the words spelled correctly? • Is the punctuation correct?	__10__/10: *The paper is free from the common errors.*
		TOTAL POINTS: __46__/50

Read and Analyze Illustration

Teaching tip Ask students to work individually, in pairs, or in groups to evaluate each of the following readings using the rubric provided.

Reading examples of illustration will help you write your own. First, two pieces of student work, a paragraph and an essay, are featured as examples. Next, the Profile of Success is paired with writing from the real world. In this profile, John D'Urso shows how he uses illustration in his work as an automobile technician. The final example is an illustration essay by Andrea Whitmer, a professional writer. As you read these selections, pay attention to the vocabulary, and answer the questions in the margin. They will help you read critically.

Student Illustration Paragraph

Casandra Palmer

Gifts from the Heart

Predict After reading the title, what do you think the paragraph will be about?

Reflect Have you ever received a gift that made you laugh or cry?

1   In our home, gift exchanges have always been meaningful items to us. We do not just give things so that everyone has lots of presents. Each item has a purpose, such as a need or something that someone has desired for a long time. Some things have been given that may have made the other person laugh or cry. I remember one Christmas, our daughter Hannah had her boyfriend, who looked a lot like Harry Potter, join us. We wanted to include him, but we did not know him well, so it was hard to know what to give him. We decided to get Hannah a Harry Potter poster and crossed

out the name Harry Potter. In place of Harry Potter, we put her boyfriend's name. Everyone thought it was funny, and we were all laughing, including Hannah's boyfriend. It was a personal gift that he knew we had thought about. For some reason, Hannah did not think it was so funny, but she will still remember it. Another meaningful gift came from watching the movie *Titanic* with my other daughter, Tabitha. We both cried hard and hugged each other. She surprised me by getting a necklace that resembled the gem known as "Heart of the Ocean." I was so touched that she gave me something to remind me of the experience we shared. These special moments have left lasting impressions on my heart.

1. Double-underline the **topic sentence**.

2. Underline the **examples** that support the main idea.

3. Circle the **transitions**.

4. Does the paragraph have the Four Basics of Good Illustration (p. 130)? Why or why not? *Answers will vary but might say that the writer could have said more about Hannah's reaction or about what the necklace looked like.*

5. Does the paragraph use a particular kind of organization, like time, space, or importance? Does that choice help the paragraph's effectiveness or not? *No. The paragraph might have been more effective if the examples had been presented in order of increasing importance.*

Student Illustration Essay

Sarah Bigler

High School Is Not Preparing Us for College

Sarah Bigler is a political science major and editor of *The Daily Eastern News* at Eastern Illinois University in Charleston, IL.

Vocabulary development   Underline these words as you see them in Sarah's essay: *hype, myriad, tedious*.

hype: exaggerated or extravagant claim
myriad: a countless or extremely great number
tedious: too long, slow, or dull

Predict   Before reading the article, what do you think some of Bigler's reasons may be? Why do you think she would say that high school doesn't prepare students for college?

1   When I first got to college I heard the same thing over and over again from professors in all of my general education classes.

2   "How do you not know this?" "What are they teaching you in high school?"

3   As a freshman, I would sort of shrug and didn't have an answer for them. I remembered analyzing a lot of literature, and vaguely remember triangles in math and dates from history. As a senior, I totally understand my professors' point. I even feel bad for them now.

Reflect In your own experience as a student, have you ever felt the "gap" that Bigler discusses? How did or does it affect you?

4   The problem everyone misses is that there's a gap in high school teaching and college teaching. High school is supposed to prepare you for college; it doesn't. It prepares you for getting into college and for little else.

5   My high school teachers used to warn us whenever we felt they were being unfairly strict that college professors wouldn't compromise with us and that we had no idea what we were in for. I don't know why they were trying to scare us, but that wasn't true. I'm a transfer student, and neither of the schools I've been to have lived up to the terrifying hype.

6   They also told us that high school was preparation for the type of study we'd experience in college. That's definitely not true. High school was all about learning for the myriad tests the government requires. It was about passing the SAT and ACT and getting a high enough GPA to apply to the particular college you wanted.

7   Basically, high school was just about getting through. It was a way station between grade school and college.

8   It wasn't about learning and knowledge, it was about memorization of facts. I look back and wonder the same thing my professors do, because it seems nothing I learned back then has an impact on my day-to-day life now.

Reflect Bigler says that high school is just about "getting through." What does she mean? Do you agree with this statement?

9   The public school system is failing us. They teach without explaining why something is important. They don't instill a sense that education is an important factor in our lives. They teach us names and dates and numbers without showing us how they will affect our decisions and ability to get good jobs in the future.

10   Take writing for an example. The way grammar is taught is tedious and mind-numbing, especially when there are just random sentences lined up on a page and covered in red markings. Every high school student complains about having to take grammar and learn all of the awful exceptions to every grammar and spelling rule in the English language.

11   But every job that requires a college degree in America will expect a good level of writing competence. Even mathematicians and scientists have to be able to write cover letters for their resumes, research grant proposals, and reports for their bosses.

Reflect Think about your chosen field or the career you would like to have. How is writing used in that field?

12   No one bothered to explain that in my high school English class, and no type of writing outside of a grocery list requires someone to line up random sentences in order.

13   But in college, the emphasis is on learning and thinking. I've had dozens of teachers emphasize critical thinking in their classes, and advisers, counselors, professors and parents suddenly want students to think for themselves. It's a huge change from high school, where students are expected to follow rules and lessons blindly.

14   Sometimes the instinct to just get by has been so embedded in students that they don't even make a serious effort in their chosen majors. These are the classes that students are supposed to feel passionately about and that they assumedly want to use for the rest of their lives.

Reflect Do you agree with Bigler's explanation about why students do not write well?

15   To use my grammar example again, I've even seen evidence of students majoring in English and journalism who do not take grammar seriously. I'm wondering why they chose those majors if they don't care about making their writing more clear and professional.

16   High school should be a time to prepare for college and for the real world. The teenage years are the beginning of finding out who each person is and what he or she wants to do with his or her life. High schools should

be promoting individuality and should be working off a more college-like atmosphere, instead of just herding teenagers through.

1. Double underline the **topic sentence**.

2. Underline the **examples** that Bigler uses to support her point.

3. Does Bigler use enough examples to make her point clear? _Answers will vary._

4. Does Bigler's essay follow the Four Basics of Good Illustration (p. 130)? _Yes._

Profile of Success
Illustration in the Real World

Background   I grew up in Warwick, Rhode Island. I was an only child, so many things came easy for me. School was not one of those things. I had no intention of continuing my education after high school, so I enrolled in the vocational program and chose auto shop as my major. I excelled and graduated at the top of my class.

After being out of school for twenty-three years, I enrolled at Rhode Island College and chose career and technical education as my major. In my previous life as a technician, I wrote reports to illustrate the repairs needed and the consequences of not performing those repairs to the service writer, who then communicated this information to customers. But as a college student, my writing skills had to become more intense to satisfy the many professors I was now dealing with in my quest for an undergraduate degree in teaching.

I graduated in 2002 and became an assistant professor at New England Tech, where I used writing to illustrate the different methods and procedures used to repair today's automobile to my many students. As an instructor, I illustrated different nomenclature and parts both with writing and drawings.

Writing at Work   In my forty-one years in the automotive field I have always viewed the pen to be one of the most important

and most used tools in my toolbox. As a technician, I used writing to illustrate repairs needed. I also used writing to illustrate repairs I had performed so I could get paid. The flat rate system pays by the repair, so the more writing I did to illustrate the work I was doing, the more I got paid.

In my tenure as an assistant professor in the automotive department I used writing in all of its forms. Because of the many different levels of students' knowledge we were seeing, it became important to be able to communicate at different levels as well. I also found myself including writing as a requirement in my courses and letting students know that writing will always be a necessary part of their life.

In my current position as a mobile fleet service technician, I serve as the service writer, the parts person, and the repair person.

I use illustration on repair orders to explain and document repairs needed and to explain and document repairs performed. I also use it to show labor charges and how they break down for the different procedures and explain the parts used to complete the repair. All of this illustrative writing must be very detailed so that the customer, who may not have knowledge of all the different parts and procedures, will more clearly understand what they are paying for.

John D'Urso
Automobile Technician

Workplace Illustration

Tasca Mobile Fleet Work Order

Date: 8/26/14   LOF (Lube, Oil & Filter) Due: 53,775

Plate: P28-6789   Company: Simmons Oil

Miles: 66,192   Trucks: 1

VIN: IFTF3TCIU66894

Repair Requested:

LOF, Air filter, TPMS (Tire Pressure Monitoring System) light on, R/S (right-side) mirror broken

Rotor Measurement	Pad Measurement	Tire Spec
LF 5 MM—RF 5 MM LR 7 MM—RR 6 MM	LF 6 MM—RF 6 MM LR 2 MM—RR 2 MM	LF 2 MM—RF 2 MM LR 8 MM—RR 7 MM

Repair Completed:

LOF

TPMS light on. Found R/F (right front) TPMS sensor broken inside.
Replaced and programmed sensor and both front tires under Spec replaced.
TPMS12x1 reprogram

Found air filter dirty. Replaced.

R/S mirror broken. Replaced.

Found rear brakes and L/F ball joints bad. Tech did not have time to repair.
Set up services on September 2, 2014 at 7 a.m.

---

1. Based on the work order above, what repairs were made on the vehicle?

   LOF, air filter, TPMS (Tire Pressure Monitoring System) light on, R/S (right-side)

   mirror broken

2. For any work order, the technician needs to provide evidence (support) to demonstrate why something needs to be repaired or replaced. Where do you see that in this work order?

   Air Filter = found dirty/replaced

   R/S mirror broken = replaced

   TPMS light on = reprogrammed sensor under both front tires

3. What is the purpose of the memo? *Answers will vary but should include some mention of providing detailed examples to the customer of what services were performed.*

Professional Illustration Essay

Andrea Whitmer

When Poor People Have Nice Things

Andrea Whitmer is a freelance writer and blogger. Most of her writing attempts to help others—mothers in particular—find the humor in everyday situations. She also hopes to share her hard-earned wisdom with others so that they can learn from and, possibly, not make some of the same choices she did. This essay first appeared on her blog, So Over This, in June of 2012.

Vocabulary development Underline these words as you see them in Andrea's essay: *graphic, circulating, indignant, scrounging.*

1   There's a graphic circulating on some of my friends' Facebook profiles that really gets on my nerves. I told myself I wouldn't write about it, but I saw it again last night and I just can't help myself. The graphic says, "Maybe someday I'll be able to afford an iPhone like the person in front of me at the grocery store. The one paying with FOOD STAMPS!"

2   Anytime that picture (or something similar) is posted, it gets about 50 "likes" and a long string of comments from indignant people who have personally witnessed a poor person owning something of value. The rage is evident—how dare someone on food stamps have a smartphone! Why should they even be allowed to have a phone at all? Our tax dollars blah blah blah blah . . .

3   Here's the thing: We can all think of at least one person who games the system. After working as a therapist for almost 7 years, I can think of quite a few. But no one knows the life situation of every single person on the planet, no matter how much they think they do.

graphic: diagrams, pictures, charts

circulating: to pass from place to place or person to person

indignant: a feeling or expressing of extreme disgust

scrounging: attempt to gather something by looking carefully or asking for the help of others.

Predict What will Whitmer's essay be about?

Reflect Has there ever been a time in your own life where you had to make a difficult financial decision? What factors did you consider before making that decision?

4   A good friend of mine got fired from her job just days after her husband was laid off. Both of them had iPhones on his parents' plan, which cost them $50 a month total. Now what makes the most sense—breaking that contract at hundreds of dollars, or scrounging up the $50 a month in hopes that one or both of them would find another job soon? They didn't have to sign up for assistance—they were both lucky to get jobs before their emergency fund was drained—but if they had, they would have been in the grocery checkout line with iPhones in their pockets.

I Speak From Experience

Reflect When you read about Whitmer's experience, what is your immediate assumption? Why?

5   The only assistance I've ever personally used was Medicaid for my son at two different times during his life. But I will tell you—during both of those times, I had cable TV. I had Internet access at home. This last time, I had an iPhone (gasp!). I also owned several items that could have been pawned or sold for a decent amount of money.

6   Was I living it up? No. Not even close. But as someone with two college degrees and tons of ambition, I also never planned to continue collecting that assistance forever. Why should I empty my house of all the things I bought with my own money, only to have to buy them again when the crisis was over? That really doesn't make sense.

Reflect Have any of Whitmer's examples affected your initial assumption?

7   Now, I could understand it if I had a Lamborghini or two in my garage. But when you're used to a fairly middle-class existence and something happens to you (no matter what it is), you assume that your situation will improve at some point. It's not like the poverty police come take all your stuff in the middle of the night. You still own all the things you did before. If you had nice clothes, you'll still have nice clothes. If your cousin bought you an expensive handbag last Christmas, you'll still have that handbag. No one drops off a tattered, dirty wardrobe for you to put on before you leave your house.

I Know What You're Thinking

8   I can just hear the comments now. "Well, I know someone who did X and Y," or "I saw a lady buy Z at the mall." I know. I've seen it too. That's not the point.

Reflect Has there ever been a time where someone has judged you without knowing you? Or have you judged someone else and found out you were incorrect?

9   The point is, some people are in situations that we know nothing about. Some people own nice things from a better time in their lives and choose to keep those things during a setback. And some people make choices after becoming poor that we wouldn't personally make. Talking smack about those people on Facebook isn't doing anything to eradicate poverty or to change the fact that there is widespread abuse of our current system.

10   If you get upset when you see a poor person with nice things like smartphones, all I ask is that you consider this:

Maybe they just got laid off last month and they already owned the iPhone.

Maybe a family member pays the phone bill.

Maybe they're picking up groceries for a disabled neighbor with the neighbor's food stamp card.

Maybe the phone was a gift and it's on a prepaid plan.

Maybe you should worry less about what someone else has and more about yourself.

11   To many people, I could be considered "poor" right now (even though my bills are paid and I'm saving money). And guess what? I own several nice things. Some of you will judge me for that, and there's nothing I can do about it. But I will continue to be disgusted when people criticize another person's choices, especially when they can't possibly know the full set of circumstances.

Evaluate Based on Whitmer's observations, do you think we have become too comfortable making judgments based only on appearance?

1. In your own words, state Whitmer's main idea. *Answers will vary. Possible answers: People with low incomes are not necessarily taking advantage of government programs.*

Tip For reading advice, see Chapter 1.

2. Underline the examples Whitmer provides to support her main idea.

3. What type of order is the author using? *Order of importance.*

4. What do you think of this essay? Do you have a better understanding of why some people may appear to have nicer things than they can afford? *Answers will vary.*

Respond to one of the following assignments in a paragraph or essay.

1. Write about a time when someone made a snap judgment about you. This could be because of where you work, how you speak, or how you dress. How did you find out about it? How did it make you feel? How close to being accurate was it? Why do you think that person made those assumptions?

2. With social networking and its primary focus on images and short text, it has become easier than ever to publicly humiliate or bully others. Do you think that social networking has created more bullying and caused more harm than there was before media like Facebook, Instagram, Twitter, and other platforms existed?

3. In your opinion, why is it important to question our assumptions about other people? How can that benefit both ourselves and other people?

Write Your Own Illustration

In this section, you will write your own illustration based on one of the following assignments. For help, refer to the How to Write Illustration checklist on page 149.

ASSIGNMENT OPTIONS   **Writing about college, work, and everyday life**

Write an illustration paragraph, essay, or other document (as described below) on one of the following topics or on one of your own choice.

College
- Describe your goals for this course, making sure to explain the benefits of achieving each goal.
- If you are still deciding on a degree program or major, identify at least two areas of study that interest you. To get some ideas, you might refer to a course catalog. Also, consider visiting a counselor at your college's guidance office or career center. The counselor might be able to recommend some study programs to you based on your goals and interests. Next, write about the areas of study that appeal to you the most, giving examples of what you would learn and explaining how each of your choices matches your goals and interests.
- Produce a one- or two-page newsletter for other students in your class on one of the following topics. Make sure to describe each club, opportunity, and event in enough detail for readers. Also, include contact information, as well as hours and locations for events and club meetings.
  - Student clubs
  - Volunteer opportunities
  - Upcoming campus events (such as lectures, movies, and sports events)
  - Upcoming events in the larger community

Work
- What is the best or worst job you have ever had? Give examples of what made it the best or worst job.
- Thinking like a television producer, find a category of jobs—such as "dirty jobs," the name of a popular cable show—that a TV audience would find strange and interesting. Then, give examples of jobs in the category. (Examples of professions covered in the show *Dirty Jobs* include maggot farming, camel ranching, and bologna making.) Give enough details about each job to make it clear why that job is unusual. To get some ideas, you might type "strange jobs" into a search engine.
- Think of the job you would most like to have after graduation. Then, write a list of your skills—both current ones and ones you will be building in college—that are relevant to the job. To identify skills you will be building

through your degree program, you might refer to a course catalog. To identify relevant work skills, consider your past or present jobs as well as internships or other work experiences you would like to have before graduation. Finally, write a cover letter explaining why you are the best candidate for your ideal job. Be sure to provide several examples of your skills, referring to the list that you prepared.

Everyday life
- Write about stresses in your life or things that you like about your life. Give plenty of details for each example.

- Give examples of memories that have stayed with you for a long time. For each memory, provide enough details so that readers will be able to share your experience.

- Identify at least three public improvements you think would benefit a significant number of people in your community, such as the addition of sidewalks in residential areas to encourage exercise. These improvements should not include changes, such as the creation of a boat dock on a local lake, that would benefit only a small portion of the community. Then, in a letter to the editor of your local paper, describe each suggested improvement in detail, and explain why it would be an asset to the community.

Teaching tip Have students pair up and exchange drafts of their cover letters. Next, ask them to read each other's letters, paying special attention to the examples. They should mark any examples that are not clear or that could be developed in more detail.

ASSIGNMENT OPTIONS   **Reading and writing critically**

Complete one of the following assignments, which ask you to apply the critical thinking, reading, and writing skills discussed in Chapter 1.

WRITING CRITICALLY ABOUT READINGS

Both Andrea Whitmer's *When Poor People Have Nice Things* (pp. 143–45) and Joshua Boyce's *Conditioning* (pp. 277–78) illustrate the assumptions that people make about others around them on a daily basis. Read or review both of these pieces, and then follow these steps:

1. **Summarize** Briefly summarize the works, listing major examples.

2. **Analyze** What questions do the essays raise for you? Are there any other issues you wish they had covered?

3. **Synthesize** Using examples from both Whitmer's and Boyce's essays and from your own experience, discuss why we make these assumptions about others or how it feels to have others make assumptions about you.

4. **Evaluate** Which essay, Whitmer's or Boyce's, do you think is more effective? Why? Does the writers' use of clear examples get their points across? Why or why not? In writing your evaluation, you might look back on your responses to step 2.

Tip For a reminder of how to summarize, analyze, synthesize, and evaluate, see the Reading and Writing Critically box on page 21.

Teaching tip If time is short, students might complete just one or two steps of this assignment.

WRITING ABOUT IMAGES

Study the photograph below, and complete the following steps.

MARTIN KIRCHNER/laif/REDUX

1. **Read the image** Ask yourself: What details does the photographer focus on? How do the colors and lights affect you as a viewer? What main impression does the picture make? (For more information on reading images, see Chapter 1.)

2. **Write an illustration** The photograph shows a luxury liner whose bright, colorful lights attract onlookers and potential customers. Write an illustration paragraph or essay about businesses that draw customers with colorful displays, loud music, or some other appeal to the senses. Include the types of details you examined in step 1.

WRITING TO SOLVE A PROBLEM

Read or review the discussion of problem solving in Chapter 1 (pp. 28–30). Then, consider the following problem.

> Your college is increasing its tuition by $500 next year, and you do not think that you can continue. You have done well so far, and you really want to get a college degree.

Assignment Rather than just giving up and dropping out next year, as many students do, working in a small group or on your own, make a list of resources you could consult to help you, and explain how they might help. You might want to start with the following sentence:

Before dropping out of school for financial reasons, students should

consult _____ because _____.

For a paragraph: Name your best resource, and give examples of how this person or office might help you.

For an essay: Name your three best resources, and give examples of how they might help you.

CHECKLIST

How to Write Illustration

Steps	Details
☐ Narrow and explore your topic. See Chapter 3.	• Make the topic more specific. • Prewrite to get ideas about the narrowed topic.
☐ Write a topic sentence (paragraph) or thesis statement (essay). See Chapter 3.	• State what you want your readers to understand about your topic.
☐ Support your point. See Chapter 4.	• Come up with examples and details to show, explain, or prove your main idea to readers.
☐ Write a draft. See Chapter 5.	• Make a plan that puts examples in a logical order. • Include a topic sentence (paragraph) or thesis statement (essay) and all the supporting examples and details.
☐ Revise your draft. See Chapter 5.	• Make sure it has *all* the Four Basics of Good Illustration. • Make sure you include transitions to move readers smoothly from one example to the next.
☐ Edit your revised draft. See Parts 3 through 6.	• Correct errors in grammar, spelling, word use, and punctuation.

Chapter Review

1. Illustration is writing that *uses examples to show, explain, or prove a point.*

2. What are the Four Basics of Good Illustration? *It has a point. It gives specific examples that show, explain, or prove the point. It gives details to support the examples. It uses enough examples to get the point across to the reader.*

3. Write sentences using the following vocabulary words: *hype, myriad, tedious, graphic, circulating, indignant,* and *scrounging.* *Answers will vary.*

REFLECTING ON THE JOURNEY

Skills Learned

Now that you've completed the chapter, share what you've learned about each skill by completing the following chart.

Skill	What I learned about this skill
Write a paper with one specific idea	
Identify the best possible support details to show, explain, or prove the main idea	
Provide examples to support the main idea	
Provide enough details and examples to get the idea across to the readers	

8

Description
Writing That Creates Pictures in Words

READING ROADMAP

Learning Objectives

Chapter Goal: Learn how to write a descriptive paper.

Tools to Achieve the Goal:

- Four Basics of Good Description (p. 152)
- Diagram: Paragraphs and Essays in Description (pp. 156–57)
- Sample Description Paragraph and Rubric (p. 160)
- Student Description Paragraph: Alessandra Cepeda, *Bird Rescue* (p. 161)
- Student Description Essay: Brian Healy, *First Day in Fallujah* (p. 162)
- Profile of Success and Workplace Description: Celia Hyde (p. 165)
- Professional Description Essay: Oscar Hijuelos, *Memories of New York City Snow* (p. 166)
- Checklist: How to Write Description (p. 171)

Key Terms

Skim Chapter 8 before reading. Find these words or terms in **bold** type. Put a check mark next to each once you locate it.

_____ description
_____ main idea
_____ support
_____ order of time
_____ order of space
_____ order of importance
_____ transitions

Guided Reading for Chapter 8

Fill out the following chart before you begin reading. For each skill, write what you know about that skill and what you would like to know upon completing the chapter. At the end of the chapter, you will be asked to share what you learned about each skill.

Skill	When I have used this skill	What I want to know about this skill
Write a paper using descriptive detail		
Describe something using the five senses		
Generate support for a description paper		
Relate support and description details directly to the main idea of the paper		

151

LaunchPadSolo

Visit **LaunchPad Solo for Readers and Writers > Reading > Patterns of Organization** for more tutorials, videos, and practice with patterns of organization.

Understand What Description Is

Description is writing that creates a clear and vivid impression of a person, place, or thing, often by appealing to the physical senses.

Four Basics of Good Description

1 It creates a main impression—an overall effect, feeling, or image—about the topic.

2 It uses specific examples to support the main impression.

3 It supports those examples with details that appeal to the five senses: sight, hearing, smell, taste, and touch.

4 It brings a person, place, or physical object to life for the reader.

In the following student paragraph, the numbers and colors correspond to the Four Basics of Good Description.

Teaching tip If you have covered narration, point out to students that this description also uses narration.

Scars are stories written on a person's skin and sometimes on his heart. **1** My scar is not very big or very visible. **2** It is only about three inches long and an inch wide. It is on my knee, so it is usually covered, unseen. **3** It puckers the skin around it, and the texture of the scar itself is smoother than my real skin. It is flesh-colored, almost like a raggedy bandage. The story on my skin is a small one. **1** The story on my heart, though, is much deeper. **2** It was night, very cold, **3** my breath pluming into the frigid air. I took deep breaths that smelled like winter, piercing through my nasal passages and into my lungs as I walked to my car. I saw a couple making out against the wall of a building I was nearing. **2** I smiled and thought about them making their own heat. **3** I thought I saw steam coming from them, but maybe I imagined that. As I got near, I heard a familiar giggle: my girlfriend's. Then I saw her scarlet scarf, one I had given her, along with soft red leather gloves. I turned and ran, before they could see me. There was loud pounding in my ears, from the inside, sounding and feeling as if my brain had just become the loudest bass I had ever heard. My head throbbed, and slipping on some ice, I crashed to the ground, landing on my hands and knees, ripping my pants. I knew my knee was bleeding, even in the dark. I didn't care: **4** That scar would heal. The other one would take a lot longer.

Being able to describe something or someone accurately and in detail is important in many situations.

College	On a physical therapy test, you describe the symptoms you observed in a patient.
Work	You write a memo to your boss describing how the office could be arranged for increased efficiency.
Everyday life	You describe something you lost to the lost-and-found clerk at a store.

In college assignments, the word *describe* may mean *tell about* or *report*. When an assignment asks you to actually describe a person, place, or thing, however, you will need to use the kinds of specific descriptive details discussed later in this chapter.

Main Idea in Description

In description, the **main idea** is the main impression you want to create for your readers. To help you discover your main idea, complete the following sentence:

Main idea in description	**What is most interesting, vivid, and important to me about this topic is . . .**

If you do not have a main impression about your topic, think about how it smells, sounds, looks, tastes, or feels.

> **PRACTICE 1**   **Finding a main impression**
>
> For the following general topics, jot down impressions that appeal to you, and circle the one you would use as a main impression. Base your choice on what is most interesting, vivid, and important to you.
>
> **Example:**
>
> **Topic: A vandalized car**
>
>   **Impressions:** *wrecked, smashed, damaged, battered* _____
>
> 1. Topic: A fireworks display
>
>   Impressions: *Answers will vary* _____
>
> 2. Topic: A football player
>
>   Impressions: _____
>
> 3. Topic: The room you are in
>
>   Impressions: _____

The topic sentence (paragraph) or thesis statement (essay) in description usually contains both your narrowed topic and your main impression. Here is a topic sentence for a description paragraph:

Topic	+	Main impression	=	Topic sentence

The view from the shore of Fisher Lake calms me every time I see it.

Remember that a topic for an essay can be a little broader than one for a paragraph.

Topic	+	Main impression	=	Thesis statement

The views from my sky-high welding jobs are more stunning than any seen through an office window.

Tip Sometimes, the same main idea can be used for a paragraph and an essay, but the essay must develop this point in more detail. (See pp. 68–69.)

Whereas the topic sentence is focused on just one location and view, the thesis statement sets up descriptions of different views from different sites.

To be effective, your topic sentence or thesis statement should be specific. You can make it specific by adding details that appeal to the senses.

PRACTICE 2   **Writing a statement of your main impression**

For two of the items from Practice 1, write the topic and your main impression. Then, write a statement of your main impression. Finally, revise the statement to make the main impression sharper and more specific.

Example:

Topic/main impression: _A vandalized car/battered_

Statement: _The vandalized car on the side of the highway was battered._

More specific: _The shell of a car on the side of the road was dented all over, apparently from a bat or club, and surrounded by broken glass._

1. Topic/main impression: _Answers will vary._

    Statement: _____

    More specific: _____

    _____

    _____

2. Topic/main impression: _____

    Statement: _____

    More specific: _____

    _____

    _____

Support in Description

In description, **support** consists of the specific examples and details that help readers experience the sights, sounds, smells, tastes, and textures of your topic. Your description should get your main impression across to readers. Here are some qualities to consider.

Sight	Sound	Smell
Colors?	Loud/soft?	Sweet/sour?
Shapes?	Piercing/soothing?	Sharp/mild?
Sizes?	Continuous/off and on?	Good? (Like what?)
Patterns?	Pleasant/unpleasant? (How?)	Bad? (Rotten?)
Shiny/dull?		New? (New what? Leather? Plastic?)
Does it look like anything else?	Does it sound like anything else?	Old?
		Does it smell like anything else?

Taste	Touch
Good? (What does "good" taste like?)	Hard/soft?
Bad? (What does "bad" taste like?)	Liquid/solid?
Bitter/sugary? Metallic?	Rough/smooth?
Burning? Spicy?	Hot/cold?
Does it taste like anything else?	Dry/oily?
	Textures?
	Does it feel like anything else?

The paragraph and essay models on pages 156–57 use the topic sentence (paragraph) and thesis statement (essay) from the Main Idea section of this chapter. Both models include the support used in all descriptive writing—examples that communicate the writer's main impression, backed up by specific sensory details. In the essay model, however, the major support points (examples) are topic sentences for individual paragraphs.

> **PRACTICE 3**   **Finding details to support a main impression**
>
> Read the statements on page 158, and write four sensory details you might use to support the main impression.
>
> **Example: The physical sensations of a day at the beach are as vivid as the visual ones.**
>
> a. *softness of the sand*
>
> b. *push and splash of waves*
>
> c. *chill of the water*
>
> d. *smoothness of worn stones and beach glass*

Teaching tip Put students in small groups, and give each group an object to describe using the questions in the text. It can be a small toy, an object from the classroom or elsewhere on campus, a photo, or a piece of paper that has a unique design on it. For more interaction, ask another group to try to identify what was described based only on the writing.

Tip When writing descriptions, consider this advice from writer Rhys Alexander: "Detail makes the difference between boring and terrific writing. It's the difference between a pencil sketch and a lush oil painting. As a writer, words are your paint. Use all the colors."

Paragraphs vs. Essays in Description

For more on the important features of description, see the Four Basics of Good Description on page 152.

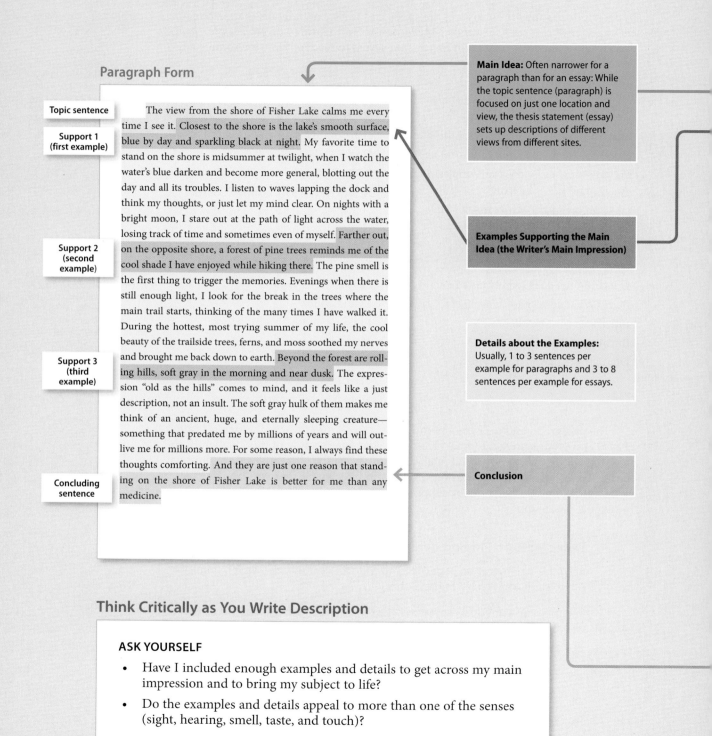

Paragraph Form

Topic sentence

Support 1 (first example)

Support 2 (second example)

Support 3 (third example)

Concluding sentence

The view from the shore of Fisher Lake calms me every time I see it. Closest to the shore is the lake's smooth surface, blue by day and sparkling black at night. My favorite time to stand on the shore is midsummer at twilight, when I watch the water's blue darken and become more general, blotting out the day and all its troubles. I listen to waves lapping the dock and think my thoughts, or just let my mind clear. On nights with a bright moon, I stare out at the path of light across the water, losing track of time and sometimes even of myself. Farther out, on the opposite shore, a forest of pine trees reminds me of the cool shade I have enjoyed while hiking there. The pine smell is the first thing to trigger the memories. Evenings when there is still enough light, I look for the break in the trees where the main trail starts, thinking of the many times I have walked it. During the hottest, most trying summer of my life, the cool beauty of the trailside trees, ferns, and moss soothed my nerves and brought me back down to earth. Beyond the forest are rolling hills, soft gray in the morning and near dusk. The expression "old as the hills" comes to mind, and it feels like a just description, not an insult. The soft gray hulk of them makes me think of an ancient, huge, and eternally sleeping creature—something that predated me by millions of years and will outlive me for millions more. For some reason, I always find these thoughts comforting. And they are just one reason that standing on the shore of Fisher Lake is better for me than any medicine.

Main Idea: Often narrower for a paragraph than for an essay: While the topic sentence (paragraph) is focused on just one location and view, the thesis statement (essay) sets up descriptions of different views from different sites.

Examples Supporting the Main Idea (the Writer's Main Impression)

Details about the Examples: Usually, 1 to 3 sentences per example for paragraphs and 3 to 8 sentences per example for essays.

Conclusion

Think Critically as You Write Description

ASK YOURSELF

- Have I included enough examples and details to get across my main impression and to bring my subject to life?
- Do the examples and details appeal to more than one of the senses (sight, hearing, smell, taste, and touch)?

Essay Form

Introductory paragraph

1

I have worked in many places, from a basement-level machine shop to a cubicle in a tenth-floor insurance office. Now that I am in the construction industry, I want to sing the praises of one en[**Thesis statement**] benefit that does not get enough attention: The views from my sky-high welding jobs have been more stunning than any seen through an office window.

From a platform at my latest job, on a high-rise, the streets below look like scenes from a miniature village. The cars and trucks—even th[**Topic sentence 1 (first example)**] people—remind me of my nephews' moto Sometimes, the breeze carries up to me one of the few reminders that what I see is real: the smell of sausage or roasting chestnuts from street vendors, the honking of taxis or the scream of sirens, the dizzying clouds of diesel smoke. Once, the streets below me were taken over for a fair, and during my lunch break, I sat on a beam and watched the scene below. I spotted the usual things—packs of people strolling by concession stands or game tents, and bands playing to crowds at different ends of the fair. As I finished my lunch, I saw two

2

small flames near the edge of one band stage, nothing burning, nothing to fear. It was, I soon realized, an acrobat carrying two torches. I watched her climb high and walk a rope, juggling the torc[**Topic sentence 2 (second example)**] crowd looked up and I looked down, fascin

Even more impressive are the sights from an oil rig. Two years ago, I worked on a rig in Prudhoe Bay, Alaska, right at the water's edge. In the long days of summer, I loved to watch the changing light in the sky and on the water: bright to darker blue as the hours passed, and at day's end, a dying gold. At the greatest heights I could see white dots of ships far out at sea, and looking inland, I might spot musk ox or bears roaming in the distance. In the long winter dark, we worked by spotlights, which blotted the views below. But I still remember one time near nightfall when the spotlights suddenly flashed off. As my eyes adjusted, a crowd of caribou emerged below like gh[**Topic sentence 3 (third example)**] snuffled the snow for food, oblivious to us.

To me, the most amazing views are those from bridges high over rivers. In 2006, I had the privilege of

3

briefly working on one of the tallest bridge-observatories in the world, over the Penobscot River in Maine. As many tourists now do, I reached the height of the observatory's top deck, 437 feet. Unlike them, however, my visits were routine and labor-intensive, giving me little time to appreciate the beauty all around me. But on clear days, during breaks and at the end of our shift, my coworkers and I would admire the wide, sapphire-colored river as it flowed to Penobscot Bay. Looking south, we would track the Maine coast's winding to the Camden Hills. Looking east, we would spot Acadia National Park, the famous Mount Desert Island offshore in the mist. Each sight made up a panoramic view that I will never forget.

Concluding paragraph

My line of work roots me in no one place, and it has a generous share of discomforts and dangers. But there are many reasons I would never trade it for another, and one of the biggest is the height from which it lets me see the world. For stretches of time, I feel nearly super human.

1. My favorite meal smells as good as it tastes.

    a. *Possible answers: sweetness of baked yams*

    b. *sage in stuffing*

    c. *buttery roasting turkey*

    d. *apple pie with cinnamon*

2. The new office building has a contemporary look.

    a. *Possible answers: lots of glass*

    b. *concrete*

    c. *steel*

    d. *tall*

3. A classroom during an exam echoes with the "sounds of silence."

    a. *Possible answers: people coughing*

    b. *rustle of papers*

    c. *radiator hissing*

    d. *sounds of pens scratching paper*

Organization in Description

Tip For more on these orders of organization, see pages 76–78.

Description can use any of the orders of organization—**time**, **space**, or **importance**—depending on your purpose. If you are writing to create a main impression of an event (for example, a description of fireworks), you might use time order. If you are describing what someone or something looks like, you might use space order, the strategy used in the paragraph model on page 156. If one detail about your topic is stronger than the others, you could use order of importance and leave that detail for last. This approach is taken in the essay model on page 157.

Order	Sequence
Time	first to last/last to first, most recent to least recent/least recent to most recent
Space	top to bottom/bottom to top, right to left/left to right, near to far/far to near
Importance	end with detail that will make the strongest impression

Use **transitions** to move your readers from one sensory detail to the next. Usually, transitions should match your order of organization.

Common Transitions in Description

Time

as	finally	next	then
at last	first	now	when
before/after	last	second	while
during	later	since	
eventually	meanwhile	soon	

Space

above	beneath	inside	over
across	beside	near	to the left/right
at the bottom/top	beyond	next to	to the side
behind	farther/further	on top of	under/underneath
below	in front of	opposite	where

Importance

especially	more/even more	most vivid
in particular	most	strongest

PRACTICE 4   **Using transitions in description**

Read the paragraph that follows, and fill in the blanks with transitions.
Answers may vary. Possible answers are shown.

      I saw the kitchen at Morley's Place on my first day assisting the town restaurant inspector. __Inside__, Morley's was empty of customers, which made sense for 3 p.m. on a Tuesday. __When__ my boss and I saw the kitchen, we hoped the restaurant would stay empty. __Across__ from the kitchen entrance was the food-prep counter, which was covered with a faint layer of grime. __On top of__ the counter were three food bins. __As__ I aimed my flashlight into one bin, numerous roaches scuttled away from the light. __Next to, Beside, To the left of, To the right of__ the counter, a fan whirred loudly in an open window. __Behind__ the stove, we discovered a mousetrap holding a shriveled, long-dead mouse. Because of the violations, the Health Department closed Morley's Place.

Evaluate Description

Teaching tip If you have samples from a previous class, bring in full papers or paragraphs and ask the students to use either this rubric or the Four Basics of Good Description to "grade" the assignments. When they have done so, ask them to pair up and work in groups to see whether they all came up with the same score and to determine where the areas of consensus and disagreement are.

To become a more successful writer, it is important not only to understand the Four Basics of Good Description but to read and evaluate examples as well. In this section, you will have the opportunity to use a sample rubric to analyze or evaluate the samples of descriptive writing provided. By using this rubric, you will gain a better understanding of how the components of good description work together to create a successful paragraph or essay. Additionally, reading examples of description will help you write your own.

Read the following sample description paragraph. Using the Four Basics of Good Description and the sample grading rubric, decide what grade this paragraph would earn. Explain your answer.

Assignment: Identify one moment in your life that remains clear and vivid in your mind. In no more than a paragraph, use the five senses to share that experience with the reader. Your goal is to be so descriptive that readers feel as though they are experiencing it with you.

> The day I graduated from high school was very important to me. When I arrived at the football field to line up, I began to notice how hot it was. Unfortunately, there wasn't any wind. I looked around and noticed that all of my friends were grouped together and talking about all of the parties that they would attend later that day. Finally, I heard the music start, and I began to line up to make my way down the aisle and take my seat. It was truly a wonderful day.

Analysis of Sample Paragraph: *The sample paragraph is a below-average paragraph. Comments on each point may vary but should include the following:*

Sample rubric

Element	Grading criteria	Point: Comment
Appropriateness	• Did the student follow the assignment directions?	__2__/5: *Student followed some of the instructions, but the story is not detailed or descriptive*
Main idea	• Does the paper clearly state a strong main idea in a complete sentence?	__10__/10: *There is a clear main idea.*
Support	• Is the main idea developed with specific support, including specific details and examples? • Is there enough support to make the main idea evident to the reader? • Is all the support directly related to the main idea?	__5__/10: *The main idea has some support but not enough to describe the event fully to the readers. It does not include all sensory details.*
Organization	• Is the writing logically organized? • Does the student use transitions (*also, for example, sometimes,* and so on) to move the reader from one point to another?	__7__/10: *Writing appears in logical order but does not use transitions.*

Element	Grading criteria	Point: Comment
Conclusion	• Does the conclusion remind the reader of the main idea? • Does it make an observation based on the support?	__5__/5: *The conclusion adds information that reinforces the main idea.*
Grammar	• Is the writing free of the four most serious errors? (See Chapters 16-19.) • Is the sentence structure clear? • Does the student choose words that clearly express his or her meaning? • Are the words spelled correctly? • Is the punctuation correct?	__10__/10: *The paper is free from the common errors but is not descriptive.*
		TOTAL POINTS: __39__/50

Read and Analyze Description

Reading examples of description will help you write your own. The first two examples are by students; one is a shorter paragraph, and the second is a longer essay. In the third example, the Profile of Success, police chief Celia Hyde shows how she uses description in a crime scene report. Last is an example of a professional description essay by Oscar Hijuelos. As you read, pay attention to the vocabulary, and answer the questions in the margin. They will help you read critically.

Teaching tip Ask students to work individually, in pairs, or in groups to evaluate each of the following readings using the rubric provided.

Student Description Paragraph

Alessandra Cepeda

Bird Rescue

1   When the owner opened the empty storage unit, we could not believe that any living creature could have survived under such horrible conditions. The inside was complete darkness, with no windows and no ventilation. The air hit us with the smell of rot and decay. A flashlight revealed three birds, quiet and huddled in the back corner. They were quivering and looked sickly. Two of the birds had injured wings, hanging from them uselessly at odd angles, obviously broken. They were exotic birds that should have had bright and colorful feathers, but the floor of the unit was covered in the feathers they had molted. We entered slowly and retrieved the abused birds. I cried at how such beautiful and helpless creatures had been mistreated. We adopted two of them, and our Samantha is now eight years old, with beautiful green feathers topped off with a brilliant blue and red head. She

talks, flies, and is a wonderful pet who is dearly loved and, I admit, very spoiled. She deserves it after such a rough start to her life.

1. Double-underline the topic sentence.

2. What main impression does the writer create? _Answers will vary. Possible_ _answer: that the storage unit was a cruel and messy place unfit for the_ _birds_

3. Underline the sensory details (sight, sound, smell, taste, texture) that create the main impression.

4. Does the paragraph have the Four Basics of Good Description (p. 152)? Why or why not? _Yes. Specific answers will vary, but students should be able to give_ _examples of the Four Basics._

Student Description Essay

Brian Healy

First Day in Fallujah

Brian Healy served in Iraq and later pursued a degree in business management at Florida Community College. Although a typical writing process includes submitting a piece to several rounds of revision, Healy decided to "revise this essay as little as possible." He says, "I felt that given the topic, I should go with what I first wrote so that it would show more dirty truth than be polished to perfection." He values the role of emotion in writing and exhorts others not to "write for the sake of writing, [but to] write because you are passionate about it."

Vocabulary development Underline these words as you read them in Healy's essay: *wasteland, squandered, battalion, craters, torso, severed, fog of war, objective, wrath, relentless, grenades, trance, tracer rounds*

1   The year was 2004, and I was a young, 21-year-old U.S. Marine corporal on my second tour of Iraq. I had been in the country for five months and was not enjoying it any more than I had the first time. From the first time I set foot in Iraq, I perceived it as a foul-smelling wasteland where my youth and, as I would soon find out, my innocence were being squandered. I had been in a number of firefights, roadside bomb attacks, and mortar and rocket attacks; therefore, I had thought I had seen it all. So when the word came down that my battalion was going to Fallujah to drive through the center of the city, I was as naïve as a child on the first day of school. The lesson of that first day would be taught with blood, sweat, and tears, learned through pain and suffering, and never forgotten.

---

wasteland: an area that is uncultivated and barren or devastated by natural disasters or war

squandered: wasted; not used to good advantage

battalion: an army unit

craters: shallow, bowl-shaped depressions on a surface, caused by an impact or explosion

torso: the trunk of a human body

severed: cut or divided

fog of war: a term describing the general uncertainty that soldiers experience during military operations

objective: a goal or target

wrath: strong, fierce anger; angry vengeance

relentless: steady; persistent; unyielding

grenades: handheld explosives

trance: a dazed or bewildered condition; a state seemingly between sleeping and waking.

tracer rounds: ammunition containing a substance that causes bullets or rounds to trail

Predict What type of experience will Healy be describing?

2   At 2:00 in the morning on November 10, the voice of my commander pierced the night: "Mount up!" Upon hearing these words, I boarded the Amtrak transport. I heard a loud "clank, clank," the sound of metal hitting metal as the ramp closed and sealed us in. Sitting shoulder to shoulder, we had no more room to move than sardines in a pitch-dark can. The diesel fumes choked our lungs and burned our throats. There was a sudden jolt as the metal beast began to move, and with each bump and each turn, I was thrown from side to side inside the beast's belly with only the invisible bodies of my comrades to steady myself. I thought back to my childhood, to a time of carefree youth. I thought how my father would tell me how I was the cleanest of his sons. I chuckled as I thought, "If only he could see me now, covered in sweat and dirt and five days away from my last shower."

3   I was violently jerked back into the present with three thunderous explosions on the right side of the Amtrak vehicle. We continued to move faster and faster with more intensity and urgency than before. My heart was racing, pounding as if it were trying to escape from my chest when we came to a screeching halt.

4   With the same clank that sealed us in, the ramp dropped and released us from our can. I ran out of the Amtrak nearly tripping on the ramp. There was no moon, no streetlight, nothing to pierce the blanket of night. Therefore, seeing was almost completely out of the question. However, what was visible was a scene that I will never forget. The massive craters from our bombs made it seem as if we were running on the surface of the moon. More disturbing were the dead bodies of those enemies hit with the bombs. Their bodies were strewn about in a frenzied manner: a leg or arm here, torso there, a head severed from its body. Trying to avoid stepping on them was impossible. Amidst all this and the natural "fog of war," we managed to get our bearings and move toward our objective. We were able to take the entrance to a government complex located at the center of the city, and we did so in fine style. "Not so tough," we all thought. We would not have to wait long until we would find out how insanely foolish we were.

5   As the sun began to rise, there were no morning prayers, no loudspeakers, and no noise at all. This, of course, was odd since we had become accustomed to the sounds of Iraq in the morning. However, this silence did not last long and was shattered as the enemy released hell's wrath upon us. The enemy was relentless in its initial assault but was unable to gain the advantage and was slowly pushed back.

6   As the day dragged on, the enemy fought us in an endless cycle of attack and retreat. There was no time to relax as rocket-propelled grenades whistled by our heads time and time again. Snipers' bullets skipped off the surface of the roof we were on. While some bullets tore through packs, radios, and boots and clothing, a lucky few found their mark and ripped through flesh like a hot knife through butter.

Reflect What specific sounds, sights, and feelings does Healy use when describing transportation? Why does he want the reader to be able to feel like they are sharing this experience with him?

Reflect Have you ever had an experience where you were anxious about something because you did not know what was about to happen? What did it feel like? Use your five senses to describe.

Reflect Healy takes a lot of time to describe the evening, the day, and the afternoon. Why does he do this? What may be about to happen?

7   Suddenly, there was a deafening crack as three 82-millimeter mortars rained upon us, throwing me to the ground. The dust blacked out the sun and choked my lungs. I began to rise only to be thrown back down by a rocket-propelled grenade whizzing just overhead, narrowly missing my face. At this point, it seemed clear to me that there was no end to this enemy. In the windows, out the doorways, through alleyways, and down streets, they would run. We would kill one, and another would pop up in his stead, as if some factory just out of sight was producing more and more men to fight us.

8   As the sun fell behind the horizon, the battle, which had so suddenly started, ended just as swiftly. The enemy, like moths to light, were nowhere to be seen. The rifles of the Marines, which were so active that day, were silent now. We were puzzled as to why it was so quiet. My ears were still ringing from that day's events when the order came down to hole up for the night. There was no sleep for me that night; the events of the day made sure of that. I sat there that cold November night not really thinking of anything. I just sat in a trance, listening to small firefights of the battle that were still raging: a blast of machine gun fire, tracer rounds, and air strikes. Artillery flying through the air gave the appearance of a laser light show. Explosions rattling the earth lit my comrades' faces. As I looked over at them, I did not see my friends from earlier in the day; instead, I was looking at old men who were wondering what the next day would bring. I wondered if I would survive the next day.

9   The battle for Fallujah would rage on for another three weeks. The Marines of the First Battalion Eighth Marine Regiment would continue to fight with courage and honor. As each day of the battle passed, I witnessed new horrors and acts of bravery, of which normal men are not capable. However, none of those days would have the impact on me that that first day did.

10   The battle is over, but for the men who were there, it will never end. It is fought every day in their heads and in voices of friends long gone, all the while listening to the screams and taunts of people who know nothing of war but would call these men terrorists.

Reflect Healy says that his friends had become "old men" in one day. How did that happen? What caused it?

Reflect What effect does this essay have on you?

Reflect Have you ever had an experience that made you feel frightened or overwhelmed? What did you do to work through that situation or try to deal with it?

Summarize What particular ideas went through Healey's mind as he found himself in the middle of the firefight?

1. What is the main impression of Healy's essay? _Answers may vary but should include the following: Combat is intense and frightening and its effects change soldiers._

2. Underline the sensory details.

3. Circle any transitional words or phrases Healy uses.

4. What senses does Healy use in his essay? _Healy uses all five senses throughout the essay._

5. Is Healy's paper organized by space, time, or importance? _Time order._

Profile of Success
Description in the Real World

Celia Hyde
Chief of Police

Background   When I graduated from high school, I was not interested in academics. I took some courses at a community college but then dropped out to travel. After traveling and trying several colleges, I returned home. The police chief in town was a family friend and encouraged me to think about law enforcement. I entered that field and have been there since.

College   Greenfield Community College, Mt. Wachusett Community College, Fort Lauderdale Community College, Western New England College

Employer   Town of Bolton, Massachusetts

Writing at work   As chief of police, I do many kinds of writing: policies and procedures for the officers to follow; responses to attorneys' requests for information; letters, reports, and budgets; interviews with witnesses; statements from victims and criminals; accident reports. In all of the writing I do, detail, clarity, and precision are essential. I have to choose my words carefully to avoid any confusion or misunderstanding.

Workplace Description

The following report is one example of the descriptive reports Celia writes.

Report, breaking and entering scene

Response to burglar alarm, 17:00 hours

The house at 123 Main Street is situated off the road with a long, narrow driveway and no visible neighbors. The dense fir trees along the drive block natural light, though it was almost dusk and getting dark. There was snow on the driveway from a recent storm. I observed one set of fresh tire marks entering the driveway and a set of footprints exiting it.

The homeowner, Mr. Smith, had been awakened by the sounds of smashing glass and the squeaking of the door as it opened. He felt a cold draft from the stairway and heard a soft shuffle of feet crossing the dining room. Smith descended the stairs to investigate and was met at the bottom by the intruder, who shoved him against the wall and ran out the front door.

While awaiting backup, I obtained a description of the intruder from Mr. Smith. The subject was a white male, approximately 25–30 years of age and 5'9"–5'11" in height. He had jet-black hair of medium length, and it was worn slicked back from his forehead. He wore a salt-and-pepper, closely shaved beard and had a birthmark on his neck the size of a dime. The subject was wearing a black nylon jacket with some logo on it in large white letters, a blue plaid shirt, and blue jeans.

165

1. What is your **main impression** of the scene and of the intruder? *a dark,*
   isolated crime scene/an ordinary-looking man

2. Underline the **details** that support the main impression.

3. What senses do the details appeal to? *sight, hearing, touch*

4. How is the description organized? *time order*

Professional Description Essay

Oscar Hijuelos

Memories of New York City Snow

circa: [taken] around

aloft: high

trestles: support structures

girded: reinforced

burlesque houses: theaters that offer live, often humorous performances and/or strip-tease acts

palatial: palace-like

perilous: dangerous

nary: not even

stint: brief job

toque: hat

to the hilt: completely, to the maximum extent possible

nostalgia: a longing for something from the past

connotation: meaning or association

inaccessible divinity: unreachable god

Predict Why might snow be significant to the author's father and godfather?

1. **Oriente Province:** a former province of Cuba, in the eastern part of the country

Oscar Hijuelos, the son of Cuban immigrants, was born in New York City in 1951. After receiving undergraduate and master's degrees from the City University of New York, he took a job at an advertising firm and wrote fiction at night. Since then, he has published numerous novels. His first, *The Mambo Kings Play Songs of Love* (1989), was awarded the Pulitzer Prize for fiction, making Hijuelos the first Hispanic writer to receive this honor. His most recent novels include *A Simple Habana Melody* (2002), *Dark Dude* (2008), and *Beautiful Maria of My Soul* (2010). Hijuelos has also published a memoir, *Thoughts without Cigarettes* (2011).

The following essay was taken from the anthology *Metropolis Found* (2003). In it, Hijuelos describes a New York City winter from the perspective of new immigrants, noting the emotions that the season inspired in them.

Vocabulary development Underline these words as you read the description essay: *circa, aloft, trestles, girded, burlesque houses, palatial, perilous, nary, stint, toque, to the hilt, nostalgia, connotation, inaccessible divinity*

1   For immigrants of my parents' generation, who had first come to New York City from the much warmer climate of Cuba in the mid-1940s, the very existence of snow was a source of fascination. A black-and-white photograph that I have always loved, circa 1948, its surface cracked like that of a thawing ice-covered pond, features my father, Pascual, and my godfather, Horacio, fresh up from **Oriente Province**,[1] posing in a snow-covered meadow in Central Park. Decked out in long coats, scarves, and black-rimmed hats, they are holding, in their be-gloved hands, a huge chunk of hardened snow. Trees and their straggly witch's hair branches, glimmering with ice and frost, recede into the distance behind them. They stand on a field of whiteness, the two men seemingly afloat in midair, as if they were being held aloft by the magical substance itself.

2   That they bothered to have this photograph taken—I suppose to send back to family in Cuba—has always been a source of enchantment for me. That something so common to winters in New York would strike them as an object of exotic admiration has always spoken volumes about the newness—and innocence—of their

immigrants' experience. How thrilling it all must have seemed to them, for their New York was so very different from the small town surrounded by farms in eastern Cuba that they hailed from. <u>Their New York was a fanciful and bustling city of endless sidewalks and unimaginably high buildings; of great bridges and twisting outdoor elevated train trestles; of walkup tenement houses with mysteriously dark basements, and subways that burrowed through an underworld of girded tunnels; of dancehalls, burlesque houses, and palatial department stores with their complement of Christmas Salvation Army Santa Clauses on every street corner. Delightful and perilous, their New York was a city of incredibly loud noises, of police and air raid sirens and factory whistles and subway rumble</u>; a city where people sometimes shushed you for speaking Spanish in a public place, or could be unforgiving if you did not speak English well or seemed to be of a different ethnic background. (My father was once nearly hit by a garbage can that had been thrown off the rooftop of a building as he was walking along La Salle Street in upper Manhattan.)

3   Even so, New York represented the future. The city meant jobs and money. Newly arrived, an aunt of mine went to work for Pan Am; another aunt, as a Macy's saleslady. My own mother, speaking nary a word of English, did a stint in the garment district as a seamstress. During the war some family friends, like my godfather, were eventually drafted, while others ended up as factory laborers. Landing a job at the Biltmore Men's Bar, my father joined the hotel and restaurant workers' union, paid his first weekly dues, and came home one day with a <u>brand new white chef's toque</u> in hand. Just about everybody found work, often for low pay and ridiculously long hours. And while the men of that generation worked a lot of overtime, or a second job, they always had their day or two off. Dressed to the hilt, they'd leave their uptown neighborhoods and make an excursion to another part of the city— perhaps to one of the grand movie palaces of Times Square or to beautiful Central Park, as my father and godfather, and their ladies, had once done, in the aftermath of a snowfall.

4   Snow, such as it can only fall in New York City, was not just about the cold and wintry differences that mark the weather of the north. It was about a <u>purity that would descend upon the grayness of its streets like a heaven of silence</u>, the city's complexity and bustle abruptly subdued. But as beautiful as it could be, it was also something that provoked nostalgia; I am certain that my father would miss Cuba on some bitterly cold days. I remember that whenever we were out on a walk and it began to snow, my father would stop and look up at the sky, with wonderment—what he was seeing I don't know. Perhaps that's why to this day my own associations with a New York City snowfall have a mystical connotation, as if the presence of snow really meant that some kind of inaccessible divinity had settled his breath upon us.

1. Double-underline the **thesis statement**.

2. Underline the **sensory details** (sight, sound, smell, taste, texture).

Reflect What main impression do these descriptions of the city create?

Reflect What types of weather do you associate with particular feelings or moods?

Tip For reading advice, see Chapter 1.

3. Circle the **transitions**.

4. Does the essay create a clear picture of New York City in the winter? Why or why not? _Answers will vary._

Respond to one of the following assignments in a paragraph or essay.

1. Describe a place that is important to you or associated with significant memories. It might be a city, a favorite park, a friend's or relative's home, or a vacation spot.

2. Describe an outdoor scene from your favorite season. You might work from a personal photograph taken during that season.

3. Describe a person who has played a major role in your life. Try to include sensory details that go beyond the person's appearance. For instance, you might describe the sight of his or her usual surroundings, the sound of his or her voice, or the texture of a favorite piece of clothing.

Write Your Own Description

ESL tip Have students describe a famous place or popular meal in their native countries.

In this section, you will write your own description based on one of the following assignments. For help, refer to the How to Write Description checklist on page 171.

ASSIGNMENT OPTIONS   **Writing about college, work, and everyday life**

Write a description paragraph or essay on one of the following topics or on one of your own choice.

College
- Describe the sights, sounds, smells, and tastes in the cafeteria or another dining spot on campus.
- Find a place where you can get a good view of your campus (for instance, a window on an upper floor of one of the buildings). Then, describe the scene using space order (p. 158).
- Think back on a place or scene on campus that has made a strong sensory impression on you. Then, describe the place or scene with specific examples and details, and explain why it made such an impression on you.

Work
- Describe your workplace, including as many sensory details as you can.
- Describe your boss or a colleague you work with closely. First, think of the main impression you get from this person. Then, choose details that would make your impression clear to readers.
- Have you ever worked with anyone who creates a mess in their office environment? If so, describe the person's workspace and/ or messes in detail.

Everyday life
- Describe a favorite photograph, using as many details as possible. For a good example of a photograph description, see the first paragraph of Oscar Hijuelos's essay (p. 166).

- Describe a holiday celebration from your past, including as many sensory details as possible. Think back on the people who attended, the food served, the decorations, and so on.

- Visit an organization that serves your community, such as an animal shelter or a food pantry. During your visit, take notes about what you see. Later, write a detailed description of the scene.

ASSIGNMENT OPTIONS   **Reading and writing critically**

Complete one of the following assignments, which ask you to apply the critical thinking, reading, and writing skills discussed in Chapter 1.

WRITING CRITICALLY ABOUT READINGS

Both Oscar Hijuelos's "Memories of New York City Snow" (p. 166) and Amy Tan's "Fish Cheeks" (p. 123) describe scenes from the past. Read or review both of these pieces, and then follow these steps:

1. **Summarize** Briefly summarize the works, listing major examples and details.

2. **Analyze** Tan uses humor to make her point, whereas Hijuelos's essay is more serious. Why do you think the authors might have chosen these different approaches?

3. **Synthesize** Using examples from both Tan's and Hijuelos's essays and from your own experience, discuss the types of details that make certain things in our lives (such as an event or a photograph) so memorable.

Tip For a reminder of how to summarize, analyze, synthesize, and evaluate, see the Reading and Writing Critically box on page 21.

4. **Evaluate** Which essay, Tan's or Hijuelos's, do you think is more effective? Why? In writing your evaluation, you might look back on your responses to step 2.

WRITING ABOUT IMAGES

Study the photographs on page 170, and complete the following steps.

1. **Read each image** Ask yourself: What part of the photograph draws your attention the most, and why? What main impression does each picture create, and what details contribute to this impression? (For more information on reading images, see Chapter 1.)

2. **Write a description** Write a paragraph or essay that describes each photograph and explains the main impression it gives. Include the details and reactions from step 1.

Teaching tip News photographs can make good subjects for descriptions. Ask students to choose and describe a photograph from a print or online news source.

ALEX E. PROIMOS/GETTY IMAGES

DENNIS OSWALD/GETTY IMAGES

WRITING TO SOLVE A PROBLEM

Read or review the discussion of problem solving in Chapter 1 (pp. 28–30). Then, consider the following problem:

An abandoned house on your street is a safety hazard for the children in the neighborhood. Although you and some of your neighbors have called the local Board of Health, nothing has been done. Finally, you and your neighbors decide to write to the mayor.

Assignment Working in a small group or on your own, write to the mayor describing why this house is a safety hazard. Thoroughly describe the house (outside and inside). Imagine a place that is not just ugly; it must also pose safety problems to children. You might start with the following sentence:

Not only is the abandoned house at 45 Main Street an eyesore, but it is also _____ .

For a paragraph: Describe in detail one room on the first floor of the house or just the exterior you can see from the street.

For an essay: Describe in detail at least three rooms in the house or the exterior you can see if you walk entirely around the house.

CHECKLIST

How to Write Description

Steps	Details
☐ Narrow and explore your topic. See Chapter 3.	• Make the topic more specific. • Prewrite to get ideas about the narrowed topic.
☐ Write a topic sentence (paragraph) or thesis statement (essay). See Chapter 3.	• State what is most interesting, vivid, and important about your topic.
☐ Support your point. See Chapter 4.	• Come up with examples and details that create a main impression about your topic.
☐ Write a draft. See Chapter 5	• Make a plan that puts examples in a logical order. • Include a topic sentence (paragraph) or thesis statement (essay) and all the supporting examples and details.
☐ Revise your draft. See Chapter 5.	• Make sure it has *all* the Four Basics of Good Description. • Make sure you include transitions to move readers smoothly from one detail to the next.
☐ Edit your revised draft. See Parts 3 through 6.	• Correct errors in grammar, spelling, word use, and punctuation

Chapter Review

1. Description is writing that *creates a clear and vivid impression of the topic.*

   _____

2. What are the Four Basics of Good Description?

   It creates a main impression about the topic.

   It uses specific examples to support the main impression.

   It supports those examples with details that appeal to the five senses.

   It brings a person, place, or physical object to life for the reader.

3. The topic sentence in a description paragraph or the thesis statement in a description essay includes what two elements? <u>*a narrowed topic and main*</u> <u>*impression about that topic*</u>

4. Write sentences using the following vocabulary words: *objective, wrath, relentless, grenades, trance, girded, circa, aloft, trestle, nary, connotation, aloft, palatial, perilous, stint, nostalgia.* <u>Answers will vary.</u>

_____

REFLECTING ON THE JOURNEY

Skills Learned

Now that you've completed the chapter, share what you've learned about each skill by completing the following chart.

Skill	What I learned about this skill
Write a paper using descriptive detail	
Describe something using the five senses	
Generate support for a descriptive paper	
Relate support and descriptive details directly to the main idea of the paper	

9

Process Analysis

Writing That Explains How Things Happen

Learning Objectives

Chapter Goal: Learn how to write a process analysis paper.

Tools to Achieve the Goal:

- Four Basics of Good Process Analysis (p. 174)
- Diagram: Paragraphs and Essays in Process Analysis (pp. 178–79)
- Sample Process Analysis Paragraph and Rubric (p. 180)
- Student Process Analysis Paragraph: Charlton Brown, *Buying a Car at Auction* (pp. 181–82)
- Student Process Analysis Essay: Daniel Bird, *What's Appropriate: How to Talk to Children about Disasters* (pp. 182–84)
- Profile of Success and Workplace Process Analysis: Monique Rizer (p. 184)
- Professional Process Analysis Essay: Kathy Stevens, *10 Tips to Ease into Plant-Based Eating* (pp. 186–88)
- Checklist: How to Write Process Analysis (pp. 192–93)

READING ROADMAP

Key Terms

Skim Chapter 9 before reading. Find these words or terms in **bold** type. Put a check mark next to each once you locate it.

_____ process analysis
_____ purpose
_____ main idea
_____ support
_____ time order
_____ transitions

Guided Reading for Chapter 9

Fill out the following chart before you begin reading. For each skill, write what you know about that skill and what you would like to know upon completing the chapter. At the end of the chapter, you will be asked to share what you learned about each skill.

Skill	When I have used this skill	What I want to know about this skill
Describe the steps of a process		
Include all of the significant steps in a process		
Generate support for a process analysis paper		
Relate support directly to the main idea of the paper in a logical order		
Read and analyze a process analysis paper		

LaunchPadSolo

Visit **LaunchPad Solo for Readers and Writers > Reading > Patterns of Organization** for more tutorials, videos, and practice with patterns of organization.

Understand What Process Analysis Is

Process analysis either explains how to do something (so that your readers can do it) or explains how something works (so that your readers can understand it).

Four Basics of Good Process Analysis

> **1** It tells readers what process the writer wants them to know about and makes a point about it.
>
> **2** It presents the essential steps in the process.
>
> **3** It explains the steps in detail.
>
> **4** It presents the steps in a logical order (usually time order).

In the following paragraph, the numbers and colors correspond to the Four Basics of Good Process Analysis.

4 Time order is used.

The poet Dana Gioia once said, "Art delights, instructs, consoles. It educates our emotions." **1** Closely observing paintings, sculpture, and other forms of visual art is a great way to have the type of experience that Gioia describes, and following a few basic steps will help you get the most from the experience. **2** First, choose an art exhibit that interests you. **3** You can find listings for exhibits on local museums' Web sites or in the arts section of a newspaper. Links on the Web sites or articles in a newspaper may give you more information about the exhibits, the artists featured in them, and the types of work to be displayed. **2** Second, go to the museum with an open mind and, ideally, with a friend. **3** While moving through the exhibit, take time to examine each work carefully. As you do so, ask yourself questions: What is my eye most drawn to, and why? What questions does this work raise for me, and how does it make me feel? How would I describe it to someone over the phone? Ask your friend the same questions, and consider the responses. You might also consult an exhibit brochure for information about the featured artists and their works. **2** Finally, keep your exploration going after you have left the museum. **3** Go out for coffee or a meal with your friend. Trade more of your thoughts and ideas about the artwork, and discuss your overall impressions. If you are especially interested in any of the artists or their works, you might look for additional information or images on the Internet, or you might consult books at the library. Throughout the whole experience, put aside the common belief that only artists or cultural experts "get" art. The artist Eugène Delacroix described paintings as "a bridge between the soul of the artist and that of the spectator." Trust your ability to cross that bridge and come to new understandings.

You use process analysis in many situations:

College	In a science course, you explain photosynthesis.
Work	You write instructions to explain how to operate something (the copier, the fax machine).
Everyday life	You write out a recipe for an aunt.

In college, a writing assignment may ask you to *describe the process of,* but you might be asked to *describe the stages of* _____ or *explain how* _____ *works.* Whenever you need to identify and explain the steps or stages of anything, you will use process analysis.

Main Idea in Process Analysis

In process analysis, your **purpose** is to explain how to do something or how something works. Your **main idea** should tell readers what process you are describing and what you want readers to know about it.

To help you discover the main idea for your process analysis, complete the following sentence:

Main idea in process analysis **What I want readers to know about this process is that . . .**

Here is an example of a topic sentence for a paragraph:

Process	+	Main idea	=	Topic sentence

Sealing windows against the cold is an easy way to reduce heating bills.

Remember that the topic for an essay can be a little broader than one for a paragraph.

Process	+	Main idea	=	Thesis statement

Improving a home's energy efficiency can actually be done fairly easily, significantly lowering utility bills.

Whereas the topic sentence focuses on just one method to improve energy efficiency, the thesis statement sets up a discussion of multiple methods.

Tip Sometimes, the same main idea can be used for a paragraph and an essay, but the essay must develop this point in more detail. (See pp. 68–69.)

Support in Process Analysis

The paragraph and essay models on pages 178–79 use the topic sentence (paragraph) and thesis statement (essay) from the Main Idea section of this chapter. Both models include the **support** used in all writing about processes: the steps in the process backed up by details about these steps. In the essay model, however, the major support points (steps) are topic sentences for individual paragraphs.

PRACTICE 1 **Finding and choosing the essential steps**

Teaching tip Students might be comforted to learn that the most productive and rewarding writing process is rarely neat or linear. You might share with them some insights from composition scholar and writer Mina Shaughnessy. According to Shaughnessy, the best writers avoid a "tight, well-ordered, but empty paper"; make a path through "a wilderness of possibilities"; and explore "alternate routes and . . . unexpected places when that seems wise or important."

For each of the following topics, write the essential steps in the order you would perform them.

1. Making (your favorite food) is simple.
   Answers will vary.

   _____

2. I think I could teach anyone how to _____.

   _____

3. Operating a _____ is _____.

   _____

   _____

PRACTICE 2 **Adding details to essential steps**

Tip If you have written a narration paragraph already, you will notice that narration and process analysis are alike in that they both usually present events or steps in time order—the order in which they occur. The difference is that narration reports what happened, whereas process analysis describes how to do something or how something works.

Choose one of the topics from Practice 1. In the spaces that follow, first copy down that topic and the steps you wrote for it in Practice 1. Then, add a detail to each of the steps. If the process has more than three steps, you might want to use a separate sheet of paper.

Topic: _Answers will vary._____

Step 1: _____

  Detail: _____

Step 2: _____

  Detail: _____

Step 3: _____

  Detail: _____

Step 4: _____

  Detail: _____

Organization in Process Analysis

Process analysis is usually organized by **time order** because it explains the steps of the process in the order in which they occur. This is the strategy used in the paragraph and essay models on pages 178–79.

 Transitions move readers smoothly from one step to the next.

Tip For more on time order, see pages 76–77.

Common Transitions in Process Analysis

after	eventually	meanwhile	since
as	finally	next	soon
at last	first	now	then
before	last	once	when
during	later	second	while

PRACTICE 3   **Using transitions in process analysis**

Read the paragraph that follows, and fill in the blanks with transitions. *Answers may vary. Possible answers are shown.*

 Scientists have discovered that, like something from a zombie movie, a mind-controlling fungus attacks certain carpenter ants. ___*Then*___, as if following the fungus's orders, the ants help their invader reproduce. The process begins when an ant is infected. ___*Next*___, the ant begins to act strangely. For instance, instead of staying in its home high in the trees, it drops to the forest floor. ___*While*___ wandering, it searches for a cool, moist place. ___*Once*___ the zombie-ant finds the right place, it clamps its jaws to a leaf and dies. ___*Eventually*___, the fungus within the ant grows until it bursts from the insect's head, and more ants are infected. By studying this process, researchers may find better ways to control the spread of carpenter ants.

Evaluate Process Analysis

To become a more successful writer, it is important not only to understand the Four Basics of Good Process Analysis but to read and evaluate examples as well. In this section, you will have the opportunity to use a sample rubric to analyze or evaluate the samples of process analysis writing provided. By using this rubric, you will gain a better understanding of how the components of good process analysis work

Teaching tip Often, process analysis is best understood visually. Ask your students to find step-by-step instructions to something online to bring in and share with the course; remind them that this could include putting together furniture, installing software on a computer, playing a game, or even learning a skill like riding a bike. For a more hands-on approach, bring in some basic materials (clay, popsicle sticks, Legos) and ask the students to build an object. Then, individually or in pairs, ask students to carefully write down the process so that another group can replicate the object. Asking students to switch "handbooks" and try to build another group's object can help identify any difficulty or misunderstanding with the instructions.

Teaching tip If you have samples from a previous class, bring in full papers or paragraphs and ask the students to use either this rubric or the Four Basics of Good Process Analysis to "grade" the assignments. When they have done so, ask them to pair up and work in groups to see if they all came up with the same score and to determine where the areas of consensus and disagreement are.

Paragraphs vs. Essays in Process Analysis

For more on the important features of process analysis, see the Four Basics of Good Process Analysis on page 174.

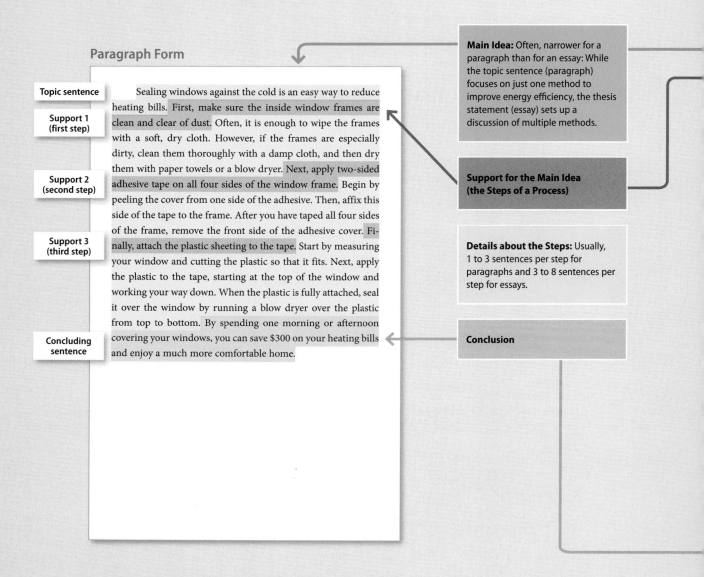

Paragraph Form

Topic sentence

Support 1 (first step)

Support 2 (second step)

Support 3 (third step)

Concluding sentence

Sealing windows against the cold is an easy way to reduce heating bills. First, make sure the inside window frames are clean and clear of dust. Often, it is enough to wipe the frames with a soft, dry cloth. However, if the frames are especially dirty, clean them thoroughly with a damp cloth, and then dry them with paper towels or a blow dryer. Next, apply two-sided adhesive tape on all four sides of the window frame. Begin by peeling the cover from one side of the adhesive. Then, affix this side of the tape to the frame. After you have taped all four sides of the frame, remove the front side of the adhesive cover. Finally, attach the plastic sheeting to the tape. Start by measuring your window and cutting the plastic so that it fits. Next, apply the plastic to the tape, starting at the top of the window and working your way down. When the plastic is fully attached, seal it over the window by running a blow dryer over the plastic from top to bottom. By spending one morning or afternoon covering your windows, you can save $300 on your heating bills and enjoy a much more comfortable home.

Main Idea: Often, narrower for a paragraph than for an essay: While the topic sentence (paragraph) focuses on just one method to improve energy efficiency, the thesis statement (essay) sets up a discussion of multiple methods.

Support for the Main Idea (the Steps of a Process)

Details about the Steps: Usually, 1 to 3 sentences per step for paragraphs and 3 to 8 sentences per step for essays.

Conclusion

Think Critically as You Write Process Analysis

ASK YOURSELF

- Have I included all the steps necessary for others to complete or understand the process?
- Would any information from experts make my description of the process clearer?

Essay Form

1

Many people are intimidated by the work necessary to make their homes more energy [Thesis statement] and they do not see it as a do-it-yourself job. However, improving a home's energy efficiency can actually be done fairly easily, significantly lowering utility bills.

First, seal air leaks around windows and doors. To seal air leaks around windows, apply cau[Topic sentence 1 (first step)] window frames and walls. Also, if you fashioned windows that are not weather-proof, cover them with plastic before the cold temperatures set in. This process involves affixing two-sided adhesive tape to the window frames and then attaching plastic sheeting, which is sealed with the use of a blow dryer. Next, look for drafty spots around doors. Many air leaks at the top or sides of doors can be sealed with adhesive-backed foam strips. Leaks under doors can be stopped with foam draft guards. Alternatively, a rolled-up blanket, rug, or towel can keep the cold from coming in. All of these measures can save up to $600 per season on heating bills.

2

Second, install water-saving shower heads and faucet aerators. These fixtures are inexpens[Topic sentence 2 (second step)] available in most hardware stores. Also, th to install. First, unscrew the old shower or faucet head. Then, follow the package instructions for affixing the new shower head or aerator. In some cases, you might have to use pipe tape or a rubber washer to ensure a good seal. After this step, run the water to make sure there are no leaks. If you find any leaks, use pliers to tighten the seal. In time, you will discover that the new shower heads and aerators will cut your w[Topic sentence 3 (third step)] and the cost of water heating by up to 50 p

Finally, look for other places where energy efficiency could be increased. One simple improvement is to replace traditional light bulbs with compact fluorescent bulbs, which use up to 80 percent less energy. Also, make sure your insulation is as good as it can be. Many utilities now offer free assessments of home insulation, identifying places where it is missing or inadequate. In some cases, any necessary insulation improvements may be subsidized by the utilities or by

3

government agencies. It is well worth considering such improvements, which, in the case of poorly insulated homes, can save thousands of dollars a year, quickly covering any costs. Although some people prefer to have professionals blow insulating foam into their walls, it is not difficult to add insulation to attics, where a large amount of heat can be lost [Concluding paragraph] months.

Taking even one of these steps can make a significant financial difference in your life and also reduce your impact on the environment. My advice, though, is to improve your home's energy efficiency as much as possible, even if it means doing just a little at a time. The long-term payoff is too big to pass up.

together to create a successful paragraph or essay. Additionally, reading examples of process analysis will help you write your own.

Read the following sample process analysis paragraph. Using the Four Basics of Good Process Analysis and the sample grading rubric, decide what grade this paragraph would earn. Explain your answer.

Assignment Please write a paragraph about how to take better notes when reading and studying. You should make sure that your instructions are careful and deliberate: what steps should be taken, what is involved in each step, and in what order a student should proceed.

Learning to take effective notes in class can be very easy once a student understands what they need to do. Too often, a student will start taking notes as they read. This becomes a problem because the student does not know what the main idea or most significant ideas of the reading are because they have not read the entire assignment yet. In order to avoid extra work or overly lengthy notes it is best to preview the reading: look at the title, any subheadings, and any bold or italicized words. After previewing, read the entire article from start to finish. Once you have completed those two steps, highlight or underline. In this way, your notes will be clearer and easier to read. It is also less likely they will contain too much extra information.

Analysis of Sample Paragraph: *The sample paragraph is slightly above average. Comments on each point may vary but should include the following:*

Sample rubric

Element	Grading criteria	Point: Comment
Appropriateness	• Did the student follow the assignment directions?	__4__/5: *Student followed most of the instructions. Toward the end, the writer seemed to skip some steps.*
Main Idea	• Does the paper clearly state a strong main idea in a complete sentence?	__10__/10: *There is a clear main idea.*
Support	• Is the main idea developed with specific support, including specific details and examples? • Is there enough support to make the main idea evident to the reader? • Is all the support directly related to the main idea?	__7__/10: *There is a main idea, and it is almost always supported. After the writer mentions "highlighting" or "underlining," he or she should have gone a bit further to explain how to do this or why it is important.*
Organization	• Is the writing logically organized? • Does the student use transitions (*also, for example, sometimes,* and so on) to move the reader from one point to another?	__9__/10: *Writing is in logical order and typically uses transitions.*

Element	Grading criteria	Point: Comment
Conclusion	• Does the conclusion remind the reader of the main idea? • Does it make an observation based on the support?	__5__ /5: *The conclusion adds information that reinforces the main idea.*
Grammar	• Is the writing free of the four most serious errors? (See Chapters 16-19.) • Is the sentence structure clear? • Does the student choose words that clearly express his or her meaning? • Are the words spelled correctly? • Is the punctuation correct?	__10__ /10: *The paper is free from the common errors.*
		TOTAL POINTS: __45__ /50

Read and Analyze Process Analysis

Reading examples of process analysis will help you write your own. The first two examples of process analysis are a paragraph from a student writer and a student essay. In the Profile of Success, Monique Rizer outlines a process she uses in her career, and the final example is a professional essay by Kathy Stevens. As you read, pay attention to the vocabulary, and answer the questions in the margin. They will help you read critically.

Teaching tip Ask students to work individually, in pairs, or in groups to evaluate each of the following readings using the rubric provided.

Student Process Analysis Paragraph

Charlton Brown

Buying a Car at an Auction

Vocabulary development Underline these words as you read: *legitimate, savvy, bid,* and *thorough.*

legitimate: lawful; genuine; real

savvy: knowledgeable; well informed

bid: an offer, in this case, of a price

thorough: complete; detailed

1   Buying a car at an auction is a good way to get a cheap car, but buyers need to be prepared. First, decide what kind of vehicle you want to buy. Then, find a local auction. Scams are common, though, so be careful. Three top sites that are legitimate are www.gov-auctions.org, www.carauctioninc.com, and www.seizecars.com. When you have found an auction and a vehicle you are interested in, become a savvy buyer. Make sure you know the car's actual market value. You can find this out from Edmunds.com, Kellybluebook.com, or NADA (the National Automobile Dealers Association).

Predict What preparation do you think Charlton will say buyers need before attending a car auction?

Because bidding can become like a competition, decide on the highest bid you will make, and stick to that. Do not get drawn into the competition. On the day of the auction, get to the auction early so that you can look at the actual cars. If you do not know about cars yourself, bring someone who does with you to the auction so that he or she can examine the car. Next, begin your thorough examination. Check the exterior; especially look for any signs that the car has been in an accident. Also, check the windshield because many states will not give an inspection sticker to cars with any damage to the windshield. Check the interior and try the brakes. Start the engine and listen to how it sounds. Check the heat and air conditioning, the CD player, and all other functions. As a final check before the bidding, look at the car's engine and transmission. Finally, get ready to place your bid, and remember, do not go beyond the amount you settled on earlier. Good luck!

Summarize What steps are necessary to buy a car at auction?

1. Double-underline the **topic sentence**.

2. What is Charlton's **main idea**? _Buyers should be prepared before buying a car at an auction._

3. Underline the **major steps**.

4. Circle the words that signal when Charlton moves from one step to the next.

5. Does Charlton's paragraph follow the Four Basics of Good Process Analysis (p. 174)? Why or why not? _Yes. Answers will vary._

news cycle: 24-hour investigation and reporting

graphically: giving a clear and effective picture

screen time: the amount of time someone spends in front of technology: television, tablets, computers, cell phones, etc.

severity: harshness or intensity

adjunct: an employee, typically at a college or university, without full-time status

therapeutic: treating or curing

dynamics: motivating or driving forces

Predict Before reading the article, what do you think may be some ways to help a child handle a disaster?

Student Process Analysis Essay

Daniel Bird

What's Appropriate: How to Talk to Children about Disasters

Daniel Bird is a student at Skyline College in California. His focus is journalism. The following essay was published in the school newspaper, the *Skyline View*, in May 2013.

Vocabulary Development Underline these words as you read: *news cycle, graphically, screen time, severity, adjunct, therapeutic,* and *dynamics.*

1   Sandy Hook Elementary. The Boston Marathon. Hurricane Sandy.

2   Whether natural disasters or acts of terrorism, these horrific events have been told and retold within the constant news cycle. Being an adult and

trying to take all of the distressing news in is difficult enough, <u>but for a child it could be life-shattering.</u> The child in your life, be it son, daughter, cousin, niece, nephew, will need your help.

3   <u>The first step you should take in order to help the child in your life is to scale down all of the information for them to take in.</u> Keep everything age appropriate, meaning don't give them information they cannot understand. For younger children, tell them generally what happened (not graphically), for older children give them more details, but not graphic ones.

4   <u>Secondly, you want to limit their screen time, meaning turn off the media that they can see.</u> You may want to see what the newest information is, but while that news comes in, older information is being replayed on the constant news cycle. Sylvia Ford, Early Childhood Education professor at Skyline told me about her opinion of news images and children.

5   "They don't benefit from graphic images," Ford said.

6   We still see these images because according to her, "blood sells." After a traumatic event, children will knowingly be out of their routine. It is the family's job to make sure we are able to protect and help our loved ones process at this time. <u>Depending on the severity of the disaster, parents should alter their routine in order to adjust them to what has happened.</u> It may be best for an immediate family member to spend extra time with them.

7   Parents and family should not feel completely alone with their issues around this subject. The National Association for the Education of Young Children (NAEYC) has specific instructions on how to explain disasters to children. <u>Children benefit from physical comfort, and comfort around them.</u> Comfort is extremely important at this point in time.

8   <u>Adjunct faculty and Early Childhood Education Professor Shawna Whitney told me families need to plan for a disaster in the same way as you would an emergency.</u> This includes making a plan, have a kit filled with comforting items (favorite toy, fuzzy pajamas, etc.). Adults being prepared will help the children as best as possible.

9   Helping your children can often be a therapeutic without having to have a long discussion. <u>Sometimes the most effective thing to do for children is to escape what has immediately happened.</u>

10   "Getting them involved in an activity that's a little bit distracting right after, when they might be particularly fearful," Early Childhood Education Program Supervisor Cece Rebele said. "Use things like puppets and books that might explain it at their level of understanding."

11   Dynamics within an area often change after a disaster. This includes all of the helpers that come out to aid those in need such as firefighters, police officers, Red Cross volunteers, etc. <u>Make sure to discuss who these people are and what jobs they do.</u> Let your children know that these people are always there to help them if they need it.

12   Having children in your family does not mean you are the parents; most of us have younger siblings, cousins, nieces, or nephews and talking to them as someone who is not their parent is important. While most parents

Reflect Before reading any further, what are your own initial thoughts or reactions when you think of these events?

Identify Bird refers to providing information that is "age appropriate." What specific ideas or events would you share to a younger child? Why limit those ideas or events? What might an older child be able to understand more clearly?

Reflect If you were asked to turn off your technology or limit your screen time, especially after a disaster, would you be able to do it? Explain your answer.

Reflect What does Ford mean when she says "blood sells?" Do you agree or disagree with this statement?

Identify Other than books or puppets, what may be some other ways to help a child deal with a disaster?

Profile of Success
Process Analysis in the Real World

Monique Rizer
Chief of Staff

Background   I was the oldest of six children, and before my mother married my stepfather, she was on welfare. She homeschooled me for five years until I begged her to let me go to a public high school. There I made friends with some people who expected to go to college, and I realized I wanted to go, too. I started at Green River Community College, but just then my parents' financial situation got really bad, and the eight of us had to move to a trailer. I stopped going to school until I met my future husband, who was going to a community college and encouraged me to go back. Several months later, I became pregnant with my first son. I was determined to stay in college, so I completed one year at Highline Community College. That summer, I had my son, got married, and found loans to transfer to Pacific Lutheran University. While there, I received a Gates Millennium Scholarship, which made continuing college possible. Although I moved a few times, I graduated from college and went on to graduate school. After I finished graduate school, I had another son.

Degrees/Colleges   B.A., Gonzaga University; M.S., Syracuse University

Employer   Be the Change, Inc.

Writing at Work   Writing is the one skill I use every day at work. As chief of staff, I'm responsible for supporting our fundraising efforts, managing our board, leading staff meetings, and other special projects. So, I am often writing to staff within the organization, my leadership, our board members, or people outside our organization with whom we are developing a relationship. I usually communicate through e-mail and I've learned it's so important to keep an e-mail short and to the point, but also friendly. Write, "Good morning" or write "Thank you" or "My best." These are small ways to keep e-mail communication personal through what can be a very impersonal technology, especially with people you don't see very often. Also, when I have to e-mail someone with a criticism or difficult message, I always try to start that e-mail with a positive note or thanks. Finally, I think very carefully about sending an e-mail when a phone call or face-to-face conversation is better. We rely on e-mail and text a lot, and we have to really try to keep those writing forums professional. But sometimes a phone call or a face-to-face conversation is more appropriate depending on the message or purpose. As I've grown in my career, I find my writing to be more important. I also have been responsible for hiring new staff and I pay close attention to how they represent themselves in writing.

I represent my leaders often in writing and so I'm very careful about what I am writing and how it will reflect on them and my organization. Sometimes I'll also write or edit something in the voice of my leadership as well. So, reading their writing and learning their "voice" has become an important skill along with writing. Finally, I draft my writing and have someone look it over or let it sit and look at it later—even a few minutes—just to get some distance and look at it with fresh eyes. Getting some distance or having a fresh view almost always improves my writing.

are able to talk to them one on one, other older family members should be prepared to. Use the tips listed above and speak to the parents if you feel the child may need more answers.

13   "Books with disasters in them that way she could be more aware of what might happen," sophomore Brittney Jacobs said about talking with her four-year-old sister about a disaster.

14   Your child wants to be reassured that they're going to be alright, and that even though bad things happen we still go on with our lives. If your child doesn't respond to verbal communication, don't get discouraged. Ask them to use puppets, books, or even a song to communicate what they feel.

1. Double underline the topic sentence.

2. Underline the steps and ways to encourage or comfort a child that Bird outlines in this article.

3. Does Bird use enough examples to make his point clear? _Answers will vary._

4. Does Bird's essay follow the Four Basics of Good Process Analysis (p. 174)? _Yes._

Workplace Process Analysis

The following is an example of an e-mail Rizer would send to her staff.

Dear team,

Thank you for your time and effort to help make the staff retreat a success. It was amazing to see how much interest there was during your presentations.

How did you feel the day went? I would love to get your thoughts.

After such a successful retreat, there are some concrete steps we need to take to keep the positive momentum going. Some can wait until our next monthly meeting, but some are immediate.

Here's what's coming up:

Monthly in-person leadership meetings: We'd like to start meeting in person as a leadership team every month. We can rotate between our two office locations and build around existing schedules.

Task Force: We scratched the surface on collaborating around a new project. Leadership would like you three to lead this continued conversation and recommend folks from your teams to support. We will discuss more in December.

Asset mapping: Several of the staff commitments referenced our organization assets, grassroots relationships, communication functions, etc. We'd like your recommendations for who should do this work in a short-term work group.

Finally, please incorporate the feedback from the meeting and share your updates. Please have those updates by **end of day Dec. 1.**

Again, we appreciate your time, thoughts, and work as we move forward.

Best,

Monique

1. What is the purpose being outlined in the e-mail above? _Identifies a timeline of ideas and projects within a department._

2. How does Rizer ensure that everyone understands this process? _She provides a process that defines each step as they move forward in the office._

3. Where did the information for this e-mail come from, and how does she create a process for moving forward? _After discussing some basic ideas at a retreat, Rizer identifies the key concepts for moving forward and provides a brief discussion/some questions about how to continue working on these projects._

Professional Process Analysis Essay

Kathy Stevens

Ten Tips to Ease into Plant-Based Eating

Kathy Stevens is the founder and director of one of the nation's leading sanctuaries for animals, Catskill Animal Sanctuary. Although she is a vegan herself, she understands that not everyone is comfortable with the idea behind a vegan lifestyle and the seemingly enormous changes that are required to eat food that does not consist of any animal products at all. Her overwhelming message in all of her writing and speaking engagements is "kindness to all."

In the following process analysis essay, which appeared in the *Huffington Post* in April 2014, Stevens presents a step-by-step process to help people learn to add more plant-based foods into their diet without feeling deprived.

vegan: one who refrains from consuming animal products, including but not limited to, meat, eggs, butter, and milk

laden: heavily loaded or weighted down

cuisine: a style of cooking practices that is often associated with a particular culture

Predict What are some reasons or steps that Stevens may use to help people ease into a plant-based diet?

Vocabulary development Underline these words as you read: *vegan, laden,* and *cuisine.*

1 At the end of a tour of Catskill Animal Sanctuary last year, a visitor who'd just been kissed by cows and held chickens in his lap said to me, "OK. I get it. How do I start?" The question came up again last night, when I was discussing my most recent post with my dad. "I've been eating one way for a long time," he said. "It's hard to change."

2 Not if you do it one step at a time, I said to him. In legions, Americans are opening their eyes, minds, and hearts to the personal, environmental, and ethical horrors of growing animals to feed humans. Moving toward a kinder and healthier way of eating needn't feel drastic if you simply *ease into it.* Here are ten tips for doing just that!

1. Eat vegan in the a.m.

3 Oatmeal. Berries and granola with almond milk. English muffin with jam and nondairy butter. Fruit and soy-yogurt smoothies. Green smoothies. Toast with peanut butter. Lots of your favorite cereals—Chex, Corn Flakes, and Special K, for starters—are vegan. Pancakes (there's no difference in taste between vegan pancakes and the ones you're used to). Tofu scramble and vegan sausage: Can you say yum?

4 Now come on . . . was that hard?

2. Switch to nondairy milk.

5   From soy to coconut to rice to almond, plant-based milks abound! With fewer calories and no cholesterol, they're arguably healthier. And the impact on animals if America went nondairy is staggering! Here's the math: In 2010, the average American drank more than 20 gallons of milk, which translates to more than 6 billion gallons of milk annually. If each cow produces 2,500 gallons, it takes 2.5 million cows to produce the milk America consumes. If we switched to nondairy milk, 2.5 million animals each year would be spared a life that consists of forcible impregnation, growth hormones and antibiotics, the stealing of their babies immediately after birth, intensive confinement and milk production for much of their lives, and slaughter at just a few years old when their wracked bodies are worn out. Many cows are too broken to stand when they arrive at the slaughterhouse. As "downed cows," they are simply shoved onto a pile and left to die.

Reflect How much of this information do you think the general population is aware of? Why might that be?

3. Go Meatless Mondays.

6   Cut back at dinner by joining the Meatless Mondays movement. If all Americans participated in this popular trend, 1.4 billion animals per year would be spared.

4. Bake without animal products

7   The reasons to bake without eggs and dairy abound. First, a single egg contains more than half the recommended maximum intake of cholesterol for a healthy person. Second, many believe that the egg and dairy industries are the cruelest industries that have ever existed. Finally, you can't taste the difference between a vegan quiche, cake, or cookie and one laden with butter and eggs. Get started here!

Identify What key steps to the plant-based eating process are outlined in this paragraph?

5. Try one new vegan product a week.

8   If you don't want to give up the taste and texture of meat and dairy, *you don't have to*. You won't like all of these foods, but when you find ones you do, use them as substitutes in your meat and dairy-based recipes. Here are some favorites: Trader Joe's vegan Meatless Meatballs, Field Roast Frankfurters, Gardein Beefless Burger, Beyond Meat Beef-free Crumbles, Tofurky Deli Slices, Daiya cheese, Treeline soft cheeses, Kite-hill cheese, Whole Soy yogurt, Almond Dream yogurt.

6. Ditch McDonald's.

9   McDonald's is the largest buyer of eggs in North America, and purchases its eggs from hens kept in battery cages. Grinding up all newborn male chicks is a standard industry practice. Another? Leaving dead birds in cages for months at a time. According to an undercover investigator at a McDonald's egg supplier, "[Dead] birds . . . were left in the cages . . . decomposing for weeks or months at a time . . . with birds who were still alive and laying eggs for human

consumption." Think conditions at McDonald's beef, chicken, and fish suppliers are any better?

Reflect How likely is it that someone would make these choices or substitutions? Why do you think that?

10   Choose Loving Hut, Native Foods, Moe's, or Chipotle instead for more humane options. Loving Hut and Native Foods, 100 percent vegan fast food chains, may not be as widespread as McDonald's, but their presence is growing. Loving Hut is now in more than forty locations across the United States, and Native Foods plans on adding 200 new restaurants in the next five years. Moe's and Chipotle also have many delicious vegan options. Fill your Moe's burrito with tofu or beans, or try the tasty new Chipotle Sofritas, a burrito with organic braised tofu.

7. When choosing restaurants or recipes, think ethnic.

11   America created the meat- and dairy-based diet that is making us all sick and fat. Most other cuisines are healthier than ours; the ones that seem to have a tremendous number of delicious plant-based choices are Indian, Japanese, Greek, Chinese, Thai, Spanish, and Mexican, so eat the foods you already love that happen to be vegan! There are also hundreds, literally, of vegan cookbooks on the market. Check Amazon or the cooking section of your favorite bookstore. My current favorite is *Big Vegan*.

8. Give up one animal a month.

12   If you're a typical American eater, you likely eat chickens, cows, pigs, and fish all the time. You drink milk and eat eggs. All these animals suffer mightily for the benefit of our taste buds. Cutting out one animal per month is a painless way to do a whole lot of good for the animals, your health, and the planet we all share.

9. Make friends!

13   Join a meet-up group and see how "seasoned" vegans live—it's helpful, inspiring . . . and fun!

10. Visit an animal sanctuary.

Reflect Have you ever followed any of the steps described in this essay?

14   *Huh?* Yep. In my view, this might be the most important tip of all. Catskill Animal Sanctuary is just two hours from Manhattan, an hour from Albany, four from Boston. We're also in the exquisite mid–Hudson Valley, a prime vacation destination. Most important, hundreds of animals, including some free-rangers who may hop into your car when you pull up to the barn, are here to work their way into your hearts. We open for the season in April—I will be there with a big smile on my face, as will Arthur the goat. Hope to see you soon. And if you can't get to CAS, find a reputable sanctuary near you. **Fair warning: Be prepared to fall in love, and be prepared for a new way of eating to begin feeling much easier than you ever imagined.**

1. The second paragraph contains the **thesis statement**. Double-underline it.

Tip For reading advice, see Chapter 1.

2. Now, look at this sentence from the last paragraph: **"Be prepared to fall in love, and be prepared for a new way of eating to begin feeling much easier than you ever imagined."** Does this sentence imply that people can skip steps 1 through 9 and only experience step 10 in their process of moving toward a vegan lifestyle? Explain your answer. *Answers will vary. Possible answers: Probably not. Most people are inundated with these facts and images and do little more than stop briefly and think "how terrible." A person who has already slowly made the switch to a vegan-based diet may find that their choice is reinforced after visiting a sanctuary, however.*

3. Rather than using typically transitional words, Stevens chooses to number each step in the process. Why do you think she chose that organizational strategy? *Answers will vary.*

4. Does this essay follow the Four Basics of Good Process Analysis (p. 174)? Why or why not? *Yes. Answers will vary.*

Respond to one of the following assignments in a paragraph or essay.

1. Identify another process that many people are a part of daily (pumping gas, taking long showers, leaving lights on around the house) which could be changed easily if there was a simple reminder or process in place to change those behaviors. Then, write that process.

2. Although Stevens is a vegan, she describes herself as "passionate but patient," meaning that she never forces her ideas on someone else, no matter how frustrating it may be to her. Identify another process that you find frustrating, and write a detailed description of it.

3. Describe to a beginner how to do something that you do well.

Write Your Own Process Analysis

In this section, you will write your own process analysis based on one of the following assignments. For help, refer to the How to Write Process Analysis checklist on pages 192–93.

ASSIGNMENT OPTIONS | **Writing about college, work, and everyday life**

Write a process analysis paragraph or essay on one of the following topics or on one of your own choice.

College
- Describe the process of preparing for an exam.
- Attend a tutoring session at your college's writing center. Afterward, describe the process: What specific things did the tutor do to help you? Also, explain what you learned from the process.
- Interview a college graduate about how he or she achieved success in school. During the interview, ask about the steps of specific processes. For example, one question might be, "What steps did you follow to take good notes?" After the interview, describe the processes in writing.

Work
- Describe how to make a positive impression at a job interview.
- Think of a challenging task you had to accomplish at work. What steps did you go through to complete it?
- Identify a job that you would like to have after graduation. Then, investigate the process of getting this job, including the courses you need to take, any exams or certifications that are required, the search stage, and the interview. To gather information, visit the Web site of your college's career center. Better yet, make an appointment to speak with a career counselor. After you have completed your research, describe the process in writing.

Everyday life
- Describe the process of making something, such as a favorite meal, a set of shelves, or a sweater.
- Think of a challenging process that you have completed successfully, such as fixing a leak under the sink, applying for a loan, or finding a good deal on a car or an apartment. Describe the steps specifically enough so that someone else could complete the process just as successfully.
- Take part in a community activity, such as a fund-raising event for a charity, a neighborhood cleanup, or food preparation at a homeless shelter. Then, describe the process you went through.

ASSIGNMENT OPTIONS | **Reading and writing critically**

Complete one of the following assignments, which ask you to apply the critical thinking, reading, and writing skills discussed in Chapter 1.

WRITING CRITICALLY ABOUT READINGS

Although both Charlton Brown's "Buying a Car at Auction" (pp. 181–82) and Kathy Steven's "Ten Tips for Easing into Plant-Based Eating" (pp. 186–89)

ESL tip Suggest that students write about a process they used in their native country or culture but don't use where they live now.

describe processes, Steven's process analysis is listed out step by step. Read or review both of these pieces, and then follow these steps:

1. **Summarize** Briefly summarize the works, listing steps in the processes described.

2. **Analyze** Are there any other steps or details that the authors might have included?

3. **Synthesize** Using examples from both Brown's and Steven's writings and from your own experience, discuss (1) processes that would be easier to outline step by step and (2) processes that are easier to describe in full paragraphs.

4. **Evaluate** Which piece, Brown's or Steven's, do you think is more effective? Why? In writing your evaluation, you might look back on your responses to step 2.

Tip For a reminder of how to summarize, analyze, synthesize, and evaluate, see the Reading and Writing Critically box on page 21.

Teaching tip If time is short, students might complete just one or two steps of this assignment.

WRITING ABOUT IMAGES

ELENABSL/ SHUTTERSTOCK

Study this visual recipe for apple pie, and complete the following steps.

1. **Read the images** Ask yourself: How is the process broken apart into a step-by-step process? What changes do you notice from illustration to illustration? What is the purpose of showing this process? (For more information on reading images, see Chapter 1.) Is it as simple to read and comprehend this visual process as it would be if there were detailed written instructions? Why or why not?

2. **Write a process analysis** Write a paragraph or essay that describes the process shown in this illustration. In your description, include the changes you observed in step 1.

WRITING TO SOLVE A PROBLEM

Read or review the discussion of problem solving in Chapter 1 (pp. 28–30). Then, consider the following problem.

Midway through a course you are taking, your instructor asks the class to tell her how she could improve the course. You have not been happy with the class because the instructor is always late, comes in seeming rushed and tense, and ends up releasing class late because of material she forgot to cover. During class, she uses PowerPoint slides and reads to the class from them, seldom adding new information. Then, after handing out an assignment for students to work on, she returns to her desk to grade papers. You are afraid to ask questions about the lecture or assignment because the instructor does not seem overly helpful. You want to tell the instructor how the course could be better, but you do not want to offend her.

Assignment Working in a small group or on your own, write to your instructor about how she could improve the course. Think of how the class could be structured differently so that you could learn more. Begin with how the class could start. Then, describe how the rest of the class period could proceed, suggesting specific activities if you can. State your suggestions in positive terms. For example, instead of telling the instructor what *not* to do, make suggestions using phrases like *you could, we could,* or *the class could.* Be sure to use formal English. You might start in this way:

Several simple changes might improve our learning. At the start of each class, _____

At the end, remember to thank your instructor for asking for students' suggestions.

CHECKLIST	
How to Write Process Analysis	
Steps	**Details**
☐ Narrow and explore your topic See Chapter 3.	• Make the topic more specific. • Prewrite to get ideas about the narrowed topic and how you will explain the steps to your audience. • Make sure your topic can be covered in the space given.

Steps	Details
☐ Write a topic sentence (paragraph) or thesis statement (essay) See Chapter 3.	• Decide what you want readers to know about the process you are describing.
☐ Support your point See Chapter 4.	• Include the steps in the process, and explain the steps in detail.
☐ Write a draft See Chapter 5.	• Make a plan that puts the steps in a logical order (often chronological). • Include a topic sentence (paragraph) or thesis statement (essay) and all the supporting details about each step.
☐ Revise your draft See Chapter 5.	• Make sure it has *all* the Four Basics of Good Process Analysis. • Read to make sure all the steps are present. • Make sure you include transitions to move readers smoothly from one step to the next.
☐ Edit your revised draft See Parts 3 through 6.	• Correct errors in grammar, spelling, word use, and punctuation.

Chapter Review

1. Process analysis is writing that _either explains how to do something or explains how something works._

2. What are the Four Basics of Good Process Analysis?
   It tells readers what process you want them to know about and makes a point about it.
   It presents the essential steps in the process.
   It explains the steps in detail.
   It presents the steps in a logical order (usually time order).

3. Write sentences using the following vocabulary words: *legitimate, savvy, bid, thorough, vegan, laden, cuisine.* Answers will vary.

REFLECTING ON THE JOURNEY

Skills Learned

Now that you've completed the chapter, share what you've learned about each skill by completing the following chart.

Skill	What I learned about this skill
Describe the steps of a process	
Include all of the significant steps in a process	
Generate support for a process analysis paper	
Relate support directly to the main idea of the paper in a logical order	
Read and analyze a process analysis paper	

10

Classification
Writing That Sorts Things into Groups

READING ROADMAP

Learning Objectives

Chapter Goal: Learn how to write a classification paper.

Tools to Achieve the Goal:

- Four Basics of Good Classification (p. 196)
- Diagram: Paragraphs and Essays in Classification (pp. 202–03)
- Sample Classification Paragraph and Rubric (p. 204)
- Student Classification Paragraph: Lorenza Mattazi, *All My Music* (p. 205)
- Student Classification Essay: Kelly Hultgren, *Pick Up the Phone to Call, Not Text* (p. 206)
- Profile of Success and Workplace Classification: Grant Grebner (p. 208)
- Professional Classification Essay: Stephanie Ericsson, *The Ways We Lie* (p. 209)
- Checklist: How to Write Classification (p. 215)

Key Terms

Skim Chapter 10 before reading. Find these words or terms in **bold** type. Put a check mark next to each once you locate it.

_____ classification
_____ organizing principle
_____ space order (or order of importance)
_____ support
_____ time order
_____ transitions

Guided Reading for Chapter 10

Fill out the following chart before you begin reading. For each skill, write what you know about that skill and what you would like to know upon completing the chapter. At the end of the chapter, you will be asked to share what you learned about each skill.

Skill	When I have used this skill	What I want to know about this skill
Group items into categories		
Identify similarities and differences		
Generate detailed examples of what a category may contain		
Relate examples or explanations to categories		
Read and analyze a classification paper		

@LaunchPad Solo

Visit **LaunchPad Solo for Readers and Writers > Reading > Patterns of Organization** for more tutorials, videos, and practice with patterns of organization.

Understand What Classification Is

Classification is writing that organizes, or sorts, people or items into categories. It uses an **organizing principle**: *how* the people or items are sorted. The organizing principle is directly related to the purpose for classifying. For example, you might sort clean laundry (your purpose) using one of the following organizing principles: by ownership (yours, your roommate's) or by where it goes (the bedroom, the bathroom).

Four Basics of Good Classification

> **1** It makes sense of a group of people or items by organizing them into categories.
>
> **2** It has a purpose for sorting the people or items.
>
> **3** It categorizes using a single organizing principle.
>
> **4** It gives detailed explanations or examples of what fits into each category.

In the following paragraph, the numbers and colors correspond to the Four Basics of Good Classification.

1 In researching careers I might pursue, I have learned that there are three major types of workers, **2** each having different strengths and preferences. **3** The first type of worker is a big-picture person, who likes to look toward the future and think of new businesses, products, and services. **4** Big-picture people might also identify ways to make their workplaces more successful and productive. Often, they hold leadership positions, achieving their goals by assigning specific projects and tasks to others. Big-picture people may be drawn to starting their own businesses, or they might manage or become a consultant for an existing business. **3** The second type of worker is a detail person, who focuses on the smaller picture, whether it be a floor plan in a construction project, a spreadsheet showing a business's revenue and expenses, or data from a scientific experiment. **4** Detail people take pride in understanding all the ins and outs of a task and doing everything carefully and well. Some detail people prefer to work with their hands, doing such things as carpentry or electrical wiring. Others prefer office jobs, such as accounting or clerical work. Detail people may also be drawn to technical careers, such as scientific research or engineering. **3** The third type of worker is a people person, who gets a lot of satisfaction from reaching out to others and helping meet their needs. **4** A people person has good social skills and likes to get out in the world to use them. Therefore, this type of worker is unlikely to be happy sitting behind a desk. A successful people person often shares qualities of the other types of workers; for example, he or she may show leadership potential. In addition, his or her job may require careful attention to detail. Good jobs for a people person include teaching, sales, nursing, and other health-care positions. Having evaluated my own strengths and preferences, I believe that I am equal parts big-picture person and people person. I am happy to see that I have many career options.

You use classification anytime you want to organize people or items.

College	In a health class, you are asked to group foods into the correct category based on the food pyramid.
Work	For a sales presentation, you classify the kinds of products your company produces.
Everyday life	You classify your typical monthly expenses to make a budget.

In college, writing assignments probably will not use the word *classification.* Instead, you might be asked to *describe the types of* _____ or *explain the types or kinds of* _____. You might also be asked, *How is* _____ *organized?* or *What are the parts of* _____? These are the words and phrases that signal that you need to sort things into categories.

Main Idea in Classification

The **main idea** in classification uses a single **organizing principle** to sort items in a way that serves your purpose. The categories should help you achieve your purpose.

To help you discover the organizing principle for your classification, complete the following sentences:

Main idea in classification	**My purpose for classifying my topic is to explain to _____ readers.**
	It would make most sense to my readers if I sorted this topic by . . .

PRACTICE 1   Using a single organizing principle

For each topic that follows, one of the categories does not fit the same organizing principle as the rest. Circle the letter of the category that does not fit, and, in the space provided, write the organizing principle that the rest follow. *Answers may vary. Possible answers are shown.*

Example:

Topic: Sports

Categories:

a. Basketball   (b.) Gymnastics   c. Football   d. Baseball

Organizing principle: *sports played on a team/sports using balls*

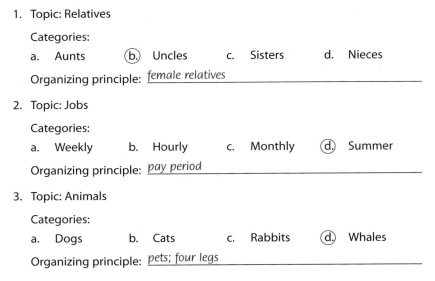

Teaching tip Turn this practice around by presenting a few different organizing principles to the class, such as *special celebrations, motor vehicles,* and *awkward moments.* Then, have students break into small groups, and ask each group to come up with at least four categories of things that would fit each organizing principle. Finally ask the groups to share their categories.

1. Topic: Relatives

    Categories:

    a.   Aunts   (b.)   Uncles   c.   Sisters   d.   Nieces

    Organizing principle: *female relatives*

2. Topic: Jobs

    Categories:

    a.   Weekly   b.   Hourly   c.   Monthly   (d.)   Summer

    Organizing principle: *pay period*

3. Topic: Animals

    Categories:

    a.   Dogs   b.   Cats   c.   Rabbits   (d.)   Whales

    Organizing principle: *pets; four legs*

Sometimes, it helps to think of classification in diagram form. Here is a diagram of the paragraph on pages 196–97.

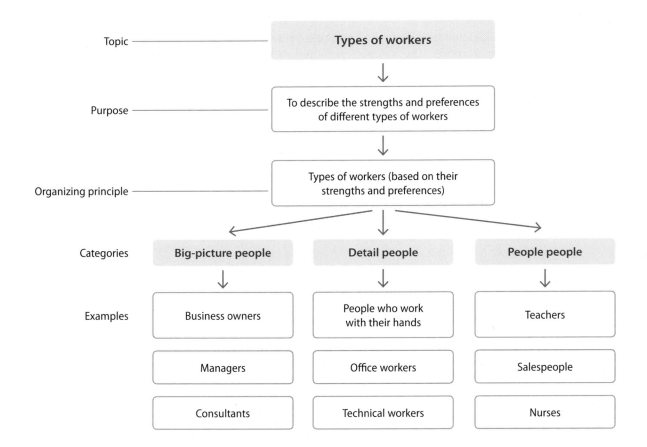

In classification, the main idea may or may not state the organizing principle directly. Look at the following examples:

Topic   Organizing principle

The columns of ancient Greek buildings can be classified into three major types.

Topic   Categories (indicating the organizing principle)

The most impressive structures in ancient Greece were stadiums, theaters, and temples.

In both main ideas, the organizing principle is *types* of things—columns in the case of the paragraph and buildings in the case of the essay. The thesis statement does not state this principle directly, however. Instead, the categories—stadiums, theaters, and temples—make the principle clear.

Also, notice that the topic for the essay is broader than the one for the paragraph. Whereas the topic sentence focuses on just one part of ancient Greek buildings— the columns—the thesis statement considers entire groups of structures.

Make sure that the categories in your classification serve your purpose. In the previous thesis statement, the categories serve the purpose of presenting impressive structures in ancient Greece.

Tip Sometimes, the same main idea can be used for a paragraph and an essay, but the essay must develop this point in more detail. (See pp. 68–69.)

Teaching tip Walk students through this step. Use a simple topic (stores in town or at a local mall, clothing students are wearing, courses offered at the college), and demonstrate how you would classify it. Or break the class into small groups, and give each group a topic. Then, call on students from each group to tell what they did.

PRACTICE 2   **Choosing categories**

In the items that follow, you are given a topic and a purpose for sorting. For each item, list three categories that serve your purpose. (There are more than three correct categories for each item.)

Example:

Topic: Pieces of paper in my wallet

Purpose for sorting: To get rid of what I do not need

Categories:

a. *Things I need to keep in my wallet*

b. *Things I can throw away*

c. *Things I need to keep, but not in my wallet*

1. Topic: College courses

   Purpose for sorting: To decide what I will register for

   Categories: *Answers will vary. Possible answers:*

   a. English

   b. Accounting

   c. Math

2. Topic: Stuff in my notebook

   Purpose for sorting: To organize my schoolwork

   Categories: _Answers will vary. Possible answers:_

   a. _Homework_

   b. _Notes_

   c. _Class handouts_

3. Topic: Wedding guests

   Purpose for sorting: To arrange seating at tables

   Categories: _Answers will vary. Possible answers:_

   a. _Family members_

   b. _Neighbors_

   c. _Friends_

4. Topic: Tools for home repair

   Purpose for sorting: To make them easy to find when needed

   Categories: _Answers will vary. Possible answers:_

   a. _Plumbing tools_

   b. _Carpentry tools_

   c. _Painting tools_

Support in Classification

The paragraph and essay models on pages 202–03 use the topic sentence (paragraph) and thesis statement (essay) from the Main Idea section of this chapter. Both models include the **support** used in all classification writing: categories backed up by explanations or examples of each category. In the essay model, however, the major support points (categories) are topic sentences for individual paragraphs.

Organization in Classification

Tip For more on the orders of organization, see pages 76–78.

Classification can be organized in different ways (**time order**, **space order**, or **order of importance**) depending on its purpose.

Purpose	Likely Organization
to explain changes or events over time	time
to describe the arrangement of people/items in physical space	space
to discuss parts of an issue or problem, or types of people or things	importance

Order of importance is used in the essay model on page 203.

As you write your classification, use **transitions** to move your readers smoothly from one category to another.

Common Transitions in Classification

another	for instance
another kind	last
first, second, third, and so on	one example/another example
for example	

PRACTICE 3   **Using transitions in classification**

Read the paragraph that follows, and fill in the blanks with transitions. You are not limited to the ones listed in the preceding box. *Answers may vary. Possible answers are shown.*

Every day, I get three kinds of e-mail: work, personal, and junk. The _first kind_ of e-mail, work, I have to read carefully and promptly. Sometimes, the messages are important ones directed to me, but mostly they are group messages about meetings, policies, or procedures. _For example, For instance_, it seems as if the procedure for leaving the building during a fire alarm is always changing. _The second kind, Another kind_ of e-mail, personal, is from friends or my mother. These I read when I get a chance, but I read them quickly and delete any that are jokes or messages that have to be sent to ten friends for good luck. _The third kind, The last kind_ of e-mail is the most common and most annoying: junk. I get at least thirty junk e-mails a day, advertising all kinds of things that I do not want, such as life insurance or baby products. Even when I reply asking that the company stop sending me these messages, they keep coming. Sometimes, I wish e-mail did not exist.

Evaluate Classification

Read the sample classification paragraph on page 204. Using the Four Basics of Good Classification and the sample grading rubric, decide what grade this paragraph would earn. Explain your answer.

Assignment   Write a paragraph that classifies the types of classes a student usually has to pass to earn a degree in a particular field.

Teaching tip If you have samples from a previous class, bring in full papers or paragraphs and ask the students to use either this rubric or the Four Basics of Good Classification to "Grade" the assignments. When they have done so, ask them to pair up and work in groups to see if they all came up with the same score and to determine where the areas of consensus and disagreement are.

Paragraphs vs. Essays in Classification

For more on the important features of classification, see the Four Basics of Good Classification on page 196.

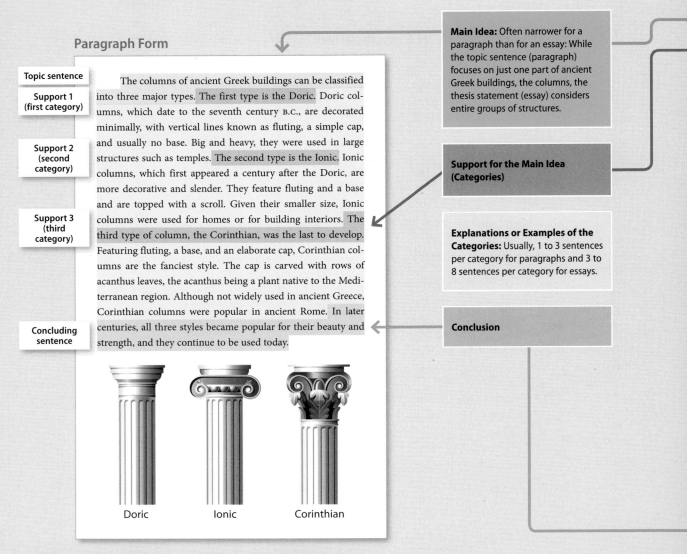

Paragraph Form

Topic sentence	The columns of ancient Greek buildings can be classified into three major types. The first type is the Doric. Doric columns, which date to the seventh century B.C., are decorated minimally, with vertical lines known as fluting, a simple cap, and usually no base. Big and heavy, they were used in large structures such as temples. The second type is the Ionic. Ionic columns, which first appeared a century after the Doric, are more decorative and slender. They feature fluting and a base and are topped with a scroll. Given their smaller size, Ionic columns were used for homes or for building interiors. The third type of column, the Corinthian, was the last to develop. Featuring fluting, a base, and an elaborate cap, Corinthian columns are the fanciest style. The cap is carved with rows of acanthus leaves, the acanthus being a plant native to the Mediterranean region. Although not widely used in ancient Greece, Corinthian columns were popular in ancient Rome. In later centuries, all three styles became popular for their beauty and strength, and they continue to be used today.
Support 1 (first category)	
Support 2 (second category)	
Support 3 (third category)	
Concluding sentence	

Doric   Ionic   Corinthian

Main Idea: Often narrower for a paragraph than for an essay: While the topic sentence (paragraph) focuses on just one part of ancient Greek buildings, the columns, the thesis statement (essay) considers entire groups of structures.

Support for the Main Idea (Categories)

Explanations or Examples of the Categories: Usually, 1 to 3 sentences per category for paragraphs and 3 to 8 sentences per category for essays.

Conclusion

Think Critically As You Write Classification

ASK YOURSELF

- Will readers be clear about my organizing principle even if my main idea doesn't state it directly?
- Do the categories that make up the support for my main idea go with my organizing principle? If not, does it make sense to rethink the categories, the organizing principle, or both?
- Are all the explanations or examples for each category relevant?

Essay Form

1

Ancient Greek civilization produced a wealth of architectural wonders that were both bea[**Thesis statement**] lasting. The most impressive structures were stadiums, theaters, and temples.

The stadiums were designed to hold thousands of spectators. These open-air spaces we[**Topic sentence 1 (first category)**] hillsides so that the seating, often ston would rise up from the central space, giving all spectators a decent view. One of the most famous stadiums, built in Delphi in the fifth century B.C., seated audiences of about 7,000 people. Many stadiums featured ornamental details such as dramatic arches, and some of the more sophisticated examples included heated bathhouses with heated floors. Most often, the stadiums hosted sporting events, such as foot races. A common racing distance was the "stade," equaling one length of the stadium.

Another type of structure, the theater, was also a popular public gathering place. Like sta[**Topic sentence 2 (second category)**] theaters were open-air sites that were set int But instead of sports, they featured plays, musical

2

performances, poetry readings, and other cultural events. In the typical Greek theater, a central performance area was surrounded by semicircular seating, which was often broken into different sections. Wooden, and later stone, stages were set up in the central area, and in front of the stage was a space used for singing and dancing. This space was known as the "orchestra." Among the most famous ancient Greek theaters is the one at Epidaurus, built in the fourth century B.C. and seating up to 14,000 peop[**Topic sentence 3 (third category)**] mances still take place there.

The most beautiful structures were the temples, with their grand entrances and large open spaces. Temples were rectangular in shape, and their outer walls as well as some interior spaces were supported by columns. Their main structures were typically made of limestone or marble, while their roofs might be constructed of terra-cotta or marble tiles. Temples were created to serve as "homes" for particular gods or goddesses, who were represented by statues. People left food or other offerings to these gods or goddesses

3

to stay in their good graces, and communities often held festivals and other celebrations in their honor. Temples tended to be built in either the Doric or Ionic style, with Doric temples featuring simple, heavy columns and Ionic temples featuring slightly more ornate columns. The most famous temple, in the Doric style, is the Parthenon in Athens.

[**Concluding paragraph**] Turning to the present day, many modern stadiums, theaters, and columned civic buildings show the influence of ancient Greek buildings. Recognizing the lasting strength and beauty of these old structures, architects and designers continue to return to them for inspiration. I predict that this inspiration will last at least a thousand more years.

As a student, we are required to take a lot of classes. Some of them are interesting, and some are not. Usually, in the first year or two there are some basic courses. These include math, history, science, and writing. Sometimes there are some other types of courses you can take, like psychology or music, but not always. These classes don't really relate to a particular major. When everyone has to take them. Then, when you finish those basic courses you can finally take classes about material that interests you. For instance, I want to be a math teacher. To take classes about education and how to teach. I would also get to take classes about how to teach math. These courses are more important to me because they are useful for my career.

Analysis of Sample Paragraph: *The sample paragraph is an average paragraph. Comments on each point may vary but should include the following:*

Sample rubric

Element	Grading criteria	Point: Comment
Appropriateness	• Did the student follow the assignment directions?	_5_ /5: *Student followed the instructions.*
Main Idea	• Does the paper clearly state a strong main idea in a complete sentence?	_8_ /10: *There is a clear main idea.*
Support	• Is the main idea developed with specific support, including specific details and examples? • Is there enough support to make the main idea evident to the reader? • Is all the support directly related to the main idea?	_5_ /10: *The supporting ideas are listed, but only some of them are explained.*
Organization	• Is the writing logically organized? • Does the student use transitions (*also, for example, sometimes,* and so on) to move the reader from one point to another?	_8_ /10: *The writer defines courses as either "important" or "basic" depending on how useful they seem to be. There are some good transitions.*
Conclusion	• Does the conclusion remind the reader of the main idea?	_5_ /5: *The conclusion appears to be a logical conclusion to the paragraph.*
Grammar	• Is the writing free of the four most serious errors? (See Chapters 16–19.) • Is the sentence structure clear? • Does the student choose words that clearly express his or her meaning? • Are the words spelled correctly? • Is the punctuation correct?	_8_ /10: *The paper has sentence fragments.*
		TOTAL POINTS: _39_ /50

Read and Analyze Classification

Reading examples of classification will help you write your own. In the first example, Lorenza Mattazi uses classification to talk about her experiences with music. In the next example, student Kelly Hultgren classifies the various types of texters. The Profile of Success highlights Professor Grant Grebner's methods of classification. Finally, in the last essay, professional writer Stephanie Ericsson lists the number of ways in which we lie.

As you read these pieces, pay attention to the vocabulary, and answer the questions in the margin. They will help you read critically.

Teaching tip Ask students to work individually, in pairs, or in groups to evaluate each of the following readings using the rubric provided.

Student Classification Paragraph

Lorenza Mattazi

All My Music

1   From the time I was young, I have always loved music, all kinds of music. My first experience of music was the opera that both of my parents always had playing in our house. I learned to understand the drama and emotion of operas. My parents both spoke Italian, and they told me the stories of the operas and translated the words sung in Italian to English so that I could understand. Because hearing opera made my parents happy, and they taught me about it, I loved it, too. Many of my friends think I am weird when I say I love opera, but to me it is very emotional and beautiful. When I was in my early teens, I found rock music and listened to it no matter what I was doing. I like the music with words that tell a story that I can relate to. In that way, rock can be like opera, with stories that everyone can relate to, about love, heartbreak, happiness, and pain. The best rock has powerful guitars and bass, and a good, strong drumbeat. I love it when I can feel the bass in my chest. Rock has good energy and power. Now, I love rap music, too, not the rap with words that are violent or disrespectful of women, but the rest. The words are poetry, and the energy is so high that I feel as if I just have to move my body to the beat. That rhythm is so steady. I have even written some good rap, which my friends say is really good. Maybe I will try to get it published, even on something like Helium, or I could start a blog. I will always love music because it is a good way to communicate feelings and stories, and it makes people feel good.

1. Double-underline the **topic sentence**.

2. What **categories** of music does Lorenza write about? *opera, rock, rap*

3. Circle the **transitions**.

4. Does the paragraph have the Four Basics of Good Classification (p. 196)? Why or why not? <u>Answers will vary, but the paragraph could use some more detailed examples.</u>

5. What kind of organization does Lorenza use? <u>time</u>

Student Classification Essay

Kelly Hultgren

Pick Up the Phone to Call, Not Text

Kelly Hultgren is studying journalism, communication, and anthropology at the University of Arizona. In addition to contributing articles to the *Arizona Daily Wildcat,* the student newspaper in which the following essay first appeared, Hultgren also enjoys writing creative nonfiction.

Guiding question What are the different types of texters?

Vocabulary development Underline these words as you read: *scrutinized, facilitates, embarking, discourse, emoticons, inherently, subsequently, hypothetical, separation anxiety, inept, barricade,* and *refrain.*

scrutinized: closely observed or studied
facilitates: makes something easier
embarking: starting out on
discourse: communication; discussion
emoticons: tiny electronic images or punctuation group-ings meant to imitate facial expressions and thus to convey emotions
inherently: by its very nature
subsequently: afterward
hypothetical: theoretical; sup-posed or imagined
separation anxiety: emo-tional upset caused by being separated from someone or something
inept: clumsy or lacking in skill
barricade: barrier
refrain: to resist a temptation; to avoid doing something

1   "So, I met this guy last week and I thought he really liked me, because he was texting me all the time, and then suddenly he started taking longer to respond. I think he's not interested anymore. You better believe I am not texting him until he texts me first. I can't believe he led me on like that."

2   Does that sound familiar? That's because you've probably heard someone say it or have said it yourself. Perhaps not word for word, but please raise your hand if you've ever made assumptions at the beginning of a relationship, based solely on texts. My hand just hit the ceiling.

3   Once upon a time, people pursuing potential mates evaluated each other on personality, looks, lifestyle, and how the person felt he or she was being treated. People always will base their opinions on the categories listed above, but now, a more relevant and scrutinized trait is a person's texting habits. People, especially we college students, rely on texting to get to know someone. Both men and women are equally guilty of this. We are all busy, and texting is quick and convenient and facilitates communication throughout the day. I've used those arguments too. <u>But instead of spending three hours on Facebook or watching TV, pick up the damn phone, call, and meet in person.</u>

4   For budding relationships, texting is used not only as a screening device but also as a deal-breaker. It sounds absolutely ridiculous because it is. From simply looking to get some action to embarking on a long-lasting romantic journey, cellular discourse is now crucial in the process. Take my starting quote, for example. The hypothetical girl first assumed the

hypothetical guy liked her and then assumed he didn't based only on his texting frequency. What if the poor guy was having phone issues or was working? You're just getting started; don't expect him to drop the whole world just to send back a response to your simple "hey" text message.

5   This example addresses some aspects of texting: You don't know what the person is physically doing, and you cannot tell the person's mood (emoticons do not count). Therefore, one of every student's favorite forms of interaction is inherently deceiving. At the start of a relationship, why do we communicate and subsequently put so much emphasis on texting, when it's not a reliable way to get to know someone?

Reflect Have you ever made an incorrect assumption about a texter based on his or her message or a lack of response to one of your own texts?

6   As I mentioned before, texting can be a deal-breaker. Let's classify some different types of texters and how they can create problems.

7   First up, we have Lazy Texters. Lazy Texters often initiate the conversation and then leave the responsibility of carrying on the conversation with the other person, rarely asking questions and usually responding with one-word answers.

Identify Underline the different types of texters Hultgren describes.

8   Then we have the Minimalists. Minimalists make their texts short and concise, and they often take longer to respond. They are also notorious for ignoring people, but you would never know this, because you didn't call. This leads us to another bittersweet characteristic of texting: You really don't know if someone has seen your text or not (unless you have Blackberry Messenger; then, your cover is blown).

9   The next type is the Stage Five Clinger, who will constantly blow up your phone wanting to know what you're doing, where you're going, and where you live. This texter sometimes sends text after text, even when you're not responding. Creepy.

10   A less creepy yet still consistent type of texter is the Text-a-holic. They are constantly texting, and they experience separation anxiety when away from their phones.

11   The use of texting to get acquainted with someone is really just a small portion of humanity's increasing problem of becoming socially inept. I said socially inept, not social-networking inept, as in not being able to communicate with someone face to face. The next time you meet someone and get that warm and fuzzy feeling in your tummy, break through the technological barricade and get to know the person in person. And, please refrain from sending the emoticon with hearts for its eyes.

Reflect Do you plan to take any of Hultgren's advice? Why or why not?

1.   Double-underline the **topic sentence**.

2.   What **categories** of texters does Kelly write about? _Lazy, Minimalist, Stage-Five Clinger, Text-a-Holic._

3.   Circle the **transitions**.

4.   Does the paragraph have the Four Basics of Good Classification (p. 196)? Why or why not? _Answers will vary._

5.   What kind of organization does Kelly use? _Types of texters_

Profile of Success
Classification in the Real World

COURTESY OF DAVID CROSSETT

Grant Grebner
Professor of Agriculture

Background I studied animal science at the University of Illinois where I earned both my bachelor's and master's degrees. After college, I returned to our family farm where I worked on our diversified grain and livestock operation with two brothers. Today as a professor of agriculture, I find that both my education and my real-world experiences on the farm help me provide a better classroom and learning experience for my students since I can share both textbook and real-life examples through personal experience and knowledge.

Degrees/Colleges B.S., Animal Science, University of Illinois—Urbana-Champaign; M.S., Non-Ruminant Nutrition, University of Illinois—Urbana-Champaign

Employer Professor and Teaching Chair, Agriculture, Illinois Central College

Writing at work My writing is extensive and varied at work. On a daily basis, I write e-mails to students, colleagues, and administrators. I also write to agricultural businesses and farmers to seek their assistance by providing worksite locations for student interns or by providing a laboratory experience for one of our agriculture classes. In addition, I write e-mails or letters to respond to high school students who express an interest in our programs. Other writing includes thank you letters or notes to the many people who support our various classes and activities.

We learn about the ways to categorize beef cattle breeds in our introductory animal science course. Students in this course learn to identify eighty breeds in five different species of livestock. Being able to classify these breeds makes them easier to learn and distinguish.

Workplace Classification

Classification of Cattle

Beef cattle can be divided into two basic classifications, *Bos taurus* and *Bos indicus*. Cattle are not native to the Western Hemisphere.

The *Bos taurus* cattle originated in the British Isles and western continental Europe and offer high-quality meat. *Bos taurus* also have strong milking ability to nourish their calves. Examples of *Bos taurus* cattle include the breeds of Angus and Hereford.

Bos indicus originated in south-central Asia and are recognizable by the large hump at the top of their shoulder as well as their large, pendulous ears. They are known for heat tolerance and hardiness and are most commonly utilized in the arid conditions of the southwestern United States. Examples include the Brahman and Santa Gertrudis breeds.

A breed can be described as animals of common genetic origin that possess distinguishing characteristics that are passed on from parent to offspring. Currently, more than 80 breeds of beef cattle can be registered in the United States.

1. Double-underline the **main idea** of the article.

2. What categories does Grant break the cattle into? *Bos taurus and Bos indicus*

3. Does the article have the Four Basics of Good Classification (p. 196)? *Yes.*
   Specific answers may vary.

Professional Classification Essay

Stephanie Ericsson

The Ways We Lie

Stephanie Ericsson was born in 1953 and raised in San Francisco. She has lived in a variety of places, including New York, Los Angeles, London, Mexico, the Spanish island of Ibiza, and Minnesota, where she currently resides. Ericsson's life took a major turn when her husband died suddenly; she was two months pregnant at the time. She began a journal to help her cope with the grief and loss, and she later used her writing to help others with similar struggles. An excerpt from her journal appeared in the *Utne Reader*, and her writings were later published in a book titled *Companion through the Darkness: Inner Dialogues on Grief* (1993).

In "The Ways We Lie," which also appeared in the *Utne Reader* and is taken from her follow-up work, *Companion into the Dawn: Inner Dialogues on Loving* (1994), Ericsson continues her search for truth by examining and classifying our daily lives.

Vocabulary Development   Underline these words as you read: *haggard, minimize, confrontation, indulge, keels, travails, hedging, penance, misdemeanors, frank, arrogance, pittance, facades, plethora, ecclesiastical, pedophilia, diocese, context, coperpetrator, nanoseconds, obliterated, refute, sleight, pious, embellish, shrouds,* and *reticent.*

Guiding question   As you read this essay, pay attention to the examples Ericsson provides. What examples of lying can you think of from your own experience?

1   The bank called today, and I told them my deposit was in the mail, even though I hadn't written a check yet. It'd been a rough day. The baby I'm pregnant with decided to do aerobics on my lungs for two hours, our three-year-old daughter painted the living-room couch with lipstick, the IRS put me on hold for an hour, and I was late to a business meeting because I was tired.

2   I told my client that the traffic had been bad. When my partner came home, his haggard face told me his day hadn't gone any better than mine, so when he asked,

haggard: drawn, worn out

minimize: to reduce

confrontation: an argumentative meeting

indulge: to become involved in

keels: falls over

travails: painful efforts; tribulations

hedging: avoiding the question

penance: a penalty to make up for an action

misdemeanors: minor violations of rules

frank: honest; direct

arrogance: belief in one's superiority

pittance: a small amount

facades: masks

plethora: excess

ecclesiastical: relating to a church

pedophilia: sexual abuse of children

diocese: a district or churches under the guidance of a bishop

context: a surrounding situation

coperpetrator: the helper of a person who commits an action

nanoseconds: billionths of a second

obliterated: wiped out

refute: to deny

sleight: a skillful trick

pious: religious

embellish: to decorate

shrouds: covers, conceals

reticent: reserved; silent; reluctant

"How was your day?" I said, "Oh, fine," knowing that one more straw might break his back. A friend called and wanted to take me to lunch. I said I was busy. Four lies in the course of a day, none of which I felt the least bit guilty about.

3   We lie. We all do. We exaggerate, we minimize, we avoid confrontation, we spare people's feelings, we conveniently forget, we keep secrets, we justify lying to the big-guy institutions. <u>Like most people, I indulge in small falsehoods and still think of myself as an honest person.</u> Sure I lie, but it doesn't hurt anything. Or does it?

4   I once tried going a whole week without telling a lie, and it was paralyzing. I discovered that telling the truth all the time is nearly impossible. It means living with some serious consequences: The bank charges me $60 in overdraft fees, my partner keels over when I tell him about my travails, my client fires me for telling her I didn't feel like being on time, and my friend takes it personally when I say I'm not hungry. There must be some merit to lying.

5   But if I justify lying, what makes me any different from slick politicians or the corporate robbers who raided the S&L industry? Saying it's OK to lie one way and not another is hedging. I cannot seem to escape the voice deep inside me that tells me: When someone lies, someone loses.

6   What far-reaching consequences will I, or others, pay as a result of my lie? Will someone's trust be destroyed? Will someone else pay *my* penance because I ducked out? We must consider the *meaning of our actions.* Deception, lies, capital crimes, and misdemeanors all carry meanings. *Webster's* definition of *lie* is specific:

1. a false statement or action especially made with the intent to deceive;
2. anything that gives or is meant to give a false impression.

7   A definition like this implies that there are many, many ways to tell a lie. Here are just a few.

The White Lie

8   The white lie assumes that the truth will cause more damage than a simple, harmless untruth. Telling a friend he looks great when he looks like hell can be based on a decision that the friend needs a compliment more than a frank opinion. But, in effect, it is the liar deciding what is best for the lied to. Ultimately, it is a vote of no confidence. It is an act of subtle arrogance for anyone to decide what is best for someone else.

9   Yet not all circumstances are quite so cut and dried. Take, for instance, the sergeant in Vietnam who knew one of his men was killed in action but listed him as missing so that the man's family would receive indefinite compensation instead of the lump-sum pittance the military gives widows and children. His intent was honorable. Yet for twenty years this family kept their hopes alive, unable to move on to a new life.

Facades

10   We all put up facades to one degree or another. When I put on a suit to go to see a client, I feel as though I am putting on another face, obeying the expectation

Reflect Think of another common human behavior. Break it into categories, and give examples for each category.

Identify In the first two paragraphs, the author provides four examples of lies she has told. Put an X by these examples.

Reflect Do you agree that there "must be some merit to lying"? Why or why not?

that serious businesspeople wear suits rather than sweatpants. But I'm a writer. Normally, I get up, get the kid off to school, and sit at my computer in my pajamas until four in the afternoon. When I answer the phone, the caller thinks I'm wearing a suit (although the UPS man knows better).

11   <u>But facades can be destructive because they are used to seduce others into an illusion.</u> For instance, I recently realized that a former friend was a liar. He presented himself with all the right looks and the right words and offered lots of new consciousness theories, fabulous books to read, and fascinating insights. Then I did some business with him, and the time came for him to pay me. He turned out to be all talk and no walk. I heard a plethora of reasonable excuses, including in-depth descriptions of the big break around the corner. In six months of work, I saw less than a hundred bucks. When I confronted him, he raised both eyebrows and tried to convince me that I'd heard him wrong, that he'd made no commitment to me. A simple investigation into his past revealed a crowded graveyard of disenchanted former friends.

Ignoring the Plain Facts

12   In the sixties, the Catholic Church in Massachusetts began hearing complaints that Father James Porter was sexually molesting children. Rather than relieving him of his duties, the ecclesiastical authorities simply moved him from one parish to another between 1960 and 1967, actually providing him with a fresh supply of unsuspecting families and innocent children to abuse. After treatment in 1967 for pedophilia, he went back to work, this time in Minnesota. The new diocese was aware of Father Porter's obsession with children, but they needed priests and recklessly believed treatment had cured him. More children were abused until he was relieved of his duties a year later. By his own admission, Porter may have abused as many as a hundred children.

13   Ignoring the facts may not in and of itself be a form of lying, but consider the context of this situation. If a lie is *a false action done with the intent to deceive*, then the Catholic Church's conscious covering for Porter created irreparable consequences. The church became a coperpetrator with Porter.

Stereotypes and Clichés

14   Stereotype and cliché serve a purpose as a form of shorthand. Our need for vast amounts of information in nanoseconds has made the stereotype vital to modern communication. Unfortunately, it often shuts down original thinking, giving those hungry for truth a candy bar of misinformation instead of a balanced meal. The stereotype explains a situation with just enough truth to seem unquestionable.

15   All the *isms*—racism, sexism, ageism, et al.—are founded on and fueled by the stereotype and the cliché, which are lies of exaggeration, omission, and ignorance. They are always dangerous. They take a single tree and make it a landscape. They destroy curiosity. They close minds and separate people. The single mother on

Teaching tip Have small groups diagram the essay. Discuss whether all the categories in the essay are really lies (for example, is stereotyping really a lie?). What other categories should the author have included? Have students record the ways they lie and share their responses at the next class meeting (anonymously, if necessary). Classify the responses according to category.

Identify Underline the main idea of this paragraph. What example does Ericsson use to support it?

Summarize In your own words, summarize the example in this paragraph in one or two sentences.

welfare is assumed to be cheating. Any black male could tell you how much of his identity is obliterated daily by stereotypes. Fat people, ugly people, beautiful people, old people, large-breasted women, short men, the mentally ill, and the homeless all could tell you how much more they are like us than we want to think. I once admitted to a group of people that I had a mouth like a truck driver. Much to my surprise, a man stood up and said, "I'm a truck driver, and I never cuss." Needless to say, I was humbled.

Out-and-Out Lies

Predict Pause just as you start the "Out-and-Out Lies" section. How do you think Ericsson might define such lies?

16   Of all the ways to lie, I like this one the best, probably because I get tired of trying to figure out the real meanings behind things. At least I can trust the bald-faced lie. I once asked my five-year-old nephew, "Who broke the fence?" (I had seen him do it.) He answered, "The murderers." Who could argue?

17   At least when this sort of lie is told it can be easily confronted. As the person who is lied to, I know where I stand. The bald-faced lie doesn't toy with my perceptions— it argues with them. It doesn't try to refashion reality; it tries to refute it. *Read my lips* . . . No sleight of hand. No guessing. If this were the only form of lying, there would be no such thing as floating anxiety or the adult-children of alcoholics movement.

18   These are only a few of the ways we lie. Or are lied to. As I said earlier, it's not easy to entirely eliminate lies from our lives. No matter how pious we may try to be, we will still embellish, hedge, and omit to lubricate the daily machinery of living. But there is a world of difference between telling functional lies and living a lie. Martin Buber once said, "The lie is the spirit committing treason against itself." Our acceptance of lies becomes a cultural cancer that eventually shrouds and reorders reality until moral garbage becomes as invisible to us as water is to a fish.

19   How much do we tolerate before we become sick and tired of being sick and tired? When will we stand up and declare our *right* to trust? When do we stop accepting that the real truth is in the fine print? Whose lips do we read this year when we vote for president? When will we stop being so reticent about making judgments? When do we stop turning over our personal power and responsibility to liars?

Reflect Think back on your answer to the question on page 210 about whether lying ever has any merit. Have your views on this issue changed? Why or why not?

20   Maybe if I don't tell the bank the check's in the mail I'll be less tolerant of the lies told to me every day. A country song I once heard said it all for me: "You've got to stand for something or you'll fall for anything."

1. Double underline the thesis statement.

2. How many categories does Ericsson use to classify types of lying? What does she call those categories? _5: White lies, facades, ignoring plain facts, stereotypes and clichés, and out-and-out lies_

3. Do you agree with these categories? If not, which ones don't seem to be labeled appropriately or should she create a new category for some of the examples? *Answers will vary.*

4. How does Ericsson organize her essay? *Order of importance*

5. What is Ericsson's attitude toward lying? What examples in the essay support your answer? *Answers will vary.*

Write Your Own Classification

In this section, you will write your own classification based on one of the following assignments. For help, refer to the How to Write Classification checklist on page 216.

ESL teaching tip Suggest to students that they write about something unique to their native cultures: foods, holidays, stores, vacation spots, housing, and so on.

ASSIGNMENT OPTIONS   **Writing about college, work, and everyday life**

Write a classification paragraph or essay on one of the following topics or on one of your own choice.

College
- Classify the types of resources available in your college's library, giving examples of things in each category. If you don't have time to visit the library, spend time looking at its Web site. (Some library Web sites include virtual tours.)
- Classify the course requirements for your program into different categories, such as easy, challenging, and very challenging. Your purpose could be to help a future student in the program understand what to expect.
- Classify the types of students at your college, giving explanations and examples for each category. You might classify students by such things as their interests, their level of dedication to school, and their backgrounds (for example, *older students returning to college* and *young students*).

Work
- Classify the different types of bosses or employees, giving explanations and examples for each category.
- Classify the types of skills you need in your current job or a job you held in the past. Give explanations and examples for each category of skill.
- Look back at the paragraph on pages 196–97 that illustrates the Four Basics of Good Classification. Based on your own experiences, think of at least two other ways in which workers might be classified. In writing about your classification, give examples of the types of jobs these workers would like and dislike.

Everyday life
- Using Lorenza Mattazi's paragraph as a guide (see p. 205), classify the types of music you enjoy.
- Write about the types of challenges you face in your everyday life, giving explanations and examples for each category.
- Find out about social-service volunteer opportunities in your community. Write about the types of opportunities that are available. Or research an organization that interests you, and write about the kinds of things it does.

ASSIGNMENT OPTIONS   ## Reading and writing critically

Complete one of the following assignments, which ask you to apply the critical thinking, reading, and writing skills discussed in Chapter 1.

WRITING CRITICALLY ABOUT READINGS

Both Stephanie Ericsson's "The Ways We Lie" (pp. 209–12) and Kelly Hultgren's "Pick Up the Phone to Call, Not Text" (pp. 206–07) describe certain behaviors (lying or stretching the truth in certain circumstances and refusing to call a person and speak to them). Read or review both of these essays, and then follow these steps:

Tip For a reminder of how to summarize, analyze, synthesize, and evaluate, see the Reading and Writing Critically box on page 21.

Teaching tip If time is short, students might complete just one or two steps of this assignment.

1. **Summarize** Briefly summarize the works, listing examples they include.

2. **Analyze** Are there any other examples or details that the authors might have provided?

3. **Synthesize** Using examples from both Ericsson's and Hultgren's essays and from your own experience, discuss various types of behaviors, annoying or endearing, and explain why you feel that way about them.

4. **Evaluate** Which piece, Ericsson's or Hultgren's, do you think is more effective? Why? In writing your evaluation, you might look back on your responses to step 2.

WRITING ABOUT IMAGES

Study the visual below, and complete the following steps.

KRISTIAN SEKULIC/GETTY IMAGES

1. **Read the image** Ask yourself: What purpose does the visual serve? How do the faces, clothing, and positions of the bodies in it help viewers understand how people feel in this image? (For more information on reading images, see Chapter 1.)

2. **Write a classification** Write a paragraph or essay classifying the types of behaviors that send signals to others. The signals can be from a pet or from a person. You might include or expand on the types of behaviors described in the visual.

WRITING TO SOLVE A PROBLEM

Read or review the discussion of problem solving in Chapter 1 (pp. 28–30). Then, consider the following problem.

You need a car loan. The loan officer gives you an application that asks for your monthly income and expenses. Because you find yourself short on money every month, you realize that you need to see how you spend your money. You decide to make a monthly budget that categorizes the kinds of expenses you have.

Assignment: Working with a group or on your own, break your monthly expenses into categories, thinking of everything that you spend money on. Then, review the expenses carefully to see which ones might be reduced. Next, write a classification paragraph or essay for the loan officer that classifies your monthly expenses, with examples, and ends with one or two suggestions about how you might reduce your monthly spending. You might start with this sentence:

My monthly expenses fall into _____*(number)*_____ **basic categories:**
_____, _____, **and** _____.

Chapter Review

1. Classification is writing that _organizes/sorts people or items into categories._

2. The organizing principle is _how you sort the people or items._

3. What are the Four Basics of Good Classification?

   It makes sense of a group of people or items by organizing them into categories.

   It has a purpose for sorting the people or items.

   It categorizes using a single organizing principle.

   It gives detailed examples or explanations of what fits into each category.

4. Write sentences using the following vocabulary words: *discourse, inept, keels, travails, hedging, facades, perpetrator,* and *reticent.* _Answers will vary._

   _____

   _____

CHECKLIST

How to Write Classification

Steps	Details
☐ Narrow and explore your topic. See Chapter 3.	• Make the topic more specific. • Prewrite to get ideas about the narrowed topic.
☐ Write a topic sentence (paragraph) or thesis statement (essay). See Chapter 3.	• State your topic and your organizing principle or categories.
☐ Support your point. See Chapter 4.	• Come up with explanations/examples to support each category.
☐ Write a draft. See Chapter 5.	• Make a plan that puts the categories in a logical order. • Include a topic sentence (paragraph) or thesis statement (essay) and all the supporting categories with explanations and examples.
☐ Revise your draft. See Chapter 5.	• Make sure it has *all* the Four Basics of Good Classification. • Make sure you include transitions to move readers smoothly from one category to the next.
☐ Edit your revised draft. See Parts 3 through 6.	• Correct errors in grammar, spelling, word use, and punctuation.

REFLECTING ON THE JOURNEY

Skills Learned

Now that you've completed the chapter, share what you've learned about each skill by completing the following chart.

Skill	What I learned about this skill
Group items into categories	
Identify similarities and differences to create groups	
Generate detailed examples of what a category may contain	
Relate examples or explanations to categories	
Read and analyze a classification paper	

11

Definition
Writing That Tells What Something Means

Learning Objectives

Chapter Goal: Learn how to write a definition paper.

Tools to Achieve the Goal:

- Four Basics of Good Definition (p. 219)
- Diagram: Paragraphs and Essays in Definition (pp. 222–23)
- Student Definition Paragraph: Corin Costas, *What Community Involvement Means to Me* (pp. 226–27)
- Student Definition Essay: Vidette Editorial Board, *ISU Restroom Change Shows Commitment to Diversity* (pp. 227–30)
- Profile of Success and Workplace Definition: Moses Maddox (pp. 228–29)
- Professional Definition Essay: Elizabeth Renter, *Napping Can Dramatically Increase Memory, Learning, Awareness, and More* (pp. 232–33)
- Checklist: How to Write Definition (p. 236)

READING ROADMAP

Key Terms

Skim Chapter 11 before reading. Find these words or terms in **bold** type. Put a check mark next to each once you locate it.

_____ definition
_____ main idea
_____ support
_____ order of importance
_____ transitions

Guided Reading for Chapter 11

Fill out the following chart before you begin reading. For each skill, write what you know about that skill and what you would like to know upon completing the chapter. At the end of the chapter, you will be asked to share what you learned about each skill.

Skill	When I have used this skill	What I want to know about this skill
Define a word or concept		
Provide examples to explain the definition of a word or concept		
Provide enough details to support the definition of a word or concept		
Read, analyze, and evaluate a definition		

Understand What Definition Is

Definition is writing that explains what a term or concept means.

Four Basics of Good Definition

> **1** It tells readers what is being defined.
> **2** It presents a clear definition.
> **3** It uses examples to show what the writer means.
> **4** It gives details to support the examples.

In the following paragraph, the numbers and colors correspond to the Four Basics of Good Definition.

A **1** stereotype **2** is a conventional idea or image that is simplistic—and often wrong, particularly when it is applied to people or groups of people. Stereotypes can prevent us from seeing people as they really are because stereotypes blind us with preconceived notions about what a certain type of person is like. **3** For example, I had a stereotyped notion of Native Americans until I met my friend Daniel, a Chippewa Indian. **4** I thought all Indians wore feathers and beads, had long black hair, and avoided all contact with non–Native Americans because they resented their land being taken away. Daniel, however, wears jeans and T-shirts, and we talk about everything—even our different ancestries. After meeting him, I understood that my stereotype of Native Americans was completely wrong. **3** Not only was it wrong, but it set up an us-them concept in my mind that made me feel that I, as a non–Native American, would never have anything in common with Native Americans. My stereotype would not have allowed me to see any Native American as an individual: I would have seen him or her as part of a group that I thought was all alike, and all different from me. From now on, I won't assume that any individual fits my stereotype; I will try to see that person as I would like them to see me: as myself, not a stereotyped image.

You can use definition in many practical situations.

College	On a math exam, you are asked to define *exponential notation*.
Work	On a job application, you are asked to choose one word that describes you and explain why.
Everyday life	In a relationship, you define for your partner what you mean by *commitment* or *communication*.

LaunchPadSolo

Visit **LaunchPad Solo for Readers and Writers > Reading > Patterns of Organization** for more tutorials, videos, and practice with patterns of organization.

Teaching tip This chapter is a good place to emphasize the benefits of vocabulary building and keeping a list of new words. Reinforce this practice by giving students a new word at the end of each class and challenging them to use the word during the next class. In addition, discuss tools like a thesaurus or dictionary. Some students may not have heard about or ever used these resources. Make sure you discuss how to use the appropriate word, synonym, or antonym.

Tip Once you have a basic statement of your definition, try revising it to make it stronger, clearer, or more interesting.

In college, writing assignments may include the word *define,* but they might also use phrases such as *explain the meaning of* _____ and *discuss the meaning of* _____. In these cases, use the strategies discussed in this chapter to complete the assignment.

Main Idea in Definition

In definition, the **main idea** usually defines a term or concept. The main idea is related to your purpose: to help your readers understand the term or concept as you are using it.

When you write your definition, do not just copy the dictionary definition; write it in your own words as you want your readers to understand it. To help you, you might first complete the following sentence:

Main idea in definition   **I want readers to understand that this term means . . .**

Then, based on your response, write a topic sentence (paragraph) or thesis statement (essay). These main-idea statements can take the following forms.

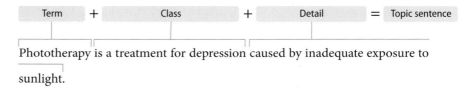

Phototherapy is a treatment for depression caused by inadequate exposure to sunlight.

In this example, "Class" is the larger group the term belongs to. Main-idea statements do not have to include a class, however. For example:

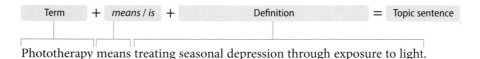

Phototherapy means treating seasonal depression through exposure to light.

Now, look at this thesis statement about a related topic.

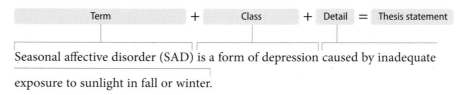

Seasonal affective disorder (SAD) is a form of depression caused by inadequate exposure to sunlight in fall or winter.

Tip Sometimes, the same main idea can be used for a paragraph and an essay, but the essay must develop this point in more detail. (See pp. 68–69.)

The thesis statement is broader in scope than the topic sentences because it sets up a discussion of the larger subject of seasonal affective disorder. In contrast, the topic sentences consider one particular treatment for this disorder (phototherapy).

PRACTICE 1   **Writing a statement of your definition**

For each of the following terms, write a definition statement using the pattern indicated in brackets. You may need to use a dictionary.

Example:

Cirrhosis [term + class + detail]:

Cirrhosis is a liver disease often caused by alcohol abuse.

Answers will vary. Possible answers are shown.

1. Stress [term + class + detail]: *Stress is an emotionally upsetting condition that can have physical effects.*

2. Vacation [term + *means /is* + definition]: *Vacation means taking time off to relax.*

3. Confidence [term + class + detail]: *Confidence is a feeling of trust or faith.*

4. Conservation [term + *means /is* + definition]: *Conservation means preserving something from damage, loss, or neglect.*

5. Marriage [term + *means /is* + definition]: *Marriage is a union that requires respect, communication, and the ability to compromise.*

Support in Definition

The paragraph and essay models on pages 222–23 use one topic sentence (paragraph) and the thesis statement (essay) from the Main Idea section in this chapter. Both models include the **support** used in all definition writing: examples that explain what a term or concept means backed up by details about these examples. In the essay model, however, the major support ideas (examples) are topic sentences for individual paragraphs.

Teaching tip In computer classrooms, have students type one example into their computers and then move to the next computer, add an example for the topic there, and move to the next computer until there are three examples for each definition.

PRACTICE 2   **Selecting examples and details to explain the definition**

List three examples or pieces of information you could use to explain each of the following definitions.

Example:

Insomnia means sleeplessness.

a. *hard to fall asleep*

b. *wake up in the middle of the night*

c. *wake up without feeling rested in the morning*

Answers will vary. Possible answers are shown.   *(Continued on page 224.)*

Paragraphs vs. Essays in Definition

For more on the important features of definition, see the Four Basics of Good Definition on page 219.

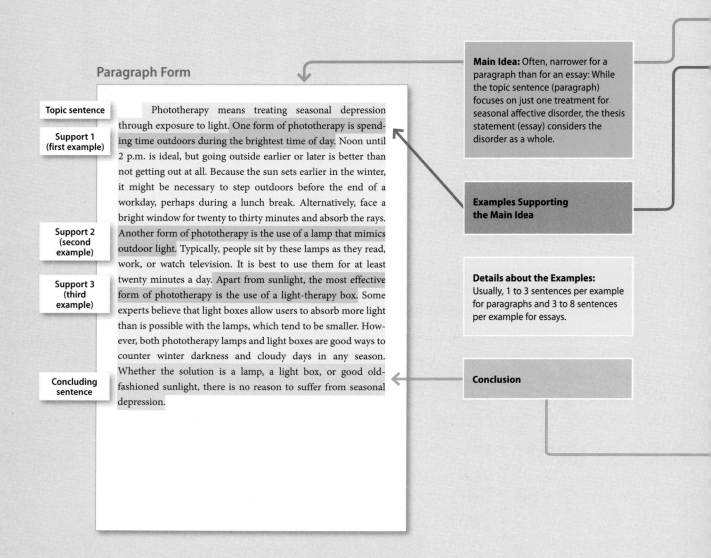

Paragraph Form

Topic sentence

Support 1 (first example)

Support 2 (second example)

Support 3 (third example)

Concluding sentence

Phototherapy means treating seasonal depression through exposure to light. One form of phototherapy is spending time outdoors during the brightest time of day. Noon until 2 p.m. is ideal, but going outside earlier or later is better than not getting out at all. Because the sun sets earlier in the winter, it might be necessary to step outdoors before the end of a workday, perhaps during a lunch break. Alternatively, face a bright window for twenty to thirty minutes and absorb the rays. Another form of phototherapy is the use of a lamp that mimics outdoor light. Typically, people sit by these lamps as they read, work, or watch television. It is best to use them for at least twenty minutes a day. Apart from sunlight, the most effective form of phototherapy is the use of a light-therapy box. Some experts believe that light boxes allow users to absorb more light than is possible with the lamps, which tend to be smaller. However, both phototherapy lamps and light boxes are good ways to counter winter darkness and cloudy days in any season. Whether the solution is a lamp, a light box, or good old-fashioned sunlight, there is no reason to suffer from seasonal depression.

Main Idea: Often, narrower for a paragraph than for an essay: While the topic sentence (paragraph) focuses on just one treatment for seasonal affective disorder, the thesis statement (essay) considers the disorder as a whole.

Examples Supporting the Main Idea

Details about the Examples: Usually, 1 to 3 sentences per example for paragraphs and 3 to 8 sentences per example for essays.

Conclusion

Think Critically As You Write Definition

ASK YOURSELF

- Have I examined different definitions of this term or concept? (If not, research them and consider broadening or narrowing your definition based on what you learn.)

- Would someone who is unfamiliar with this term or concept understand it based on my definition and my supporting details and examples?

Essay Form

1

Thesis statement

Seasonal affective disorder (SAD) is a form of depression caused by inadequate exposure to sunlight in fall or winter. It can seriously affect the daily life of those who suffer from it.

One consequence of SAD is sleepiness and a lack of energy. SAD sufferers may find that they **Topic sentence 1 (first example)** ing longer yet are still drowsy during the day during the afternoon. Connected to the drowsiness may be moodiness and an inability to concentrate. The latter effect can result in poorer performance at work and at other tasks. Those affected by SAD may also find that they move more slowly than usual and that all types of physical activity are more challenging than they used to be. All these difficulties can be a source of frustration, sometimes worsening the depression. Another consequence of SAD is loss of interest in work, hobbies, and other activities. To some ex **Topic sentence 2 (second example)** symptoms may be connected to a lack of ene however, the feelings run deeper than that. Activities that once lifted one's spirits may have the opposite effect. For instance, a mother who at one time never

missed her child's soccer games might now see attending them as a burden. Someone who was once a top performer at work may find that it is all he or she can do to show up in the morning. Such changes in one's outlook can contribute to a feeling of hopelessness.

The most serious consequence of SAD is withdrawal from interactions with others. SAI **Topic sentence 3 (third example)** may find that they are no longer intereste out with friends, and they may turn down requests to get together for movies, meals, or social events. They may even withdraw from family members, engaging less frequently in conversation or even spending time alone in their room. Furthermore, they may postpone or cancel activities, such as vacation trips, that might require them to interact with family for hours at a time. Withdrawal symptoms may also extend to the workplace, with SAD sufferers becoming less vocal at meetings or avoiding lunches or conversations with colleagues. Concern that family members or coworkers may be noticing such personality changes can cause or worsen anxiety in those with SAD.

3

Concluding paragraph

Because the effects of SAD can be so significant, it is important to address them as soon as possible. Fortunately, there are many good therapies for the condition, from drug treatment to greater exposure to sunlight, whether real or simulated through special lamps or light boxes. Often, such treatments have SAD sufferers feeling better quickly.

1. A good workout makes you feel better.

    a.   *You focus on your strengths.*

    b.   *You feel yourself getting stronger.*

    c.   *You can work out frustrations through activities.*

2. A real friend is not just someone for the fun times.

    a.   *sticks up for you*

    b.   *helps when you need it*

    c.   *likes you for who you are*

Teaching tip Ask students, "How has the definition of *family* changed in the last decade?"

3. A family is a group you always belong to, no matter what.

    a.   *You can always count on family.*

    b.   *Distance, divorce, even death will not change it.*

    c.   *Sometimes you might want to escape, but you cannot.*

4. Beauty is an important element in life that a viewer needs to be always looking for, even in unlikely places.

    a.   *It is not perfect, but always contains a flaw or a potential to fade.*

    b.   *It is always changing across peoples' ages, locations, or lives.*

    c.   *It depends on each person being attentive.*

Organization in Definition

Tip For more on order of importance, see page 78.

The examples in definition are often organized by **order of importance**, meaning that the example that will have the most effect on readers is saved for last. This strategy is used in the paragraph and essay models on pages 222–23.

    Transitions in definition move readers from one example to the next. Here are some transitions you might use in definition, although many others are possible, too.

> ## Common Transitions in Definition
>
> | | |
> |---|---|
> | alternately | first, second, third, and so on |
> | another; one/another | for example |
> | another kind | for instance |

> **PRACTICE 3**   **Using transitions in definition**

Read the paragraph that follows, and fill in the blanks with transitions. You are not limited to the ones listed in the preceding box. *Answers may vary. Possible answers are shown.*

    Each year, *Business Week* publishes a list of the most family-friendly

companies to work for. The magazine uses several factors to define the organizations as family-friendly. __One__ factor is whether the company has

flextime, allowing employees to schedule work hours that better fit family needs.

___For example___, a parent might choose to work from 6:30 a.m. to 2:30 p.m. to

be able to spend time with children. ___Alternately___, a parent might split his

or her job with a colleague, so each person thus has more time for child care.

___Another, A second___ factor is whether family leave programs are encouraged.

In addition to maternity leaves, ___for example___, does the company encourage

paternity leaves and leaves for care of elderly parents? Increasingly, companies

are trying to become more family-friendly to attract and keep good employees.

Evaluate Definition

Read the following sample definition paragraph. Using the Four Basics of Good Definition and the sample grading rubric, decide what grade this paragraph would earn. Explain your answer.

Teaching tip If you have samples from a previous class, bring in full papers or paragraphs and ask the students to use either this rubric or the Four Basics of Good Definition to "grade" the assignments. When they have done so, ask them to pair up and work in groups to see if they all came up with the same score and to determine where the areas of consensus and disagreement are.

Assignment Define one character trait that you would look for in a best friend.

> **Finding a best friend isn't always easy because it's important to make sure to know the person well. When I first meet a person and begin to spend time with them, I want to make sure that we have enough in common to be good friends. If we can't agree on places to go or what to do, then that may mean that we do not really share enough interests to spend a lot of time together. What if I always want to go to sporting events and they always want to go to a movie? That makes it hard for us to hang out because we just don't find the same things entertaining. Therefore, if we are not spending a lot of time together, then we probably are not a great fit as best friends.**

Analysis of Sample Paragraph: *The sample paragraph is an above average paragraph. Comments on each point may vary but should include the following:*

Sample rubric

Element	Grading criteria	Point: Comment
Appropriateness	• Did the student follow the assignment directions?	__5__/5: *Student followed the instructions.*
Main idea	• Does the paper clearly state a strong main idea in a complete sentence?	__10__/10: *There is a clear main idea.*
Support	• Is the main idea developed with specific support, including specific details and examples? • Is there enough support to make the main idea evident to the reader? • Is all the support directly related to the main idea?	__10__/10: *The supporting details are listed and explained in good detail.* ►

Element	Grading criteria	Point: Comment
Organization	• Is the writing logically organized according to a basic principle (order of importance)? • Does the student use transitions (*also, for example, sometimes,* and so on) to move the reader from one point to another?	__8__ /10: *The writer does use order of importance as she or he starts by identifying the quality and then providing examples and details to support that definition.*
Conclusion	• Does the conclusion remind the reader of the main idea?	__5__ /5: *The conclusion appears to be a logical ending to the paragraph.*
Grammar	• Is the writing free of the four most serious errors? (See Chapters 16–19.) • Is the sentence structure clear? • Does the student choose words that clearly express his or her meaning? • Are the words spelled correctly? • Is the punctuation correct?	__10__ /10: *The paper is free from major errors.*
		TOTAL POINTS: __48__ /50

Read and Analyze Definition

Teaching tip Ask students to work individually, in pairs, or in groups to evaluate each of the following readings using the rubric provided above.

Reading examples of definition will help you write your own. The first example is a student paragraph by Corin Costas about a community service group in which he is involved. An essay by the Vidette Editorial Board explores a controversial issue on campus. In the Profile of Success, Moses Maddox describes how he uses definition in his career. Finally, a professional essay by Elizabeth Renter defines "napping" and how it can positively affect a person's performance in everyday life. As you read these pieces, pay attention to the vocabulary, and answer the questions in the margin. They will help you read critically.

Student Definition Paragraph

Corin Costas

What Community Involvement Means to Me

SHOCWAVES is a student organization at Bunker Hill Community College. SHOCWAVES stands for Students Helping Our Community with Activities, and its mission is to get students involved with the community—to become part of it by actively working in it in positive ways. Each year, SHOCWAVES is assigned a budget by the Student Activities Office, and it spends that budget in activities that help the community in a variety of ways. Some of the money is spent, for example, in fund-raising events for community causes. We have money to plan and launch a fund-raiser, which raises far more than we spend. In the process, other students and members of the community also become involved in the helping effort. We get to know lots of people, and we usually have a lot of fun—all while helping others. Recently, we have worked as part of the Charles River Cleanup, the Walk for Hunger, collecting toys for sick and needy children, and Light One Little Candle. While SHOCWAVES's mission is to help the community, it also benefits its members. Working in the community, I have learned so many valuable skills, and I always have something I care about to write about for my classes. I have learned about budgeting, advertising, organizing, and managing. I have also developed my creativity by coming up with new ways to do things. I have networked with many people, including people who are important in the business world. SHOCWAVES has greatly improved my life, and my chances for future success.

1. Double-underline the **topic sentence**.

2. Underline the **examples** of what SHOCWAVES does for the community.

3. Double-underline the sentence that makes a final observation about the topic.

4. Does this paragraph follow the Four Basics of Good Definition (p. 219)? Why or why not? *Yes. Answers will vary.*

Student Definition Essay

ISU's Restroom Change Shows Commitment to Diversity

The following article is an editorial published by the Illinois State University student newspaper, *The Daily Vidette*.

Vocabulary development Underline these words as you read: *garner, dubbing, baffled, rendition, dismay, transgender, bewilderment, empathize, profound,* and *ideology*.

1   When Illinois State University changed their "Family Restroom" signs to "All Gender," they most likely did not expect the switch to garner national attention. As it turns out, however, Fox News has a keen eye for such changes.

2   Dubbing the new signs as a product of the "P.C. Police," Fox News was both confused and even amused by the concept of such a restroom.

3   The news channel was so baffled by the idea that it even took to the streets asking random people outside of the studio if they understood the meaning of the "All Gender" sign.

4   A Fox News representative carried a large rendition of the sign, a figure that is half male and half female, and gave those they interviewed twenty

garner: to gather, collect, or hoard

dubbing: to give a nickname

baffled: frustrated or confused

rendition: an interpretation

dismay: to alarm or dishearten

transgender: a person appearing to or attempting to be of the opposite sex

bewilderment: confused

empathize: sympathize

profound: going beyond what is obvious

ideology: the belief that guides a group

Predict Why might such a change create headlines nationwide? What do you think the article will be about?

Reflect What do you think Fox News meant by the term, "P.C. Police?"

Profile of Success
Definition in the Real World

Moses Maddox

Fellowship Specialist at The Mission Continues

Background   When I was pursuing my degree, I struggled with writing. It wasn't that I didn't enjoy writing, but with my program being in social sciences I had concentrations in sociology, political science, and history, and I also pursued a minor in philosophy because, well, why not? The struggle with having four different focuses was that all four subjects had different tones in writing. When writing a paper in history, you had to present facts and analysis of those facts, and there was little room for personality or creativity beyond the presentation of those facts. In philosophy, one had to be careful of what one was writing so that one didn't commit any logical fallacies. In philosophy, it will take you four pages to write something that would be one page in history because you have to be careful that the reader understands your premise before you get to your point. It was a tough learning experience to get a "C" on a history paper because I "didn't write a history paper." That happened a lot.

What I learned through experiences like that was to understand my audience. Sometimes people just want the facts and your presentation of those facts; however, in my current position, if I just presented facts, it would impact how seriously a person would take this program. I have also learned how to find my voice through my writing. I was encouraged by my professors to experiment, to look at writing as my true expression of self. People will forget what you've said, but what you write can last forever. I was taught to write so that if someone one hundred years from now read something I'd written, they would get a sense of who I am, as though I was able to communicate with a person in the future. Writing is that powerful.

Degrees/Colleges   B.A. Social Sciences with Philosophy Minor from California State University, San Marcos; A.A. Arts & Humanities, Social & Behavioral Sciences, Sociology from Palomar College, San Marcos, CA

---

seconds to see if they could determine its meaning. Likely to their dismay, not only were none of the people confused by the signs, but even the child that was asked completely understood what the sign was supposed to mean.

5   The reaction by Fox News really should not be surprising. The program has a long history of being insensitive to the transgender community as well as any group they perceive as "different."

6   Their laughter and utter bewilderment of ISU's new direction only reflects their inability to understand diversity or to empathize with other cultures. Complete disconnect.

7   Such a reaction, though, is not tolerable, especially in this day and age. As we attempt to push our country into a more progressive and an all-encompassing state, such attitudes simply have no place. If anything, Illinois State should be lauded for its attempt to create a more understanding community.

8   In the Fox News segment, Heather Nauert claimed that ISU students didn't ask for these changes. This is true to some extent, but the reality is we

Identify   The writers claim that FOX News reacted without empathy when it reported this story. What specific examples do the writers give to support that claim?

228

Writing at work What I do at The Mission Continues is manage returning post-9/11 veterans as they navigate through their six-month Fellowships. A Fellowship with The Mission Continues resembles more of an executive internship where Fellows pick the nonprofit organization they want to serve, but as they pick that organization, it has to fulfill some sort of qualitative and quantitative goals. That means that they have to fulfill a professional goal, a continued education goal, or a continued service goal, and they have to generate data. What Fellows accomplish throughout their Fellowships serves as resume fodder for many of them, who have a ton of leadership experience from the military but do not necessarily have the relevant work experience to be marketable in the civilian job market.

Veterans are really good at the "how" part of life. If you give military members a job to do, they will do it and do it well. However, if you ask them why they are doing the job, many don't know the answer. My position is to facilitate our curriculum, where we focus on personal and professional development through goal setting, finding allies, identifying role models, identifying driving force, and creating personal mission statements. The overarching goal is for our veterans to be in a place where they can go out into the world and understand what they are looking for in a career and understand how their military experience applies to the nonmilitary world. We feel that service is a vehicle through a successful transition, and my job is to hold the Fellows accountable for the goals that they set and push them to explore their inner selves so that they can move on and find joy in their lives.

As such, writing is a huge part of my job. Although the writing is mainly conversational in tone, creating the correct message is important. Things such as punctuation are important because there is a difference between "You're doing a great job." and "You're doing a great job!" It is part of the job to remain positive, as well as approachable, in all of my interactions. In covering rather deep philosophical conversations, if one approaches the topic in a completely academic tone, then people will check out. If one approaches it in a conversational tone, people are more receptive. One e-mail—in fact, one sentence—can mean the difference between a successful Fellowship or someone giving up completely. So focusing on writing is one of the key competencies of my work.

did not need to. To be a student at Illinois State means entering an inclusive community, one that tries to recognize the perspectives of all people.

9   The changes themselves may be small, as they only affect 10 restrooms, but their meaning is incredibly profound. They represent an attitude that is held by the university: Everyone is welcome and ISU is committed to the needs of every student. Such an ideology shouldn't be confusing to anyone.

10   Ideally, these changes will inspire other universities to do the same. This country suffers a lack of empathy for the transgender community, and introducing gender-neutral restrooms could be an important step in creating such understanding.

11   Even for those that do object to the philosophy behind a gender-neutral restroom, it is not as if the changes will dramatically affect anyone in a negative way. Again, the "All-Gender" restrooms make up only a small portion of those found on campus and will still function in the same way that the "Family Restrooms" did.

12   Ultimately, though, these new restrooms are the beginning of a bold new direction that ISU is taking. Regardless of the opinions of Fox News,

Identify What exactly, is an "All-Gender" restroom, and why did ISU believe it was an important change to make on the campus?

these changes make ISU a better university. Students here should be proud that their university is truly a school for everyone.

1. What is the term being defined in this essay? <u>*Answers may vary but should*</u>
   <u>*focus on the "All-Gender" aspect of the restroom and whether or not it is a*</u>
   <u>*confusing term.*</u>

2. Underline the specific examples the article gives to support the inclusion of this type of facility on campus.

3. Circle any transitions used throughout the paper.

4. Does this article meet all the requirements of the Four Basics of Good Definition on p. 219? _____

Workplace Definition

The following is an e-mail Moses sent out to his clients at The Mission Continues.

Hello Fellows,

First: amazing work! Thanks each and every single one of you for getting me your written assignments on time. Your candid responses have let me know that you are taking this seriously and have given me a look into the impact you all want to make. All of your goals are achievable, and all of your fears can be overcome!

<u>In Month 2, we talk more about overcoming fear and identifying allies</u>. In a few minutes, I will share some tips and tricks to get the most out of Month 2. First, I want to recap the two main terms I went over with all of you in Month 1:

Eudaimonia: gotta love the work that goes into "well-being" or "being well." My goal for all of you is to find your joy and be well.

10,000 Hours: Malcolm Gladwell stated that it takes 10,000 hours of deliberate practice to become an expert at something. The actual research (attached) suggests that it takes 10 years. I think most of us have agreed that achieving 10,000 hours of deliberate practice helps you master the basics. We have also agreed that for many of you, due to your time in the military, you have devoted more than 10,000 hours of your life to service, and your Fellowships add to your tally.

Month 2:

Month 2 is less intimidating, but just as deep. Here are the terms that I enjoyed researching, and the stuff we will talk about over the month.

Mental Rehearsal: The best way to face your fears is to think about them, visualize the worst-case scenario, and then in your visualization, come up with a way to solve your worst-case scenario. In philosophy, we call this a thought experiment. Einstein famously used thought experimentation during his development of the theory of special relativity. Long story short, with enough practice, mental rehearsal can be a great tool.

Finding Allies: You will read (or have read) an excerpt from Reid Hoffman from his book *The Start-Up of You*. The summary I attached is basically a CliffsNotes version of the book. Also, *How to Win Friends and Influence People* was mentioned, and I included the entire book mainly because it is such an amazing and enlightening read.

Remember that no person is an island, so when you are thinking about your allies, the reading states that "allies can be friends, spouses, colleagues, family, supervisors, mentors," which I agree with. However, don't pick your spouse as an ally just because he or she is there. Choose allies that share your goals, offer something of their own, and are willing to be helped. Also remember that an ally is:

- Someone you consult regularly for advice.
- Someone with whom you share opportunities and collaborate.

Cheers,
Mo

1. Double-underline the **topic sentence**.

2. Maddox includes many terms and definitions in his e-mail. Define each of the following using context clues:

    Eudaimonia: *Happiness or well-being*

    Thought experiment: *visualizing a worst-case scenario of your fears and coming up with a way to solve it*

    Allies: *someone you regularly consult for advice; someone with whom you share opportunities and collaborate*

3. Maddox notes that, "allies can be friends, spouses, colleagues, family, supervisors, mentors;" however, he also warns his readers about choosing someone just because they are close in proximity. Why do you think he does this? What does he want his readers to do as they choose an ally? *Answers will vary, but he wants to remind his readers that working through these concepts and ideas may require honest and thoughtful discussion. Relying on someone, such as a spouse, may hinder that process because that person may not have had similar experiences that allow him or her to reflect on the topic in a similar way.*

4. Maddox notes that he is always aware of his audience and how they will perceive his work. Who do you think he is writing to in this e-mail? What clues do you see that help you identify that reader? *Answers will vary but should note that he is writing to veterans and that he is enthusiastic in his tone, acknowledges the time these readers spent in the military, and reminds them of what an "ally" is.*

Professional Definition Essay

Elizabeth Renter

Napping Can Dramatically Increase Learning, Memory, Awareness, More . . .

siesta: a midday or afternoon rest or nap (from Spanish)

circadian rhythm: the body's natural sleep-wake cycle

affirmed: to confirm

reboot: to restart

defragged: to improve performance

grogginess: dazed and weakened by lack of sleep

Elizabeth Renter is a freelance writer and editor whose works have appeared in *The Huffington Post*, *FOX Health*, *Lifehacker*, and *Natural Society*, among other publications. After graduating from Bellevue University with a B.S. in Criminal Justice Administration, she now writes a variety of articles that are typically focused on topics of social justice/injustice and natural living.

The following essay, which appeared in *Natural Society* in 2014, outlines and defines the benefits of napping.

Vocabulary development Underline these words as you read: *siesta, circadian rhythm, affirmed, reboot, defragged,* and *grogginess.*

How Long to Nap

10 to 20 Minutes

This power nap is ideal for a boost in alertness and energy, experts say. This length usually limits you to the lighter stages of non-rapid eye movement (NREM) sleep, making it easier to hit the ground running after waking up.

30 Minutes

Some studies show sleeping this long may cause sleep inertia, a hangover-like groggy feeling that lasts for up to 30 minutes after waking up, before the nap's restorative benefits become apparent.

60 Minutes

This nap is best for improvement in remembering facts, faces and names. It includes slow-wave sleep, the deepest type. The downside: some grogginess upon waking up.

90 Minutes

This is a full cycle of sleep, meaning the lighter and deeper stages, including REM (rapid eye movement) sleep, typically likened to the dreaming stage. This leads to improved emotional and procedural memory (i.e. riding a bike, playing the piano) and creativity. A nap of this length typically avoids sleep inertia, making it easier to wake up.

Summarize In your own words, describe how napping is beneficial for a person.

Predict Before reading the article, what reasons can you think of that may support the idea that napping is good for a person?

1   In some places, towns essentially shut down in the afternoon while everyone goes home for a siesta. Unfortunately, in the U.S.—more bound to our corporate lifestyles than our health—a mid-day nap is seen as a luxury and, in some cases, a sign of pure laziness. But before you feel guilty about that weekend snooze or falling asleep during a movie, rest assured that napping is actually good for you and a completely natural phenomena in the circadian (sleep-wake cycle) rhythm.

2   As our day wears on, even when we get enough sleep at night, our focus and alertness degrade. While this can be a minor inconvenience in modern times, it may have meant life or death for our ancestors. Whether you are finishing up a project for work or hunting for your livelihood, a nap can rekindle your alertness and have your neurons back up and firing on high in as little as 15 to 20 minutes.

3   Big name (and high-dollar) companies recognize this. Google and Apple are just a few that allow employees to have naptime. Studies have affirmed that short naps can improve awareness and productivity. Plus, who wouldn't love a boss that lets you get a little shut-eye before the afternoon push?

4   A study from the University of Colorado Boulder found that children who missed their afternoon nap showed less joy and interest, more anxiety, and poorer problem-solving skills than other children. The same can be seen in adults that benefit from napping.

5   Researchers with Berkeley found an hour nap to dramatically increase learning ability and memory. Naps sort of provide a reboot, where the short-term memory is cleared out and our brain becomes refreshed with new defragged space.

6   Experts say a 10 to 20 minute "power nap" is best for refreshing your mind and increasing energy and alertness. The sleep isn't as deep as longer naps, which allows you to get right back at your day upon waking.

7   A 30-minute nap can lead to 30 minutes of grogginess, as you are often waking just as your body enters the deeper stages of sleep. You'll experience some of that same fogginess if you sleep for an hour, but 60-minute naps are good for memory boosting.

8   The longest naps—around 90 minutes—are good for those people who just don't get enough sleep at night. It's a complete sleep cycle and can improve emotional memory and creativity.

9   Naps are good for you—physically and mentally. But don't sacrifice night time zzz's for an afternoon snooze; take your nap in addition to a good night's sleep.

1. Double-underline the **thesis statement**.

2. Circle the **transitions** used to introduce examples.

3. Do the writers provide enough examples to demonstrate why napping is a benefit? If not, where could more examples be added? _Answers will vary._

_____

4. Look back at the final paragraph. Why do you suppose the authors chose to conclude in that way? _Answers will vary. Possible answers: to show that even though a nap can be beneficial, it is no substitute for a good night's sleep._

_____

Reflect How often do you actually feel rested in the morning? What causes you to feel sleepy or why are you often awake too long to be well rested?

Reflect Many people believe that these kinds of "perks" offered by companies such as Google and Apple are a step forward and lead to healthy, happy workers, while others believe it is a waste of time and hurts productivity. What is your opinion: would such a policy be taken advantage of, or would it improve work quality?

Identify Looking at the previous two studies and the infographic, what is the ideal naptime? Why?

Tip For reading advice, see Chapter 1.

Respond to one of the following assignments in a paragraph or essay.

1. Are you the type of person who needs a nap to make it through your day, or are you one who either can't or won't nap? What are your reasons for your answer? (In other words, if you "need" a nap, why and how does it help you? If you choose not to nap, why not? What happens if you do try to nap?)

2. Napping isn't the only way that humans attempt to make up for "lost time." Can you think of any other parts of our day or our life where we try to catch up for something we missed? For example, cramming for a test rather than creating a schedule for studying in advance.

3. Define "full night's sleep" and provide reasons and examples to support making time to sleep at night, rather than napping during the day.

Write Your Own Definition

In this section, you will write your own definition based on one of the following assignments. For help, refer to the How to Write Definition checklist on page 236.

ASSIGNMENT OPTIONS   **Writing about college, work, and everyday life**

Write a definition paragraph or essay on one of the following topics or on one of your own choice.

College
- How would you define effective study habits and noneffective study habits? Give examples to explain your definition.
- Identify a difficult or technical term from a class you are taking. Then, define the term, and give examples of different ways in which it might be used.
- Define *learning,* not only in terms of school but in terms of all the ways in which it can occur. You might start by writing down the different types of learning that go on both in school and in other settings. Then, (1) write a main idea that defines learning in a broader way, and (2) support your definition with the examples you came up with.

Work
- Define a satisfying job, giving explanations and examples.
- If you have ever held a job that used unusual or interesting terminology, write about some of the terms used, what they meant, and their function on the job.
- In many businesses, it's common for workers to use jargon, which can be defined either as insider language or as vague, empty, or overused expressions. Some examples are "going the extra mile," "being on the same page," and "thinking outside the box." Give examples of work jargon that you've heard of, provide definitions, and explain why the jargon is vague or ineffective. Then, for each expression, suggest more specific words.

Everyday life
- What does it mean to be a good friend? Provide a definition, giving explanations and examples.
- What does it mean to be a good parent? Provide a definition, giving explanations and examples.
- Ask three (or more) people to tell you what they think *community service* means. Take notes on their responses, and then write a paragraph or an essay combining their definitions with your own.

ASSIGNMENT OPTIONS   Reading and writing critically

Complete one of the following assignments, which ask you to apply the critical thinking, reading, and writing skills discussed in Chapter 1.

WRITING CRITICALLY ABOUT READINGS

Both Kathy Stevens's "Ten Tips to Ease into Plant-Based Eating" (p. 186) and Elizabeth Renter's "Napping Can Dramatically Increase Memory, Learning, Awareness, and More" (p. 232) define a situation (eating and napping) and explain that definition through evidence and examples. Read or review both of these essays, and then follow these steps:

1. **Summarize** Briefly summarize the works, listing examples they include.

2. **Analyze** What questions do the essays raise for you?

3. **Synthesize** Using examples from both essays and from your own experience, describe ways in which you have redefined a common term or concept for your own life. For example, just as one can nap for different lengths with different outcomes, consider how eating many small meals during a day may affect a person.

4. **Evaluate** Which essay do you think is more effective? Why? In writing your evaluation, look back on your responses to step 2.

> **Teaching tip** *Critical thinking* is a term that encompasses many definitions and instructional approaches. For insightful articles and other resources on these topics, visit **www.criticalthinking.org.**

> **Tip** For a reminder of how to summarize, analyze, synthesize, and evaluate, see the Reading and Writing Critically box on page 21.

WRITING ABOUT IMAGES

Study the photograph to the right, and complete the following steps.

1. **Read the image** A phobia is a fear, and one that many people share is coulrophobia: a fear of clowns. You could explain to a friend your fear of clowns, or you could show your friend the picture to the right. What makes this photograph such a striking visual definition? (For more on reading images, see Chapter 1.)

2. **Write a definition** Write a paragraph or essay that explains what a visual definition is. To support your definition, use examples of any types of images you are familiar with—signs, advertisements, photographs, and so on.

SAMULI SULTANEN/GETTY IMAGES

WRITING TO SOLVE A PROBLEM

Read or review the discussion of problem solving in Chapter 1 (pp. 28–30). Then, consider the following problem.

A recent survey asked business managers what skills or traits they value most in employees. The top five responses were (1) motivation, (2) interpersonal skills, (3) initiative, (4) communication skills, and (5) maturity.

    You have a job interview next week, and you want to be able to present yourself well. Before you can do that, though, you need to have a better understanding of the five skills and traits noted above and what examples you might be able to give to demonstrate that you have them.

Assignment Working in a group or on your own, come up with definitions of three of the five terms, and think of some examples of how the skills or traits

---

CHECKLIST

How to Write Definition

Steps	Details
☐ Narrow and explore your topic. See Chapter 3.	• Make the topic more specific. • Prewrite to get ideas about the narrowed topic.
☐ Write a topic sentence (paragraph) or thesis statement (essay). See Chapter 3.	• State the term that you are focusing on, and provide a definition for it.
☐ Support your point. See Chapter 4.	• Come up with examples and details to explain your definition.
☐ Write a draft. See Chapter 5.	• Make a plan that puts the examples in a logical order. • Include a topic sentence (paragraph) or thesis statement (essay) and all the supporting examples and details.
☐ Revise your draft. See Chapter 5.	• Make sure it has *all* the Four Basics of Good Definition. • Make sure you include transitions to move readers smoothly from one example to the next.
☐ Edit your revised draft. See Parts 3 through 6.	• Correct errors in grammar, spelling, word use, and punctuation.

could be used at work. Then, do one of the following assignments. You might begin with the following sentence:

I am a person who is (or has) _____

_____ .

For a paragraph: Choose one of the terms, and give examples of how you have demonstrated the trait.

For an essay: Write about how you have demonstrated the three traits.

Chapter Review

1. Definition is writing that *explains what a term or concept means.* _____

2   What are the Four Basics of Good Definition?

    It tells readers what is being defined. _____

    It presents a clear definition. _____

    It uses examples to show what the writer means. _____

    It gives details to support the examples. _____

3. Write sentences using the following vocabulary words: *garner, dubbing, rendition, dismay, empathize, profound, ideology.* *Answers will vary.* _____

    _____

REFLECTING ON THE JOURNEY

Skills Learned

Now that you've completed the chapter, share what you've learned about each skill by completing the following chart.

Skill	What I learned about this skill
Define a word or concept	
Provide examples to explain the definition of a word or concept	
Provide enough details to support the definition of a word or concept	
Read, analyze, and evaluate a definition	

12

Comparison and Contrast

Writing That Shows Similarities and Differences

READING ROADMAP

Learning Objectives

Chapter Goal: Learn how to write compare-and-contrast documents.

Tools to Achieve the Goal:

- Four Basics of Good Comparison and Contrast (p. 239)
- Sample Comparison and Contrast Paragraph and Rubric (pp. 247–48)
- Student Comparison/Contrast Paragraph: Said Ibrahim, *Eyeglasses vs. Laser Surgery: Benefits and Drawbacks* (p. 249)
- Student Comparison/Contrast Essay: Armand Powell-Archie, *Pirate vs. Poet* (pp. 250–251)
- Profile of Success and Workplace Comparison and Contrast: Darin Adams (p. 252)
- Professional Comparison/Contrast Essay: John Tierney, *Yes, Money Can Buy Happiness* (pp. 257–58)
- Checklist: How to Write Good Comparison and Contrast (p. 262)

Key Terms

Skim Chapter 12 before reading. Find these words or terms in **bold** type. Put a check mark next to each once you locate it.

_____ comparison
_____ contrast
_____ main idea
_____ support
_____ point by point
_____ whole to whole
_____ order of importance
_____ transitions

Guided Reading for Chapter 12

Fill out the following chart before you begin reading. For each skill, write what you know about that skill and what you would like to know upon completing the chapter. At the end of the chapter, you will be asked to share what you learned about each skill.

Skill	When I have used this skill	What I want to know about this skill
Compare two or more objects to identify similarities		
Contrast two or more objects to identify differences		
Identify topics that have enough in common to be compared or contrasted		
Present logical points to support the comparison or contrast		
Arrange points in a logical order		
Read and analyze compare and contrast documents		

Understand What Comparison and Contrast Are

LaunchPadSolo

Visit **LaunchPad Solo for Readers and Writers > Reading > Patterns of Organization** for more tutorials, videos, and practice with patterns of organization.

Comparison is writing that shows the similarities among subjects—people, ideas, situations, or items; **contrast** shows the differences. In conversation, people often use the word *compare* to mean either compare or contrast, but as you work through this chapter, the terms will be separated.

Compare	=	Similarities
Contrast	=	Differences

Teaching tip Point out to students that some professors in other disciplines ask for comparison when they really mean *both* comparison and contrast. Suggest that they ask professors to clarify questions that ask for comparisons.

Four Basics of Good Comparison and Contrast

1 It uses subjects that have enough in common to be compared or contrasted in a useful way.

2 It serves a purpose—to help readers make a decision, to help them understand the subjects, or to show your understanding of the subjects.

3 It presents several important, parallel points of comparison and contrast.

4 It arranges points in a logical order.

In the following paragraph, written for a biology course, the numbers and colors correspond to the Four Basics of Good Comparison and Contrast.

Tip This paragraph uses point-by-point organization. For more information, see page 244.

1 Although frogs and toads are closely related, 2 they differ in appearance, habitat, and behavior. 3 The first major difference is in the creatures' physical characteristics. Whereas most frogs have smooth, slimy skin that helps them move through water, toads tend to have rough, bumpy skin suited to drier surroundings. Also, whereas frogs have long, muscular hind legs that help them leap away from predators or toward food, most toads have shorter legs and, therefore, less ability to move quickly. Another physical characteristic of frogs and toads is their bulging eyes, which help them see in different directions. This ability is important because neither creature can turn its head to look for food or spot a predator. However, frogs' eyes may protrude more than toads'. The second major difference between frogs and toads is their choice of habitat. Frogs tend to live in or near ponds, lakes, or other sources of water. In contrast, toads live mostly in drier areas, such as gardens, forests, and fields. But, like frogs, they lay their eggs in water. The third major difference between frogs and toads concerns their behavior. Whereas frogs may be active during the day or at night, most toads keep a low profile until nighttime. Some biologists believe that it is nature's way of making up for toads' inability to escape from danger as quickly as frogs can. At night, toads are less likely to be spotted by predators. Finally, although both frogs and toads tend to live by themselves, toads, unlike frogs, may form groups while they are hibernating. Both creatures can teach us a lot about how animals adapt to their environments, and studying them is a lot of fun.

4 Points arranged in a logical order

College	In a pharmacy course, you compare and contrast the side effects of two drugs prescribed for the same illness.
Work	You are asked to contrast this year's sales with last year's.
Everyday life	At the supermarket, you contrast brands of the same food to decide which to buy.

In college, writing assignments may include the words *compare and contrast*, but they might also use phrases such as *discuss similarities and differences, how is X like (or unlike) Y?*, or *what do X and Y have in common?* Also, assignments may use only the word *compare*.

Main Idea in Comparison and Contrast

The **main idea** should state the subjects you want to compare or contrast and help you achieve your purpose. (See the second of the Four Basics of Good Comparison and Contrast, p. 239.)

To help you discover your main idea, complete the following sentence:

Main idea in comparison and contrast	**I want my readers to _____ after reading my comparison or contrast.**

Then, write a topic sentence (paragraph) or thesis statement (essay) that identifies the subjects and states the main idea you want to make about them. Here is an example of a topic sentence for a paragraph:

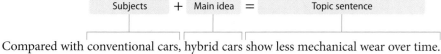

Subjects + Main idea = Topic sentence

Compared with conventional cars, hybrid cars show less mechanical wear over time.

[Purpose: to help readers understand mechanical differences between conventional cars and hybrids.]

Remember that the topic for an essay can be a little broader than one for a paragraph.

Subjects + Main idea = Thesis statement

A hybrid car is a better choice than a conventional car, even one with low gas mileage.

[Purpose: to help readers decide which type of car to buy.]

Tip Sometimes, the same main idea can be used for a paragraph and an essay, but the essay must develop this point in more detail. (See pp. 68–69.)

Whereas the topic sentence focuses on the mechanical advantages of hybrid cars, the thesis statement sets up a broader discussion of these cars' benefits.

Support in Comparison and Contrast

The paragraph and essay models on pages 242–43 use the topic sentence (paragraph) and thesis statement (essay) from the Main Idea section in this chapter. Both models include the **support** used in all comparison and contrast writing: points of comparison/contrast backed up by details. In the essay model, however, the points of comparison/contrast are topic sentences for individual paragraphs.

The support in comparison/contrast should show how your subjects are the same or different. To find support, many people make a list with two columns, one for each subject, with parallel points of comparison or contrast.

TOPIC SENTENCE/THESIS STATEMENT: The two credit cards I am considering offer different financial terms.

Big card	Mega card
no annual fee	$35 annual fee
$1 fee per cash advance	$1.50 fee per cash advance
30 days before interest charges begin	25 days before interest charges begin
15.5% finance charge	17.9% finance charge

Teaching tip You might mention that credit card offers provide a good opportunity for students to practice their critical-thinking skills. Card Hub (**www.cardhub.com**) has tools for comparing credit cards, as well as advice for college students about identifying the cards that best suit their budgets and needs.

Choose points that will be convincing and understandable to your readers. Explain your points with facts, details, or examples.

> **PRACTICE 1**   **Finding points of contrast**

Each of the following items lists some points of contrast. Fill in the blanks with more points.

Example:

Contrast hair lengths

Long hair	**Short hair**
takes a long time to dry	**dries quickly**
can be worn a lot of ways	*only one way to wear it*
does not need to be cut often	**needs to be cut every five weeks**
gets tangled, needs brushing	*low maintenance*

1. Contrast sports

Baseball	**Soccer**
runs = points	goals = points
Answers will vary but should focus	ball is kicked
on differences.	

(Continued on page 244.)

Paragraphs vs. Essays in Comparison and Contrast

For more on the important features of comparison and contrast, see the Four Basics of Good Comparison and Contrast on page 239.

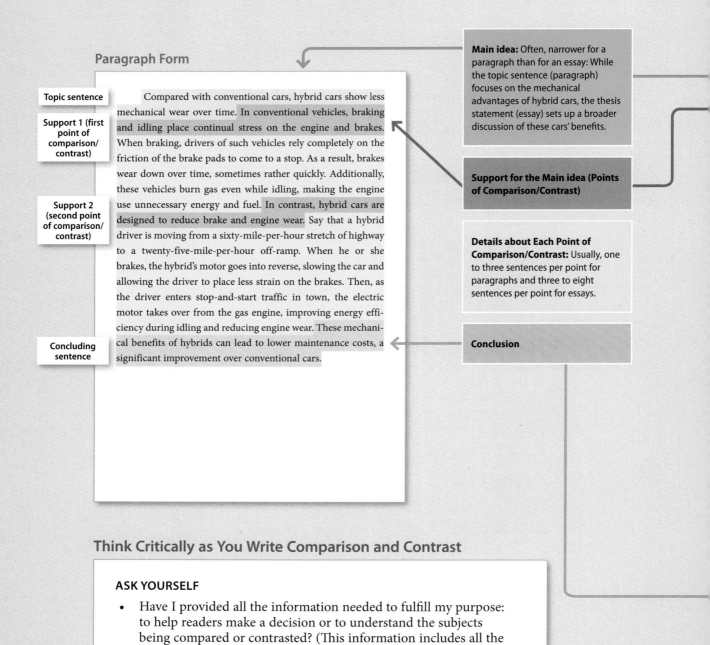

Paragraph Form

Topic sentence

Support 1 (first point of comparison/contrast)

Support 2 (second point of comparison/contrast)

Concluding sentence

Compared with conventional cars, hybrid cars show less mechanical wear over time. In conventional vehicles, braking and idling place continual stress on the engine and brakes. When braking, drivers of such vehicles rely completely on the friction of the brake pads to come to a stop. As a result, brakes wear down over time, sometimes rather quickly. Additionally, these vehicles burn gas even while idling, making the engine use unnecessary energy and fuel. In contrast, hybrid cars are designed to reduce brake and engine wear. Say that a hybrid driver is moving from a sixty-mile-per-hour stretch of highway to a twenty-five-mile-per-hour off-ramp. When he or she brakes, the hybrid's motor goes into reverse, slowing the car and allowing the driver to place less strain on the brakes. Then, as the driver enters stop-and-start traffic in town, the electric motor takes over from the gas engine, improving energy efficiency during idling and reducing engine wear. These mechanical benefits of hybrids can lead to lower maintenance costs, a significant improvement over conventional cars.

Main idea: Often, narrower for a paragraph than for an essay: While the topic sentence (paragraph) focuses on the mechanical advantages of hybrid cars, the thesis statement (essay) sets up a broader discussion of these cars' benefits.

Support for the Main idea (Points of Comparison/Contrast)

Details about Each Point of Comparison/Contrast: Usually, one to three sentences per point for paragraphs and three to eight sentences per point for essays.

Conclusion

Think Critically as You Write Comparison and Contrast

ASK YOURSELF

- Have I provided all the information needed to fulfill my purpose: to help readers make a decision or to understand the subjects being compared or contrasted? (This information includes all the important similarities or differences between the subjects, as well as details about these similarities or differences.)

- If my information about similarities or differences feels "thin," might consulting outside sources help me find new details?

Essay Form

1

Introductory paragraph

For the past two years, while trying to keep my dying 1999 Chevy on the road, these words have popped into my head every time I have thought about purchasing a hybrid car. But now that I **Thesis statement** some research, I am finally convinced: A hybrid car is a better choice than a conventional car, even one with low gas mileage.

The first advantage of hybrid cars over conventional cars is that buyers can get tax breaks and other hybrid-specific benefits. Although federal **Topic sentence 1 (first point of comparison/ contrast)** for hybrid purchasers expired in 2010, sev including Colorado, Louisiana, Maryland, Mexico, continue to offer such credits. Also, in Arizona, Florida, and several other states, hybrid drivers are allowed to use the less congested high-occupancy vehicle (HOV) lanes even if the driver is the only person on board. Additional benefits for hybrid drivers include longer warranties than those offered for conventional cars and, in some states and cities, rebates, reduced licensing fees, and free parking. None of these benefits are offered to drivers of conventional cars.

2

The second advantage of hybrid cars over conventional cars is that they save money over the long term. In addition to using less fuel, hybrid **Topic sentence 2 (second point of comparison/ contrast)** mechanical wear over time, reducing m costs. When braking, drivers of convention completely on the friction of the brake pads to come to a stop. As a result, brakes wear down over time, sometimes rather quickly. Additionally, these vehicles burn gas even while idling, making the engine use unnecessary energy and fuel. In contrast, when hybrid drivers hit the brakes, the car's motor goes into reverse, slowing the car and allowing the driver to place less strain on the brakes. Then, as the driver enters stop-and-start traffic in town, the electric motor **Topic sentence 3 (third point of comparison/ contrast)** from the gas engine, improving energy during idling and reducing engine wear.

The most important benefit of hybrid cars over conventional cars is that they have a lower impact on the environment. Experts estimate that each gallon of gas burned by conventional motor vehicles produces 28 pounds of carbon dioxide (CO_2), a greenhouse gas

that is a major contributor to global warming. Because hybrid cars use about half as much gas as conventional vehicles, they reduce pollution and greenhouse gases by at least 50 percent. Some experts estimate that they reduce such emissions by as much as 80 percent. The National Resources Defense Council says that if hybrid vehicles are widely adopted, annual reductions in emissions could reach 450 million metric tons by the year 2050. This reduction would be equa **Concluding paragraph** 82.5 million cars off the road.

Although hybrid cars are more expensive than conventional cars, they are well worth it. From an economic standpoint, they save on fuel and maintenance costs. But, to me, the best reasons for buying a hybrid are ethical: By switching to such a vehicle, I will help reduce my toll on the environment. So goodbye, 1999 Chevy, and hello, Toyota Prius!

2. Contrast pets

Dogs	Cats
bark	_____
_____	independent
_____	_____

PRACTICE 2   **Finding points of comparison**

Each of the following items lists some points of comparison. Fill in the blanks with more.

1. Compare sports

Baseball	Soccer
team sport	team sport
Answers will vary but should focus	_____
on similarities.	_____

2. Compare pets

Dogs	Cats
shed fur	_____
common household pet	_____
_____	_____

Organization in Comparison and Contrast

Teaching tip Point out that in a whole-to-whole essay, there usually needs to be a strong transition when the essay moves from subject 1 to subject 2.

Comparison/contrast can be organized in one of two ways: A **point-by-point** organization presents one point of comparison or contrast between the subjects and then moves to the next point. (See the essay model on page 243.) A **whole-to-whole** organization presents all the points of comparison or contrast for one subject and then all the points for the next subject. (See the paragraph model on page 242.) Consider which organization will best explain the similarities or differences to your readers. Whichever organization you choose, stay with it throughout your writing.

PRACTICE 3   **Organizing a comparison/contrast**

The first outline that follows is for a comparison paper using a whole-to-whole organization. Reorganize the ideas and create a new outline (outline 2) using a point-by-point organization. The first blank has been filled in for you. The third outline is for a contrast paper using a point-by-point organization. Reorganize the ideas, and create a new outline (outline 4) using a whole-to-whole organization. The first blank in outline 4 has been filled in for you.

1. Comparison paper using whole-to-whole organization

   Main idea: My daughter is a lot like I was at her age.

   a.   Me

   Not interested in school

   Good at sports

   Hard on myself

   b.   My daughter

   Does well in school but doesn't study much or do more than the minimum

   Plays in a different sport each season

   When she thinks she has made a mistake, she gets upset with herself

2. Comparison paper using point-by-point organization

   Main idea: My daughter is a lot like I was at her age.

   a.   Interest in school

   Me: _Not interested in school_____

   My daughter: _____

   b.   _____

   Me: _____

   My daughter: _____

   c.   _____

   Me: _____

   My daughter: _____

3. Contrast paper using point-by-point organization

   Main idea: My new computer is a great improvement over my old one.

   a.   Weight and portability

   New computer: _small and light_____

   Old computer: _heavy, not portable_____

   b.   _Speed_____

   New computer: _fast_____

   Old computer: _slow_____

c. _Cost_ _____

   New computer: _inexpensive_ _____

   Old computer: _expensive_ _____

4. Contrast paper using whole-to-whole organization

   Main idea: My new phone is a great improvement over my old one.

   a. New phone

      More apps _____

      Better battery life _____

      _____

   b. Old phone

      _____

      _____

      _____

Tip For more on order of importance, see page 78.

Comparison/contrast is often organized by **order of importance**, meaning that the most important point is saved for last. This strategy is used in the essay model on page 243.

Transitions in comparison/contrast move readers from one subject to another and from one point of comparison or contrast to the next.

Common Transitions in Comparison and Contrast

Comparison	Contrast
both	in contrast
like/unlike	most important difference
most important similarity	now/then
one similarity/another similarity	one difference/another difference
similarly	unlike
	while

PRACTICE 4   **Using transitions in comparison and contrast**

Read the paragraph that follows, and fill in the blanks with transitions. You are not limited to the ones listed in the preceding box. _Answers may vary. Possible answers are shown._

Modern coffee shops share many similarities with the coffeehouses

that opened hundreds of years ago in the Middle East and Europe.

One similarity is that the coffeehouses of history, like modern cafés, were popular places to socialize. In sixteenth-century Constantinople (now Istanbul, Turkey) and in seventeenth- and eighteenth-century London, customers shared stories, information, and opinions about current events, politics, and personal matters. The knowledge shared at London coffeehouses led customers to call these places "Penny Universities," a penny being the price of admission. _Another similarity_ is that the old coffeehouses, like today's coffee shops, were often places of business. However, although most of today's coffee-shop customers work quietly on their laptops, customers of the old shops openly, and sometimes loudly, discussed business and sealed deals. In fact, for more than seventy years, traders for the London Stock Exchange operated out of coffeehouses. _The most important_ similarity between the old coffeehouses and modern coffee shops is that they both increased the demand for coffee and places to drink it. In 1652, a former servant from western Turkey opened the first coffeehouse in London. As a result of its popularity, many more coffeehouses soon sprouted up all over the city, and within a hundred years there were more than 500 coffeehouses in London. _Similarly_, in recent years the popularity of Starbucks, and its shops, spread rapidly throughout the United States.

Evaluate Comparison and Contrast

Read the following sample comparison and contrast paragraph. Using the Four Basics of Good Comparison and Contrast and the sample grading rubric, decide what grade this paragraph would earn. Explain your answer.

Teaching tip If you have samples from a previous class, bring in full papers or paragraphs and ask the students to use either this rubric or the Four Basics of Good Comparison and Contrast to "grade" the assignments. When they have done so, ask them to pair up and work in groups to see if they all came up with the same score and to determine where the areas of consensus and disagreement are.

Assignment Describe one significant difference between your classes in high school and ones you are enrolled in at college.

> **High school and college are completely different in many ways. When I was in high school, I didn't have a lot of choices about what courses I wanted to take and I didn't really need to think about what classes I was taking because it didn't really apply to my future or job or anything. When I got to college I found out that everything was different. Although a lot of classes were required. Some of them were choices that I got to make on my own. The biggest change is the amount of homework, time I have to spend on it all.**

Analysis of Sample Paragraph: *The sample paragraph is a below-average paragraph. Comments on each point may vary but should include the following:*

Sample rubric

Element	Grading criteria	Point: Comment
Appropriateness	• Did the student follow the assignment directions?	__2__/5: *Student followed some of the instructions but did not focus on one main difference or similarity.*
Main idea	• Does the paper clearly state a strong main idea in a complete sentence? • Do the two topics have enough in common to be compared and contrasted?	__5__/10: *The subjects do have enough in common to be compared and contrasted, but the paragraph doesn't focus on just one idea.*
Support	• Is the main idea developed with specific support, including specific details and examples? • Is there enough support to make the main idea evident to the reader? • Is all the support directly related to the main idea?	__5__/10: *The main idea has some support, but not enough to describe one main difference or similarity.*
Organization	• Is the writing in order of importance? • Is it apparent that the writer is using point to point or whole to whole as their organizational pattern?	__2__/10: *Writing does not have a clear logical order.*
Conclusion	• Does the conclusion remind the reader of the main idea? • Does it make an observation based on the support?	__1__/5: *The conclusion presents new information rather than wrapping up the main idea.*
Grammar	• Is the writing free of the four most serious errors? (See Chapters 16–19.) • Is the sentence structure clear? • Does the student choose words that clearly express his or her meaning? • Are the words spelled correctly? • Is the punctuation correct?	__5__/10: *The paper has several errors that affect the writing and comprehension.*
		TOTAL POINTS: __20__/50

Read and Analyze Comparison and Contrast

Teaching tip Ask students to work individually, in pairs, or in groups to evaluate each of the following readings using the rubric provided.

Reading examples of comparison and contrast will help you write your own. The first example is a paragraph by a student writer, followed by an essay by a student writer. Following those examples are two examples of résumés—one from Darin

Adams, a working professional, and one from Calysta Will, a student. Finally, John Tierney's essay is an example of professional comparison and contrast.

Student Comparison/Contrast Paragraph

Said Ibrahim

Eyeglasses versus Laser Surgery: Benefits and Drawbacks

Vocabulary development   Underline these words as you read: *laser, reasonably,* and *forgo.*

laser: a concentrated beam of light; in this case, it is used to reshape part of the eye

reasonably: not excessively

forgo: go without

1   Although both eyeglasses and laser surgery can successfully address vision problems, each approach has particular benefits and drawbacks. Whereas one pair of eyeglasses is reasonably priced in comparison with laser surgery,[1] eyeglass prescriptions often change over time, requiring regular lens replacements. As a result,[2] over the wearer's lifetime, costs of eyeglasses can exceed $15,000. On the positive side,[3] an accurate lens prescription results in clear vision with few or no side effects. Furthermore,[4] glasses of just the right shape or color can be a great fashion accent. In contrast to eyeglasses,[1] laser vision correction often has to be done only once. Consequently,[2] although the costs average $2,500 per eye, the patient can save thousands of dollars over the following years. On the downside,[3] some recipients of laser surgery report difficulties seeing at night, dry eyes, or infections. Fortunately, these problems are fairly rare.[4] The final advantage of laser surgery applies to those who are happy to forgo the fashion benefits of eyeglasses. Most laser-surgery patients no longer have to wear any glasses other than sunglasses until later in life. At that point, they may need reading glasses. All in all, we are fortunate to live in a time when there are many good options for vision correction. Choosing the right one is a matter of carefully weighing the pros and cons of each approach.

1. Double-underline the **topic sentence**.

2. Is the **purpose** of the paragraph to help readers make a decision, to help them understand the subjects better, or both? *both*

3. Underline **each point of contrast** in the sample paragraph. Give each parallel, or matched, point the same number.

4. Which organization (point by point or whole to whole) does Ibrahim use? *whole to whole*

5. Circle the **transitions** in the paragraph.

Student Comparison/Contrast Essay

Armand Powell-Archie

Pirate vs. Poet

valiant: possessing or showing determination or courage

convey: transport or carry

hostile: unfriendly

articulate: express an idea clearly and coherently

hail: one's home or origin

harassing: to disturb persistently; to torment

vulgar: indecent or obscene

brash: hasty

Predict What may the author use to compare or contrast these two musicians?

Armand Powell-Archie is a twenty-year-old communications student. Aside from school, Armand is an aspiring writer who is passionate about music and composes both poetry and song lyrics. He also works with children at an after-school program and for UPS as a preloader. He wrote this essay as an assignment for his English class and said it was "very easy" because most of his conversations are about music and hip-hop. He says, "For me to actually compose the essay, I gathered all my thoughts and feelings, and from there everything flowed naturally. It's all genuine and authentic."

Vocabulary development Underline these words as you read: *valiant, convey, hostile, articulate, hail, harassing, vulgar,* and *brash.*

1   In the genre of hip-hop, there have been many artists, or emcees (as they're known in the genre), to step behind a microphone and make valiant efforts to convey messages to the people. Personally, however, there are two individuals who convey a message deeper than the average person and stand on a higher podium to do so because their messages are more efficient. Nas and The Notorious B.I.G. (also known as Biggie, Biggie Smalls, Frank White, etc.) are vocal prophets, and anybody willing to lend their ears for three minutes can easily understand why.

2   Both Biggie and Nas bring a unique, unmatched, and unparalleled style to the hip-hop community and to the world of music. Through tough times such as being raised by struggling single mothers, being financially limited, and growing up in hostile environments, both artists are thoroughly able to articulate their experiences to the point where you practically envision their hardships and feel them as your own. Both of these greats hail from the Empire State (New York) and grew up in the seventies and eighties. Not only did they grown up during the crack epidemic, which had a significant role in the lives of both Nas and B.I.G., facing financial tribulations, both men sold drugs including crack to earn some sort of profit.

Reflect It is clear that the writer believes that the background of each person plays a significant role in his music. Do you agree with that assessment? Why or why not?

3   With the drug game comes the responsibility of being armed to protect themselves and their product, but also being paranoid as a result of the life they live. Their paranoia comes from the worry of somebody trying to handle them in the street and from law enforcement trying to lock them up. Law enforcement in these times were best known for harassing young black men. All of this came with the territory of drug dealing and hustling, which both men were well aware of and were able to share in the stores they told. But with the many similarities these emcees share, there are just as many differences to differentiate them.

4   If you were to sit down and listen to a story from both Biggie and Nas, you'd probably be more amazed and astonished listening to that story from Biggie's perspective. With vivid yet vulgar language, the Notorious B.I.G. can vocally illustrate a brash, blunt, and straight to the point picture. The Bed-Stuy, Brooklyn, native possesses a delivery so very forceful and

hard-hitting like a brick through a windshield. Although at times his stories consisted of his lavish come up, his many escapades, and how much of a Casanova he was, Biggie viewed the world through a more pessimistic lens.

5   His debut album titled *Ready to Die* is ironically how Frank White lived his life, enjoying and working every day like it was his last. With songs like *Suicidal Thoughts* and *Things Done Changed* he stresses to us both intentionally and unintentionally his reasoning for being so volatile. Biggie Smalls tells the story exactly how he sees it. His raw wit and his rugged style makes it easier for me to label him the Pirate.

6   Now if you're listening to that same story narrated by Nas, you'd be more intrigued and fascinated than anything else. "God's Son," as he's well known, uses colorful and descriptive vocabulary that creates an image of both triumph and hope. Through his frustrations of being poor, black, and a target for police brutality, the Queens, New York, representative displays vocal and lyrical finesse to spread his message. His deep thought process and his compassion for the people make him relatable to a politician; however, his policies won't suit everybody: Only people who have shared the same struggle as he such as the thugs, the gangsters, the frustrated, and those who wish to find a way.

Identify Looking at the previous and following paragraphs, what similarities do the two men share? What differences are there?

7   Nas is a combination of a political activist and a cold-blooded criminal, which ultimately makes it easy for him to be labeled a Political Gangster. However, his intellect is prominent, and he uses phrases to make us sit back and reflect "people fear what they don't understand/hate what they can't conquer guess it's just the theory of man." His style is sharp, clever, and crisp, and even with his thug persona he remains polished and punctual. While Biggie is known for telling it how it is in black and white, Nas shares what he envisions and what he hopes to see. Songs like "The World Is Yours,' "If I Ruled the World," and "Rule" solidify and confirm that. Nas's intellect, his wordplay, and his overall way of expression make it easy for me to label him the Poet.

8   From whomever you hear the story, you are guaranteed to have a thorough understanding of what's being told. Both Nas and the Notorious give clear insight to the daily and everyday struggles of somebody living in the inner city. They also portray the message of a man in America—just trying to make his own way for both he and his family. A shared message one being told from the angle of a Pirate. "If I said it I meant it, bite my tongue for no one call me evil or unbelievable." And the other being told from the angle of a Poet "we should take time to think, bombs and war leave mankind extinct." Although Biggie is our Pirate and Nas is our Poet, it can easily be inferred that both individuals are profound prophets in the world of music and inspiration to anybody who can relate.

Summarize Briefly restate the main ideas of this essay.

1. Underline the topic sentence.

2. What are the main criteria being compared and contrasted in this article?

     Answers should include the following: their background, their initial careers as

     drug dealers, their use of language in their music, their personal style, and their

     outlook on life.

Profile of Success
Comparison and Contrast in the Real World

Darin Adams

Claims Representative

COURTESY OF DARIN ADAMS

Background   I almost didn't graduate high school on time, and the only reason I was able to walk was due to an English teacher that was gracious enough to allow me to redo an assignment. When I graduated high school, I left with a GPA of 1.83, which at the time was the lowest GPA allowable by the state. I initially went to Hawkeye Community College when I graduated and had to take developmental classes because of my low GPA. I failed horribly and decided to join the military. After my time in the military, I went back to college and had the best English teacher one could ever have. She laid the foundation for my success throughout the remainder of my life.

I studied Liberal Arts at Hawkeye Community College and transferred to the University of Northern Iowa to finish out my education. I graduated in 2013 with my degree in criminology with a cumulative GPA of 3.07. I finished my education in 3.5 years while working 35+ hours a week at PepsiCo, serving in the U.S. Army Reserve, and somehow finding time to be a husband.

Degrees/Colleges   A.A., Hawkeye Community College; B.A., University of Northern Iowa

Writing at work   I work for the Social Security Administration as a claims representative. My job in some ways is hard to describe because the scope of work is pretty vast. I'm a mix between a lawyer, disability examiner, benefits expert, fraud/waste/misuse criminal investigator, and in some situations also a judge.

On a day-to-day basis, I help the public with the process of applying for benefits and ensuring they are entitled to benefits according to state/local/federal laws. The scope of benefits that I process are Retirement, Survivors, Hospital Insurance, Disability, and Auxiliary (children/spouses) Benefits. In addition to my daily tasks, there are other workloads where I use what I learned in college. When I'm looking at a case of fraud/waste/misuse of benefits, I have to look back to my training as a criminologist and ensure I'm following the law correctly. If I do find fraud/waste/misuse, I have to make the determination if the case should be moved forward for official criminal action or if the case should be subject to administrative sanctions. If the case is subject to administrative sanctions, I have to look at which parties are liable and sanction them accordingly. On a typical day, I will communicate with the public via letters, e-mails, and other forms of written correspondence.

3. Does the author use enough examples to make his point clear? *Answers will vary.*

4. Does this essay follow the Four Basics of Good Comparison and Contrast (p. 239)? *Yes.*

Workplace Comparison and Contrast

The following is Darin's professional résumé, which he used to secure his job at the Social Security Administration.

1111 Newcastle Road
Newburg, IA
(111) 500-0123
adams@uni.edu
Darin Adams

Education	B.A. Criminology: December 2013
	University of Northern Iowa, Cedar Falls, IA
	A.A. Liberal Arts: May 2012
	Hawkeye Community College, Waterloo, IA

Experience

Assistant Manager, Wal-Mart, Marshalltown, IA
May 2013–Present

- Manage 150 employees in a constantly changing diverse operational environment.
- Utilize and train conflict resolution solutions to assist in managing customer complaints, concerns, and suggestions.
- Facilitated the hiring, termination, coaching, development, and promotion of a wide range of associates in multiple management positions.
- Train more than 30 associates with tasks relevant to their career choices.

Merchandiser, Pepsi Beverages Company, Waterloo, IA
March 2010–April 2013

- Trained a group of high-performing merchandisers to perform as a team, operate independently, and incorporate the values of Pepsi Beverages Company.
- Arranged and coordinated displays to showcase Pepsi products to increase product visibility and drive bottom-line sales.
- Resolved customer and client complaints on-site to reduce workload on salesmen and the PepsiCo warehouse.

Computer Administrator U.S. Army Reserve, Fort McCoy, WI
December 2009–June 2013

- Managed a computer network of 100 terminals used by multiple U.S. Army Reserve Battalions.
- Ensured the 11th of the 100th Military Intelligence Battalion had the resources necessary to accomplish USAR missions.

Yellow Ribbon Program Coordinator, Fort McCoy, WI

December 2009–June 2013

- Designed and coordinated biannual presentations detailing the complexity and vast number of VA resources available to service members and veterans.
- Developed and managed multiple Yellow Ribbon Program sessions for soldiers of the 11th of the 100th and multiple other battalions at Fort McCoy, Wisconsin.

Infantryman, U.S. Army, Fort Wainwright, AK

January 2005–December 2009

- Performed duties as a Team Leader during drills and live combat; aided in the mobilization of vehicles, troops, weaponry, equipment, and assisted in reconnaissance missions, use, maintenance, and storage of various combat weaponry and equipment.
- Maintained the operational capability of more than $4 million worth of military equipment with zero inventory loss and constant operational use.
- Lead a team of communication experts to ensure the communication capability over 60 km of land space in hostile territory.

Volunteerism and Leadership

Employer Representative, Employer Support of the Guard and Reserve, Department of Defense

June 2013–Present

- Coordinate multiple training sessions for Wal-Mart assistant managers, comanagers, and store mangers covering the Uniformed Services Employment and Reemployment Rights Act.
- Setup multiple on-the-job training locations at Wal-Mart stores for veterans to use their education benefits to attain their career goals.
- Coordinate a mentorship program for veterans pursuing educational and career goals within Wal-Mart.

Committee Member, Veteran Student Services Committee, University of Northern Iowa

January 2011–May 2013

- Created the first veterans scholarship called Boots to Books at the University of Northern Iowa, which is funded for the next several years to provide a $1000 scholarship to student veterans.
- Assisted in developing specialized brochures that were targeted at veteran recruitment and resulted in showcasing the resources, facilities, and empowering faculty at the university.
- Secured the support of dozens of businesses and nonprofits in the Waterloo/Cedar Valley area for the Veteran Upward Bound Program Grant.
- Worked with faculty, university leadership, and student government to secure a student center for veterans on campus.

Member, UNI Proud, University of Northern Iowa

September 2012–May 2013

- Coordinated the first NOH8 at My School photo shoot in the United States with more than 500 participants.
- Facilitated the creation of the first lesbian-gay-bisexual-transgender (LGBT) Scholarship at the University of Northern Iowa.
- Drove an initiative to create an LGBT Center at UNI that opened in December 2013.
- Raised private capital to bring a speaker to UNI to discuss the ramifications of the repeal of Don't Ask, Don't Tell and his military service.

SVA Hawkeye Community College Chapter, Hawkeye Community College

January 2010–May 2012—Founder and President

- Founded the first Veterans Club at Hawkeye Community College and was elected as the first president.
- Grew the Veterans Club to be the largest student group at Hawkeye Community College.
- Partnered with the UNI Veterans Association during September 2011 to assist in the development of their organization, and developed resources to assist UNI and the veterans on their campus.
- Facilitated an open discussion with Senator Tom Harkin regarding the Post 9/11 GI Bill and resources for veterans at universities and at the Veterans Administration.

Student Veteran Advisor, Veterans Task Force, Hawkeye Community College

December 2009–May 2012

- Coordinated with Hawkeye Community College Grant Office to assist in the pursuit of grants for veterans.
- Identified areas of opportunity for Hawkeye regarding the veteran population at the institution.
- Coordinated a veterans forum to identify the needs of veterans at Hawkeye Community College with the participation of 35% of student veterans on campus.

Skills   Proficient in Microsoft Office, Adobe Acrobat, Android Operating System, Active Directory, VA Once; knowledgeable on veteran employment programs and veteran education programs.

Decorations   The Diversity Matters Award from the University of Northern Iowa, Combat Infantrymen's Badge, Two Army Commendation Medals, Three Good Conduct Medals, Presidential Unit Citation

References   Available on request.

The next résumé is an example of a student résumé, from Calysta Will, a student at Illinois State University.

Calysta Will

555 N. Oak Terrace, Normal, IL 60052 | (111) 555-5678 | cwill@ilstu.edu

Education

Bachelor of Arts | May 2015 | Illinois State University

Major: Public Relations

Lorenze de' Medici University | Spring 2013 | Florence, Italy

Skills & Abilities

Communication and computer skills

Microsoft Word and Power Point: Proficient

Excel: Intermediate

Spanish: Proficient

Italian: Basic, conversational, and reading

Leadership

Social Chair, Public Relations Student Society of America, Illinois State University
August 2014–May 2015

Experience

Academic Peer Advisor | Illinois State University—University College | May 2014–Present

- Advise first-year students with academic planning and major exploration in partnership with a University College Professional Advisor
- Assist in the delivery of University College programs and services
- Maintain accurate, detailed record of all advising contacts

Marketing and Communications Intern | Special Olympics Illinois | January–May 2014

- Created various publications for Special Olympics events
- Planned and executed Special Olympics events
- Facilitated creative projects to be featuring Special Olympics Illinois athletes
- Supported and promoted accomplishments of Special Olympics athletes

Communications Intern | Illinois State University Dean of Students | January–May 2014

- Conducted research to define needs of members of the Student Government Association
- Reconstructed operations manual for Student Government Association
- Edited and condensed various documents included in the operations manual

Peer Instructor | Illinois State University Success 101 Program | August 2012–January 2014

- Provided academic support to first-year students
- Created lesson plans focused on important skills necessary to being successful in higher education
- Planned and facilitated social events for students

1. What are the main similarities between the two résumés? What about the differences? _Answers will vary but should include mention of contact information, education, and related experience. Differences include the length and type of job experience._

2. According to the Four Basics of Good Comparison and Contrast, there are only a few possible purposes. What is the purpose of these résumés? _Answers will vary but should include the following: help readers make a hiring decision and help readers understand more about the applicant and his or her qualifications._

3. Does the article have the Four Basics of Good Comparison and Contrast (p. 239)? _Yes; specific answers will vary._

4. What organization does each résumé use, and is it effective? _Specific answers will vary but should include mention of the clear, logical order of each._

Professional Comparison/Contrast Essay

John Tierney

Yes, Money Can Buy Happiness . . .

John Tierney is a columnist for the Science Times section of the *New York Times*. He has also written for many other science publications such as *Discovery, Hippocrates,* and *Science 86.* According to his biography, "he's using TierneyLab to check out new research and rethink conventional wisdom about science and society. The Lab's work is guided by two founding principles: Just because an idea appeals to a lot of people doesn't mean it's wrong. But that's a good working theory."

This essay originally appeared in his TierneyLab column in the *New York Times* in 2008.

Vocabulary development   Underline these words as you read: *correlated, prosocially,* and *derive.*

correlated: to be related in some sense
prosocially: good for society
derive: to trace from a source

1   Yes, money can buy happiness, but probably not in the way you imagined. Spending it on yourself may not do much for your spirits, but spending it on others will make you happier, according to a report from a team of social psychologists in the new issue of *Science*.

2   The researchers confirmed the joys of giving in three separate ways. First, by surveying a national sample of more than 600 Americans, they found that spending more on gifts and charity correlated with greater happiness, whereas spending more

money on oneself did not. Second, by tracking 16 workers before and after they received profit-sharing bonuses, the researchers found that that the workers who gave more of the money to others ended up happier than the ones who spent more of it on themselves. In fact, how the bonus was spent was a better predictor of happiness than the size of the bonus.

3   The final bit of evidence came from an experiment in which 46 students were given either $5 or $20 to spend by the end of the day. The ones who were instructed to spend the money on others—they bought toys for siblings, treated friends to meals and made donations to the homeless—were happier at the end of the day than the ones who were instructed to spend the money on themselves.

4   "These experimental results," the researchers conclude, "provide direct support for our causal argument that spending money on others promotes happiness more than spending money on oneself." The social psychologists—Elizabeth Dunn and Lara Aknin of the University of British Columbia, Vancouver, and Michael Norton of Harvard Business School—also conclude that "how people choose to spend their money is at least as important as how much money they make."

5   I asked Dr. Dunn if she had any advice for Lab readers on how much to spend on others. Her reply:

> I think even minor changes in spending habits can make a difference. In our experiment with college students, we found that spending just $5 prosocially had a substantial effect on happiness at the end of the day. But I wouldn't say that there's some fixed amount that everyone should spend on others. Rather, the best bet might be for people to think about whether they can push themselves to devote just a little more of their money to helping others.

6   But why wouldn't people be doing that already? Because most people don't realize the personal benefits of charity, according to Dr. Dunn and her colleagues. When the researchers surveyed another group of students, they found that most of the respondents predicted that personal spending would make them happier than spending the money on other people.

7   Perhaps that will change as word of these experiments circulates—although that prospect raises another question, which I put to Dr. Dunn: If people started giving away money chiefly in the hope of making themselves happier, as opposed to wanting to help others, would they still derive the same happiness from it?

8   "This is a fascinating question," she replied. "I certainly hope that telling people about the emotional benefits of prosocial spending doesn't completely erase these benefits; I would hate to be responsible for the downfall of joyful prosocial behavior."

9   Do you have any theories on the joys of giving? Any reports of your own experiments? Or any questions you'd like to ask the researchers? Dr. Dunn, in keeping with the results of her experiments, has generously offered to provide some answers free of charge.

1. Double-underline the **thesis statement**.

2. What type of organization does this essay use (point by point or whole to whole)? _Point by point_

3. Why do you suppose each group of people had different outcomes from spending money? _Answers will vary._

4. Why is it that even though spending money on others makes people happier, more people don't give to charity? _Answers will vary._

Tip For reading advice, see Chapter 1.

Respond to one of the following assignments in a paragraph or essay.

1. The main idea of the article involves our intent: whether we spend money on others or ourselves, we feel differently about the experience. Why do you suppose the students instructed to spend money on others felt better than those who spent it on themselves?

2. In paragraph 8, Tierney asks Dr. Dunn if people would still feel happy when spending money on others if they knew that it would make them happier? What do you think? Explain your answer.

Write Your Own Comparison and Contrast

In this section, you will write your own comparison and contrast based on one of the following assignments. For help, refer to the How to Write Comparison and Contrast checklist on page 262.

| ASSIGNMENT OPTIONS | **Writing about college, work, and everyday life** |

Write a comparison/contrast paragraph or essay on one of the following topics or on one of your own choice.

College
- Describe similarities and differences between high school and college, and give examples.
- Compare two approaches you have used to study, such as studying in a group and studying on your own using notes or other aids. Explain whether you prefer one approach over the other or like to use both methods.
- If you are still deciding on a major area of study, see if you can sit in on a class or two in programs that interest you. Then, compare and contrast the classes. If this process helped you decide on a program, explain the reasons for your choice.

Work
- Compare a job you liked with one you did not like, and give reasons for your views.
- Have you had experience working for both a bad supervisor and a good one? If so, compare and contrast their behaviors, and explain why you preferred one supervisor to another.
- Work styles tend to differ from employee to employee. For instance, some like to work in teams, whereas others prefer to complete tasks on their own. Some like specific directions on how to do things, whereas others want more freedom. Contrast your own work style with someone else's, whose approach and preferences are quite different from yours.

Everyday life
- Compare your life now with the way you would like it to be in five years.
- Have your experiences changed how you see your surroundings? If so, discuss your experiences, and give examples.
- Participate in a cleanup effort in your community, and then compare and contrast how the area looked before the cleanup with how it looked afterward.

ASSIGNMENT OPTIONS   **Reading and writing critically**

Complete one of the following assignments, which ask you to apply the critical thinking, reading, and writing skills discussed in Chapter 1.

WRITING CRITICALLY ABOUT READINGS

Both Amy Tan's "Fish Cheeks" (p. 123) and Liz Riggs "What It's Like to Be the First Person in Your Family to Go to College" (p. 278) present an unfamiliar scene or a time that the writer felt concerned about fitting in. Read or review both of these pieces, and then follow these steps:

1. **Summarize** Briefly summarize the works, listing major events.

2. **Analyze** What questions do the pieces raise for you?

3. **Synthesize** Sometimes we approach new experiences tentatively, as in Riggs's piece, and other times we are embarrassed by them, as in Tan's. Using examples from these writings and from your own experience, discuss which types of changes are positive, which types are negative, and why.

4. **Evaluate** Which piece did you connect with more, and why? In writing your evaluation, you might look back on your responses to step 2.

WRITING ABOUT IMAGES

Study the photographs on page 261, and complete the following steps.

1. **Read the images** Ask yourself: What details are you drawn to in each photograph? What differences do you notice as you move from the 1973 model to the 1985 model and from these cell-phone ancestors to the 1991–2014 phones? (For more on reading images, see Chapter 1.)

Tip For a reminder of how to summarize, analyze, synthesize, and evaluate, see the Reading and Writing Critically box on page 21.

Teaching tip If time is short, students might complete just one or two steps of this assignment.

2. **Write a comparison and contrast** Choose two or more of the photographs to compare and contrast, and write a paragraph or essay about the changing looks of mobile phones. You might want to address how changes in mobile phones represent larger changes in society and culture. Also, answer this question: What do you think phones will look like in another ten years? In writing your comparison/contrast, include the details and differences you identified in step 1.

ANCESTORS OF MODERN CELL PHONES, 1973 AND 1985

Above left: Martin Cooper, chairman and CEO of ArrayComm, holds a Motorola DynaTAC, a 1973 prototype of the first handheld cellular telephone. Thirty years before this photograph was taken, on April 2, 2003, the first call was made from a cellular phone.
Above right: The Vodafone mobile phone, introduced in 1985. Marketed by Racal-Vodac Limited, this phone was aimed at busy professionals and regular travelers, for portable use or for use in their cars. This phone came with a battery charger and an antenna for use in areas with poor reception.

Teaching tip Industry experts predict that mobile phones will continue to evolve rapidly. For example, some expect that phones of the near future will be physically flexible and waterproof and that people will use their phones—not cash or credit cards—to pay for things. Ask students what improvements or changes they would most like to see in mobile phones. Will we laugh someday at how antiquated the iPhone looks?

CELL PHONES FROM 1991 TO 2011

Brands from left to right: Motorola (1991), Nokia (1999), LG (2005/2006), and Motorola Droid 2 Global (2011).

The Apple iPhone 6 (2014).

WRITING TO SOLVE A PROBLEM

Read or review the discussion of problem solving in Chapter 1 (pp. 28–30). Then, consider the following problem:

You need a new smartphone, and you want the best one for your money. Before ordering, you do some research.

Assignment Consult a Web site that rates smartphones, such as www.pcworld.com. Identify three features covered by the ratings, and make notes about why each feature is important to you. Then, choose a model based on these features. Finally, write a contrast paragraph or essay that explains your decision and contrasts your choice versus another model. Make sure to support your choice based on the three features you considered.

CHECKLIST

How to Write Comparison and Contrast

Steps	Details
☐ **Narrow and explore your topic.** See Chapter 3.	• Make the topic more specific. • Prewrite to get ideas about the narrowed topic.
☐ **Write a topic sentence (paragraph) or thesis statement (essay).** See Chapter 3.	• State the main idea you want to make in your comparison/contrast.
☐ **Support your point.** See Chapter 4.	• Come up with points of comparison/contrast and with details about each one.
☐ **Write a draft.** See Chapter 5.	• Make a plan that sets up a point-by-point or whole-to-whole comparison/contrast. • Include a topic sentence (paragraph) or thesis statement (essay) and all the support points.
☐ **Revise your draft.** See Chapter 5.	• Make sure it has *all* the Four Basics of Good Comparison and Contrast. • Make sure you include transitions to move readers smoothly from one subject or comparison/contrast point to the next.
☐ **Edit your revised draft.** See Parts 3 through 6.	• Correct errors in grammar, spelling, word use, and punctuation.

Chapter Review

1. What are the Four Basics of Good Comparison and Contrast? _It uses subjects that_ _have enough in common to be compared/contrasted in a useful way. It serves a_ _purpose—to help readers make a decision, to help them understand the subjects, or_ _to show your understanding of the subjects. It presents several important, parallel_ _points of comparison/contrast. It arranges points in a logical order._

2. The topic sentence (paragraph) or thesis statement (essay) in comparison/contrast should include what two parts? _the subjects being compared or contrasted and the_ _main idea of the comparison/ contrast_

3. What are the two ways to organize comparison/contrast? _point by point and_ _whole to whole_

4. In your own words, explain the two ways of organizing comparison/contrast. _Answers will vary._

5. Write sentences using the following vocabulary words: _laser, reasonably, forgo, valiant, convey, hostile, articulate, hail, harassing, vulgar, brash, correlated, prosocially,_ and _derive._ _Answers will vary._

REFLECTING ON THE JOURNEY

Skills Learned

Now that you've completed the chapter, share what you've learned about each skill by completing the following chart.

Skill	What I learned about this skill
Compare two or more objects to identify similarities	
Contrast two or more objects to identify differences	
Identify topics that have enough in common to be compared or contrasted	
Present logical points to support the comparison or contrast	
Arrange points in a logical order	
Read and analyze compare-and-contrast documents	

13

Cause and Effect
Writing That Explains Reasons or Results

Learning Objectives

Chapter Goal: Learn how to write a good cause-and-effect paper

Tools to Achieve the Goal:

- Four Basics of Good Cause-and-Effect (p. 266)
- Sample Cause-and-Effect Paragraph and Grading Rubric (pp. 272–73)
- Student Cause-and-Effect Paragraph: Caitlin Prokop, *A Difficult Decision with a Positive Outcome* (p. 274)
- Student Cause-and-Effect Essay: Stephanie Alaimo and Mark Koester, *The Backdraft of Technology* (pp. 275–76)
- Profile of Success and Workplace Cause and Effect: Joshua Boyce (p. 277)
- Professional Cause-and-Effect Essay: Liz Riggs, *What It's Like to Be the First Person in Your Family to Go to College* (pp. 278–81)
- Checklist: How to Write Cause-and-Effect (p. 284)

READING ROADMAP

Skim Chapter 13 before reading. Find these words or terms in **bold** type. Put a check mark next to each once you locate it.

_____ cause
_____ effect
_____ main idea
_____ support
_____ transitions

Guided Reading for Chapter 13

Fill out the following chart before you begin reading. For each skill, write what you know about that skill and what you would like to know upon completing the chapter. At the end of the chapter, you will be asked to share what you learned about each skill.

Skill	When I have used this skill	What I want to know about this skill
Identify the causes of events		
Identify the effects of events		
Express causes, effects, or both through writing		
Provide specific examples to support those causes and effects		
Read and analyze cause and effect		

LaunchPadSolo

Visit **LaunchPad Solo for Readers and Writers > Reading > Patterns of Organization** for more tutorials, videos, and practice with patterns of organization.

Understand What Cause and Effect Are

A **cause** is what made an event happen. An **effect** is what happens as a result of the event.

Four Basics of Good Cause and Effect

1. The main idea reflects the writer's purpose: to explain causes, effects, or both.
2. If the purpose is to explain causes, the writing presents real causes.
3. If the purpose is to explain effects, it presents real effects.
4. It gives readers detailed examples or explanations of the causes or effects.

Teaching tip Explain to students the differences between *effect* (noun) and *affect* (verb).

In the following paragraph, the numbers and colors correspond to the Four Basics of Good Cause and Effect.

1 Although the thought of writing may be a source of stress for college students, researchers have recently found that it can also be a potent stress reliever. In the winter of 2008, during a time when many people catch colds or the flu or experience other symptoms of ill health, two psychologists conducted an experiment with college students to find out if writing could have positive effects on their minds and/or their bodies. After gathering a large group of college students, a mix of ages, genders, and backgrounds, the psychologists explained the task. The students were asked to write for only two minutes, on two consecutive days, about their choice of three kinds of experiences: a traumatic experience, a positive experience, or a neutral experience (something routine that happened). The psychologists did not give more detailed directions about the kinds of experiences, rather just a bad one, a good one, or one neither good nor bad. A month after collecting the students' writing, the psychologists interviewed each of the students and asked them to report any symptoms of ill health, such as colds, flu, headaches, or lack of sleep. **3** What the psychologists found was quite surprising. **4** Those students who had written about emotionally charged topics, either traumatic or positive, all reported that they had been in excellent health, avoiding the various illnesses that had been circulating in the college and the larger community. The students who had chosen to write about routine, day-to-day things that didn't matter to them reported the ill health effects that were typical of the season, such as colds, flu, poor sleep, and coughing. From these findings, the two psychologists reported that writing about things that are important to people actually has a positive effect on their health. Their experiment suggests the value to people of regularly recording their reactions to experiences, in a journal of some sort. If writing can keep you well, it is worth a good try. The mind-body connection continues to be studied because clearly each affects the other.

Teaching tip Have students try the experiment, or just have them write about either negative or positive experiences.

When you are writing about causes and effects, make sure that you do not confuse something that happened before an event with a real cause or something that happened after an event with a real effect. For example, if you have pizza on Monday and get the flu on Tuesday, eating the pizza is not the cause of the flu just because it happened before you got the flu, nor is the flu the effect of eating pizza. You just happened to get the flu the next day.

You use cause and effect in many situations.

College	In a nutrition course, you are asked to identify the consequences (effects) of poor nutrition.
Work	Sales are down in your department or branch, and you have to explain the cause.
Everyday life	You explain to your child why a certain behavior is not acceptable by warning him or her about the negative effects of that behavior.

In college, writing assignments might include the words *discuss the causes (or effects) of*, but they might also use phrases such as *explain the results of, discuss the impact of,* and *how did X affect Y?* In all these cases, use the strategies discussed in this chapter.

Main Idea in Cause and Effect

The **main idea** introduces causes, effects, or both. To help you discover your main idea, complete the following sentence:

Main idea in cause and effect	**(Your topic) causes (or caused)** . . .
	(Your topic) resulted in (or results in) . . .

Here is an example of a topic sentence for a paragraph:

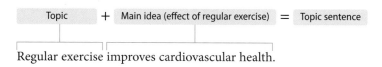

Topic   +   Main idea (effect of regular exercise)   =   Topic sentence

Regular exercise improves cardiovascular health.

Remember that the main idea for an essay can be a little broader than one for a paragraph.

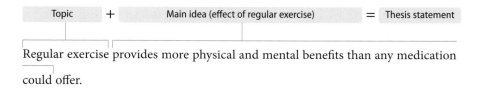

Topic   +   Main idea (effect of regular exercise)   =   Thesis statement

Regular exercise provides more physical and mental benefits than any medication could offer.

Whereas the topic sentence focuses on just one major benefit of regular exercise, the thesis statement considers multiple benefits.

Teaching tip You might point out that mistaken causes or effects are just one type of logical fallacy and that avoiding such errors in reasoning is an important part of critical thinking. One Web site that offers excellent explanations and examples of logical fallacies is Fallacy Files, at **www.fallacyfiles.org**.

Teaching tip Ask students to bring in images that show causes, effects, or both.

Tip If the writer wanted to explore causes, he or she might look into the factors that motivate people to exercise.

Tip Sometimes, the same main idea can be used for a paragraph and an essay, but the essay must develop this point in more detail. (See pp. 68–69.)

PRACTICE 1   **Stating your main idea**

For each of the following topics, make notes about possible causes and effects on a separate sheet of paper. Then, in each of the spaces below, write a sentence that states a main idea. First, look at the following example.

Example:

Topic: Bankruptcy

Main idea: *Although many different kinds of people declare bankruptcy each year, the causes of bankruptcy are often the same.*

1. Topic: A fire in someone's home

    Main idea: *Answers will vary.*

2. Topic: An "A" in this course

    Main idea: _____

3. Topic: Waking up late in the morning

    Main idea: _____

Support in Cause and Effect

The paragraph and essay models on pages 270–71 use the topic sentence (paragraph) and thesis statement (essay) from the Main Idea section of this chapter. Both models include the **support** used in all cause-effect writing: statements of cause or effect backed up by detailed explanations or examples. In the essay plan, however, the major support points (statements of cause/effect) are topic sentences for individual paragraphs.

PRACTICE 2   **Giving examples and details**

Write down two causes or two effects for two of the three topics from Practice 1. Then, give an example or detail that explains each cause or effect.

Example:

Topic: Bankruptcy

Cause 1: *Overspending*

    Example/Detail: *bought a leather jacket I liked and charged it*

Cause 2: *Poor budgeting*

    Example/Detail: *not tracking monthly expenses versus income*

1. Topic: A fire in someone's home

    Cause/Effect 1: *Answers will vary.*

        Example/Detail: _____

    Cause/Effect 2: _____

        Example/Detail: _____

2. Topic: An "A" in this course

Cause/Effect 1: _____

Example/Detail: _____

Cause/Effect 2: _____

Example/Detail: _____

3. Topic: Waking up late in the morning

Cause/Effect 1: _____

Example/Detail: _____

Cause/Effect 2: _____

Example/Detail: _____

Organization in Cause and Effect

Cause and effect can be organized in a variety of ways, depending on your purpose.

Tip For more on the different orders of organization, see pages 76–78.

Main Idea	Purpose	Organization
The "Occupy" protests of 2011 brought attention to the economic difficulties faced by low- and middle-income citizens.	To explain the effects of the protests	Order of importance, saving the most important effect for last
A desire to remain at a protest site for an extended period led "Occupy" protesters to create miniature towns, with food service, libraries, and more.	To describe the places where protesters camped out	Space order
The "Occupy" protests in New York City inspired other protests throughout the country.	To describe the spread of the protest movement over time	Time order

NOTE: If you are explaining both causes and effects, you would present the causes first and the effects later.

Use **transitions** to move readers smoothly from one cause to another, from one effect to another, or from causes to effects. Because cause and effect can use any method of organization depending on your purpose, the following list shows just a few of the transitions you might use.

Common Transitions in Cause and Effect

also	more important/serious cause or effect
as a result	most important/serious cause or effect
because	one cause/effect; another cause or effect
the final cause or effect	a primary cause; a secondary cause
the first, second, third cause or effect	a short-term effect; a long-term effect

Paragraphs vs. Essays in Cause and Effect

For more on the important features of cause and effect, see the Four Basics of Good Cause and Effect on page 266.

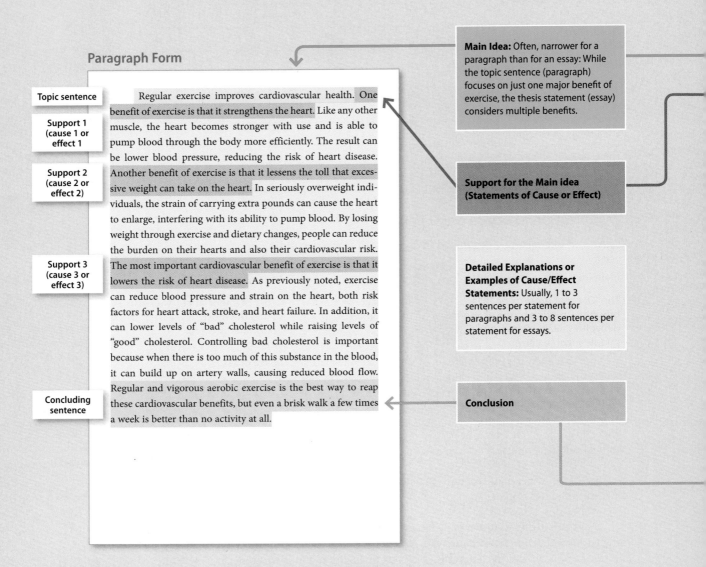

Paragraph Form

Topic sentence

Support 1 (cause 1 or effect 1)

Support 2 (cause 2 or effect 2)

Support 3 (cause 3 or effect 3)

Concluding sentence

Regular exercise improves cardiovascular health. One benefit of exercise is that it strengthens the heart. Like any other muscle, the heart becomes stronger with use and is able to pump blood through the body more efficiently. The result can be lower blood pressure, reducing the risk of heart disease. Another benefit of exercise is that it lessens the toll that excessive weight can take on the heart. In seriously overweight individuals, the strain of carrying extra pounds can cause the heart to enlarge, interfering with its ability to pump blood. By losing weight through exercise and dietary changes, people can reduce the burden on their hearts and also their cardiovascular risk. The most important cardiovascular benefit of exercise is that it lowers the risk of heart disease. As previously noted, exercise can reduce blood pressure and strain on the heart, both risk factors for heart attack, stroke, and heart failure. In addition, it can lower levels of "bad" cholesterol while raising levels of "good" cholesterol. Controlling bad cholesterol is important because when there is too much of this substance in the blood, it can build up on artery walls, causing reduced blood flow. Regular and vigorous aerobic exercise is the best way to reap these cardiovascular benefits, but even a brisk walk a few times a week is better than no activity at all.

Main Idea: Often, narrower for a paragraph than for an essay: While the topic sentence (paragraph) focuses on just one major benefit of exercise, the thesis statement (essay) considers multiple benefits.

Support for the Main idea (Statements of Cause or Effect)

Detailed Explanations or Examples of Cause/Effect Statements: Usually, 1 to 3 sentences per statement for paragraphs and 3 to 8 sentences per statement for essays.

Conclusion

Think Critically As You Write Cause and Effect

ASK YOURSELF

- Have I examined a variety of possible causes and/or effects related to my topic? (If not, research them, and consider revising your main idea and support based on what you learn.)
- Am I certain that my causes are real causes and my effects real effects? (For help with answering this question, see p. 267.)

270

Essay Form

1

Most people know how hard it is to start and stick with an exercise program. However, there is a good reason to build a significant amount **Thesis statement** activity into every week: Regular exercise provides more physical and mental benefits than any medication could offer.

First, exercise helps people achieve and maintain a healthy weight. A nutritious diet **Topic sentence 1 (cause 1 or effect 1)** excessive in calories has a greater effect loss than exercise does. However, regular exercise— ideally, interspersed throughout the day—can make an important contribution. For instance, people trying to lose weight might walk to work or to other destinations instead of driving. Or, they might take the stairs to their office instead of the elevator. If they **Topic sentence 2 (cause 2 or effect 2)** go the gym at the end of the day, so much Added up, all these efforts can make a dif

Second, exercise boosts mood and energy levels. For example, exercise causes the body to release endorphins, chemicals that give us a sense of well-being, even happiness. Accordingly, exercise can help

2

reduce stress and combat depression. In addition, because exercise can make people look and feel more fit, it can improve their self-esteem. Finally, by improving strength and endurance, exercise gives individuals more energy to go about their lives.

The most important benefit of exercise is that it can help prevent disease. For example, e **Topic sentence 3 (cause 3 or effect 3)** improve the body's use of insulin and, as lier, help people maintain a healthy weight. Therefore, it can help prevent or control diabetes. Additionally, exercise can lower the risk of heart attacks, strokes, and heart failure. For instance, exercise strengthens the heart muscle, helping it pump blood more efficiently and reducing high blood pressure, a heart disease risk factor. Also, exercise can lower levels of "bad" cholesterol while raising levels of "good" cholesterol. Controlling levels of bad cholesterol is important because when there is too much of this substance in the blood, it can build up in the walls of arteries, possibly blocking blood flow. Finally, some research suggests that regular exercise

3

can reduce the risk of certain cancers, including breast, colon, and lung cancer.

In my own life, exercise has made a huge difference. Before starting a regular exercise program, I was close to needing prescription medications to lower my blood pressure and cholesterol. Thanks to regular physical activity, however, both my blood pressure and cholesterol levels are now in the normal range, and I have never felt better. Every bit of time spent at the gym or exchanging a ride in an elevator for a walk up the stairs has been well worth it.

PRACTICE 3   **Using transitions in cause and effect**

Read the paragraph that follows, and fill in the blanks with transitions.
Answers may vary. Possible answers are shown.

Recently, neuroscientists, who have long been skeptical about meditation, confirm that it has numerous positive outcomes. ___One, The first___ is that people who meditate can maintain their focus and attention longer than people who do not. This ability to stay "on task" was demonstrated among students who had been practicing meditation for several weeks. They reported more effective studying and learning because they were able to pay attention. ___Another, A second___ positive outcome was the ability to relax on command. Many people lead busy, stressful lives with multiple pressures on them—family responsibilities, work duties, financial worries, and uncertainties about the future. While meditating, people learned how to reduce their heart rates and blood pressure so that they could relax more easily in all kinds of situations. ___A third, The most important___ outcome was a thickening of the brain's cortex. Meditators' cortexes were uniformly thicker than nonmeditators'. Because the cortex enables memorization and the production of new ideas, this last outcome is especially exciting, particularly in fighting Alzheimer's disease and other dementias.

Evaluate Cause and Effect

Teaching tip If you have samples from a previous class, bring in full papers or paragraphs and ask the students to use either this rubric or the Four Basics of Good Cause and Effect to "grade" the assignments. When they have done so, ask them to pair up and work in groups to see if they all came up with the same score and to determine where the areas of consensus and disagreement are.

Read the following sample cause-and-effect paragraph. Using the Four Basics of Good Cause and Effect and the sample grading rubric, decide what grade this paragraph would earn. Explain your answer.

> **Assignment** Write a paragraph that identifies one reason (cause) that may have resulted in a poor grade on a test (effect).
>
> **Failing grades on a test can have any number of causes. For example, lack of sleep. Sleep is important to help a student perform well on tests. If tired may cause the student to not pay attention or read questions. Tired may also cause misunderstanding. When you know you have a test coming, you need to make sure that you have more than enough rest in order to focus.**

Analysis of Sample Paragraph: *The sample paragraph is an average paragraph. Comments on each point may vary but should include the following:*

Sample rubric

Element	Grading criteria	Point: Comment
Appropriateness	• Did the student follow the assignment directions?	__5__/5: *Student followed the instructions.*
Main idea	• Does the paper clearly state a strong main idea in a complete sentence?	__8__/10: *There is a clear main idea.*
Support	• Is the main idea developed with specific support, including specific details and examples? • Is there enough support to make the main idea evident to the reader? • Is all the support directly related to the main idea?	__7__/10: *The supporting ideas are listed, but only some of them are explained.*
Organization	• Does the writer clearly demonstrate how one behavior causes the end result? • Does the student use transitions (*also, for example, sometimes,* and so on) to move the reader from one point to another?	__8__/10: *The writer focuses on one cause that can result in the failing grade. There are some transitions.*
Conclusion	• Does the conclusion remind the reader of the main idea?	__3__/5: *There is a conclusion, but it is not as effective as it could be.*
Grammar	• Is the writing free of the four most serious errors? (See Chapters 16–19.) • Is the sentence structure clear? • Does the student choose words that clearly express his or her meaning? • Are the words spelled correctly? • Is the punctuation correct?	__5__/10: *The paper has some of the four most serious errors.*
		TOTAL POINTS: __36__/50

Read and Analyze Cause and Effect

Reading examples of cause and effect will help you write your own. The first example is a student cause-and-effect paragraph, followed by a student essay written about the effects of modern technology. The Profile of Success and workplace cause-and-effect essay are by blogger Joshua Boyce, and the final essay is by professional writer Liz Riggs.

Teaching tip Ask students to work individually, in pairs, or in groups to evaluate each of the following readings using the rubric provided above.

Student Cause-and-Effect Paragraph

Caitlin Prokop

A Difficult Decision with a Positive Outcome

accompany: to be with; to go with

cherish: to value highly

Vocabulary development Underline these words as you read: *accompany* and *cherish*.

When my mother made the decision to move back to New York, I made the choice to move in with my dad so that I could finish high school. This decision affected me in a positive way because I graduated with my friends, built a better relationship with my father, and had the chance to go to college without leaving home. Graduating with my friends was important to me because I have known most of them since we were in kindergarten. It was a journey through childhood that we had shared, and I wanted to finish it with them. Accomplishing the goal of graduating from high school with my close friends, those who accompanied me through school, made me a stronger and more confident person. Another good outcome of my difficult decision was the relationship I built with my dad. We never saw eye to eye when I lived with both of my parents. For example, we stopped talking for five months because I always sided against him with my mom. Living together for the past five years has made us closer, and I cherish that closeness we have developed. Every Thursday is our day, a day when we talk to each other about what is going on in our lives, so that we will never again have a distant relationship. A third good outcome of my decision is that I can go to Brevard Community College, which is right down the street. In high school, I had thought that I would want to go away to college, but then I realized that I would miss my home. By staying here, I have the opportunity to attend a wonderful college that is preparing me for transferring to a four-year college and finding a good career. I have done some research and believe I would like to become a police officer, a nurse, or a teacher. Through the school, I can do volunteer work in each of these areas. Right now, I am leaning toward becoming a teacher, based on my volunteer work in a kindergarten class. There, I can explore what grades I want to teach. In every way, I believe that my difficult decision was the right one, giving me many opportunities that I would not have had if I had moved to a new and unfamiliar place.

1. Double-underline the **topic sentence**.

2. Does Caitlin write about causes or effects? *effects* _____

3. Circle the **transitions** Caitlin uses to move readers from one point to the next.

4. Does Caitlin's paragraph include the Four Basics of Good Cause and Effect? Why or why not? *Yes. Answers will vary.* _____

_____

5. Have you made a difficult decision that turned out to be a good one? Why and how? _Answers will vary._ _____

Student Cause-and-Effect Essay

Stephanie Alaimo and Mark Koester

The Backdraft of Technology

Stephanie Alaimo and Mark Koester both graduated from DePaul University of Chicago. Alaimo was a Spanish major who volunteered as an English tutor. She is now studying sociology at the University of California, San Diego. Koester majored in philosophy and taught English in Hangzhou, China, after graduation. He is now developing software in China as an entrepreneur.

Vocabulary development Underline these words as you read: _miscellaneous, automated, entry level,_ and _mechanization._

Guiding question Do Stephanie and Mark present causes, effects, or both in their essay? Keep track of them while you read.

1   You have picked up the bread and the milk and the day's miscellaneous foodstuffs at your local grocery store. The lines at the traditional, human-operated checkouts are a shocking two customers deep. Who wants to wait? Who would wait when we have society's newest upgrade in not having to wait: the self-checkout?

2   Welcome to the automated grocery store. "Please scan your next item," a repetitively chilling, mechanical voice orders you.

3   If you have yet to see it at your nearest grocer, a new technological advance has been reached. Instead of waiting for some minimally waged, minimally educated, and, most likely, immigrant cashier to scan and bag your groceries for you, you can now do it yourself. In a consumer-driven, hyperactive, "I want" world, an increase in speed is easily accepted thoughtlessly. We're too busy. But, in gaining efficiency and ease, a number of jobs have been lost, particularly at the entry level, and a moment of personal, human engagement with actual people has vanished.

4   It seems easy enough to forget about the consequences when you are rushed and your belly is grumbling. The previously utilized checkout lanes at local grocery stores and super, mega, we-have-everything stores are now routinely left unattended during the peak hours. In these moments, your options are using the self-checkout or waiting for a real human being. Often in a hurried moment we choose the easiest, fastest, and least mentally involved option without much consideration.

5   We forget to consider that with the aid of the self-checkout, at least two jobs have been lost. As a result, a human cashier and grocery bagger are now waiting in the unemployment line. Furthermore, self-checkout

miscellaneous: random; an assortment

automated: controlled by a machine

entry level: a job at the lowest level of experience in any field

mechanization: the process of doing work with machinery

Predict Before reading the rest of the paper, consider what you may already know about this topic. What are some of the reasons Stephanie and Mark may use to support their thesis?

machines are probably not manufactured in the United States, thus shipping more jobs overseas. And sadly, the job openings are now shrinking by putting consumers to work. The wages from these jobs are stockpiled by those least in need—corporations and those who own them.

Identify What specific information do Stephanie and Mark supply about self-checkouts? Are they a cause of the problem of unemployment or an effect? Explain your answer.

6   The mechanization of the service industry has been occurring throughout our lifetimes. Gas stations were once full-service. Human bank tellers, instead of ATMs, handled simple cash withdrawals. Even video stores are being marginalized from people ordering online from companies like Netflix. And did you know that you can now order a pizza for delivery online without even talking to a person?

7   Sure, these new robots and computers reduce work, which could potentially be a really good thing. But these mechanizations have only increased profit margins for large corporations and have reduced the need to hire employees. Jobs are lost along with means of providing for one's self and family.

8   For those who find the loss of grocery store labor to be meaningless and, quite frankly, beyond impacting their future lives as accountants or lawyers, it does not seem to be entirely implausible that almost any job or task could become entirely technologically mechanized and your elitist job market nuked.

Reflect Have you seen negative publicity about self-checkouts? Has it made you consider whether you choose to use them, or did you ignore it? Explain your answer.

9   We are a society trapped in a precarious fork in the road. We can either eliminate the time and toil of the human workload and still allow people to have jobs and maintain the same standard of living, though working less, or, in a darker scenario, we can eliminate human work in terms of actual human jobs and make the situation of the lower classes more tenuous. Is it our goal to reduce the overall time that individuals spend laboring? Or is it our goal to increase corporate profits at the loss of many livelihoods?

10   At present, corporations and their executives put consumers to work, cut the cost of labor through the use of technology such as self-checkouts and ATMs, and profit tremendously. But a host of workers are now scrambling to find a way to subsist. To choose the self-checkout simply as a convenience cannot be morally justified unless these jobs remain.

Summarize Briefly restate the main ideas of this essay.

11   The choices we make on a daily basis affect the whole of our society. Choosing convenience often translates to eliminating actual jobs that provide livelihoods and opportunities to many. Think before you simply follow the next technological innovation. Maybe it could be you in their soon-to-be-jobless shoes. Say "No!" to self-checkout.

1.   Underline the **topic sentence**.

2.   Do the authors use enough examples and detail to demonstrate the causes and effects in the essay? _Answers will vary._

3.   Does this essay follow the Four Basics of Good Cause and Effect (p. 266)? _Yes._

Profile of Success
Cause and Effect in the Real World

Background   I grew up in poverty and graduated from high school not knowing how to read, write, or do any math beyond simple arithmetic. This occurred because I was wrongfully placed in special education at an early age. Upon completion of high school, I attended Job Corps. There I learned how to weld and moved to Vicksburg, Mississippi. Shortly after moving, I met Dr. Nettle, a local minister. He taught me how to read and encouraged me to pursue my GED.

After getting my GED, I enrolled full time at a two-year college where I graduated with honors. Then I attended a four-year institution and received my B.S. degree in exercise science. Currently, I am a fitness trainer and blogger. My blog, "Slim Chance Motivation," is aimed at inspiring others to dream and pursue their goals no matter what the odds are.

Degrees/Colleges   A.A. Degree/Hinds Community College; B.S./Mississippi College

Writing at work   This blog post reveals the harmful effect of wrong conditioning and challenges people to make steps to recondition their mind.

Joshua Boyce
Blogger

Workplace Cause and Effect: Conditioning

"If you make a man feel that he is inferior, you do not have to compel him to accept an inferior status, for he will seek it himself. If you make a man think that he is justly an outcast, you do not have to order him to the back door. He will go without being told; and if there is no back door, his very nature will demand one."

—Dr. Carter G. Woodson

1   Dr. Woodson's quote paints a good picture of the effect of conditioning. In athletics, conditioning is important. It is the combination of physical and mental training with the right nutritional plan. <u>The right conditioning program makes a difference between experiencing the sweet taste of victory or the bitterness of defeat, and the same applies to people and their goals.</u>

2   I was conditioned to accept failure, and this mindset wreaked havoc in my life for many years. This became even more evident when I was in Job Corp. No matter how many welding processes or techniques I learned, I still had this strong internal feeling that I was going to fail. My conditioning was preventing me from believing in my ability to weld even though I had all the proof that suggested differently.

3   There are still many enslaved by this conditioning. It leads to the acceptance of going to prison instead of college or trade school. It forces you into submission to a mindless, backbreaking job. It causes fear in doing the most simple of tasks. I have been, and I have watched too many individuals, be held down by this conditioning.

4   I was reconditioned to think otherwise by two important factors. **(1) People**—Mr. Beard, my Job Corp welding instructor, saw my ability to weld and often helped me to shake the doubts. **(2) Interpretation**—With the help of Mr. Beard, I was able to understand and accept that it was not luck but my ability to perform a task well that was producing the result. With people and good discernment, I was able to decrease the doubts and increase my confidence.

5   In the end, it is still a battle, one you cannot win on your own. I needed help, and you will also. So to make a slim chance a chance, I had to be reconditioned, and so will you.

1. Underline the main idea of the article.

2. What is Boyce's **purpose?** *To explain to readers the direct correlation between preparation and success.*

3. Identify and list the **effects of being conditioned or not being conditioned.** *Answers will vary but should include accepting (or not accepting) defeat and failure.*

4. Identify and list the causes that lead to these effects. *Answers will vary but should include people and interpretation.*

Professional Cause-and-Effect Essay

Liz Riggs

What It's Like to Be the First Person in Your Family to Go to College

immigrant: a person who comes to live permanently in a foreign country

rigorous: rigidly severe or harsh

estrangement: unfriendly or hostile

alienation: withdrawn from the rest of the world

remedial: intended to correct or improve one's skill

formidable: causing fear, apprehension, or dread

influx: flowing inward

lag: to fail to maintain a desired pace

Liz Riggs in a writer and teacher who lives in Nashville, Tennessee. Her work has appeared in *The Atlantic*, *The Huffington Post*, and *Relevant* magazine, to name just a few. This piece first appeared in *The Atlantic* in January 2014.

Vocabulary development Underline these words as you read: *immigrant, rigorous, estrangement, alienation, remedial, formidable, influx,* and *lag*.

Guiding question As you read the article, try to identify potential causes and effects for the way Harry felt during his time at school.

1   When Harry arrived at Vanderbilt University in 2008, he became the first person in his family to attend college. His parents were immigrants from Nicaragua,

and he had attended a so-called "academically and economically disadvantaged" high school on the North side of Miami. Even after completing a rigorous IB [international baccalaureate] program as a high-school student and receiving a scholarship, he arrived on campus feeling like an outsider.

2   "Never before had I truly felt such an extreme sense of estrangement and alienation," he says of his first few months. "I quickly realized that although I may look the part, my cultural and socio-economic backgrounds were vastly different from those of my predominantly white, affluent peers. I wanted to leave."

3   Harry opted to stay at Vanderbilt, but he found acclimating to the school's cultural climate to be extremely difficult. His scholarship covered books, tuition, and housing—but it didn't cover little costs like dorm move-in needs and travel costs home for breaks—expenses his classmates could typically afford that exacerbated his feelings of alienation. Eventually, he found refuge in the school's theatre department and student government.

4   "There were very few Latinos that I could connect with," he says. "[But], I got very involved in extra-curricular activities in hopes of meeting people. . . . It was in each of these organizations that I met older students that informally mentored me. . . . I would ask questions shamelessly and learn about their experiences.

5   Harry's difficult adjustment is just one example of the many obstacles first-generation and minority students confront each year that don't typically plague their second- and third-generation peers. Extensive studies show that low-income and first-generation students are more likely to be academically behind, sometimes several years in core subjects. They're more likely to live at home or off-campus. They're less likely to have gained AP [advanced placement] credit and more likely to have to take uncredited remedial courses. And they're more likely to face serious financial hurdles.

6   These challenges are sometimes so formidable that studies say that only 8 percent of low-income (many of whom are first-generation) students will graduate college by age 25. Social integration is only one piece of the puzzle for these students, and for Harry—like many other students—combating this transition can be easier with the help of older peers, teachers and guiding professors who act as mentors. While the definition of "mentor" varies, there are both informal and formal structures that have the potential to influence first-generation college persistence and graduation. Armed with this understanding, many secondary and post-secondary institutions have created programming to better support and mentor first-generation students.

7   In Chicago, The Noble Network of Charter Schools collects extensive data on their alumni to determine what students need in order to persist and graduate from college. Last year, nine of the campuses graduated seniors and each of these nine schools has a college counselor and an alumni coordinator—allowing students to have extensive support through the college application, matriculation, and transition process.

Reflect Have you ever found yourself in a situation where you felt you didn't belong or understand what was going on around you?

Identify What specific causes are identified in the previous paragraph that explain why a first-generation student may have difficulty when they begin their college education?

Reflect Do you think students would benefit from the types of mentoring and counseling these schools provide? Explain.

8   "It's very intentionally called college counseling," Matt Niksch, Noble's Chief College Officer, tells me. "They're not kids anymore, [and] a lot of it is about helping young adults determine the right choice for them."

9   Noble schools look to a college's institutional minority graduation rate as a predictor of student success, but even these statistics can't always foresee what different students will face.

Reflect In the previous paragraphs, the author identifies many causes of student success or a lack of success. Have you ever found yourself in one of these situations? What did you do about it?

10   Caroline Kelly, a college counselor at Noble's Pritzker College Prep, categorizes the challenges into "different buckets. One is financial, one is motivation, one is family, one is academics, and one is social integration."

11   Many first-generation students, like Harry, struggle socially when they arrive on a college campus only to find that they have trouble identifying with their wealthier peers, or they feel a distinct "otherness" that they didn't experience in high school. Others adjust socially but find themselves paying for their education for the first time in their lives.

12   "In high school your education was given to you for free in most cases," says Mac, a current junior at the University of Illinois at Urbana Champaign. Mac is an alumnus of a traditional public school on the Southside of Chicago, where he participated in OneGoal, a teacher-led college persistence program for low-income students that provides school-based support for students over the course of three years. OneGoal teachers begin work with students during their junior year of high school and bridge the gap between high school and college with a curriculum that continues into each student's first-year of college.

13   Despite the influx of programs on high-school and college campuses, many programs still lag in hard graduation numbers.

14   "College becomes a major expense. I have to focus a lot more on how I will pay for school before attending school each semester," he says. He has had support from the program since his junior year in high school, when OneGoal teachers helped him prepare for standardized tests, research and apply for schools and apply for financial aid. His OneGoal teacher even drove him to college on move-in day. "Before OneGoal I don't feel that college was even on my radar," he says.

15   "There's just a huge financial gap," says Thomas Dickson, the Director of Teacher Recruitment for OneGoal.

Identify Out of all the causes Riggs identifies, which do you believe is the biggest hurdle for first generation college students and why?

16   Since its official launch in 2007, 87 percent of OneGoal's high school graduates have enrolled in college, and of those who have enrolled, 85 percent are persisting in college or have graduated with a college degree.

17   OneGoal has many look-alike organizations in other cities, some of which are school-based (KIPP Through College, Achievement First's Alumni Program) and others that are independent companies such as College Forward—a non-profit college-coaching organization based in Texas that boasts 78 percent of their students as still enrolled or graduated, or InsideTrack, a for-profit coaching organization aimed at increasing college enrollment and graduation rates.

18   Despite the influx of programs on high-school and college campuses, many programs still lag in hard graduation numbers.

19   "Our four-year college graduation numbers are not even close to where we want them to be," Angela Montagna, Noble's Director of External Affairs, says. Noble says 88 percent of their students make it from their first to their second year, but don't always make it to graduation.

20   Though there isn't significant research that measures all mentoring relationships and their effects on college persistence, there is some research showing the positive effects of mentoring relationships on young kids. Colleges across the country are implementing mentoring initiatives for first-generation college students in attempts to combat the staggeringly low graduation rates.

21   And, while a degree is the ultimate goal for many parents, teachers and students, there are other results that are perhaps more important for first-generation college students, Noble's Matt Niksch says.

22   "A lot of [students] talk about college as the goal. But we also don't want them to forget that really the goal is: We want them to have happy, successful, choice-filled lives."

Summarize What is the author's main idea in this article?

1. Double-underline the **thesis statement**.

2. Does this essay present causes, effects, or both? Explain how you came to your conclusion. *Answers will vary. Possible answer: The essay presents both causes and effects. While financial and academic problems are certainly hurdles for these students, the effect of alienation or otherness are often an effect of just attending school.*

3. Does this essay follow the Four Basics of Good Cause and Effect (p. 266)? Why or why not? *Answers will vary.*

_____

_____

_____

Respond to one of the following assignments in a paragraph or essay.

Tip For reading advice, see Chapter 1.

1. At the beginning of her essay, Riggs writes about situations that may cause a student to feel uncomfortable or alienated at college because of their background. Write about a time when your past created an uncomfortable situation and how you managed to work through it.

2. In paragraph 10, Caroline Kelly identifies some causes of difficulty as a student enters college: financial, motivation, family, academics, and social integration. Which of these causes can be controlled by a student? In other words, to be

successful, students can change the effect that some of these have on their life: which would those be?

3. In paragraph 20, Riggs presents some research that shows how mentoring can have a positive effect on both children and college students. Why do you think that is?

Write Your Own Cause and Effect

In this section, you will write your own cause-and-effect paragraph or essay based on one of the following assignments. For help, refer to the How to Write Cause and Effect checklist on page 284.

| **ASSIGNMENT OPTIONS** | **Writing about college, work, and everyday life** |

Write a cause-and-effect paragraph or essay on one of the following topics or on one of your own choice.

ESL teaching tip Suggest that students write about the cause or effect of a cultural misunderstanding.

College
- Write about the causes, effects, or both of not studying for an exam.
- If you have chosen a major or program of study, explain the factors behind your decision. How do you think this choice will shape your future?
- Why do some people stay in college, while others drop out? Interview one or two college graduates about the factors behind their decision to stay in school. Also, ask them how staying in school and graduating has affected their lives. Then, write about the causes and effects they describe.

Work
- Write about the causes, effects, or both of stress at work.
- Identify a friend or acquaintance who has been successful at work. Write about the factors behind this person's success.
- Write about the causes, effects, or both of having a good or bad attitude at work.

Everyday life
- Think of a possession that has great personal meaning for you. Then, write about why you value the possession, and give examples of its importance in your life.
- Try to fill in this blank: "_____ changed my life." Your response can be an event, an interaction with a particular person, or anything significant to you. It can be something positive or negative. After you fill in the blank, explain how and why this event, interaction, or time had so much significance.
- Arrange to spend a few hours at a local soup kitchen or food pantry, or on another volunteer opportunity that interests you. (You can use a search engine to find volunteer opportunities in your area.) Write about how the experience affected you.

| ASSIGNMENT OPTIONS | **Reading and writing critically** |

Complete one of the following assignments, which ask you to apply the critical thinking, reading, and writing skills discussed in Chapter 1.

WRITING CRITICALLY ABOUT READINGS

Jelani Lynch's "My Turnaround" (p. 118), Caitlin Prokop's "A Difficult Decision with a Positive Outcome" (p. 274), and Liz Riggs's "What It's Like to Be the First Person in Your Family to Go to College" (p. 278) talk about taking control of one's life. Read or review these pieces, and then follow these steps:

1. **Summarize** Briefly summarize the works, listing major examples.

2. **Analyze** What questions do these pieces raise for you? Are there any other issues you wish they had covered?

3. **Synthesize** Using examples from Lynch, Prokop's, and Riggs's writings and from your own experience, discuss different ways—big and small—in which people can take control of their lives.

4. **Evaluate** Which of the pieces had the deepest effect on you? Why? In writing your evaluation, you might look back on your responses to step 2.

Tip For a reminder of how to summarize, analyze, synthesize, and evaluate, see the Reading and Writing Critically box on page 21.

WRITING ABOUT IMAGES

Sometimes, using language is not an effective means of communication. This can happen when a child is too young to speak, a person does not feel comfortable with written or spoken language (perhaps he or she is learning a new language and is not comfortable speaking or writing publicly), or when something, for instance, pain, makes it difficult to speak or write. Study the following images and then answer the following questions.

Teaching tip If time is short, students might complete just one or two steps of this assignment.

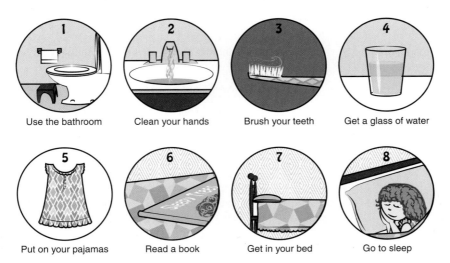

| 1 Use the bathroom | 2 Clean your hands | 3 Brush your teeth | 4 Get a glass of water |
| 5 Put on your pajamas | 6 Read a book | 7 Get in your bed | 8 Go to sleep |

It's important to make a bedtime ritual that helps children prepare to go to sleep each night.

1. **Read the images** Ask yourself: Why is it a good idea to use a series of images, instead of a single image, to help the "reader" identify what they want to say? (For more information on reading images, see Chapter 1.)

2. **Write a cause-and-effect paragraph or essay** Identify another situation in which using images to explain the cause-and-effect relationship between two situations, feelings, or actions would be as helpful or more helpful than written directions/instructions.

WRITING TO SOLVE A PROBLEM

Read or review the discussion of problem solving in Chapter 1 (pp. 28–30). Then, consider the following problem.

You have learned of a cheating ring at school that uses cell phones to give test answers to students taking the test. A few students in your math class, who are also friends of yours, think that this scheme is a great idea and are planning to cheat on a test you will be taking next week. You decide not to participate, partly because you fear getting caught, but also because you think that cheating is wrong. Now you want to convince your friends not to cheat, because you don't want them to get caught and possibly kicked out of school. How do you make your case?

(Continued on page 285.)

CHECKLIST

How to Write Cause and Effect

Steps	Details
☐ Narrow and explore your topic. See Chapter 3.	• Make the topic more specific. • Prewrite to get ideas about the narrowed topic.
☐ Write a topic sentence (paragraph) or thesis statement (essay). See Chapter 3.	• State your subject and the causes, effects, or both that your paper will explore.
☐ Support your point. See Chapter 4.	• Come up with explanations or examples of the causes, effects, or both.
☐ Write a draft. See Chapter 5.	• Make a plan that puts the support points in a logical order. • Include a topic sentence (paragraph) or thesis statement (essay) and all the supporting explanations and examples.
☐ Revise your draft. See Chapter 5.	• Make sure it has *all* the Four Basics of Good Cause and Effect. • Make sure you include transitions to move readers smoothly from one cause and effect to the next.
☐ Edit your revised draft. See Parts 3 through 6.	• Correct errors in grammar, spelling, word use, and punctuation.

Assignment Working in a group or on your own, list the various effects of cheating—both immediate and long term—you could use to convince your friends. Then, write a cause-and-effect paragraph or essay that identifies and explains some possible effects of cheating. You might start with this sentence:

Cheating on tests or papers is not worth the risks.

Teaching tip Ask students what other causes or effects might be well illustrated through a series of photos.

Chapter Review

1. A cause is _what made an event happen._

2. An effect is _what happens as a result of the event._

3. What are the Four Basics of Good Cause and Effect? _The main idea reflects the writer's purpose: to explain causes, effects, or both. If the purpose is to explain causes, it presents real causes. If the purpose is to explain effects, it presents real effects. It gives readers detailed examples or explanations of the causes or effects._

4. Write sentences using the following vocabulary words: *cherish, motives, immigrant, rigorous, estrangement, alienation, remedial, formidable, influx, lag.* _Answers will vary._

REFLECTING ON THE JOURNEY

Skills Learned

Now that you've completed the chapter, share what you've learned about each skill by completing the following chart.

Skill	What I learned about this skill
Identify the causes of events	
Identify the effects of events	
Express causes, effects, or both through writing	
Provide specific examples to support those causes and effects	
Read and analyze cause and effect	

14

Argument

Writing That Persuades

READING ROADMAP

Learning Objectives

Chapter Goal: Learn how to write an argument paper.

Tools to Achieve the Goal:

- Four Basics of Good Argument (p. 287)
- Diagram: Paragraphs and Essays in Argument (pp. 290–92)
- Sample Paragraph and Rubric (pp. 299–300)
- Profile of Success and Workplace Argument: Stacie Brown (pp. 301–02)
- Professional Argument Essay: John Hawkins, *5 Scientific Reasons that Global Warming Isn't Happening* (pp. 303–05)
- Professional Argument Essay: The Environmental Protection Agency, *Climate Change is Happening* (pp. 305–07)
- Checklist: How to Write Argument (p. 310)

Key Terms

Skim Chapter 14 before reading. Find these words or terms in **bold** type. Put a check mark next to each once you locate it.

- _____ argument
- _____ main idea
- _____ support
- _____ reasons
- _____ evidence
- _____ assumptions
- _____ order of importance
- _____ transitions

Guided Reading for Chapter 14

Fill out the following chart before you begin reading. For each skill, write what you know about that skill and what you would like to know upon completing the chapter. At the end of the chapter, you will be asked to share what you learned about each skill.

Skill	When I have used this skill	What I want to know about this skill
Identify an argument		
Identify strong points, evidence, and support for an argument		
Consider opposing views		
Read and analyze argument		

Understand What Argument Is

LaunchPadSolo

Visit **LaunchPad Solo for Readers and Writers > Reading > Patterns of Organization** for more tutorials, videos, and practice with patterns of organization.

Argument is writing that takes a position on an issue and gives supporting evidence to persuade someone else to accept, or at least consider, the position. Argument is also used to convince someone to take (or not take) an action.

Four Basics of Good Argument

1 It takes a strong and definite position.

2 It gives good reasons and supporting evidence to defend the position.

3 It considers opposing views.

4 It has enthusiasm and energy from start to finish.

In the following paragraph, the numbers and colors correspond to the Four Basics of Good Argument.

1 Even though I write this blog post on an 88-degree day, I am truly glad that I stopped using my air conditioner, and I urge you to follow my lead. 2 For one thing, going without air conditioning can save a significant amount of money. Last summer, this strategy cut my electricity costs by nearly $2,000, and I am on my way to achieving even higher savings this summer. For another thing, living without air conditioning reduces humans' effect on the environment. Agricultural researcher Stan Cox estimates that air conditioning creates 300 million tons of carbon dioxide (CO_2) emissions each year. This amount, he says, is the equivalent of every U.S. household buying an additional car and driving it 7,000 miles annually. Because CO_2 is one of the greenhouse gases responsible for trapping heat in our atmosphere, reducing CO_2 emissions is essential to curbing climate change. The final reason for going without air conditioning is that it is actually pretty comfortable. The key to staying cool is keeping the blinds down on south-facing windows during the day. It is also a good idea to open windows throughout the home for cross ventilation while turning on ceiling fans to improve air circulation. 3 Although some people argue that using fans is just as bad as switching on the air conditioner, fans use far less electricity. In closing, let me make you a promise: The sooner you give up air conditioning, the sooner you will get comfortable with the change—and the sooner you and the planet will reap the rewards.

4 Argument is enthusiastic and energetic.

Teaching tip Explain to students that argument is not like bickering or fighting. It is a reasonable defense of a position.

Knowing how to make a good argument is one of the most useful skills you can develop.

College	You argue for or against makeup exams for students who do not do well the first time.
Work	You need to leave work an hour early one day a week for twelve weeks to take a course. You persuade your boss to allow you to do so.
Everyday life	You try to negotiate a better price on an item you want to buy.

In college, writing assignments might include questions or statements such as the following: *Do you agree or disagree with* _____*? Defend or refute* _____. *Is* _____ *fair and just?* In all these cases, use the strategies discussed in this chapter.

Main Idea in Argument

Your **main idea** in argument is the position you take on the issue (or topic) about which you are writing. When you are free to choose an issue, choose something that matters to you. When you are assigned an issue, try to find some part of it that matters to you. You might try starting with a "should" or "should not" sentence:

Main idea in argument	**College football players should/should not be paid.**

If you have trouble seeing how an issue matters, talk about it with a partner or write down ideas about it using the following tips.

Tips for Building Enthusiasm and Energy

- Imagine yourself arguing your position with someone who disagrees.
- Imagine that your whole grade rests on persuading your instructor to agree with your position.
- Imagine how this issue could affect you or your family personally.
- Imagine that you are representing a large group of people who care about the issue very much and whose lives will be forever changed by it. It is up to you to win their case.

In argument, the topic sentence (in a paragraph) or thesis statement (in an essay) usually includes the issue/topic and your position about it. Here is an example of a topic sentence for a paragraph:

Subject or issue	+	Position	=	Topic sentence

Our company should make regular contributions to local food banks.

Remember that the main idea for an essay can be a little broader than one for a paragraph.

Subject or issue	+	Position	=	Thesis statement

Our company should become more active in supporting charities.

Tip Sometimes, the same main idea can be used for a paragraph and an essay, but the essay must develop this point in more detail. (See pp. 68–69.)

Whereas the topic sentence focuses on just one type of charitable organization, the thesis statement sets up a discussion of different ways to help different charities.

PRACTICE 1   **Writing a statement of your position**

Write a statement of your position for each item. *Answers will vary.*
Possible answers are shown.
Example:

Issue: Prisoners' rights

Position statement: *Prisoners should not have more rights and privileges than law-abiding citizens.*

Teaching tip Have students type some keywords about their topic into a search engine (e.g., **www.google.com**)—for instance, *animal testing* and *pros and cons*. Seeing the points others have raised about an issue can help them consider the various sides.

1. Issue: Lab testing on animals

   Position statement: *Animals should continue to be used for lab testing.*

2. Issue: Wearing seatbelts.

   Position statement: *Laws that require drivers and passengers to wear seatbelts in their vehicle save lives.*

3. Issue: Athletes' salaries

   Position statement: *Limits should be placed on major league baseball players' salaries.*

4. Issue: Treadmill desks

   Position statement: *All desk workers should be provided with treadmill desks to encourage standing and healthy exercise.*

5. Issue: GMOs

   Position statement: *Genetically modified organisms (GMOs) should be researched further to identify potential long-term effects on humans.*

Support in Argument

The paragraph and essay models on pages 290–91 use the topic sentence (paragraph) and thesis statement (essay) from the Main Idea section of this chapter. Both models include the **support** used in all argument writing: the **reasons** for the

Tip For more on evidence, see page 292.

Paragraphs vs. Essays in Argument

For more on the important features of argument, see the Four Basics of Good Argument on page 287.

Paragraph Form

Topic sentence

Support 1 (reason 1)

Support 2 (reason 2)

Support 3 (reason 3)

Concluding sentence

Our company should make regular contributions to local food banks. The first reason for making these contributions is that, as a food wholesaler, we have the resources to do so. Often, we find that we have a surplus of certain items, such as canned goods and pasta, and it would be a waste not to donate this food to organizations that need it so desperately. We could also donate food that is safe to consume but that we cannot sell to stores or institutions. These items include market-testing products from manufacturers and goods with torn labels. Second, these contributions will improve our image among clients. All other things being equal, grocers, schools, hospitals, and other institutions will be more likely to purchase food from a wholesaler that gives something back to the community than one focused on its financial interests alone. The most important reason for making these contributions is to help our company become a better corporate citizen. Especially in challenging economic times, many people see corporations as heartless and as motivated by profits alone. It is important to show not only clients but also the wider community that we are one of the "good guys." That is, we are willing to do what is right, not only within our organization but also in society. Although some question the need for a donation program, arguing that it would take too much time to organize, the good that will come from the program will far exceed the effort devoted to it.

Main Idea: Often, narrower for a paragraph than for an essay: While the topic sentence (paragraph) focuses on just one type of charitable organization, the thesis statement (essay) sets up a discussion of different ways to help different charities.

Support for the Main Idea (Reasons for the Writer's Position)

Evidence to Back Up Each Reason: Usually, 1 to 3 sentences per reason for paragraphs and 3 to 8 sentences per reason for essays.

Conclusion

Think Critically as You Write Argument

ASK YOURSELF

- Have I questioned the assumptions behind my main idea?
- Have I looked for evidence to respond to these questions and to develop support for my argument?
- Have I tested this evidence before including it in my paper? (For more on testing evidence, see pp. 294–95.)

Essay Form

1

Introductory paragraph

At the last executive meeting, we discussed several possible ways to improve our company's marketing and advertising and to increase employee morale. Since attending the meeting, I have become convinc[ed] [that an] effort would help in those areas and more: Our company should become more active in supporting charities.

Thesis statement

First, giving time and money to community organizations is a good way to promote our organization. This approach has worked well for several o[ur com]petitors. For example, Lanse Industries is v[ell known] for sponsoring Little League teams throughout the city. Its name is on the back of each uniform, and banners promoting Lanse's new products appear on the ball fields. Lanse gets free promotion of these efforts through articles in the local papers, and according to one company source quoted in the *Hillsburg Gazette*, Lanse's good works in the community have boosted its sales by 5 to 10 percent. Another competitor, Great Deals, has employees serve meals at soup kitchens over the holidays and at least once during the spring or summer. It, too, has gotten great publicity from these efforts,

Topic sentence 1 (reason 1)

including a spot on a local TV news show. It is time for our company to start reaping these kinds of benefits.

Second, activities like group volunteering will help employees feel more connected to one another and to their community. Kay Rodriguez, a manag[er at Great] Deals and a good friend of mine, organize[d our com]pany's group volunteering efforts at the soup kitchens, and she cannot say enough good things about the results. Aside from providing meals to the needy, the volunteering has boosted the morale of Great Deals employees because they understand that they are supporting an important cause in their community. Kay has also noticed that as employees work together at the soup kitchens, they form closer bonds. She says, "Some of these people work on different floors and rarely get to see each other during the work week. Or they just do not have time to talk. But while they work together on the volunteering, I see real connections forming." I know that some members of our executive committee might think it would be too time-consuming to organize companywide volunteering efforts. Kay assures

Topic sentence 2 (reason 2)

me, however, that this is not the case and that the rewards of such efforts far exceed the costs in time.

The most important reason for supporting charities is that it is the right thing to do. As a[company or] business that depends on the local comm[unity for a] large share of revenue and employees, I believe we owe that community something in return. If our home city does not thrive, how can we? By giving time and money to local organizations, we provide a real service to people, and we present our company as a good and caring neighbor instead of a faceless corporation that could not care less if local citizens went hungry, had trash and graffiti in their parks, or couldn't afford sports teams for their kids. We could make our community proud to have us around.

Topic sentence 3 (reason 3)

Concluding paragraph

I realize that our main goal is to run a profitable and growing business. I do not believe, however, that this aim must exclude doing good in the community. In fact, I see these two goals moving side by side, and hand in hand. When companies give back to local citizens, their businesses benefit, the community benefits, and everyone is pleased by the results.

writer's position backed up by **evidence**. In the essay model, however, the major support points (reasons) are topic sentences for individual paragraphs.

A good way to find strong support for an argument is to return to some of the critical-thinking strategies you learned about in Chapter 1. Let's take another look at the basics.

Four Basics of Critical Thinking

1	Be alert to assumptions made by you and others.
2	Question those assumptions.
3	Consider and connect various points of view, even those different from your own.
4	Do not rush to conclusions; instead, remain patient with yourself and others, and keep an open mind.

When writing, you may apply some of these basics while working on an argument paper for English class. Consider the following:

> While working at a local restaurant, your attention is drawn to something on the TV over the restaurant's bar. On the TV, a political commentator and a doctor were debating whether a tax on soda would help reduce obesity.
>
> You are in favor of just about any reasonable approach to fighting obesity, although you are uncertain about a tax on soda (and other sugary beverages) and whether it would work. Even the doctor on TV seemed a little unsure.
>
> After finishing your shift and thinking more about the issue, you begin to see how the pros of such a tax might outweigh the cons but decide to sleep on the issue before coming to any final conclusions. Here is the working main idea as you may write it down in a notebook before going to bed.

Main idea   Taxing sugary drinks might be a good way to reduce obesity.

QUESTIONING ASSUMPTIONS TO BUILD EVIDENCE

Tip Consider this advice from actor Alan Alda:

"Begin challenging your own assumptions. Your assumptions are your windows on the world. Scrub them off every once in a while, or the light won't come in."

The next step in this process is to use key critical-thinking strategies to explore the main idea in more depth. Specifically, it is important to identify some of the **assumptions** (unquestioned ideas or opinions) behind that main idea. You may want to write them down on one half of a sheet of notebook paper. One way to examine these assumptions is to try to put yourself in the shoes of someone opposed to beverage taxes. Then, write these questions on the other half of the notebook paper.

Assumptions behind main idea	Questions about assumptions
Sugary drinks, like soda, energy drinks, and sweetened tea, can make people fat.	*But why target sugary drinks instead of other junk food? Aren't french fries just as bad for the waistline as soda is?*
Taxes on sugary drinks would make people less likely to buy these beverages.	*Really? It's easy for me to say that this tax would work because I'm not a big fan of these drinks. But if they taxed coffee, the taxes would have to be pretty big to break my four-cups-a-day habit.*

Assumptions behind main idea	Questions about assumptions
The tax revenues would benefit the public.	*How much difference would they really make?*

To answer these questions, you will typically need to turn to some sources recommended by a college librarian, draw on results from an Internet search, and include information from your own experiences and observations. Through those methods, you may gather the following four types of evidence used most often in support of arguments.

Teaching tip Go over the concept of evidence carefully. Students' arguments are often weak because of poor evidence or lack of evidence.

- *Facts:* Statements or observations that can be proved. Statistics—real numbers from actual studies—can be persuasive factual evidence.

- *Examples:* Specific information or experiences that support your position.

- *Expert opinions:* The opinions of people considered knowledgeable about your topic because of their educational or work background, their research into the topic, or other qualifications. It is important to choose these sources carefully. For example, an economics professor might be knowledgeable about the possible benefits and drawbacks of beverage taxes. He or she probably wouldn't be the best source of information on the health effects of soda, however.

- *Predictions:* Forecasts of the possible outcomes of events or actions. These forecasts are the informed views of experts, not the best guesses of nonexperts.

The following chart shows the evidence that could be pulled together to address assumptions and questions about them. (Your original questions can be revised and expanded as you explore your topic further.)

Tip When looking for evidence about assumptions, always seek the most reliable sources of information.

Assumptions/questions to investigate	Evidence in response
To what degree do sugary drinks contribute to obesity?	**Fact:** According to the Centers for Disease Control and Prevention, about half of all Americans get a major portion of their daily calories from sweetened beverages. **Fact:** In the *Journal of Pediatrics,* Robert Murray reported that one-fourth of U.S. teenagers drink as many as four cans of soda or fruit drinks a day, each one containing about 150 calories. That translates to a total of 600 calories a day, the equivalent of an additional meal. **Expert opinion:** Dr. Richard Adamson, senior scientific consultant for the American Beverage Association, says, "Blaming one specific product or ingredient as the root cause of obesity defies common sense. Instead, there are many contributing factors, including regular physical activity."
Do sugary drinks deserve to be targeted more than other dietary factors that can contribute to obesity?	**Example (from Jess's personal experience):** My brother, his wife, and their three kids are all big soda drinkers, and they are all overweight. They also eat lots of junk food, however, so it is hard to tell how much the soda is to blame for their weight. **Fact:** The Center for Science in the Public Interest says that sugary beverages are more likely to cause weight gain than solid foods are. After eating solid food, people tend to reduce their consumption of other calorie sources. Unlike solid foods, however, sugary beverages do not make people feel full. Therefore, they may add on calories to satisfy their hunger.

Assumptions/questions to investigate	Evidence in response
To what degree would taxes on sugary drinks discourage people from buying these beverages and also reduce obesity?	**Expert opinion/fact:** Several researchers say that the taxes would have to be pretty significant to affect consumer behavior. The average national tax on a 12-ounce bottle of soda is 5 cents, and that has not provided enough discouragement. **Prediction:** In the *New England Journal of Medicine,* Kelly D. Brownell says that a penny-per-ounce tax on sugary beverages could reduce consumption of these beverages by more than 10 percent.
Would the taxes have any other benefits?	**Prediction:** Kelly D. Brownell says that by reducing the consumption of sugary beverages, the taxes could help cut public expenditures on obesity. Each year, about $79 billion goes toward the health-care costs of overweight and obese individuals. Approximately half of these costs are paid by taxpayers. **Expert opinion:** Brownell also believes that the tax revenues could and should be used for programs to prevent childhood obesity.

PRACTICE 2   Deepening the search for evidence

Come up with at least one other question that could be raised about the sugary drinks tax issue. Then, list the type(s) of evidence (such as personal examples, an expert opinion from a scientific study, or a prediction from a business leader) that could help answer the question.

Question(s): _Answers will vary._ _____

_____

Type(s) of evidence: _____

Teaching tip To aid students' critical thinking, consider sharing this quotation from Ralph Waldo Emerson: "Stay at home in your mind. Don't recite other people's opinions. . . . Tell me what you know." Even though students may be drawing on outside sources in their arguments, encourage them to be confident in the conclusions they draw from these sources and from their own observations.

In the process of investigating your assumptions, it is important to gather not only good support but also some opposing views (one of the Four Basics of Good Argument). One of the opposing views, from Dr. Richard Adamson of the American Beverage Association, may make you stop and evaluate the credibility or bias of the source. Because he represents the interests of the beverage industry, he might not offer a completely balanced opinion on the health effects of sweetened drinks, but you may decide that as long as you mentioned his affiliation with the beverage industry, his point might be worth including in the paper.

In reviewing your evidence, consider the following tips as well:

Testing evidence

Teaching tip Model the opponent's perspective in class. Put a topic and some evidence on the board. Ask for ideas about how the opposition would try to knock down the evidence.

- Consider your audience's view of the issue. Are audience members likely to agree with you, to be uncommitted, or to be hostile? Then, make sure your evidence would be convincing to a typical member of your audience.

- Reread your evidence from an opponent's perspective, looking for ways to knock it down. Anticipate your opponent's objections, and include evidence to answer them.

- Do not overgeneralize. Statements about what everyone else does or what always happens are easy to disprove. It is better to use facts (including statistics), specific examples, expert opinions, and informed predictions.

- Make sure you have considered every important angle of the issue.

- Reread the evidence to make sure it provides good support for your position. Also, the evidence must be relevant to your argument.

> **PRACTICE 3**   **Reviewing the evidence**
>
> For each of the following positions, one piece of evidence is weak: It does not support the position. Circle the letter of the weak evidence, and, in the space provided, state why it is weak.
>
> **Example:**
>
> **Position: Advertisements should not use skinny models.**
>
> **Reason: Skinny should not be promoted as ideal.**
>
> a.   **Three friends of mine became anorexic trying to get skinny.**
>
> (b.)   **Everyone knows that most people are not that thin.**
>
> c.   **A survey of girls shows that they think that they should be as thin as models.**
>
> d.   **People can endanger their health trying to fit the skinny "ideal" promoted in advertisements.**
>
> **Not strong evidence because** *"everyone knows" is not strong evidence;*
> *everyone obviously doesn't know that.*

> **Teaching tip** If you are working in a lab setting, have each student list the evidence for his or her topic on the computer. Then, have each student move to another student's computer and write down opposition to the evidence that is listed. Students should then return to their own computers and try to answer the objections.

1. Position: People who own guns should not be allowed to keep them at home.

   Reason: It is dangerous to keep a gun in the house.

   a.   Guns can go off by accident.

   b.   Keeping guns at home has been found to increase the risk of home suicides and adolescent suicides.

   c.   Just last week, a story in the newspaper told about a man who, in a fit of rage, took his gun out of the drawer and shot his wife.

   (d.)   Guns can be purchased easily.

   Not strong evidence because *it is irrelevant; it doesn't support the position.*

   _____

2. Position: Schoolchildren in the United States should go to school all year.

   Reason: Year-round schooling promotes better learning.

   ⓐ All my friends have agreed that we would like to end the long summer break.

   b. A survey of teachers across the country showed that children's learning improved when they had multiple shorter vacations rather than entire summers off.

   c. Many children are bored and restless after three weeks of vacation and would be better off returning to school.

   d. Test scores improved when a school system in Colorado went to year-round school sessions.

   Not strong evidence because *wanting it doesn't mean it should happen;*

   also this statement is a personal preference, not evidence.

3. Position: The "three strikes and you're out" law that forces judges to send people to jail after three convictions should be revised.

   Reason: Basing decisions about sentencing on numbers alone is neither reasonable nor fair.

   a. A week ago, a man who stole a slice of pizza was sentenced to eight to ten years in prison because it was his third conviction.

   b. The law makes prison overcrowding even worse.

   ⓒ Judges always give the longest sentence possible anyway.

   d. The law too often results in people getting major prison sentences for minor crimes.

   Not strong evidence because *it is a generality; not all judges act this*

   way.

After reviewing the evidence, you may need to refine the initial position.

Revised main idea   To help address the obesity crisis, states should place significant taxes on sugary beverages.

Notice the removal of the word *might* that was part of the original main idea. Having done some research, you now believe strongly that the taxes are a good idea—as long as they are high enough to make a significant dent in consumption.

Before writing a paper, create a rough outline stating the main idea and the major support points—the reasons for the position expressed in the main idea. The reasons are based on the evidence you gathered.

Rough outline

Main idea: To help address the obesity crisis, states should place significant taxes on sugary beverages.

Support/reasons:

Sugary drinks are a major contributor to obesity.

As long as they are significant, taxes on these drinks could reduce consumption.

The taxes could fund programs targeting childhood obesity.

WRITING THE CONCLUSION

Your conclusion is your last opportunity to convince readers of your position. Make it memorable and forceful. Remind readers of the stand you are taking and the rightness of this stand, even in the face of opposing views.

Before writing your conclusion, imagine that you are an attorney making a final, impassioned appeal to the judge in an important case. Then, put this energy into words with a conclusion that drives your point home. (See a sample conclusion on p. 298.)

Organization in Argument

Most arguments are organized by **order of importance**, starting with the least important evidence and saving the most convincing reason and evidence for last.

Tip For more on order of importance, see page 78.

Use **transitions** to move your readers smoothly from one supporting reason to another. Here are some of the transitions you might use in your argument.

Common Transitions in Argument

above all	more important
also	most important
best of all	one fact/another fact
especially	one reason/another reason
for example	one thing/another thing
in addition	remember
in fact	the first (second, third) point
in particular	worst of all
in the first (second, third) place	

The sample that follows uses order of importance to organize the argument in favor of taxes on sugary drinks. The transitions are highlighted in bold.

You will notice that this draft doesn't incorporate all the evidence from the chart on pages 293–94; instead, it includes only the evidence believed to offer the strongest support for the main idea. It also includes an opposing view.

To help address the obesity crisis, states should place significant taxes on sugary beverages, such as soda, sweetened tea and fruit juices, and energy drinks. These drinks are a good target for taxation because they are a major contributor to obesity. According to the Centers for Disease Control and Prevention, about half of all Americans get a major portion of their daily calories from sweetened beverages. **In addition**, the *Journal of Pediatrics* reports that one-fourth of U.S. teenagers get as many as 600 calories a day from soda or fruit drinks. This consumption is the equivalent of an additional meal. **Another reason to tax sugary drinks is that** such taxation could reduce consumption. However, it is important that these taxes be significant because taxes of just a few additional pennies per can or bottle probably wouldn't deter consumers. According to Kelly D. Brownell, director of the Rudd Center for Food Policy and Obesity, a penny-per-ounce tax on sugary beverages could cut consumption of these beverages by more than 10 percent. It could also reduce the estimated $79 billion of taxpayer money spent each year on health care for overweight and obese individuals. **The most important reason to tax sugary drinks is that** the money from such taxes could be used to prevent future cases of obesity. As Brownell notes, the taxes could fund antiobesity programs aimed at educating children about healthy diets and encouraging them to exercise. Some people who are opposed to taxing sugary beverages, such as Dr. Richard Adamson of the American Beverage Association, argue that it is unfair to blame one product for our expanding waistlines. It is true that overconsumption of soda and other sweetened beverages is just one cause of obesity. Nevertheless, targeting this one cause could play a vital, lasting role in a larger campaign to bring this major health crisis under control.

PRACTICE 4   **Using transitions in argument**

The following argument essay encourages students to get involved in service work during college. It was written by Jorge Roque, an Iraq War veteran and Miami-Dade College student who is vice president of a service fraternity.

After reading Jorge's essay, fill in the blanks with transitions. You are not limited to the ones listed in the box on page 297. *Answers may vary. Possible answers are shown.*

Even for the busiest student, getting involved in service organizations

is worth the time and effort it takes. At one point, after I had returned from

Iraq, was homeless, and was experiencing posttraumatic stress disorder, I

was referred to Veteran Love, a nonprofit organization that helps disabled

ex-soldiers, and it helped me when I needed it most. When I was back on track, I

knew that I wanted to help others. I was working and going to school with little

extra time, but getting involved has been important in ways I had not expected.

One reason for getting involved is that; In the first place, getting involved

helps you meet many new people and form a new and larger network of friends and colleagues. You also learn new skills, like organization, project management, communication, teamwork, and public speaking. The practical experience I have now is more than I could have gotten from a class, and I have met people who want to help me in my career.

Another reason for doing service work is that; In the second place,

service work lets you help other people and learn about them. You feel as if you have something valuable to give. You also feel part of something larger than yourself. So often, students are not connected to meaningful communities and work, and service helps you while you help others.

The most important reason to get involved is that; Best of all, service work makes you feel better about yourself and your abilities. What I am doing is important and real, and I feel better than I ever have because of my service involvement. If you get involved with community service of any kind, you will become addicted to it. You get more than you could ever give.

Evaluate Argument

To become a more successful writer, it is important not only to understand the Four Basics of Good Argument but also to read and evaluate examples. In this section, you will have the opportunity to use a sample rubric to analyze or evaluate the samples of argument writing provided. By using this rubric, you will gain a better understanding of how the components of good argument work together to create a successful paragraph or essay.

Read the following sample argument paragraph. Using the Four Basics of Good Argument and the sample grading rubric, decide what grade this paragraph would earn. Explain your answer.

Teaching tip If you have samples from a previous class, bring in full papers or paragraphs and ask the students to use either this rubric or the Four Basics of Good Argument to "grade" the assignments. When they have done so, ask them to pair up and work in groups to see if they all came up with the same score and to determine where the areas of consensus and disagreement are.

Assignment Concealed carry laws are becoming increasingly controversial, especially when people feel as though their rights are being restricted or that they are in danger. Write a paragraph that takes a position on the question: Should students be allowed to carry a concealed weapon on a college campus? Support your argument with specific examples and evidence.

College students should be allowed to carry concealed weapons on campus if they are legally permitted to do so. To have a firearm legally, people are required to apply for a FOID card (Firearms Owner Identification) and subject themselves to a background check. This process is meant to ensure that the people who are allowed to carry these weapons have no history of violence or mental illness that may create future problems. Although there has not been a security issue at my own campus, I would

like to know that I have the option to protect myself if a situation like this occurred. In addition, the legal age for owning specific firearms is eighteen or twenty-one, depending on what type of gun a person chooses to carry. I am safer with a weapon than without.

Analysis of Sample Paragraph: *The sample paragraph is an average paragraph. Comments on each point may vary but should include the following:*

Sample rubric

Element	Grading criteria	Point: Comment
Appropriateness	• Did the student follow the assignment directions?	__3__/5: *An outline summary should contain all of the previous material (keyword and main idea summary), but then it should add in any significant quotes, phrases, dates, names, or information that would be helpful later on.*
Main idea	• Does the paper clearly state a strong main idea in a complete sentence?	__10__/10: *There is a clear main idea.*
Support	• Is the main idea developed with specific support, including specific details and examples? • Is there enough support to make the main idea evident to the reader? • Is all the support directly related to the main idea? • Is there a counterargument present at some point?	__5__/10: *The supporting details are a bit vague, and no counterargument is addressed.*
Organization	• Is the writing logically organized? • Does the student use transitions (*also, for example, sometimes,* and so on) to move the reader from one point to another?	__5__/10: *Organization is the flaw here because ideas do not seem to follow a logical progression. Transitions are infrequent at best.*
Conclusion	• Does the conclusion remind the reader of the main idea? • Does it make an observation based on the support?	__0__/5: *There isn't a clear conclusion.*
Grammar	• Is the writing free of the four most serious errors? (See Chapters 16–19.) • Is the sentence structure clear? • Does the student choose words that clearly express his or her meaning? • Are the words spelled correctly? • Is the punctuation correct?	__10__/10: *The paper is free from the common errors.*
		TOTAL POINTS: __33__/50

Profile of Success
Argument in the Real World

Background   I grew up in an exceptionally small town (population 99) where it was easy for me to excel in high school—and I did—because all the teachers would know why I didn't do well if I didn't. After my dad died during my senior year of high school, though, school was just something I had to finish.

After high school, I couldn't settle on anything because everything seemed useless or pointless. Hoping to find my way, I enrolled in Blinn College for the first time. I ended up dropping two classes and failing the other two, one of which was English 1301. A few years later, I enrolled in a veterinary technician course, but I soon decided that also wasn't for me.

I started dating my husband a while after that and soon became pregnant. Twenty-five years old, no career plan, no college degree, baby on the way—I knew I had to get my act together. With support from family and friends, I enrolled in college for the third time.

While at Blinn College, a few encouraging teachers helped me to realize my potential, and I started writing again. (I had put the pen down after my dad died.) Indeed, I graduated Blinn College with honors. My long-term goal is to become a novelist.

After getting my associate's degree, I started my career in the administrative field as a legal assistant, and I get to use my writing and editing skills every day to communicate with clients, attorneys, courts, and other business entities. I am now situated to pursue my passion. My career has taught me that everyone has at least one remarkable story. It's up to me to write it.

Degrees/Colleges   Associate of Applied Science, Blinn College

Writing at Work   I write business e-mails, letters, memos, legal pleadings, and other legal documents. Working with clients often involves discussing uncomfortable or difficult topics. Addressing issues related to billing are necessary not only for a business to succeed but also for building a strong, successful attorney-client relationship. Many times, an attorney needs to communicate with not only a client but also the client's family member—and family members can be quite inexorable. One must respond in a firm but tactful manner.

Stacie Brown
Legal Assistant

Read and Analyze Argument

In this section, the Profile of Success illustrates how Stacie Brown uses argument in her job in a legal office. Next, two professional articles present different positions in the debate surrounding climate change. The first one makes the claim that climate change is not a problem and is not occurring at present. The second article, a piece by the Environmental Protection Agency of the United States, argues that climate change is a very real threat to the environment. Both articles present a clear position and evidence to support that position. By reading two perspectives on the same issue, you can start to understand your own position on the subject. All good arguments start with some degree of research to see what has already been written on the topic and to better inform the writer. Read these selections, pay attention to the vocabulary, and answer the questions in the margin. They will help you read critically.

Teaching tip Ask students to work individually, in pairs, or in groups to evaluate each of the following readings using the rubric provided.

Workplace Argument

The following is an example of an e-mail pertaining to billing.

Dear John Doe:

We recently sent your most recent invoice (November 2014) to the address we have in our file: 555 No Name Street, Anywhere, Texas 55555. It was returned to us as "not deliverable as addressed, unable to forward." As a result, I am e-mailing your November 2014 invoice, which is attached. If the mailing address we have on file is incorrect, please notify our office immediately of your correct mailing address.

Additionally, when we last spoke about payment arrangements, you agreed to send a money order once you received your tax return, which you indicated would be in ten to twelve days. It has been six months since that phone conversation, and our office has yet to receive payment of any kind. As you are aware, our office policy dictates that attorneys may not continue work for a client for which there is no money left in the Trust account. This means that any pending or future issues related to your case will not be considered until your balance is paid in full.

If you believe there has been an error in receiving payment, please contact our office to discuss. Otherwise, please consider this e-mail a formal demand for payment in full. If your payment is not received within fifteen days from the date of this e-mail, our office will have no choice but to begin formal collection actions. These actions will, of course, increase the amount owed to this office. I sincerely hope this will not be necessary.

Thank you,

Stacie

Stacie Brown

Legal Assistant

Law Firm

555 No Name Street

Anywhere, Texas 55555

Phone: 555.555.5555

Fax: 555.555.5556

E-mail: emailaddress@domain.net

1. Double-underline the **thesis statement**.

2. Circle the **transitions** that introduce the different reasons supporting the argument.

3. Underline the parts of the e-mail that present each supporting reason for the argument.

4. Does this workplace sample follow the Four Basics of Good Argument (p. 287)? Why or why not? _Answers will vary._

Professional Argument Essay 1: Climate Change Is Not Happening

John Hawkins

5 Scientific Reasons That Global Warming Isn't Happening

John Hawkins is a well-known writer and political commentator. Not only does Hawkins write for publications such as *The Huffington Post, Washington Examiner*, and *The Hill*, he also makes numerous regular appearances on ABC News, MSNBC, and C-Span. Throughout his career, he has spent a great deal of time interviewing and working with conservatives and he is the founder of Rightroots group, an organization that raises money to fund conservative political candidates nationwide.

This piece first appeared on TownHall.com on February 18, 2014.

Vocabulary development   Underline these words as you read: *hinging, unverifiable, skeptical, assertion, upswing, consensus, mainstream, talking point, tipping point, troposphere,* and *hasty.*

Guiding question   As you read this essay, identify what specific evidence the writer uses to support the main argument.

1   How did global warming discussions end up hinging on what's happening with polar bears, unverifiable predictions of what will happen in a hundred years, and whether people are "climate deniers" or "global warming cultists"? If this is a scientific topic, why aren't we spending more time discussing the science involved? Why aren't we talking about the evidence and the actual data involved? Why aren't we looking at the predictions that were made and seeing if they match up to the results? If this is such an open and shut case, why are so many people who care about science skeptical? Many Americans have long since thought that the best scientific evidence available suggested that man wasn't causing any sort of global warming. However, now, we can go even further and suggest that the planet isn't warming at all.

2   There hasn't been any global warming since 1997: If nothing changes in the next year, we're going to have kids who graduate from high school who will have never seen any "global warming" during their lifetimes. That's right; the temperature of the planet has essentially been flat for 17 years. This isn't a controversial assertion either. Even the former Director of the Climate Research Unit (CRU) of the University of East Anglia, Phil Jones, admits that it's true. Since the planet was cooling from 1940 to 1975 and the upswing in temperature afterward only lasted 22 years, a 17-year pause is a big deal. It also begs an obvious question: How can we be experiencing global warming if there's no actual "global warming"?

3   There is no scientific consensus that global warming is occurring and caused by man: Questions are not decided by "consensus." In fact, many scientific theories that were once widely believed to be true were made irrelevant by new evidence.

---

hinging: that something is based on or dependent on

unverifiable: not able to determine the truth of

skeptical: showing doubt

assertion: a positive statement, often without support

upswing: a marked increase or improvement

consensus: general agreement

mainstream: the dominant tendency

talking point: a fact that supports only one side

tipping point: the point at which a minor development becomes a major crisis

troposphere: the lowest layer of the atmosphere

hasty: moving or acting quickly

Predict   What reasons can you think of that may support the foregoing argument?

Teaching tip   Before starting these readings, make sure the students understand what *global warming* is and why it is an important topic. You can do this by assigning a basic Web site with information to each group within the class and ask them to report back to the whole what they have learned. As a class, discuss what the implications of global warming, whether it's happening or not, may have on the students personally. If the students cannot connect with the material, they often cannot think critically about it.

Reflect   What have you noticed about our climate? Is it becoming warmer or colder? Does that affect you?

Just to name one of many, many examples, in the early seventies, scientists believed global cooling was occurring. However, once the planet started to warm up, they changed their minds. Yet, the primary "scientific" argument for global warming is that there is a "scientific consensus" that it's occurring. Setting aside the fact that's not a scientific argument, even if that ever was true (and it really wasn't), it's certainly not true anymore. Over 31,000 scientists have signed on to a petition saying humans aren't causing global warming. More than 1000 scientists signed on to another report saying there is no global warming at all. There are tens of thousands of well-educated, mainstream scientists who do not agree that global warming is occurring at all, and people who share their opinion are taking a position grounded in science.

Identify What significance does the amount of Arctic ice have on the planet?

4   Arctic ice is up 50% since 2012: The loss of Arctic ice has been a big talking point for people who believe global warming is occurring. Some people have even predicted that all of the Arctic ice would melt by now because of global warming. Yet, Arctic ice is up 50% since 2012. How much Arctic ice really matters is an open question since the very limited evidence we have suggests that a few decades ago, there was less ice than there is today, but the same people who thought the drop in ice was noteworthy should at least agree that the increase is important as well.

5   Climate models showing global warming have been wrong over and over: These future projections of what global warming will do to the planet have been based on climate models. Essentially, scientists make assumptions about how much of an impact different factors will have; they guess how much of a change there will be and then they project changes over time. Unfortunately, almost all of these models showing huge temperature gains have turned out to be wrong.

Reflect How credible are the sources that the author is using? What makes you say that?

6   Former NASA scientist Dr. Roy Spencer says that climate models used by government agencies to create policies "have failed miserably." Spencer analyzed 90 climate models against surface temperature and satellite temperature data, and found that more than 95 percent of the models "have over-forecast the warming trend since 1979, whether we use their own surface temperature dataset (HadCRUT4), or our satellite dataset of lower tropospheric temperatures (UAH)."

Identify Can you clearly summarize what the author means by "garbage in, garbage out?" Do you agree with his statement?

7   There's an old saying in programming that goes, "Garbage in, garbage out." In other words, if the assumptions and data you put into the models are faulty, then the results will be worthless. If the climate models that show a dire impact because of global warming aren't reliable—and they're not—then the long-term projections they make are meaningless.

8   Predictions about the impact of global warming have already been proven wrong: The debate over global warming has been going on long enough that we've had time to see whether some of the predictions people made about it have panned out in the real world. For example, Al Gore predicted all the Arctic ice would be gone by 2013. In 2005, the *Independent* ran an article saying that the Arctic had entered a death spiral.

Teaching tip Although Gore's *An Inconvenient Truth* is now dated, many of the arguments seem to be coming true. Show clips to the class and ask them whether they think the world is changing in that way or whether he may have been inaccurate in his predictions.

9   Scientists fear that the Arctic has now entered an irreversible phase of warming which will accelerate the loss of the polar sea ice that has helped to keep the climate stable for thousands of years. . . . The greatest fear is that the Arctic has reached a "tipping point" beyond which nothing can reverse the continual loss of sea ice and with it the massive land glaciers of Greenland, which will raise sea levels dramatically. Of course, the highway is still there.

10   Meanwhile, Arctic ice is up 50% since 2012. James Hansen of NASA fame predicted that the West Side Highway in New York would be under water by now because of global warming.

11   If the climate models and the predictions about global warming aren't even close to being correct, wouldn't it be more scientific to reject hasty action based on faulty data so that we can further study the issue and find out what's really going on?

Tip For reading advice, see Chapter 1.

1. Double-underline the **thesis statement**.

2. In your own words, what is the main idea of this article? *To demonstrate that global warming is not being caused by humans and is not happening.*

3. Briefly summarize the article, making sure to include all main ideas. *Answers will vary.*

4. Does the author consider counterarguments? What are they? *Yes; Answers will vary.*

Respond to one of the following assignments in a paragraph or essay.

1. According to the author, what are the definitions of *global warming* and *global cooling*? What evidence does the author provide to support his claims that either one is or is not happening currently? Is enough evidence provided to support those claims?

2. In paragraph 9, Hawkins writes about Arctic ice and the claim that global warming and climate change has created an inevitable tipping point for our planet. Do you agree or disagree with this claim? Explain your answer.

Professional Argument Essay 2: Climate Change Is Happening

Environmental Protection Agency

Climate Change Is Happening

The U.S. Environmental Protection Agency (EPA) was formed in 1970 in response to concern about pollution and how it might be affecting the country. By creating this government agency, federal research, monitoring, standard-setting, and enforcement activities connected to pollution and the environment have been consolidated to "work for a cleaner, healthier environment for the American People."

The following article was posted on the EPA's Web site under the heading "Climate Change: Basic Information" on March 18, 2014.

Vocabulary development Underline these words as you read: *potentially, climate, carbon dioxide, deforestation,* and *adapted.*

Guiding question According to the EPA, how is climate change affecting humans?

1   Our Earth is warming. Earth's average temperature has risen by 1.4°F over the past century, and is projected to rise another 2 to 11.5°F over the next hundred years. Small changes in the average temperature of the planet can translate to large and potentially dangerous shifts in climate and weather.

2   The evidence is clear. Rising global temperatures have been accompanied by changes in weather and climate. Many places have seen changes in rainfall, resulting in more floods, droughts, or intense rain, as well as more frequent and severe heat waves. The planet's oceans and glaciers have also experienced some big changes— oceans are warming and becoming more acidic, ice caps are melting, and sea levels are rising. As these and other changes become more pronounced in the coming decades, they will likely present challenges to our society and our environment.

3   Humans are largely responsible for recent climate change. Over the past century, human activities have released large amounts of carbon dioxide and other greenhouse gases into the atmosphere. The majority of greenhouse gases come from burning fossil fuels to produce energy, although deforestation, industrial processes, and some agricultural practices also emit gases into the atmosphere.

4   Greenhouse gases act like a blanket around Earth, trapping energy in the atmosphere and causing it to warm. This phenomenon is called the greenhouse effect and is natural and necessary to support life on Earth. However, the buildup of greenhouse gases can change Earth's climate and result in dangerous effects to human health and welfare and to ecosystems.

5   The choices we make today will affect the amount of greenhouse gases we put in the atmosphere in the near future and for years to come.

Climate Change Affects Everyone

6   Our lives are connected to the climate. Human societies have adapted to the relatively stable climate we have enjoyed since the last ice age, which ended several thousand years ago. A warming climate will bring changes that can affect our water supplies, agriculture, power and transportation systems, the natural environment, and even our own health and safety.

7   Some changes to the climate are unavoidable. Carbon dioxide can stay in the atmosphere for nearly a century, so Earth will continue to warm in the coming

decades. The warmer it gets, the greater the risk for more severe changes to the climate and Earth's system. Although it's difficult to predict the exact impacts of climate change, what's clear is that the climate we are accustomed to is no longer a reliable guide for what to expect in the future.

8   We can reduce the risks we will face from climate change. By making choices that reduce greenhouse gas pollution, and preparing for the changes that are already underway, we can reduce risks from climate change. Our decisions today will shape the world our children and grandchildren will live in.

Summarize Write a brief summary about what you read.

Tip For reading advice, see Chapter 1.

1. Double-underline the **thesis statement**.

2. What is the main idea of this article? _Climate change can occur even with very small changes over the years._

3. What counterarguments do you see in this article? _Answers will vary._

4. How does the EPA think humans have affected climate change? _Answers will vary._

Respond to one of the following assignments in a paragraph or essay.

1. What do humans do that cause climate change? Do you think we would alter our behavior to save the planet? Explain your answer.

2. In paragraph 2, the EPA notes extreme weather patterns that could be connected to global warming. Do you agree with this connection or not? Explain your answer.

Write Your Own Argument

In this section, you will write your own argument based on one of the following assignments. For help, refer to the How to Write Argument checklist on page 310.

> **ASSIGNMENT OPTIONS**   **Writing about college, work, and everyday life**

Write an argument paragraph or essay on one of the following topics or on one of your own choice.

College   •   Take a position on a controversial issue on your campus. If you need help coming up with topics, you might consult the campus newspaper.   →

Teaching tip Organize debates on some of these topics. Poll the class on the issues, divide students into groups to develop arguments, and suggest using the library to gather evidence. Devote a class period to the debates and a discussion of the effectiveness of the arguments.

- Argue for or against the use of standardized tests or placement tests. Make sure to research different positions on the tests to support your argument and address opposing views. Many schools use placement tests for incoming students to determine what courses they are prepared to take. If your school has one, think about what it tested and how it affected your schedule or the courses you have to take. One Web site you might consult is standardizedtests.procon.org.

- Within the past few years, the media have started to discuss student loans and how they often cause a college student to enter the workforce deeply in debt. Does it cost too much to attend college? Is there a way, other than student loans, for a potential student to be able to afford a college education? Take one clear position on the issue and support that position with evidence.

Work

- Argue for a change in company policy such as a new chain of command, clearer job descriptions, or more transparency in the hiring process.

- Argue for something that you would like to get at work, such as a promotion, a raise, or a flexible schedule. Explain why you deserve what you are asking for, and give specific examples.

- Argue for an improvement in your workplace, such as the addition of a bike rack, new chairs in the break room, or a place to swap books or magazines. Make sure your request is reasonable in cost and will be beneficial to a significant number of employees.

Everyday life

- Take a position on a controversial issue in your community.
- Choose a community organization that you belong to, and write about why it is important. Try to persuade your readers to join.
- Oscar Wilde (1854–1900), a famous Irish writer, once commented, "Most people are other people. Their thoughts are someone else's opinions, their lives a mimicry,[1] their passions a quotation." Write an argument that supports or opposes Wilde's views, giving reasons and examples for your position.

1. **mimicry:** an imitation of something else

ASSIGNMENT OPTIONS   **Reading and writing critically**

Complete one of the following assignments, which ask you to apply the critical thinking, reading, and writing skills discussed in Chapter 1.

WRITING CRITICALLY ABOUT READINGS

The article from *The Daily Vidette* titled "ISU Restroom Change Shows Commitment to Diversity" (p. 227) and John Tierney's essay, "Yes, Money Can Buy Happiness" (p. 257) both take a strong position on an issue. That position can be expressed either implicitly (it requires you to use clues in the paper to determine the position) or explicitly (it is clearly identified). Read or review these pieces, and then follow these steps:

1. **Summarize** Briefly summarize the two works, listing major examples and details.

2. **Analyze** What features of argument do you see in each essay?

3. **Synthesize** Using examples from one or both of the two essays and from your own experience, describe the features that make an argument successful and convincing. Think of features beyond those in the Four Basics of Good Argument.

4. **Evaluate** In your opinion, are strongly focused arguments or subtler arguments more effective? Or do both types of writing have a place? Explain your answer.

Tip For a reminder of how to summarize, analyze, synthesize, and evaluate, see the Reading and Writing Critically box on page 21.

Teaching tip If time is short, students might complete just one or two steps of this assignment.

WRITING ABOUT IMAGES

The following image illustrates the concept of climate change as it affects animals, not just humans.

SMETEK/GETTY IMAGES

Study the photograph, and complete the following steps.

1. **Read the image** Ask yourself: What details are you drawn to, and why? What emotions or reactions does the melting glacier or stranded animals bring about in you? (For more information on reading images, see Chapter 1.)

2. **Write an argument** Write a paragraph or essay in which you respond to this image and discuss the argument you think it is making. How effective do you find the visual argument? Is it a good way to convey the effects of climate change? Why or why not? Include the details and reactions from step 1.

WRITING TO SOLVE A PROBLEM

Read or review the discussion of problem solving in Chapter 1 (pp. 28–30). Then, consider the following problem.

Your friend/child/relative has just turned sixteen and is planning to drop out of high school. He has always done poorly, and if he drops out, he can increase his hours at the restaurant where he works. You think that this idea is terrible for many reasons.

(Continued on page 311.)

CHECKLIST

How to Write Argument

Steps	Details
☐ Narrow and explore your topic. See Chapter 3.	• Make the topic more specific. • Prewrite to get ideas about the narrowed topic.
☐ Write a topic sentence (paragraph) or thesis statement (essay). See Chapter 3.	• State your position on your topic.
☐ Support your point. See Chapter 4.	• Come up with reasons and evidence to back up your position.
☐ Write a draft. See Chapter 5.	• Make a plan that puts the reasons in a logical order. • Include a topic sentence (paragraph) or thesis statement (essay) and all the reasons and supporting evidence.
☐ Revise your draft. See Chapter 5.	• Make sure it has *all* the Four Basics of Good Argument. • Make sure you include transitions to move readers smoothly from one reason to the next.
☐ Edit your revised draft. See Parts 3 through 6.	• Correct errors in grammar, spelling, word use, and punctuation.

Assignment In a group or on your own, come up with various reasons in support of your decision. Consider, too, your friend's/child's/relative's possible objections to your argument, and account for them. Then, write an argument paragraph or essay to persuade him to complete high school. Give at least three solid reasons, and support your reasons with good evidence or examples. You might start with the following sentence:

There are so many important reasons to stay in school and get your high school diploma.

Chapter Review

1. Argument is writing *that takes a position on an issue and gives evidence to* *support it.*

2. What are the Four Basics of Good Argument?
    It takes a strong and definite position.
    It gives good reasons and supporting evidence to defend the position.
    It considers opposing views.
    It has enthusiasm and energy from start to finish.

3. The topic sentence (paragraph) or thesis statement (essay) in an argument should include what two elements? *an issue and the writer's position on that issue*

4. What three types of information make good evidence? *facts, examples, expert* *opinions*

5. Why do you need to be aware of opposing views? *to anticipate attacks that may* *damage the strength of your argument*

6. Write sentences using the following vocabulary words: *hinging, unverifiable, skeptical, assertion, upswing, consensus, mainstream, talking point, tipping point, hasty, potentially, climate, deforestation,* and *adapted.* *Answers will vary.*

REFLECTING ON THE JOURNEY

Skills Learned

Now that you've completed the chapter, share what you've learned about each skill by completing the following chart.

Skill	What I learned about this skill
Identify an argument	
Identify strong points, evidence, and support for an argument	
Consider opposing views	
Read and analyze argument	

Part 3

The Four Most Serious Errors

"I write directions, instructions, captions for photographs, and descriptions of my art."

—Ali K., student

15

The Basic Sentence

The Four Most Serious Errors

This part of the book focuses first on the four grammar errors that people most often notice.

LaunchPadSolo
Visit **LaunchPad Solo for Readers and Writers > Grammar > Parts of Speech and Basic Sentences** for more tutorials, videos, and practice with crafting paragraphs.

The Four Most Serious Errors

1. Fragments (Chapter 16)

2. Run-ons (Chapter 17)

3. Problems with subject-verb agreement (Chapter 18)

4. Problems with verb form and tense (Chapter 19)

If you can edit your writing to correct these four errors, your grades will improve.

This chapter reviews the basic sentence elements you will need to understand to find and fix the four most serious errors.

GRAMMAR & MECHANICS ROADMAP

An Overview

This Chapter Identifies the Following Trouble Spots

- The four most important grammar errors to find and fix
- The basic elements of a sentence
- Essential grammar terms, including the parts of speech
- Prepositional phrases
- Different types of verbs
- Complete thoughts

Tools to Address the Trouble Spots

- List of the Four Most Serious Errors (p. 315)
- The Seven Basic Parts of Speech (p. 316)
- The Basic Sentence (p. 317)
- List of Common Linking Verbs (p. 320)
- List of Common Helping Verbs (p. 320)
- Complete Thoughts (p. 322)
- Six Basic English Sentence Patterns (p. 322)

The Parts of Speech

There are seven basic parts of speech:

1. **Noun:** names a person, place, thing, or idea (for information on making nouns plural, see p. 490). A **noun phrase** is a group of words that includes a noun, or a word that functions as a noun, and any surrounding article and modifiers.

   <u>Jaime</u> <u>dances</u>.

Tip In the examples in this chapter, subjects are underlined once, and verbs are underlined twice.

Tip For a definition of *subject,* see page 317.

2. **Pronoun:** replaces a noun in a sentence. *He, she, it, we,* and *they* are pronouns.

   <u>She</u> <u>dances</u>.

3. **Verb:** tells what action the subject does or links a subject to another word that describes it.

   <u>Jaime</u> **dances**.   [The verb *dances* is what the subject, Jaime, does.]

   <u>She</u> **is** a dancer.
   [The verb *is* links the subject, Jaime, to a word that describes her, *dancer.*]

4. **Adjective:** describes a noun or a pronoun (can also be a participle, a verb that functions as a noun).

   <u>Jaime</u> <u>is</u> **thin**.   [The adjective *thin* describes the noun *Jaime.*]

   <u>She</u> <u>is</u> **graceful**.   [The adjective *graceful* describes the pronoun *She.*]

Tip Some grammar experts consider **interjections** to be a part of speech. Interjections are words or phrases that are often used to convey emotion—for example, "Ouch!", "Oh no!", and "Good grief!"

5. **Adverb:** describes an adjective, a verb, or another adverb. Adverbs often end in *-ly*.

   <u>Jaime</u> <u>is</u> **extremely** graceful.   [The adverb *extremely* describes the adjective *graceful.*]

   <u>She</u> <u>practices</u> **often**.   [The adverb *often* describes the verb *practices.*]

   <u>Jaime</u> <u>dances</u> **quite** beautifully.

   [The adverb *quite* describes another adverb, *beautifully.*]

6. **Preposition:** connects a noun, pronoun, or verb with information about it. *Across, around, at, in, of, on,* and *out* are prepositions (there are many others).

   <u>Jaime</u> <u>practices</u> **at** the studio.

   [The preposition *at* connects the verb *practices* with the noun *studio.*]

7. **Conjunction:** connects words to each other. An easy way to remember the seven common conjunctions is to connect them in your mind to **FANBOYS:** *for, and, nor, but, or, yet, so.*

The studio is expensive **but** good.

Tip For more on coordinating conjunctions, see pages 409–11. For more on subordinating conjunctions (dependent words), see page 413.

The Basic Sentence

A **sentence** is the basic unit of written communication. A complete sentence in written standard English must have these three elements:

- A **subject**
- A **verb**
- A **complete thought**

Teaching tip Make a list of your top ten grammar pet peeves and give it to your students to use.

Subjects

The **subject** of a sentence is the person, place, thing, or idea that a sentence is about. The subject of a sentence can be a noun or a pronoun. For a list of common pronouns, see page 382.

To find the subject, ask yourself, **Whom or what is the sentence about?**

Person as subject	Isaac arrived last night.
	[**Whom** is the sentence about? *Isaac*]
Thing as subject	The restaurant has closed.
	[**What** is the sentence about? The *restaurant*]

A **compound subject** consists of two or more subjects joined by *and, or,* or *nor.*

Teaching tip Have students look back at a recent paper and underline the subjects of sentences in a few paragraphs.

| Two subjects | Kelli and Kate love animals of all kinds. |
| Several subjects | The baby, the cats, and the dog play well together. |

The subject of a sentence is *never* in a **prepositional phrase**, a word group that begins with a preposition and ends with a noun or pronoun, called the **object of a preposition**.

Preposition
Subject │ Object of preposition
Your dinner is in the oven.
Prepositional phrase

Preposition	Object	Prepositional phrase
from	the bakery	from the bakery
to	the next corner	to the next corner
under	the table	under the table

Language note: *In* and *on* can be tricky prepositions for people whose native language is not English. Keep these definitions and examples in mind:

in = inside of (in the box, in the office) or at a certain time (in January, in the fall, in three weeks)

on = on top of (on the table, on my foot), located in a certain place (on the page, on Main Street), or at a certain time (on January 31)

If you have trouble deciding which prepositions to use, see Chapter 26.

Tip For common prepositional phrases, see Chapter 26.

See if you can identify the subject of the following sentence:

One of my best friends races cars.

Although you might think that the word *friends* is the subject, it isn't. *One* is the subject. The word *friends* cannot be the subject because it is in the prepositional phrase *of my best friends*. When you are looking for the subject of a sentence, cross out the prepositional phrase.

Prepositional Phrase Crossed Out

<u>One</u> ~~of the students~~ <u>won</u> the science prize.

The <u>rules</u> ~~about the dress code~~ <u>are</u> very specific.

 Language note: The example sentences use the word *the* before the noun (*the rules, the dress code*). *The, a,* and *an* are called *articles*. If you have trouble deciding which article to use with which nouns, see Chapter 26.

PRACTICE 1 Identifying subjects and prepositional phrases

In each of the following sentences, cross out any prepositional phrases, and underline the subject of the sentence.

Example: <u>Coupons</u> ~~from newspapers and Web sites~~ are just one way to save money.

1. A <u>friend</u> ~~from my neighborhood~~ packs her lunch every day.

2. <u>Sandwiches</u> ~~in her workplace cafeteria~~ cost five dollars.

3. <u>Restaurants</u> ~~near her job~~ charge even more.

4. Therefore, <u>sandwiches</u> ~~from her own kitchen~~ are saving my friend twenty-five dollars or more each week.

5. <u>Savings</u> ~~in gasoline expenses~~ are also possible.

6. <u>Everything</u> ~~in the trunk of a car~~ increases the car's weight and gasoline usage.

7. Recently, a ~~hiker~~ <u>down the street</u> cleaned out his trunk.

8. The <u>amount</u> ~~of old hiking gear in the trunk~~ was surprisingly large.

9. The <u>result</u> ~~of his cleanup~~ was greatly reduced gasoline expenses.

10. <u>Savings</u> ~~during just one week~~ reached thirty dollars.

Verbs

Every sentence has a **main verb**, the word or words that tell what the subject does or that link the subject to another word that describes it. There are three kinds of verbs: action verbs, linking verbs, and helping verbs.

ACTION VERBS

An **action verb** tells what action the subject performs.

To find the main action verb in a sentence, ask yourself: **What action does the subject perform?**

Action verbs	The <u>band</u> <u>played</u> all night.
	The <u>alarm</u> <u>rings</u> loudly.

LINKING VERBS

A **linking verb** connects (links) the subject to another word (or group of words) that describes the subject. Linking verbs show no action. The most common linking verb is *be* (*am, is, are,* and so on). Other linking verbs, such as *seem* and *become,* can usually be replaced by a form of the verb *be,* and the sentence will still make sense.

To find linking verbs, ask yourself: **What word joins the subject and the words that describe the subject?**

Linking verbs	The <u>bus</u> <u>is</u> late.
	My new <u>shoes</u> <u>look</u> shiny. (My new <u>shoes</u> <u>are</u> shiny.)
	The <u>milk</u> <u>tastes</u> sour. (The <u>milk</u> <u>is</u> sour.)

Some words can be used as either action verbs or linking verbs, depending on how the verb is used in a particular sentence.

Action verb	<u>Justine</u> <u>smelled</u> the flowers.
Linking verb	The <u>flowers</u> <u>smelled</u> wonderful.

Tip Verbs do not always immediately follow the subject: Other words may come between the subject and the verb. **Example:** The <u>boy</u> who came in first <u>won</u> a <u>prize</u>.

Teaching tip Have a verb contest. Call out a subject, and ask students to write as many action verbs as possible to go with it. Suggest that they work through the alphabet.

Common Linking Verbs

Forms of *be*	Forms of *seem* and *become*	Forms of sense verbs
am	seem, seems, seemed	look, looks, looked
are	become, becomes, became	appear, appears, appeared
is		smell, smells, smelled
was		taste, tastes, tasted
were		feel, feels, felt

Language note: The verb *be* cannot be left out of sentences in English.

Incorrect	<u>Tonya</u> well now.
Correct	<u>Tonya</u> **is** well now.

HELPING VERBS

A **helping verb** joins the main verb in a sentence to form the **complete verb (also known as a verb phrase—the main verb and all of its helping verbs)**. The helping verb is often a form of the verb *be, have,* or *do.* A sentence may have more than one helping verb along with the main verb.

Helping verb + Main verb = Complete verb

<u>Sharon</u> <u>was listening</u> to the radio as <u>she</u> <u>was studying</u> for the test.
[The helping verb is *was*; the complete verbs are *was listening* and *was studying*.]

<u>I</u> <u>am saving</u> my money for a car.

<u>Colleen</u> <u>might have borrowed</u> my sweater.

<u>You</u> <u>must pass</u> this course before taking the next one.

<u>You</u> <u>should stop</u> smoking.

Common Helping Verbs

Forms of *be*	Forms of *have*	Forms of *do*	Other
am	have	do	can
are	has	does	could
been	had	did	may
being			might
is			must
was			should
were			will
			would

Before you begin Practice 2, look at these examples to see how action, linking, and helping verbs are different.

Action verb	<u>Kara</u> <u><u>graduated</u></u> last year.
	[The verb *graduated* is an action that Kara performed.]
Linking verbs	<u>Kara</u> <u>=</u>is a graduate.
	[The verb *is* links Kara to the word that describes her: *graduate*. No action is performed.]
Helping verb	<u>Kara</u> <u><u>is graduating</u></u> next spring.
	[The helping verb *is* joins the main verb *graduating* to make the complete verb *is graduating*, which tells what action the subject is taking.]

> **PRACTICE 2**   **Identifying the verb (action, linking, or helping verb + main verb)**

In the following sentences, underline each subject and double-underline each verb. Then, identify each verb as an action verb, a linking verb, or a helping verb + a main verb.

                 Helping verb + main verb
Example: <u>Bowling</u> <u><u>was created</u></u> a long time ago.

                  Action verb
1. The ancient <u>Egyptians</u> <u><u>invented</u></u> bowling.

              Linking verb
2. Dutch <u>settlers</u> <u><u>were</u></u> responsible for bowling's introduction to North America.

         Action verb
3. <u>They</u> <u><u>bowled</u></u> outdoors on fields of grass.

                  Helping verb + main verb
4. One <u>area</u> in New York City <u><u>is called</u></u> Bowling Green because the <u>Dutch</u>
  Action verb
<u><u>bowled</u></u> there in the 1600s.

                          Action verb
5. The first indoor bowling <u>alley</u> in the United States <u><u>opened</u></u> in 1840 in New York.

             Linking verb
6. Indoor <u>bowling</u> soon <u><u>became</u></u> popular across the country.

                    Action verb
7. The largest bowling <u>alley</u> in the United States <u><u>offers</u></u> more than a hundred lanes.

            Helping verb + main verb
8. <u>Visitors</u> to Las Vegas <u><u>can bowl</u></u> there.

          Helping verb + main verb
9. Most <u>people</u> <u><u>would</u></u> not <u><u>think</u></u> of bowling as more popular than basketball.

              Action verb
10. However, more <u>Americans</u> <u><u>participate</u></u> in bowling than in any other sport.

Complete Thoughts

A **complete thought** is an idea, expressed in a sentence that makes sense by itself, without additional words. An incomplete thought leaves readers wondering what's going on.

Incomplete thought	because my alarm did not go off
Complete thought	I <u>was</u> late because my alarm did not go off.
Incomplete thought	the people who won the lottery
Complete thought	The <u>people</u> who won the lottery <u>were</u> old.

To determine whether a thought is complete, ask yourself: **Do I have to ask a question to understand?**

Incomplete thought	in my wallet
	[You would have to ask a question to understand, so it is not a complete thought.]
Complete thought	My <u>ticket</u> <u>is</u> in my wallet.

Six Basic English Sentence Patterns

In English, there are six basic sentence patterns, some of which you have just worked through in this chapter. Although there are other patterns, they build on these six.

1. **Subject-Verb (S-V).** This pattern is the most basic one, as you have already seen.

   S   V
   <u>Babies</u> <u>cry</u>.

2. **Subject-Linking Verb-Noun (S-LV-N)**

   S   LV   N
   <u>They</u> <u>are</u> children.

3. **Subject-Linking Verb-Adjective (S-LV-ADJ)**

   S   LV   ADJ
   <u>Parents</u> <u>are</u> tired.

4. **Subject-Verb-Adverb (S-V-ADV)**

   S   V   ADV
   <u>They</u> <u>sleep</u> poorly.

5. **Subject-Verb-Direct Object (S-V-DO).** A *direct object* directly receives the action of the verb.

   S   V   DO
   <u>Teachers</u> <u>give</u> tests.   [The *tests* are given.]

6. **Subject-Verb-Direct Object-Indirect Object.** An *indirect object* does not directly receive the action of the verb.

      S   V   DO   IO
<u>Teachers</u> <u>give</u> tests to students.   [The *tests* are given; the *students* are not.]

This pattern can also have the indirect object before the direct object.

      S   V   IO   DO
<u>Teachers</u> <u>give</u> students tests.

> **PRACTICE 3**   Identifying basic sentence patterns
>
> Using the sentence pattern indicated, write a sentence for each of the following items.
>
> 1. (Subject-verb-direct object) _____
>   _____
>
> 2. (Subject-linking verb-noun) _____
>   _____
>
> 3. (Subject-verb-adverb) _____
>   _____
>
> 4. (Subject-verb-direct object-indirect object) _____
>   _____
>
> 5. (Subject-verb-indirect object-direct object) _____
>   _____

> **PRACTICE 4**   Identifying complete sentences

In this essay, underline the subject of each sentence, and double-underline the verb. Correct five incomplete thoughts. *Answers may vary. Possible edits are shown.*

(1) Space <u>travel</u> <u>fascinates</u> my grandpa Bill. (2) <u>He</u> <u>watches</u> every space movie at least a dozen times. (3) Before 1996, <u>he</u> never even <u>thought</u> about the moon, Mars, or beyond. (4) <u>He</u> <u>was</u> too old to be an astronaut. (5) Now, however, <u>he</u> <u>is</u> on board a satellite. (6) <u>It</u> <u>analyzes</u> particles in the atmosphere. (7) <u>He</u> <u>has</u> the company of millions of other people̸ *and* (8) A̶n̶d̶ me, too. (9) Truthfully, only our <u>names</u> <u>travel</u> to Mars or beyond. (10) <u>We</u> <u>are</u> happy with that.

(11) In 1996, the Planetary Society flew the names of members into
space. (12) ~~Using~~ *using* the Mars *Pathfinder*. (13) At first, individuals signed a paper.
(14) Then, Planetary Society members put the signatures into electronic form.
(15) Now, people submit names on the Internet. (16) ~~By~~ *by* filling out a form.
(17) The names go on a microchip. (18) One spacecraft to the moon had more
than a million names on board. (19) Some people have placed their names on
a spacecraft going past Pluto and out of our solar system. (20) Their names are
on a CD. (21) ~~Which~~ *which* could survive for billions of years.

(22) Grandpa and I feel good about our journey into space. (23) In a
way, we will travel to places only dreamed about. (24) After signing up, we
received colorful certificates to print out. (25) ~~To~~ *to* tell about our mission. (26) My
certificate hangs on my wall. (27) My grandpa and I travel proudly into space.

Chapter Review

1. List the seven parts of speech. *nouns, pronouns, verbs, adjectives, adverbs, prepositions, and conjunctions*

2. A sentence must have three things: *a subject, a verb, and a complete thought.*

3. A *subject* is the person, place, or thing that a sentence is about.

4. A prepositional phrase is *a word group that begins with a preposition and ends with a noun or pronoun.*

5. Write an example of a prepositional phrase (not from one of the examples presented earlier): *Answers will vary.*

6. An action verb tells *what action the subject performs.*

7. A linking verb *connects the subject to another word or group of words that describes the subject.*

8. A helping verb *joins the main verb in a sentence to form the complete verb.*

16

Fragments
Incomplete Sentences

Understand What Fragments Are

A **fragment** is a group of words that is missing one or more parts of a complete sentence: a subject, a verb, or a complete thought.

Sentence	I was hungry, so I ate some cold pizza and drank a soda.
Fragment	I was hungry, so I ate some cold pizza. *And drank a soda.*
	[*And drank a soda* contains a verb (*drank*) but no subject.]

Language note: Remember that any idea that ends with a period needs a subject and verb to be complete. As a quick review, a subject is the person, place, or thing that a sentence is about. A verb tells what the subject does, links the subject to another word that describes it, or "helps" another verb form a complete verb.

LaunchPadSolo

Visit **LaunchPad Solo for Readers and Writers > Grammar > Basic Sentences** for more tutorials, videos, and practice with crafting paragraphs.

GRAMMAR & MECHANICS ROADMAP

An Overview

This Chapter Identifies the Following Trouble Spots

- Fragments that start with a preposition
- Fragments that start with a dependent word
- Fragments that start with -*ing* words
- Fragments that start with *to* and a verb
- Fragments that are examples or explanations

Tools to Address the Trouble Spots

- Understand What Fragments Are (p. 325)
- List of Common Dependent Words (p. 328)
- Edit for Fragments exercises (p. 333)
- Finding and Fixing Fragments flowchart (p. 336)
- Chapter Review (p. 337)

In the Real World, Why Is It Important to Correct Fragments?

People outside the English classroom notice fragments and consider them major mistakes.

Teaching tip Students should underline the fragments for Practice 1 and correct them for Practice 10 (on p. 336).

Situation: Justina is interested in starting a blog to establish an online presence and attract potential employers. Here is part of an e-mail that Justina sent to a popular blogger:

I am getting in touch with you about starting a blog on dress design/ ^bBecause I have heard about the success you have had with your fashion blog. For a long time, I have designed and sewn many dresses for myself and my friends, and I have a good sense of style. On my blog, I would like to share sewing tips and patterns based on my dress designs/ ^wWhich should appeal to many readers. I would like to ask your opinion about many things/ ^eEspecially about how to write clear, interesting blog posts. I have to admit that my dream would be for my blog to catch the eye of a major fashion house looking for talent/ ^tTo come up with new looks for its dress line. Could we set up a time to talk in person?

> **YOUR TURN**
>
> What are your thoughts about Justina's e-mail?
>
> Does Justina present herself professionally in her e-mail?
>
> How could grammar and spelling mistakes in an e-mail potentially affect Justina's future as a blogger?
>
> What can Justina do to improve her e-mail?

Teaching tip Have your students read aloud and discuss Justina's e-mail in class, using Your Turn questions as guidance for the discussion. Ask students if they read blogs, and if so, what they like about that style of writing. What draws them in and makes them want to read that particular blog?

Find and Correct Fragments

To find fragments in your own writing, look for the five trouble spots in this chapter. They often signal fragments.

When you find a fragment in your own writing, you can usually correct it in one of two ways.

Teaching tip Consider having students use different-colored highlighters to indicate subjects and verbs.

Basic Ways to Correct a Fragment

- Add what is missing (a subject, a verb, or both).
- Attach the fragment to the sentence before or after it.

PRACTICE 1   Finding fragments

Find and underline the four fragments in Justina's e-mail.

1. Fragments That Start with Prepositions

Whenever a preposition starts what you think is a sentence, check for a subject, a verb, and a complete thought. If the group of words is missing any of these three elements, it is a fragment.

Tip Remember that the subject of a sentence is *never* in a prepositional phrase (see p. 317).

Fragment	<u>I</u> <u><u>pounded</u></u> as hard as I could. *Against the door.*
	[*Against the door* lacks both a subject and a verb.]

Tip In the examples in this chapter, subjects are underlined once, and verbs are underlined twice.

Correct a fragment that starts with a preposition by connecting it to the sentence either before or after it. If you connect such a fragment to the sentence after it, put a comma after the fragment to join it to the next sentence.

Common Prepositions

about	before	for	on	until
above	behind	from	out	up
across	below	in	outside	upon
after	beneath	inside	over	with
against	beside	into	past	within
along	between	like	since	without
among	by	near	through	
around	down	next to	to	
at	during	of	toward	
because of	except	off	under	

2. Fragments That Start with Dependent Words

A **dependent word** (also called a **subordinating conjunction**) is the first word in a dependent clause (a clause is a group of words that has a subject and a verb).

Sentence with a dependent word	<u>We</u> <u><u>arrived</u></u> late *because* <u>the bus</u> <u><u>was delayed</u></u>.
	[*Because* is a dependent word introducing the dependent clause *because the bus was delayed.*]

A dependent clause cannot be a sentence because it does not express a complete thought, even though it has a subject and a verb. Whenever a dependent word starts what you think is a sentence, stop to check for a subject, a verb, and a complete thought.

Teaching tip Ask students to jot down what they think the word *dependent* means in the real world and to give an example. After getting some responses, ask how *dependent* in *dependent clause* is similar to *dependent* in the real world.

Fragment	*Since I moved.* <u>I</u> <u><u>have eaten</u></u> out every day.
	[*Since I moved* has a subject (*I*) and a verb (*moved*), but it does not express a complete thought.]
Corrected	Since I moved, <u>I</u> <u><u>have</u></u> eaten out every day.

Common Dependent Words

after	if/if only	until
although	now that	what (whatever)
as/as if/as though	once	when (whenever)
as long as/as soon as	since	where (wherever)
because	so that	whether
before	that	which
even if/even though	though	while
how	unless	who/whose

When a word group starts with *who, whose,* or *which,* it is not a complete sentence unless it is a question.

Fragment   That woman is the police officer. *Who gave me a ticket last week.*

Question   *Who* gave you a ticket last week?

Fragment   He is the goalie. *Whose team is so bad.*

Question   *Whose* team are you on?

Fragment   Sherlene went to the HiHo Club. *Which serves alcohol.*

Question   *Which* club serves alcohol?

Correct a fragment that starts with a dependent word by connecting it to the sentence before or after it. If the dependent clause is joined to the sentence after it, put a comma after the dependent clause.

Tip For more on commas with dependent clauses, see Chapters 23 and 30.

PRACTICE 2   **Correcting fragments that start with prepositions or dependent words**

In the following items, circle any prepositions or dependent words that start a word group. Then, correct each fragment by connecting it to the sentence before or after it. *Answers may vary. Possible edits are shown.*

Example: **The fire at the Triangle Waist Company in New York City marked a turning point, In U.S. labor history.**

1. Before the fire occurred, on March 25, 1911, Labor activists had raised complaints against the company, a maker of women's blouses.

2. The activists demanded shorter hours and better wages, For the company's overworked and underpaid sewing-machine operators.

3. The owners refused these requests, however, ~~however/~~ **Because** they placed profits over their employees' welfare.

4. **When** activists demanded better safety measures, such as sprinkler systems, ~~systems/~~ The owners again refused to do anything.

5. **On** the day of the fire, ~~fire/~~ A scrap bin on the eighth floor of the blouse factory ignited by accident.

6. **Although** workers threw buckets of water on the flames, ~~flames/~~ Their efforts could not keep the fire from spreading to other floors.

7. **Without** access to safe or unlocked exits, ~~exits/~~ Many workers died in the smoke and flames or jumped to their deaths.

8. One hundred and forty-six workers had lost their lives, ~~lives/~~ By the end of this tragic day.

9. **After** news of the tragedy spread, ~~spread/~~ The public reacted with outrage and greater demands for better working conditions.

10. **Within** a few years of the fire, ~~fire/~~ Legislatures in New York and other states passed laws to improve workplace safety and worker rights.

PRACTICE 3 **Correcting fragments that start with prepositions or dependent words**

Read the following paragraph, and circle the ten fragments that start with prepositions or dependent words. Then, correct the fragments. *Answers may vary. Possible edits are shown.*

Staying focused at an office job can be difficult, ~~difficult/~~ Because of these jobs' many distractions. **After making just a few changes,** Workers will find that they are less distracted and more productive. A good first step is to clear away clutter, such as old files, ~~files/~~ From their desktop screen. **Once that screen is cleared,** It is helpful to make a list of the most important tasks for the day. It is best for workers to do brain-demanding tasks when they are at their best, ~~best/~~ Which is often the start of the day. Workers can take on simpler tasks, like filing, ~~filing/~~ When they are feeling less energetic. **While they are doing something especially challenging,** Workers might want to disconnect themselves from the Internet and turn off their personal cell phones. **Although it is tempting to look at social media sites and answer e-mails and phone calls immediately,** They are among the worst workplace distractions. Since social media is particularly distracting/ ^i *I*t is important to avoid it while at work/ ^b ~~B~~ecause it is not an appopriate work activity. Some people set a special electronic folder/ ^f |For personal e-mails.| They check this folder only while they are on break or between tasks. Finally, it is important for workers to remember the importance of breaks/ ^w, |Which recharge the mind and improve its focus.|

3. *Fragments That Start with* -ing *Verb Forms*

An **-*ing* verb form** (also called a **gerund**) is the form of a verb that ends in *-ing*: *walking, writing, running.* Sometimes, an *-ing* verb form is used at the beginning of a complete sentence.

> **Sentence** Walking is good exercise.
>
> [The *-ing* verb form *walking* is the subject; *is* is the verb. The sentence expresses a complete thought.]

Sometimes, an *-ing* verb form introduces a fragment. When an *-ing* verb form starts what you think is a sentence, stop and check for a subject, a verb, and a complete thought.

> **Fragment** I ran as fast as I could. *Hoping to get there on time.*
>
> [*Hoping to get there on time* lacks a subject, and it does not express a complete thought.]

Correct a fragment that starts with an *-ing* verb form either by adding whatever sentence elements are missing (usually a subject and a helping verb) or by connecting the fragment to the sentence before or after it. Usually, you will need to put a comma before or after the fragment to join it to the complete sentence.

> **PRACTICE 4** **Correcting fragments that start with *-ing* verb forms**
>
> Circle any *-ing* verb that appears at the beginning of a word group in the paragraph. Then, read the word group to see if it has a subject and a verb and expresses a complete thought. Not *all* the word groups that start with an *-ing* verb are fragments, so read carefully. In the space provided, record the numbers of the word groups that are fragments. Then, correct each fragment either by adding the missing sentence elements or by connecting it to the sentence before or after it. *Answers will vary. Possible edits are shown.*
>
> Which word groups are fragments? ___4, 7, 9, 11___
>
> (1) People sometimes travel long distances in unusual ways trying to set new world records. (2) |Walking| is one unusual way to set records. (3) In 1931, Plennie Wingo set out on an ambitious journey/ (4) ^w |Walking| backward

around the world. (5) Wearing sunglasses with rearview mirrors, he started his trip early one morning. (6) After eight thousand miles, Wingo's journey was interrupted by a war in Pakistan, (7) Ending his ambitious journey. (8) Hans Mullikan spent more than two years in the late 1970s traveling to the White House by crawling from Texas to Washington, D.C. (9) Taking time out to earn money as a logger and a Baptist minister. (10) Alvin Straight, suffering from poor eyesight, traveled across the Midwest on a lawn mower, (11) Looking for his long-lost brother.

4. Fragments That Start with to and a Verb

When what you think is a sentence begins with *to* and a verb (called the *infinitive* form of the verb), you need to make sure it is not a fragment.

Fragment	Each day, I check freecycle.org. *To see if it has anything I need.*
Corrected	Each day, I check freecycle.org to see if it has anything I need.

If a word group begins with *to* and a verb, it must have another verb; if not, it is not a complete sentence. When you see a word group that begins with *to* and a verb, first check to see if there is another verb. If there is no other verb, the word group is a fragment.

Sentence	*To run* a complete marathon was my goal.
	[*To run* is the subject; *was* is the verb.]
Fragment	Cheri got underneath the car. *To change the oil.*
	[No other verb appears in the word group that begins with *to change*.]

Language note: Do not confuse the infinitive (*to* before the verb) with *that*.

Incorrect	My brother wants *that* his girlfriend cook.
Correct	My brother wants his girlfriend *to cook*.

To correct a fragment that starts with *to* and a verb, join it to the sentence before or after it, or add the missing sentence elements.

> **PRACTICE 5** **Correcting fragments that start with *to* and a verb**
>
> Circle any *to*-plus-verb combination that appears at the beginning of a sentence in the paragraph. Then, read the word group to see if it has a subject and a verb and expresses a complete thought. Not *all* the word groups that start with *to* and a verb are fragments, so read carefully. In the space provided, record the numbers of the word groups that are fragments. Then, correct each

fragment either by adding the missing sentence elements or by connecting it to the sentence before or after it. *Answers may vary. Possible edits are shown.*

Which word groups are fragments? ___3, 7, 9, 10___

(1) For people older than twenty-five, each hour spent watching TV lowers life expectancy by nearly twenty-two minutes. (2) This finding is the result of Australian researchers' efforts / (3) To investigate the health effects of TV viewing. (4) To put it another way, watching an hour of television is about the same as smoking two cigarettes. (5) The problem is that most people are inactive while watching TV. (6) They are not doing anything, like walking or playing sports / (7) To strengthen their heart and maintain a healthy weight. (8) Fortunately, it is possible / (9) To counteract some of TV's negative health effects. (10) To increase their life expectancy by three years / (11) People need to exercise just fifteen minutes a day. (12) To accomplish this goal, they might exchange a ride in an elevator for a climb up the stairs. (13) Or they might walk around the block during a lunch break at work.

5. *Fragments That Are Examples or Explanations*

As you edit your writing, pay special attention to groups of words that are examples or explanations of information you presented in the previous sentence. They may be fragments.

Fragment	More and more <u>people</u> <u>are reporting</u> food allergies. *For example, allergies to nuts or milk.*
Fragment	My <u>body</u> <u>reacts</u> to wheat-containing foods. *Such as bread or pasta.* [*For example, allergies to nuts or milk* and *Such as bread or pasta* are not complete thoughts.]

This last type of fragment is harder to recognize because there is no single word or kind of word to look for. The following words may signal a fragment, but fragments that are examples or explanations do not always start with these words.

especially	for example	like	such as

When a group of words gives an example or explanation connected to the previous sentence, stop to check it for a subject, a verb, and a complete thought.

Tip *Such as* and *like* do not often begin complete sentences.

Fragment	<u>I</u> <u>have found</u> great things at freecycle.org. *Like a nearly new computer.*
Fragment	<u>Freecycle.org</u> <u>is</u> a good site. *Especially for household items.*
Fragment	<u>It</u> <u>lists</u> many gently used appliances. *Such as DVD players.* [*Like a nearly new computer*, *Especially for household items*, and *Such as DVD players* are not complete thoughts.]

Correct a fragment that starts with an example or explanation by connecting it to the sentence before or after it. Sometimes, you can add whatever sentence elements are missing (a subject, a verb, or both) instead. When you connect the fragment to a sentence, you may need to change some punctuation. For example, fragments that are examples are often set off by a comma.

PRACTICE 6   **Correcting fragments that are examples or explanations**

Circle word groups that are examples or explanations. Then, read the word group to see if it has a subject and verb and expresses a complete thought. In the space provided, record the numbers of the word groups that are fragments. Then, correct each fragment either by adding the missing sentence elements or by connecting it to the sentence before or after it. *Answers may vary. Possible edits are shown.*

Which word groups are fragments? __2, 4, 6, 8, 10__

(1) Being a smart consumer can be difficult. (2) Especially when making a major purchase. (3) At car dealerships, for example, important information is often in small type. (4) Like finance charges or preparation charges. (5) Advertisements also put negative information in small type. (6) Such as a drug's side effects. (7) Credit-card offers often use tiny, hard-to-read print for the terms of the card. (8) Like interest charges and late fees, which can really add up. (9) Phone service charges can also be hidden in small print. (10) Like limits on text messaging and other functions. (11) Especially now, as businesses try to make it seem as if you are getting a good deal, it is important to read any offer carefully.

Edit for Fragments

Use the chart on page 336, Finding and Fixing Fragments, to help you complete the practices in this section and edit your own writing.

PRACTICE 7   **Correcting various fragments**

In the following items, circle each word group that is a fragment. Then, correct fragments by connecting them to the previous or next sentence or by adding the missing sentence elements. *Answers will vary. Possible edits are shown.*

Example: With the high cost of producing video games, Game
                                                    , game
publishers are turning to a new source of revenue.

1. To add to their income, ~~Publishers~~ *publishers* are placing advertisements in their games.

Teaching tip Divide the class into small groups, and have each group present a corrected paragraph. Compare the different ways the groups correct the fragments.

2. Sometimes, the ads show a character using a product. [For example,
   a character might be shown
   drinking a specific brand of soda to earn health points.]

3. One character, a race-car driver, drove his ad-covered car/ [~~Across~~ the
   across
   finish line.]

4. [When a warrior character picked up a sword decorated with an athletic-
   , some
   shoe logo/] ~~Some~~ players complained.

5. [Worrying that ads are distracting/] ~~Some~~ publishers are trying to limit the
   , some
   number of ads per game.

6. But most players do not seem to mind seeing ads in video games/ [~~If~~ there
   if
   are not too many of them.]

7. These players are used to seeing ads in all kinds of places/ [~~Like~~ grocery
   like
   carts and restroom walls.]

8. [For video game publishers/] ~~The~~ goal is making a profit, but most
   , the
   publishers also care about the product.

9. [To strike a balance between profitable advertising and high game quality/]
   ~~That~~ is what publishers want.

10. [Doing market research/] ~~Will~~ help publishers find that balance.
    will

PRACTICE 8   **Editing paragraphs for fragments**

Find and correct the ten fragments in the following paragraphs.

1. Ida Lewis was born on February 25, 1842, in Newport, Rhode Island.
   Her father, Hosea, had been a coast pilot but was transferred to the
   Lighthouse Service. Although he was in failing health/ *i*n 1853, he was
   appointed lighthouse keeper at Lime Rock in Newport. Many lighthouse
   keepers were forced to leave family behind when they assumed their
   duties/ *b*ecause the lighthouses were in remote locations and the living
   situations were poor. At first, Lime Rock had only a shed/ *f*or the keeper
   and a temporary lantern for light. Appropriate housing was constructed in
   1857, and Hosea moved his family to Lime Rock.

2. Hosea was completely disabled by a stroke/ *i*n only a few months. Ida,
   who was already caring for an ill sister, took care of her father and the
   lighthouse as well/ *k*eeping the lighthouse lamp lit. At sunset, the lamp

had to be filled with oil and refilled at midnight. The reflectors needed

constant polishing, and the light had to be extinguished in the morning.

Since schools were on the mainland, Ida rowed her brothers and sisters

to school every day, ~~S~~trengthening her rowing ability, which ultimately

saved many lives. In 1872, Hosea died, and Ida's mother was appointed

keeper, ~~E~~ven though Ida did all the work. Finally, in 1879, Ida became the

keeper and received a salary of $500 a year.

3. She was the best-known lighthouse keeper because of her many rescues.

Some called her "The Bravest Woman in America," ~~Saving~~ *for saving* eighteen lives

during her time of service. In 1867, during a storm, sheepherders had

gone into the water after a lost sheep. Ida saved both the sheep and the

sheepherders. She became famous, and many important people came to

see her, ~~F~~or example, President Ulysses S. Grant. All the ships anchored in

the harbor tolled their bells, ~~T~~o honor her after her death. Later, the Rhode

Island legislature changed the name of Lime Rock to Ida Lewis Rock, the

first and only time this honor was awarded.

PRACTICE 9   Editing fragments and using formal English

Your friend wants to send this thank-you note to an employer who interviewed her for a job. She knows that the note has problems and has asked for your help. Correct the fragments in the note. Then, edit the informal English in it. *Answers will vary. Possible edits are shown.*

Tip For more advice on using formal English, see Chapter 26. For advice on choosing appropriate words, see Chapter 27.

Dear Ms. Hernandez,

(1) Thank you so much for taking the time, (2) ~~T~~o meet with me this past Wednesday. (3) I am more ~~psyched~~ *excited* than ever about the administrative assistant position at Fields Corporation. (4) Learning more about the ~~stuff I would need to do. Was very cool.~~ *challenges and requirements of the job was valuable to me.* (5) Also, I enjoyed meeting you and the other managers. (6) With my strong organizational skills, professional experience, and friendly personality, (7) I'm sure that I would be ~~awesome for the job.~~ *an asset to the company.* (8) Because ~~I'm totally jazzed about the position.~~ *of my strong interest in the position,* (9) I hope you will keep me in mind. (10) Please let me know if you need any other ~~info.~~ *information, such as*

(11) ~~Like~~ references or a writing sample. (12) ~~Thank U much,~~ *Thanks again for your time.*

Sincerely,

Terri Hammons

PRACTICE 10   **Editing Justina's e-mail**

Look back at Justina's e-mail on page 326. You may have already underlined the fragments in her e-mail; if not, do so now. Next, using what you have learned in this chapter, correct each fragment in the e-mail.

PRACTICE 11   **Editing your own writing for fragments**

Edit fragments in a piece of your own writing—a paper for this course or another one, or something you have written for work or your everyday life. Use the chart below to help you.

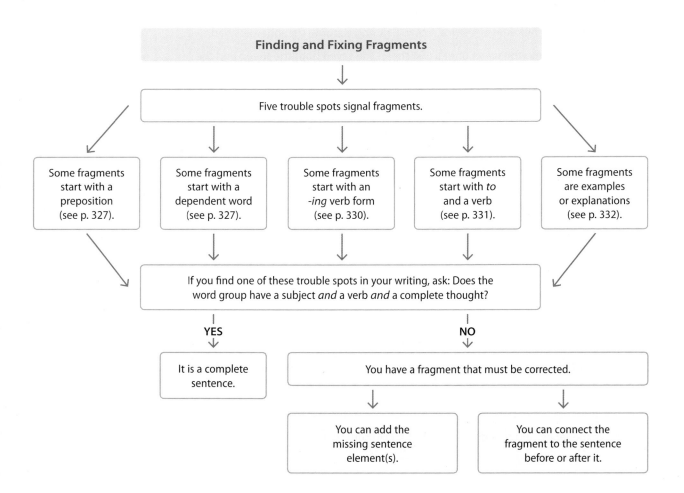

Finding and Fixing Fragments

Five trouble spots signal fragments.

Some fragments start with a preposition (see p. 327).	Some fragments start with a dependent word (see p. 327).	Some fragments start with an *-ing* verb form (see p. 330).	Some fragments start with *to* and a verb (see p. 331).	Some fragments are examples or explanations (see p. 332).

If you find one of these trouble spots in your writing, ask: Does the word group have a subject *and* a verb *and* a complete thought?

YES

It is a complete sentence.

NO

You have a fragment that must be corrected.

You can add the missing sentence element(s).

You can connect the fragment to the sentence before or after it.

Chapter Review

1. A *sentence* is a group of words that has three elements: a ___subject___ , a ___verb___ , and a ___completed thought___ .

2. A ___fragment___ seems to be a complete sentence but is only a piece of one. It lacks a ___subject___ , a ___verb___ , or a ___completed thought___ .

3. What are the five trouble spots that signal possible fragments?

   A word group that starts with a preposition

   A word group that starts with a dependent word

   A word group that starts with an -ing verb form

   A word group that starts with to and a verb

   A word group that is an example or explanation

4. What are the two basic ways to correct fragments?

   Add what is missing (a subject, a verb, or both).

   Attach the fragment to the sentence before or after it.

17

Run-Ons

Two Sentences Joined Incorrectly

 **LaunchPad**Solo

Visit **LaunchPad Solo for Readers and Writers > Grammar > Basic Sentences** for more tutorials, videos, and practice with crafting paragraphs.

Understand What Run-Ons Are

A sentence is also called an independent clause, a group of words with a subject and a verb that expresses a complete thought. Sometimes, two independent clauses can be joined to form one larger sentence.

Sentence with two independent clauses

Independent clause   Independent clause

The college offers financial aid, and it encourages students to apply.

GRAMMAR & MECHANICS ROADMAP

An Overview

This Chapter Identifies the Following Trouble Spots

- Run-ons
- Fused sentences
- Comma splices

Tools to Address Trouble Spots

- Joining two independent clauses with a period (p. 341)
- Joining two independent clauses with a semicolon (p. 341)
- Joining two independent clauses with a comma and a coordinating conjunction (p. 343)
- Joining two sentences with a dependent word (p. 344)
- Edit for Run-Ons exercises (p. 347)
- Finding and Fixing Run-Ons flowchart (p. 351)

A **run-on** is two complete sentences (independent clauses) joined incorrectly as one sentence. There are two kinds of run-ons: **fused sentences** and **comma splices**.

A **fused sentence** is two complete sentences joined without a coordinating conjunction (*for, and, nor, but, or, yet, so*) or any punctuation.

No punctuation

Independent clause | Independent clause

Fused sentence   Exercise is important it has many benefits.

A **comma splice** is two complete sentences joined by only a comma.

Comma

Independent clause | Independent clause

Comma splice   My mother jogs every morning, she runs three miles.

When you join two sentences, use the proper punctuation.

Corrections   Exercise is important; it has many benefits.

My mother jogs every morning; she runs 3 miles.

Tip To find and correct run-ons, you need to be able to identify a complete sentence. For a review, see Chapter 15.

Tip In the examples throughout this chapter, subjects are underlined once, and verbs are underlined twice.

In the Real World, Why Is It Important to Correct Run-Ons?

People outside the English classroom notice run-ons and consider them major mistakes.

Situation: Naomi is applying to a special program for returning students at Cambridge College. Here is one of the essay questions on the application, followed by a paragraph from Naomi's answer.

Statement of Purpose: In two hundred words or less, describe your intellectual and professional goals and how a Cambridge College education will assist you in achieving them.

For many years, I did not take control of my life. I just drifted without any goals. I realized one day as I met with my daughter's guidance counselor that I hoped my daughter would not turn out like me. From that moment, I decided to do something to help myself and others. I set a goal of becoming a teacher. To begin on that path, I took a math course at night school, *and* then I took another in science. I passed both courses. With hard work, I know I can do well in the Cambridge College program. I am committed to the professional goal I finally found. It has given new purpose to my whole life.

Teaching tip Students should underline the run-ons for Practice 1, page 340, and correct them for Practice 6, page 348.

> **YOUR TURN**
>
> What are your thoughts about Naomi's essay?
>
> If you were a college official looking at applications, how would you perceive Naomi as a potential student? Why?
>
> What kind of error is Naomi making most often? How does it affect the text (in other words, can you still easily read and comprehend what she wants to say? Is it harder to understand certain ideas or thoughts?)?
>
> How would you correct Naomi's essay?

Find and Correct Run-Ons

To find run-ons, focus on each sentence in your writing, one at a time, looking for fused sentences and comma splices. Pay special attention to sentences longer than two lines. By spending this extra time, your writing will improve.

> **PRACTICE 1**   **Finding run-ons**
>
> Find and underline the four run-ons in Naomi's writing on page 339.

Once you have found a run-on, there are five ways to correct it.

Five Ways to Correct Run-Ons

1. **Add a period.**

   I saw the man. *He* he did not see me.

2. **Add a semicolon.**

   I saw the man; he did not see me.

3. **Add a semicolon, a conjunctive adverb, and a comma.**

   I saw the man; *however,* he did not see me.

4. **Add a comma and a coordinating conjunction.**

   I saw the man, *but* he did not see me.

5. **Add a dependent word.**

   When I saw the man, he did not see me.

Add a Period

You can correct run-ons by adding a period to make two separate sentences. After adding the period, capitalize the letter that begins the new sentence. Reread your two sentences to make sure they each contain a subject, a verb, and a complete thought.

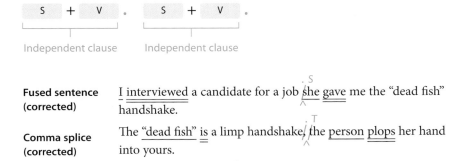

Fused sentence (corrected)	I interviewed a candidate for a job she gave me the "dead fish" handshake.
Comma splice (corrected)	The "dead fish" is a limp handshake, the person plops her hand into yours.

Add a Semicolon

A second way to correct run-ons is to use a semicolon (;) to join the two sentences. Use a semicolon only when the two sentences express closely related ideas and the words on each side of the semicolon can stand alone as a complete sentence. Do not capitalize the word that follows a semicolon unless it is the name of a specific person, place, or thing that is usually capitalized—for example, Mary, New York, or the Eiffel Tower.

Teaching tip Remind students that a semicolon balances two independent clauses. What is on either side of it must be able to stand alone as a complete sentence.

Fused sentence (corrected)	Slouching creates a terrible impression it makes a person seem uninterested, bored, or lacking in self-confidence.
Comma splice (corrected)	It is important in an interview to hold your head up, it is just as important to sit up straight.

Add a Semicolon, a Conjunctive Adverb, and a Comma

A third way to correct run-ons is to add a semicolon followed by a **conjunctive adverb** and a comma.

Common Conjunctive Adverbs

consequently	indeed	moreover	still
finally	instead	nevertheless	then
furthermore	likewise	otherwise	therefore
however	meanwhile	similarly	

Conjunctive adverb

Semicolon | Comma

I stopped by the market; however, it was closed.

Conjunctive adverb

Semicolon | Comma

Sharon is a neighbor; moreover, she is my friend.

PRACTICE 2 **Correcting run-ons by adding a period or a semicolon**

For each of the following items, indicate in the space to the left whether it is a fused sentence ("FS") or a comma splice ("CS"). Then, correct the error by adding a period or a semicolon. Capitalize the letters as necessary to make two sentences. *Answers will vary. Possible answers are shown.*

Example: __FS__ **Being a farmer can mean dealing with all types of**

;

challenges one of the biggest ones comes from the sky.

^

1. __CS__ Farmers have been trying to keep hungry birds out of their crops for

;

centuries/ the first scarecrow was invented for this reason.

^

. Other

2. __CS__ Some farmers have used a variety of chemicals/ ~~other~~ farmers have

^

tried noise, such as small cannons.

. They

3. __FS__ Recently, a group of berry farmers tried something new ~~they~~

^

brought in bigger birds called falcons.

;

4. __FS__ Small birds such as starlings love munching on berries each year

^

they destroy thousands of dollars' worth of farmers' berry crops.

5. __FS__ Because these starlings are frightened of falcons, they fly away

. They

when they see these birds of prey in the fields ~~they~~ need to get to where

^

they feel safe.

. It

6. __CS__ Using falcons to protect their crops saves farmers money/ ~~it~~ does not

^

damage the environment either.

7. __FS__ A falconer, or a person who raises and trains falcons, keeps an eye

. He

on the birds during the day ~~he~~ makes sure they only chase away the

^

starlings instead of killing them.

. They

8. __CS__ Falcons are used for protection in other places as well/ ~~they~~ are used

^

in vineyards to keep pests from eating the grapes.

9. _FS_ In recent years, the falcons have also been used in landfills to
scatter birds and other wildlife <del>some</del> ^{. Some} have even been used at large
airports to keep flocks of birds out of the flight path of landing
airplanes.

10. _FS_ Although a falconer's services are not cheap, they cost less than
some other methods that farmers have tried <del>for</del> ^{. For} example, putting nets
over a berry field can often cost more than $200,000.

Add a Comma and a Coordinating Conjunction

A fourth way to correct run-ons is to add a comma and a **coordinating conjunction**: a link that joins independent clauses to form one sentence. The seven coordinating conjunctions are *and, but, for, nor, or, so,* and *yet*. Some people remember these words by thinking of **FANBOYS**: *for, and, nor, but, or, yet, so.*

To correct a fused sentence this way, add a comma and a coordinating conjunction. A comma splice already has a comma, so just add a coordinating conjunction that makes sense in the sentence.

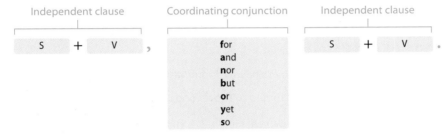

Tip Notice that the comma does not follow the conjunction. The comma follows the word before the conjunction.

Fused sentence (corrected) Nakeisha was qualified for the job ^{, but} she hurt her chances by mumbling.

Comma splice (corrected) The candidate smiled, ^{and} she waved to the crowd.

Coordinating conjunctions need to connect two independent clauses. They are not used to join a dependent and an independent clause.

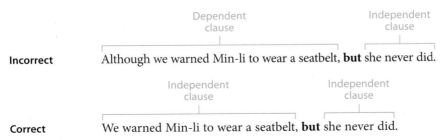

Incorrect Although we warned Min-li to wear a seatbelt, **but** she never did.

Correct We warned Min-li to wear a seatbelt, **but** she never did.

PRACTICE 3   Correcting run-ons by adding a comma and/or a coordinating conjunction

Correct each of the following run-ons by adding a comma, if necessary, and an appropriate coordinating conjunction. First, underline the subjects, and double-underline the verbs. *Answers will vary. Possible edits are shown.*

Example: Most **Americans do not like** the idea of eating certain kinds
and
of food, most **of us would** probably **reject** horse meat.

1. In most cultures, popular foods depend on availability and tradition *, so* people
tend to eat old familiar favorites.

2. Sushi shocked many Americans thirty years ago, *but* today some young
people in the United States have grown up eating raw fish.

3. In many societies, certain foods are allowed to age *, for* this process adds
flavor.

4. Icelanders bury eggs in the ground to rot for months, *and* these aged eggs are
considered a special treat.

5. As an American, you might not like such eggs *, or* the thought of eating them
might even revolt you.

6. In general, aged foods have a strong taste, *so* the flavor is unpleasant to
someone unaccustomed to those foods.

7. Many Koreans love to eat kimchee, a spicy aged cabbage, *but* Americans
often find the taste odd and the smell overpowering.

8. Herders in Kyrgyzstan drink kumiss *, and* this beverage is made of aged horse's
milk.

9. Americans on a visit to Kyrgyzstan consider themselves brave for
but
tasting kumiss, local children drink it regularly.
yet
10. We think of familiar foods as normal, favorite American foods might
horrify people in other parts of the world.

Add a Dependent Word

A fifth way to correct run-ons is to make one of the complete sentences a dependent clause by adding a dependent word (a **subordinating conjunction** or a **relative pronoun**), such as *after, because, before, even though, if, that, though, unless, when,* *who,* and *which*. (For a more complete list of these words, see the graphic below.) Choose the dependent word that best expresses the relationship between the two clauses.

Turn an independent clause into a dependent one when it is less important than the other clause or explains it, as in the following sentence:

> *When* I get *to the train station,* I will call *Josh.*

The italicized clause is dependent (subordinate) because it just explains when the most important part of the sentence—calling Josh—will happen. It begins with the dependent word *when*.

Because a dependent clause is not a complete sentence (it has a subject and verb but does not express a complete thought), it can be joined to a sentence without creating a run-on. When the dependent clause is the second clause in a sentence, you usually do not need to put a comma before it unless it is showing contrast.

Two sentences

Halloween was originally a religious holiday. People worshipped the saints.

Dependent clause: no comma needed

Halloween was originally a religious holiday *when people worshipped the saints.*

Dependent clause showing contrast: comma needed

Many holidays have religious origins, *although some celebrations have moved away from their religious roots.*

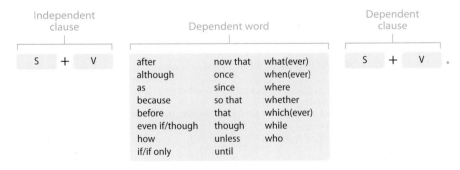

Independent clause	Dependent word			Dependent clause
S + V	after	now that	what(ever)	S + V .
	although	once	when(ever)	
	as	since	where	
	because	so that	whether	
	before	that	which(ever)	
	even if/though	though	while	
	how	unless	who	
	if/if only	until		

Fused sentence (corrected)

Your final statement should express your interest in the
, *although*
position you do not want to sound desperate.
[The dependent clause *although you do not want to sound desperate* shows contrast, so a comma comes before it.]

Comma splice (corrected)

because
It is important to end an interview on a positive note, that final impression is what the interviewer will remember.

You can also put the dependent clause first. When the dependent clause comes first, be sure to put a comma after it.

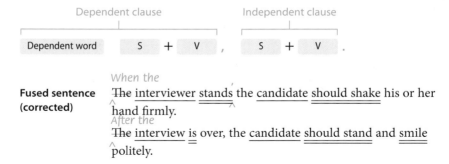

Fused sentence (corrected)

When the
~~The~~ interviewer stands the candidate should shake his or her hand firmly.

After the
~~The~~ interview is over, the candidate should stand and smile politely.

PRACTICE 4   **Correcting run-ons by adding a dependent word**

Correct run-ons by adding a dependent word to make a dependent clause. First, underline the subjects, and double-underline the verbs. Although these run-ons can be corrected in different ways, in this exercise, correct by adding dependent words. You may want to refer to the graphic on page 345. *Answers will vary. Possible edits are shown.*

Example:
When many
Many soldiers returned from Iraq and Afghanistan missing arms or legs, demand for better artificial limbs increased.

1. *Before computer*
   ~~Computer~~ chips were widely used artificial limbs remained largely unchanged for decades.

2. *Because computer*
   ~~Computer~~ chips now control many artificial limbs, these limbs have more capabilities than those of the past.

3. The i-LIMB artificial hand picks up electrical signals from nearby arm
   so that
   muscles the amputee can move individual fingers of the hand.

4. *Before lighter-weight*
   ~~Lighter-weight~~ materials were introduced artificial limbs were not as easy to move as they are today.

5. Now, the C-Leg artificial leg is popular it is lightweight, flexible, and
   because
   technically advanced.

6. *If a*
   ~~A~~ C-Leg user wants to jog, bike, or drive instead of walk he or she can program the leg for the necessary speed and motion.

7. *Though major*
   ~~Major~~ advances have been made in artificial limbs, researchers believe the technology has not reached its full potential.

8. Many will not be satisfied *until* the human brain directly controls the motion of artificial limbs.

9. ~~A~~ *Now that a* thought-controlled artificial arm is being tested on patients, that time may not be far off.

10. ~~The~~ *If the* artificial arm passes those tests it may be introduced to the market within the next few years.

A Word That Can Cause Run-Ons: Then

Many run-ons are caused by the word *then*. You can use *then* to join two sentences, but if you add it without the correct punctuation or added words, your sentence will be a run-on. Often, writers use just a comma before *then*, but that makes a comma splice.

Comma splice   I picked up my laundry, then I went home.

Some of the methods you have just practiced can be used to correct errors caused by *then*. These methods are shown in the following examples.

I picked up my laundry. *Then* I went home.

I picked up my laundry; then I went home.

I picked up my laundry, *and* then I went home.

I picked up my laundry *before* ~~then~~ I went home.
[dependent word *before* added to make a dependent clause]

Edit for Run-Ons

Use the chart on page 351, Finding and Fixing Run-Ons, to help you complete the practices in this section and edit your own writing.

> **PRACTICE 5**   **Correcting various run-ons**
>
> In the following items, correct any run-ons. Use each method of correcting such errors—adding a period; adding a semicolon; adding a semicolon, a conjunctive adverb, and a comma; adding a comma and a coordinating conjunction; or adding a dependent word—at least once. *Answers will vary. Possible edits are shown.*

Although some

Example: ~~Some~~ people doubt the existence of climate change, few can
              ∧

deny that the weather has become more extreme and dangerous.

When more

1. ~~More~~ than nine hundred tornadoes tore through the United States in
      ∧
2013, hundreds of people lost their lives.

2. That same year, parts of the Midwest experienced severe flooding droughts
                                                              , and
                                                                 ∧
in Texas cost farmers upward of 8 billion.

3. Some cities are taking steps to adapt to environmental changes / they are
                                                                    ;
                                                                    ∧
focusing on the biggest threats.

Because global

4. ~~Global~~ temperatures are rising, sea levels are also rising—a threat to
      ∧
coastal regions.

5. As a result, some coastal cities are planning to build protective walls,
    while
others are raising roadbeds.
    ∧

6. Extreme heat is another major problem / urban planners are studying
                                          ; therefore,
                                          ∧
different ways to address it.

7. New York City is painting some rooftops white / light and heat will be
                                                  so that
                                                  ∧
reflected away from the city.

8. In Chicago, landscapers are planting heat-tolerant trees / ~~these~~ trees
                                                             . These
                                                             ∧
should help cool the environment and reduce flooding during heavy rains.

9. All these efforts are encouraging most parts of the United States are
                                      , but
                                      ∧
doing little or nothing to plan for ongoing environmental changes.

10. One study reports that only fourteen states are undertaking such
                              ; meanwhile,
planning the threats of severe weather remain.
         ∧

PRACTICE 6   **Editing paragraphs for run-ons**

Find and correct the run-ons you underlined in Naomi's paragraph in
Practice 1. *More than one correct response is possible.*

PRACTICE 7   **Editing paragraphs for run-ons**

Teaching tip Have students
read the paragraphs aloud to
listen for errors.

Find and correct the six run-ons in the following paragraphs. *More than one
correct response is possible.*

(1) For the first time, monster-size squid were filmed while still in the

wild. (2) The images were caught on camera in the North Pacific Ocean / the
                                                                      ;
                                                                      ∧

site is located just off the coast of southeastern Japan. (3) A team of Japanese

scientists followed a group of sperm whales to locate the rare squids ~~the~~ *. The*

whales like to eat the eight-legged creatures. (4) Wherever the whales went,

the squids were likely to be found as well.

(5) From aboard their research ship, the team located the squids

thousands of feet under the water *. The* / ~~the~~ scientists lowered bait over the side

to attract them. (6) Next, they sent down cameras alongside the bait to catch

images of these bizarre animals as soon as they appeared.

(7) The Dana octopus squid, also known as *Taningia danae,* often grows

to the size of a human being or even larger. (8) Its eight arms are covered

in suckers, as most squid species are *; however,* / these particular types of arms end in

catlike claws. (9) Two of the arms contain special organs on the ends called

photophores. (10) These photophores produce flashing bursts of light *. They* ~~they~~ are

designed to lure and capture prey. (11) The burst of light stuns other creatures,

giving a squid a chance to capture and eat its victim. (12) When the squid isn't

hunting, it still glows. (13) Experts believe that squids remain lighted as a way

of communicating with other squids about potential dangers or as a way of

attracting mates. (14) These lights appear eerie, *but* the scientists were glad for

them, as the lights made the giant squids slightly easier to find and finally film.

PRACTICE 8   Editing run-ons and using formal English

Your brother has been overcharged for an MP3 player he ordered online, and he is
about to send this e-mail to the seller's customer-service department. Help him by
correcting the run-ons. Then, edit the informal English. *Answers will vary. Possible
edits are shown.*

> *to you because   overcharged*
> (1) I'm writing ~~2U cuz~~ I was seriously ~~ripped off~~ for the Star 3 MP3 player
> *^ You   , but*
> I ordered from your Web site last week. (2) ~~U~~ listed the price as $50 $150 was
> *If you check   ^   you ^*
> charged to my credit card. (3) ~~Check~~ out any competitors' sites, ~~U~~ will see that no
> *to pay that much money for the Star model. The*
> one expects people ~~2 cough up that much cash for the Star model, the~~ prices
> *^   Because   a large amount for this product,*
> are never higher than $65. (4) I overpaid ~~big bucks on this,~~ I want my money
> back as soon as possible.
> *Sincerely,*
> (5) ~~Seriously bummin',~~
> Chris Langley

Tip For more advice on using formal English, see Chapter 26. For advice on choosing appropriate words, see Chapter 27.

> **PRACTICE 9** **Editing your own writing for run-ons**
>
> Edit run-ons in a piece of your own writing—a paper for this course or another one, or something you have written for work or your everyday life. Use the chart on page 345 to help you.

Chapter Review

1. A sentence can also be called an ___*independent clause*___.

2. A ___*fused sentence*___ is two complete sentences joined without any punctuation.

3. A ___*comma splice*___ is two complete sentences joined by only a comma.

4. What are the five ways to correct run-ons?

   Add a period.

   Add a semicolon.

   Add a semicolon, a conjunctive adverb, and a comma.

   Add a comma and a coordinating conjunction.

   Add a dependent word.

5. What word in the middle of a sentence may signal a run-on? *then*

6. What are the seven coordinating conjunctions? *for, and, nor, but, or, yet, so*

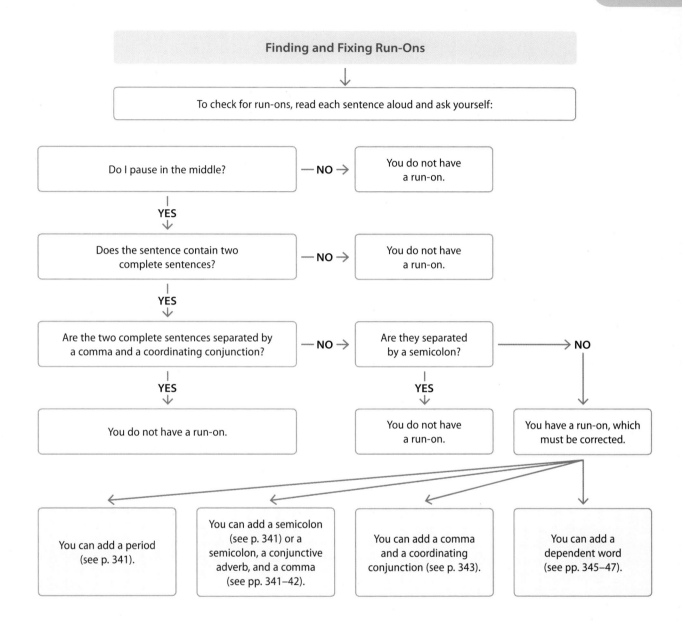

Finding and Fixing Run-Ons

↓

To check for run-ons, read each sentence aloud and ask yourself:

Do I pause in the middle?	— NO →	You do not have a run-on.

YES ↓

Does the sentence contain two complete sentences?	— NO →	You do not have a run-on.

YES ↓

Are the two complete sentences separated by a comma and a coordinating conjunction?	— NO →	Are they separated by a semicolon?	──→ NO

YES ↓ | | YES ↓ | ↓

You do not have a run-on.		You do not have a run-on.	You have a run-on, which must be corrected.

← ← ← ↓

You can add a period (see p. 341).	You can add a semicolon (see p. 341) or a semicolon, a conjunctive adverb, and a comma (see pp. 341–42).	You can add a comma and a coordinating conjunction (see p. 343).	You can add a dependent word (see pp. 345–47).

18

Problems with Subject-Verb Agreement

When Subjects and Verbs Don't Match

Visit **LaunchPad Solo for Readers and Writers > Grammar > Basic Sentences** for more tutorials, videos, and practice with crafting paragraphs.

Understand What Subject-Verb Agreement Is

In any sentence, the **subject and the verb must match—or agree**—in number. If the subject is singular (one person, place, or thing), the verb must also be singular. If the subject is plural (more than one), the verb must also be plural.

Singular	The skydiver jumps out of the airplane.
Plural	The skydivers jump out of the airplane.

GRAMMAR & MECHANICS ROADMAP

An Overview

This Chapter Identifies the Following Trouble Spots

- Agreement problems when using the verb forms *Be*, *Have*, or *Do*
- Agreement problems when using words between the subject and the verb
- Agreement problems with a compound subject
- Agreement problems when the subject is an indefinite pronoun
- Agreement problems when the verb comes before the subject

Tools to Address the Trouble Spots

- Understand What Subject-Verb Agreement Is (p. 352)
- Forms of *be* verbs (p. 354)
- Forms of *have* verbs (p. 354)
- Forms of *do* verbs (p. 354)
- List of indefinite pronouns (p. 357)
- Edit for agreement problems exercises (p. 359)
- Finding and fixing agreement problems flowchart (p. 362)

Regular Verbs, Present Tense

	Singular	**Plural**
First person	I walk.	We walk.
Second person	You walk.	You walk.
Third person	He (she, it) walks.	They walk.
	Joe walks.	Joe and Alice walk.
	The student walks.	The students walk.

no -s (bracketing the first-person and second-person singular forms)

all end in -s (bracketing the third-person singular forms)

Tip In the examples throughout this chapter, subjects are underlined, and verbs are double-underlined.

Regular verbs (with forms that follow standard English patterns) have two forms in the present tense: one that ends in *-s* and one that has no ending. The third-person subjects—*he*, *she*, *it*—and singular nouns always use the form that ends in *-s*. First-person subjects (*I*), second-person subjects (*you*), and plural subjects use the form with no ending.

In the Real World, Why Is It Important to Correct Errors in Subject-Verb Agreement?

People outside the English classroom notice subject-verb agreement errors and consider them major mistakes.

Situation: Regina Toms wrote the following brief report about a company employee whom she was sending to the employee assistance program. These programs help workers with various problems, such as alcoholism or mental illness, that may affect their job performance.

Mr. XXX, who has been a model employee of the company for five years,
has
~~have~~ recently behaved in ways that ~~is~~ *are* inappropriate. For example, last week he
was rude when a colleague asked him a question. He has been late to work several
times and has missed work more often than usual. When I spoke to him about his
has
behavior and asked if he ~~have~~ problems, he admitted that he had been drinking
understands
more than usual. I would like him to speak to someone who ~~understand~~ more
about this than I do.

Teaching tip Students should underline the errors for Practice 1 (on p. 355), and correct them for Practice 7 (on p. 361).

YOUR TURN

Did you immediately notice Regina's errors in subject-verb agreement in her report? Which ones were most obvious? Which ones did you miss?

How does a problem with subject-verb agreement affect the reader's understanding of the material?

Rewrite the report fixing all of Regina's errors.

Teaching tip Ask students to form their own impression of the student based on her writing. Create samples of reports or other classroom writing situations, even e-mails and text messages, and ask the students what impression they create after reading those messages. Reinforce the idea that writing creates an image of a person and that writing correctly is important to create the best possible image of yourself.

Find and Correct Errors in Subject-Verb Agreement

To find problems with subject-verb agreement in your own writing, look for five trouble spots that often signal these problems.

1. *The Verb Is a Form of* Be, Have, *or* Do

The verbs *be, have,* and *do* do not follow the rules for forming singular and plural forms; they are **irregular verbs**.

Forms of the Verb *Be*

Present Tense	Singular	Plural
First person	I am	we are
Second person	you are	you are
Third person	she, he, it is	they are
	the student is	the students are

Past tense		
First person	I was	we were
Second person	you were	you were
Third person	she, he, it was	they were
	the student was	the students were

Forms of the Verb *Have*, Present Tense

	Singular	Plural
First person	I have	we have
Second person	you have	you have
Third person	she, he, it has	they have
	the student has	the students have

Forms of the Verb *Do*, Present Tense

	Singular	Plural
First person	I do	we do
Second person	you do	you do
Third person	she, he, it does	they do
	the student does	the students do

These verbs cause problems for writers who in conversation use the same form in all cases: *He do the cleaning; they do the cleaning.* People also sometimes use the word *be* instead of the correct form of *be: She be on vacation.*

In college and at work, use the correct forms of the verbs *be, have,* and *do* as shown in the charts on page 354.

are
They <u>is</u> sick today.

has
Joan <u>have</u> the best jewelry.

does
Carlos <u>do</u> the laundry every Wednesday.

> **PRACTICE 1**   **Identifying problems with subject-verb agreement**
>
> Find and underline the four problems with subject-verb agreement in Regina Toms's report on page 353.

2. Words Come between the Subject and the Verb

When the subject and verb are not directly next to each other, it is more difficult to find them to make sure they agree. Most often, either a prepositional phrase or a dependent clause comes between the subject and the verb.

PREPOSITIONAL PHRASE BETWEEN THE SUBJECT AND THE VERB

A **prepositional phrase** starts with a preposition and ends with a noun or pronoun: I took my bag *of books* and threw it *across the room.*

The subject of a sentence is never in a prepositional phrase. When you are looking for the subject of a sentence, you can cross out any prepositional phrases.

A <u>volunteer</u> ~~in the Peace Corps~~ (serve/<u>serves</u>) two years.

Tip For a list of common prepositions, see page 327.

DEPENDENT CLAUSE BETWEEN THE SUBJECT AND THE VERB

A **dependent clause** has a subject and a verb, but it does not express a complete thought. When a dependent clause comes between the subject and the verb, it usually starts with the word *who, whose, whom, that,* or *which.*

The subject of a sentence is never in a dependent clause. When you are looking for the subject of a sentence, you can cross out any dependent clauses.

The <u>coins</u> ~~that I found last week~~ (<u>seem</u>/seems) valuable.

> **PRACTICE 2**   **Making subjects and verbs agree when they are separated by a dependent clause**

In each of the following sentences, cross out any dependent clauses. Then, correct any problems with subject-verb agreement. If the subject and the verb agree, write "OK" next to the sentence.

have

Example: My cousins, ~~who immigrated to this country from Ecuador,~~ has jobs in a fast-food restaurant.
                                                              ^

is

1. The restaurant ~~that hired my cousins are~~ not treating them fairly.

have ^

2. People ~~who work in the kitchen~~ has to report to work at 7:00 a.m.
                                     ^

3. The boss ~~who supervises the morning shift~~ tells the workers not to punch in until 9:00 a.m.   OK

4. The benefits ~~that full-time workers earn~~ have not been offered to my cousins.   OK

s

5. Ramón, ~~whose hand was injured slicing potatoes,~~ need to have physical therapy.
                                                       ^

6. No one ~~who works with him~~ has helped him file for worker's compensation.   OK

7. The doctors ~~who cleaned his wound and put in his stitches at the hospital~~ expects̸ him to pay for the medical treatment.

8. The managers ~~who run the restaurant~~ insists̸ that he is not eligible for medical coverage.

9. My cousins, ~~whose English is not yet perfect,~~ feels̸ unable to leave their jobs.

10. The restaurant ~~that treats them so badly~~ offers the only opportunity for them to earn a living.   OK

3. The Sentence Has a Compound Subject

A **compound subject** is two (or more) subjects joined by *and, or,* or *nor.*

Tip Whenever you see a compound subject joined by *and,* try replacing it in your mind with *they.*

And/Or Rule: If two subjects are joined by *and,* use a plural verb. If two subjects are joined by *or* (or *nor*), they are considered separate, and the verb should agree with whatever subject it is closer to.

Plural subject = Plural verb

The teacher *and* her aide grade all the exams.

Subject *or* Singular subject = Singular verb

Either the <u>teacher</u> *or* <u>her aide</u> <u>grades</u> all the exams.

Subject *or* Plural subject = Plural verb

The <u>teacher</u> *or* <u>her aides</u> <u>grade</u> all the exams.

Subject *nor* Plural subject = Plural verb

Neither the <u>teacher</u> *nor* <u>her aides</u> <u>grade</u> all the exams.

4. The Subject Is an Indefinite Pronoun

An **indefinite pronoun** replaces a general person, place, or thing or a general group of people, places, or things. Indefinite pronouns are often singular, although there are some exceptions, as shown in the following chart.

Singular	<u>Everyone</u> <u>wants</u> the semester to end.
Plural	<u>Many</u> <u>want</u> the semester to end.
Singular	<u>Either</u> of the meals <u>is</u> good.

Often, an indefinite pronoun is followed by a prepositional phrase or dependent clause. Remember that the verb of a sentence must agree with the subject of the sentence, and the subject of a sentence is *never in a prepositional phrase or dependent clause*. To choose the correct verb, cross out the prepositional phrase or dependent clause.

<u>Everyone</u> ~~in all the classes~~ (want/<u>wants</u>) the term to end.

<u>Several</u> ~~who have to take the math exam~~ (is/<u>are</u>) studying together.

Indefinite Pronouns

Always singular			May be singular or plural
another	everybody	no one	all
anybody	everyone	nothing	any
anyone	everything	one (of)	none
anything	much	somebody	some
each (of)*	neither (of)*	someone	
either (of)*	nobody	something	

*When one of these words is the subject, mentally replace it with *one*. *One* is singular and takes a singular verb.

5. *The Verb Comes before the Subject*

Teaching tip Divide the class down the middle. One side should ask questions (have students go in turns according to where they are sitting). The other side should turn the questions around (anyone can answer by raising his or her hand or calling out the answer). Keep a fairly fast pace.

In most sentences, the subject comes before the verb. Two kinds of sentences often reverse the usual subject-verb order: questions and sentences that begin with *here* or *there*. In these two types of sentences, check carefully for errors in subject-verb agreement.

QUESTIONS

In questions, the verb or part of the verb comes before the subject. To find the subject and verb, you can turn the question around as if you were going to answer it.

> Where is the bookstore?/The bookstore is . . .
>
> Are you excited?/You are excited.

 Language note: For reference charts showing how to form questions, see pages 450–51 and pages 452–55, in Chapter 26.

Note: Sometimes the verb in a sentence appears before the subject even in sentences that are not questions:

> Most inspiring of all were her speeches on freedom.

SENTENCES THAT BEGIN WITH *HERE* OR *THERE*

When a sentence begins with *here* or *there*, the subject often follows the verb. Turn the sentence around to find the subject and verb.

> Here is your key to the apartment./Your key to the apartment is here.
>
> There are four keys on the table./Four keys are on the table.

PRACTICE 3   **Correcting a sentence when the verb comes before the subject**

Correct any problem with subject-verb agreement in the following sentences. If a sentence is already correct, write "OK" next to it.

          does
Example: **What electives do the school offer?**
                        ^

        is
1. What ~~are~~ the best reason to study music?
        ^*are*
2. There ~~is~~ several good reasons.
        ^

3. There is evidence that music helps students with math. OK

4. What is your favorite musical instrument? OK
        are
5. Here ~~is~~ a guitar, a saxophone, and a piano.
        ^

are
6. There ~~is~~ very few people with natural musical ability.
   ^

do
7. What time of day ~~does~~ you usually practice?
   ^

8. There is no particular time. OK

do
9. What musician ~~does~~ you admire most?
   ^

is
10. Here ~~are~~ some information about the importance of regular practice.
    ^

Edit for Subject-Verb Agreement Problems

Use the chart on page 362, Finding and Fixing Problems with Subject-Verb Agreement, to help you complete the practices in this section and edit your own writing.

> **PRACTICE 4**   **Correcting various subject-verb agreement problems**
>
> In the following sentences, identify any verb that does not agree with its subject. Then, correct the sentence using the correct form of the verb.
>
> *wake*
> **Example: Some twenty-somethings in Washington, D.C., wakes before dawn to read the news.**
> ^

do
1. They ~~does~~ so not out of interest in current events.
   ^

require
2. Instead, their jobs in government and business ~~requires~~ them to read and
   ^
   summarize the latest information related to these jobs.

needs
3. Each of their bosses ~~need~~ this information early in the morning to be
   ^
   prepared for the day.

wants
4. For example, a politician who introduces new legislation ~~want~~ to know
   ^
   the public's reaction as soon as possible.

gives
5. Learning of new complaints about such legislation by 8 a.m. ~~give~~ the
   ^
   politician time to shape a thoughtful response for a 10 a.m. news
   conference.

are
6. What ~~is~~ the benefits of the reading-and-summarizing job?
   ^*are*

7. There ~~is~~ several, according to the young people who do such work.
   ^

go
8. Information and power ~~goes~~ together, some of them say.
   ^

9. A reputation for being in-the-know ~~help~~ ^{*helps*} them rise through the ranks at their workplaces.

10. Also, they ~~has~~ ^{*have*} a chance to build skills and connections that can lead to other jobs.

PRACTICE 5 **Editing paragraphs for subject-verb agreement**

Find and correct six problems with subject-verb agreement in the following paragraphs.

(1) You probably ~~does~~ *do* not have a mirror at your computer desk, but if you did, you might notice something about yourself you had not been aware of before. (2) As you sit there, hour after hour, your shoulders are rounded, your back is slumped, and your posture ~~are~~ *is* awful.

(3) Do not worry; you are not alone. (4) Most students spend hours in front of a computer monitor with terrible posture. (5) Then, they make things worse by getting up and heading off to school with painfully heavy backpacks on their backs. (6) Young people who carry a heavy burden ~~is~~ *are* forced to hunch forward even more to balance the weight, adding strain to already seriously fatigued muscles. (7) Everyone who studies these trends ~~are~~ *is* concerned.

(8) The study of people and their surroundings is known as *ergonomics*. (9) Improperly slouching at the computer and toting around a heavy backpack are both examples of poor ergonomics. (10) These bad habits ~~is~~ *are* two causes of chronic back pain that can interfere with school, work, and sports. (11) Everyone, according to experts, ~~need~~ *needs* to sit up straight while at the computer, take frequent breaks to get up and walk around, and carry less in his or her backpack.

PRACTICE 6 **Editing subject-verb agreement errors and using formal English**

A friend of yours has been turned down for a course because of high enrollment, even though she registered early. She knows that her e-mail to the instructor teaching the course has a few problems in it. Help her by correcting any subject-verb agreement errors. Then, edit the informal English in the e-mail. *Answers will vary. Possible answers are shown.*

(1) ~~Hey Prof~~ *Dear Professor* Connors,

(2) I am e-mailing you to make sure you ~~gets~~ *got* the e-mail I sent before about registering for your Business Writing course this semester.

Tip For more advice on using formal English, see Chapter 26. For advice on choosing appropriate words, see Chapter 27.

(3) ~~IMHO,~~ ^{*In my humble opinion,*} it is one of the best classes this college offers. (4) I ~~does~~ ^{*did*} not miss the deadline; I signed up on the first day, in fact. (5) I ~~plans~~ ^{*plan*} to graduate with a degree in business and economics, so your class is important to me. (6) Could you please check ~~yur~~ ^{*your*} class roster to see if I was somehow skipped or missed? (7) I would sure appreciate it ~~a ton, LOL.~~ [.] (8) ~~Plz~~ ^{*Please*} let me know what you ~~finds~~ ^{*find*} out. (9) If I cannot get into your class this semester, I will have to rearrange my schedule so that I can ~~takes~~ ^{*take*} it next semester instead.

(10) I look forward to taking your class and learning all about business writing. (11) ~~You rocks, prof.~~ ^{*You are great, professor.*}

(12) Sincerely,

Cameron Taylor

PRACTICE 7   **Editing Regina's report**

Look back at Regina Toms's report on page 353. You may have already underlined the subject-verb agreement errors; if not, do so now. Next, using what you have learned in this chapter, correct each error.

PRACTICE 8   **Editing your own writing for subject-verb agreement**

Edit for subject-verb agreement problems in a piece of your own writing—a paper for this course or another one, or something you have written for work or your everyday life. Use the chart on page 362 to help you.

Chapter Review

1. The __subject__ and the __verb__ in a sentence must agree (match) in terms of number. They must both be __singular__, or they must both be plural.

2. Five trouble spots can cause errors in subject-verb agreement:

   • When the verb is a form of __be__, __have__, or __do__.

   • When a __prepositional phrase__ or a __dependent clause__ comes between the subject and the verb.

   • When the sentence has a __compound__ subject joined by *and, or,* or *nor.*

   • When the subject is an __indefinite__ pronoun.

   • When the __verb__ comes __before__ the subject.

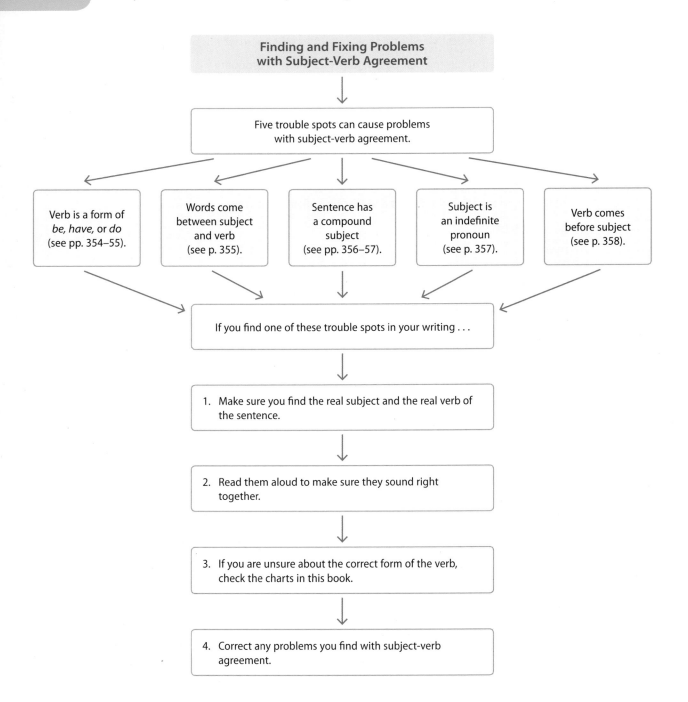

Finding and Fixing Problems with Subject-Verb Agreement

Five trouble spots can cause problems with subject-verb agreement.

Verb is a form of *be, have,* or *do* (see pp. 354–55).

Words come between subject and verb (see p. 355).

Sentence has a compound subject (see pp. 356–57).

Subject is an indefinite pronoun (see p. 357).

Verb comes before subject (see p. 358).

If you find one of these trouble spots in your writing . . .

1. Make sure you find the real subject and the real verb of the sentence.

2. Read them aloud to make sure they sound right together.

3. If you are unsure about the correct form of the verb, check the charts in this book.

4. Correct any problems you find with subject-verb agreement.

19

Verb Tense
Using Verbs to Express Different Times

Understand What Verb Tense Is

Verb tense tells *when* an action happened or will happen: in the past, in the present, or in the future. Verbs change their **base form** or use the helping verbs *have, be,* or *will* to indicate different tenses.

Present tense	Rick hikes every weekend.
Past tense	He hiked 10 miles last weekend.
Future tense	He will hike again on Saturday.

LaunchPadSolo

Visit **LaunchPad Solo for Readers and Writers > Grammar > Basic Sentences** for more tutorials, videos, and practice with crafting paragraphs.

GRAMMAR & MECHANICS ROADMAP

An Overview

This Chapter Identifies the Following Trouble Spots

- Regular verb problems with present-tense endings
- Regular verb problems with past-tense endings
- Regular verb problems with past-participle endings
- Irregular verb problems in the present tense
- Irregular verb problems in the past tense
- Irregular verb problems in the past-participle tense
- Irregular verb problems in the past-perfect tense

Tools to Address the Trouble Spots

- Understanding verb tense (p. 363)
- Present tense endings for regular verbs (p. 365)
- Past-tense endings for regular verbs (p. 366)
- Past-participle endings for regular verbs (p. 366)
- List of irregular verbs (pp. 366–69)
- Verb forms of *be* and *have* (p. 369)
- Edit for Verb Problems exercises (p. 374)
- Chapter Review (p. 376)
- Finding and fixing verb tenses flowchart (p. 377)

Language note: Remember to include needed endings on present-tense and past-tense verbs, even if they are not noticed in speech.

Present tense	Nate listen**s** to his new iPod wherever he go**es**.
Past tense	Nate listen**ed** to his iPod while he walk**ed** the dog.

In the Real World, Why Is It Important to Use the Correct Verb Tense?

People outside the English classroom notice errors in verb tense and consider them major mistakes.

Situation: Cal is a summer intern in the systems division of a large company. He would like to get a part-time job there during the school year because he is studying computer science and knows that the experience would help him get a job after graduation. He sends this e-mail to his supervisor.

I have work hard since coming to Technotron and learn many new things. Mr. Joseph tell me that he like my work and that I shown good motivation and teamwork. As he know, I ~~spended~~ many hours working on a special project for him. I would like to continue my work here beyond the summer.

Therefore, I hope that you will consider me for future employment.

Sincerely,

Cal Troppo

YOUR TURN

What are your thoughts about Cal's e-mail?

Does Cal present himself professionally in this e-mail?

How could verb errors affect Cal's potential career or how he is perceived as an applicant for a job?

What can Cal do to improve his e-mail? Rewrite it so it has no verb errors.

Practice Using Correct Verbs

This section will teach you about verb tenses and give you practice with using them. The best way to learn how to use the various verb tenses correctly, however, is to read, write, and speak them as often as possible.

Teaching tip Students should underline the verb errors in Cal's e-mail for Practice 1.

Teaching tip The *Instructor's Manual for Real Writing* contains tests and supplemental practice exercises for this chapter.

Tip To find and correct problems with verbs, you need to be able to identify subjects and verbs. For a review, see Chapter 15. Some students have a tendency to forget these basic sentence parts unless they are often reinforced; make sure to go over them again if you haven't done so recently.

> **PRACTICE 1**   **Identifying verb errors**
>
> Find and underline the seven verb errors in Cal's e-mail.

Regular Verbs

Most verbs in English are **regular verbs** that follow standard rules about what endings to use to express time.

PRESENT-TENSE ENDINGS: -*S* AND NO ENDING

The **present tense** is used for actions that are happening at the same time that they are being written about (the present) and for things that happen all the time. Present-tense, regular verbs either end in -*s* or have no ending added.

-*s* ending	No ending
jumps	jump
walks	walk
lives	live

Use the -*s* ending when the subject is *he, she, it,* or the name of one person or thing. Use no ending for all other subjects.

Regular Verbs in the Present Tense

	Singular	**Plural**
First person	I jump.	We jump.
Second person	You jump.	You jump.
Third person	She (he, it) jumps.	They jump.
	The child jumps.	The children jump.

Do not confuse the simple present tense with the **present progressive**, which is used with a form of the helping verb *be* to describe actions that are in progress right now.

Simple present	I eat a banana every day.
Present progressive	I am eating a banana.

 Language note: Some languages do not use progressive tenses. If you have trouble using progressive tenses, see Chapter 26.

Tip A complete verb, also known as a verb phrase, is made up of the main verb and all of its helping verbs.

Teaching tip A common error is using only the present tense in writing. If your students do so, ask why. A common answer is that they know the present form and are less certain about others. Point out that using the present-tense form of a verb where the past tense is correct is as serious an error as using an incorrect past form.

Tip For more about making verbs match subjects, see Chapter 18.

Tip In the examples throughout this chapter, subjects are underlined, and verbs are double-underlined.

ONE REGULAR PAST-TENSE ENDING: -ED

The **past tense** is used for actions that have already happened. An -ed ending is needed on all regular verbs in the past tense.

Tip If a verb already ends in -e, just add -d: dance/danced. If a verb ends in -y, usually the -y changes to -i when -ed is added: spy/spied; try/tried.

	Present tense	Past tense
First person	I avoid her.	I avoided her.
Second person	You help me.	You helped me.
Third person	He walks quickly.	He walked quickly.

ONE REGULAR PAST-PARTICIPLE ENDING: -ED

The **past participle** is a verb that is used with a helping verb (also called a modal auxiliary), such as *have* or *be*. For all regular verbs, the past-participle form is the same as the past-tense form: It uses an -ed ending. (To learn about when past participles are used, see pp. 371–73.)

Tip The modal auxiliary verbs are *can, could, may, might, must, shall, should, will,* and *would.*

Past tense	Past participle
My kids watched cartoons.	They have watched cartoons before.
George visited his cousins.	He has visited them every year.

Irregular Verbs

Irregular verbs do not follow the simple rules of regular verbs, which have just two present-tense endings (-s or -es) and two past-tense endings (-d or -ed). Irregular verbs show past tense with a change in spelling, although some irregular verbs, such as *cost, hit,* and *put,* do not change their spelling. The most common irregular verbs are *be* and *have* (see p. 369). As you write and edit, use the following chart to make sure you use the correct form of irregular verbs.

Note: What is called "present tense" in the chart that follows is sometimes called the "base form of the verb."

ESL tip It is helpful for students to *hear* the verb forms, particularly for irregular verbs. If you have access to a language lab, you might have them listen to verb recordings. If students can record, have them record personalized examples for one another.

Irregular Verbs

Present tense (base form of verb)	Past tense	Past participle (used with helping verb)
be (am/are/is)	was /were	been
become	became	become
begin	began	begun
bite	bit	bitten
blow	blew	blown
break	broke	broken
bring	brought	brought
build	built	built
buy	bought	bought

Teaching tip Give students a few minutes in class, or, as a homework assignment, ask them to review the list of irregular verbs and underline the fifteen verbs they use most frequently.

Present tense (base form of verb)	Past tense	Past participle (used with helping verb)
catch	caught	caught
choose	chose	chosen
come	came	come
cost	cost	cost
dive	dived, dove	dived
do	did	done
draw	drew	drawn
drink	drank	drunk
drive	drove	driven
eat	ate	eaten
fall	fell	fallen
feed	fed	fed
feel	felt	felt
fight	fought	fought
find	found	found
fly	flew	flown
forget	forgot	forgotten
get	got	gotten
give	gave	given
go	went	gone
grow	grew	grown
have/has	had	had
hear	heard	heard
hide	hid	hidden
hit	hit	hit
hold	held	held
hurt	hurt	hurt
keep	kept	kept
know	knew	known
lay	laid	laid
lead	led	led
leave	left	left
let	let	let
lie	lay	lain
light	lit	lit
lose	lost	lost
make	made	made
mean	meant	meant
meet	met	met ►

Present tense (base form of verb)	Past tense	Past participle (used with helping verb)
pay	paid	paid
put	put	put
quit	quit	quit
read	read	read
ride	rode	ridden
ring	rang	rung
rise	rose	risen
run	ran	run
say	said	said
see	saw	seen
seek	sought	sought
sell	sold	sold
send	sent	sent
shake	shook	shaken
show	showed	shown
shrink	shrank	shrunk
shut	shut	shut
sing	sang	sung
sink	sank	sunk
sit	sat	sat
sleep	slept	slept
speak	spoke	spoken
spend	spent	spent
stand	stood	stood
steal	stole	stolen
stick	stuck	stuck
sting	stung	stung
strike	struck	struck, stricken
swim	swam	swum
take	took	taken
teach	taught	taught
tear	tore	torn
tell	told	told
think	thought	thought
throw	threw	thrown
understand	understood	understood

Present tense (base form of verb)	Past tense	Past participle (used with helping verb)
wake	woke	woken
wear	wore	worn
win	won	won
write	wrote	written

PRESENT TENSE OF BE AND HAVE

The present tense of the verbs *be* and *have* is irregular, as shown in the following chart.

Present Tense of *Be* and *Have*

Be		*Have*	
I am	we are	I have	we have
you are	you are	you have	you have
he, she, it is	they are	he, she, it has	they have
the editor is	the editors are		
Beth is	Beth and Christina are		

PAST TENSE OF BE

The past tense of the verb *be* is tricky because it has two forms: *was* and *were*.

Past Tense of *Be*

	Singular	Plural
First person	I was	we were
Second person	you were	you were
Third person	she, he, it was	they were
	the student was	the students were

PRACTICE 2   **Using irregular verbs in the past tense**

In the following paragraph, replace any incorrect present-tense verbs with the correct past tense of the verb. If you are unsure of the past-tense forms of irregular verbs, refer to the chart on pages 366–69.

(1) For years, Homer and Langley Collyer ~~are~~ *were* known for their strange living conditions. (2) Neighbors who passed by the brothers' New York City townhouse ~~see~~ *saw* huge piles of trash through the windows. (3) At night, Langley roamed the streets in search of more junk. (4) In March 1947, an anonymous caller ~~tells~~ *told* the police that someone had died in the Collyers' home. (5) In response, officers ~~break~~ *broke* through a second-floor window and tunneled through mounds of newspapers, old umbrellas, and other junk. (6) Eventually, they ~~find~~ *found* the body of Homer Collyer, who seemed to have died of starvation. (7) But where was Langley? (8) In efforts to locate him, workers ~~spend~~ *spent* days removing trash from the house—more than one hundred tons' worth in total. (9) They ~~bring~~ *brought* a strange variety of items to the curb, including medical equipment, bowling balls, fourteen pianos, and the frame of a Model T car. (10) In early April, a worker finally discovered Langley's body. (11) It ~~lies~~ *lay* just 10 feet from where Homer had been found. (12) Apparently, Langley died while bringing food to his disabled brother. (13) As he tunneled ahead, a pile of trash ~~falls~~ *fell* on him and crushed him. (14) This trash was part of a booby trap that Langley had created to stop intruders. (15) Not long after the brothers' deaths, the city demolished their former home. (16) In 1965, community leaders ~~do~~ *did* something that might have surprised Homer and Langley: Where the trash-filled home once ~~stands~~ *stood*, workers created a neat and peaceful park. (17) In the 1990s, this green space ~~becomes~~ *became* the Collyer Brothers Park.

For irregular verbs, the past participle is often different from the past tense.

	Past tense	Past participle
Regular verb	I walked home.	I have walked home before.
Irregular verb	I drove home.	I have driven home before.

It is difficult to predict how irregular verbs form the past participle. Until you are familiar with them, find them in the chart on pages 366–69.

Past Participles

A **past participle**, by itself, cannot be the main verb of a sentence. When a past participle is combined with another verb, called a **helping verb**, however, it can be used to make the present perfect tense and the past perfect tense.

Tip For more about using perfect-tense verbs, see Chapter 26.

Teaching tip As you introduce this section, remind students that the purpose of this chapter is not to memorize the terms but to use verbs correctly in writing.

> *Have/Has* + Past participle = Present perfect tense

The **present perfect** tense is used for an action that began in the past and either continues into the present or was completed at some unknown time in the past.

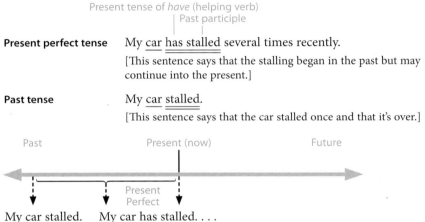

Present tense of *have* (helping verb)
Past participle

Present perfect tense   My car has stalled several times recently.

[This sentence says that the stalling began in the past but may continue into the present.]

Past tense   My car stalled.

[This sentence says that the car stalled once and that it's over.]

Past   Present (now)   Future

Present Perfect

My car stalled.   My car has stalled. . . .

Present Perfect Tense

	Singular	**Plural**
First person	I have laughed.	We have laughed.
Second person	You have laughed.	You have laughed.
Third person	She /he /it has laughed.	They have laughed.
	The baby has laughed.	The babies have laughed.

Language note: Be careful not to leave out *have* when it is needed for the present perfect. Time-signal words such as *since* and *for* may mean that the present perfect is required.

Incorrect	I drive since 1985.	We wait for 2 hours.
Correct	I **have** driven since 1985.	We **have** waited for 2 hours.

| Had | + | Past participle | = | Past perfect tense |

Use *had* plus the past participle to make the **past perfect tense**. The past perfect tense is used for an action that began in the past and ended before some other past action.

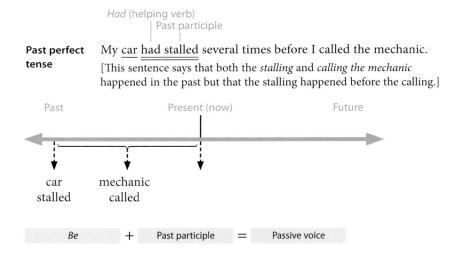

Had (helping verb)
Past participle

Past perfect tense   My car had stalled several times before I called the mechanic.

[This sentence says that both the *stalling* and *calling the mechanic* happened in the past but that the stalling happened before the calling.]

| Past | Present (now) | Future |

car stalled   mechanic called

| Be | + | Past participle | = | Passive voice |

A sentence that is written in the **passive voice** has a subject that does not perform an action. Instead, the subject is acted on. To create the passive voice, combine a form of the verb *be* with a past participle.

Form of *be* (helping verb)
Past participle

Passive   The newspaper was thrown onto the porch.

[The subject, *newspaper,* did not throw itself onto the porch. Some unidentified person threw the newspaper.]

Most sentences should be written in the **active voice**, which means that the subject performs the action.

Active   The delivery person threw the newspaper onto the porch.

[The subject, *delivery person,* performed the action: He or she threw the newspaper.]

Use the passive voice when no one person performed the action, when you do not know who performed the action, or when you want to emphasize the receiver of the action. When you know who performed the action, it is usually preferable to identify the actor.

Active   The bandleader chose Kelly to do a solo.

Passive   Kelly was chosen to do a solo.

[If you wanted to emphasize Kelly's being chosen rather than the bandleader's choice, you might decide to use the passive voice.]

PRACTICE 3   **Changing the passive voice to the active voice**

Rewrite the following sentences, changing them from the passive voice to the active voice. *Answers will vary. Possible answers are shown.*

The legislature cut funding

Example: **Funding for animal shelters was cut by the legislature.**
                                        ^   ^

The owners were going to close some
1. Some shelters were going to be closed by the owners.
       ^   ^

No one knew what
2. What would become of the animals was unknown.
       ^   ^

Animal lovers started a
3. A campaign was started by animal lovers.
       ^   ^

The owners and volunteers at shelters gave interviews.
4. Interviews were given by the owners and volunteers at shelters.
       ^

News teams filmed the
5. The animals were filmed by news teams.
       ^   ^

All the local television stations aired the
6. The stories were aired on all the local television stations.
       ^   ^

Animal lovers across the state staged a
7. A protest was staged by animal lovers across the state.
       ^   ^

People held fund-raisers
8. Fund-raisers of all sorts were held.
       ^   ^

The legislature restored some
9. Some funds were restored by the legislature.
       ^   ^

People raised enough
10. Enough money was raised to keep the shelters open.
       ^

Consistency of Verb Tense

Consistency of verb tense means that all actions in a sentence that happen (or happened) at the same time are in the same tense. If all the actions happen in the present or happen all the time, use the present for all verbs in the sentence. If all the actions happened in the past, use the past tense for all verbs.

| | Past tense | Present tense |
| | | | | |

Inconsistent   The <u>movie</u> <u>started</u> just as <u>we</u> <u>take</u> our seats.

[The actions both happened at the same time, but *started* is in the past tense, and *take* is in the present tense.]

| | Past tense | Present tense |
| | | | | |

Consistent, past tense   The <u>movie</u> <u>started</u> just as <u>we</u> <u>took</u> our seats.

[The actions *started* and *took* both happened in the past, and both are in the past tense.]

Use different tenses only when you are referring to different times.

My <u>daughter</u> <u>hated</u> math as a child, but now <u>she</u> <u>loves</u> it.

[The sentence uses two tenses because the first verb (*hated*) refers to a past condition, whereas the second verb (*loves*) refers to a present one.]

| PRACTICE 4 | **Using consistent verb tense** |

In each of the following sentences, double-underline the verbs, and correct any unnecessary shifts in verb tense. Write the correct form of the verb in the blank space provided.

Example: ___*have*___ Although some people dream of having their picture taken by a famous photographer, not many had the chance.

1. ___*wants*___ Now, special stores in malls take magazine-quality photographs of anyone who wanted one.

2. ___*heard*___ The founder of one business got the idea when she hear friends complaining about how bad they looked in family photographs.

3. ___*decided*___ She decide to open a business to take studio-style photographs that did not cost a lot of money.

4. ___*offered*___ Her first store included special lighting and offers different sets, such as colored backgrounds and outdoor scenes.

5. ___*want*___ Now, her stores even have makeup studios for people who wanted a special look for their pictures.

Edit for Verb Problems

Use the chart on page 377, Finding and Fixing Verb-Tense Errors, to help you complete the practices in this section and edit your own writing.

Teaching tip If you are going to ask your students to write a narration, description, or illustration paper during the course of your semester, consider covering this material at the same time. Some students have a tendency to shift verb tenses when working with those particular types of papers and making this a specific lesson may help with that problem. Have students write a summary of their morning or their weekend and identify any places where their verb tenses shifted out of past or present tense. Help them see these changes in their own writing.

| PRACTICE 5 | **Correcting various verb problems** |

In the following sentences, find and correct any verb problems.

Example: Sheena *is* be tired of the tattoo on her left shoulder.

1. Sheena had never consider*ed* a tattoo until several of her friends got them.

2. Sheena was twenty-two when she *went* goes to the tattoo parlor.

3. After looking at many designs, she chose choose a purple rose design, which she gave to the tattoo artist.

4. Her sister liked the tattoo, but her mother faint*ed*.

5. Like Sheena, many people who now *have* reached their thirties want to get rid of their old tattoos.

6. A few years ago, when a person ~~decides~~ *decided* to have a tattoo removed,
   doctors had to cut out the design.

7. That technique ~~leaved~~ *left* scars.

8. Today, doctors ~~using~~ *use* laser light to break up the ink molecules in
   the skin.

9. Six months ago, Sheena start*ed* to have treatments to remove her tattoo.

10. The procedure ~~hurted~~ every time she saw the doctor, but she hoped it
    would be worth the pain.

PRACTICE 6   **Editing paragraphs for verb problems**

Find and correct seven problems with verb tense in the following
paragraphs.

(1) When you ~~thought~~ *think* about a farm, you probably imagine acres
of cornfields and stalls full of noisy animals. (2) Although that is an
understandable vision, it may not be a particularly accurate one in the near
future. (3) Some experts ~~believes~~ *believe* that farms of the future will be found inside
the top floors of a city's tallest skyscrapers. (4) This concept ~~have~~ *has* been referred
to as "vertical gardening."

(5) Indoor city gardening not only would help make places become more
self-sufficient but also could provide new uses for the variety of abandoned
buildings that are ~~finded~~ *found* scattered throughout large cities. (6) Experts ~~has~~ *have*
suggested that the water used for these small farms and gardens could
be recycled from indoor fishponds. (7) False sunlight could be created
through the use of artificial lights. (8) Thermostats could control the indoor
temperatures.

(9) Although this technology is not currently available, architects ~~has~~ *have*
been toying with possible designs. (10) In the future, farms will most likely
include everything from solar panels and windmills to generators that run
on biofuels. (11) It ~~is~~ *will be* about five to ten years before all these ideas will be
commonplace.

> **PRACTICE 7** **Editing verb problems and using formal English**

Your sister has a bad case of laryngitis and wants to bring a note about her condition to her doctor. Help her by correcting the verb problems in the note. Then, edit the informal English. *Answers will vary. Possible edits are shown.*

Dear Dr. Kerrigan,

(1) ~~What's up, Doc Kerrigan?~~

asked
(2) Your assistant ~~ask~~ me to tell you about my symptoms, so I will describe
became
them as well as I can. (3) I ~~becomed~~ sick about a day ago. (4) Now, my throat
hurts   have
~~hurt~~ every time I swallow~~ed~~, and I cannot speak. (5) Also, I ~~has~~ a high fever,
am very   have   felt   bad
and I ~~be wicked~~ tired. (6) I do not think I ~~has~~ ever ~~feeled~~ so ~~crappy~~ before.
look
(7) I ~~looked~~ forward to seeing you during my appointment.

Thank you very much,
(8) ~~Thanks mucho,~~

Corrine Evans

> **PRACTICE 8** **Editing your own writing for verb problems**

Edit verb-tense problems in a piece of your own writing—a paper for this course or another one, or something you have written for work or your everyday life. Use the chart on page 377 to help you.

Chapter Review

1. Verb _____tense_____ indicates when the action in a sentence happens (past, present, or future).

2. What are the two present-tense endings for regular verbs? _____-s and no ending_____

3. How do regular verbs in the past tense end? _____-ed or -d_____

4. The past participle is used with a _____helping_____ verb.

5. Verbs that do not follow the regular pattern for verbs are called _____irregular_____.

6. An action that started in the past but might continue into the present uses the _____present perfect tense_____.

7. An action that happened in the past before something else that happened in the past uses the _____past perfect tense_____.

8. You should usually avoid using the _____passive_____ voice, which has a subject that performs no action but is acted upon.

9. Verb tenses are consistent when actions that happen at the same _____time_____ are in the same _____tense_____.

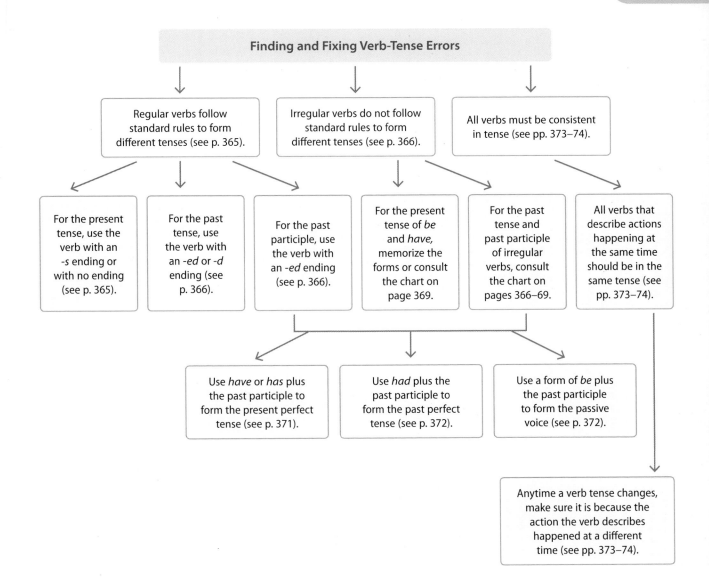

Finding and Fixing Verb-Tense Errors

Regular verbs follow standard rules to form different tenses (see p. 365).

Irregular verbs do not follow standard rules to form different tenses (see p. 366).

All verbs must be consistent in tense (see pp. 373–74).

For the present tense, use the verb with an -s ending or with no ending (see p. 365).

For the past tense, use the verb with an -ed or -d ending (see p. 366).

For the past participle, use the verb with an -ed ending (see p. 366).

For the present tense of *be* and *have,* memorize the forms or consult the chart on page 369.

For the past tense and past participle of irregular verbs, consult the chart on pages 366–69.

All verbs that describe actions happening at the same time should be in the same tense (see pp. 373–74).

Use *have* or *has* plus the past participle to form the present perfect tense (see p. 371).

Use *had* plus the past participle to form the past perfect tense (see p. 372).

Use a form of *be* plus the past participle to form the passive voice (see p. 372).

Anytime a verb tense changes, make sure it is because the action the verb describes happened at a different time (see pp. 373–74).

Part 4

Other Grammar Concerns

"I write to persuade and to make connections."

—John F., student

20

Pronouns
Using Substitutes for Nouns

Understand What Pronouns Are

A **pronoun** is used in place of a noun or other pronoun mentioned earlier. Pronouns enable you to avoid repeating those nouns or other pronouns mentioned earlier.

Sheryl got into ~~Sheryl's~~ *her* car.

I like Mario. ~~Mario~~ *He* is a good dancer.

The noun or pronoun that a pronoun replaces is called the **antecedent**. In most cases, a pronoun refers to a specific antecedent nearby.

I picked up my new glasses. They are cool.

Antecedent — my new glasses

Pronoun replacing antecedent — They

LaunchPadSolo

Visit **LaunchPad Solo for Readers and Writers > Grammar > Parts of Speech** for more tutorials, videos, and practice with crafting paragraphs.

GRAMMAR & MECHANICS ROADMAP

An Overview

This Chapter Identifies the Following Trouble Spots

- Pronoun agreement
- Indefinite pronouns
- Collective nouns
- Vague and ambiguous pronouns
- Subject, object, and possessive pronouns
- Point of view pronouns

Tools to Address the Trouble Spots

Practice Using Pronouns Correctly

Identify Pronouns

Before you practice finding and correcting common pronoun errors, it is helpful to practice identifying pronouns.

Common Pronouns

Personal pronouns	Possessive pronouns	Indefinite pronouns	
I	my	all	much
me	mine	any	neither (of)
you	your/yours	anybody	nobody
she/he	hers/his	anyone	none (of)
her/him	hers/his	anything	no one
it	its	both	nothing
we	our/ours	each (of)	one (of)
us	our/ours	either (of)	some
they	their/theirs	everybody	somebody
them	their/theirs	everyone	someone
		everything	something
		few (of)	

PRACTICE 1 **Identifying pronouns**

In each of the following sentences, circle the pronoun, underline the noun it refers to, and draw an arrow from the pronoun to the noun.

Example: People can have a hard time seeing stars at night if they live in or near a big city.

1. Each night, the stars fill the skies, but in many large cities, they are impossible to see.

2. The huge amount of light coming from homes, businesses, and streets creates a type of pollution, and it makes seeing the stars difficult.

3. The average night sky has approximately 2,500 stars in it, and they can be seen with the human eye.

4. In many neighborhoods, however, only two hundred or three hundred stars can be spotted, whereas in a big city, only about a dozen of them can be seen.

5. The International Dark Sky Association focuses on reducing light pollution as its main goal and has several recommendations.

6. Pointing lights down toward the ground instead of allowing them to shine up toward the sky is one suggestion.

7. To help battle light pollution, some cities and towns have passed laws limiting what lights they will allow.

8. Experts have been studying light pollution, and they have reported that it can affect many things, including wildlife and even human health.

9. Migrating birds sometimes fly over brightly lit cities and, confused by the unnatural light, fly in circles until they become exhausted.

10. Too much light has also been shown to be harmful to humans, and studies are being done to determine just how this overexposure affects them.

ESL teaching tip ESL students may have particular trouble with pronouns and benefit from extra practice exercises.

Check for Pronoun Agreement

A pronoun must agree with (match) the noun or pronoun it refers to in number. It must be either singular (one) or plural (more than one).

If a pronoun is singular, it must also match the noun or pronoun it refers to in gender (*he, she,* or *it*).

Consistent Magda sold *her* old television set.

[*Her* agrees with *Magda* because both are singular and feminine.]

Consistent The Wilsons sold *their* old television set.

[*Their* agrees with *the Wilsons* because both are plural.]

Watch out for singular, general nouns. If a noun is singular, the pronoun that refers to it must be singular as well.

Inconsistent Any student can tell you what *their* least favorite course is.

[*Student* is singular, but the pronoun *their* is plural.]

Consistent Any student can tell you what *his* or *her* least favorite course is.

[*Student* is singular, and so are the pronouns *his* and *her*.]

To avoid using the awkward phrase *his or her*, make the subject plural when you can.

Consistent   Most students can tell you what *their* least favorite course is.

Two types of words often cause errors in pronoun agreement: indefinite pronouns and collective nouns.

Indefinite Pronouns

An **indefinite pronoun** does not refer to a specific person, place, or thing: It is general. Indefinite pronouns often take singular verbs. Whenever a pronoun refers to an indefinite pronoun, check for agreement.

The monks got up at dawn. Everybody had ~~their~~ *his* chores for the day.

Indefinite Pronouns

Always singular			May be plural or singular
another	everyone	nothing	all
anybody/anyone	everything	one (of)	any
anything	much	somebody	none
each (of)	neither (of)	someone	some
either (of)	nobody	something	
everybody	no one		

Teaching tip Have students focus on the "significant seven" indefinite pronouns: *any, each, either,* and *neither* and words ending in *-one, -thing,* or *-body.*

Note: Many people object to the use of only the masculine pronoun *he* when referring to a singular indefinite pronoun, such as *everyone*. Although grammatically correct, using the masculine form alone to refer to an indefinite pronoun is considered sexist. Here are two ways to avoid this problem:

Teaching tip Students can use the find or search function on their computer to check each use of *their* in their own writing and make sure that this pronoun matches the noun that it refers to in number.

1. Use *his or her.*

    Someone posted *his or her* e-mail address to the Web site.

2. Change the sentence so that the pronoun refers to a plural noun or pronoun.

    Some students posted *their* e-mail addresses to the Web site.

Teaching tip Doing this practice orally will help students hear the correct choice.

> **PRACTICE 2**   **Using indefinite pronouns**

Circle the correct pronoun or group of words in parentheses.

(1) Anyone who wants to start (their/ his or her) own business had better be prepared to work hard. (2) One may find, for example, that (his or her)

their) work is never done. (3) Something is always waiting, with (its/their) own peculiar demands. (4) Nothing gets done on (their/its) own. (5) Anybody who expects to have more freedom now that (he or she no longer works/they no longer work) for a boss may be disappointed. (6) After all, when you work as an employee for a company, someone above you makes decisions as (they see/he or she sees) fit. (7) When you are your own boss, no one else places (themselves/himself or herself) in the position of final responsibility.

(8) Somebody starting a business may also be surprised by how much tax (they/he or she) must pay. (9) Each employee at a company pays only about half as much toward social security as what (they/he or she) would pay if self-employed. (10) Neither medical nor dental coverage can be obtained as inexpensively as (it/they) can when a person is an employee at a corporation.

Collective Nouns

A **collective noun** names a group that acts as a single unit.

Common Collective Nouns

audience	company	group
class	crowd	jury
college	family	society
committee	government	team

Collective nouns are usually singular, so when you use a pronoun to refer to a collective noun, it is also usually singular.

its

The team had ~~their~~ sixth consecutive win of the season.

If the people in a group are acting as individuals, however, the noun is plural and should be used with a plural pronoun.

The class brought *their* papers to read.

Make Pronoun Reference Clear

In an **ambiguous pronoun reference**, the pronoun could refer to more than one noun.

Ambiguous	Enrico told Jim that *he* needed a better résumé.
	[Did Enrico tell Jim that Enrico himself needed a better résumé? Or did Enrico tell Jim that Jim needed a better résumé?]
Edited	Enrico advised Jim to revise his résumé.

Teaching tip
Criticalthinking.org provides excellent suggestions for integrating critical thinking into grammar instruction. To access this material, type "integrated grammar" into the "search" box on the Web site.

Ambiguous	I put the glass on the shelf, even though it was dirty.
	[Was the glass dirty? Or was the shelf dirty?]
Edited	I put the dirty glass on the shelf.

In a **vague pronoun reference**, the pronoun does not refer clearly to any particular person, place, or thing. To correct a vague pronoun reference, use a more specific noun instead of the pronoun.

Vague	When Tom got to the clinic, they told him it was closed.
	[Who told Tom the clinic was closed?]
Edited	When Tom got to the clinic, the nurse told him it was closed.
Vague	Before I finished printing my report, it ran out of paper.
	[What ran out of paper?]
Edited	Before I finished printing my report, the printer ran out of paper.

PRACTICE 3   **Avoiding ambiguous or vague pronoun references**

Edit each sentence to eliminate ambiguous or vague pronoun references. Some sentences may be revised in more than one way. *Answers may vary. Possible edits are shown.*

Example: I am always looking for good advice on controlling my weight, but
experts
they have provided little help.
  ^

Teaching tip Ask students to highlight the pronouns they used in their written work and circle or underline the subjects that those pronouns refer to. Make sure that the pronoun is always clear to the reader. Another way to make sure that these references are clear is to ask another student to read the paper and to circle any pronouns that are unclear to the reader.

1. My doctor referred me to a physical therapist, ~~and she~~ *who* said that I needed

   to exercise more.

2. I joined a workout group and did exercises with the members, but ~~it~~ *exercising* did

   not solve my problem.

3. I tried a lower-fat diet along with the exercising, but ~~it~~ *this combination* did not really work

   either.

4. ~~They~~ *Some nutritionists* used to say that eliminating carbohydrates is the easiest way to

   lose weight.

5. Therefore, I started eating fats again and stopped consuming carbs,

   but ~~this was~~ *these methods were* not a permanent solution.

6. Although I lost weight and loved eating fatty foods, ~~it~~ *this low-carb diet* did not keep me

   from eventually gaining the weight back.

7. Last week, I overheard my Uncle Kevin talking to my brother, and

   ~~he~~ *my uncle* explained how he stayed slender even while traveling a lot.

8. Uncle Kevin eats fruit and vegetables instead of junk food while traveling,
   this diet
   and ~~it~~ has kept off the pounds.
   ^

9. He says that it is not hard to pack carrots or apples for a trip, so anyone
   plan in advance
   can ~~do this~~.
   ^

10. I now try to plan better, eat less at each meal, and ignore all diet books,
    these three strategies work
    and I hope ~~it works~~.
    ^

In a **repetitious pronoun reference**, the pronoun repeats a reference to a noun rather than replacing the noun.

The nurse at the clinic ~~he~~ told Tom that it was closed.

The newspaper~~ it~~ says that the new diet therapy is promising.

PRACTICE 4   **Avoiding repetitious pronoun references**

Correct any repetitious pronoun references in the following sentences.

Example: Car commercials they want viewers to believe that buying a certain brand of car will bring happiness.

1. Young people ~~they~~ sometimes take advertisements too literally.
   A
2. ~~In a~~ beer advertisement~~ it~~ might suggest that drinking alcohol makes
   ^
   people more attractive and popular.

3. People who see or hear an advertisement ~~they~~ have to think about the message.

4. Parents should help their children understand why advertisements ~~they~~ do not show the real world.

5. A recent study~~ it~~ said that parents can help kids overcome the influence of advertising.

Use the Right Type of Pronoun

Three important types of pronouns are **subject pronouns**, **object pronouns**, and **possessive pronouns**. Notice their uses in the following sentences.

Object Subject
pronoun pronoun

The dog barked at *him*, and *he* laughed.

Possessive pronoun

As Josh walked out, *his* phone started ringing.

ESL teaching tip
Repetitious pronoun reference is a common error among ESL students. Read aloud some sentences with this problem (from their own writing, if possible), and ask students to raise their hands when they hear a repetitious pronoun reference.

Tip Never put an apostrophe in a possessive pronoun.

Pronoun Types

	Subject	Object	Possessive
First-person singular/plural	I/we	me/us	my, mine/our, ours
Second-person singular/plural	you/you	you/you	your, yours/your, yours
Third-person singular	he, she, it who	him, her, it whom	his, her, hers, its whose
Third-person plural	they who	them whom	their, theirs whose

 Language note: Notice that pronouns have gender (*he/she, him/her, his/her/hers*). The pronoun must agree with the gender of the noun to which it refers.

Incorrect   Carolyn went to see *his* boyfriend.

Correct   Carolyn went to see *her* boyfriend.

Also, notice that English has different forms for subject and object pronouns, as shown in the previous chart.

Read the following sentence, and replace the underlined nouns with pronouns. Notice that all the pronouns are different.

When Andreas made an A on ~~Andreas's~~ ^{his} final exam, ~~Andreas~~ ^{he} was proud of himself, and the teacher congratulated ~~Andreas~~ ^{him}.

SUBJECT PRONOUNS

Subject pronouns serve as the subject of a verb.

You live next door to a coffee shop.

I opened the door too quickly.

OBJECT PRONOUNS

Tip For a list of common prepositions, see page 327.

Object pronouns either receive the action of a verb or are part of a prepositional phrase.

Object of the verb   Jay gave *me* his watch.

Object of the preposition   Jay gave his watch to *me*.

POSSESSIVE PRONOUNS

Possessive pronouns show ownership.

> Dave is *my* uncle.

Three trouble spots make it difficult to know which type of pronoun to use; compound subjects and objects, comparisons, and sentences that need *who* or *whom*.

OTHER TYPES OF PRONOUNS

Intensive pronouns emphasize a noun or other pronoun. **Reflexive pronouns** are used when the performer of an action is also the receiver of the action. Both types of pronouns end in *-self* or *-selves*.

> **Reflexive**   He taught *himself* how to play the guitar.
>
> **Intensive**   The club members *themselves* have offered to support the initiative.

Relative pronouns refer to a noun already mentioned, and introduce a group of words that describe this noun (*who, whom, whose, which, that*).

> Tomatoes, *which* are popular worldwide, were first grown in South America.

Interrogative pronouns are used to begin questions (*who, whom, whose, which, what*).

> *What* did the senator say at the meeting?

Demonstrative pronouns specify which noun is being referred to (*this, these, that, those*).

> Use *this* simple budgeting app, not *that* complicated one.

Reciprocal pronouns refer to individuals when the antecedent is plural (*each other, one another*).

> My friend and I could not see *one another* in the crowd.

PRONOUNS USED WITH COMPOUND SUBJECTS AND OBJECTS

A **compound subject** has more than one subject joined by *and* or *or*. A **compound object** has more than one object joined by *and* or *or*.

> **Compound subject**   *Chandler and I* worked on the project.
>
> **Compound object**   My boss gave the assignment to *Chandler and me*.

Tip When you are writing about yourself and someone else, always put yourself after everyone else. *My friends and I went to a club,* not *I and my friends went to a club.*

To decide which type of pronoun to use in a compound construction, try leaving out the other part of the compound and the *and* or *or*. Then, say the sentence aloud to yourself.

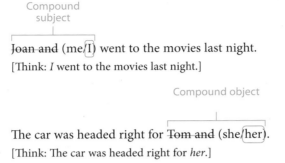

<u>Joan and</u> (me/I) went to the movies last night.

[Think: *I* went to the movies last night.]

The car was headed right for <u>Tom and</u> (she/her).

[Think: The car was headed right for *her*.]

If a pronoun is part of a compound object in a prepositional phrase, use an object pronoun.

I will keep that information just between you and (I/me).

[*Between you and me* is a prepositional phrase, so an object pronoun, *me*, is required.]

Tip Many people make the mistake of using *I* in the phrase *between you and I*. The correct pronoun with *between* is the object *me*.

> **PRACTICE 5**   **Editing pronouns in compound constructions**
>
> Correct any pronoun errors in the following sentences. If a sentence is already correct, write a "C" next to it.
>
> **Example: Marie Curie made several major contributions to science, but**
> *she*
> **in 1898, ~~her~~ and her husband, Pierre Curie, announced their greatest**
> **achievement: the discovery of radium.**
>
> 1. Before this discovery, Marie and Pierre understood that certain substances
>   *they*
>   gave off rays of energy, but ~~them~~ and other scientists were just beginning
>   to learn why and how.
>
> 2. Eventually, the Curies made a discovery that intrigued ~~they~~ and, soon
>   *them*
>   afterward, hundreds of other researchers.
>
> 3. Two previously unknown elements, radium and polonium, were
>   responsible for the extra radioactivity; fascinated by this finding, Marie
>   began thinking about the consequences of the work that she and her
>   husband had done. C

4. As ~~them~~ *they* and other researchers were to discover, radium was especially

   valuable because it could be used in X-rays and for other medical

   purposes.

5. Marie was deeply moved when, in 1903, the scientific community

   honored ~~she~~ *her* and Pierre with the Nobel Prize in physics.

PRONOUNS USED IN COMPARISONS

Using the right type of pronoun in comparisons is particularly important because using the wrong type changes the meaning of the sentence. Editing comparisons can be tricky because they often imply (suggest the presence of) words that are not actually included in the sentence.

> Bob trusts Donna more than *I*.
>
> [This sentence means that Bob trusts Donna more than I trust her. The implied words are *trust her*.]
>
> Bob trusts Donna more than *me*.
>
> [This sentence means that Bob trusts Donna more than he trusts me. The implied words are *he trusts*.]

To decide whether to use a subject or object pronoun in a comparison, try adding the implied words and saying the sentence aloud.

> The registrar is much more efficient than (us/**we**).
>
> [Think: The registrar is much more efficient than *we are*.]
>
> Susan rides her bicycle more than (**he**/him).
>
> [Think: Susan rides her bicycle more than *he does*.]

CHOOSING BETWEEN *WHO* AND *WHOM*

Who is always a subject; *whom* is always an object. If a pronoun performs an action, use the subject form *who*. If a pronoun does not perform an action, use the object form *whom*.

> **Who = subject**   I would like to know <u>who</u> <u><u>delivered</u></u> this package.
>
> **Whom = object**   He told me to *whom* <u>I</u> <u><u>should report</u></u>.

In sentences other than questions, when the pronoun (*who* or *whom*) is followed by a verb, use *who*. When the pronoun (*who* or *whom*) is followed by a noun or pronoun, use *whom*.

> The pianist (**who**/whom) <u><u>played</u></u> was excellent.
>
> [The pronoun is followed by the verb *played*. Use *who*.]
>
> The pianist (who/**whom**) <u>I</u> <u><u>saw</u></u> was excellent.
>
> [The pronoun is followed by another pronoun: *I*. Use *whom*.]

Teaching tip Have each student write a sentence that uses implied words in a comparison. Then, have the students read the sentences aloud and ask other class members to supply the missing words.

Tip To find comparisons, look for the word *than* or *as*.

Tip Add the additional words to the comparison when you speak and write. Then, others will not think you are incorrect.

Tip In the examples here, subjects are underlined, and verbs are double-underlined.

Tip *Whoever* is a subject pronoun; *whomever* is an object pronoun.

Make Pronouns Consistent in Person

Person is the point of view a writer uses—the perspective from which he or she writes. Pronouns may be in first person (*I* or *we*), second person (*you*), or third person (*he, she,* or *it*). (See the chart on p. 388.)

Inconsistent	As soon as *a shopper* walks into the store, *you* can tell it is a weird place.
	[The sentence starts with the third person (*a shopper*) but shifts to the second person (*you*).]
Consistent, singular	As soon as *a shopper* walks into the store, *he* or *she* can tell it is a weird place.
Consistent, plural	As soon as *shoppers* walk into the store, *they* can tell it is a weird place.

Edit for Pronouns

> **PRACTICE 6**   **Correcting various pronoun problems**

In the following sentences, find and correct problems with pronoun use. You may be able to revise some sentences in more than one way, and you may need to rewrite some sentences to correct errors. *Answers may vary. Possible edits are shown.*

Example: Everyone with a busy schedule has *(Students with busy schedules have)* probably been tempted to take shortcuts on their coursework.

1. My class received ~~its~~ *their* term paper grades yesterday.

2. My friend Gene and ~~me~~ *I* were shocked to see that he had gotten an F on his paper.

3. I usually get better grades than ~~him~~ *he*, but he does not usually fail.

4. Mr. Padilla, the instructor, ~~who~~ *whom* most students consider strict but fair, scheduled an appointment with Gene.

5. When Gene went to the department office, ~~they~~ *the office assistant* told him where to find Mr. Padilla.

6. Mr. Padilla ~~told Gene that he did not think he~~ *did not think Gene* had written the paper.

7. The paper ~~it~~ contained language that was unusual for Gene.

8. The instructor said that ~~you~~ *he* could compare Gene's in-class writing with this paper and see differences.

9. Mr. Padilla, ~~whom~~ had typed some passages from Gene's paper into a

    search engine, found two online papers containing sentences that were

    also in Gene's paper.

10. Gene ~~told Mr. Padilla~~ that he had made a terrible mistake.

    ^admitted^

11. Gene told my girlfriend and ~~I~~ later that he did not realize that borrowing

    ^me^

    sentences from online sources was plagiarism.

12. We looked at the paper, and ~~you~~ could tell that parts of it did not sound

    ^we^

    like Gene's writing.

13. Anyone doing Internet research must be especially careful to document

    ~~their~~ sources, as Gene now knows.

    ^his or her^

14. The department decided ~~that they would~~ not suspend Gene from school.

    ^to^

15. Mr. Padilla will let Gene take the class again and will help him avoid

    accidental plagiarism, and Gene said that no one had ever been more

    relieved than ~~him~~ to hear that news.

    ^he^

PRACTICE 7   Editing paragraphs for pronoun problems

Find and correct seven errors in pronoun use in the following paragraphs.
Answers may vary. Possible edits are shown.

(1) Ask anyone who has moved to a city, and ~~they~~ will tell you: At first, life
^he or she^

can feel pretty lonely. (2) Fortunately, it is possible to make friends just about

anywhere. (3) One good strategy is to get involved in a group that interests

you, such as a sports team or arts club. (4) In many cases, a local baseball team

or theater group will open ~~their~~ arms to new talent. (5) Joining in on practices,
^its^

games, or performances is a great way to build friendships with others ~~whom~~
^who^

have interests like yours. (6) Also, most community organizations are always

in need of volunteers. (7) ~~It~~ is a great way to form new friendships while doing
^Volunteering^

something positive for society.

(8) Getting a pet or gardening~~, it~~ is another great way to meet new

people. (9) In many cities, you can walk down the street for a long time and

never be greeted by another person. (10) If you are walking a dog, though, it is

likely that others will say hello. (11) Some may even stop to talk with you and

pet your dog. (12) Also, gardeners tend to draw other gardeners. (13) If you are

Teaching tip Have students underline every pronoun in their paragraphs and draw an arrow to the word or words each pronoun refers to.

they

planting flowers and other flower growers stop by to chat, ~~them~~ and you will
                                                                   ^

have plenty to talk about.

(14) To sum up, newcomers to any city do not have to spend all their

They

nights alone in front of the TV. (15) ~~You~~ have plenty of opportunities to get out
                                         ^

and feel more connected.

PRACTICE 8   **Editing your own writing for pronoun problems**

Edit pronoun errors in a piece of your own writing—a paper for this course
or another one, or something you have written for work or your everyday life.
Use the chart on page 395 to help you.

Chapter Review

1. Pronouns replace ___*nouns*___ or other ___*pronouns*___ in a sentence.

2. A pronoun must agree with (match) the noun or pronoun it replaces in ___*number*___
   and ___*gender*___.

3. In an ___*ambiguous*___ pronoun reference, the pronoun could refer to more than one
   noun.

4. Subject pronouns serve as the subject of a verb. Write a sentence using a subject
   pronoun. *Answers will vary. Possible answer: We went to the movies last night.*

   _____

5. What are two other types of pronouns? *object pronouns and possessive pronouns*

6. What are three trouble spots in pronoun use?

   compound subjects and objects

   comparisons

   sentences that need who or whom

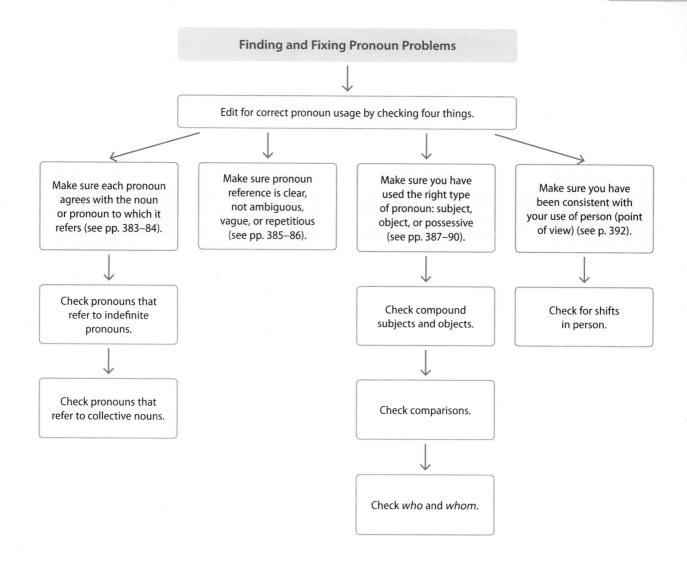

21

Adjectives and Adverbs
Using Descriptive Words

Visit **LaunchPad Solo for Readers and Writers > Grammar > Basic Sentences** for more tutorials, videos, and practice with crafting paragraphs.

Tip To understand this chapter on adjectives and adverbs, you need to know what nouns and verbs are. For a review, see Chapter 15.

Understand What Adjectives and Adverbs Are

Adjectives describe or modify nouns (words that name people, places, things, or ideas) and pronouns (words that replace nouns). They add information about *what kind*, *which one*, or *how many*.

The *final* exam was today.

It was *long* and *difficult*.

The *three shiny new* coins were on the dresser.

> **Language note:** In English, adjectives do not indicate whether the words they describe are singular or plural.

Incorrect The three babies are *adorables*.

[The adjective *adorables* should not end in *-s*.]

Correct The three babies are *adorable*.

GRAMMAR & MECHANICS ROADMAP

An Overview

This Chapter Identifies the Following Trouble Spots

- Choosing between adjectives and adverbs
- Using adjectives and adverbs in comparisons
- Using *good*, *well*, *bad*, and *badly*

Tools to Address the Trouble Spots

- Understand What Adjectives and Adverbs Are (p. 396)
- Forming Comparatives and Superlatives (p. 399)
- Edit for Adjectives and Adverbs exercises (p. 400)
- Chapter Review (p. 401)
- Editing for Correct Usage of Adjectives and Adverbs flowchart (p. 401)

Adverbs describe or modify verbs (words that tell what happens in a sentence), adjectives, or other adverbs. They add information about *how, how much, when, where, why*, or *to what extent*.

Modifying verb	Sharon *enthusiastically* accepted the job.
Modifying adjective	The *very* young lawyer handled the case.
Modifying another adverb	The team played *surprisingly* well.

Adjectives usually come before the words they modify; adverbs come before or after. You can use more than one adjective or adverb to modify a word.

> **Language note:** The *-ed* and *-ing* forms of adjectives are sometimes confused. Common examples include *bored/boring, confused/confusing, excited/exciting*, and *interested/interesting*.
>
> Often, the *-ed* form describes a person's reaction, whereas the *-ing* form describes the thing to which a person is reacting.

Incorrect	Janelle is interesting in ghosts and ghost stories.
Correct	Janelle is interested in ghosts and ghost stories.
Correct	Janelle finds ghosts and ghost stories interesting.

Practice Using Adjectives and Adverbs Correctly

Choosing between Adjectives and Adverbs

Many adverbs are formed by adding *-ly* to the end of an adjective.

adjective	adverb
She received a *quick* answer.	Her sister answered *quickly*.
Our *new* neighbors just got married.	The couple is *newly* married.
That is an *honest* answer.	Please answer *honestly*.

To decide whether to use an adjective or an adverb, find the word being described. If that word is a noun or pronoun, use an adjective. If it is a verb, adjective, or another adverb, use an adverb.

Teaching tip To get students focused on adjectives and adverbs, provide a few sentences containing adjectives, with students in the class as the subjects (e.g., *Dan is wearing a black leather jacket*). Ask the student named in the sentence what the adjectives in the sentence are.

Teaching tip Find an item in the classroom or bring an item in with you. Ask students to write down as many adjectives as they can to describe that item. You can do the same with adverbs; bring in a picture or demonstrate an activity, and then ask them to list as many adverbs as they can think of. You may choose to do this as a group activity and create a competition with points for the most creative adjectives and adverbs as well as the longest list. Try to get the students to think beyond the ordinary words we would use; thinking creatively will help them in their writing.

PRACTICE 1   **Choosing between adjectives and adverbs**

In each sentence, underline the word in the sentence that is being described or modified. Then, circle the correct word in parentheses.

Example People are (common/*commonly*) aware that smoking causes health risks.

1. Many <u>smokers</u> are (*stubborn*/stubbornly) about refusing to quit.

2. Others who are thinking about quitting may <u>decide</u> (sudden/*suddenly*) that the damage from smoking has already been done.

3. In such cases, the (*typical*/typically) <u>smoker</u> sees no reason to stop.

4. The news about secondhand smoke may have made some smokers <u>stop</u> (quick/*quickly*) to save the health of their families.

5. Research now shows that pet lovers who smoke can have a (*terrible*/terribly) <u>effect</u> on their cats.

6. Cats who live with smokers (frequent/*frequently*) <u>develop</u> cancer.

7. Veterinarians point out that the cats of smokers may <u>smell</u> (strong/*strongly*) of smoke.

8. Cats like to have their <u>fur</u> (*clean*/cleanly), and they lick the fur to groom themselves.

9. When they are grooming, cats may inhale a (*large*/largely) <u>dose</u> of tobacco smoke.

10. Perhaps some smokers who believe that it is too late for their own health will (serious/*seriously*) <u>consider</u> quitting for the sake of their pets.

Using Adjectives and Adverbs in Comparisons

To compare two people, places, or things, use the **comparative** form of adjectives or adverbs. Comparisons often use the word *than*.

> Carol ran *faster* than I did.
>
> Johan is *more intelligent* than his sister.

To compare three or more people, places, or things, use the **superlative** form of adjectives or adverbs.

> Carol ran the *fastest* of all the women runners.
>
> Johan is the *most intelligent* of the five children.

If an adjective or adverb is short (one syllable), add the endings *-er* to form the comparative and *-est* to form the superlative. Also use this pattern for adjectives that end in *-y* (but change the *-y* to *-i* before adding *-er* or *-est*).

For all other adjectives and adverbs, add the word *more* to make the comparative and the word *most* to make the superlative.

Tip Some people refer to the correct use of comparatives and superlatives as *appropriate degree forms*.

Forming Comparatives and Superlatives

Adjective or adverb	Comparative	Superlative
Adjectives and adverbs of one syllable		
tall	taller	tallest
fast	faster	fastest
Adjectives ending in -*y*		
happy	happier	happiest
silly	sillier	silliest
Other adjectives and adverbs		
graceful	more graceful	most graceful
gracefully	more gracefully	most gracefully
intelligent	more intelligent	most intelligent
intelligently	more intelligently	most intelligently

Use either an ending (-*er* or -*est*) or an extra word (*more* or *most*) to form a comparative or superlative—not both at once.

This park is known for the ~~most~~ greatest hiking trails.

Using Good, Well, Bad, *and* Badly

Four common adjectives and adverbs have irregular forms: *good, well, bad,* and *badly*.

Tip *Irregular* means not following a standard rule.

Forming Irregular Comparatives and Superlatives

	Comparative	Superlative
Adjective		
good	better	best
bad	worse	worst
Adverb		
well	better	best
badly	worse	worst

Teaching tip The words *good* and *well* are often confused for many writers. Have students create paragraphs using these words and then ask them to switch with a partner. Did they use the words correctly in their paragraphs? As a class, discuss any instances where the words were not used correctly. To make students more comfortable, it may be best to work in groups or partners. Another possibility would be to provide prewritten paragraphs and ask the students to edit them before discussing them as a group.

People often get confused about whether to use *good* or *well*. *Good* is an adjective, so use it to describe a noun or pronoun. *Well* is an adverb, so use it to describe a verb or an adjective.

Adjective   She has a *good* job.

Adverb   He works *well* with his colleagues.

Well can also be an adjective to describe someone's health: I am not *well* today.

Edit for Adjectives and Adverbs

PRACTICE 2   **Editing paragraphs for correct adjectives and adverbs**

Find and correct seven adjective and adverb errors in the following paragraphs. *Answers may vary. Possible edits are shown.*

(1) Every day, many people log on to play one of the ~~popularest~~ *most popular* computer games of all time, *World of Warcraft*. (2) This multiplayer game was first introduced by Blizzard Entertainment in 1994 and has grown ~~quick~~ *quickly* ever since. (3) More than 11 million players participate in the game every month, according to the ~~recentest~~ *most recent* figures.

(4) Computer game experts call *World of Warcraft* a "massively multiplayer online role-playing game," or MMORPG for short. (5) Players of this game select a realm in which to play. (6) They choose from among four ~~differently~~ *different* realms. (7) Each realm has its own set of rules and even its own language. (8) Players also choose if they want to be members of the Alliance or the Horde, which are groups that oppose each other. (9) Each side tends to think that it is ~~gooder~~ *better* than the other one.

(10) In *World of Warcraft,* questing is one of the ~~funnest~~ *most fun* activities. (11) Questing players undertake special missions or tasks to earn experience and gold. (12) The goal is to trade these earnings for better skills and equipment. (13) Players must proceed ~~careful~~ *carefully* to stay in the game and increase their overall power and abilities.

PRACTICE 3   **Editing your own writing for correct adjectives and adverbs**

Edit a piece of your own writing for correct use of adjectives and adverbs. It can be a paper for this course or another one, or choose something you have written for work or your everyday life. Use the chart on page 401 to help you.

Teaching tip Take an article from an online newspaper or other source, and have students find all the adjectives and adverbs, drawing arrows from the modifiers to the words they modify. This activity can be done in small groups in class or assigned as homework and gone over the next day in class.

Chapter Review

1. Adjectives modify ___nouns___ and ___pronouns___ .

2. Adverbs modify ___verbs___ , ___adjectives___ , or ___other adverbs___ .

3. Many adverbs are formed by adding an ___-ly___ ending to an adjective.

4. The comparative form of an adjective or adverb is used to compare how many people, places, things, or ideas? ___two___

5. The superlative form of an adjective or adverb is used to compare how many people, places, things, or ideas? ___three or more___

6. What four words have irregular comparative and superlative forms?
   ___good, well, bad, badly___

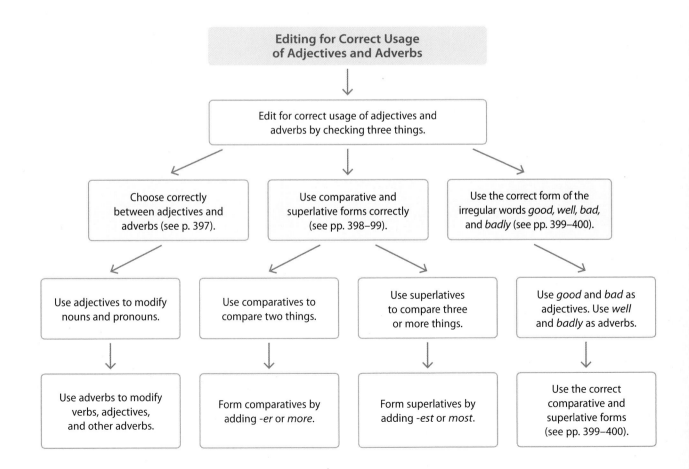

22

Misplaced and Dangling Modifiers

Avoiding Confusing Descriptions

LaunchPadSolo

Visit **LaunchPad Solo for Readers and Writers > Grammar > Basic Sentences** for more tutorials, videos, and practice with crafting paragraphs.

Understand What Misplaced Modifiers Are

Modifiers are words or word groups that describe other words in a sentence. Modifiers should be near the words they modify; otherwise, the sentence can be unintentionally funny. A **misplaced modifier**, because it is in the wrong place, describes the wrong word or words.

Tip For a review of basic sentence elements, see Chapter 15.

Misplaced	Linda saw the White House *flying over Washington, D.C.*
	[Was the White House flying over Washington?]
Clear	*Flying over Washington, D.C.,* Linda saw the White House.

GRAMMAR & MECHANICS ROADMAP

An Overview

This Chapter Identifies the Following Trouble Spots

- Modifiers such as *only, almost, hardly, nearly,* and *just*
- Modifiers that are prepositional phrases
- Modifiers that start with *-ing* verbs
- Modifier clauses that start with *who, whose, that,* or *which*
- Dangling modifiers

Tools to Address the Trouble Spots

- Understand What Misplaced Modifiers Are (p. 402)
- Understand What Dangling Modifiers Are (p. 404)
- Edit for Misplaced and Dangling Modifiers exercises (p. 406)
- Chapter Review (p. 407)
- Editing for Misplaced and Dangling Modifiers flowchart (p. 407)

To correct a misplaced modifier, place the modifier as close as possible to the word or words it modifies, often directly before it.

Wearing my bathrobe,
I went outside to get the paper. ~~wearing my bathrobe.~~
^   ^

Four constructions often lead to misplaced modifiers.

1. Modifiers such as *only, almost, hardly, nearly,* and *just.* These words need to be immediately before—not just close to—the words or phrases they modify.

   only
   I ~~only~~ found two old photos in the drawer.
   ^

   [The intended meaning is that just two photos were in the drawer.]

   almost
   Joanne ~~almost~~ ate the whole cake.
   ^

   [Joanne actually ate; she did not "almost" eat.]

   nearly
   Thomas ~~nearly~~ spent 2 hours waiting for the bus.
   ^

   [Thomas spent close to 2 hours waiting; he did not "nearly" spend them.]

2. Modifiers that are prepositional phrases.

   from the cash register
   The cashier found money on the floor. ~~from the cash register.~~
   ^   ^

   in plastic cups
   Jen served punch to the seniors. ~~in plastic cups.~~
   ^   ^

3. Modifiers that start with *-ing* verbs.

   Using jumper cables,
   Darlene started the car. ~~using jumper cables.~~
   ^   ^

   [The car was not using jumper cables; Darlene was.]

   Wearing flip-flops,
   Javier climbed the mountain. ~~wearing flip-flops.~~
   ^   ^

   [The mountain was not wearing flip-flops; Javier was.]

4. Modifier clauses that start with *who, whose, that,* or *which.*

   that was infecting my hard drive
   Joel found the computer virus attached to an e-mail message. ~~that was infecting my hard drive.~~
   ^   ^

   [The e-mail did not infect the hard drive; the virus did.]

   who was crying
   The baby on the bus ~~who was crying~~ had curly hair.
   ^

   [The bus was not crying; the baby was.]

Teaching tip The *Instructor's Manual for Real Writing* contains tests and supplemental practice exercises for this chapter.

Teaching tip As homework, have each student write a sentence that is funny because of a misplaced or dangling modifier. Collect the sentences and read some aloud, asking the class for corrections.

Practice Correcting Misplaced Modifiers

PRACTICE 1 Correcting misplaced modifiers

Find and correct misplaced modifiers in the following sentences.

Example I write things in my blog that I used to ~~only~~ tell my best friends. *^only*

1. I used to write about all kinds of personal things and private observations *^in a diary* . ~~in a diary.~~

2. Now, I ~~nearly~~ write *^nearly* the same things in my blog.

3. Any story *^that is entertaining* might show up in my blog. ~~that is entertaining.~~

4. The video I was making was definitely something I wanted to write about *^of my cousin Tim's birthday* in my blog. ~~of my cousin Tim's birthday.~~

5. *Wanting the video to be funny,* I had invited to the birthday party my loudest, wildest friends. ~~wanting the video to be funny.~~

6. We jumped off tables, had mock swordfights, and ~~almost~~ used ten cans of *^almost* whipped cream in a food fight.

7. Unfortunately, the battery in the smartphone died. ~~that I was using to make the video.~~ *^that I was using to make the video*

8. ~~I told my friends~~ *Apologizing to my friends, I told them* that I would write a blog post about the party anyway. ~~apologizing to them.~~

9. I explained how I would include the funny story about the failed video session. ~~in the blog post.~~ *^in the blog post*

10. My friends ~~hardly~~ said that they could wait until we tried again to make *^hardly* the video.

Understand What Dangling Modifiers Are

Teaching tip Have students highlight introductory phrases in their writing. Then, ask them to look at the first word after the phrase to make sure it is the noun or pronoun the phrase describes.

A **dangling modifier** "dangles" because the word or word group it modifies is not in the sentence. Dangling modifiers usually appear at the beginning of a sentence and seem to modify the noun or pronoun that immediately follows them, but they are really modifying another word or group of words.

Dangling	*Rushing to class,* the books fell out of my bag.
	[The books were not rushing to class.]
Clear	*Rushing to class,* I dropped my books.

There are two basic ways to correct dangling modifiers. Use the one that makes more sense. One way is to add the word being modified immediately after the opening modifier so that the connection between the two is clear.

Trying to eat a hot dog, ~~my bike~~ swerved.
I ^   *on my bike* ^

Another way is to add the word being modified in the opening modifier itself.

While I was trying
~~Trying~~ to eat a hot dog, my bike swerved.
^

Practice Correcting Dangling Modifiers

PRACTICE 2   **Correcting dangling modifiers**

Find and correct any dangling modifiers in the following sentences. If a sentence is correct, write a "C" next to it. It may be necessary to add new words or ideas to some sentences. *Answers may vary. Possible edits are shown.*

Because I had invited
Example: ~~Inviting~~ my whole family to dinner, the kitchen was filled with all
^

kinds of food.

While I was preparing
1. ~~Preparing~~ a big family dinner, the oven suddenly stopped working.
^

2. In a panic, we searched for Carmen, who can solve any problem. C

With everyone trying
3. ~~Trying~~ to help, the kitchen was crowded.
^

we could see that
4. Looking into the oven, the turkey was not done.
^

we almost canceled dinner.
5. Discouraged, ~~the dinner was about to be canceled.~~
^

As I was staring
6. ~~Staring~~ out the window, a pizza truck went by.
^

7. Using a credit card, Carmen ordered six pizzas. C

One   *and*
8. ~~With one~~ quick phone call, six large pizzas solved our problem.
^   ^

When I returned
9. ~~Returning~~ to the crowd in the kitchen, family members still surrounded
^

the oven.

they cheered.
10. Delighted with Carmen's decision, ~~cheers filled the room.~~
^

Edit for Misplaced and Dangling Modifiers

PRACTICE 3   **Editing paragraphs for misplaced and dangling modifiers**

Find and correct any misplaced or dangling modifiers in the following paragraphs. *Answers may vary. Possible edits are shown.*

(1) Carrying overfilled backpacks is a common habit, but not necessarily a good one. (2) Bulging with books, water bottles, and sports equipment and weighing an average of fourteen to eighteen pounds, ~~students' backs~~ *backpacks can* ~~can gradually become damaged.~~ *gradually damage students' backs.* (3) Because ~~they~~ *students* have to plan ahead for the whole day and often need books, extra clothes, and on-the-go meals, *their* backpacks get heavier and heavier. (4) An increasing number of medical professionals, primarily physical therapists, are seeing young people with chronic back problems.

(5) Researchers have recently invented a new type of backpack. *from the University of Pennsylvania and the Marine Biological Laboratory* ~~from the University of Pennsylvania and the Marine Biological Laboratory.~~ (6) Designed with springs, the backpack moves up and down as a person walks. (7) This new backpack creates energy, which is then collected and transferred to an electrical generator. (8) Experiencing relief from the wear and tear on muscles, *wearers of the new packs find that* the springs make the pack more comfortable.

(9) What is the purpose of the electricity generated by these new backpacks? (10) Needing electricity for their night-vision goggles, ~~the backpacks~~ *soldiers use the backpacks to* could solve a problem. ~~for soldiers.~~ (11) Soldiers could benefit from such an efficient energy source to power their global positioning systems and other electronic gear. (12) ~~Instead of being battery operated, the soldiers~~ *They* could use the special backpacks and would not have to carry additional batteries *for their battery-operated gear*. (13) For the average student, these backpacks might one day provide convenient energy for video games, television, and music players, all at the same time. (14) ~~Designed~~ *Wearing backpacks designed* with this technology, kids would just have to look both ways before crossing the street.

PRACTICE 4   **Editing your own writing for misplaced and dangling modifiers**

Edit a piece of your own writing for misplaced and dangling modifiers. It can be a paper for this course or another one, or it could be something you have written for work or your everyday life. You may want to use the chart on page 407.

Chapter Review

1. __Modifiers__ are words or word groups that describe other words in a sentence.

2. A __misplaced modifier__ describes the incorrect word or word group because it is in the wrong place in a sentence.

3. When an opening modifier does not modify any word in the sentence, it is a __dangling modifier__.

4. Which four constructions often lead to misplaced modifiers?
   modifiers such as "only," "almost," "hardly," "nearly," and "just"; modifiers that are _prepositional phrases; modifiers that start with "-ing" verbs; and modifier clauses_ _that start with "who," "whose," "that," or "which"_

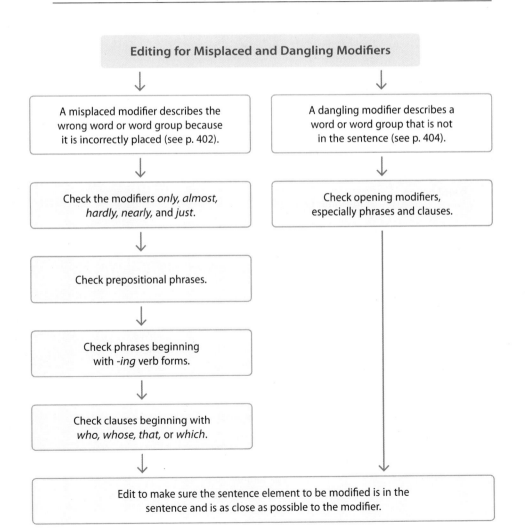

Editing for Misplaced and Dangling Modifiers

A misplaced modifier describes the wrong word or word group because it is incorrectly placed (see p. 402).

A dangling modifier describes a word or word group that is not in the sentence (see p. 404).

Check the modifiers _only, almost, hardly, nearly,_ and _just._

Check opening modifiers, especially phrases and clauses.

Check prepositional phrases.

Check phrases beginning with _-ing_ verb forms.

Check clauses beginning with _who, whose, that,_ or _which._

Edit to make sure the sentence element to be modified is in the sentence and is as close as possible to the modifier.

23

Coordination and Subordination

Joining Sentences with Related Ideas

Understand What Coordination Is

Coordination is used to join two sentences with related ideas, and it can make your writing less choppy. The sentences remain complete and independent, but they are joined with a comma and a coordinating conjunction.

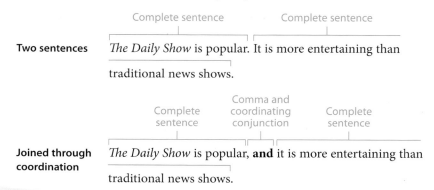

Tip To understand this chapter, you need to be familiar with basic sentence elements. For a review, see Chapter 15.

Teaching tip It is always best to remind students of the basic elements of a sentence before beginning a more complex lesson.

	Complete sentence	Complete sentence
Two sentences	*The Daily Show* is popular.	It is more entertaining than traditional news shows.

	Complete sentence	Comma and coordinating conjunction	Complete sentence
Joined through coordination	*The Daily Show* is popular,	**and**	it is more entertaining than traditional news shows.

GRAMMAR & MECHANICS ROADMAP

An Overview

This Chapter Identifies the Following Trouble Spots

- Joining sentences using coordinating conjunctions
- Joining sentences using semicolons
- Joining sentences using a subordinating conjunction

Practice Using Coordination

Using Coordinating Conjunctions

Conjunctions join words, phrases, or clauses. **Coordinating conjunctions** join ideas of equal importance. (You can remember them by thinking of **FANBOYS**—*for, and, nor, but, or, yet, so.*) To join two sentences through coordination, put a comma and one of these conjunctions between the sentences. Choose the conjunction that makes the most sense for the meaning of the two sentences.

Teaching tip The *Instructor's Manual for Real Writing* contains tests and supplemental practice exercises for this chapter.

Complete sentence		Complete sentence
	, for	
	, and	
	, nor	
	, but	
	, or	
	, yet	
	, so	

Wikipedia is a popular encyclopedia	, for [*For* indicates a reason or cause.]	it is easily available online.
The encyclopedia is open to all	, and [*And* simply joins two ideas.]	anyone can add information to it.
Often, inaccurate entries cannot be stopped	, nor [*Nor* indicates a negative.]	is there any penalty for them.
People have complained about errors	, but [*But* indicates a contrast.]	the mistakes may or may not be fixed.
Some people delete information	, or [*Or* indicates alternatives.]	they add their own interpretations.
Many people know that Wikipedia is flawed	, yet [*Yet* indicates a contrast or possibility.]	they continue to use it.
Wikipedia now has trustees	, so [*So* indicates a result.]	perhaps it will be monitored more closely.

Tip For more on the use of commas, see Chapter 30.

Teaching tip Emphasize that conjunctions are not interchangeable (*but* can't fill in for *so*, for example). Write two independent clauses on the board (*Tom was hungry/he had a sandwich*). Ask students which conjunctions would work. Ask how the sentence would have to change to use others.

| PRACTICE 1 | **Combining sentences with coordinating conjunctions** |

Combine each pair of sentences into a single sentence by using a comma and a coordinating conjunction. In some cases, there may be more than one correct answer. *Answers may vary. Possible edits are shown.*

Example: In business, e-mails can make a good or bad impression. *, so people* **People should mind their e-mail manners.**

1. Many professionals use e-mail to keep in touch with clients and contacts. *, so they* ~~They~~ must be especially careful not to offend anyone with their e-mail messages.

2. However, anyone who uses e-mail should be cautious. *, for it* ~~It~~ is dangerously easy to send messages to the wrong person.

3. Employees may have time to send personal messages from work. *, but they* ~~They~~ should remember that employers often have the ability to read their workers' messages.

4. R-rated language and jokes may be deleted automatically by a company's server. *, or they* ~~They~~ may be read by managers and cause problems for the employee sending or receiving them.

5. No message should be forwarded to everyone in a sender's address book. *, and senders* ~~Senders~~ should ask permission before adding someone to a mass-mailing list.

6. People should check the authenticity of mailings about lost children, dreadful diseases, and terrorist threats before passing them on. *, for most* ~~Most~~ such messages are hoaxes.

7. Typographical errors and misspellings in e-mail make the message appear less professional. *, yet using* ~~Using~~ all capital letters—a practice known as *shouting*— is usually considered even worse.

8. People who use e-mail for business want to be taken seriously. *, so they* ~~They~~ should make their e-mails as professional as possible.

Using Semicolons

A **semicolon** is a punctuation mark that can join two sentences through coordination. Use semicolons *only* when the ideas in the two sentences are closely related. Do not overuse semicolons.

Complete sentence	;	Complete sentence
Antarctica is a mystery	;	few people know much about it.
Its climate is extreme	;	few people want to endure it.
My cousin went there	;	he loves to explore the unknown.

A semicolon alone does not tell readers much about the relationship between the two ideas. To give more information about the relationship, use a **conjunctive adverb** after the semicolon. Put a comma after the conjunctive adverb.

Complete sentence	; also, ; as a result, ; besides, ; furthermore, ; however, ; in addition, ; in fact, ; instead, ; moreover, ; still, ; then, ; therefore,	Complete sentence

Tip When you connect two sentences with a conjunctive adverb, the statement following the semicolon remains a complete thought. If you use a subordinating word such as *because,* however, the second statement becomes a dependent clause, and a semicolon is not needed: *The desert is cold at night because sand does not store heat well.*

Antarctica is largely unexplored	; as a result,	it is unpopulated.
It receives little rain	; also,	it is incredibly cold.
It is a huge area	; therefore,	scientists are becoming more interested in it.

> **PRACTICE 2** **Combining sentences with semicolons and conjunctive adverbs**

Combine each pair of sentences by using a semicolon and a conjunctive adverb. In some cases, there may be more than one correct answer. *Answers may vary. Possible edits are shown.*

Example: More and more people are researching their family history,

or genealogy. ; in fact, this **~~This~~ type of research is now considered one of the**

fastest-growing hobbies in North America.

1. Before the Internet, genealogy researchers had to contact public

   offices to get records of ancestors' births, marriages, occupations,

   and deaths. ; in addition, some **~~Some~~** visited libraries to search for old newspaper articles

   mentioning the ancestors.

2. There was no quick and easy way to search records or article data-

   bases. ; however, with **~~With~~** the rise of the Internet and new digital tools, genealogy

   research has become much simpler.

3. These tools allow people to search a wide range of records with key
   words. *; therefore, researchers* ~~Researchers~~ can gather details about their ancestors' lives much
   more quickly and efficiently.

4. Recently, people have started using social-networking tools to find
   out about living and dead relatives. *; as a result, some* ~~Some~~ of them are getting more
   information even more quickly.

5. One researcher, Lauren Axelrod, used Ancestry.com to gather some
   information on the birth mother of her husband, who had been
   adopted. *; then, using* ~~Using~~ this information, she searched for his birth mother
   on Facebook.

6. The entire search, wich ended successfully, took only 2 hours. *; moreover, in* ~~In~~ less
   than a week, Axelrod's husband was talking on the phone with his birth
   mother.

7. Not everyone thinks that genealogy research has to be a purely serious
   hobby. *; instead, some* ~~Some~~ people see it as a great way to have fun.

8. In the online Family Village Game, players create characters, or avatars,
   representing their ancestors. *; also, using* ~~Using~~ genealogical records, they add
   background information on these ancestors.

9. Players have a lot of fun creating the characters and their worlds. *; furthermore, they* ~~They~~ get
   additional genealogical information by following the research suggestions
   provided by the game.

10. Some parents play Family Village Game with their children. *; as a result, the* ~~The~~ children
    see their connection to the past.

Understand What Subordination Is

Like coordination, **subordination** is a way to join short, choppy sentences with related ideas into a longer sentence. With subordination, you put a dependent word (such as *after*, *although*, *because*, or *when*) in front of one of the sentences, which then becomes a dependent clause and is no longer a complete sentence.

	Complete sentence	Complete sentence
Two sentences	Patti is proud of her son.	He was accepted into the Officer Training Program.

Complete sentence   Dependent clause

Joined through subordination   Patti is proud of her son **because** he was accepted into the Officer Training Program.

Practice Using Subordination

To join two sentences through subordination, use a **subordinating conjunction**. Choose the conjunction that makes the most sense with the two sentences. Here are some of the most common subordinating conjunctions.

Complete sentence	after	now that	Dependent clause
	although	once	
	as	since	
	as if	so that	
	because	unless	
	before	until	
	even if/	when	
	though	whenever	
	if	where	
	if only	while	

I love music   because   it makes me relax.

It is hard to study at home   when   my children want my attention.

When a dependent clause ends a sentence, it usually does not need to be preceded by a comma unless it is showing a contrast.

When the dependent clause begins a sentence, use a comma to separate it from the rest of the sentence.

Subordinating conjunction	Dependent clause	,	Complete sentence
When	I eat out	,	I usually have steak.
Although	it is harmful	,	young people still smoke.

PRACTICE 3   Combining sentences through subordination

Combine each pair of sentences into a single sentence by using an appropriate subordinating conjunction either at the beginning of or between the two sentences. Use a conjunction that makes sense with the two sentences, and add commas where necessary. *Answers may vary. Possible edits are shown.*

Example: *If someone* ~~Someone~~ told you that you share DNA with humans' extinct relatives, the Neanderthals, *you* ~~You~~ might be surprised.

1. In fact, scientists have found that mating between humans and Neander-thals occurred *after groups* ~~Groups~~ of humans migrated north and east from Africa.

Teaching tip Write two sentences on the board, and have students suggest how the sentences would have to change to accommodate different subordinating conjunctions.

Teaching tip Point out that unlike the conjunctive adverbs on page 411, these subordinating conjunctions are never used with a semicolon in front of them and a comma after.

Teaching tip This practice is a good one to do orally.

2. ~~Scientists~~ *When scientists* examined the DNA of modern humans~~.~~ *, they* ~~They~~ made a startling discovery: 1 to 4 percent of all non-Africans' DNA is Neanderthal DNA.

3. ~~Old~~ *Because old* illustrations present Neanderthals as bent over and primitive looking~~.~~ *, it* ~~It~~ may be hard to believe that humans would want to mate with them.

4. However, *if* a Neanderthal man got a good shave and a nice set of clothes~~.~~ *, he* ~~He~~ might pass for a modern man.

5. ~~Researchers~~ *Although researchers* are learning more about Neanderthals~~.~~ *, many* ~~Many~~ mysteries remain.

6. ~~Researchers~~ *As researchers* continue their investigations~~.~~ *, they* ~~They~~ are trying to answer one key question: What are the specific genetic differences between humans and Neanderthals?

7. They have started sequencing the entire Neanderthal genome~~.~~ *, so that they* ~~They~~ can answer this question.

8. ~~The~~ *Because the* genome is the entire set of genetic material for an organism~~.~~ *, comparing* ~~Comparing~~ the Neanderthal genome to the human one might help researchers identify a number of differences between the two species.

9. ~~These~~ *Although these* differences have yet to be identified~~.~~ *, scientists* ~~Scientists~~ are growing more and more certain about the answer to one question: Why did Neanderthals become extinct?

10. ~~Humans~~ *Even though humans* mated with Neanderthals~~.~~ *, they* ~~They~~ also contributed to Neanderthals' extinction, either by killing them or by outcompeting them for food and other resources.

PRACTICE 4   **Combining sentences through coordination and subordination**

Join each of the following sentence pairs in two ways, first by coordination and then by subordination. *Answers may vary. Possible edits are shown.*

Example: Rick has many talents. He is still deciding what to do with his life.

Joined by coordination: *Rick has many talents, but he is still deciding what to do with his life.*

Joined by subordination: *Although Rick has many talents, he is still deciding what to do with his life.*

1. Rick rides a unicycle. He can juggle four oranges.

   Joined by coordination: *Rick rides a unicycle, and he can juggle four oranges.*

   Joined by subordination: *While Rick rides a unicycle, he can juggle four oranges.*

2. A trapeze school opened in our town. Rick signed up immediately.

   Joined by coordination: *A trapeze school opened in our town, so Rick signed up immediately.*

   Joined by subordination: *When a trapeze school opened in our town, Rick signed up immediately.*

3. Rick is now at the top of his class. He worked hard practicing trapeze routines.

   Joined by coordination: *Rick is now at the top of his class, for he worked hard practicing trapeze routines.*

   Joined by subordination: *Rick is now at the top of his class because he worked hard practicing trapeze routines.*

4. Rick asks me for career advice. I try to be encouraging.

   Joined by coordination: *Rick asks me for career advice, and I try to be encouraging.*

   Joined by subordination: *Whenever Rick asks me for career advice, I try to be encouraging.*

5. He does not want to join the circus. He could study entertainment management.

   Joined by coordination: *He does not want to join the circus, but he could study entertainment management.*

   Joined by subordination: *If he does not want to join the circus, he could study entertainment management.*

Edit for Coordination and Subordination

PRACTICE 5   **Editing paragraphs for coordination and subordination**

In the following paragraphs, combine the six pairs of underlined sentences. For three of the sentence pairs, use coordination. For the other three sentence pairs, use subordination. Do not forget to punctuate correctly, and keep in mind that there may be more than one way to combine each sentence pair. *Answers may vary. Possible edits are shown.*

   (1) Washington, D.C., was the first city in the United States to offer a public bicycle-sharing program*, but the* (2) ~~The~~ idea has been popular in Europe for years. (3) In fact, Paris has more than twenty thousand bikes available for people to rent and ride around the city. (4) Called Capital Bikeshare, the Washington program costs citizens $7 a day, $25 a month, or $75 a year to join. (5) For that fee, they have access to more than one thousand bikes available at 110 stations set up all over Washington and in Arlington, Virginia. (6) After using the bikes, people must return them to one of the stations*, for other* (7) ~~Other~~ riders might be waiting for one. (8) Regular users have come to depend on Capital Bikeshare for short trips and errands*, and the* (9) ~~The~~ popularity of the program is growing.

   (10) Throughout the United States, cycling has become much more popular in recent years*, since gasoline* (11) ~~Gasoline~~ prices have increased. (12) A number of other cities are now considering bike-sharing programs*, because studies* (13) ~~Studies~~ show that these programs can reduce city traffic by 4 to 5 percent. (14) Some companies are already creating similar programs to encourage their employees to exercise more and drive less. (15) Company leaders are aware that fit employees and a healthier environment are important goals to achieve*, even if it* (16) ~~It~~ means that the company spends a little extra time, money, and effort to start and run a bike-sharing program.

PRACTICE 6   **Editing your own writing for coordination and subordination**

Edit a piece of your own writing for coordination and subordination. It can be a paper for this course or another one, or it can be something you have written for work or your everyday life. You may want to use the chart on page 417.

Chapter Review

1. What are the two ways to join sentences through coordination?

   Use a comma and a coordinating conjunction, a semicolon alone, or use a semicolon

   and a conjunctive adverb followed by a comma.

2. Use a semicolon *only* when the sentences are   *closely related* .

3. Write two sentences using coordination. *Answers will vary. One possibility: I worked*

   until midnight, and I was paid overtime.

4. With subordination, you put a   *dependent word*   in front of one of two related

   sentences.

5. Write two sentences using subordination. *Answers will vary. One possibility: Because*

   I worked until midnight, I am tired today.

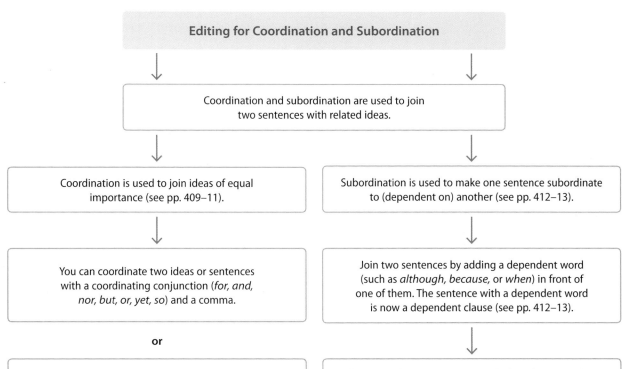

Editing for Coordination and Subordination

Coordination and subordination are used to join
two sentences with related ideas.

Coordination is used to join ideas of equal
importance (see pp. 409–11).

Subordination is used to make one sentence subordinate
to (dependent on) another (see pp. 412–13).

You can coordinate two ideas or sentences
with a coordinating conjunction (*for, and,
nor, but, or, yet, so*) and a comma.

Join two sentences by adding a dependent word
(such as *although, because,* or *when*) in front of
one of them. The sentence with a dependent word
is now a dependent clause (see pp. 412–13).

or

You can coordinate two ideas or sentences with a
semicolon or with a semicolon and a conjunctive adverb
(such as *also, however,* or *instead*) followed by a comma.

If the complete sentence comes before the dependent
clause, a comma is usually not needed. If the
complete sentence comes after the dependent
clause, add a comma after the dependent clause.

24

Parallelism
Balancing Ideas

LaunchPadSolo

Visit **LaunchPad Solo for Readers and Writers > Grammar > Basic Sentences** for more tutorials, videos, and practice with crafting paragraphs.

Understand What Parallelism Is

Parallelism in writing means that similar parts in a sentence have the same structure: Their parts are balanced. Use nouns with nouns, verbs with verbs, and phrases with phrases.

Not parallel	I enjoy <u>basketball</u> more than <u>playing video games</u>.
	[*Basketball* is a noun, but *playing video games* is a phrase.]
Parallel	I enjoy <u>basketball</u> more than <u>video games</u>.
Parallel	I enjoy <u>playing basketball</u> more than <u>playing video games</u>.
Not parallel	Last night, I <u>worked</u>, <u>studied</u>, and <u>was watching</u> television.
	[Verbs must be in the same tense to be parallel. *Was watching* has a different structure from *worked* and *studied*.]
Parallel	Last night, I <u>worked</u>, <u>studied</u>, and <u>watched</u> television.
Parallel	Last night, I was <u>working</u>, <u>studying</u>, and <u>watching</u> television.

GRAMMAR & MECHANICS ROADMAP

An Overview

This Chapter Identifies the Following Trouble Spots

- Parallelism in pairs and lists
- Parallelism in comparisons
- Parallelism with certain paired words

Tools to Address Trouble Spots

- Understand What Parallelism Is (p. 418)
- List of commonly paired words (p. 421)
- Edit for Parallelism exercises (p. 423)
- Chapter Review (p. 424)
- Editing for Parallelism flowchart (p. 424)

Not parallel	This weekend, we can go <u>to the beach</u> or <u>walking in the mountains</u>.
	[*To the beach* should be paired with another prepositional phrase: *to the mountains.*]
Parallel	This weekend, we can go <u>to the beach</u> or <u>to the mountains</u>.

Tip To understand this chapter, you need to be familiar with basic sentence elements, such as nouns and verbs. For a review, see Chapter 15.

Practice Writing Parallel Sentences

Parallelism in Pairs and Lists

When two or more items in a series are joined by *and* or *or,* use a similar form for each item.

Not parallel	The professor assigned <u>readings</u>, <u>practices to do</u>, and <u>a paper</u>.
Parallel	The professor assigned <u>readings</u>, <u>practices</u>, and <u>a paper</u>.
Not parallel	The story was <u>in the newspaper</u>, <u>on the radio</u>, and <u>the television</u>.
	[*In the newspaper* and *on the radio* are prepositional phrases. *The television* is not.]
Parallel	The story was <u>in the newspaper</u>, <u>on the radio</u>, and <u>on the television</u>.

> **PRACTICE 1**   **Using parallelism in pairs and lists**
>
> In each sentence, underline the parts of the sentence that should be parallel. Then, edit the sentence to make it parallel. *Answers may vary. Possible edits are shown.*
> **Example: Coyotes roam the <u>western mountains</u>, <u>the central plains</u>, and ~~they~~**
> *suburbs.*
> **~~are in the suburbs~~ of the East Coast of the United States.**
> ^

1. Wild predators, such as wolves, are vanishing because people <u>hunt</u> them
   take
   and <u>~~are taking~~</u> over their land.
   ^
2. Coyotes are <u>surviving</u> and ~~they do~~ well in the modern United States.
   doing
   ^
3. The success of the coyote is due to its <u>varied diet</u> and ~~adapting easily.~~
   adaptability.
   ^
4. Coyotes are sometimes <u>vegetarians</u>, sometimes <u>scavengers</u>, and
   hunters.
   sometimes ~~they hunt.~~
   ^
5. Today, they are <u>spreading</u> and ~~populate~~ the East Coast for the first time.
   populating
   ^
6. The coyotes' appearance <u>surprises</u> and ~~is worrying~~ many people.
   worries
   ^
7. The animals have chosen an area ~~that is more populated and it's not as~~
   more populated and less wild than
   ^
   ~~wild as~~ their traditional home.

Teaching tip The *Instructor's Manual for Real Writing* contains tests and supplemental practice exercises for this chapter.

Teaching tip Doing this practice orally allows students to hear problems with parallelism. The same is true of Practices 2, 3, and 5.

8. Coyotes can adapt to rural, suburban, and ~~even living in a city.~~ *urban life.*

9. One coyote was identified, tracked, and ~~they~~ captured ~~him~~ in Central Park in New York City.

10. Suburbanites are getting used to the sight of coyotes. *and sound* ~~and hearing them.~~

Parallelism in Comparisons

Comparisons often use the word *than* or *as*. When you edit for parallelism, make sure the items on either side of those words have parallel structures.

Not parallel	Taking the bus downtown is as fast as the drive there.
Parallel	Taking the bus downtown is as fast as driving there.
Not parallel	To admit a mistake is better than denying it.
Parallel	To admit a mistake is better than to deny it.
	Admitting a mistake is better than denying it.

Sometimes you need to add or delete a word or two to make the parts of a sentence parallel.

Not parallel	A tour package is less expensive than arranging every travel detail yourself.
Parallel, word added	*Buying* a tour package is less expensive than arranging every travel detail yourself.
Not parallel	The sale price of the shoes is as low as paying half of the regular price.
Parallel, words dropped	The sale price of the shoes is as low as half of the regular price.

PRACTICE 2   **Using parallelism in comparisons**

In each sentence, underline the parts of the sentence that should be parallel. Then, edit the sentence to make it parallel. *Answers may vary. Possible edits are shown.*

Example: Leasing a new car may be less expensive than ~~to buy~~ one. *buying*

1. Car dealers often require less money down for leasing a car than for ~~the purchase of~~ one. *purchasing*

2. The monthly payments for a leased car may be as low as ~~paying for a loan.~~ *loan payments.*

3. You should check the terms of leasing to make sure they are as favorable as ~~to buy.~~ *the terms of buying.*

4. You may find that ~~to lease~~ _leasing_ is a safer bet than <u>buying</u>.

5. You will be making less of a financial commitment <u>by leasing</u> a car than ~~to own~~ _by owning_ it.

6. <u>Buying</u> a car may be better than ~~a lease on~~ _leasing_ one if you plan to keep it for several years.

7. <u>A used car</u> can be more economical than ~~getting~~ <u>a new one</u>.

8. However, ~~maintenance of~~ _maintaining_ <u>a new car</u> may be easier than <u>taking care of a used car</u>.

9. <u>A used car</u> may not be as impressive as ~~buying~~ <u>a brand-new vehicle</u>.

10. <u>To get a used car</u> from a reputable source can be a better decision than ~~to buy~~ _to buy_ <u>a new vehicle</u> that loses value the moment you drive it home.

Parallelism with Certain Paired Words

Certain paired words, called **correlative conjunctions**, link two equal elements and show the relationship between them. Here are the paired words:

both . . . and   neither . . . nor   rather . . . than

either . . . or   not only . . . but also

Make sure the items joined by these paired words are parallel.

Not parallel   Bruce wants _both_ <u>freedom</u> _and_ <u>to be wealthy</u>.

[_Both_ is used with _and_, but the items joined by them are not parallel.]

Parallel   Bruce wants _both_ <u>freedom</u> _and_ <u>wealth</u>.

Parallel   Bruce wants _both_ <u>to have freedom</u> _and_ <u>to be wealthy</u>.

Not parallel   He can _neither_ <u>fail the course</u> and <u>quitting his job</u> is also impossible.

Parallel   He can _neither_ <u>fail the course</u> _nor_ <u>quit his job</u>.

> **PRACTICE 3**   **Using parallelism with certain paired words**
>
> In each sentence, circle the paired words, and underline the parts of the sentence that should be parallel. Then, edit the sentence to make it parallel. You may need to change one of the paired elements to make the sentence parallel.
>
> _Answers may vary. Possible edits are shown._
>
> **Example:** A cell phone can be (either) a lifesaver (or) ~~it can be annoying~~ _an annoyance_.

1. Twenty years ago, most people (neither) <u>had cell phones</u> (nor) ~~did they want~~ _wanted_ <u>them</u>.

Teaching tip Students can use the find or search function to locate the first word in correlative conjunctions. They should read the sentences with those constructions carefully to make sure the second word is present and parallel structure is used.

2. Today, cell phones are ⌈not only⌉ used by people of all ages ⌈but also⌉ ~~are~~ carried everywhere.

3. Cell phones are not universally popular: Some commuters would ⌈rather⌉
   be
   ban cell phones on buses and trains ⌈than⌉ ~~being~~ forced to listen to other
                                             ∧
   people's conversations.

   convenient.
4. No one denies that a cell phone can be ⌈both⌉ useful ⌈and⌉ ~~convenience is a~~
                                                              ∧
   ~~factor.~~

5. A motorist stranded on a deserted road would ⌈rather⌉ have a cell phone
   ___ *be forced*
   ⌈than⌉ to walk to the nearest gas station.
        ∧

6. When cell phones were first introduced, some people feared that they
   ⌈either⌉ caused brain tumors ⌈or⌉ ~~they~~ were a dangerous source of radiation.

7. Most Americans today ⌈neither⌉ worry about radiation from cell phones ⌈nor⌉
   fear
   other injuries.
   ∧

8. The biggest risk of cell phones is ⌈either⌉ that drivers are distracted by them
   ___ *that people get*
   ⌈or⌉ ~~people getting~~ angry at someone talking too loudly in public on a cell
        ∧
   phone.

9. Cell phones probably do not cause brain tumors, but some experiments
   on human cells have shown that energy from the phones may ⌈both⌉ affect
   people's reflexes ⌈and⌉ ~~it might~~ alter the brain's blood vessels.

10. Some scientists think that these experiments show that cell phone use
                                                     also mental ones.
    might have ⌈not only⌉ physical effects on human beings ⌈but⌉ ~~it also~~ ~~could~~
                                                                         ∧
    ~~influence mental processes.~~

PRACTICE 4   **Completing sentences with paired words**

For each sentence, complete the correlative conjunction, and add more
information. Make sure the structures on both sides of the correlative
conjunction are parallel. *Answers may vary. Possible answers are shown.*

Example: I am both impressed by your company *and enthusiastic to work for*
you .

1. I could bring to this job not only youthful enthusiasm *but also relevant*
   experience .

2. I am willing to work either in your main office *or in your San Francisco office* .

3. My current job neither encourages initiative *nor allows flexibility* .

4. I would rather work in a challenging job *than work in a boring one* .

5. In college, I learned a lot both from my classes *and from other students* .

Edit for Parallelism

> **PRACTICE 5** **Editing paragraphs for parallelism problems**

Find and correct five parallelism errors in the following paragraphs.

(1) On a mountainous island between Norway and the North Pole
is a special underground vault. (2) It contains neither gold ~~and~~ currency.
                                           nor
(3) Instead, it is full of a different kind of treasure: seeds. (4) They are being
saved for the future in case something happens to the plants that people need
to grow for food.

(5) The vault has the capacity to hold 4.5 million types of seed samples.
(6) Each sample contains an average of five hundred seeds, which means that
up to 2.25 billion seeds can be stored in the vault. (7) ~~To store~~ them is better
                               Storing
than planting them. (8) Stored, they are preserved for future generations to
plant. (9) On the first day that the vault's storage program began, 268,000
different seeds were deposited, put into sealed packages, and ~~collecting~~ into
                            collected
sealed boxes. (10) Some of the seeds were for maize (corn), and others were
for rice, wheat, and barley.

(11) Although some people call it the "Doomsday Vault," many others
see it as a type of insurance policy against starvation in the case of a terrible
natural disaster. (12) The vault's location keeps it safe from floods, earthquakes,
and ~~storming.~~ (13) Carefully storing these seeds will help ensure not only that
   storms.   *but also that*
people have food to eat important crops never go extinct.

> **PRACTICE 6** **Editing your own writing for parallelism**

Edit a piece of your own writing for parallelism. It can be a paper for this
course or another one, or it can be something you have written for work or
your everyday life. You may want to use the chart on page 424.

Teaching tip Have students form small groups. Then, have each group write five sentences that are not parallel. Each group should exchange sentences with another group and correct the other group's sentences.

Chapter Review

1. Parallelism in writing means that <u>similar parts in a sentence have the same</u>
    <u>structure</u>.

2. In what three situations do problems with parallelism most often occur? <u>with pairs</u>
    <u>and lists, with comparisons, and with certain paired words</u>

3. What are two pairs of correlative conjunctions? <u>Possible answers: both/and,</u>
    <u>neither/nor</u>

4. Write two sentences using parallelism. <u>Answers will vary. One possibility: He was</u>
    <u>walking to the store and whistled all the way.</u>

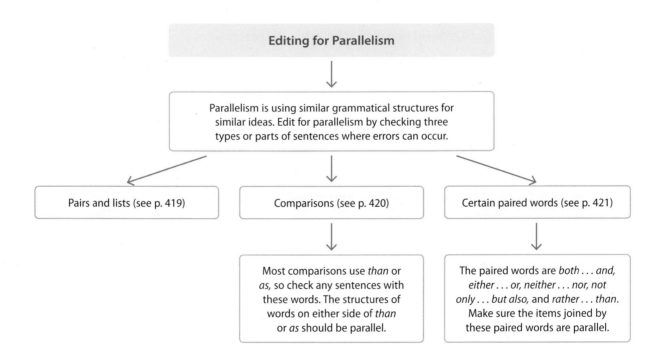

Editing for Parallelism

Parallelism is using similar grammatical structures for similar ideas. Edit for parallelism by checking three types or parts of sentences where errors can occur.

Pairs and lists (see p. 419)

Comparisons (see p. 420)

Certain paired words (see p. 421)

Most comparisons use *than* or *as,* so check any sentences with these words. The structures of words on either side of *than* or *as* should be parallel.

The paired words are *both . . . and, either . . . or, neither . . . nor, not only . . . but also,* and *rather . . . than.* Make sure the items joined by these paired words are parallel.

25

Sentence Variety
Putting Rhythm in Your Writing

Understand What Sentence Variety Is

Sentence variety means using different sentence patterns and lengths to give your writing good rhythm and flow. Notice how the first of the following examples does not have any rhythm.

LaunchPadSolo

Visit **LaunchPad Solo for Readers and Writers > Grammar > Style and Mechanics** for more tutorials, videos, and practice with crafting paragraphs.

With short, simple sentences

Many people do not realize how important their speaking voice and style are. Speaking style can make a difference, particularly in a job interview. What you say is important. How you say it is nearly as important. Your speaking voice creates an impression. Mumbling is a bad way of speaking. It makes the speaker appear sloppy and lacking in confidence. Mumbling also makes it difficult for the interviewer to hear what is being said. Talking too fast is another bad speech behavior. The speaker runs his or her ideas together. The interviewer cannot follow them or distinguish what is important. A third common bad speech behavior concerns verbal "tics." Verbal tics are empty filler phrases like "um,"

GRAMMAR & MECHANICS ROADMAP

An Overview

This Chapter Identifies the Following Trouble Spots

- Starting sentences with adverbs
- Joining ideas using an *-ing* verb
- Joining ideas using a past participle
- Joining ideas using an appositive
- Joining ideas using an adjective clause

Tools to Address Trouble Spots

- Understand What Sentence Variety Is (p. 425)
- Edit for Sentence Variety exercises (p. 435)
- Chapter Review (p. 436)
- Editing for Sentence Variety flowchart (p. 437)

"like," and "you know." Practice for an interview. Sit up straight. Look the person to whom you are speaking directly in the eye. Speak up. Slow down. One good way to find out how you sound is to leave yourself a voice-mail message. If you sound bad to yourself, you need practice speaking aloud. Do not let poor speech behavior interfere with creating a good impression.

With sentence variety

Many people do not realize how important their speaking voice and style are, particularly in a job interview. What you say is important, but how you say it is nearly as important in creating a good impression. Mumbling is a bad way of speaking. Not only does it make the speaker appear sloppy and lacking in confidence, but mumbling also makes it difficult for the interviewer to hear what is being said. Talking too fast is another bad speech behavior. The speaker runs his or her ideas together, and the interviewer cannot follow them or distinguish what is important. A third common bad speech behavior is called verbal "tics," empty filler expressions such as "um," "like," and "you know." When you practice for an interview, sit up straight, look the person to whom you are speaking directly in the eye, speak up, and slow down. One good way to find out how you sound is to leave yourself a voice-mail message. If you sound bad to yourself, you need practice speaking aloud. Do not let poor speech behavior interfere with creating a good impression.

Practice Creating Sentence Variety

Teaching tip The *Instructor's Manual for Real Writing* contains tests and supplemental practice exercises for this chapter.

Most writers tend to write short sentences that start with the subject, so this chapter focuses on techniques for starting with something other than the subject and for writing a variety of longer sentences. Two additional techniques for achieving sentence variety—coordination and subordination—are covered in Chapter 23.

Start Some Sentences with Adverbs

Tip For more about adverbs, see Chapter 22.

Adverbs are words that describe verbs, adjectives, or other adverbs; they often end with *-ly*. As long as the meaning is clear, adverbs can be placed at the beginning of a sentence instead of in the middle. Adverbs at the beginning of a sentence are usually followed by a comma.

Adverb in middle	Stories about haunted houses *frequently* surface at Halloween.
Adverb at beginning	*Frequently*, stories about haunted houses surface at Halloween.
Adverb in middle	These stories *often* focus on ship captains lost at sea.
Adverb at beginning	*Often*, these stories focus on ship captains lost at sea.

PRACTICE 1   **Starting sentences with an adverb**

Edit each sentence so that it begins with an adverb. *Answers may vary.*

Unfortunately, rabies ....*Possible answers are shown.*

Example: Rabies unfortunately remains a problem in the United States.

Once, rabies
1. ~~Rabies once~~ was a major threat to domestic pets in this country.

Now, the
2. ~~The~~ disease is ~~now~~ most deadly to wildlife such as raccoons, skunks, and bats.

Frequently, people
3. ~~People frequently~~ fail to have their pets vaccinated against rabies.

Mistakenly, they believe
4. ~~They believe mistakenly~~ that their dogs and cats are no longer in danger.

Thankfully, an
5. ~~An~~ oral vaccine that prevents rabies in raccoons and skunks has been developed~~, thankfully~~.

PRACTICE 2   **Writing sentences that start with an adverb**

Write three sentences that start with an adverb. Use commas as necessary. Choose among the following adverbs: *often, sadly, amazingly, luckily, lovingly, aggressively, gently, frequently, stupidly.*

1. __Answers will vary._____

2. _____

3. _____

Teaching tip Explain to students that in their own writing, they will need to consider the context when deciding which sentence contains the more important idea. Ask them to bring in their own writing and use the strategy of starting with an adverb in at least one sentence in a paragraph. Have them trade with one another or read out loud and discuss how well that transition or new sentence worked in context with the rest of the paragraph.

Join Ideas Using an -ing *Verb*

One way to combine sentences is to add *-ing* to the verb in the less important of the two sentences and to delete the subject, creating a phrase.

Two sentences	A pecan roll from our bakery is not a health food. It contains 800 calories.
Joined with *-ing* **verb form**	*Containing* 800 calories, a pecan roll from our bakery is not a health food.

You can add the *-ing* phrase to the beginning or the end of the other sentence, depending on what makes more sense.

, equaling
The fat content is also high. ~~It equals~~ the fat in a huge country breakfast.

If you add the *-ing* phrase to the beginning of a sentence, you will usually need to put a comma after it. If you add the phrase to the end of a sentence, you will usually need to put a comma before it. A comma should *not* be used only when the *-ing* phrase is essential to the meaning of the sentence.

Two sentences	Experts examined the effects of exercise on arthritis patients. The experts found that walking, jogging, or swimming could reduce pain.
Joined without commas	Experts examining the effects of exercise on arthritis patients found that walking, jogging, or swimming could reduce pain. [The phrase *examining the effects of exercise on arthritis patients* is essential to the meaning of the sentence.]

Tip For more on finding and correcting dangling modifiers, see Chapter 22, and for more on joining ideas, see Chapter 23.

If you put a phrase starting with an *-ing* verb at the beginning of a sentence, be sure the word that the phrase modifies follows immediately. Otherwise, you will create a dangling modifier.

Two sentences	I ran through the rain. My raincoat got all wet.
Dangling modifier	Running through the rain, my raincoat got all wet.
Edited	Running through the rain, I got my raincoat all wet.

PRACTICE 3   Joining ideas using an *-ing* verb

Teaching tip Doing this practice orally will help students hear the correct formation. The same is true of Practices 5, 7, 8, and 10.

Combine each pair of sentences into a single sentence by using an *-ing* verb. Add or delete words as necessary. *Answers may vary. Possible edits are shown.*

Example: Some people read faces amazingly well. They ~~interpret~~ nonverbal
                                                            , *interpreting*
cues that other people miss.

1. A recent study ~~tested~~ children's abilities to interpret facial expressions. ~~The~~
                  testing
    ~~study~~ made headlines.

2. ~~Physically~~ abused children ~~participated in the study. They~~ saw
    Participating in the study, physically
    photographs of faces changing from one expression to another.

3. The children told researchers what emotion was most obvious in each
    face. ~~The children chose~~ among fear, anger, sadness, happiness, and other
        , *choosing*
    emotions.

4. The study also included nonabused children. ~~They served~~ as a control
                                               , *serving*
    group for comparison with the other children.

5. All the children in the study were equally good at identifying most
    emotions. ~~They all responded~~ similarly to happiness or fear.
            , *responding*

6. Battered children were especially sensitive to one emotion on the
   , identifying
   faces/~~These children identified~~ anger much more quickly than the

   other children could.
   Having
7. ~~The abused children have~~ learned to look for anger/~~They~~ protect
   the abused children

   themselves with this early-warning system.

8. Their sensitivity to anger may not help the abused children later in life/
   perhaps hurting
   ~~It perhaps hurts~~ them socially.
   Tending
9. ~~The abused children tend~~ to run from anger they observe/~~They~~ have
   , abused children

   difficulty connecting with people who exhibit anger.
   , often hanging
10. The human brain works hard to acquire useful information/~~It often hangs~~

    on to the information after its usefulness has passed.

PRACTICE 4   **Joining ideas using an *-ing* verb**

Write two sets of sentences, and join them using an *-ing* verb form.

Example:

a. _Carol looked up._____

b. _She saw three falling stars in the sky._____

Combined: _Looking up, Carol saw three falling stars in the sky._____

1. a. ___Answers will vary._____

   b. _____

   Combined: _____

2. a. _____

   b. _____

   Combined: _____

Join Ideas Using a Past Participle

Another way to combine sentences is to use a past participle (often, a verb ending in *-ed*) to turn the less important of the two sentences into a phrase.

Tip For more on helping verbs, see Chapters 15 and 19. Chapter 19 also covers past participles.

Two sentences	Henry VIII was a powerful English king. He is *remembered* for his many wives.
Joined with a past participle	*Remembered* for his many wives, Henry VIII was a powerful English king.

Past participles of irregular verbs do not end in -ed; they take different forms.

Two sentences	Tim Treadwell was *eaten* by a grizzly bear. He showed that wild animals are unpredictable.
Joined with a past participle	*Eaten* by a grizzly bear, Tim Treadwell showed that wild animals are unpredictable.

Notice that sentences can be joined this way when one of them has a form of *be* along with a past participle (*is remembered* in the first Henry VIII example and *was eaten* in the first Tim Treadwell example).

To combine sentences this way, delete the subject and the *be* form from the sentence that has the *be* form and the past participle. You now have a phrase that can be added to the beginning or the end of the other sentence, depending on what makes more sense.

Pronoun changed to a noun

Subject | *be* form | Past participle

~~Henry VIII was~~ determined to divorce one of his wives. He created the Church of
                                                                              , Henry VIII
England because Catholicism does not allow divorce.

Tip If you put a phrase starting with a past participle at the beginning of a sentence, be sure the word that the phrase modifies follows immediately. Otherwise, you will create a dangling modifier.

If you add a phrase that begins with a past participle to the beginning of a sentence, put a comma after it. If you add the phrase to the end of the sentence, put a comma before it.

> **PRACTICE 5**   **Joining ideas using a past participle**

Combine each pair of sentences into a single sentence by using a past participle. *Answers may vary. Possible edits are shown.*

                          Forced
Example: ~~The oil company was forced~~ to take the local women's
                                       , the oil
objections seriously. ~~The company~~ had to close for ten days during

their protest.

1. *Angered by British colonial rule in 1929, the*
   ~~The~~ women of southern Nigeria ~~were angered by British colonial rule in 1929. They~~ organized a protest.

2. *Covered with pipelines and oil wells,*
   Nigeria is now one of the top ten oil-producing countries. ~~The nation is covered with pipelines and oil wells.~~

3. *Pumped*
   ~~The oil is pumped~~ by American and other foreign oil companies. ~~The~~ oil *, the* often ends up in wealthy Western economies.

4. *Stolen by corrupt rulers in many cases, the*
   ~~The~~ money from the oil seldom reaches Nigeria's local people. ~~The cash is stolen by corrupt rulers in many cases.~~

5. *Polluted*
   ~~The Nigerian countryside is polluted~~ by the oil industry/ ,*the Nigerian countryside* ~~The land then~~

   becomes a wasteland.

6. *Insulted*
   ~~Many Nigerians are insulted~~ by the way the oil industry treats them/ ,*many Nigerians* ~~They~~

   want the oil companies to pay attention to their problems.

7. *Inspired*
   ~~Local Nigerian women were inspired~~ by the 1929 women's protests/ ,*local Nigerian women* ~~They~~

   launched a series of protests against the oil industry in the summer of

   2002.

8. The women prevented workers from entering or leaving two oil company

   offices/ ~~The offices were~~ located in the port of Warri.

9. *Concerned*
   ~~Workers at the oil company were concerned~~ about the women's threat

   to take off their clothes/ ,*many workers at the oil company* ~~Many workers~~ told company officials that such a

   protest would bring a curse on the company and shame to its employees.

10. The company eventually agreed to hire more local people and to invest in

    local projects/ ~~The projects are~~ intended to supply electricity and provide

    the villagers with a market for fish and poultry.

PRACTICE 6 **Joining ideas using a past participle**

Write two sets of sentences, and join them with a past participle.

Example:

a. *Chris is taking intermediate accounting.*

b. *It is believed to be the most difficult course in the major.*

Combined: *Chris is taking intermediate accounting, believed to be the most difficult course in the major.*

1. a. *Answers will vary.*

   b. _____

   Combined: _____

   _____

2. a. _____

   b. _____

   Combined: _____

   _____

Teaching tip Say aloud a sentence that has as its subject something familiar to students in the class (for example, the president, a celebrity). Ask them to suggest a good appositive.

Tip Usually, you will want to turn the less important of the two sentences into an appositive.

Join Ideas Using an Appositive

An **appositive** is a noun or noun phrase that renames a noun or pronoun. Appositives can be used to combine two sentences into one.

Two sentences	Brussels sprouts can be roasted for a delicious flavor. They are a commonly disliked food.
Joined with an appositive	Brussels sprouts, a commonly disliked food, can be roasted for a delicious flavor.

[The phrase *a commonly disliked food* renames the noun *brussels sprouts*.]

Notice that the sentence that renames the noun was turned into a noun phrase by dropping the subject and the verb (*They* and *are*). Also, commas set off the appositive.

> **PRACTICE 7**   **Joining ideas using an appositive**

Combine each pair of sentences into a single sentence by using an appositive. Be sure to use a comma or commas to set off the appositive. *Answers may vary. Possible edits are shown.*

Example: Levi's jeans have looked the same for well over a century. ~~They are perhaps the most famous work clothes in the world.~~ *; perhaps the most famous work clothes in the world,*

1. Jacob Davis, ~~was~~ a Russian immigrant working in Reno, Nevada, ~~He was~~ the inventor of Levi's jeans.

2. Davis came up with an invention that made work clothes last longer. *, the riveted seam,* ~~The invention was the riveted seam.~~

3. Davis bought denim from a wholesaler. ~~The wholesaler was~~ Levi Strauss.

4. In 1870, he offered to sell the rights to his invention to Levi Strauss for the price of the patent. ~~Patents then cost~~ about $70.

5. Davis joined the firm in 1873 and supervised the final development of its product. ~~The product was~~ the famous Levi's jeans.

6. Davis oversaw a crucial design element. ~~The jeans all had~~ orange stitching.

7. *Another* ~~The curved stitching on the back pockets was another~~ choice Davis made. ~~It~~ also survives in today's Levi's. *, the curved stitching on the back pockets,*

8. *A* ~~The stitching on the pockets has been a~~ trademark since 1942. ~~It~~ is very recognizable. *the stitching on the pockets*

9. During World War II, Levi Strauss temporarily stopped adding the pocket stitches because they wasted thread/, ~~It was~~ a valuable resource.
   _∧

10. Until the war ended, the pocket design was added with a less valuable material/, ~~The company used~~ paint.
    _∧

Join Ideas Using an Adjective Clause

An **adjective clause** is a group of words with a subject and a verb that describes a noun. An adjective clause often begins with the word *who, which,* or *that,* and it can be used to combine two sentences into one.

Tip For more about adjectives, see Chapter 21.

Two sentences	Lauren has won many basketball awards. She is captain of her college team.
Joined with an adjective clause	Lauren, *who is captain of her college team,* has won many basketball awards.

To join sentences this way, use *who, which,* or *that* to replace the subject in a sentence that describes a noun in the other sentence. You now have an adjective clause that you can move so that it follows the noun it describes. The sentence with the more important idea (the one you want to emphasize) should become the main clause. The less important idea should be in the adjective clause.

```
        Main clause                    Adjective clause
┌──────────────┴──────────────┐  ┌──────────┴──────────┐
                                      , which
Leigh got an internship because of her blog/ It caught the eye of people in the
└──────────────────────────┘              ∧
fashion industry.
```

[The more important idea here is that Leigh got an internship because of her blog. The less important idea is that the blog caught the eye of people in the fashion industry.]

Tip Use *who* to refer to a person, *which* to refer to places or things (but not to people), and *that* for places or things.

NOTE: If an adjective clause can be taken out of a sentence without completely changing the meaning of the sentence, put commas around it.

Lauren, *who is captain of her college team,* has won many basketball awards.

[The phrase *who is captain of her college team* adds information about Lauren, but it is not essential.]

If an adjective clause is an essential part of a sentence, do not put commas around it.

Lauren is an award-winning basketball player who overcame childhood cancer.

[*Who overcame childhood cancer* is an essential part of this sentence.]

> **PRACTICE 8**   Joining ideas using an adjective clause

Combine each pair of sentences into a single sentence by using an adjective clause beginning with *who, which,* or *that.* *Answers will vary. Possible edits are shown.*

Example: My friend Erin had her first child last June. *, who has been going to college for the past three years,* ~~She has been going to college for the past three years.~~

1. While Erin goes to classes, her baby boy stays at a day-care center. *, which* ~~The day-care center~~ costs Erin about $100 a week.

2. Twice when her son was ill, Erin had to miss her geology lab. *, which* ~~The lab~~ is an important part of her grade for that course.

3. Occasionally, Erin's parents *, who live about 70 miles away,* come up and watch the baby while Erin is studying. ~~They live about 70 miles away.~~

4. Sometimes Erin feels discouraged by the extra costs. *that* ~~The costs~~ have come from having a child.

5. She believes that some of her professors are not very sympathetic. *who have never been parents themselves* ~~These professors are the ones who have never been parents themselves.~~

6. Erin *, who wants to be a good mother and a good student,* understands that she must take responsibility for both her child and her education. ~~She wants to be a good mother and a good student.~~

7. Her grades *, which were once straight A's,* have suffered somewhat since she had her son. ~~They were once straight A's.~~

8. Erin wants to graduate with honors. *, who hopes to go to graduate school someday,* ~~She hopes to go to graduate school someday.~~

9. Her son *, who is the most important thing to her,* is more important than an A in geology. ~~He is the most important thing to her.~~

10. Erin still expects to have a high grade point average. *, who* ~~She~~ has simply given up expecting to be perfect.

> **PRACTICE 9**   Joining ideas using an adjective clause

Fill in the blank in each of the following sentences with an appropriate adjective clause. Add commas, if necessary. *Answers may vary. Possible edits are shown.*

Example: The firefighters ___*who responded to the alarm*___ **entered the burning building.**

Teaching tip If your students have written a full-length paper, ask them to go through and incorporate each of these sentence variety strategies at least one time. Then, have them highlight the area where they did so. Have them trade papers or talk about them as a class—did the sentence variety strategies make the paper more interesting? Did the strategies help them connect or combine ideas together to help with the flow of the paper?

1. A fire ___*that was probably caused by faulty wiring*___ began in our house in the middle of the night.

2. The members of my family ___*who were home at the time of the fire*___ were all asleep.

3. My father ___*, who has always been a light sleeper,*___ was the first to smell smoke.

4. He ran to our bedrooms ___*, which were on the second floor,*___ and woke us up with his shouting.

5. The house ___*, which was the only home I had ever lived in,*___ was damaged, but everyone in my family reached safety.

Edit for Sentence Variety

PRACTICE 10   Editing paragraphs for sentence variety

Create sentence variety in the following paragraphs by joining at least two sentences in each of the paragraphs. Use several of the techniques covered in this chapter. More than one correct answer is possible. *Answers may vary. Possible edits are shown.*

(1) Few people would associate the famous English poet and playwright William Shakespeare with prison. (2) However, Shakespeare has taken on an important role in the lives of certain inmates/ *who* (3) ~~They~~ are serving time at the Luther Luckett Correctional Complex in Kentucky. (4) ~~These inmates were brought~~ *Brought* together by the Shakespeare Behind Bars program/ *, these inmates* (5) ~~They~~ spend nine months preparing for a performance of one of the great writer's plays.

(6) Recently, prisoners at Luckett performed *The Merchant of Venice*/ (7) ~~It is~~ one of Shakespeare's most popular plays. (8) Many of the actors identified with Shylock/ (9) ~~He is~~ a moneylender who is discriminated against because he is Jewish. (10) When a rival asks Shylock for a loan to help a friend, Shylock drives a hard bargain/ *demanding* (11) ~~He demands~~ a pound of the rival's flesh if the loan is not repaid. (12) ~~One inmate shared~~ *Sharing* his views of this play with a newspaper reporter/ *, one* (13) ~~The~~ inmate said, "It deals with race. It deals with discrimination. It deals with gambling, debt, cutting people. It deals with it all. And we were all living that someway, somehow."

(14) Through the Shakespeare performances, the inmates form bonds not only with the characters but also with one another. (15) Additionally,

they are able to explore their own histories and their responsibility for the

crimes they committed. (16) Many feel changed by their experience on

the stage. (17) ~~One actor was affected~~ deeply by his role in *The Merchant*
Affected

of Venice, (18) ~~He~~ said, "You feel like you're in a theater outside of here. You
one actor

don't feel the razor wire."

PRACTICE 11   **Editing your own writing for sentence variety**

Add more sentence variety to a piece of your own writing—a paper for this
course or another one, or choose something you have written for work or your
everyday life. You may want to use the chart on page 437.

Chapter Review

1. Having sentence variety means *using different sentence patterns and lengths to give
    your writing good rhythm and flow* .

2. If you tend to write short, similar-sounding sentences, what five techniques should
    you try? *starting some sentences with adverbs, joining sentences using an "-ing"
    verb, joining sentences using a past participle, joining sentences using an appositive,
    and joining sentences using an adjective clause* .

3. An ___*appositive*___ is a noun or noun phrase that renames a noun.

4. An ___*adjective*___ clause often starts with *who,* ___*which*___, or ___*that*___. It describes a
    noun or pronoun.

5. Use commas around an adjective clause when the information in it is
    (essential/not essential) to the meaning of the sentence.

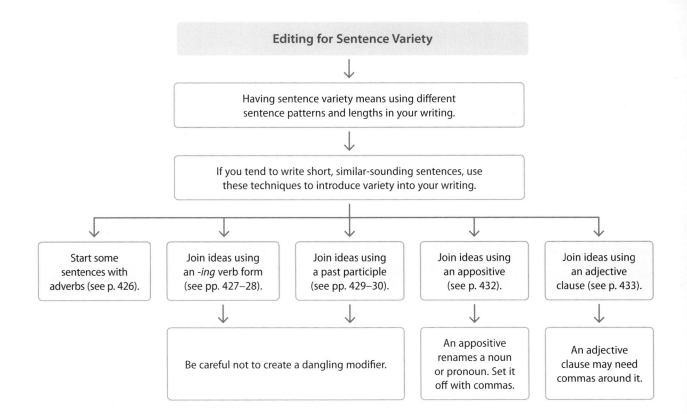

Editing for Sentence Variety

Having sentence variety means using different sentence patterns and lengths in your writing.

↓

If you tend to write short, similar-sounding sentences, use these techniques to introduce variety into your writing.

Start some sentences with adverbs (see p. 426).

Join ideas using an *-ing* verb form (see pp. 427–28).

Join ideas using a past participle (see pp. 429–30).

Join ideas using an appositive (see p. 432).

Join ideas using an adjective clause (see p. 433).

Be careful not to create a dangling modifier.

An appositive renames a noun or pronoun. Set it off with commas.

An adjective clause may need commas around it.

26

Formal English and ESL Concerns
Grammar Trouble Spots for Multilingual Students

LaunchPadSolo

Visit **LaunchPad Solo for Readers and Writers > Grammar > Resources for Multilingual Writers** for more tutorials, videos, and practice with crafting paragraphs.

Tip In this chapter, we use the word *English* to refer to formal English. Throughout the chapter, subjects are underlined, and verbs are double-underlined.

Teaching tip For additional support and exercises for ESL students, see *The Bedford/St. Martin's ESL Workbook,* Second Edition, available with this text.

Academic, or formal, English is the English you will be expected to use in college and in most work situations, especially in writing. If you are not accustomed to using formal English or if English is not your native language, this chapter will help you avoid the most common problems with key sentence parts.

Basic Sentence Patterns

Statements

Every sentence in English must have at least one subject and one verb **(S-V)** that together express a complete idea. The subject performs the action, and the verb names the action, as in the sentence that follows.

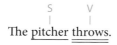

The pitcher throws.

GRAMMAR & MECHANICS ROADMAP

An Overview

This Chapter Identifies the Following Trouble Spots

- Sentence patterns and word order
- Pronouns
- Negatives
- Questions
- *There is* and *there are*
- Confusing subject and object pronouns
- Verbs
- Articles
- Count and noncount nouns
- Prepositions

Tools to Address Trouble Spots

- Understand Basic Sentence Patterns (p. 438)
- List of common negatives and helping verbs (pp. 440–41)
- List of Pronoun Types (p. 444)
- Coverage of verbs and verb tenses (p. 445)
- List of Modal (Helping) Verbs (pp. 452–55)
- List of verbs commonly followed by a gerund or infinitive (pp. 457–58)
- List of Count and Noncount Nouns (p. 460)
- Common verb/preposition combinations (p. 462)
- Chapter Review (p. 463)

Other English sentence patterns build on that structure. One of the most common patterns is subject-verb-object **(S-V-O)**.

Teaching tip You may wish to assign this chapter to your class as a whole, especially if you have native students who speak nonstandard English. Even if they know the parts of speech, many students need extra practice with how those parts function in writing.

```
        S      V        O
        |      |        |
The pitcher throws the ball.
```

There are two kinds of objects.
   Direct objects receive the action of the verb.

```
        S      V        DO
        |      |        |
The pitcher throws the ball.
```

[The ball directly receives the action of the verb *throws*.]

Indirect objects do not receive the action of the verb. Instead, the action is performed *for* or *to* the person.

```
        S      V    IO    DO
        |      |    |      |
The pitcher throws me the ball.
```

> **PRACTICE 1**   **Sentence patterns**
>
> Label the subject (S), verb (V), direct object (DO), and indirect object (IO), if any, in the following two sentences.
>
> ```
>          S     V      DO
>          |     |      |
> 1.  John sent the letter.
>          S     V    IO     DO
>          |     |    |      |
> 2.  John sent Beth the letter.
> ```

Another common sentence pattern is subject-verb-prepositional phrase. In standard English, the prepositional phrase typically follows the subject and verb.

Tip For more on the parts of sentences, see Chapter 15.

```
                Prepositional
   S    V          phrase
   |    |     |-------------|
Lilah went to the movies.
```

> **PRACTICE 2**   **Using correct word order**
>
> Read each of the sentences that follow. If the sentence is correct, write "C" in the blank to the left of it. If it is incorrect, write "I"; then, rewrite the sentence using correct word order.
>
> **Example:** __I__ **My friend to me gave a present.**
>
>   **Revision:** *My friend gave me a present.* _____
>
> 1. __I__ Presents I like very much.
>
>   Revision: *I like presents very much.* _____

2. ___I___ To parties I go often.

   Revision: _I go to parties often._

3. ___I___ To parties, I always bring a present.

   Revision: _I always bring a present to parties._

4. ___C___ At my parties, people bring me presents, too.

   Revision: _____

5. ___I___ Always write to them a thank-you note.

   Revision: _I always write them a thank-you note._

Negatives

To form a negative statement, use one of the words listed here, often with a helping verb such as *can/could, does/did, has/have,* or *should/will/would.*

never	nobody	no one	nowhere
no	none	not	

Notice in these examples that the word *not* comes *after* the helping verb.

Sentence	Dina can sing.
Negative	Dina <del>no</del> can sing. ^*cannot*
Sentence	The store sells cigarettes.
Negative	The store <del>no</del> sells cigarettes. ^*does not*
Sentence	Bruce will call.
Negative	Bruce <del>no</del> will call. ^*not*
Sentence	Caroline walked.
Negative	Caroline <del>no</del> did walk. ^*not*

Tip For more on helping verbs and their forms, see Chapter 15.

The helping verb cannot be omitted in expressions using *not.*

Incorrect	The store *not sell* cigarettes.
Correct	The store *does not sell* cigarettes.
	[*Does,* a form of the helping verb *do,* must come before *not.*]
Correct	The store *is not selling* cigarettes.
	[*Is,* a form of *be,* must come before *not.*]

Common Helping Verbs

Forms of *be*	Forms of *have*	Forms of *do*	Other verbs
am	have	do	can
are	has	does	could
is	had	did	may
been			might
being			must
was			should
were			will
			would

Double negatives are not standard in English.

Incorrect	Shane *does not have* no ride.
Correct	Shane *does not have* a ride.
Correct	Shane *has no* ride.

When forming a negative in the simple past tense, use the past tense of the help-ing verb *do*.

| *did* | + | *not* | + | Base verb without an *-ed* | = | Negative past tense |

Sentence	I *talked* to Jairo last night.
	[*Talked* is the past tense.]
Negative	I *did not* talk to Jairo last night.
	[Notice that *talk* in this sentence does not have an *-ed* ending because the helping verb *did* conveys the past tense.]

PRACTICE 3   **Forming negatives**

Rewrite the sentences to make them negative.

Example: Hassan's son is ^not^ talking now.

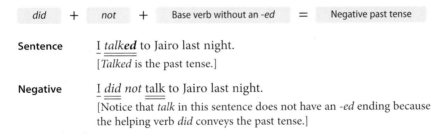

1. He ~~can~~ ^cannot^ say several words.

2. Hassan ^does not^ remembers when his daughter started talking.

3. He ^does not^ thinks it was at the same age.

4. His daughter was ^not^ an early speaker.

5. Hassan ^does not^ expects his son to be a talkative adult.

Questions

Tip Sometimes the verb appears before the subject in sentences that are not questions: *Behind the supermarket is the sub shop.*

To turn a statement into a question, move the helping verb so that it comes before the subject. Add a question mark (**?**) to the end of the question.

Statement	Johan *can go* tonight.
Question	*Can* Johan *go* tonight?

If the only verb in the statement is a form of *be*, it should be moved before the subject.

Statement	Jamie *is* at work.
Question	*Is* Jamie at work?

If the statement does not contain a helping verb or a form of *be*, add a form of *do* and put it before the subject. Be sure to end the question with a question mark (**?**).

Statement	Norah sings in the choir.	Tyrone goes to college.
Question	*Does* Norah sing in the choir?	*Does* Tyrone go to college?
Statement	The building burned.	The plate broke.
Question	*Did* the building burn?	*Did* the plate break?

Notice that the verb changed once the helping verb *did* was added.

Do is used with *I, you, we,* and *they. Does* is used with *he, she,* and *it.*

Examples	*Do* [I/you/we/they] practice every day?
	Does [he/she/it] sound terrible?

> **PRACTICE 4   Forming questions**
>
> Rewrite the sentences to make them into questions.
>
> ~~~Does~~~   ?
> Example: Brad knows how to cook.
>
>   Does he   ?
> 1. He makes dinner every night for his family.
>   Does he go   ?
> 2. He goes to the grocery store once a week.
>   Does he   ?
> 3. He uses coupons to save money.
>   Does   ?
> 4. Brad saves a lot of money using coupons.

There Is *and* There Are

English sentences often include *there is* or *there are* to indicate the existence of something.

> *There is* a <u>man</u> at the door.
> [You could also say, *A man is at the door.*]
>
> *There are* many <u>men</u> in the class.
> [You could also say, *Many men are in the class.*]

When a sentence includes the words *there is* or *there are*, the verb (*is, are*) comes before the noun it goes with (which is actually the subject of the sentence). The verb must agree with the noun in number. For example, the first sentence above uses the singular verb *is* to agree with the singular noun *man*, and the second sentence uses the plural verb *are* to agree with the plural noun *men*.

In questions, *is* or *are* comes before *there*.

Statements	*There is* <u>plenty</u> to eat.
	There are some <u>things</u> to do.
Questions	*Is there* <u>plenty</u> to eat?
	Are there some <u>things</u> to do?

Pronouns

Pronouns replace nouns or other pronouns in a sentence so that you do not have to repeat them. There are three types of pronouns: subject pronouns, object pronouns, and possessive pronouns.

Subject pronouns serve as the subject of the verb (and remember that every English sentence *must* have a subject).

> <u>Rob</u> <u>is</u> my cousin. ^{He}<u>Rob</u> <u>lives</u> next to me.

Object pronouns receive the action of the verb or are part of a prepositional phrase.

> <u>Rob</u> <u>asked</u> *me* for a favor.
> [The object pronoun *me* receives the action of the verb *asked*.]
>
> <u>Rob</u> <u>lives</u> next door *to me*.
> [*To me* is the prepositional phrase; *me* is the object pronoun.]

Possessive pronouns show ownership.

> <u>Rob</u> <u>is</u> *my* cousin.

Tip For more on pronouns, see Chapter 20.

Use the following chart to check which type of pronoun to use.

Pronoun Types

Subject		Object		Possessive	
Singular	**Plural**	**Singular**	**Plural**	**Singular**	**Plural**
I	we	me	us	my/mine	our/ours
you	you	you	you	your/yours	your/yours
he/she/it	they	him/her/it	them	his/her/hers/its	theirs

Relative Pronouns

who, which, that

The singular pronouns *he/she, him/her,* and *his/hers* show gender. *He, him,* and *his* are masculine pronouns; *she, her,* and *hers* are feminine.

Here are some examples of common pronoun errors, with corrections.

Confusing Subject and Object Pronouns

Use a subject pronoun for the word that *performs* the action of the verb, and use an object pronoun for the word that *receives* the action.

<u>Tashia</u> is a good student. <u>Her</u> gets all A's. *She*

[The pronoun performs the action *gets,* so it should be the subject pronoun, *she.*]

<u>Tomas</u> <u>gave</u> the keys to she. <u>Banh</u> <u>gave</u> the coat to he. *her* ... *him*

[The pronoun receives the action of *gave,* so it should be the object pronoun, *her* or *him.*]

Confusing Gender

Use masculine pronouns to replace masculine nouns, and use feminine pronouns to replace feminine nouns.

<u>Nick</u> <u>is</u> sick. <u>She</u> <u>has</u> the flu. *He*

[*Nick* is a masculine noun, so the pronoun must be masculine.]

The <u>jacket</u> <u>belongs</u> to Jane. <u>Give</u> it to him. *her*

[*Jane* is feminine, so the pronoun must be feminine.]

Leaving Out a Pronoun

Some sentences use the pronoun *it* as the subject or object. Do not leave *it* out of the sentence.

It is
~~Is~~ a holiday today.

It will
Maria will bring the food. ~~Will~~ be delicious.

it
I tried calamari last night and liked very much.

Using a Pronoun to Repeat a Subject

A pronoun *replaces* a noun, so do not use both a subject noun and a pronoun.

My father ~~he~~ is very strict.

[*Father* is the subject noun, so the sentence should not also have the subject pronoun *he.*]

The bus ~~it~~ was late.

[*Bus* is the subject noun, so the sentence should not also have the subject pronoun *it.*]

Using Relative Pronouns

The words *who, which,* and *that* are **relative pronouns**. Use relative pronouns in a clause that gives more information about the subject.

- Use *who* to refer to a person or people.

  The man *who* lives next door plays piano.
- Use *which* or *that* to refer to nonliving things.

  The plant, *which* was a gift, died.

  The phone *that* I bought last week is broken.

Verbs

Verbs have different tenses to show when something happened: in the past, present, or future.

This section contains time lines, examples, and common errors for the simple and perfect tenses; coverage of progressive tenses; and more. See Chapter 19 for full coverage of the simple tenses and the perfect tenses, as well as practice exercises.

The Simple Tenses

SIMPLE PRESENT

Use the simple present to describe situations that exist now.

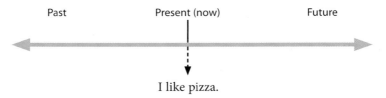

I like pizza.

I/You/We/They <u>like</u> pizza.
She/He <u>likes</u> pizza.

The third-person singular (*she/he*) of regular verbs ends in *-s* or *-es*. For irregular verb endings, see pages 366–69.

SIMPLE PAST

Use the simple past to describe situations that began and ended in the past.

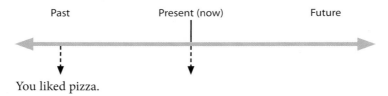

You liked pizza.

I/You/She/He/We/They <u>like**d**</u> pizza.

For regular verbs, the simple past is formed by adding either *-d* or *-ed* to the verb. For the past forms of irregular verbs, see the chart on pages 366–69.

SIMPLE FUTURE

Use the simple future to describe situations that will happen in the future. It is easier to form than the past tense. Use this formula for forming the future tense.

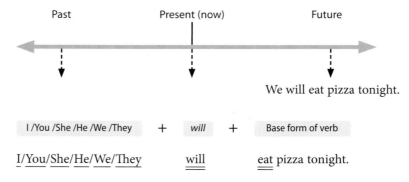

We will eat pizza tonight.

| I /You /She /He /We /They | + | *will* | + | Base form of verb |

I/You/She/He/We/They   <u>will</u>   <u>eat</u> pizza tonight.

COMMON ERRORS IN USING SIMPLE TENSES

Following are some common errors in using simple tenses.

Simple present. Forgetting to add *-s* or *-es* to verbs that go with third-person singular subjects (*she/he/it*)

Tip The subject and the verb must agree in number. For more on subject-verb agreement, see Chapter 18.

Incorrect	She know the manager.
Correct	She knows the manager.

Simple past. Forgetting to add *-d* or *-ed* to regular verbs

Incorrect	Gina work late last night.
Correct	Gina worked late last night.

Forgetting to use the correct past forms of irregular verbs (see the chart of irregular verb forms on pages 366–69)

Incorrect	Gerard speaked to her about the problem.
Correct	Gerard **spoke** to her about the problem.

Forgetting to use the base verb without an ending for negative sentences

Tip Double negatives (*Johnetta will **not** call **no one***) are not standard in English. One negative is enough (*Johnetta will **not** call **anyone***).

Incorrect	She does not wants money for helping.
Correct	She does not **want** money for helping.

The Perfect Tenses

PRESENT PERFECT

Use the present perfect to describe situations that started in the past and either continue into the present or were completed at some unknown time in the past.

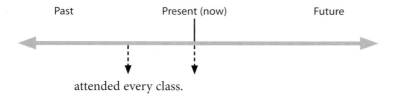

attended every class.

To form the present perfect tense, use this formula:

Subject	+	*has/have*	+	Past participle of base verb

She/He	*has*	*attended* every class.
I/We/They	*have*	*attended* every class.

Notice that *I/We/They* use *have* and that *She/He* use *has*.

PAST PERFECT

Use the past perfect to describe situations that began and ended before some other situation happened.

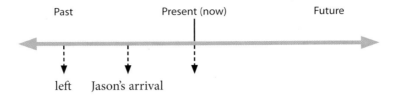

To form the past perfect tense, use this formula:

I/You/She/He/We/They   _had_   _left_ before Jason arrived.

FUTURE PERFECT

Use the future perfect to describe situations that begin and end before another situation begins.

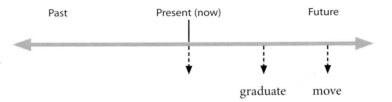

Use this formula to form the future perfect tense:

I/You/She/He/We/They   _will have_   _graduated_ before moving.

COMMON ERRORS IN FORMING THE PERFECT TENSE

Using _had_ instead of _has_ or _have_ for the present perfect

Incorrect	We **had** lived here since 2003.
Correct	We **have** lived here since 2003.

Forgetting to use past participles (with *-d* or *-ed* endings for regular verbs)

Incorrect	She has attend every class.
Correct	She has attend**ed** every class.

Using *been* between *have* or *has* and the past participle of a base verb

Incorrect	I have **been** attended every class.
Correct	I have attended every class.
Incorrect	I will have **been** graduated before I move.
Correct	I will have graduated before I move.

The Present Progressive Tenses

The progressive tense is used to describe ongoing actions in the present, past, or future. Following are some common errors in using the present progressive tense.

Forgetting to add *-ing* to the verb

Incorrect	I am type now. She/he is not type now.
Correct	I am typ**ing** now. She/he is not typ**ing** now.

Forgetting to include a form of *be* (*am/is/are*)

Incorrect	He typing now. They typing now.
Correct	He **is** typing now. They **are** typing now.

Forgetting to use a form of *be* (*am/is/are*) to start questions

Incorrect	They typing now?
Correct	**Are** they typing now?

The following charts show how to use the present, past, and future progressive tenses in regular statements, negative statements, and questions.

THE PROGRESSIVE TENSES

Tense

Present Progressive

Time line: a situation that is happening now but started in the past

Past	Present (now)	Future

I am typing.

STATEMENTS

Present of *BE* (*am/is/are*) + Base verb ending in *-ing*

I **am typing**.	We **are typing**.
You **are typing**.	They **are typing**.
She/he **is typing**.	

NEGATIVES

Present of *BE* (*am/is/are*) + *not* + Base verb ending in *-ing*

I **am not typing**.	We **are not typing**.
You **are not typing**.	They **are not typing**.
She/he **is not typing**.	

QUESTIONS

Present of *BE* (*am/is/are*) + Subject + Base verb ending in *-ing*

Am I **typing**?	**Are** we **typing**?
Are you **typing**?	**Are** they **typing**?
Is she/he **typing**?	

Past Progressive

Time line: a situation that was going on in the past

Past	Present (now)	Future

raining — arrival at restaurant

STATEMENTS

Past of *BE* (*was/were*) + Base verb ending in *-ing*

It **was raining** when I got to the restaurant at 7:00.

The students **were studying** all night.

NEGATIVES

Past of *BE* (*was/were*) + *not* + Base verb ending in *-ing*

It **was not raining** when I got to the restaurant at 7:00.

The students **were not studying** all night.

QUESTIONS

Past of *BE* (*was/were*) + Subject + Base verb ending in *-ing*

Was it **raining** when I got to the restaurant at 7:00?

Were the students **studying** all night?

Tense		
Future Progressive		

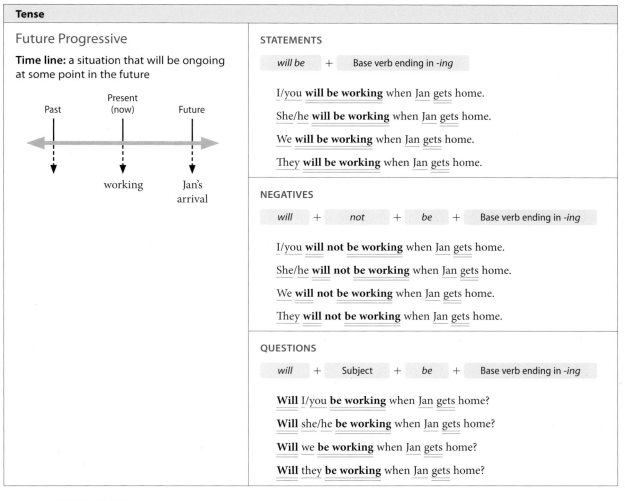

Future Progressive

Time line: a situation that will be ongoing at some point in the future

Past — Present (now) — Future

working   Jan's arrival

STATEMENTS

| will be | + | Base verb ending in *-ing* |

I/you **will be working** when Jan gets home.

She/he **will be working** when Jan gets home.

We **will be working** when Jan gets home.

They **will be working** when Jan gets home.

NEGATIVES

| will | + | not | + | be | + | Base verb ending in *-ing* |

I/you **will not be working** when Jan gets home.

She/he **will not be working** when Jan gets home.

We **will not be working** when Jan gets home.

They **will not be working** when Jan gets home.

QUESTIONS

| will | + | Subject | + | be | + | Base verb ending in *-ing* |

Will I/you **be working** when Jan gets home?

Will she/he **be working** when Jan gets home?

Will we **be working** when Jan gets home?

Will they **be working** when Jan gets home?

PRACTICE 5   **Forming negative statements and questions**

Rewrite the following sentences as indicated.

1. Betsy is golfing today. *Make the sentence a question:*

   Is Betsy golfing today?

2. It was snowing when we got up. *Make the sentence a negative statement:*

   It was not snowing when we got up.

3. You are going to the mall. *Make the sentence a question:*

   Are you going to the mall?

4. They are losing the game. *Make the sentence a negative statement:*

   They are not losing the game.

5. Meriam was eating when you arrived. *Make the sentence into a question:*

   Was Meriam eating when you arrived?

Modal (Helping) Verbs

Tip For more on helping verbs, see Chapter 15.

Modal verbs (or modal auxiliary verbs) are helping verbs that express the writer's attitude about an action. You do not have to learn too many modal verbs—just the eight in the chart that follows.

MODAL (HELPING) VERBS	
General Formulas For all modal verbs	**STATEMENTS** Present: Subject + Modal verb + Base verb Dumbo can fly. Past: Forms vary.
	NEGATIVES Present: Subject + Modal verb + *not* + Base verb Dumbo cannot fly. Past: Forms vary.
	QUESTIONS Present: Modal verb + Subject + Base verb Can Dumbo fly? Past: Forms vary.
Can Means *ability*	**STATEMENTS** Present: Beth **can** work fast. Past: Beth **could** work fast.
	NEGATIVES Present: Beth **can**not work fast. Past: Beth **could** not work fast.
	QUESTIONS Present: **Can** Beth work fast? Past: **Could** Beth work fast? →

MODAL (HELPING) VERBS

Could

Means *possibility*. It can also be the past tense of *can*.

STATEMENTS

Present: Beth **could** work quickly if she had more time.

Past: Beth **could** have worked quickly if she had had more time.

NEGATIVES

Can is used for present negatives. (See above.)

Past: Beth **could** not have worked quickly.

QUESTIONS

Present: Could Beth work quickly?

Past: Could Beth have worked quickly?

May

Means *permission*
For past-tense forms, see *might*.

STATEMENTS

Present: You **may** borrow my car.

NEGATIVES

Present: You **may** not borrow my car.

QUESTIONS

Present: May I borrow your car?

Might

Means *possibility*. It can also be the past tense of *may*.

STATEMENTS

Present (with *be*): Lou **might** be asleep.

Past (with *have* + past participle of *be*): Lou **might** have been asleep.

Future: Lou **might** sleep.

NEGATIVES

Present (with *be*): Lou **might** not be asleep.

Past (with *have* + past participle of *be*): Lou **might** not have been asleep.

Future: Lou **might** not sleep.

QUESTIONS

Might in questions is very formal and not often used.

→

MODAL (HELPING) VERBS	
Must Means *necessary*	**STATEMENTS** **Present:** We **must** try. **Past** (with *have* + past participle of base verb): We **must** have tried. **Past** (with *had* + *to* + base verb): We **had to** try.
	NEGATIVES **Present:** We **must** not try. **Past** (with *have* + past participle of base verb): We **must** not have tried.
	QUESTIONS **Present: Must** we try? Past-tense questions with *must* are unusual.
Should Means *duty* or *expectation*	**STATEMENTS** **Present:** They **should** call. **Past** (with *have* + past participle of base verb): They **should** have called.
	NEGATIVES **Present:** They **should** not call. **Past** (with *have* + past participle of base verb): They **should** not have called.
	QUESTIONS **Present: Should** they call? **Past** (with *have* + past participle of base verb): **Should** they have called?
Will Means *intend to* (future) For past-tense forms, see *would*.	**STATEMENTS** **Future:** I **will** succeed.
	NEGATIVES **Future:** I **will** not succeed.
	QUESTIONS **Future: Will** I succeed? →

MODAL (HELPING) VERBS

Would

Means *prefer* or used to start a future request. It can also be the past tense of *will*.

STATEMENTS

Present: I **would** like to travel.

Past (with *have* + past participle of base verb):
I **would** have traveled if I had had the money.

NEGATIVES

Present: I **would** not like to travel.

Past (with *have* + past participle of base verb):
I **would** not have traveled if it had not been for you.

QUESTIONS

Present: Would you like to travel?

Or to start a request: **Would** you help me?

Past (with *have* + past participle of base verb):
Would you have traveled with me if I had asked you?

COMMON ERRORS WITH MODAL VERBS

Following are some common errors in using modal verbs.

Using more than one helping verb

Incorrect	They **will can** help.
Correct	They **will** help. (future intention)
	They **can** help. (are able to)

Using *to* between the modal verb and the main (base) verb

| Incorrect | Emilio **might to** come with us. |
| Correct | Emilio **might** come with us. |

Using *must* instead of *had to* to form the past tense

| Incorrect | She **must** work yesterday. |
| Correct | She **had to** work yesterday. |

Forgetting to change *can* to *could* to form the past negative

Incorrect	Last night, I **can**not sleep.
Correct	Last night, I **could** not sleep.

Forgetting to use *have* with *could/should/would* to form the past tense

Incorrect	Tara **should** called last night.
Correct	Tara **should have** called last night.

Using *will* instead of *would* to express a preference in the present tense

Incorrect	I **will** like to travel.
Correct	I **would** like to travel.

> **PRACTICE 6**   **Using the correct tense**
>
> Fill in the blanks with the correct form of the verbs in parentheses, adding helping verbs as needed. Refer to the verb charts if you need help. *Answers may vary. Possible answers are shown.*
> **Example:** ___*Have*___ you ___*heard*___ (hear) of volcano boarding?

(1) In a November 5, 2002, article in *National Geographic Today*, Zoltan Istvan ___*reported*___ (report) on a new sport: volcano boarding. (2) Istvan first ___*got*___ (get) the idea in 1995, when he ___*was sailing*___ (sail) past Mt. Yasur, an active volcano on an island off the coast of Australia. (3) For centuries, Mt. Yasur ___*has had*___ (have) the reputation of being a dangerous volcano. (4) For example, it regularly ___*spits*___ (spit) out lava bombs. (5) These large molten rocks ___*have*___ often ___*struck*___ (strike) visitors on the head.

(6) There is a village at the base of Mt. Yasur. (7) When Istvan arrived with his snowboard, the villagers ___*did*___ not ___*know*___ (know) what to think. (8) He ___*made*___ (make) his way to the volcano, ___*hiked*___ (hike) up the highest peak, and rode his board all the way down. (9) After he ___*reached*___ (reach) the bottom, Istvan admitted that volcano boarding is more difficult than snowboarding. (10) Luckily, no lava bombs ___*fell*___ (fall) from the sky, although the volcano ___*had erupted*___ (erupt) seconds before his descent. (11) Istvan hopes that this new sport ___*will become*___ (become) popular with snowboarders around the world.

Gerunds and Infinitives

A **gerund** is a verb form that ends in *-ing* and acts as a noun. An **infinitive** is a verb form that is preceded by the word *to*. Gerunds and infinitives cannot be the main verbs in sentences; each sentence must have another word that is the main verb.

Gerund	Mike loves **swimming**.
	[*Loves* is the main verb, and *swimming* is a gerund.]
Infinitive	Mike loves **to run**.
	[*Loves* is the main verb, and *to run* is an infinitive.]

How do you decide whether to use a gerund or an infinitive? The decision often depends on the main verb in a sentence. Some verbs can be followed by either a gerund or an infinitive.

Verbs That Can Be Followed by Either a Gerund or an Infinitive

begin	hate	remember	try
continue	like	start	
forget	love	stop	

Sometimes, using a gerund or an infinitive after one of these verbs results in the same meaning.

Gerund	Joan likes **playing** the piano.
Infinitive	Joan likes **to play** the piano.

Other times, however, the meaning changes depending on whether you use a gerund or an infinitive.

Infinitive	Carla stopped **helping** me.
	[This wording means Carla no longer helps me.]
Gerund	Carla stopped **to help** me.
	[This wording means Carla stopped what she was doing and helped me.]

Tip To improve your ability to write and speak standard English, read print or online articles, and listen to television and radio news programs. Also, reading articles aloud will help your pronunciation.

Verbs That Are Followed by a Gerund

admit	discuss	keep	risk
avoid	enjoy	miss	suggest
consider	finish	practice	
deny	imagine	quit	

The <u>politician</u> <u>risked</u> **losing** her supporters.
<u>Sophia</u> <u>considered</u> **quitting** her job.

Verbs That Are Followed by an Infinitive

agree	decide	need	refuse
ask	expect	offer	want
beg	fail	plan	
choose	hope	pretend	
claim	manage	promise	

<u>Aunt Sally</u> <u>wants</u> **to help**.
<u>Cal</u> <u>hopes</u> **to become** a millionaire.

Do not use the base form of the verb when you need a gerund or an infinitive.

Incorrect, base verb	*Swim* is my favorite activity.
	[*Swim* is the base form of the verb, not a noun; it cannot be the subject of the sentence.]
Correct, gerund	*Swimming* is my favorite activity.
	[*Swimming* is a gerund that can be the subject of the sentence.]
Incorrect, base verb	My goal is *graduate* from college.
Correct, gerund	My goal is *graduating* from college.
Correct, infinitive	My goal is *to graduate* from college.
Incorrect, base verb	I need *stop* at the store.
	[*Need* is the verb, so there cannot be another verb that shows the action of the subject, *I*.]
Correct, infinitive	I need *to stop* at the store.

PRACTICE 7   **Using gerunds and infinitives**

Read the paragraphs, and fill in the blanks with either a gerund or an infinitive as appropriate. *Answers may vary. Possible answers are shown.*

Example: **If you want** ___to be___ **(be) an actor, be aware that the profession is not all fun and glamour.**

(1) When you were a child, did you pretend ___to be___ (be) famous people? (2) Did you imagine ___playing___ (play) roles in movies or on television? (3) Do you like ___to take___ (take) part in plays? (4) If so, you might want ___to make___ (make) a career out of acting.

(5) Be aware of some drawbacks, however. (6) If you hate ___working___ (work) with others, acting may not be the career for you. (7) Also, if you do not enjoy ___repeating___ (repeat) the same lines over and over, you will find acting dull. (8) You must practice ___speaking___ (speak) lines to memorize them. (9) Despite these drawbacks, you will gain nothing if you refuse ___to try___ (try). (10) Anyone who hopes ___to become___ (become) an actor has a chance at succeeding through hard work and determination.

Teaching tip Have students submit (anonymously, if they prefer) paragraphs from one of their rough drafts. Then, copy and distribute the paragraphs, and, as a whole class, edit the paragraphs with attention to verb forms.

Articles

Articles announce a noun. English uses only three articles—*a*, *an*, and *the*—and the same articles are used for both masculine and feminine nouns.

Definite and Indefinite Articles

The is a **definite article** and is used before a specific person, place, or thing. *A* and *an* are **indefinite articles** and are used with a person, place, or thing whose specific identity is not known.

Definite article	*The* car crashed into the building.
	[A specific car crashed into the building.]
Indefinite article	*A* car crashed into the building.
	[Some car, we don't know which one exactly, crashed into the building.]

When the word following the article begins with a vowel (*a, e, i, o, u*), use *an* instead of *a*.

An **o**ld car crashed into the building.

To use the correct article, you need to know what count and noncount nouns are.

Count and Noncount Nouns

Count nouns name things that can be counted, and they can be made plural, usually by adding -s or -es. **Noncount nouns** name things that cannot be counted, and they are usually singular. They cannot be made plural.

Count noun/singular	I got a **ticket** for the concert.
Count noun/plural	I got two **tickets** for the concert.
Noncount noun	The Internet has all kinds of **information**.
	[You would not say, *The Internet has all kinds of informations.*]

Here is a brief list of several count and noncount nouns. In English, all nouns are either count or noncount.

Count	Noncount	
apple/apples	beauty	milk
chair/chairs	flour	money
dollar/dollars	furniture	postage
letter/letters	grass	poverty
smile/smiles	grief	rain
tree/trees	happiness	rice
	health	salt
	homework	sand
	honey	spaghetti
	information	sunlight
	jewelry	thunder
	mail	wealth

Use the chart that follows to determine when to use **a, an, the**, or no article.

Articles with Count and Noncount Nouns

Count nouns	Article used
Singular	
Specific →	*the*
	I want to read **the** book on taxes that you recommended.
	[The sentence refers to one particular book: the one that was recommended.]
	I cannot stay in **the** sun very long.
	[There is only one sun.]
Not specific →	*a* or *an*
	I want to read **a** book on taxes.
	[It could be any book on taxes.] ▶

Count nouns Plural		Article used
Specific	→	*the*
		I enjoyed the books that we read.
		[The sentence refers to a particular group of books: the ones that we read.]
Not specific	→	no article or *some*
		I usually enjoy books.
		[The sentence refers to books in general.]
		She found some books.
		[I do not know which books she found.]

Noncount nouns Singular		Article used
Specific	→	*the*
		I put away the food that we bought.
		[The sentence refers to particular food: the food that we bought.]
Not specific	→	no article or *some*
		There is food all over the kitchen.
		[The reader does not know what food the sentence refers to.]
		Give some food to the neighbors.
		[The sentence refers to an indefinite quantity of food.]

Prepositions

A **preposition** is a word (such as *of, above, between,* or *about*) that connects a noun, pronoun, or verb with information about it. The correct preposition to use is often determined by common practice rather than by the preposition's actual meaning.

Tip For more on prepositions, see Chapter 15.

Prepositions after Adjectives

Adjectives are often followed by prepositions. Here are some common examples.

afraid of	full of	scared of
ashamed of	happy about	sorry about/sorry for
aware of	interested in	tired of
confused by	proud of	
excited about	responsible for	

Peri is afraid ~~to~~ *of* walking alone.

We are happy ~~of~~ *about* Dino's promotion.

Prepositions after Verbs

Many verbs consist of a verb plus a preposition. The meaning of these combinations is not usually the meaning that the verb and the preposition would each have on its own. Often, the meaning of the verb changes completely depending on which preposition is used with it.

You must **take out** the trash.   [*take out* = bring to a different location]

You must **take in** the exciting sights of New York City.   [*take in* = observe]

Here are a few common verb/preposition combinations.

call in (telephone)	You can *call in* your order.
call off (cancel)	They *called off* the party.
call on (ask for a response)	The teacher always *calls on* me.
drop in (visit)	*Drop in* the next time you are around.
drop off (leave behind)	Juan will *drop off* the car for service.
drop out (quit)	Many students *drop out* of school.
fight against (combat)	He tried to *fight against* the proposal.
fight for (defend)	We will *fight for* our rights.
fill out (complete)	Please *fill out* the form.
fill up (make full)	Do not *fill up* with junk food.
find out (discover)	Did you *find out* the answer?
give up (forfeit)	Do not *give up* your chance to succeed.
go by (visit, pass by)	I may *go by* the store on my way home.
go over (review)	Please *go over* your notes before the test.
grow up (mature)	All children *grow up*.
hand in (submit)	Please *hand in* your homework.
lock up (secure)	*Lock up* the apartment before leaving.
look up (check)	*Look up* the meaning in the dictionary.
pick out (choose)	*Pick out* a good apple.
pick up (take or collect)	Please *pick up* some drinks.
put off (postpone)	Do not *put off* starting your paper.
sign in (register)	*Sign in* when you arrive.
sign out (borrow)	You can *sign out* a book from the library.
sign up (register for)	I want to *sign up* for the contest.
think about (consider)	Simon *thinks about* moving.
turn in (submit)	Please *turn in* your homework.

PRACTICE 8 Editing paragraphs for preposition problems

Edit the following paragraphs to make sure the correct prepositions are used.

about

Example: At some point, many people think ~~out~~ having a more flexible
^
work schedule.

for

(1) If they are responsible ~~in~~ child care, they might want to get home
^

in

from work earlier than usual. (2) Or they might be interested ~~on~~ having one
^

workday a week free for studying or other activities. (3) Employees shouldn't

of

be afraid ~~to~~ asking a supervisor about the possibility of a flexible schedule.
^

(4) For instance, the supervisor might be willing to allow the employee to do

40 hours of work in four days instead of five days. (5) Or a worker who wants to

up

leave a little earlier than usual might give ~~out~~ half of a lunch hour to do so.
^

(6) The wide use of computers also allows for flexibility. (7) For example,

busy parents might use their laptops to work from home a day or two a

week. (8) They can stay in touch with the office by e-mailing supervisors or

in

coworkers, or they might call ~~on~~.
^

out

(9) Often, employers who allow more flexibility find ~~in~~ that they benefit,
^

about

too. (10) Workers are happy ~~on~~ having more control over their own time;
^

therefore, they are less stressed out and more productive than they would

have been on a fixed schedule.

Chapter Review

1. What is a pronoun? *a word that replaces a noun or another pronoun*

    What are the three types of pronouns in English? *subject, object, possessive*

2. Rewrite this sentence in the simple past and the simple future:

    Melinda picks flowers every morning.

    Past: *Melinda picked flowers yesterday. (or another past time)*

    Future: *Melinda will pick flowers tomorrow. (or another future time)*

3. Rewrite this sentence so that it uses the perfect tense correctly:

    They have call an ambulance. *They have called an ambulance.*

4. Using the progressive tenses, first rewrite this sentence as a question:

    Chris is learning Spanish.

    Then, rewrite the question in the past tense and in the future tense.

    Question: *Is Chris learning Spanish?*

    Past: *Was Chris learning Spanish?*

    Future: *Will Chris be learning Spanish?*

5. Rewrite these sentences so that they use the modal verb correctly:

    Jennifer should to help her mother. *Jennifer should help her mother.*

    Yesterday, I cannot work. *Yesterday, I could not work.*

6. What is a gerund? *a verb form that ends in "-ing" and acts as a noun*

    Write a sentence with a gerund in it. *Answers will vary.*

7. What is an infinitive? *a verb form that is preceded by the word "to"*

    Write a sentence with an infinitive in it. *Answers will vary.*

8. Give an example of a count noun. *Answers will vary.*

    Give an example of a noncount noun. *Answers will vary.*

9. What is a preposition? *a word that connects a noun, pronoun, or verb with information about it*

    Write a sentence using a preposition. *Answers will vary.*

"I write presentations for work and school."

—Katie F., student

27

Word Choice

Using the Right Words

Understand the Importance of Choosing Words Carefully

In conversation, you show much of your meaning through facial expression, tone of voice, and gestures. In writing, you have only the words on the page to make your point, so you must choose them carefully. If you use vague or inappropriate words, your readers may not understand you.

Two resources will help you find the best words for your meaning: a dictionary and a thesaurus.

Dictionary

Dictionaries give you all kinds of useful information about words: spelling, division of words into syllables, pronunciation, parts of speech, other forms of words, definitions, and examples of use. Following is a sample dictionary entry.

Spelling and end-of-line division | Pronunciation | Parts of speech | Other forms

con • crete (kon′krēt, kong′-, kon-krēt′), *adj., n., v.* **-cret • ed, -cret • ing,**
adj. **1.** constituting an actual thing or instance; real; perceptible; substantial: *concrete proof.* **2.** pertaining to or concerned with realities or actual instances

— Definition
— Example

LaunchPadSolo
Visit **LaunchPad Solo for Readers and Writers > Grammar > Style and Mechanics** for more tutorials, videos, and practice with crafting paragraphs.

Tip A number of good dictionaries are now available free online. An excellent resource is at **www.dictionary.com.**

GRAMMAR & MECHANICS ROADMAP

An Overview

This Chapter Identifies the Following Trouble Spots
- Choosing the correct word
- Vague and abstract words
- Slang
- Wordy language
- Clichés

Tools to Address Trouble Spots
- Dictionary (p. 467)
- Thesaurus (p. 468)
- List of Vague and Abstract Words (p. 468)
- List of Common Wordy Expressions (p. 471)
- List of Common Clichés (p. 472)
- Edit for Word Choice exercises (p. 474)
- Chapter Review (p. 475)
- Editing for Word Choice flowchart (p. 475)

rather than abstractions; particular as opposed to general: *concrete proposals.*
3. referring to an actual substance or thing, as opposed to an abstract quality: The words *cat, water,* and *teacher* are concrete, whereas the words *truth, excellence,* and *adulthood* are abstract.

— *Random House Webster's College Dictionary*

Thesaurus

A thesaurus gives **synonyms** (words that have the same meaning) for the word you look up. Use a thesaurus when you cannot find the right word for what you mean. Be careful, however, to choose a word that has the precise meaning you intend. Following is a sample thesaurus entry.

> **Concrete**, *adj.* 1. Particular, specific, single, certain, special, unique, sole, peculiar, individual, separate, isolated, distinct, exact, precise, direct, strict, minute; definite, plain, evident, obvious; pointed, emphasized; restrictive, limiting, limited, well-defined, clear-cut, fixed, finite; determining, conclusive, decided.

—J. I. Rodale, *The Synonym Finder*

Practice Avoiding Four Common Word-Choice Problems

Four common problems with word choice may make it hard for readers to understand your point.

Vague and Abstract Words

Vague and abstract words are too general. They do not give your readers a clear idea of what you mean. Here are some common vague and abstract words.

Vague and Abstract Words

a lot	cute	nice	stuff
amazing	dumb	OK (okay)	terrible
awesome	good	old	thing
bad	great	pretty	very
beautiful	happy	sad	whatever
big	huge	small	young

When you see one of these words or another general word in your writing, replace it with a concrete or more specific word or description. A **concrete** word names something that can be seen, heard, felt, tasted, or smelled. A **specific** word names a particular person or quality. Compare these two sentences:

Vague and abstract	An old man crossed the street.
Concrete and specific	An eighty-seven-year-old priest stumbled along Main Street.

The first version is too general to be interesting. The second version creates a clear, strong image. Some words are so vague that it is best to avoid them altogether.

Vague and abstract	It is awesome.
	[This sentence is neither concrete nor specific.]

Teaching tip Take students to a spot on campus, and have each student write a description of the same scene. Then, have them compare what they wrote, noting the use of concrete and specific language as well as of vague and abstract words.

PRACTICE 1   Avoiding vague and abstract words

In the following sentences, underline any words that are vague or abstract. Then, edit each sentence by replacing the vague or abstract words with concrete, specific ones. You may invent details or base them on brief online research into physician assistant careers. *Answers may vary. Possible edits are shown.*

Example: It would be <u>cool</u> to be a physician assistant (PA). *It would be rewarding to be a physician assistant (PA).*

1. I am drawn to this career because it would let me <u>do neat things</u> for others. *I am drawn to this career because it would let me help others by providing them with medical care.*

2. I know that becoming a PA would require <u>tons of work</u>. *I know that becoming a PA would require years of study and practice with patients.*

3. Also, each day in the classroom or clinic would be <u>long</u>. *Also, each day in the classroom or clinic would last 10 to 12 hours.*

4. Furthermore, I would have to be able to tolerate <u>some rough sights</u>. *Furthermore, I would have to be able to tolerate the sight of blood and injuries.*

5. However, I would learn <u>a lot</u>. *However, I would learn how to examine patients and how to diagnose and treat various conditions.*

6. And in meetings with patients, I would be able to apply my <u>great</u> listening skills. *And in meetings with patients, I would be able to apply my ability to listen to others carefully.*

7. All this stuff would be interesting. *My time in the classroom or with patients would be interesting.*

8. I am confident that my PA education would have a good outcome. *I am confident that my PA education would help me get a job soon after graduation.*

9. Also, my starting salary would be decent. *Also, my starting salary would be at least $60,000 a year.*

10. Getting accepted into a PA program would be awesome. *Getting accepted into a PA program would help me get started on a career that I would love.*

Slang

Teaching tip Students can collaborate to list slang words and then translate them into formal English.

Slang, informal and casual language, should be used only in informal situations. Avoid it when you write, especially for college classes or at work. Use language that is appropriate for your audience and purpose.

Slang	Edited
S'all good.	Everything is going well.
Dawg, I don't deserve this grade.	Professor, I don't deserve this grade.

> **PRACTICE 2** **Avoiding slang**
>
> In the following sentences, underline any slang words. Then, edit the sentences by replacing the slang with language appropriate for a formal audience and purpose. Imagine that you are writing to a boss where you work. *Answers may vary. Possible edits are shown.*
>
> Example: *Hello,* ~~Yo,~~ Randy, I need to talk *to* at you for a minute.
>
> 1. That reference letter you wrote for me was ~~really awesome sweet~~ *helpful and much appreciated*.
> 2. I am grateful because the one my English instructor did for me ~~sucked~~ *was not helpful*.
> 3. She said that ~~I thought~~ I was ~~all that~~ *conceited*, but that is not true.
> 4. I would be ~~down with doing~~ *happy to do* a favor for you in return if you need it.
> 5. Maybe you and I could ~~hang sometime~~ *spend time together* one of these weekends?
> 6. I know that we cannot be best ~~buds~~ *friends*, but we could ~~shoot some hoops or something~~ *play basketball*.
> 7. You could let me know ~~whazzup~~ *what you have planned* when I see you at work next week.
> 8. If you are too stressed, do not ~~go all emo on me~~ *get upset*.
> 9. Just ~~chill out,~~ *relax* and forget about it.
> 10. ~~Text~~ *Contact* me when you get ~~a mo.~~ *a chance*

Wordy Language

People sometimes use too many words to express their ideas. They may think that using more words will make them sound smart, but too many words can weaken a writer's point.

Wordy   I am not interested *at this point in time.*

Edited   I am not interested *now.*

> [The phrase *at this point in time* uses five words to express what could be said in one word: *now.*]

Common Wordy Expressions

Wordy	Edited
As a result of	Because
Due to the fact that	Because
In spite of the fact that	Although
It is my opinion that	I think *(or just make the point)*
In the event that	If
The fact of the matter is that	*(Just state the point.)*
A great number of	Many
At that time	Then
In this day and age	Now
At this point in time	Now
In this paper, I will show that . . .	*(Just make the point; do not announce it.)*
Utilize	Use

PRACTICE 3   **Avoiding wordy language**

In the following sentences, underline the wordy or repetitive language. Then, edit each sentence to make it more concise. Some sentences may contain more than one wordy phrase. *Answers may vary. Possible edits are shown.*

Example: Sugar substitutes are a popular diet choice for people ~~of all ages~~
                                                                        reduce
when they are searching for ways to ~~cut down on all~~ **the calories they ingest**
each day
~~on a daily basis.~~
ᴧ

                                    Dieting
1. ~~It is a well-known fact that~~ ~~dieting~~ is difficult for most people.
   Because
            ᴧ
2. ~~Due to the fact that~~ people are trying to cut calories, sugar substitutes are
   ᴧ
   used in sodas, snacks, and other products.
                                These
3. ~~The fact of the matter is that these~~ substitutes provide a sweet taste, but
                                    ᴧ
   without the calories of sugar or honey.

    Many
4. ~~A great number of~~ researchers have stated ~~at this time~~ that such substitutes are not ~~necessarily~~ safe or healthy to use in large quantities.

    Current   *believe*
5. ~~Some of the current~~ experts ~~on the matter are of the opinion~~ that sugar substitutes can cause cancer, allergies, and other serious health problems.

    Other
6. ~~At this point in time, other~~ experts ~~on the same subject~~ believe that using these substitutes maintains a person's addiction to sugar and leads people to eat more junk food.

7. Despite these warnings/ ~~negative evaluations, and critical opinions~~ from the experts, nearly 200 million people consume sugar-free or low-calorie products each year.

    People
8. ~~In this day and age, people~~ are consuming an average of four of these items each day.

    Although
9. ~~In spite of the fact that~~ people know sugar is bad for them, their tastes
                        soon
will probably not change ~~anytime in the near future~~.

              It
10. ~~It is my opinion that it~~ would be better if people just learned to consume foods that do not contain sweeteners of any kind.

Clichés

Clichés are phrases used so often that people no longer pay attention to them. To get your point across and to get your readers' attention, replace clichés with fresh and specific language.

Clichés	Edited
I cannot *make ends meet*.	I do not have enough money to live on.
My uncle *worked his way up the corporate ladder*.	My uncle started as a shipping clerk but ended up as a regional vice president.
This roll is *as hard as a rock*.	This roll is so hard I could bounce it.

Common Clichés

as big as a house	few and far between	spoiled brat
as light as a feather	hell on earth	starting from scratch
better late than never	last but not least	sweating blood/bullets
break the ice	no way on earth	too little, too late
crystal clear	110 percent	24/7
a drop in the bucket	playing with fire	work like a dog
easier said than done		

PRACTICE 4   **Avoiding clichés**

In the following sentences, underline the clichés. Then, edit each sentence by replacing the clichés with fresh and specific language. *Answers will vary. Possible edits are shown.*

Tip Hundreds of clichés exist. To check if you have used one, go to **www.clichesite.com**.

excruciating
Example: Riding a bicycle 100 miles a day can be hell on earth unless you
work extremely hard
are willing to give 110 percent.

devote every bit of your strength to the challenge
1. You have to persuade yourself to sweat blood and work like a dog for up to 10 hours.

It is impossible to
2. There's no way on earth you can do it without extensive training.

the very last mile,   *an enormously difficult*
3. Staying on your bike until the bitter end, of course, is easier said than
task
done.

maintain your determination
4. It is important to keep the fire in your belly and keep your goal of finishing
always present
the race crystal clear in your mind.

5. No matter how long it takes you to cross the finish line, remind yourself
finishing at all is a tremendous achievement
that it's better late than never.

6. Even if you are not a champion racer, training for a bike race will keep you
in top physical condition
fit as a fiddle.

continue to
7. It may take discipline to make yourself train, but you should keep your
work hard
nose to the grindstone.

protect themselves
8. Bike racers should always play it safe by wearing helmets.

watch carefully
9. When you train for road racing, keep an eye peeled for cars.

injured   *killed*
10. You do not want to end up flat on your back in the hospital or six feet
under!

A final note: Language that favors one gender over another or that assumes that only one gender performs a certain role is called *sexist*. Such language should be avoided.

Tip See Chapter 20 for more advice on using pronouns.

Sexist	A doctor should politely answer *his* patients' questions.
	[Not all doctors are male, as suggested by the pronoun *his*.]
Revised	A doctor should politely answer *his or her* patients' questions.
	Doctors should politely answer *their* patients' questions.
	[The first revision changes *his* to *his or her* to avoid sexism. The second revision changes the subject to a plural noun (*Doctors*) so that a genderless pronoun (*their*) can be used. Usually, it is preferable to avoid *his or her*.]

Edit for Word Choice

PRACTICE 5   **Editing paragraphs for word choice**

Find and edit six examples of vague or abstract language, slang, wordy language, or clichés in the following paragraphs. *Answers may vary. Possible edits are shown.*

(1) Imagine spending almost two weeks living in the ~~coolest~~ [most unusual] home in the world. (2) That is what scientist Lloyd Godson did when he lived at the bottom of a lake in Australia for thirteen days. (3) Although ~~there is no way on earth~~ I would want to do that, it ~~sure~~ [not] sounds fascinating.

(4) Godson's home was an 8-by-11-foot-long yellow steel box that he dubbed the BioSUB. (5) His air supply came from the algae plants growing inside the BioSUB. (6) Divers brought him food, water, and other ~~junk~~ [supplies] through a manhole built in the bottom of his underwater home. (7) To keep busy, he rode on an exercise bicycle, which created electricity for him to recharge his laptop and run the lights for his plants. (8) He used his computer to talk to students all over the world and to watch movies.

(9) Godson paid for this experiment with money he had won in the "Live Your Dream" contest. (10) ~~At this point in time, I have to say that for~~ [For] most people, the BioSUB home would be less appealing than a regular, aboveground room, apartment, or house. (11) Indeed, by the time his two weeks were over, Godson was ready to come up [and] feel the sunshine and wind on his face again~~, and "smell the roses."~~

PRACTICE 6   **Editing your own writing for word choice**

Edit a piece of your own writing for word choice. It can be a paper for this course or another one, or choose something you have written for work or your everyday life. You may want to use the chart on page 475.

Chapter Review

1. What two resources will help you choose the best words to get your ideas across in writing? *a dictionary and a thesaurus*

2. What are four common word-choice problems? *vague and abstract words, slang, wordy language, and clichés*

3. Replace vague and abstract words with *concrete* and *specific* words.

4. When is it appropriate to use slang in college writing or in writing at work? *never*

5. Give two examples of wordy expressions. *Answers will vary.*

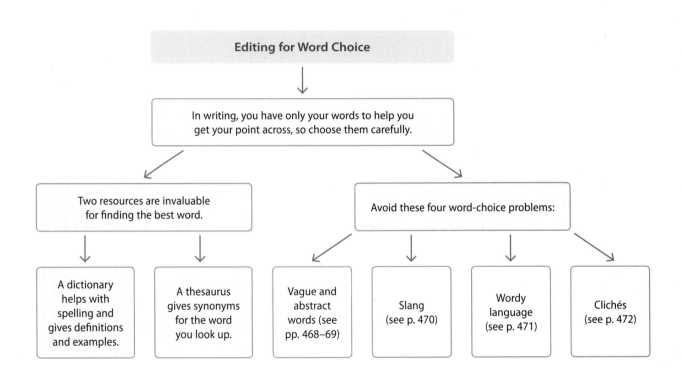

Editing for Word Choice

↓

In writing, you have only your words to help you get your point across, so choose them carefully.

Two resources are invaluable for finding the best word.

Avoid these four word-choice problems:

A dictionary helps with spelling and gives definitions and examples.

A thesaurus gives synonyms for the word you look up.

Vague and abstract words (see pp. 468–69)

Slang (see p. 470)

Wordy language (see p. 471)

Clichés (see p. 472)

28

Commonly Confused Words
Avoiding Mistakes with Soundalike Words

Visit **LaunchPad Solo for Readers and Writers > Grammar > Style and Mechanics** for more tutorials, videos, and practice with crafting paragraphs.

Understand Why Certain Words Are Commonly Confused

People often confuse certain words in English because they sound alike and may have similar meanings. In speech, words that sound alike are not a problem. In writing, however, words that sound alike may be spelled differently, and readers rely on the spelling to understand what you mean. Edit your writing carefully to make sure you have used the correct words.

- **Proofread carefully,** using the techniques discussed on page 487.
- **Use a dictionary** to look up any words you are unsure about.
- **Focus on finding and correcting mistakes** you make with the twenty-seven sets of commonly confused words covered in this chapter.
- **Develop a personal list of soundalike words** you confuse often. Record words that you confuse in your writing and their meanings. Before you turn in any piece of writing, consult your personal word list to make sure you have used words correctly.

GRAMMAR & MECHANICS ROADMAP

An Overview

This Chapter Identifies the Following Trouble Spots
- 27 sets of commonly confused words

Tools to Address Trouble Spots
- Definition of each set of words and how they should be used (p. 477)
- Edit for Commonly Confused Words exercises (p. 484)
- Chapter Review (p. 485)

Practice Using Commonly Confused Words Correctly

Study the different meanings and spellings of these twenty-seven sets of commonly confused words. Complete the sentence after each set of words, filling in each blank with the correct word.

Tip Some commonly confused words sound similar but not exactly alike, such as *conscience* and *conscious*, *loose* and *lose*, and *of* and *have*. To avoid confusing these words, practice pronouncing them correctly.

A/AN/AND

a: used before a word that begins with a consonant sound

> *A* friend of mine just won the lottery.

an: used before a word that begins with a vowel sound

> *An* old friend of mine just won the lottery.

and: used to join two words

> My friend *and* I went out to celebrate.

A friend *and* I ate at *an* Italian restaurant.

Other lottery winners were __*an*__ algebra teacher __*and a*__ bowling team.

ACCEPT/EXCEPT

accept: to agree to receive or admit (verb)

> I will *accept* the job offer.

except: but, other than

> All the stores are closed *except* the Quik-Stop.

I *accept* all the job conditions *except* the low pay.

Do not __*accept*__ gifts from clients __*except*__ those who are also personal friends.

ADVICE/ADVISE

advice: opinion (noun)

> I would like your *advice* before I make a decision.

advise: to give an opinion (verb)

> Please *advise* me what to do.

Please *advise* me what to do; you always give me good *advice*.

If you do not like my __*advice*__, please __*advise*__ me how to proceed.

AFFECT/EFFECT

affect: to make an impact on, to change something (verb)

> The whole city was *affected* by the hurricane.

Tip Thinking *"the effect"* will help you remember that *effect* is a noun.

effect: a result (noun)

> What *effect* will the hurricane have on the local economy?

Although the storm will have many negative *effects*, it will not *affect* the price of food.

The ___effect___ of the disaster will ___affect___ many people.

ARE/OUR

Teaching tip It is helpful to complete these sentences as a class or to assign them as homework and then go over them in class. Have students read the sentences aloud so that they can focus on differences in pronunciation.

are: a form of the verb *be*

> The workers *are* about to go on strike.

our: a pronoun showing ownership

> The children played on *our* porch.

My relatives *are* staying at *our* house.

___Our___ new neighbors ___are___ moving in today.

BY/BUY/BYE

by: next to, before, or past

> Meet me *by* the entrance.
>
> Make sure the bill is paid *by* the fifteenth of the month.
>
> The motorcycle raced *by* me.

buy: to purchase (verb)

> I would like to *buy* a new laptop.

bye: an informal way to say *goodbye*

> "Bye, Grandma!"

I said "___Bye___" from the window as we drove ___by___ our friends, who were standing next to the house I wanted to ___buy___.

Tip Remember that one of the words is *con-science*; the other is not.

CONSCIENCE/CONSCIOUS

conscience: a personal sense of right and wrong (noun)

> Jake's *conscience* would not allow him to cheat.

conscious: awake, aware (adjective)

> The coma patient is now *conscious*.
>
> I am *conscious* that it is getting late.

The judge was *conscious* that the accused had acted according to his *conscience* even though he had broken the law.

The man said that he was not ___conscious___ that what he had done was illegal, or his ___conscience___ would not have let him do it.

FINE/FIND

fine: of high quality (adjective); feeling well (adjective); a penalty for breaking a law (noun)

This jacket is made of *fine* leather.

After a day in bed, Jacob felt *fine*.

The *fine* for exceeding the speed limit is $50.

find: to locate, to discover (verb)

Did Clara *find* her glasses?

I *find* gardening to be a *fine* pastime.

Were you able to __*find*__ a place to store your __*fine*__ jewelry?

ITS/IT'S

its: a pronoun showing ownership

The dog chased *its* tail.

it's: a contraction of the words *it is*

It's about time you got here.

It's very hard for a dog to keep *its* teeth clean.

__*It's*__ no surprise that the college raised __*its*__ tuition.

> **Tip** If you are not sure whether to use *its* or *it's* in a sentence, try substituting *it is*. If the sentence does not make sense with *it is*, use *its*.

KNEW/NEW/KNOW/NO

knew: understood; recognized (past tense of the verb *know*)

I *knew* the answer, but I could not think of it.

new: unused, recent, or just introduced (adjective)

The building has a *new* security code.

know: to understand; to have knowledge of (verb)

I *know* how to bake bread.

no: used to form a negative

I have *no* idea what the answer is.

I never *knew* how much a *new* car costs.

The __*new*__ teacher __*knew*__ many of her students already.

There is __*no*__ way Tom could __*know*__ where Celia is hiding.

I __*know*__ that there is __*no*__ cake left.

LOOSE/LOSE

loose: baggy; relaxed; not fixed in place (adjective)

In hot weather, people tend to wear *loose* clothing.

lose: to misplace; to forfeit possession of (verb)

> Every summer, I *lose* about three pairs of sunglasses.

If the ring is too *loose* on your finger, you might *lose* it.

I __*lose*__ my patience with the __*loose*__ rules on Wall Street.

MIND/MINE

mind: to object to (verb); the thinking or feeling part of one's brain (noun)

> Toby does not *mind* if I borrow his tool chest.
>
> Estela has a good *mind,* but often she does not use it.

mine: belonging to me (pronoun); a source of ore and minerals (noun)

> That coat is *mine.*
>
> My uncle worked in a coal *mine* in West Virginia.

That writing problem of *mine* was on my *mind.*

If you do not __*mind*__, the gloves you just took are __*mine*__.

OF/HAVE

of: coming from; caused by; part of a group; made from (preposition)

> The leader *of* the band played bass guitar.

have: to possess (verb; also used as a helping verb)

> I *have* one more course to take before I graduate.
>
> I should *have* started studying earlier.

The president *of* the company should *have* resigned.

Sidney could __*have*__ been one __*of*__ the winners.

Note: Do not use *of* after *would, should, could,* and *might.* Use *have* after those words (*would have, should have*).

PASSED/PAST

passed: went by or went ahead (past tense of the verb *pass*)

> We *passed* the hospital on the way to the airport.

past: time that has gone by (noun); gone by, over, just beyond (preposition)

> In the *past*, I was able to stay up all night and not be tired.
>
> I drove *past* the burning warehouse.

This *past* school year, I *passed* all my exams.

Trish __*passed*__ me as we ran __*past*__ the 1-mile marker.

PEACE/PIECE

peace: no disagreement; calm

Could you quiet down and give me a little *peace*?

piece: a part of something larger

May I have a *piece* of that pie?

The feuding families found *peace* after they sold the *piece* of land.

To keep the ___*peace*___, give your sister a ___*piece*___ of candy.

PRINCIPAL/PRINCIPLE

principal: main (adjective); head of a school or leader of an organization (noun)

Brush fires are the *principal* risk in the hills of California.

Ms. Edwards is the *principal* of Memorial Elementary School.

Corinne is a *principal* in the management consulting firm.

principle: a standard of beliefs or behaviors (noun)

Although tempted, she held on to her moral *principles*.

The *principal* questioned the delinquent student's *principles*.

The ___*principal*___ problem is that you want me to act against my ___*principles*___.

QUIET/QUITE/QUIT

quiet: soft in sound; not noisy (adjective)

The library was *quiet*.

quite: completely; very (adverb)

After cleaning all the windows, Alex was *quite* tired.

quit: to stop (verb)

She *quit* her job.

After the band *quit* playing, the hall was *quite quiet*.

If you would ___*quit*___ shouting and be ___*quiet*___, you would find that the scenery is ___*quite*___ pleasant.

> **Teaching tip** Tell students that although a spell checker won't help them with the spelling of most of these words, they can use the search or find function to find every instance of the words they have trouble with.

RIGHT/WRITE

right: correct; in a direction opposite from left (adjective)

You definitely made the *right* choice.

When you get to the stoplight, make a *right* turn.

write: to put words on paper (verb)

Will you *write* your phone number for me?

Please *write* the *right* answer in the space provided.

You were __*right*__ to __*write*__ to the senator.

SET/SIT

set: a collection of something (noun); to place an object somewhere (verb)

Paul has a complete *set* of Johnny Cash records.

Please *set* the package on the table.

sit: to rest in a chair or other seat-like surface; to be located in a particular place

I need to *sit* on the sofa for a few minutes.

The shed *sits* between the house and the garden.

If I *sit* down now, I will not have time to *set* the plants outside.

Before you __*sit*__ on that chair, __*set*__ the magazines on the floor.

SUPPOSE/SUPPOSED

suppose: to imagine or assume to be true

I *suppose* you would like something to eat.

Suppose you won a million dollars.

supposed: past tense of *suppose*; intended

Karen *supposed* Thomas was late because of traffic.

I *suppose* you know that Rita was *supposed* to be home by 6:30.

I __*suppose*__ you want to leave soon because we are __*supposed*__ to arrive before the guests.

THAN/THEN

than: a word used to compare two or more people, places, or things

It is colder inside *than* outside.

then: at a certain time; next in time

I got out of the car and *then* realized the keys were still in it.

Clara ran more miles *than* she ever had before, and *then* she collapsed.

Back __*then*__, I smoked more __*than*__ three packs a day.

THEIR/THERE/THEY'RE

Tip If you are not sure whether to use *their* or *they're*, substitute *they are*. If the sentence does not make sense, use *their*.

their: a pronoun showing ownership

I borrowed *their* clippers to trim the hedges.

there: a word indicating location or existence

Just put the keys *there* on the desk.

There are too many lawyers.

they're: a contraction of the words *they are*

> *They're* about to leave.

There is a car in *their* driveway, which indicates that *they're* home.

___Their___ beach house is empty except for the one week that ___they're___

vacationing ___there___.

THOUGH/THROUGH/THREW

though: however; nevertheless; in spite of (conjunction)

> *Though* he is short, he plays great basketball.

through: finished with (adjective); from one side to the other (preposition)

> I am *through* arguing with you.

> The baseball went right *through* the window.

threw: hurled; tossed (past tense of the verb *throw*)

> She *threw* the basketball.

Even *though* it was illegal, she *threw* the empty cup *through* the window onto the road.

___Though___ she did not really believe it would bring good luck, Jan ___threw___ a

penny ___through___ the air into the fountain.

TO/TOO/TWO

to: a word indicating a direction or movement (preposition); part of the infinitive form of a verb

> Please give the message *to* Sharon.

> It is easier *to* ask for forgiveness than *to* get permission.

too: also; more than enough; very (adverb)

> I am tired *too*.

> Dan ate *too* much and felt sick.

> That dream was *too* real.

two: the number between one and three (noun)

> The lab had only *two* computers.

They went *to* a restaurant and ordered *too* much food for *two* people.

When Marty went ___to___ pay for his meal, the cashier charged him ___two___

times, which was ___too___ bad.

USE/USED

use: to employ or put into service (verb)

> How do you plan to *use* that blueprint?

Tip Writing *use to* instead of *used to* is a common error. Train yourself not to make that mistake.

used: past tense of the verb *use. Used to* can indicate a past fact or state, or it can mean "familiar with."

> He *used* his lunch hour to do errands.
>
> He *used* to go for a walk during his lunch hour.

She *used* to be a chef, so she knows how to *use* all kinds of kitchen gadgets.

She is also *used* to improvising in the kitchen.

Tom ___used___ the prize money to buy a boat; his family hoped he would

___use___ the money for his education, but Tom was ___used___ to getting his way.

WHO'S/WHOSE

Tip If you are not sure whether to use *whose* or *who's*, substitute *who is*. If the sentence does not make sense, use *whose*.

who's: a contraction of the words *who is*

> *Who's* at the door?

whose: a pronoun showing ownership

> *Whose* car is parked outside?

Who's the person *whose* car sank in the river?

The student ___whose___ name is first on the list is the one ___who's___ in charge.

YOUR/YOU'RE

Tip If you are not sure whether to use *your* or *you're*, substitute *you are*. If the sentence does not make sense, use *your*.

your: a pronoun showing ownership

> Did you bring *your* wallet?

you're: a contraction of the words *you are*

> *You're* not telling me the whole story.

You're going to have *your* third exam tomorrow.

___Your___ teacher says that ___you're___ good with numbers.

Edit for Commonly Confused Words

> **PRACTICE 1**   **Editing paragraphs for commonly confused words**

Edit the following paragraphs to correct eighteen errors in word use.

1 More and more women are purchasing handguns, against the ~~advise~~ *advice*

of law enforcement officers. 2 Few of these women are criminals or plan to

commit crimes. 3 They ~~no~~ *know* the risks of guns, and they ~~except~~ *accept* those risks. 4 They

buy weapons primarily because ~~their~~ *they're* tired of feeling like victims. 5 They do not

want to contribute ~~too~~ *to* the violence in ~~are~~ *our* society, but they also realize that

women are the victims of violent attacks far ~~to~~ *too* often. 6 Many women ~~loose~~ *lose*

their
~~they're~~ lives because they cannot fight off ~~there~~ attackers. 7 Some women
^   *conscious*   ^
have made a ~~conscience~~ decision to arm themselves for protection.
                   ^
                                                    than
          8 But does buying a gun make things worse rather ~~then~~ better? 9 Having
            your   ^
a gun in ~~you're~~ house makes it three times more likely that someone will
         ^

be killed there—and that someone is just as likely to be you or one of your

children as a criminal. 10 Most young children cannot tell the difference
                                          find   *there*
between a real gun and a toy gun when they ~~fine~~ one. 11 Every year, ~~their~~
                                           ^   ^
are tragic examples of children who accidentally shoot and even kill other
                                                      whose
youngsters while they are playing with guns. 12 A mother ~~who's~~ children are
                                                         ^
injured while playing with her gun will never again think that a gun provides
peace   *our*
~~piece~~ of mind. 13 Reducing the violence in ~~are~~ society may be a better
^   ^
solution.

PRACTICE 2   **Editing your own writing for commonly confused words**

Edit a piece of your own writing for commonly confused words. It can be a
paper for this course or another one, or choose something you have written
for work or your everyday life.

Teaching tip Ask students for a few more commonly confused words. Start them off by putting one set on the board; then, list others they suggest.

Chapter Review

1. What are four strategies you can use to avoid confusing words that sound alike or
    have similar meanings? _Proofread carefully, use a dictionary to look up any words_
    you are unsure about, find and correct mistakes you make with the twenty-seven sets
    of commonly confused words, and develop a personal list of soundalike words you
    confuse often.

2. What are the top five commonly confused words on your personal list? _Answers_
    will vary.

29

Spelling
Using the Right Letters

 LaunchPadSolo

Visit **LaunchPad Solo for Readers and Writers > Grammar > Style and Mechanics** for more tutorials, videos, and practice with crafting paragraphs.

Finding and Correcting Spelling Mistakes

Some extremely smart people are poor spellers. Unfortunately, spelling errors are easy for readers to spot, and they make a bad impression. Learn to find and correct spelling mistakes in your writing by using the following strategies.

Use a Dictionary

When proofreading your papers, consult a dictionary whenever you are unsure about the spelling of a word. *Checking a dictionary is the single most important thing you can do to improve your spelling.*

Use a Spell Checker—with Caution

Use a spell checker after you have completed a piece of writing but before you print it out. This word-processing tool finds and highlights a word that may be misspelled, suggests other spellings, and gives you the opportunity to change the spelling of the word.

Tip Online dictionaries, such as **www.merriam-webster.com**, can help you spell because they often allow you to type in an incorrectly spelled word and get the correct spelling.

Teaching tip Keep at least two dictionaries in the classroom. Let students know where the dictionaries are, but also emphasize that students should buy their own.

GRAMMAR & MECHANICS ROADMAP

An Overview

This Chapter Identifies the Following Trouble Spots

- Common spelling mistakes

Tools to Address Trouble Spots

- Dictionary (p. 486)
- Spell Checker (p. 486)
- Proofreading Techniques (p. 487)
- Personal Spelling List (p. 487)
- Six Basic Spelling Rules (p. 488)
- List of Commonly Misspelled Words (p. 491)
- Chapter Review (p. 492)

However, never rely on a spell checker to do your editing for you. It ignores anything it recognizes as a word, so it will not help you find misused words or misspellings that are also words. For example, a spell checker would not highlight any of the problems in these phrases:

Just *to* it.	(Correct: Just *do* it.)
pain in the *nick*	(Correct: pain in the *neck*)
my writing *coarse*	(Correct: my writing *course*)

Teaching tip The *Instructor's Manual for Real Writing* contains tests and supplemental exercises for this chapter.

Use Proofreading Techniques

Use some of the following proofreading techniques to focus on the spelling of one word at a time. Try them all. Then, decide which ones work best for you.

- Print out your paper before proofreading. (Many writers find it easier to detect errors on paper than on a computer screen.)

- Put a piece of paper under the line that you are reading.

- Proofread your paper backward, one word at a time.

- Print out a version of your paper that looks noticeably different: Make the words larger, make the margins larger, triple-space the lines, or make all these changes.

- Read your paper aloud. This strategy will help you if you tend to leave out words.

- Exchange papers with a partner and proofread each other's papers, identifying only possible misspellings.

Make a Personal Spelling List

Set aside a section of your course notebook for your spelling list. Every time you edit a paper, write down the words that you misspelled. Every couple of weeks, go back to your spelling list to see whether your problem words have changed. Are you misspelling fewer words in each paper?

For each word on your list, create a memory aid or silly phrase to help you remember the correct spelling. For example, if you often misspell *a lot*, you could remember that "*a lot* is a lot of words."

Teaching tip Telling students that they will have to turn in their spelling lists reinforces the importance of making a list. If you have time, you can make up individualized spelling quizzes.

Strategies for Becoming a Better Speller

Here are three good strategies for becoming a better speller.

Master Commonly Confused Words

Chapter 28 covers twenty-seven sets of words that are commonly confused because they sound similar, such as *write* and *right*. If you can master these commonly confused words, you will avoid many spelling mistakes.

Learn Six Spelling Rules

If you can remember the following six rules, you can correct many of the spelling errors in your writing.

First, here is a quick review of vowels and consonants.

Vowels: *a, e, i, o,* and *u*

Consonants: *b, c, d, f, g, h, j, k, l, m, n, p, q, r, s, t, v, w, x,* and *z*

The letter *y* can be either a vowel or a consonant. It is a vowel when it sounds like the *y* in *fly* or *hungry*. It is a consonant when it sounds like the *y* in *yellow*.

Rule 1. "*I* before *e,* except after *c.* Or when sounded like *a,* as in *neighbor* or *weigh*."

Many people repeat this rhyme to themselves as they decide whether a word is spelled with an *ie* or an *ei*.

Teaching tip For each rule, have students give three additional examples of words that follow the rule. This exercise can be done in small groups or pairs.

> pie**ce** (*i* before *e*)
>
> rec**ei**ve (except after *c*)
>
> **ei**ght (sounds like *a*)

Exceptions: *either, neither, foreign, height, seize, society, their, weird*

Rule 2. **Drop the final *e*** when adding an ending that begins with a vowel.

> hop**e** + ing = hoping
>
> imagin**e** + ation = imagination

Keep the final *e* when adding an ending that begins with a consonant.

> achiev**e** + ment = achievement
>
> definit**e** + ly = definitely

Exceptions: *argument, awful, judgment, simply, truly,* and others

Rule 3. When adding an ending to a word that ends in *y,* **change the *y* to *i*** when a consonant comes before the *y.*

> lone**ly** + est = loneliest   apolo**gy** + ize = apologize
>
> hap**py** + er = happier   like**ly** + hood = likelihood

Do not change the *y* when a vowel comes before the *y.*

> **boy** + ish = boyish   sur**vey** + or = surveyor
>
> **pay** + ment = payment   **buy** + er = buyer

Exceptions:

1. When adding *-ing* to a word ending in *y*, always keep the *y*, even if a consonant comes before it: stu**dy** + ing = stud**y**ing.

2. Other exceptions include *daily, dryer, said,* and *paid*.

Rule 4. When adding an ending that starts with a vowel to a one-syllable word, follow these rules.

Double the final consonant only if the word ends with a consonant-vowel-consonant.

trap + ed = tra**pp**ed	**knit** + ed = kni**tt**ed
drip + ed = dri**pp**ed	**fat** + er = fa**tt**er

Do not double the final consonant if the word ends with some other combination.

Vowel-vowel-consonant	Vowel-consonant-consonant
cl**ean** + est = cleanest	sl**ick** + er = slicker
p**oor** + er = poorer	t**each** + er = teacher
cl**ear** + ed = cleared	l**ast** + ed = lasted

Rule 5. When adding an ending that starts with a vowel to a word with two or more syllables, follow these rules.

Double the final consonant only if the word ends with a consonant-vowel-consonant and the stress is on the last syllable.

sub**mit** + ing = submi**tt**ing

pre**fer** + ed = prefe**rr**ed

Do not double the final consonant in other cases.

underst**and** + ing = understanding

of**fer** + ed = offered

Rule 6. Add *-s* to most nouns to form the plural, including words that end in *o* preceded by a vowel.

Most words	Words that end in vowel plus *o*
book + **s** = book**s**	vid**eo** + **s** = videos
college + **s** = college**s**	ster**eo** + **s** = stereos

Add *-es* to words that end in *o* preceded by a consonant and words that end in *s*, *sh*, *ch*, or *x*.

Words that end in consonant plus *o*	Words that end in *s*, *sh*, *ch*, or *x*
pota**to** + **es** = pota**toes** he**ro** + **es** = he**roes**	cla**ss** + **es** = cla**sses** pu**sh** + **es** = pu**shes** ben**ch** + **es** = ben**ches** fa**x** + **es** = fa**xes**

Exceptions When Forming Plurals

A **compound noun** is formed when two nouns are joined, with a hyphen (*in-law*), a space (*life vest*), or no space (*keyboard, stockpile*). Plurals of compound nouns are generally formed by adding an *-s* to the end of the last noun (*in-laws, life vests*) or to the end of the combined word (*keyboards, stockpiles*). Some hyphenated compound words such as *mother-in-law* or *hole-in-one* form plurals by adding an *-s* to the chief word (*mothers-in-law, holes-in-one*).

Some words form plurals in different ways, as in the list below.

Different Types of Plurals

Singular	Plural	Singular	Plural
analysis	analyses	louse	lice
bacteria	bacterium	loaf	loaves
bison	bison	medium	media
cactus	cacti	man	men
calf	calves	mouse	mice
child	children	phenomenon	phenomena
deer	deer	roof	roofs
die	dice	sheep	sheep
foot	feet	shelf	shelves
focus	foci	tooth	teeth
goose	geese	thief	thieves
half	halves	vertebra	vertebrae
hoof	hooves	wife	wives
knife	knives	wolf	wolves
leaf	leaves	woman	women

Consult a List of Commonly Misspelled Words

Use a list like the one that follows as an easy reference to check your spelling.

One Hundred Commonly Misspelled Words

absence	dollar	ninety
achieve	eighth	noticeable
across	embarrass	occasion
aisle	environment	perform
a lot	especially	physically
already	exaggerate	prejudice
analyze	excellent/excellence	probably
answer	exercise	psychology
appetite	fascinate	receive
argument	February	recognize
athlete	finally	recommend
awful	foreign	restaurant
basically	friend	rhythm
beautiful	government	roommate
beginning	grief	schedule
believe	guidance	scissors
business	harass	secretary
calendar	height	separate
career	humorous	sincerely
category	illegal	sophomore
chief	immediately	succeed
column	independent	successful
coming	interest	surprise
commitment	jewelry	truly
conscious	judgment	until
convenient	knowledge	usually
cruelty	license	vacuum
daughter	lightning	valuable
definite	loneliness	vegetable
describe	marriage	weight
develop	meant	weird
dictionary	muscle	writing
different	necessary	written
disappoint		

Chapter Review

1. What are two important tools for finding and correcting spelling mistakes?

   Answers should include two of the following: a dictionary, a spell checker, a

   proofreading tool/technique, a spelling list.

2. What three strategies can you use to become a better speller? *Master commonly*

   confused words, learn the six spelling rules, and consult a list of commonly misspelled

   words.

Part 6

Punctuation and Capitalization

"I write e-mails to clients, asking them questions to help them figure out what they want."

—Daniel B., student

30

Commas

Understand What Commas Do

Commas (,) are punctuation marks that help readers understand a sentence. Read the following three sentences aloud. How does the use of commas change the meaning?

No comma	When you call Sarah I will start cooking.
One comma	When you call Sarah, I will start cooking.
Two commas	When you call, Sarah, I will start cooking.

To get your intended meaning across to your readers, it is important that you understand when and how to use commas.

Visit **LaunchPad Solo for Readers and Writers > Grammar > Style and Mechanics** for more tutorials, videos, and practice with crafting paragraphs.

GRAMMAR & MECHANICS ROADMAP

An Overview

This Chapter Identifies the Following Trouble Spots

- Commas between items in a series
- Commas between coordinate adjectives
- Commas in compound sentences
- Commas after introductory words
- Commas around appositives and interrupters
- Commas around adjective clauses
- Commas with quotation marks
- Commas with dates
- Commas with addresses
- Commas with names

Tools to Address Trouble Spots

- Understand What Commas Do (p. 495)
- List of coordinating conjunctions (p. 497)
- Understand introductory words and phrases (p. 497)
- Understand appositives and interrupters (p. 498)
- Identify adjective clauses (p. 500)
- Edit for Commas exercises (p. 502)
- Chapter Review (p. 503)

Practice Using Commas Correctly

Commas between Items in a Series

Use commas to separate the items in a series (three or more items), including the last item in the series, which usually has *and* before it.

Item , Item , Item , and Item

To get from South Dakota to Texas, we will drive through *Nebraska, Kansas,* and *Oklahoma.*

We can *sleep in the car, stay in a motel,* or *camp outside.*

As I drive, I see many beautiful sights, such as *mountains, plains,* and *prairies.*

Tip How does a comma change the way you read a sentence aloud? Many readers pause when they come to a comma.

Note: Writers do not always use a comma before the final item in a series (this comma is known as the Oxford comma or serial comma). In college writing, however, it is best to include it.

Commas between Coordinate Adjectives

Coordinate adjectives are two or more adjectives that independently modify the same noun and are separated by commas.

Conor ordered a *big, fat, greasy* burger.

The diner food was *cheap, unhealthy,* and *delicious.*

Do *not* use a comma between the final adjective and the noun it describes.

Incorrect   Joelle wore a *long, clingy, red,* dress.

Correct   Joelle wore a *long, clingy, red* dress.

Cumulative adjectives describe the same noun but are not separated by commas because they form a unit that describes the noun. You can identify cumulative adjectives because separating them by *and* does not make any sense.

The store is having its *last storewide clearance* sale.

[Putting *and* between *last* and *storewide* and between *storewide* and *clearance* would make an odd sentence: The store is having its *last* and *storewide* and *clearance* sale. The adjectives in the sentence are cumulative adjectives and should not be separated by commas.]

In summary:

Teaching tip Write this incorrectly punctuated sentence on the board: *My daughter is a fast aggressive, and competitive soccer player.* Read it aloud (as if it were correctly punctuated), and ask students if they can hear where the missing comma should go.

- **Do** use commas to separate two or more **coordinate adjectives**.
- **Do not** use commas to separate **cumulative adjectives**.

Commas in Compound Sentences

A **compound sentence** contains two complete sentences joined by a coordinating conjunction: *and, but, for, nor, or, so, yet*. Use a comma before the joining word to separate the two complete sentences.

> **Tip** Remember the coordinating conjunctions with *FANBOYS: for, and, nor, but, or, yet,* and *so*. For more information, see Chapter 23.

Sentence	,	and, but, for, nor, or, so, yet	Sentence.

I called my best friend, and she agreed to drive me to work.

I asked my best friend to drive me to work, but she was busy.

I can take the bus to work, or I can call another friend.

> **Language note:** A comma alone cannot separate two sentences in English. Doing so creates a run-on (see Chapter 17).

Commas after Introductory Words

Use a comma after an introductory word, phrase, or clause. The comma lets your readers know when the main part of the sentence is starting.

Introductory word or word group	,	Main part of sentence.

Introductory word	*Yesterday,* I went to the game.
Introductory phrase	*By the way,* I do not have a babysitter for tomorrow.
Introductory clause	*While I waited outside,* Susan went backstage.

> **PRACTICE 1** **Using commas after introductory word groups**

In each item, underline introductory words or word groups. Then, add commas after introductory word groups where they are needed. If a sentence is already correct, put a "C" next to it.

Example: <u>In the 1960s</u>␠John Mackey became famous for his speed and strength as a tight end for the Baltimore Colts football team.

1. <u>In his later years</u>, the National Football League Hall-of-Famer was in the news for another reason: He suffered from dementia possibly linked to the head blows he received on the football field.

2. <u>According to medical experts</u>, repeated concussions can severely damage the brain over time, and they are especially harmful to young people, whose brains are still developing. C

3. Based on these warnings and on stories like John Mackey's‸athletic associations, coaches, and parents of young athletes are taking new precautions.

4. For example‸more football coaches are teaching players to tackle and block with their heads up, reducing the chance that they will receive a blow to the top of the head.

5. Also‸when players show signs of a concussion—such as dizziness, nausea, or confusion—more coaches are taking them out of the game.

6. Ideally‸coaches then make sure injured players receive immediate medical attention.

7. Once concussion sufferers are back home, they should take a break from sports until the symptoms of their injury are gone. C

8. During their recovery‸they should also avoid any activity that puts too much stress on the brain; these activities can include playing video games, studying, and driving.

9. When concussion sufferers feel ready to get back into the game‸a doctor should confirm that it is safe for them to do so.

10. As a result of these new precautions‸young athletes may avoid experiencing anything like the long‸difficult decline of John Mackey, who died in 2011.

Commas around Appositives and Interrupters

Tip For more on appositives, see Chapter 25

An **appositive** comes directly before or after a noun or pronoun and renames it.

> Lily, *a senior,* will take her nursing exam this summer.
>
> The prices are outrageous at Beans, *the local coffee shop.*

An **interrupter** is an aside or transition that interrupts the flow of a sentence and does not affect its meaning.

> My sister, *incidentally,* has good reasons for being late.
>
> Her child had a fever, *for example.*

Putting commas around appositives and interrupters tells readers that these elements give extra information but are not essential to the meaning of a sentence. If an appositive or interrupter is in the middle of a sentence, set it off with a pair of commas, one before and one after. If an appositive or interrupter comes at the beginning or end of a sentence, separate it from the rest of the sentence with one comma.

> *By the way,* your proposal has been accepted.
>
> Your proposal, *by the way,* has been accepted.
>
> Your proposal has been accepted, *by the way.*

Note: Sometimes, an appositive is essential to the meaning of a sentence. When a sentence would not have the same meaning without the appositive, the appositive should not be set off with commas.

> The actor *Leonardo DiCaprio* has never won an Oscar.
>
> [The sentence *The actor has never won an Oscar* does not have the same meaning.]

PRACTICE 2 **Using commas to set off appositives and interrupters**

Underline all the appositives and interrupters in the following sentences. Then, use commas to set them off.

Example: Harry, an attentive student, could not hear his teacher because the radiator in class made a constant rattling.

1. Some rooms, in fact, are full of echoes, dead zones, and mechanical noises that make it hard for students to hear.

2. The American Speech-Language-Hearing Association, experts on how noise levels affect learning abilities, has set guidelines for how much noise in a classroom is too much.

3. The association recommends that background noise, the constant whirring or whining sounds made by radiators, lights, and other machines, be no more than thirty-five decibels.

4. That level, thirty-five decibels, is about as loud as a whispering voice 15 feet away.

5. One study found a level of sixty-five decibels, the volume of a vacuum cleaner, in a number of classrooms around the country.

6. Other classroom noises came, for example, from ancient heating systems, whirring air-conditioning units, rattling windows, humming classroom computers, buzzing clocks, and the honking of traffic on nearby streets.

7. An increasing number of school districts are beginning to pay more attention to acoustics, the study of sound, when they plan new schools.

8. Some changes, such as putting felt pads on the bottoms of chair and
   desk legs to keep them from scraping against the floor, are simple and
   inexpensive.

9. Other changes, however, can be costly and controversial; these changes
   include buying thicker drapes, building thicker walls, or installing specially
   designed acoustic ceiling tiles.

10. School administrators, often parents themselves, hope that these
    improvements will result in a better learning environment for students.

Commas around Adjective Clauses

An **adjective clause** is a group of words that begins with *who, which,* or *that*; has a
subject and a verb; and describes a noun right before it in a sentence.

If an adjective clause can be taken out of a sentence without completely changing the meaning of the sentence, put commas around the clause.

> Lily, *who is my cousin,* will take her nursing exam this summer.
>
> Beans, *which is the local coffee shop,* charges outrageous prices.
>
> I complained to Mr. Kranz, *who is the shop's manager.*

If an adjective clause is essential to the meaning of a sentence, do not put commas around it. You can tell whether a clause is essential by taking it out and seeing
if the meaning of the sentence changes significantly, as it would if you took the
clauses out of the following examples.

> The only grocery store *that sold good bread* went out of business.
>
> Students *who do internships* often improve their hiring potential.
>
> Salesclerks *who sell liquor to minors* are breaking the law.

Noun	Adjective clause essential to meaning	Rest of sentence.

Noun	,	Adjective clause not essential to meaning	,	Rest of sentence.

Teaching tip Ask students to explain what is meant by *essential* in this context. Help them see that essential (restrictive) phrases and clauses generally answer the question, "Which one?" If a phrase or clause is taken out, the meaning of the sentence can change completely.

PRACTICE 3   Using commas to set off adjective clauses

In each item, underline the adjective clauses. Then, put commas around
these clauses where they are needed. Remember that if an adjective clause
is essential to the meaning of a sentence, commas are not necessary. If a
sentence is already correct, put a "C" next to it.

Example: Daniel Kish, who has been blind since the age of one, has changed
many people's ideas about what blind people can and cannot do.

1. Kish, who runs the organization World Access for the Blind, regularly rides his bike down busy streets and goes on long hikes.

2. His system for "seeing" his surroundings, which is known as echolocation, uses sound waves to create mental pictures of buildings, cars, trees, and other objects.

3. As Kish bikes around his neighborhood or hikes to sites that are deep in the wilderness, he clicks his tongue and listens to the echoes. C

4. The echoes, which differ depending on the distance and physical features of nearby objects, allow him to map his surroundings in his mind.

5. This mental map, which he constantly revises as he moves ahead, helps him avoid running into cars, trees, and other obstacles.

6. Researchers who recently investigated Kish's echolocation made some interesting discoveries. C

7. They found that Kish's visual cortex, which is the part of the brain that processes visual information, was activated during his sessions of mapping with sound.

8. This finding, which received a lot of attention in the scientific community, suggests that Kish's way of seeing the world is indeed visual.

9. Other blind people who have been trained in echolocation have learned to be as active and independent as Kish is. C

10. The successes that they and Kish have achieved offer additional proof that blindness does not equal helplessness. C

Other Uses for Commas

COMMAS WITH QUOTATION MARKS

Quotation marks are used to show that you are repeating exactly what someone said. Use commas to set off the words inside quotation marks from the rest of the sentence.

Tip For more on quotation marks, see Chapter 32.

"Let me see your license," demanded the police officer.

"Did you realize," she asked, "that you were going 80 miles per hour?"

I exclaimed, "No!"

Notice that a comma never comes directly after a quotation mark.

When quotations are not attributed to a particular person, commas may not be necessary.

"Pretty is as pretty does" never made sense to me.

COMMAS IN ADDRESSES

Use commas to separate the elements of an address included in a sentence. However, do not use a comma before a zip code.

> My address is 2512 Windermere Street, Jackson, Mississippi 40720.

If a sentence continues after a city-state combination or after a street address, put a comma after the state or the address.

> I moved here from Detroit, Michigan, when I was eighteen.
> I've lived at 24 Heener Street, Madison, since 1989.

COMMAS IN DATES

Separate the day from the year with a comma. If you give just the month and year, do not separate them with a comma.

> My daughter was born on November 8, 2004.
> The next conference is in August 2014.

If a sentence continues after the date, put a comma after the date.

> On April 21, 2013, the contract will expire.

COMMAS WITH NAMES

Put a comma after (and sometimes before) the name of someone being addressed directly.

> Don, I want you to come look at this.
> Unfortunately, Marie, you need to finish the report by next week.

COMMAS WITH *YES* OR *NO*

Put a comma after the word *yes* or *no* in response to a question.

> Yes, I believe that you are right.

Edit for Commas

> **PRACTICE 4**   **Editing paragraphs for commas**
>
> Edit the following paragraphs by adding commas where they are needed.
>
> (1) By the end of 2011, communities in California, Texas, Washington, and several other states had banned the use of plastic bags. (2) One grocery

store chain, Whole Foods Market, was an early leader in restricting the use of these bags. (3) As of April 22, 2008, Whole Foods stopped asking customers if they wanted paper bags or plastic bags. (4) The store, which cares about environmental issues, now offers only paper bags made from recycled paper.

(5) The president of Whole Foods stated, "We estimate we will keep 100 million new plastic grocery bags out of our environment between Earth Day and the end of this year." (6) The company also sells cloth bags, hoping to encourage shoppers to bring their own reusable bags with them when they go shopping.

(7) Experts believe that plastic bags do a great deal of damage to the environment. (8) They clog drains, harm wildlife, and take up an enormous amount of space in the nation's landfills. (9) According to the experts, it takes more than a thousand years for a plastic bag to break down, and Americans use 100 billion of them every single year.

> **PRACTICE 5**   **Editing your own writing for commas**
>
> Edit a piece of your own writing for comma usage. It can be a paper for this course or another one, or something you have written for work or your everyday life.

Chapter Review

1. A comma (,) is a ___punctuation mark___ that helps readers understand a sentence.

2. How do you use commas in these three situations?

   In a series of items, _use commas to separate three or more items_ .

   In a compound sentence, _use a comma and a coordinating conjunction to make two_
   sentences into one .

   With introductory words, _use a comma after the word, clause, or phrase_

   _____ .

3. An appositive comes before or after a noun or pronoun and _renames the noun or_
   pronoun .

4. An interrupter is an ___aside or transition___ that interrupts the flow of a sentence.

5. Put commas around an adjective clause when it is ___not essential___ to the meaning of a sentence.

31

Apostrophes

Understand What Apostrophes Do

An **apostrophe (')** is a punctuation mark that either shows ownership (*Susan's*) or indicates that a letter has been intentionally left out to form a contraction (*I'm, that's, they're*).

Practice Using Apostrophes Correctly

Apostrophes to Show Ownership

Add -'s to a singular noun to show ownership even if the noun already ends in -s.

> *Karen's* apartment is on the South Side.
>
> *James's* roommate is looking for him.

GRAMMAR & MECHANICS ROADMAP

An Overview

This Chapter Identifies the Following Trouble Spots

- Apostrophes to show ownership
- Apostrophes in contractions
- Apostrophes with letters, numbers, and time

Tools to Address Trouble Spots

If a noun is plural and ends in -*s*, just add an apostrophe. If it is plural but does not end in -*s*, add -'*s*.

My *books'* covers are falling off.

[More than one book]

The *twins'* father was building them a playhouse.

[More than one twin]

The *children's* toys were broken.

The *men's* locker room is being painted.

Tip Use apostrophes to show ownership for abbreviations: *The NBA's playoff system has changed.*

The placement of an apostrophe makes a difference in meaning.

My *sister's* six children are at my house for the weekend.

[One sister who has six children]

My *sisters'* six children are at my house for the weekend.

[Two or more sisters who together have six children]

Do not use an apostrophe to form the plural of a noun.

Gina went camping with her *sister/s* and their children.

All the *highway/s* to the airport are under construction.

Do not use an apostrophe with a possessive pronoun. These pronouns already show ownership (possession).

Is that bag *your/s*?   No, it is *our/s*.

Teaching tip Using an apostrophe with a possessive pronoun is a common error; tell students to be especially careful of this problem when they edit. You may also want to have students discuss why this error is so common.

Possessive Pronouns

my	his	its	their
mine	her	our	theirs
your	hers	ours	whose
yours			

Teaching tip If some students often misuse apostrophes in possessive pronouns, advise them to use the find or search function to find and check all uses of -'s in papers before turning them in. Tell them to write "checked for -'s" at the top of each paper.

The single most common error with apostrophes and pronouns is confusing *its* (a possessive pronoun) with *it's* (a contraction meaning "it is"). Whenever you write *it's*, test correctness by replacing it with *it is* and reading the sentence aloud to hear if it makes sense.

Apostrophes in Contractions

Tip Ask your instructor if contractions are acceptable in papers.

A **contraction** is formed by joining two words and leaving out one or more of the letters. When writing a contraction, put an apostrophe where the letter or letters have been left out.

> *She's* on her way. = *She is* on her way.
>
> *I'll* see you there. = *I will* see you there.

Be sure to put the apostrophe in the correct place.

Tip To shorten the full year to only the final two numbers, replace the first two numbers: The year 2016 becomes '16.

> It *doesn't* really matter.

Common Contractions

aren't = are not	she'll = she will
can't = cannot	she's = she is, she has
couldn't = could not	there's = there is
didn't = did not	they'd = they would, they had
don't = do not	they'll = they will
he'd = he would, he had	they're = they are
he'll = he will	they've = they have
he's = he is, he has	who'd = who would, who had
I'd = I would, I had	who'll = who will
I'll = I will	who's = who is, who has
I'm = I am	won't = will not
I've = I have	wouldn't = would not
isn't = is not	you'd = you would, you had
it's = it is, it has	you'll = you will
let's = let us	you're = you are
she'd = she would, she had	you've = you have

Apostrophes with Letters, Numbers, and Time

Use -'s to make letters and numbers plural. The apostrophe prevents confusion or misreading.

> In Scrabble games, there are more *e's* than any other letter.
>
> In women's shoes, size *8's* are more common than size *10's*.

Use an apostrophe or -'s in certain expressions in which time nouns are treated as if they possess something.

> She took four *weeks'* maternity leave after the baby was born.
>
> This *year's* graduating class is huge.

Edit for Apostrophes

PRACTICE 1   **Editing paragraphs for apostrophes**

Edit the following paragraphs by adding two apostrophes where needed and crossing out five incorrectly used apostrophes.

(1) Have you noticed many honeybee's when you go outside? (2) If not, it is~~n't~~ surprising. (3) For reasons that scientists still don't quite understand, these bees have been disappearing all across the country. (4) This mass disappearance is a problem because bees are an important part of growing a wide variety of flowers, fruits, vegetables, and nuts as they spread pollen from one place to another.

(5) In the last year, more than one-third, or billions, of the honeybees in the United States/ have disappeared. (6) As a consequence, farmers have been forced either to buy or to rent beehives for their crops. (7) Typically, people who are in the bee business ship hives to farmers' fields by truck. (8) The hives often have to travel hundreds of miles.

(9) Scientist's have been trying to find out what happened to the once-thriving bee population. (10) They suspect that either a disease or chemicals harmed the honeybee's.

PRACTICE 2   **Editing your own writing for apostrophes**

Edit a piece of your own writing for apostrophes. It can be a paper for this course or another one, or choose something you have written for work or your everyday life.

Chapter Review

1. An apostrophe (') is a punctuation mark that either shows __*ownership*__ or indicates that a letter or letters have been intentionally left out to form a __*contraction*__ .

2. To show ownership, add __'s__ to a singular noun, even if the noun already ends in -s. For a plural noun, add an __*apostrophe*__ alone if the noun ends in -s; add __'s__ if the noun does not end in -s.

3. Do not use an apostrophe with a __*possessive*__ pronoun.

4. Do not confuse *its* and *it's*. *Its* shows __*ownership*__ ; *it's* is a __*contraction*__ meaning "it is."

5. A __*contraction*__ is formed by joining two words and leaving out one or more of the letters.

32

Quotation Marks

Visit **LaunchPad Solo for Readers and Writers > Grammar > Style and Mechanics** for more tutorials, videos, and practice with crafting paragraphs.

Understand What Quotation Marks Do

Quotation marks (" ") always appear in pairs. Quotation marks have two common uses in college writing:

- They are used with direct quotations, which exactly repeat, word for word, what someone said or wrote. (Nick said, "You should take the downtown bus.")
- They are used to set off **titles**. (My favorite song is "Sophisticated Lady.")

Practice Using Quotation Marks Correctly

Quotation Marks for Direct Quotations

When you write a direct quotation, use quotation marks around the quoted words. Quotation marks tell readers that the words used are exactly what was said or written.

1. "I do not know what she means," I said to my friend Lina.
2. Lina asked, "Do you think we should ask a question?"

GRAMMAR & MECHANICS ROADMAP

An Overview

This Chapter Identifies the Following Trouble Spots

- Quotation marks for direct quotations
- Quotation marks for certain titles

Tools to Address the Trouble Spots

- Understand What Quotation Marks Do (p. 508)
- Guidelines for Capitalization and Punctuation (p. 509)
- Setting Off a Quotation within Another Quotation (p. 510)
- No Quotation Marks for Indirect Quotations (p. 511)
- Edit for Quotation Marks exercises (p. 512)
- Chapter Review (p. 513)

3. "Excuse me, Professor Soames," I called out, "but could you explain that again?"

4. "Yes," said Professor Soames. "Let me make sure you all understand."

5. After further explanation, Professor Soames asked, "Are there any other questions?"

When you are writing a paper that uses outside sources, use quotation marks to indicate where you quote the exact words of a source.

Teaching tip The *Instructor's Manual for Real Writing* contains tests and supplemental exercises for this chapter.

> We all need to become more conscientious recyclers. A recent editorial in the *Bolton Common* reported, "When recycling volunteers spot-checked bags that were supposed to contain only newspaper, they found a collection of nonrecyclable items such as plastic candy wrappers, aluminum foil, and birthday cards."

When quoting, writers usually use words that identify who is speaking, such as *I said to my friend Lina* in the first example in the "Quotation Marks for Direct Quotations" section. The identifying words can come after the quoted words (example 1), before them (example 2), or in the middle of them (example 3). Here are some guidelines for capitalization and punctuation.

Guidelines for Capitalization and Punctuation

- Capitalize the first letter in a complete sentence that is being quoted, even if it comes after some identifying words (example 2 on the previous page).

- Do not capitalize the first letter in a quotation if it is not the first word in a complete sentence (*but* in example 3).

- If it is a complete sentence and it is clear who the speaker is, a quotation can stand on its own (second sentence in example 4).

- Identifying words must be attached to a quotation; they cannot be a sentence on their own.

- Use commas to separate any identifying words from quoted words in the same sentence.

- Always put quotation marks after commas and periods. Put quotation marks after question marks and exclamation points if they are part of the quoted sentence.

Teaching tip As you go over the first two rules on capitalization, put a sentence on the board without any quotation marks. Ask students where the quotation marks should go and which letters should be capitalized.

Quotation mark   Quotation mark

Lina asked, "Do you think we should ask a question?"

Comma   Question mark

Tip For more on commas with quotation marks, see Chapter 30.

- If a question mark or exclamation point is part of your own sentence, put it after the quotation mark.

Quotation mark   Quotation mark

What did she mean when she said, "All tests are graded on a curve"?

Comma   Question mark

Setting Off a Quotation within Another Quotation

Sometimes, when you quote someone directly, part of what that person said quotes words that someone else said or wrote. Put single quotation marks (' ') around the quotation within a quotation so that readers understand who said what.

The student handbook says, "Students must be given the opportunity to make up work missed for legitimate reasons."

Terry told his instructor, "I am sorry I missed the exam, but that is not a reason to fail me for the term. Our student handbook says, 'Students must be given the opportunity to make up work missed for legitimate reasons,' and I have a good reason."

PRACTICE 1 **Punctuating direct quotations**

Edit the following sentences by adding quotation marks and commas where needed.

Example: A radio journalist asked a nurse at a critical-care facility, Do you believe that the medical community needlessly prolongs the life of the terminally ill?"

1. "If I could answer that question quickly," the nurse replied, "I would deserve an honorary degree in ethics."

2. She added, "But I see it as the greatest dilemma we face today."

3. "How would you describe that dilemma?" the reporter asked the nurse.

4. The nurse said, "It is a choice of when to use our amazing medical technology and when not to."

5. The reporter asked, "So there are times when you would favor letting patients die on their own?"

6. "Yes," the nurse replied, "I would."

7. The reporter asked, "Under what circumstances should a patient be allowed to die?"

8. "I cannot really answer that question because so many variables are involved," the nurse replied.

9. "Is this a matter of deciding how to allocate scarce resources?" the reporter asked.

10. "In a sense, it is," the nurse replied. "As a colleague of mine says, 'We should not try to keep everyone alive for as long as possible just because we can.'"

No Quotation Marks for Indirect Quotations

When you report what someone said or wrote but do not use the person's exact words, you are writing an **indirect quotation.** Do not use quotation marks for indirect quotations. Indirect quotations often begin with the word *that.*

Indirect quotation	Direct quotation
Sam said that there was a fire downtown.	Sam said, "There was a fire downtown."
The police told us to move along.	"Move along," directed the police.
Tara told me that she is graduating.	Tara said, "I am graduating."

PRACTICE 2   **Punctuating direct and indirect quotations**

Edit the following sentences by adding quotation marks where needed and crossing out quotation marks that are used incorrectly. If a sentence is already correct, put a "C" next to it.

Example: **Three days before her apartment was robbed, Jocelyn told a friend, "I worry about the safety of this building."**

1. "Have you complained to the landlord yet?" her friend asked.

2. "Not yet," Jocelyn replied, "although I know I should."

3. Jocelyn phoned the landlord and asked him to install a more secure lock on the front door. C

4. The landlord said that "he believed that the lock was fine the way it was."

5. When Jocelyn phoned the landlord after the burglary, she said, "I know this burglary would not have happened if that lock had been installed."

6. "I am sorry," the landlord replied, "but there is nothing I can do about it now."

7. Jocelyn asked a tenants' rights group whether she had grounds for a lawsuit. C

8. The person she spoke to said that "she probably did."

9. "If I were you," the person said, "I would let your landlord know about your plans."

10. When Jocelyn told her landlord of the possible lawsuit, he said that he would reimburse her for the stolen items. C

Quotation Marks for Certain Titles

When you refer to a short work such as a magazine or newspaper article, a chapter in a book, a short story, an essay, a song, or a poem, put quotation marks around the title of the work.

Newspaper article	"Volunteers Honored for Service"
Short story	"The Awakening"
Essay	"Why Are We So Angry?"

Usually, titles of longer works, such as novels, books, magazines, newspapers, movies, television programs, and albums, are italicized. The titles of sacred books such as the Bible or the Koran are neither underlined nor surrounded by quotation marks.

Book	*To Kill a Mockingbird*
Newspaper	*Washington Post*

Do not italicize or capitalize the word *the* before the name of a newspaper or magazine, even if it is part of the title: I saw that article in the *New York Times*. But do capitalize *The* when it is the first word in titles of books, movies, and other sources.

If you are writing a paper with many outside sources, your instructor will probably refer you to a particular system of citing sources. Follow that system's guidelines when you use titles in your paper.

Note: Do not enclose the title of a paragraph or an essay that you have written in quotation marks when it appears at the beginning of your paper. Do not italicize it either.

Edit for Quotation Marks

PRACTICE 3   **Editing paragraphs for quotation marks**

Edit the following paragraphs by adding twelve sets of quotation marks where needed and crossing out the two sets of incorrectly used quotation marks. Correct any errors in punctuation.

(1) When Ruiz first came into my office, he told me that he was a poor student. (2) I asked, "What makes you think that?"

(3) Ruiz answered, "I have always gotten bad grades, and I do not know how to get any better." (4) He shook his head. (5) "I have just about given up."

(6) I told him that "there were some resources on campus he could use and that we could work together to help him."

(7) "What kind of things are you talking about?" asked Ruiz. (8) "What exactly will I learn?"

(9) I said, "There are plenty of programs to help you. (10) You really have no excuse to fail."

(11) "Can you be a little more specific?" he asked.

(12) "Certainly," I said. (13) I told him about the survival skills program. (14) I also pulled out folders on study skills, such as managing time, improving memory, taking notes, and having a positive attitude. (15) "Take a look at these," I said.

(16) Ruiz said, "No, I am not interested in that. (17) And I do not have time."

(18) I replied, "That is your decision, Ruiz, but remember that education is one of the few things that people are willing to pay for and not get." (19) I paused and then added, "It sounds to me like you are wasting the money you spent on tuition. (20) Why not try to get what you paid for?"

(21) Ruiz thought for a moment, while he looked out the window, and finally told me that he would try.

(22) "Good," I said. (23) "I am glad to hear it."

> **PRACTICE 4**   **Editing your own writing for quotation marks**
>
> Edit a piece of your own writing for quotation marks. It can be a paper for this course or another one, or choose something you have written for work or your everyday life.

Chapter Review

1. Quotation marks look like _____ " " ____. They always appear in (pairs/threes).

2. A direct quotation exactly __repeats__ what someone (or some outside source) said or wrote. (Use/Do not use) quotation marks around direct quotations.

3. An indirect quotation _restates what someone said or wrote, but not word for word_. (Use/Do not use) quotation marks with indirect quotations.

4. To set off a quotation within a quotation, use _____ single quotation marks _____.

5. Put quotation marks around the titles of short works such as (give four examples) _Answers will vary. Possible answers: short stories, poems, songs, articles_.

6. For longer works such as magazines, novels, books, newspapers, and so on, ____italicize____ the titles.

33

Other Punctuation

LaunchPadSolo

Visit **LaunchPad Solo for Readers and Writers > Grammar > Style and Mechanics** for more tutorials, videos, and practice with crafting paragraphs.

Understand What Punctuation Does

Punctuation helps readers understand your writing. If you use punctuation incorrectly, you send readers a confusing—or, even worse, a wrong—message. This chapter covers five punctuation marks that people sometimes use incorrectly because they are not quite sure what these marks are supposed to do.

GRAMMAR & MECHANICS ROADMAP

An Overview

This Chapter Identifies the Following Trouble Spots

- Semicolons
- Parenthesis
- Dash
- Hyphen

Practice Using Punctuation Correctly

Semicolon ;

SEMICOLONS TO JOIN CLOSELY RELATED SENTENCES

Use a semicolon to join two closely related sentences into one sentence.

> In an interview, hold your head up and do not slouch; it is important to look alert.

> Make good eye contact; looking down is not appropriate in an interview.

 Language note: Using a comma instead of a semicolon to join two sentences would create a run-on (see Chapter 17).

SEMICOLONS WHEN ITEMS IN A LIST CONTAIN COMMAS

Use semicolons to separate items in a list that itself contains commas. Otherwise, it is difficult for readers to tell where one item ends and another begins.

> For dinner, Bob ate an order of onion rings; a 16-ounce steak; a baked potato with sour cream, bacon bits, and cheese; a green salad; and a huge bowl of ice cream with fudge sauce.

Because one item, *a baked potato with sour cream, bacon bits, and cheese*, contains its own commas, all items need to be separated by semicolons.

Colon :

COLONS BEFORE LISTS

Use a colon after an independent clause to introduce a list. An independent clause contains a subject, a verb, and a complete thought. It can stand on its own as a sentence.

> The software conference fair featured a vast array of products: financial-management applications, games, educational CDs, college-application programs, and so on.

COLONS BEFORE EXPLANATIONS OR EXAMPLES

Use a colon after an independent clause to let readers know that you are about to provide an explanation or example of what you just wrote.

> The conference was overwhelming: too much hype about too many things.

One of the most common misuses of colons is to use them after a phrase instead of an independent clause. Watch out especially for colons following the phrases *such as* and *for example*.

Tip See Chapter 30 (Commas), Chapter 31 (Apostrophes), and Chapter 32 (Quotation Marks) for coverage of these punctuation marks. For more information on using semicolons to join sentences, see Chapter 23.

Incorrect	Tonya enjoys sports that are sometimes dangerous. For example: white-water rafting, wilderness skiing, rock climbing, and motorcycle racing.
Correct	Tonya enjoys sports that are sometimes dangerous: white-water rafting, wilderness skiing, rock climbing, and motorcycle racing.
Incorrect	Jeff has many interests. They are: bicycle racing, sculpting, and building musical instruments.
Correct	Jeff has many interests: bicycle racing, sculpting, and building musical instruments.

COLONS IN BUSINESS CORRESPONDENCE AND BEFORE SUBTITLES

Use a colon after a greeting (called a *salutation*) in a business letter and after the standard heading lines at the beginning of a memorandum.

Dear Mr. Hernandez:

To: Pat Toney

From: Susan Anker

Colons should also be used before subtitles—for example, "Running a Marathon: The Five Most Important Tips."

Parentheses ( )

Use parentheses to set off information that is not essential to the meaning of a sentence. Parentheses are always used in pairs and should be used sparingly.

My grandfather's most successful invention (and also his first) was the electric blanket.

When he died (at the age of ninety-six), he had more than 150 patents registered.

Dash --

Dashes can be used like parentheses to set off additional information, particularly information that you want to emphasize. Make a dash by writing or typing two hyphens together. Do not put extra spaces around a dash.

The final exam--worth 25 percent of your total grade--will be next Thursday.

A dash can also indicate a pause, much like a comma does.

My uncle went on long fishing trips--without my aunt and cousins.

Hyphen -

HYPHENS TO JOIN WORDS THAT FORM A SINGLE DESCRIPTION

Writers often join two or more words that together form a single description of a person, place, or thing. To join the words, use a hyphen.

> Being a stockbroker is a high-risk career.
>
> Jill is a lovely three-year-old girl.

When writing out two-word numbers from twenty-one to ninety-nine, put a hyphen between the two words.

> Seventy-five people participated in the demonstration.

HYPHENS TO DIVIDE A WORD AT THE END OF A LINE

Use a hyphen to divide a word when part of the word must continue on the next line.

> Critics accused the tobacco industry of increasing the amounts of nico-
> tine in cigarettes to encourage addiction and boost sales.

If you are not sure where to break a word, look it up in a dictionary. The word's main entry will show you where you can break the word: *dic • tio • nary*. If you still are not confident that you are putting the hyphen in the correct place, do not break the word; write it all on the next line.

Tip Most word-processing programs automatically put an entire word on the next line rather than hyphenating it. When you write by hand, however, you need to hyphenate correctly.

Edit for Other Punctuation Marks

> **PRACTICE 1** **Editing paragraphs for other punctuation marks**

Edit the following paragraphs by adding semicolons, colons, parentheses, dashes, and hyphens when needed. In some places, more than one type of punctuation may be acceptable. *Answers may vary. Possible answers shown.*

(1) When John Wood was on a backpacking trip to Nepal in 1998, he discovered something he had not expected: only a few books in the nation's schools. (2) He knew that if the students did not have the materials they needed, it would be much harder for them to learn. (3) They did not need high-tech supplies as much as they needed old-fashioned books. (4) Wood decided that he would find a way to get those books.

(5) Two years later, Wood founded Room to Read, an organization dedicated to shipping books to students who needed them. (6) Since then, the group has donated more than three million books. (7) One of Wood's first shipments was carried to students on the back of a yak. (8) Many others arrived in a Cathay Pacific Airlines plane.

(9) Along with the books, Room to Read has also built almost three hundred schools and has opened five thousand libraries. (10) Different companies donate books to the organization; Scholastic, Inc., recently sent
^
400,000 books to Wood's group. (11) Money to fund all these efforts comes through various fund-raisers: read-a-thons, auctions, and coin drives.
^

> **PRACTICE 2**   **Editing your own writing for punctuation**
>
> Edit a piece of your own writing for semicolons, colons, parentheses, dashes, and hyphens. It can be a paper for this course or another one, or choose something you have written for work or your everyday life. You may want to try more than one way to use these punctuation marks in your writing.

Chapter Review

1. Semicolons (;) can be used to *join closely related sentences into one sentence*

   and to *separate items in a list that itself contains commas*   .

2. Colons (:) can be used in what three ways? *after an independent clause to introduce*

   a list; after an independent clause to provide an explantion or example of what you

   just wrote; after a greeting in a business letter, after heading lines in a memo, and

   before subtitles.

3. A colon in a sentence must always be used after an *independent clause*   .

4. Parentheses ( ) set off information that is *not essential* to a sentence.

5. *Dashes (--)* also set off information in a sentence, usually information that you
   want to emphasize.

6. Hyphens (-) can be used to join two or more words that together *form a single*
    description and to *break* a word at the end of a line.

34

Capitalization
Using Capital Letters

Understand Three Rules of Capitalization

Capital letters (A, B, C, etc.) are generally bigger than lowercase letters (a, b, c, etc.), and they may have a different form. To avoid the most common errors of capitalization, follow these three rules:

Capitalize the first letter

- Of every new sentence.
- In names of specific people, places, dates, and things (also known as proper nouns).
- Of important words in titles.

LaunchPadSolo

Visit **LaunchPad Solo for Readers and Writers > Grammar > Style and Mechanics** for more tutorials, videos, and practice with crafting paragraphs.

Practice Capitalization

Capitalization of Sentences

Capitalize the first letter of each new sentence, including the first word of a direct quotation.

> The superintendent was surprised.
> He asked, "What is going on here?"

GRAMMAR & MECHANICS ROADMAP

An Overview

This Chapter Identifies the Following Trouble Spots

- Capitalization of sentences
- Capitalization of names of specific people, places, dates, and things
- Capitalization of titles

Tools to Address Trouble Spots

- Understanding capitalization (p. 519)
- Chapter Review (p. 522)

Capitalization of Names of Specific People, Places, Dates, and Things

The general rule is to capitalize the first letter in names of specific people, places, dates, and things. Do not capitalize a generic (common) name such as *college* as opposed to the specific name: *Carroll State College*. Look at the examples for each group.

PEOPLE

Capitalize the first letter in names of specific people and in titles used with names of specific people.

Specific	Not specific
Jean Heaton	my neighbor
Professor Fitzgerald	your math professor
Dr. Cornog	the doctor
Aunt Pat, Mother	my aunt, your mother

The name of a family member is capitalized when the family member is being addressed directly: Happy Birthday, *Mother*. In other instances, do not capitalize: It is my *mother's* birthday.

The word *president* is not capitalized unless it comes directly before a name as part of that person's title: *President* Barack Obama.

PLACES

Capitalize the first letter in names of specific buildings, streets, cities, states, regions, and countries.

Specific	Not specific
Bolton Town Hall	the town hall
Arlington Street	our street
Dearborn Heights	my hometown
Arizona	this state
the South	the southern region
Spain	that country

Do not capitalize directions in a sentence.

Drive *south* for five blocks.

DATES

Capitalize the first letter in the names of days, months, and holidays. Do not capitalize the names of the seasons (winter, spring, summer, fall).

Specific	Not specific
Wednesday	tomorrow
June 25	summer
Thanksgiving	my birthday

 Language note: Some languages, such as Spanish, French, and Italian, do not capitalize days, months, and languages. In English, such words must be capitalized.

Incorrect	I study russian every monday, wednesday, and friday from january through may.
Correct	I study **Russian** every **Monday**, **Wednesday**, and **Friday** from **January** through **May**.

ORGANIZATIONS, COMPANIES, AND GROUPS

Specific	Not specific
Taft Community College	my college
Microsoft	that software company
Alcoholics Anonymous	the self-help group

LANGUAGES, NATIONALITIES, AND RELIGIONS

Specific	Not specific
English, Greek, Spanish	my first language
Christianity, Buddhism	your religion

The names of languages should be capitalized even if you aren't referring to a specific course.

I am taking psychology and *Spanish*.

COURSES

Specific	Not specific
Composition 101	a writing course
Introduction to Psychology	my psychology course

COMMERCIAL PRODUCTS

Specific	Not specific
Diet Pepsi	a diet cola
Skippy peanut butter	peanut butter

Capitalization of Titles

Tip For more on punctuating titles, see Chapter 32. For a list of common prepositions, see page 327.

When you write the title of a book, movie, television program, magazine, newspaper, article, story, song, paper, poem, and so on, capitalize the first word and all important words. The only words that do not need to be capitalized (unless they are the first word) are *the, a, an,* coordinating conjunctions (*and, but, for, nor, or, so, yet*), and prepositions.

> *I Love Lucy* was a long-running television program.
>
> Both *USA Today* and the *New York Times* are popular newspapers.
>
> "Once More to the Lake" is one of Chuck's favorite essays.

Chapter Review

1. Capitalize the ___first letter___ of every new sentence.

2. Capitalize the first letter in names of specific ___people___, ___places___, ___dates___, and ___things___.

3. Capitalize the first word and all ___important words___ in titles.

Editing Review Test 1
The Four Most Serious Errors (Chapters 15–19)

Directions: Each of the underlined word groups contains one or more errors. As you locate and identify each error, write its item number on the appropriate line below. Then, edit the underlined word groups to correct the errors. If you need help, turn back to the chapters indicated. *Answers may vary. Possible edits are shown.*

Two fragments 2, 9 _____   Two verb problems 10, 16 _____

Two run-ons 8, 15 _____   Four subject-verb
                                            agreement errors 4, 6, 11, 14 _____

You

1 Every time you step outside, you are under attack. 2 ~~Which you~~ may not know what is hitting you, but the attack is truly happening. 3 Invisible storms of sky dust rain down on you all the time.

is

4 It does not matter if the sun is shining and the sky ~~are~~ bright blue. 5 The dust is still there.

consists

6 Sky dust ~~consist~~ of bug parts, specks of hair, pollen, and even tiny chunks of comets. 7 According to experts, 6 million pounds of space dust settle on the earth's surface every year. 8 You will never

.

notice it/ scientists, however, are collecting it in order to learn more about weather patterns and

Scientists use

pollution. 9 ~~Using~~ sophisticated equipment like high-tech planes and sterile filters to collect dust

samples.

begun

10 Dan Murray, a geologist at the University of Rhode Island, has ~~began~~ a new project that invites students and teachers to help collect samples of cosmic dust. 11 Murray says that collecting the dust

is

particles ~~are~~ quite simple. 12 It starts with a researcher setting up a small, inflatable swimming pool.

13 Next, this investigator leaves the pool out in the open for 48 hours. 14 Finally, the researcher uses

has

a special type of tape to pick up whatever ~~have~~ settled over time. 15 The tape is put into a beaker of

. A   found

water to dissolve / microscope is used to analyze what comes off the tape. 16 The information ~~finded~~

there will help scientists predict insect seasons, measure meteor showers, or even catch signs of global

warming.

Editing Review Test 2

The Four Most Serious Errors (Chapters 15–19)

2

Directions: Each of the underlined word groups contains one or more errors. As you locate and identify each error, write its item number on the appropriate line below. Then, edit the underlined word groups to correct the errors. If you need help, turn back to the chapters indicated. *Answers may vary. Possible edits are shown.*

Two fragments _5, 12_____   Two verb problems _4, 16_____

Three run-ons _6, 9, 14_____   Three subject-verb
                                      agreement errors _1, 8, 17_____

1 Most people spend many hours a day indoors, so windows and natural light is [*are*] important to their health. 2 Light helps people feel connected to the world around them. 3 However, traditional windows allow the loss of heat in winter and of cool air in summer; the result is high energy costs to maintain office buildings and homes at comfortable temperatures. 4 Architects and designers knowed [*know*] this fact, so they have developed energy-efficient "smart windows." 5 Shifting [*Smart windows shift*] from clear to dark and back again. 6 Some smart windows change from clear to dark with a touch of a button [;] others change automatically in response to the intensity of the outside light.

7 Their design and engineering make smart windows *chromogenic,* or able to change colors. 8 Smart windows shifts [*shift*] to darker colors when they are given a small electrical charge. 9 The darker the room, the more it remains cool the [*. The*] sun does not warm it. 10 Smart windows take only a minute or so to darken.

11 Although these smart windows save energy, they may not be ready for the market [*for*] 12 For a few more years. 13 At present, designers face some resistance from potential customers who distrust the technology. 14 Another obstacle is the price tag [*. This*] this new technology remains expensive. 15 To deal with both of these issues, developers are starting small. 16 They were [*are*] creating motorcycle and ski helmets with face masks that switch between dark and clear. 17 They hopes [*hope*] that handy products like these helmets will help the new technology gain wide acceptance.

Editing Review Test 3

The Four Most Serious Errors (Chapters 15–19)
Other Grammar Concerns (Chapters 20–26)

3

Directions: Each of the underlined word groups contains one or more errors. As you locate and identify each error, write its item number on the appropriate line below. Then, edit the underlined word groups to correct the errors. If you need help, turn back to the chapters indicated. *Answers may vary. Possible edits are shown.*

Two fragments 3, 6 _____   Two verb problems 1, 5 _____

One run-on 10 _____   Two pronoun errors 2, 8 _____

One adjective error 11 _____   One parallelism error 13 _____

Two subject-verb
agreement errors 16, 17 _____

    1 Flying an airplane across the Atlantic Ocean may have been a miracle almost a century ago, but

                is

today it ~~be~~ quite commonplace. 2 When a man named Maynard Hill decided to do it, however, most
            ^   *it*   *He gave*

people told him that ~~he~~ simply could not be done. 3 ~~Giving~~ it a try despite everyone's doubts. 4 His

persistence was rewarded when TAM-5, his 11-pound model airplane, flew from Canada to Ireland in
                                     set

approximately 39 hours. 5 TAM-5's flight ~~sat~~ world records not only for the longest distance but also
                              ^   *It followed*

for the longest time ever flown by this type of airplane. 6 ~~Following~~ the same path as the first nonstop

flight across the ocean in 1919.

    7 This successful trip was not Hill's first attempt, by any means. 8 He started ~~its~~ project a decade
                                             his

ago, and he lost several planes trying to complete the journey. 9 Finally, in August 2003, he made a

fifth attempt. 10 He tossed the TAM-5 into the air once airborne, it was guided by remote control on
                   best

the ground. 11 It was the ~~most best~~ version he had made. 12 It soared to a cruising altitude of almost a

thousand feet, and at that point a computerized autopilot took over.
                                      hoped

    13 For days, the flight crew watched the clock, followed the TAM-5's progress, and ~~hopes~~ for the

best. 14 A crowd of fifty people waited on the shore in Ireland to watch the TAM-5's landing. 15 When
                                          remember

the plane appeared on the horizon, a cheer went up. 16 Today, model plane enthusiasts ~~remembers~~ his
          was

feat. 17 Even though the plane ~~were~~ made out of nothing more than balsa wood, fiberglass, and plastic

film, it flew right into history that August afternoon.

Editing Review Test 4

4

The Four Most Serious Errors (Chapters 15–19)
Other Grammar Concerns (Chapters 20–26)

Directions: Each of the underlined word groups contains one or more errors. As you locate and identify each error, write its item number on the appropriate line below. Then, edit the underlined word groups to correct the errors. If you need help, turn back to the chapters indicated. *Answers may vary. Possible edits are shown.*

Two fragments <u>11, 14</u>   One run-on <u>13</u>

One subject-verb agreement error <u>15</u>   One pronoun error <u>8</u>

One misplaced/dangling modifier <u>3</u>   Two coordination/
                                              subordination errors <u>4, 7</u>
One use of inappropriately
informal or casual language <u>10</u>

1 Early on May 1, 2011, Sohaib Athar, an IT consultant in Pakistan, was surprised to hear helicopters flying over his house. 2 Soon, he sent a Twitter message about it: "Helicopter hovering above Abbottabad at 1 a.m. (is a rare event)." 3 *For the next half hour, he* ~~He~~ continued to tweet about what he was hearing ~~for the next half hour~~, attracting many Twitter followers.

4 *Although* ~~Because~~ he didn't know it at the time, Athar became the first person to publicize the raid in which Osama bin Laden was captured and assassinated. 5 For this reason, Athar also became one of the most famous of a growing number of so-called citizen journalists. 6 Unlike most traditional news gatherers, citizen journalists aren't trained in journalism. 7 They follow events and trends that interest them, *and* ~~but~~ they send their observations to others through Facebook, Twitter, and other social media.

8 Certain media critics argue, however, that if someone tweets about something newsworthy, *he or she doesn't* ~~they don't~~ necessarily deserve to be called a journalist. 9 That is the view of Dan Miller, a reporter who had the following reaction to Athar's famous reports: "Wondering on Twitter why there are helicopters flying around your neighborhood isn't journalism." 10 According to Miller, traditional media, not Athar, got the *news* ~~411~~ about bin Laden's capture out to the whole world, 11 *not* ~~Not~~ to just some Twitter followers.

12 Others say that Athar provided a more valuable service. 13 For example, he communicated with people who were following him and tried to answer their questions*. He* ~~he~~ sought out other sources of information and shared them. 14 Also, *he* tried to analyze what he observed himself and what he learned from other sources.

15 Whether or not Athar deserves to be called a journalist, one thing is clear: More people *are* ~~is~~ feeling driven to tweet, text, or blog from their particular corners of the world.

Editing Review Test 5

The Four Most Serious Errors (Chapters 15–19)
Other Grammar Concerns (Chapters 20–26)
Word Use (Chapters 27–29)

5

Directions: Each of the underlined word groups contains one or more errors. As you locate and identify each error, write its item number on the appropriate line below. Then, edit the underlined word groups to correct the errors. If you need help, turn back to the chapters indicated. *Answers may vary. Possible edits are shown.*

One run-on _13_____   One verb problem _5_____
One word-choice error _11_____   Two pronoun errors _2, 8_____
One adjective error _9_____   One spelling error _16_____
One subject-verb agreement error _4_____   One misplaced/dangling modifier _15_____
Two commonly
confused word errors _13, 18_____

    1 How do you celebrate the New Year? 2 <u>Some people watch television on New Year's Eve so that</u>
they
<u>~~he~~ can see the glittering ball drop in New York's Times Square.</u> 3 Others invite friends and family over
  ^

to celebrate with special foods or fireworks.
              is
    4 <u>The New Year ~~are~~ celebrated all over the world in a variety of ways.</u> 5 <u>For example, in Australia,</u>
      spend   ^
<u>people ~~spended~~ the day in fun, outdoor activities, such as picnics, trips to the beach, and rodeos.</u>
    ^

6 After all, it is summertime there in January. 7 In Spain, people eat a dozen grapes at midnight. 8 <u>They</u>
                              they
<u>eat one each time the clock chimes because ~~she~~ believe that it will bring good luck for the New Year.</u>
                 an unusual ^
9 The people of Denmark have ~~the unusualest~~ tradition. 10 On New Year's Eve, they throw old dishes
                        ^   *dishes*
at the doors of their friends' homes. 11 <u>If you find a lot of broken ~~junk~~ in front of your house in the</u>
                                         ^

<u>morning, you are well liked.</u> 12 Wearing all new clothes is the way many Koreans celebrate the start of
                           their   ;
the New Year. 13 <u>In Germany, people leave food on ~~there~~ plates/ this practice is meant to ensure that</u>
                               ^   ^

<u>their kitchens will be full of food for the coming New Year.</u>

    14 Not all countries celebrate the New Year on January 1. 15 ~~Setting off firecrackers, the~~ holiday
                                       The
                       , by setting off firecrackers.   ^
<u>is celebrated later by the Chinese people/</u> 16 <u>The date of the Chinese New Year depends on the lunar</u>
calendar   ^
<u>~~calander~~ and usually falls somewhere between January 21 and February 20.</u> 17 The Chinese often have
^

a big parade with colorful floats of dancing dragons. 18 <u>The mythical creatures are supposed to be</u>
symbols
<u>~~cymbals~~ of wealth and long life.</u>
^

527

Editing Review Test 6

6

The Four Most Serious Errors (Chapters 15–19)
Other Grammar Concerns (Chapters 20–26)
Word Use (Chapters 27–29)

Directions: Each of the underlined word groups contains one or more errors. As you locate and identify each error, write its item number on the appropriate line below. Then, edit the underlined word groups to correct the errors. If you need help, turn back to the chapters indicated. *Answers may vary. Possible edits are shown.*

One run-on <u>4</u>_____

One subject-verb agreement error <u>8</u>_____

One parallelism error <u>1</u>_____

Two commonly
confused word errors <u>3, 13</u>_____

One use of inappropriately
informal or casual language <u>6</u>_____

One verb problem <u>2</u>_____

One pronoun error <u>9</u>_____

Two spelling errors <u>7, 14</u>_____

1 The idea of being able to unlock your car, turn on a light, or ~~starting~~ ^{start} your computer just by waving your hand sounds like something out of a science-fiction novel. 2 Thanks to advancements in technology, the futuristic idea has ~~became~~ ^{become} a reality. 3 Some people are ~~all ready~~ ^{already} able to accomplish routine actions in this unusual way. 4 They do not have special powers[;] they have special computer chips embedded inside their bodies. 5 These high-tech chips help people do daily tasks with little or no effort.

6 Known as RFIDs, which stands for "radio frequency identification devices," the chips are ~~way~~ ^{extremely} small. 7 They are as tiny as a ~~peice~~ ^{piece} of rice, have small antennas that send signals, and can be painlessly implanted and worn under the skin. 8 Health-care workers ~~uses~~ ^{use} the chips in a variety of life-saving ways. 9 For example, emergency medical workers can scan the chips in accident victims to determine ~~his~~ ^{their} blood type or allergies.

10 For security reasons, some parents have their children wear RFIDs on backpacks, bracelets, or ID tags. 11 Through a cell-phone signal, the chips automatically let the parents know when their children have reached and left school or other destinations. 12 Even some pets are now equipped with these computer chips. 13 If the pet runs away or gets lost, ~~than~~ ^{then} its owners can track down their pet more easily by using the chip. 14 Although many people think that these chips have great ~~potental,~~ ^{potential,} others worry that the government will eventually use them to spy on people.

Editing Review Test 7

The Four Most Serious Errors (Chapters 15–19)
Other Grammar Concerns (Chapters 20–26)
Word Use (Chapters 27–29)
Punctuation and Capitalization (Chapters 30–34)

7

Directions: Each of the underlined word groups contains one or more errors. As you locate and identify each error, write its item number on the appropriate line below. Then, edit the underlined word groups to correct the errors. If you need help, turn back to the chapters indicated. *Answers may vary. Possible edits are shown.*

One run-on 7 _____   One verb problem 13 _____

One apostrophe error 3 _____   One pronoun error 10 _____

One adverb error 2 _____   One quotation mark error 9 _____

One subject-verb agreement error 11 _____   One capitalization error 4 _____

One comma error 8 _____   One semicolon error 5 _____

1 In response to the ongoing economic crisis, more high schools are teaching financial literacy:

how to create a budget, save money, and stay out of debt. 2 <u>Although most experts agree that</u>

<u>teaching these skills is a good idea, some recommend that such education begin ~~more~~ earlier—even</u>

<u>in preschool.</u> 3 <u>This way, young people have more time to learn good habit's, save money, and plan for</u>

<u>their financial future.</u>
                          t
        4 <u>The Moonjar is one ̃Tool for teaching children good money skills.</u> 5 <u>It consists of three tin boxes̷</u>

<u>each of which is labeled "spend," "save," or "share."</u> 6 Children are encouraged to divide allowances

or gifts of money equally among the boxes. 7 <u>As the weeks pass by, they watch their savings grow,</u>
                                                        . They
<u>helping them see the benefits of saving money over time̷ ~~they~~ also learn discipline about spending.</u>
                                        ,
8 <u>For example a child who is shopping with a parent might ask for a pack of candy or a small toy.</u>
                                                                            ?"
9 <u>The parent can reply, "Do you have enough money in your spend box"?</u> 10 <u>Exchanges like that</u>
                                                          he or she spends
<u>one help the child understand the consequences of financial decisions; if ~~they spend~~ money on</u>

<u>one item now, less money will be available for other purchases in the future.</u>
                                                                    s
        11 <u>Mary Ryan Karges, who is in charge of sales for Moonjar LLC, recommend that financial skills</u>

<u>be emphasized as much as other basic skills taught to young children.</u> 12 She says, "If we teach save,

spend, share with the same vigor that we teach stop, look, listen, we won't run into so many financial
                                    seen
problems." 13 <u>Once children have ~~seed~~ the benefits of good financial choices, they are on their way to a</u>

<u>better future.</u>

Editing Review Test 8

8

The Four Most Serious Errors (Chapters 15–19)
Other Grammar Concerns (Chapters 20–26)
Word Use (Chapters 27–29)
Punctuation and Capitalization (Chapters 30–34)

Directions: Each of the underlined word groups contains one or more errors. As you locate and identify each error, write its item number on the appropriate line below. Then, edit the underlined word groups to correct the errors. If you need help, turn back to the chapters indicated. *Answers may vary. Possible edits are shown.*

One run-on ⁵ _____   One semicolon error ¹ _____
One pronoun error ¹³ _____   One verb problem ⁴ _____
One comma error ¹⁴ _____   One adverb error ¹⁰ _____
One apostrophe error ⁹ _____   One spelling error ¹¹ _____
One use of inappropriately   One parallelism error ¹² _____
informal or casual language ¹¹ _____   One hyphen error ⁷ _____
One capitalization error ⁶ _____

1 If it seems as though places in the United States are more crowded lately⟋ it might be because the country's population recently hit three hundred million. 2 The nation has the third-largest population in the world. 3 Only China and India have more people. 4 Experts ~~belief~~ *believe* that by 2043 there will be four hundred million people in the United States.

5 The country is growing rapidly because people are having more babies *and* more people are moving to the United States. 6 The ~~northeast~~ *Northeast* is the most populated area within the country. 7 It took ~~fifty two~~ *fifty-two* years for the country's population to go from one hundred million to two hundred million. 8 It took only thirty-nine years to rise from two hundred million to its current three hundred million. 9 If ~~experts~~ *experts'* statistics are correct, it will take even less time for the population of the United States to reach four hundred million.

10 Some people worry that the United States is growing too ~~quick~~ *quickly*. 11 Researchers predict some *frightening possibilities* ~~super scary possibilitys~~. 12 They state that if the population grows too large, it will stress available land, deplete water resources, and ~~it can~~ increase air pollution. 13 *Their* ~~Its~~ concerns are valid ones; in the meantime, the population just keeps growing. 14 Although this country is large⟋ future generations may be squeezed in more tightly than the present generation can imagine.

Editing Review Test 9

The Four Most Serious Errors (Chapters 15–19)
Other Grammar Concerns (Chapters 20–26)
Word Use (Chapters 27–29)
Punctuation and Capitalization (Chapters 30–34)

9

Directions: Each of the underlined word groups contains one or more errors. As you locate and identify each error, write its item number on the appropriate line below. Then, edit the underlined word groups to correct the errors. If you need help, turn back to the chapters indicated. *Answers may vary. Possible edits are shown.*

One fragment _7_____   One spelling error _9_____
One run-on _10_____   One hyphen error _4_____
One pronoun error _13_____   One semicolon error _8_____
One parallelism error _14_____ One parenthesis error _12_____
One commonly   One word-choice error _2_____
confused word error _3_____

1 Whenever you have to write a paper, a letter, or any other document for work or school, you
probably head toward the computer. 2 *Today,* ~~In this day and age,~~ most people reach for keyboards faster
than they pick up pens. 3 At one elementary school in Scotland, however, the *principal,* ~~principle,~~ Bryan Lewis, is
taking a different approach. 4 He believes that neat handwriting is still an important skill, so he has his
students write not only by hand but also with *old-fashioned* ~~old fashioned~~ fountain pens.

5 Fountain pens were used in schools long ago and lately have been regaining popularity because
they are refillable. 6 A writer using a fountain pen dips the point into a little ink bottle*,* 7 *drawing* ~~Drawing~~ ink
up into the barrel of the pen, as needed. 8 Today, a writer simply throws an empty pen away*,* and gets
a new one.

9 So far, Principal Lewis is pleased with the results of his *experiment* ~~experimint.~~ 10 He reports that students
are taking more care with their work*;* their self-esteem has improved as well. 11 He stresses to teachers
all over the world that the ability to produce legible handwriting remains a necessary skill. 12 Lewis is
happy with the improvement he sees in his students' writing (and in his own writing, too*)*. 13 He knows
that computers are here to stay and that *they* ~~it~~ will not disappear. 14 However, he believes that the practice
with fountain pens helps students focus, write faster, and ~~they can~~ feel proud of themselves.

Editing Review Test 10

The Four Most Serious Errors (Chapters 15–19)
Other Grammar Concerns (Chapters 20–26)
Word Use (Chapters 27–29)
Punctuation and Capitalization (Chapters 30–34)

10

Directions: Each of the underlined word groups contains one or more errors. As you locate and identify each error, write its item number on the appropriate line below. Then, edit the underlined word groups to correct the errors. If you need help, turn back to the chapters indicated. *Answers may vary. Possible edits are shown.*

One subject-verb agreement error ___11_____   One spelling error ___7_____

One pronoun error ___4_____   One comma error ___14_____

One coordination/subordination error ___2_____   One semicolon error ___13_____

One colon error ___9_____   One apostrophe error ___12_____

One commonly confused word error ___15_____

1 When Shaun Ellis decided that he wanted to learn more about wolves, he made a radical life
                                                                              and
change. 2 He decided to live with the wolves ~~yet~~ imitate their wild lifestyle as closely as he possibly
                                                        ∧
could. 3 For eighteen months, he lived with three wolf pups that had been abandoned. 4 <u>He pretended</u>
          their
<u>to be ~~its~~ mother in many ways.</u> 5 He worked to teach them the skills they would need to survive in the
            ∧
wild. 6 It certainly was not an easy way to live. 7 <u>Ellis shared an outdoor pen with the pups, and it had</u>
                    bedding
<u>no heat or ~~beding.~~</u> 8 To keep warm on the cold nights, he had to snuggle with the young wolves.
              ∧

    9 <u>To communicate with them, Ellis learned how to̸ growl, snarl, and howl.</u> 10 He also learned how

to use body positions and facial expressions in order to get a message across to the animals. 11 <u>While</u>
                                                              tried
<u>living with the wolves, he also ~~try~~ to eliminate any emotion because animals do not feel things as human</u>
                    man's   ∧
<u>beings do.</u> 12 <u>This ~~mans~~ transition back to regular life was quite difficult for him.</u>
                  ∧

    13 <u>Ellis's unorthodox methods have earned him criticism from his colleagues̸ but he firmly</u>
                                                                              ∧
<u>believes that his techniques led to valuable knowledge about wolves.</u> 14 <u>He has founded̸ the Wolf Pack</u>
                                                                                        ∧
<u>Management organization in England.</u> 15 <u>Its goal is to get captive wolves released back into the wild</u>
                then
<u>and ~~than~~ use what was learned to help the animals avoid future conflicts with humans.</u>
          ∧

Appendix
Problem Solving in Writing

Some writing assignments, both in English and in other subjects, will require you to use problem-solving skills. Such assignments will ask you to read and analyze a problem to develop possible solutions, often by synthesizing information from various sources.

Problem-solving skills are necessary not only in college but also—and even more so—in the work world. Often, managers assign a team to work on and pose possible solutions to a problem that the organization faces. Also, problem-solving skills will help you in your everyday life when you run into a situation that you want to change.

Each of the chapters in Part 2 includes problem-based writing assignments ("Writing to Solve a Problem"). These assignments offer you the opportunity to solve real-world problems by working alone or as part of a team. Use the following section to complete those assignments or to address any problem you may face in college, at work, or in your everyday life.

Problem Solving

Problem solving is the process of identifying a problem and figuring out a reasonable solution.

Problems range from minor inconveniences like finding a rip in the last clean shirt you have when you're running late to more serious problems such as being laid off from your job. Although such problems disrupt our lives, they also give us opportunities to tackle difficult situations with confidence.

Too often, people are paralyzed by problems because they don't have strategies for attacking them. However, backing away from a problem rarely helps solve it. When you know how to approach a challenging situation, you are better able to take charge of your life.

Problem solving consists of five basic steps, which can be used effectively by both individuals and groups of people.

The Problem-Solving Process

Understand the problem.

You should be able to say or write it in a brief statement or question.

> **EXAMPLE:** Your ten-year-old car needs a new transmission, which will cost at least $1500. Do you keep the car or buy a new one?

Identify people or information that can help you solve the problem (resources).

EXAMPLES

- Your mechanic
- Friends who have had similar car problems
- Car advice from print or Web sources

List the possible solutions.

EXAMPLES

- Pay for the transmission repair.
- Buy a new car.

Evaluate the possible solutions.

1. Identify the steps each solution would require.

2. List possible obstacles for each solution (like money or time constraints).

3. List the advantages and disadvantages of the solutions.

> **EXAMPLES (considering only advantages and disadvantages):**
> - Pay for the transmission repair.
>   *Advantage:* This would be cheaper than buying a new car.
>   *Disadvantage:* The car may not last much longer, even with the new transmission.
> - Buy a new car.
>   *Advantage:* You will have a reliable car.
>   *Disadvantage:* This option is much more expensive.

Choose the most reasonable solution.

Choose the solution that is realistic—the simpler the better. Be able to give reasons for your choice.

> *Solution:* Pay for the transmission repair.
>
> *Reasons:* You do not have money for a new car, and you do not want to assume more debt. Opinions from two mechanics indicate that your car should run for three to five more years with the new transmission. At that point, you will be in a better position to buy a new car.

Acknowledgments

Sarah Bigler. "High School Is Not Preparing Us for College." *Daily Eastern News*, October 10, 2010. Reprinted by permission.

Daniel Bird. "What's Appropriate: How to Talk to Children about Disasters." *The Skyline View*, May 16, 2013. Reprinted by permission.

Environmental Protection Agency. "Climate Change Is Happening." Courtesy of the Environmental Protection Agency.

Stephanie Ericsson. "The Ways We Lie." Copyright © 1992 by Stephanie Ericsson. Originally published by the *Utne Reader*. Reprinted by permission of Dunham Literary as agents for the author.

John Hawkins. "5 Scientific Reasons That Global Warming Isn't Happening." *Townhall.com*, February 18, 2014. Reprinted by permission.

Oscar Hijuelos. "Memories of New York City Snow." *Metropolis Found: New York Is Book Country 25th Anniversary Collection* (New York: New York Is Book Country, 2003). Copyright © 2003 by Oscar Hijuelos. Reprinted with the permission of the Jennifer Lyons Literary Agency, LLC for the author.

Kelly Hultgren. "Pick Up the Phone to Call, Not Text." Dailywildcat.com, August 31, 2011.

Amanda Jacobowitz. "A Ban on Water Bottles: A Way to Bolster the University's Image." Posted by Amanda Jacobowitz on April 28, 2010. Forum Staff Columnists.

Elizabeth Renter. "Napping Can Dramatically Increase Learning, Memory, Awareness, and More." *Natural Society*, March 17, 2014. Reprinted by permission. Illustration courtesy of Remie Geoffroi. www.remgeo.com.

Liz Riggs. "What It's Like to Be the First Person in Your Family to Go to College." *The Atlantic*, January 13, 2014. Reprinted by permission.

Caroline Bunker Rosdahl and Mary T. Kowalski. Excerpt from *Textbook of Basic Nursing*, 9th ed. © 2008 Wolters Kluwer Health | Lippincott Williams & Wilkins.

Kathy Stevens. "Ten Tips for Easing into Plant-Based Eating." *Huffington Post*, April 18, 2014. Reprinted by permission.

Amy Tan. "Fish Cheeks." © 1987 by Amy Tan. First appeared in *Seventeen* Magazine. Reprinted by permission of the author and the Sandra Dijkstra Literary Agency.

John Tierney. "Yes, Money Can Buy Happiness." *The New York Times*, March 20, 2008. © 2008 *The New York Times*. All rights reserved. Used by permission and protected by the laws of the United States. The printing, copying redistribution, or transmission of the material without express permission is prohibited.

Vidette Editorial Board. "ISU's Restroom Change Shows Commitment to Diversity." *Vidette*, July 14, 2014. Used by permission.

Andrea Whitmer. "When Poor People Have Nice Things." sooverthis.com, June 18, 2012. Reprinted by permission.

Index

Missing something?

Instructors may assign the online materials that accompany this text. To access them, visit **macmillanhighered.com/launchpadsolo/readwrite/**.

Inside *LaunchPad Solo for Readers and Writers*

	Video	LearningCurve	Pre/Post MC	Quizbank
Welcome				
Teaching and Learning Advice				
Diagnostics				
Grammar			●	
Reading			●	
Reading	●			
Topics and Main Ideas	●	●	●	●
Topic Sentences and Supporting Details	●	●	●	●
Patterns of Organization	●	●	●	
Vocabulary	●	●	●	
Active Reading	●		●	
Critical Reading	●	●	●	
Interpretive Reading	●		●	
Reading Tutorials	●			
25 Reading Quizzes			●	
Writing Process	●			
Purpose, Audience, and Topic	●		●	
Prewriting	●		●	
Thesis Statements	●		●	●
Drafting	●		●	●
Revising	●		●	
Editing	●		●	
Digital Writing Tutorials	●			
Integrated Reading and Writing	●			
Argument	●	●	●	
Summarizing	●		●	●
Research	●			
Working with Sources	●	●	●	●
Documentation Guides				
Search and Citation Tutorials	●			
Grammar: Parts of Speech	●	●	●	●
Grammar: Basic Sentences	●	●	●	●
Grammar: Style and Mechanics	●	●	●	●
Grammar: Resources for Multilingual Writers		●		●